D1217565

Does Atlas Shrug?

Does Atlas Shrug?

The Economic Consequences
of Taxing the Rich

Joel B. Slemrod

EDITOR

RUSSELL SAGE FOUNDATION
New York

HARVARD UNIVERSITY PRESS
Cambridge, Massachusetts, and London, England

Library of Congress Cataloging-in-Publication Data

Does atlas shrug?: the economic consequences of taxing the rich / Joel B. Slemrod, editor.

    p.   cm.

Includes bibliographical references and index.

ISBN 0-674-00154-0

1. Tax incidence—United States.   2. Wealth tax—United States.
3. Wealth—United States.   4. Income distribution—United States.
I. Title: Economic consequences of taxing the rich.   II. Slemrod, Joel.

HJ2322.A3 D64 2000   99–057238
336.24–dc21   CIP

The paper used in this publication meets the minimum requirements of American National Standard for Information Sciences—Permanence of Paper for Printed Library Materials. ANSI Z39.48-1992.

Text design by Suzanne Nichols.

10 9 8 7 6 5 4 3 2 1

Contents

Preface

Joel B. Slemrod

This volume contains fifteen papers that were prepared as part of a research project on the economic consequences of taxing the rich sponsored by the Office of Tax Policy Research (OTPR) at the University of Michigan Business School.[1] The papers examine the history and current environment of U.S. tax policy toward the affluent, address the impact of taxation on a wide range of economic behavior, and challenge the conceptual models used by economists to address these issues. Most of the papers were presented at a conference attended by academics, policymakers, and journalists held in Ann Arbor, Michigan, in October of 1997.

I would like to thank The Ford Foundation, The Lynde and Harry Bradley Foundation, the KPMG Peat Marwick Foundation, and the Russell Sage Foundation for financial support of this project. Mary Ceccanese, administrative assistant of OTPR, was indispensable to its success and completion.

NOTE

1. The Office of Tax Policy Research is a research office of the University of Michigan Business School. OTPR supports and disseminates academic research on all aspects of the tax system, with the goal of informing discussion about the future course of policy. The organization is nonpartisan and does not advocate any policies. More information about OTPR activities is available at www.otpr.org.

Part I
History and Background

The Economics of Taxing the Rich

Joel B. Slemrod

> To show, for example, the obvious advantages of enabling men to enjoy securely the "fruits of their labor" is not to justify all forms of property or its present distribution—any more than the manifold examples of property gained without labor justify the counter-generalization that all property is theft.
> —Josiah Wedgwood, *The Economics of Inheritance* (1929, 62)

Ayn Rand's *Atlas Shrugged*, published in 1957, depicts a world in which the "prime movers" go on strike[1] in order to demonstrate how essential their contribution is to society and to expose the obstacles that society places in their way. Each prime mover decides "not to work in his own profession, not to give the world the benefit of his mind" (747).

In 1957 the top marginal tax rate under the U.S. federal individual income tax was 91 percent, beginning at taxable incomes of $400,000, equivalent to $2,276,000 in 1997 dollars.[2] Very high (by today's standards) marginal rates started at lower levels of taxable income: at $100,000 (in 1957 dollars) the marginal rate was 75 percent; at $140,000 it was 81 percent. The high tax rates in this era were undoubtedly one of the obstacles to the prime movers that enraged Ayn Rand, as they did another high earner of those years, Ronald Reagan.

Notably, 1957 lies in the middle of a period of extraordinary U.S. economic growth—the average annual rate of productivity growth was 3.1 percent over the period 1951 through 1963, compared to about 1.5 percent since 1981. The fact that the golden years of modern American economic growth occurred during the apex of marginal tax rates is, at a minimum, an embarrassing coincidence for those who believe that avoiding such a policy is the key to economic success. But this correspondence is surely not convincing in itself, because arguably the postwar growth could have been even higher if the tax rates had been lower.

THE CONSEQUENCES OF TAXING THE RICH

Economic controversies are rarely disposed of, and this one is no exception. How the tax system affects the behavior of the affluent and the impact of these behavioral changes on economic performance are still controversial questions for the design of tax policy. Surprisingly little hard evidence on the impact of the tax system on the behavior of the very affluent, or the contribution of the affluent to overall economic performance, has been uncovered.

In spite of, or perhaps because of, the paucity of evidence, strong opinions on these issues abound. George Gilder (1981) states bluntly that "a successful economy depends on the proliferation of the rich" (245), and that "to help the poor and middle classes, one must cut the taxes of the rich" (188). In contrast, the noted author Peter Drucker, quoted in Robert Lenzner and Stephen Johnson (1997), dismisses the economic importance of the rich: "If all the super-rich disappeared, the world economy would not even notice. The super-rich are irrelevant to the economy." He also predicts that in the next economic downturn "there will be an outbreak of bitterness and contempt for the super corporate chieftains who pay themselves millions. In every major economic downturn in U.S. history the 'villains' have been the 'heroes' in the preceding boom" (124).

Pressing policy issues cannot be put off until these questions are settled. The setting of appropriate rates of income tax for affluent households periodically surfaces as a hot policy issue, as it did during the recent discussion of the flat tax. The capital gains tax is a perennial topic and, given the great concentration of realized and unrealized gains among the affluent, inevitably involves these same questions. Recently the estate and gift tax, which directly affects less than 1 percent of all families, has made it onto the federal policy agenda; the exemption level was increased in the 1997 tax bill, and many Republican legislators favor abolishing it entirely.

Today's tax policy debate must be seen in the context of two historical trends. First, the top federal income tax rates are quite low by post–World War II standards. The 90-plus percentage rates in the era of Ayn Rand and the actor Ronald Reagan are long gone. The top rate was cut to 70 percent by the 1964 Tax Act, and to 50 percent in the first year of the first term of Ronald Reagan's presidency. It was further cut to 28 percent in the second year of Reagan's second term, marking an extraordinary decline in the span of slightly more than two decades. By 1993 the top rate had returned to 39.6 percent, still low by historical standards. As W. Elliot Brownlee discusses in this volume, the average effective tax rate on the most affluent never reached nearly as high as the top statutory rates would indicate, but it probably has declined as well.

Second, there is near-unanimity that since 1970 the distribution of pre-tax income has become more unequal. While the real earnings of the broad swath of the population have stagnated, the real income of the most affluent Americans has risen considerably. A fierce debate rages among economists about the source of this phenomenon; the leading candidates are skill-biased technological change and greater integration of the world economy, but no theory has satisfactorily explained the twenty-five-year trend. The role of the tax system has received some attention. Edward Gramlich, Richard Kasten, and Frank Sammartino (1993) and others have shown that the federal income tax system has neither offset the increased inequality of pre-tax incomes by increased progressivity nor significantly exacerbated it. More controversial is the extent to which the income growth at the top has been the result of increased labor supply, entrepreneurial activity, and other aspects of a reduced aversion to receiving taxable income coaxed out by lower taxes. Understanding the answer to this last question is critical to the policy issues, for it sheds light on the economic consequences of the attempt to tax the affluent.

The chapters in this book begin to fill the gaps in our understanding of these key issues. This chapter provides some conceptual background for these investigations and their policy implications.

Who Are the Rich?

Who is rich and who is not? The answer to that question depends on the measure of affluence chosen, and on the dividing line chosen. Some candidates for a measure of affluence are annual income, annual consumption, wealth, lifetime income, and lifetime consumption; depending on the issue at hand, different measures may be more or less appropriate. Although conceptually attractive, a lack of data that track people over a lifetime precludes empirical examination of the latter two measures, although longitudinal data sets that follow people over a decade or more are now available.

Data on measures of annual income are readily available but may be misleading for two reasons. First, the top fractile of income earners inevitably includes some households that had one great year of unusually high income; this problem is exacerbated if capital gains realizations are included in income. However, several studies (for example, Slemrod 1992b) suggest that a snapshot of a single year's income distribution is not highly misleading as a representative of several years' average income, the closest measure we have to lifetime income. Second, focusing on the skewness of annual income is also potentially misleading to the extent that it reflects life-cycle effects; if income naturally rises as individuals age, a snapshot of people at every age may overstate the concentration of lifetime income. This concern turns out not to be quantitatively important. In 1995 the top 1 percent received 14.4 percent of adjusted gross income (AGI). If one classifies people by age,[3] the share of the top 1 percent is 7.9 percent, 11.8 percent, 15.2 percent, 17.8 percent, and 19.4 percent for the age groups twenty-five to thirty-four, thirty-five to forty-four, forty-five to fifty-four, fifty-five to sixty-four, and over sixty-five, respectively.[4] Clearly, within-age-group skewness rises with age, and the overall share in fact understates the concentration of income among the groups with the highest average income, those between forty-five and sixty-four.

Another useful indicator of affluence is wealth. It has the advantage of being less subject to transitory fluctuations, but it may misclassify high-income, high-spending households as nonaffluent. It is also subject to the potential problem that a single-year snapshot, because of the natural life cycle of wealth accumulation, overstates inequality.

Annual consumption data should be less subject to the problem of fluctuating incomes, given people's tendency to smooth consumption across high- and low-income periods. If consumption depends primarily on permanent or lifetime income, then it is an ideal indicator of well-being. This has led some researchers (for example, Cutler and Katz 1992) to focus on this measure of well-being; unfortunately, it is not well measured by surveys.

Whatever measure of affluence is chosen, one has to decide on a cutoff level that distinguishes the rich from the non-rich. This is an arbitrary choice, but one that affects the nature of the group under investigation; after all, the rich family with $200,000 a year is quite different from the "super-rich" family with $200 million a year. Many researchers have focused on the top 1 percent, but others also separate out the top 0.5 percent, top 0.1 percent, and even the top 5 percent. What does it take to make the top 1 percent? In the tax year 1995 it took an adjusted gross income of $218,220. According to Edward Wolff (this volume), in 1992 the 1 percent cutoff for a family's net worth was $2.42 million.

These cutoffs may or may not correspond to what most Americans mean by "rich." In a 1990 Gallup poll (Gallup and Newport 1990), less than 0.5 percent of respondents considered themselves rich (another 7 percent admitted to being "upper-income"), but on average respondents said that 21 percent of all Americans are in fact rich. To a question about what income it takes to be rich, the median response was $95,000. Because in 1990 only about 4 percent of all households had income at least that high, it is clear that a correct perception of the actual distribution of income is not widely shared.

The Economic Importance of the Rich

Why focus on the rich? For one thing, it's where the money is. In 1994 the 1 percent of taxpayers with the highest AGI received 13.8 percent of total income and remitted 28.7 percent of total federal personal income tax. Increasing these payments by 25 percent would generate $38.2 billion more in tax revenue and could finance a 10 percent across-the-board tax cut for everyone else (Tax Foundation 1996).

Their role in the economy is also disproportionate to their numbers, and for that reason policymakers must be wary of the potential adverse consequences of taxation. Robert Avery and Arthur Kennickell (1991) report that the top 1 percent of wealth-holders owned 31.9 percent of net wealth in 1983, and 30.4 percent in 1986. Wolff (this volume) reports that in 1992, 35.9 percent of total net worth and 45.6 percent of financial wealth (net wealth excluding house and auto) was held by the wealthiest 1 percent in that category. According to Wolff, both measures of concentration had increased from 1983, when the figures were 32.6 percent and 42.9 percent, respectively.[5]

The distribution of net saving by wealth class is also apparently quite concentrated.[6] According to Avery and Kennickell (1991), the top 1 percent of 1983 wealth-holders did 13 percent of net saving between 1983 and 1986; when ranked by 1986 wealth-holders, the top 1 percent did 53.7 percent of net real saving! The striking difference in results is due to the endogeneity of 1986 wealth to realized savings between 1983 and 1986—those who successfully saved are, other things equal, bound to become wealthier.

Not only do the rich account for a large fraction of personal saving, but it is undoubtedly true, as Ayn Rand emphasized, that they provide tangible and intangible skills that are critical to economic performance.[7] The question of whether they are compensated in line with their social contribution, and the correlation between affluence and talent, are taken up later. In any event, the extent to which these talents are withheld from the economy because of the tax system is of great import.

Clearly, the economic stakes in taxing the rich are enormous. The potential contribution of the rich to tax revenue is large, and probably growing in importance. But also large is the potential cost of diverting their wealth and talents into socially unproductive uses.

How Much Tax Do the Rich Pay?

Before discussing how much tax the rich ought to pay, it helps to talk about how much tax they pay now, and the average tax rate that results. This turns out to be a harder question than it might seem. Here are some facts. In 1994 the top 1 percent of taxpayers in terms of adjusted gross income remitted taxes totaling $152.7 billion, which was 27.9 percent of their total AGI of $546.7 billion (Tax Foundation 1996).

For a few reasons, the 27.9 percent number is an inadequate measure of the average tax rate of the affluent. For one thing, it includes neither state and local income taxes nor other kinds of taxes levied by all governments, including sales taxes, property taxes, corporate income tax, and estate and gift taxes. Another reason is that the person who *remits* money to the IRS is not necessarily the person who "pays" the tax in the sense of being worse off because of the tax; through price adjustments, the tax may be shifted onto someone else. How much shifting occurs depends on the supply and demand characteristics of the economy and is a highly controversial subject among economists, especially with regard to the corporate income tax.

Controversy notwithstanding, several attempts have been made recently to assess the burden of taxes, using reasonable assumptions about incidence. The Congressional Budget Office (CBO) (1994) estimated the average (federal only) tax rate on the top 1 percent of families, ranked by income, to be 33.2 percent, compared to a 23.7 percent average for all families. The Office of Tax Analysis (OTA) of the Treasury Department (1996) estimated the average tax rate on the top 1 percent to be 24.5 percent, compared to 19.7 percent for all taxpayers.[8] Although the two estimates differ somewhat, they both find the federal tax system to be slightly, but not overwhelmingly, progressive overall, and taxes other than the income tax to be much less progressive than the income tax, or even regressive.

Besides the difficulty of assessing the true incidence of taxes, estimated average tax rates are subject to error because they are based on income reported to the Internal Revenue Service (IRS). In the words of Gabriel Kolko (1962, 9): "Since [the social scientist] is getting the same information as the tax collector, he is confronted with essentially the same barriers of the deception and silence in approaching . . . a good number of the wealthy." The CBO makes no adjustment at all for nonreporting, but James Nunns (1995) reports that the OTA uses information from the Taxpayer Compliance Measurement Program (TCMP) of the IRS to correct reported income for noncompliance. Although Nunns does not spell out how this correction is made or how large it is, the TCMP data suggest that any correction is small. As Charles Christian (1994) documents, in the 1988 TCMP data the voluntary compliance rate (reported income as a percentage of true income) is actually higher for the highest income class (AGI over $500,000) than for any other income group, at 97.1 percent; in comparison, it is 92.4 percent for those with income between $25,000 and $50,000. It may be that these data confirm the old saying that "the poor evade, and the rich avoid," but it may also be that the TCMP auditors are unable to detect the kind of sophisticated evasion in which some upper-income people engage.

How Much Should They Pay? What Americans Think

In 1993, when Congress was considering President Clinton's proposed tax increase on upper-income people, several polls found overwhelming support for increasing taxes on the affluent. For instance, in an April 1993 Gallup poll, 75 percent of respondents said that "upper-income" people paid less than their "fair share" in taxes. Similarly, a February 1993 *Time*/CNN poll found support among 79 percent of respondents for increasing the personal income tax for families making more than $200,000 a year.

It is, however, a bit difficult to interpret these poll results in light of the results of another poll, taken in 1986 by Roper. People were asked to estimate how much personal income tax was actually paid by families at various income levels. The median estimate of taxes paid for a family with $200,000 income was only $15,000, or 7.5 percent, at a time when the actual average tax rate was about 21 percent. Furthermore, a 1987 survey showed that people on average believe that 45 percent of millionaires paid no income tax at all, although IRS statistics showed the actual figure was less than 2 percent. Thus, the professed desire for more progressivity may in part stem from a lack of understanding of how progressive the system really is.

The next sections lay out the underlying non-economic and economic arguments for using the tax system to redistribute income. I stress the role played in these arguments by the economic consequences of taxing the rich.

NON-ECONOMIC ARGUMENTS
The Case for Equality

What have the "second-handers" (as Ayn Rand described those who impede the "prime movers") got against the rich anyway? More generally, what are the arguments for progressive tax systems that redistribute income away from the most affluent members of society?

In a classic passage, Henry Simons (1938, 24) refers to inequality of income as "unlovely"; he characterizes the objection to extreme affluence in the presence of poverty as almost aesthetic, and certainly a value judgment about a society with unequal outcomes. Many would subscribe to an "ability to pay" principle, under which tax burden is related to a family's ability to bear a tax burden or, in other words, to tolerate a sacrifice. Reasoning from the plausible idea that each dollar paid is a lesser sacrifice for a well-to-do family than for a poor family, an equal sacrifice requires higher tax payments from a well-to-do family. After all, $100 more in taxes may induce an affluent family to cut back on magazine subscriptions, but it may induce a poor family to have less to eat. Although this is a sensible, and even compelling, proposition, it is also one that is impossible to quantify, because the magnitude of sacrifice cannot be compared across individuals. Thus, the ability-to-pay principle stands as an intuitively appealing defense of linking tax liability to some measure of well-being, but it does not offer concrete guidance on just how progressive a tax system ought to be.

Others argue that economic inequality is undesirable because it inevitably leads to inequality of political power, which is itself undesirable. From another perspective, arguing about the principles underlying the proper post-fisc distribution of income is irrelevant, because that will be determined by the distribution of political power in the society, which may depend on the degree of economic inequality. The origins of the modern, redistributive welfare state can be traced to Bismarckian Germany, when the explicit objective was to counter the appeal of the Communist call for an even more radical redistribution of resources through an overthrow of the capitalist system entirely. Friedrich Hayek (1960, 311) stresses the political function of the *appearance* of progressivity: "It would probably be true . . . to say that the illusion that by means of progressive taxation the burden can be shifted substantially onto the shoulders of the wealthy has been the chief reason why taxation has increased as fast as it has done, and that, under the influence of this illusion, the masses have come to accept a much heavier burden than they would have done otherwise."

The Case Against Equality and Redistribution

The central philosophical argument against redistribution is that individuals have a *right* to what they earn. Governments should not redistribute income because they have no income to redistribute; they can only confiscate the income of some and confer it on others. A modern form of this argument, introduced by Robert Nozick (1974), is that only *processes* of income generation can be judged to be just or not; if incomes are obtained through a just process, then the resulting distribution of income is unassailable.

The difficulty with this type of argument is ascertaining what people would earn in the absence of government. Certainly the level and ordering of income would be much different under anarchy compared to a situation in which the government supports property rights. To what income do people have a right? Beyond basic property rights all governments undertake a host of programs that affect incomes. The practical reality is that it is impossible to determine what a nonredistributive tax policy would be. This is also the response to those who argue that redistribution is politically divisive; this may be so, but there is no way for any government to wash its hands of the redistributive implications of its policies.

There is a long history to the argument that only the super-rich can and will support cultural activities. Bertrand de Jouvenel (1990, 42) laments that in the society that would result from radical redistribution, "the production of all first-quality goods would cease. . . . The production of artistic and intellectual goods would be affected first and foremost. Who could buy paintings? Who even could buy books other than pulp?" Clive Bell (1928, 175, 179) cites the historical association, arguing that "civilization requires the existence of a leisured class, and a leisure class requires the existence of slaves. . . . On inequality all civilizations have stood. The Athenians had their slaves: the class that gave Florence her culture was maintained by a voteless proletariat." Josiah Wedgwood (1939, 269) restates the argument disapprovingly: "The surplus income of society has never been sufficient to secure the refinements and culture of civilisation for all, that these would vanish if everybody had to earn their daily bread, and that it is better that a few should achieve a high level of civilisation than that all should remain in barbarism."

Accepting the importance of cultural activities to a community, the argument here rests on two empirical claims: that the marginal propensity to consume cultural activities is higher for the rich than for others, and that publicly funded cultural activities cannot provide the appropriate level of cultural activities. Econometric evidence casts doubt on the former claim, because the income elasticity of total giving is generally estimated to be positive, but less than 1; it may, however, be greater than 1 for particular kinds of giving, such as contributions to "high" culture. Note also that, because contributions are deductible for most high-income households, a redistribution to the rich effected by lowering marginal tax rates would, through a price effect, tend to reduce giving.

ECONOMIC ARGUMENTS
The Modern Theory of Optimal Progressivity

The approach of mainstream modern public finance economics to these issues has been to accept, for the sake of argument, the right of government to redistribute income through the tax system (and other means); to sidestep the ethical arguments about assessing the value of a more equal distribution of economic outcomes; and to instead investigate the implications of various value judgments for the design of the tax system. Front and center comes the fact that greater redistribution of income requires higher marginal tax rates, which may provide disincentives to work, save, take risks, and invest in human and physical capital. The essential problem, then, is to describe the inherent trade-offs between the distribution of income and economic performance.

James Mirrlees (1971) initiated the modern literature formalizing this trade-off. In his formulation, the government must choose an income tax schedule to raise a given amount of total revenue, with the goal of maximizing a utilitarian social welfare function. This function implicitly trades off the welfare of individuals at different income levels but assumes that social welfare increases when any member of society (including the richest) is better off, holding others' welfare constant. It therefore precludes envy as the basis of tax policy.[9] Mirrlees first investigated what characterizes the optimal income tax for any set of assumptions about the social welfare function, the distribution of endowments, and the behavioral response (utility) functions.[10] He concluded that in this general case only very weak conditions characterize the optimal tax structure, conditions that offer little concrete guidance in the construction of a tax schedule.

In the absence of general results, the approach has been to make specific assumptions about the key elements of the model and then to calculate the parameters of the optimal income tax system. The purpose of this approach is to suggest the characteristics of the optimal income tax under reasonable assumptions and to investigate how these characteristics depend on the elements of the model. Mirrlees also pioneered this approach in his 1971 article and concluded that the optimal tax structure is approximately linear (that is, it has a constant marginal tax rate and an exemption level below which tax liability is negative) and has marginal tax rates that were quite low by then-current standards, usually between 20 and 30 percent and almost always less than 40 percent.[11] This was a stunning and unexpected result—

even, it seems, to Mirrlees himself—and especially in an era when top rates of 70 percent or more were the norm.

Subsequent work investigated the sensitivity of the optimal income tax to the parametric assumptions. Mirrlees (1976) has shown that widening the distribution of skill, assumed equal to wage rates, increased the optimal marginal tax rates, though he considered the dispersion of skills necessary to imply much higher rates to be unrealistic.[12] Anthony Atkinson (1973) explores the effect of increasing the egalitarianism of the social welfare function. Even in the extreme case of John Rawls's (1971) "maximin" social welfare function, where social welfare is judged solely on the basis of how well off the worst-off class of people is, the model generated optimal tax rates not much higher than 50 percent. Finally, Nicholas Stern (1976) demonstrates that the key parameter is the degree of labor supply responsiveness; he argues that Mirrlees's assumption is excessive and thereby overstates the costs of increasing tax progressivity. This is true because the larger the responsiveness, the larger the social waste (in this case, people whose labor productivity exceeds their valuation of leisure, but who do not work) per dollar of revenue raised. Stern shows that when what he considers a more reasonable estimate of labor supply responsiveness is used, the value of the optimal tax rate exceeds 50 percent-approximately twice as high as what Mirrlees found.[13]

In sum, simple models of optimal income taxation do not necessarily point to sharply progressive tax structures, even if the objective function puts relatively large weight on the welfare of less well-off individuals. This conclusion does, however, depend critically on the sensitivity of labor supply to the after-tax wage rate; low elasticities, which imply a low marginal cost of redistributing income through the tax system, can imply highly progressive tax structures, so that lack of consensus about elasticities precludes consensus about optimal progressivity. One objective of the contributions to this volume is to sharpen our understanding of the elasticity of response to taxation among the rich.

There is one other—truly startling—result of this early literature. Jesus Seade (1977) and Efraim Sadka (1976) have proved that, under certain conditions, the marginal tax rate at the highest level of income should be precisely zero! This is true regardless of the form of the social welfare function, provided that the welfare of the most well-off individual carries some positive weight, and provided that there is a known upper bound to the income distribution. To see the intuition behind the result, first consider an income tax schedule in which the marginal rate applicable to the highest observed income is positive. Now consider a second tax schedule that is identical to the first except that it allows the highest-earning household to pay no taxes on any excess of income over what it would have earned under the first tax schedule. When faced with the second tax schedule, this household is certainly better off, works more hours, and pays no less tax than under the first schedule; all other households are at least as well off. In other words, raising the marginal tax at the top above zero distorts the labor supply decision of the highest earner but raises no revenue. All other households may be strictly better off compared to a high-tax-at-the-top regime if the top marginal tax rate is set to be just slightly positive and the increased revenue from the highest-earning household is used to allow a reduction in average tax rates in the lower brackets.

This result calls to mind Francis Edgeworth's (undated, 9) comment about Marshall's discovery of the Giffen good: "Only a very clever man would discover that exceptional case; only a very foolish man would take it as the basis of a rule for general practice." The result does not imply that marginal taxes should be zero or very low near the top, only precisely at the top. In fact, numerical calculations by Mirrlees (1976, 340) suggest that zero "is a bad approximation to the [optimal] marginal tax rate even within most of the top . . . percentiles."

Although I feel that this result should not be taken seriously as a practical guide to tax policy, it does provide some insight into the question of optimal tax progressivity. It highlights the possibility that a utilitarian social objective function, even one that places a large weight on the welfare of the poor, is not necessarily maximized through high marginal tax rates on the rich. This issue is difficult to explore in the post-Mirrlees numerical simulation tradition, which for simplicity assumes that the tax-and-transfer system must have a flat rate plus a fixed grant received by all household units, and which finds only the optimal setting of these two parameters. My colleagues and I (Slemrod, Yitzhaki, Mayshar, and Lundholm 1994) generalize the problem by allowing a two-bracket system. We find that, for most parameter assumptions, the optimal income tax structure features a top marginal rate that is indeed lower than the first marginal rate, even though, because of the grant, the average tax rate is generally increasing with income.[14]

This result is driven by two considerations. First, an increase in the marginal tax rate applying only to income above a cutoff generates less revenue than an across-the-board increase for a given (uncompensated) elasticity of response to the marginal rate. This happens because the increase in the top rate does not increase the tax raised on the inframarginal income up to the cutoff. Second, recall that tax increases reduce labor supply through a substitution effect (leisure is cheaper) but also probably increase labor supply through an income effect (worse-off people work more). For given income and substitution effects, a tax change that applies only to the top tax bracket produces a more negative supply elasticity than would an across-the-board change. This occurs because, compared to an across-the-board tax increase, the decline in income is lower, so that there will be less of a positive income effect on labor supply to offset the negative substitution effect.

These results have all been derived in the context of a very stylized model. In particular, in the standard formulation of the optimal progressivity problem, the rich are different from the poor in only one way: they are endowed with the ability to command a higher market wage rate, which is presumed to reflect a higher real productivity of their labor effort. In fact, there are a variety of other reasons why some people end up affluent and others do not, with vastly different policy implications.

The rich may have been lucky. The influential study of Christopher Jencks et al. (1972, 227) concludes that, in addition to on-the-job competence, economic success depends primarily on luck,[15] but that "those who are lucky tend, of course, to impute their success to skill, while those who are inept believe that they are merely unlucky."[16]

If there is income uncertainty that is uncorrelated across individuals and for which private insurance markets do not exist, then taxation becomes a form of social insurance; a more progressive system, by narrowing the dispersion in after-tax income, provides more social insurance than a less progressive tax system. The optimally progressive tax system then balances the gains from social insurance (and perhaps also redistribution) against the incentive costs. As Hal Varian (1980) points out, introducing luck eliminates the Sadka-Seade result about a marginal rate of zero at the top of the income distribution. He argues that, in the presence of substantial uncertainty or opportunities for the free play of luck, the optimal marginal tax rate should in all likelihood be high, because high realized income is probably the result of a good draw of the random component of income and taxing an event probably largely due to luck has minimal disincentive effects.

The rich may have different tastes, either for goods compared to leisure (working harder) or for future consumption. In the former case, even with homogenous wage rates, some people have higher incomes by virtue of working more, but the higher income is offset by less leisure time. In this case, a progressive tax system is not necessarily redistributing from the better-off to the worse-off, but capriciously according to tastes.

The rich may have inherited more, either in financial resources or in human capital broadly defined. If inherited endowment is the principal source of inequality (so that, inter alia, people do not differ in what they make of their endowments), from a one-generation perspective there is little potential economic cost from a tax system that redistributes the fruits of this endowment. A longer horizon is required, however, because the incentive of parents to leave an endowment would arguably be affected by such taxation and so could affect the incentive of potential bequeathers to work and to save.

The rich may have skills different from those of everyone else, rather than more of the same kind of skills. This characterization certainly rings true: the affluent tend to supply "skilled" rather than "unskilled" labor, that is, they tend to be entrepreneurs, professionals, or "symbolic analysts," in Robert Reich's (1991) terminology.

Why does this matter for optimal progressivity? For one thing, as Martin Feldstein (1973) first investigated, when there are two distinct types of labor, the relative wage rate depends on the relative supply to the market of the two kinds of labor, which in turn depends on the tax system chosen. Thus, the tax system redistributes income directly through differential tax liabilities but also indirectly by altering the wage structure. Although Feldstein argues that this does not substantially alter optimal progressivity, Franklin Allen (1982) disagrees, arguing that it could be important enough that an increase in the statutory progressivity of an income tax system could actually make members of the lower-ability, lower-income group worse off by reducing their before-tax wage rate.

But what if the affluent offer to the economy a particularly essential ingredient? George Gilder (1981, 245) certainly thinks so, arguing that "a successful economy depends on the proliferation of the rich, on creating a large class of risk-taking men [*sic*] who are willing to shun the easy channels of a comfortable life in order to create new enterprise." If entrepreneurial talent is priced appropriately by the market, then the standard optimal progressivity framework still applies: the extent to which taxes discourage its supply is a social cost. But there may be more to it than this if there are important spillovers of information from entrepreneurial activity whose social value cannot be captured by the entrepreneurs themselves. In economics jargon, there are positive externalities of innovation. These kinds of externalities are the building blocks of many "new growth" theories. Propounded by Paul Romer (1990) among others, such theories argue that policy can have persistent effects on economic growth rates, not just on the level of economic performance. Gilder (1981, 245) appears to believe this, asserting that "most successful entrepreneurs contribute far more to society than they ever recover, and most of them win no riches at all."

To the extent that the activities of the affluent have positive externalities because of their entrepreneurial nature, this argues for lower taxation at the top than otherwise. But the argument is not crystal clear. Although it is true that, compared to the overall population, a larger fraction of the rich classify themselves as professional or managerial (48.5 percent versus 27 percent in 1982, according to Slemrod [1996]), it is also true that a larger than average fraction (12 percent versus 1 percent) are lawyers and accountants, professions that some have argued are detrimental to economic growth, because they are concerned with rent-seeking rather than income creation. Stephen Magee, William Brock, and Leslie Young (1989) present evidence that countries with more lawyers grow more slowly.

Because appropriate policy depends on the process that determines how and why the affluent become affluent, one objective of economic research is to clarify that process. A second research objective, on which the chapters in this book concentrate, is to understand better how the affluent (and those who aspire to affluence) respond to attempts to tax away some of their affluence. In the context of the modern optimal progressivity model, it is precisely the behavioral response to taxation that limits the appropriateness of progressivity: other things equal, the greater the response, the less progressivity is appropriate.

Of course, measuring the behavioral response has dominated empirical tax research for at least two decades; there have been scores, probably even hundreds, of studies investigating the response to taxation of labor supply, savings, portfolio choice, business investment, and other aspects of individual and firm choices. However, very few of these studies have focused on the affluent, primarily because of the paucity of data that focus on this segment of the population.

There are, moreover, sensible reasons to suspect that the potential behavioral response of the affluent would be larger, and of a different nature, than that of everyone else, owing, for example, to their greater flexibility in work arrangements and the sophistication of the financial advice and options available to them. The popular conception that the affluent are able to manipulate the tax system to avoid much of its intended burden relies on this notion.

On the surface, there seems to be a conceptual distinction between the question of whether the rich *should* be taxed a lot and that of whether they *can* be taxed a lot. Similarly, there may seem to be some incompatibility between two classes of economic objections to taxing the rich—that there are negative economic consequences, and that it is infeasible. If the rich are able to to avoid paying the nominal taxes imposed on them, how could the deleterious effects be large? However, according to the modern public finance tradition, these pairs of questions are intimately linked because it is precisely the difficulty of taxing the rich—the "can" question—that circumscribes its appropriateness. It is all of the actions taken by the rich to reduce their tax burden—be it reducing work effort, reducing saving, hiring high-priced accountants, or chancing evasion—that raises the social cost per dollar of revenue actually collected. There is some controversy as to whether, for policy purposes, it matters what kind of behavioral response is predominant. I return to that issue in the concluding section. In what follows, I briefly review some evidence about the economic consequences of taxing the rich.

Aggregate Evidence

U.S. History   In highly influential work that stimulated much empirical investigation, Simon Kuznets (1955) argues that income inequality first increases, then decreases, with development. American economic historians have looked to the period of industrialization for evidence to shed light on the relationship between inequality and growth. Frederick Turner (1920) stresses high saving rates of the well-to-do and the dependence of sustained growth on either capital deepening or the introduction of a radically new generation of technologies and capital equipment. Opponents of this view have stressed that greater equality stimulates growth by encouraging the evolution of more extensive networks of markets, including that for labor, and commercialization in general, and that economic growth is not driven by the actions of a narrow elite but rather is the cumulative impact of incremental advances made by individuals throughout the economy. For example, Kenneth Sokoloff (1986) argues that advances in productivity during the early stages of industrialization were largely based on changes in organization, methods, and designs that did not require much in the way of capital deepening or dramatically new capital equipment. Rather, technological advances and productivity improvements seem to have been stimulated by the extension of markets.

As mentioned, one key aspect of this argument is that inappropriate tax policy can reduce the saving rate of the affluent. If a high level of national saving is the key to economic growth, and if the rich have a higher marginal propensity to save than the non-rich, then any redistribution of income from the rich to the poor hampers growth. If such redistribution is implemented in a way that reduces the after-tax return to saving, the negative impact is exacerbated to the extent that a lower return depresses saving.

Adam Smith maintained this connection, and it was central to growth models of the 1950s and 1960s, such as Arthur Lewis's (1954) and Nicholas Kaldor's (1956). Lewis maintains that the central problem during industrial revolutions was increasing the saving rate, and that one key source of increased savings was the rise in the profits share—that is, a shift in the distribution of income. However, the connection between income inequality and aggregate saving has been challenged on both empirical and theoretical grounds. Several studies find that redistribution from the poor to the rich has little impact on the aggregate saving rate. That is the conclusion of Alan Blinder (1980) on the postwar United States, of William Cline (1972) on Latin America, and of Philip Musgrove (1980) on international cross-sections. Although saving rates and growth increased concomitantly during the industrial revolutions of the United States and the United Kingdom, Jeffery Williamson

(1991) argues that these correlations are spurious and do not support the Smithian trade-off between equality and growth.

Moreover, in the context of a pure life-cycle model, there is no presumption that the marginal propensity to save differs across people with different lifetime incomes: because all individuals spend all of their income over their lifetime, higher saving rates in the saving years are offset by higher dissaving rates in the retirement years.[17] Savings differences arise, though, if the life-cycle model is enriched to include income-elastic bequests. This implies that, within a life-cycle framework, saving is increased not by redistribution across income groups but rather through redistribution to the young (savers) from the elderly (dissavers). There is, however, a clear positive correlation between income and age, at least within the set of working families, so that any increase in the progressivity of the tax system (measured annually) may on average effect a redistribution of income toward the young (savers), and for that reason would imply an increase in aggregate savings.

Cross-Country Evidence   A large, recent literature has examined the cross-country evidence on this question. There is substantial agreement that across countries more inequality is correlated with lower subsequent growth. There is less agreement, however, on the structural relationship between inequality and growth.

Roberto Perotti (1996) usefully classifies the theoretical underpinnings into four categories: the fiscal policy approach, in which inequality leads to redistributive, distortionary fiscal policy that reduces growth; the sociopolitical instability approach, in which inequality engenders sociopolitical instability, which reduces investment and growth; the borrowing constraints approach, in which inequality reduces investment in human capital among those with little wealth, thus reducing growth; and the joint education-fertility approach, in which inequality not only decreases investment in human capital among the nonwealthy but also increases fertility, both of which decrease per capita growth. Perotti's empirical investigation of the cross-country data finds support for all but the fiscal policy approach; Klaus Deininger and Lyn Squire (1998) agree, but Torsten Persson and Guido Tabellini (1994) argue that the postwar OECD data weakly support the fiscal policy approach.

This ongoing controversy is not directly relevant to the question at hand, because it concerns the link between *pre-tax* inequality and economic performance. We are not concerned with the political economy question of whether more inequality engenders a more redistributive tax and transfer policy, but instead on the economic consequences of such policies, whatever their origin. In the sociopolitical approach, presumably it is the extent of inequality in after-tax incomes that would create incentives for organized individuals to pursue their interests outside normal market activities or the usual political channels, so that this factor, ominously alluded to by Peter Drucker at the beginning of this chapter, still applies. The human capital approaches rely on spreading wealth more broadly, not specifically on which sections of society the redistributed wealth is taken from.

Of more relevance would be the link between economic performance and attempts by government to redistribute income by taxing the rich.[18] I am not aware of any cross-country study that examines this link. The evidence linking the level or rate of growth of prosperity to the overall level of taxes is, however, quite fragile.

As I argue in Slemrod (1995), there are inherent problems in attempting to separate out the effects of tax policy on prosperity and to determine the extent to which prosperity facilitates the collection of taxes.

Micro Evidence

Earlier Survey Evidence   There were several descriptive and analytical studies of the impact of taxes on the behavior of the rich in an earlier generation. One particularly influential study (Barlow, Brazer, and Morgan 1966) was the result of an extensive field study, conducted in 1964 by the University of Michigan Survey Research Center, of 957 individuals who had yearly incomes in 1961 of $10,000 or more. Of the respondents, 69 percent (48 percent if income-weighted) had 1961 incomes between $10,000 and $15,000, and less than 0.5 percent (6 percent if income-weighted) had incomes over $100,000. Correspondingly, 77 percent of the sample (60 percent if income-weighted) faced marginal tax rates of 39 percent or less, and only 6 percent (17 percent if income-weighted) faced a marginal tax rate over 50 percent.

This study found that the tax system had little impact on economic decisions. Only one-eighth of the sample said they had curtailed their work effort because of the income tax, and those facing the highest marginal tax rates reported work disincentives only a little more frequently than did those facing the lowest rates. Very few reported that their wives' participation in the labor force or the timing of retirement was affected by taxes. Sensitivity to taxes appeared widespread in two investment situations: when income could be received in the form of capital gains, there was a noticeable "lock-in" effect on gains and a tax-related tendency to realize losses; and when it was possible to transfer assets to relatives and reduce one's tax liabilities by so doing, the timing of large gifts to children and other relatives appeared to be dominated by tax considerations. Between one-fourth and one-third of the respondents were definitely unaware of their marginal tax rates; furthermore, the awareness of preferential tax treatment and the inclination to take advantage of it appeared to be confined to a small minority, with the exception of the tax advantages of capital gains.

Modern Economic Evidence   Today economists tend to devalue this type of evidence, preferring to analyze data on actual behavior rather than rely on people's stated intentions and motivations. There is a large literature on many of the critical aspects of behavior—labor supply, saving, entrepreneurship—although little of it focuses on, or even treats, the behavior of the affluent. I do not have space here to review all that has been learned in these fields. Taken together, the chapters in this volume review much of the relevant literature. Alan Auerbach and I (Auerbach and Slemrod 1997) discuss what evidence was unearthed by the Tax Reform Act of 1986 (TRA86). We argue that the evidence from TRA86 is consistent with the notion of a hierarchy of behavioral responses to taxation, as suggested in Slemrod (1992a, 1996). At the top of the hierarchy—the most clearly responsive to tax incentives— is the timing of economic transactions. The pattern of capital gains realizations before and after TRA86 is the best example, but there are many others. Foreign direct investment into the United States climbed to $16.3 billion in the fourth quarter of 1986, more than double the rate of adjacent quarters, as investors raced to beat the expiration of tax rules favoring mergers and acquisitions. In these and other instances, for many people the opportunity to achieve temporarily available tax savings obviously dominated the cost of accelerating transactions.

In the second tier of the hierarchy are financial and accounting responses. There is substantial evidence of the reshuffling of individuals' portfolios and repackaging of firms' financial claims in response to the tax cuts of 1981 and TRA86, and clear evidence (discussed in Gordon and MacKie-Mason 1990) of a post-TRA86 shift of small and medium-sized businesses out of C corporation status into S corporation status. There are many other examples, such as the speed with which individuals changed the form of much of their debt away from newly nondeductible personal loans after TRA86 and into still-deductible mortgage debt.

At the bottom of the hierarchy is the response of the real activities chosen by individuals or firms. On this issue, the evidence is mixed. The aggregate values of labor supply and saving apparently responded very little, but it is not clear whether this reflects a low elasticity of substitution or the fact that TRA86 did not in fact effect a large change in the relevant relative prices. Furthermore, for some aspects of real behavior, such as multifamily housing starts and investment in equipment, TRA86 apparently did generate a significant response.

The striking response of the set of behaviors that might be characterized as avoidance—in that they do not involve individuals altering their consumption bundle or firms altering their inputs or outputs—suggests a need to pay more attention to these aspects in the future. A pervasive issue is the difficulty of disentangling the real response from the financial, accounting, and timing responses that accompany it. In most of the simple theoretical models of taxation that underlie empirical investigation, only a real response is possible. For example, in models of labor supply the choice facing the consumer is between (possibly dated) leisure and consumption; alternative methods of avoidance and increased noncompliance thus are not allowed as possible responses to higher marginal tax rates. In these cases and others, the statutory tax rate is not a reliable measure of how the tax system affects the opportunities of individuals and firms, and the true budget set reflects not only the apparent relative prices that would prevail in the absence of avoidance but also how real behavior facilitates avoidance and vice versa. A first step toward a generalized model of behavioral response, in which individuals choose both their real consumption activity and avoidance expenditures, is taken in Slemrod (forthcoming).

What difference to policy is made by how (as opposed to how much) the rich respond to taxation? If, for example, the hypothetical revenue gain from a tax increase assuming no behavioral response were reduced by $1 billion owing to such a response, does it matter whether the response is in the form of reduced labor supply, intensified use of accountants, or increased evasion?

Martin Feldstein (1999) has argued that, for the purpose of calculating the marginal efficiency cost of taxation—a critical parameter for optimal progressivity as well as the size of government—all one needs to know is the elasticity of taxable income; the origin of that elasticity is irrelevant. However, because Feldstein derives this conclusion in a model that allows real substitution response but neither avoidance nor evasion, the question remains whether knowing taxable income elasticity is sufficient.

Joel Slemrod and Shlomo Yitzhaki (1996, 1999) demonstrate that Feldstein's assertion does generalize to a world with avoidance and evasion, but subject to several provisos. One is that taxable income needs to be defined comprehensively so as to take account of shifts across tax bases and time periods. For example, there is evidence that the lowering of the top personal rate below the top corporation income tax rate by the TRA86 induced many small corporations to reorganize as S corporations, which are not subject to the entity-level corporation income tax; with the corporation so classified, the shareholders' income is subject to personal tax as accrued, in the same way a partnership is taxed. To the extent this occurred, some of the post-TRA86 increase in individual taxable income and revenue was offset by a decline in corporate income tax revenue. Furthermore, the tax base must be defined in present value terms. If taxable income is realized at a different time because of a tax change, the revenue of other periods cannot be disregarded. For example, the taxable income response to an anticipated future decrease in tax rates must consider the lost revenue in the period before the tax rate change. Similarly, if a tax change causes an increase in deferred compensation, the increased future tax liability (discounted) must be netted against any decline in current tax payments.

Second, this conclusion applies only when the cost borne by taxpayers in the process of reducing tax liability is also a social cost. This presumption is reasonable in many situations, such as when the private cost takes the form of a distorted consumption basket. But in some cases, the private cost is not identical to the social cost. A straightforward example occurs when the action of the taxpayer causes some externality.

Fines (but not imprisonment) for tax evasion bring up a more subtle example of the potential divergence between the private and social costs of tax-reducing activities. The possibility of a fine for detected tax evasion is certainly viewed as a cost by the taxpayer, but from society's point of view it is merely a transfer.

Third, the conclusion presumes that the rich and the poor are linked only through the collection and redistribution of tax revenue. The salience of positive externality arguments certainly depend on the nature of the behavioral response. If, for example, the rich supply entrepreneurial services that have spillover effects, a tax increase that increases avoidance but not effort will be better than one that inhibits effort.

Finally, although labor supply or savings elasticities are presumably ineluctable aspects of people's preferences, avoidance and evasion elasticities depend critically on the institutional details of tax law enforcement. If, for example, enforcement instruments are set suboptimally, so that the marginal cost of raising revenue is higher than it need be, the optimal tax rate appears lower than if the enforcement parameters are set optimally: the optimal progressivity can be properly assessed only simultaneously with the instruments the government uses to control avoidance and evasion.[19]

DOES ATLAS SHRUG?

How much and how to tax high-income individuals are questions at the core of many recent proposals for incremental as well as fundamental tax reform. The right answers depend in part on value judgments to which economic analysis has little to contribute, but it also depends on standard economic concerns, such as the process that generates income, and on whether high-income individuals' efforts generate positive externalities. How much and how to tax the rich also depends critically on how they will respond to attempts to tax them because, other things equal, it is wise to limit the extent to which they are induced to pursue less socially productive activities in order to avoid taxes. We can be sure that most of the rich, like most everyone else, entertain ways to rearrange their affairs to reduce their taxes. Some Atlases do shrug, depending on the burden they are asked to bear. The real questions are, alas, less literary than the ones Ayn Rand considered forty years ago: How much does Atlas shrug, under what circumstances, and how much is too much to ask?

The remaining chapters of this book address these questions. The core of the book, in part II, consists of original research on how the rich react to alternative tax systems, and part III offers some new perspectives on how to think about that issue. Part I provides some context for these studies. First, W. Elliot Brownlee paints a vivid historical study of how U.S. tax policy toward the rich has unfolded since the founding of the republic. His chapter is devoted largely to understanding the ideals of the American architects of tax policy, and how those architects have acted on their ideals, balancing expectations of republican virtue with a desire to achieve a wide range of social goals, only one of which was the advancement of capitalism. Brownlee also reflects in his chapter on the reactions of the rich to progressive policies that have singled them out for heavy taxation. He argues that in the interwar period, when progressive assaults were most ambitious and threatening, the rich generally reacted, not by shrugging and going "on strike," as Ayn Rand proposed, but rather by staying in both the economic and political marketplaces and struggling to turn back the assaults. By the late 1940s, concludes Brownlee, they had largely succeeded in removing the redistributional fangs from the movement for progressive taxation.

Brownlee's account brings us right up to the present. The rate structure of the federal personal income tax is graduated, with a top rate now of 39.6 percent. The top rate was 70 percent as recently as 1980, fell to 28 percent by 1988, and has since crept back up. But the nominal rate structure is only one aspect of the tax structure. Equally important is how the tax base is defined. For example, capital gains are taxed at a preferential rate, are taxed only on realization (usually the sale of the asset), and are excused on the death of the owner.

The principal motivation for levying particularly high rates of tax on the affluent—achieving a just sharing of the tax burden—cannot be evaluated independently of the pattern of distribution of pre-tax income and wealth. In his chapter, Edward N. Wolff offers a demographic portrait of the rich in 1983 and 1992, focusing on the changes in the portrait over that decade. As mentioned earlier, he first notes that the late-twentieth-century United States is marked by an extreme concentration of wealth: in 1992 the richest 1 percent of households owned 35.9 percent of total wealth, up from 32.6 percent in 1983. In 1992 the top 20 percent owned 84 percent of wealth. Moreover, the inequality of income rose even more substantially than wealth over this period. The share of total income received by the top 1 percent of income earners increased from 12.8 percent in 1983 to 15.7 percent in 1992, a truly remarkable rise. More recent data suggest that the concentration has continued to increase in the mid-1990s. Clearly, the rich are getting richer, not only in absolute terms but also compared to everyone else. They are not a static bunch, however. One would expect a certain amount of movement into and out of the ranks of the rich, defined, for example, by those in the top 1 percent of the wealth distribution. But Wolff shows that there were systematic differences in demographic makeup in 1992 compared to 1983. There was, for instance, a notable increase in the number of young families—the fraction of household heads under forty-five rose from 10 to 15 percent. Strikingly, the labor earnings (including wages, salary, and self-employment income) of the top wealth percentile jumped from 51 to 69 percent over this period. There was also a huge increase in the number of self-employed people among the rich, and a corresponding decline in the number of salaried managers and professionals. Property income of all forms declined sharply, from 46 to 27 percent of the total income of the top wealth percentile and from 36 to 30 percent of the top income percentile.

In his chapter, Douglas A. Shackelford characterizes the complicated tax environment facing the wealthy and the reality of substantial avoidance opportunities. He notes that the tax environment is a complex composite of income and transfer incentives that vary with the source and use of wealth. Without tax planning, many wealthy individuals would face very heavy tax burdens; in the most tax-disadvantaged conditions he analyzes, there would be no difference when bequeathing the wealth derived from labor income to one's children between a single wage tax of 91 percent (!) and the current tax system. However, tax planners have responded to this situation with a variety of products that successfully mitigate income and transfer-tax payments. These plans include a diverse set of transactions (for example, shorting against the box and like-kind exchanges), products (such as derivatives and life insurance) and organizational structures (for example, family partnerships and investment companies). Customized to individual needs and circumstances, the plans are capable of lowering the actual marginal tax rates faced by wealthy individuals enough that marginal rates approaching zero are not implausible. In this way, wealthy individuals exchange large tax levies for smaller avoidance fees. Clearly, any serious student of the tax system needs to go beyond the statutory provisions and carefully consider the available avoidance opportunities.

This, then, is the context. But it is only context, because the critical trade-offs in tax policy are concerned with the consequences of attempting to tax the rich, and the consequences hinge on how the rich respond to the attempt. The chapters of part II all represent state-of-the-art economic research about various aspects of this question. No one study can draw conclusions about the tax system's entire range of effects, but each study can shed light on some important aspects of the question.

Of all the potential margins of behavioral response, labor supply is perhaps the most important. If high taxes encourage people to work fewer hours, devote less effort to work, or invest less in themselves, this is worrisome. If the tax system has this effect on the most talented members of society (who are not necessarily, as noted earlier, the same as the most affluent), it is particularly worrisome. In their chapter, Robert A. Moffitt and Mark Wilhelm investigate the impact of taxation on the labor supply of the affluent. To do so, they focus on the Tax Reform Act of 1986, which reduced marginal tax rates for the affluent more than for other taxpayers. If labor supply is responsive to tax rates, one would expect that the labor supply of the affluent would increase more for the affluent than for others. To examine this idea, they study data from the 1983 and 1989 Survey of Consumer Finances, which brackets the 1986 tax reform. Using instrumental-variables methods with a variety of identifying variables, Moffitt and Wilhelm find essentially no responsiveness of the hours of work of high-income men to the tax reduction. They do find, however, that hourly wage rates of such men increased over this period, and that the total reported income of these households increased at a much higher rate.

The Moffitt-Wilhelm findings are consistent with a scenario in which, although the responsiveness of male labor supply to tax rates is small, the response of the other behaviors reflected in taxable income is not small. This is consistent with an influential literature, discussed earlier, in which it is claimed that the elasticity of taxable income with respect to the net-of-tax share is very high, possibly exceeding 1. To quantify this elasticity, the studies of this genre have conducted "natural experiments" comparing the behavior of the rich to that of other income groups, assuming that they are the same except for changes in their tax rates. (The Moffitt-Wilhelm study is an example of this genre, although its econometric specification is the sine qua non of the field.)

The chapter by Austan Goolsbee tests the natural experiment assumption using data on the compensation of several thousand corporate executives. He concludes that it is clearly false, for three reasons. First, the very rich have incomes that recently have been trending upward at a faster rate than others' incomes; thus, natural experiments conducted over periods in which the relative tax rates of the rich are declining confound the secular trend with the effect of taxes themselves. Second, the rich are much more sensitive to demand conditions than are others; surging income in good times that also feature tax cuts may thus be misinterpreted as an indication of behavioral response when it is not. Finally, the compensation of the rich is much more likely to be in a form whose timing can be shifted in the short run. As a result, observed changes in taxable income that occur around anticipated tax changes may reflect retiming of taxable income rather than a behavioral response that will persist. Goolsbee estimates that taking account of these three factors may reduce previously estimated elasticities by 75 percent or more.

Although Goolsbee's chapter suggests that caution is in order in making conclusions about behavioral response elasticities from time-series data, other chapters in the book investigate margins of response that do seem to be responsive to tax rates. The chapter by Gerald E. Auten, Charles T. Clotfelter, and Richard L. Schmalbeck investigates the tax effect on charitable giving by the wealthy. They conclude that the current tax system does stimulate some charitable giving, compared to a system in which contributions are not deductible from either the income or estate tax. However, their analysis suggests that the sensitivity of giving to tax changes perceived to be permanent is somewhat smaller than previous researchers had concluded. They also argue that as a result of high tax rates and serpentine provisions, the wealthy engage in much more elaborate arrangements associated with their charitable donations, at the cost of valuable human resources.

The chapter by Alan J. Auerbach, Leonard E. Burman, and Jonathan M. Siegel provides new evidence on the effect of capital gains taxation on the financial behavior of the wealthy. They focus on the question of whether high-income people can shelter all or most of their capital gains with the judicious realization of capital losses. They conclude that such avoidance is not prevalent, although it increased after 1986, so that most high-income people realize gains that are not sheltered by losses. Their findings dispel two contentions about the fairness of capital gains taxation: that high-income people can avoid the tax at will, subverting the slight progressivity designed into long-term capital gains tax rates; and that the loss limitation is especially unfair to lower-income taxpayers with only a single asset who therefore never are able to deduct fully a catastrophic loss against other gains or income.

The chapter by Roger H. Gordon and myself investigates whether the large recent increase in reported individual income by the most affluent taxpayers is partly due to a tax-induced shift from the corporate tax base to the individual base caused by the narrowing of the differential in the corporate and individual rates. Under this hypothesis, a decrease in personal tax rates should result in a decrease in reported corporate income as well as a rise in reported personal income. The Gordon-Slemrod chapter focuses on one particular avenue of income shifting—where compensation of labor is reported and therefore taxed. Our analysis leads us to conclude that substantial shifting of this kind has in fact occurred, and that this phenomenon is a part of the story of increased reported personal income and declining taxable reported corporate profits over the last decade or two.

The chapter by James Poterba explores the effect of estate and gift taxes on the rate of return earned by savers. He argues that the estate tax can be viewed as a tax on capital income, with the effective tax rate depending on the statutory tax rate as well as the potential taxpayer's mortality risk. Because mortality rates rise with age, the effective estate tax burden is therefore greater for older than for younger individuals. Poterba calculates that the estate tax adds approximately 0.3 percentage points to the average burden on capital income for households headed by individuals between the ages of fifty and fifty-nine. However, for households headed by someone between the ages of seventy and seventy-nine, the estate tax increases the tax burden on capital income by approximately three percentage points. The chapter also concludes that actual levels of inter vivos giving are much lower than one would expect if households were taking full advantage of this estate tax avoidance technique.

The chapter by Andrew A. Samwick looks at another aspect of behavior potentially distorted by the tax system—portfolio choice. Samwick makes use of comprehensive wealth data from recent Surveys of Consumer Finances to analyze the effects of tax changes on the portfolio holdings of households, particularly those at the top of the wealth distribution. He concludes that although marginal tax rates do explain some of the cross-sectional differences in portfolio allocations, the role of tax changes is more limited in determining observed changes over time in household portfolios relative to the market portfolio. Evidence on the changes in portfolio allocations by marginal tax rate also fails to support an important time-series role for marginal tax rates. Samwick concludes that the responsiveness of the portfolios of the rich to taxation appears to be limited, perhaps because of the systematic risk that makes it worthwhile for the rich to hold a portfolio that is not optimal based on tax considerations alone.

Rather than focusing on one aspect of behavior, the chapter by James Alm and Sally Wallace examines a wide range of taxpayer reporting decisions over the past decade by households in the top percentile of the distribution of income. They conclude that not only do the rich respond to tax changes, but that they differ from the average population in how they respond. They suggest that that these differential responses are due largely to the greater control and flexibility of the rich in overall financial matters, especially in the form of their compensation. This finding is consistent with the Gordon-Slemrod conclusion that the affluent exploit through income shifting differences in how a given stream of income is taxed.

The critical role of the entrepreneur in economic growth is widely accepted. To what extent does the tax system discourage and divert individuals away from entrepreneurial activities? The chapter by Robert Carroll, Douglas Holtz-Eakin, Mark Rider, and Harvey S. Rosen studies one aspect of this question: how the income tax influences entrepreneurs' capital investment decisions. Their research examines the income tax returns of a sample of sole proprietors before and after the Tax Reform Act of 1986 in order to determine how the substantial reductions in marginal tax rates for the relatively affluent associated with that law affected their decisions to invest in physical capital. They find that individual income taxes had a large negative effect, implying that a five-percentage point increase in marginal tax rates would reduce the proportion of entrepreneurs who make capital investment and mean investment expenditures by approximately 10 percent. In their words, these particular Atlases do indeed shrug.

Taken as a whole, however, the evidence of part II is more mixed on the question of how, and how much, today's Atlases shrug. In the face of substantial tax rates (ignoring, for the moment, avoidance opportunities), the rich appear not to alter significantly either their supply of labor or their portfolios. They do seem to be induced to be more charitable than they otherwise would be, and the investment decisions of the sole proprietors among them seem to be sensitive to tax rates. In terms of financial or accounting responses, the evidence is also somewhat mixed. Techniques to avoid capital gains taxes do not seem to be fully utilized and inter vivos gifts to minimize estate taxes are not widely used, although differential taxes levied on individuals and corporations do appear to generate shifts of taxable income between those tax bases. The timing of certain taxable activities, such as the receipt of executive compensation, is highly sensitive to anticipated tax changes, corroborating a large literature on this topic. All in all, these studies do not suggest anything like the complete withdrawal of productive energies that Ayn Rand warned of. Nevertheless, the tax system clearly induces people to rearrange their affairs and change their behavior, and these changes are evidence of an unseen but real cost of levying taxes.

For the most part, modern economics is predicated on the belief that economic data can be made sense of only in the context of a model. The empirical research presented in part II all rests on the standard economic model of individuals who value consumption of goods and services over their lifetime and perhaps also the consumption and happiness of their families and favored charities. The two chapters of part III challenge the standard model and offer two alternatives.

The chapter by Christopher Carroll argues that the saving behavior of the richest households, in particular the fact that households with higher levels of lifetime income have higher lifetime saving rates, cannot be explained by models in which the only purpose of wealth accumulation is to finance future consumption, either their own or that of their heirs. The simplest model that explains the relevant facts, he proposes, is one in which consumers regard the accumulation of wealth as an end in itself, or one in which unspent wealth yields a flow of services, such as power or social status.

The book closes with a plea for an even more radical recasting of the underlying model of economic decision-making. Robert H. Frank argues that individuals' well-being depends not only on their (and possibly their heirs') leisure and level of consumption but also on their consumption *relative* to that of others. This gives rise to "positional externalities," under which an increase in one's own consumption reduces the satisfaction of others whose consumption ranking declines. In this context, the effect of a tax on wages is, as in conventional models, to lower the reward for selling leisure. In conventional models this introduces a distortion, but in Frank's model it mitigates an existing distortion. Moreover, he argues that virtually all top-decile earners in the United States are participants in labor markets in which rewards are heavily based on relative performance. In such markets income taxation can improve efficiency because it reduces overcrowding in the market in which reward depends on rank. One implication of these models is that there may not be a trade-off between equity and efficiency, and the same tax policies that promote equity may also promote efficiency.

Frank's argument is intriguing but has yet to displace the predominant view among economists that there is indeed a trade-off between the equity and economic cost of a tax system. To make that trade-off wisely, one should be informed about its terms. This requires more of the kind of careful research that follows.

I am grateful for comments on an earlier draft from Paul Courant, Julie Cullen, Bill Gale, Roger Gordon, Ned Gramlich, and Jim Hines.

NOTES

1. While Rand was writing the novel, the working title was "The Strike." *Atlas Shrugged* did not become the title until 1956, at the suggestion of Rand's husband.

2. This calculation assumes that 1997 CPI-U will be 160, or 5.67 times higher than its value in 1957.

3. For a married couple, age is defined as that of the "primary" taxpayer, that is, the one listed first on the tax form.

4. These figures are based on tabulations of the tax database of the Office of Tax Analysis, U.S. Treasury Department. I am grateful to Gerald Auten for providing them to me.

5. This claim that the concentration of wealth increased substantially between 1983 and 1992 is controversial. See John Weicher (1996), who argues that the distribution of wealth in 1992 was about the same as in 1983 and, in fact, the same as in 1962.

6. Note that high-wealth families tend to be older and thus more likely to be in their declining saving years.

7. Characterizing the focus of this volume as "the rich" is certainly provocative; consider the difference in emphasis if the subtitle were "The Economic Consequences of Taxing the Talented," or,

"The Economic Consequences of Taxing the Successful." From another perspective, one colleague of mine offered that the title of the conference should have been "Does Atlas Shirk?" instead of "Does Atlas Shrug?"

8. The Treasury's average tax rates are lower than the CBO's mainly because their methodology adopts a broader definition of income as the denominator in calculating the average tax rate.

9. Martin Feldstein (1976) offers an excellent review of these issues.

10. Because a tax schedule may feature rebates rather than taxes at some levels of income, it is really the optimal tax-and-transfer system that is at issue in the optimal progressivity literature.

11. Note that, although the marginal tax rate is approximately constant, the average tax rate (tax liability divided by income) increases with income owing to the presence of the positive exemption level. Mirrlees (1971) assumed that the government needed to raise 20 percent of national income in taxes.

12. This conclusion is extremely relevant to current policy issues, debated in the midst of near-unanimous agreement that the distribution of pre-tax earnings has been widening at least since 1970.

13. The revenue requirement in this example was about 20 percent of net output.

14. Peter Diamond (1998), however, shows that certain combinations of assumptions about the utility function and distribution of skills can generate a U-shaped pattern of optimal marginal tax rates.

15. The authors of this study admit, however, that their conclusions do not apply to the "very rich," defined as those with assets exceeding $10 million (1972 dollars).

16. Lester Thurow (1975) offers a similar view.

17. With a growing population, positive saving rates occur because there are always more young savers than older dissavers. Thus, if the rich accumulate and de-accumulate wealth more rapidly than the non-rich, they would contribute to a higher aggregate saving rate.

18. This is one part of the fiscal approach linking pre-tax inequality to reduced growth.

19. I have constructed an example (Slemrod 1994) in which, at given suboptimal settings of the enforcement parameter, it is optimal to reduce that progressivity, while the true global optimum features more enforcement and more progressivity.

REFERENCES

Allen, Franklin. 1982. "Optimal Linear Income Taxation with General Equilibrium Effects on Wages." *Journal of Public Economics* 17: 135–43.

Atkinson, Anthony B. 1973. "How Progressive Should Income Tax Be?" In *Essays in Modern Economics*, edited by Michael Parkin and Arelino Romeo Nobay. London: Longman.

Auerbach, Alan J., and Joel Slemrod. 1997. "The Economic Effects of the Tax Reform Act of 1986." *Journal of Economic Literature* 35: 589–632.

Avery, Robert, and Arthur Kennickell. 1991. "Household Saving in the United States." *Review of Income and Wealth* 37(4): 409–32.

Barlow, Robin, Harvey E. Brazer, and James N. Morgan. 1966. *Economic Behavior of the Affluent*. Washington, D.C.: Brookings Institution.

Bell, Clive. 1928. *Civilization*. New York: Harcourt, Brace.

Blinder, Alan S. 1980. "The Level and Distribution of Economic Well-being." In *The American Economy in Transition*, edited by Martin Feldstein. Chicago: University of Chicago Press.

Christian, Charles W. 1994. "Voluntary Compliance with the Individual Income Tax: Results from the 1988 TCMP Study." *IRS Research Bulletin* (1993–94), publication 1500. Washington, D.C.: Internal Revenue Service.

Cline, William R. 1972. *Potential Effects of Income Distribution on Economic Growth: Latin American Cases*. New York: Praeger.

Congressional Budget Office. 1994. "An Economic Analysis of the Provisions of OBRA-93." Working paper. Washington, D.C.: Congressional Budget Office.

Cutler, David M., and Lawrence F. Katz. 1992. "Rising Inequality?: Changes in the Distribution of Income and Consumption in the 1980s." *American Economic Review* 82(2): 946–51.

Deininger, Klaus, and Lyn Squire. 1998. "New Ways of Looking at Old Issues: Inequality and Growth." *Journal of Development Economics* 57: 259–87.

De Jouvenel, Bertrand. 1990. *The Ethics of Redistribution*. Indianapolis: Liberty Press.

Diamond, Peter. 1998. "Optimal Income Taxation: An Example with a U-Shaped Pattern of Optimal Marginal Tax Rates." *American Economic Review* 88: 83–95.

Edgeworth, Francis Y. Undated. *On the Relations of Political Economy to War*. London: Oxford University Press.

Feldstein, Martin. 1973. "On the Optimal Progressivity of the Income Tax." *Journal of Public Economics* 2: 357–76.

———. 1976. "On the Theory of Tax Reform." *Journal of Public Economics* 6: 7–64.

———. 1999. "Tax Avoidance and the Deadweight Loss of the Income Tax." *Review of Economics and Statistics*, forthcoming.

Gallup, George Jr., and Frank Newport. 1990. "Americans Widely Disagree on What Constitutes 'Rich.'" *Gallup Poll Monthly* (July): 28–36.

Gilder, George. 1981. *Wealth and Poverty*. New York: Basic Books.

Gordon, Roger, and Jeffrey MacKie-Mason. 1990. "Effects of the Tax Reform Act of 1986 on Corporate Financial Policy and Organizational Form." In *Do Taxes Matter?: The Impact of the Tax Reform Act of 1986*, edited by Joel Slemrod. Cambridge, Mass.: MIT Press.

Gramlich, Edward M., Richard Kasten, and Frank Sammartino. 1993. "Growing Inequality in the 1980s: The Role of Federal Taxes and Cash Transfers." In *Uneven Tides: Rising Inequality in America*, edited by Sheldon Danziger and Peter Gottschalk. New York: Russell Sage Foundation.

Hayek, Friedrich A. 1960. *The Constitution of Liberty*. Chicago: University of Chicago Press.

Jencks, Christopher, with Marshall Smith, Henry Aulands, Mary Jo Bane, David Cohen, Herbert Gintis, Barbara Heyns, and Stephan Michelson. 1972. *Inequality: A Reassessment of the Effect of Family and Schooling in America*. New York: Basic Books.

Kaldor, Nicholas. 1956. "Alternative Theories of Distribution." *Review of Economic Studies* 23: 83–100.

Kolko, Gabriel. 1962. *Wealth and Power in America*. New York: Praeger.

Kuznets, Simon. 1955. "Economic Growth and Income Inequality." *American Economic Review* 45: 1–28.

Lenzner, Robert, and Stephen S. Johnson. 1997. "Seeing Things as They Really Are." *Forbes*, March 10: 122–28.

Lewis, W. Arthur. 1954. "Economic Development with Unlimited Supplies of Labour." *Manchester School* 22: 139–91.

Magee, Stephen P., William A. Brock, and Leslie Young. 1989. *Black Hole Tariffs and the Endogenous Policy Theory*. Cambridge: Cambridge University Press.

Mirrlees, James A. 1971. "An Exploration in the Theory of Optimum Income Taxation." *Review of Economic Studies* 38: 175–208.

———. 1976. "Optimal Tax Theory: A Synthesis." *Journal of Public Economics* 6: 327–58.

Musgrove, Philip. 1980. "Income Distribution and the Aggregate Consumption Function." *Journal of Political Economy* 88: 504–25.

Nozick, Robert. 1974. *Anarchy, State, and Utopia*. New York: Basic Books.

Nunns, James R. 1995. "Distributional Analysis at the Office of Tax Analysis." In *Distributional Analysis of Tax Policy*, edited by David F. Bradford. Washington, D.C.: AEI Press.

Perotti, Roberto. 1996. "Growth, Income Distribution, and Democracy: What the Data Say." *Journal of Economic Growth* 1: 149–87.

Persson, Torsten, and Guido Tabellini. 1994. "Is Inequality Harmful for Growth?" *American Economic Review* 84(3): 600–21.

Rand, Ayn. 1957. *Atlas Shrugged*. New York: Random House.

Rawls, John. 1971. *A Theory of Justice*. Cambridge, Mass.: Harvard University Press.

Reich, Robert B. 1991. *The Work of Nations: Preparing Ourselves for Twenty-first-Century Capitalism*. New York: Alfred A. Knopf.

Romer, Paul. 1990. "Capital, Labor, and Productivity." *Brookings Papers on Economic Activity* (special issue): 337–420.

Sadka, Efraim. 1976. "On Income Distribution, Incentive Effects, and Optimal Income Taxation." *Review of Economic Studies* 43(June): 261–68.

Seade, Jesus. 1977. "On the Shape of Optimal Tax Schedules." *Journal of Public Economics* 7: 203–36.

Simons, Henry. 1938. *Personal Income Taxation*. Chicago: University of Chicago Press.

Slemrod, Joel. 1990. "Optimal Taxation and Optimal Tax Systems." *Journal of Economic Perspectives* 4: 157–78.

———. 1992a. "Do Taxes Matter?: Lessons from the 1980s." *American Economic Review* 83(2): 250–56.

———. 1992b. "Taxation and Inequality: A Time-Exposure Perspective." In *Tax Policy and the Economy*, edited by James M. Poterba, vol. 6. Cambridge, Mass.: MIT Press.

———. 1994. "Fixing the Leak in Okun's Bucket: Optimal Tax Progressivity When Avoidance Can Be Controlled." *Journal of Public Economics* 51: 41–51.

———. 1995. "What Do Cross-Country Studies Teach About Government Involvement, Prosperity, and Economic Growth?" *Brookings Papers on Economic Activity* 2: 373–431.

———. 1996. "High-Income Families and the Tax Changes of the 1980s: The Anatomy of Behavioral Response." In *Empirical Foundations of Household Taxation*, edited by Martin Feldstein and James Poterba. Chicago: University of Chicago Press and National Bureau of Economic Research.

Slemrod, Joel, and Shlomo Yitzhaki. 1999. "Tax Avoidance, Evasion, and Administration." Unpublished paper. University of Michigan, Ann Arbor.

———. 1996. "The Cost of Taxation and the Marginal Efficiency Cost of Funds." *International Monetary Fund Staff Papers* 43(1): 172–98.

———. Forthcoming. "A General Model of the Behavioral Response to Taxation." *International Tax and Public Finance*.

Slemrod, Joel, Shlomo Yitzhaki, Joram Mayshar, and Michael Lundholm. 1994. "The Optimal Two-Bracket Linear Income Tax." *Journal of Public Economics* 53: 269–90.

Sokoloff, Kenneth. 1986. "Productivity Growth in Manufacturing During Early Industrialization: Evidence from the American Northwest, 1820 to 1860." In *Long-term Factors in American Economic Growth*, edited by Stanley Engerman and Robert E. Gallman. Chicago: University of Chicago Press.

Stern, Nicholas H. 1976. "On the Specification of Models of Optimum Income Taxation." *Journal of Public Economics* 6: 123–62.

Tax Foundation. 1996. "Latest Data Shows Trend Reversal: Top 1 Percent Not Paying Larger Share of Federal Income Taxes." *Tax Features*, 40(8): 1–2.

Thurow, Lester. 1975. *Generating Inequality*. New York: Basic Books.

Turner, Frederick J. 1920. *The Frontier in American History*. New York: Henry Holt & Co.

U.S. Treasury Department, Office of Tax Analysis. 1996. "'New' Armey-Shelby Flat Tax Would Lose Money, Treasury Finds." *Tax Notes*, January 22: 451–61.

Varian, Hal. 1980. "Redistributive Taxation as Social Insurance." *Journal of Public Economics* 14: 49–68.

Wedgwood, Josiah. 1929. *The Economics of Inheritance*. London: G. Routledge & Sons.

Weicher, John C. 1996. "The Distribution of Wealth, 1983–1992: Secular Growth, Cyclical Stability." Working paper 96-012A. St. Louis: Federal Reserve Bank Research Division.

Williamson, Jeffery G. 1991. *Inequality, Poverty, and History: The Kuznets Memorial Lectures*. Oxford: Basil Blackwell.

2

Historical Perspective on
U.S. Tax Policy Toward the Rich

W. Elliot Brownlee

The goal of taxing America's richest citizens has made the nation's tax system unique.[1] In the twentieth century, to tax the rich, the federal government adopted sharply progressive personal and corporate income rates, a highly progressive system of estate and gift taxation, and an income tax that has generally taxed capital income at higher rates than "earned" income. However, the federal tax code has also embraced a wide variety of "tax expenditures," many of which served to reduce the progressivity of the American tax system. The two most distinctive features of American taxation are the resulting complexity joined with a highly progressive rate structure. Uncovering the meaning of these features requires an exploration of the history of taxation, and especially the taxation of the rich, from the origins of the new republic during the late eighteenth century.[2]

Since the time of the constitutional crisis in which the republic took shape, American governments have taxed the rich not only to raise revenue but also to foster internal social order. Historians of American taxation generally agree on this point. They agree as well on the importance of the symbolism of taxation of the rich—that is, on the historic imperative felt by American governments to tax the rich at rates that appear to equal or surpass those applied to individuals and families of lesser means.

Historians disagree widely, however, on the purposes underlying this symbolism and on the intimately related questions of how serious and how effective America's political leaders have been in making the reality of the tax code reflect the progressive symbolism.

Some historians view the taxation of the rich, including the introduction of progressive income taxation, as nothing more than empty rhetoric. One such historian, Robert Stanley (1993, viii–ix), describes the early history of the federal income tax (from the Civil War through 1913) as an expression of capitalist desire "to preserve imbalances in the structure of wealth and opportunity, rather than to ameliorate or abolish them, by strengthening the status quo against the more radical attacks on that structure by the political left and right." Consistent with Stanley's history of the income tax is Mark Leff's (1984) history of New Deal tax reform. He argues that Franklin D. Roosevelt looked only for cosmetic tax reform and was never willing to confront capitalist power by undertaking a serious program of income and wealth redistribution through taxation. Thus, Stanley and Leff regard income tax initiatives before World War II as hollow, almost entirely symbolic efforts designed by the protectors of capitalism to appease the forces of democracy.

I take a very different point of view. My study locates the symbolism that led to "progressive" taxation deep in the nation's republican traditions. The central concern for promoting civic virtue among the republic's citizens had a powerful impact on traditional republican ways of taxing the rich, as well as on the formation of new tax regimes. I argue that American republicanism was concerned with far more than the preservation of capitalism, and that for two centuries republicanism has been the most important determinant of American taxation of the rich. Moreover, I suggest that republicanism has brought about substantial taxation of the nation's richest citizens, especially during great national emergencies, which spawned America's distinctive tax regimes. During the last two hundred years, Americans have taxed the wealthy at high levels, despite the social value they have attached to the accumulation of private capital, and despite their reluctance to throw up governmental barriers to individuals' "pursuit of happiness."[3]

This chapter is devoted largely to understanding the ideals of American architects of tax policy, and how those architects have acted on their ideals, balancing expectations of republican virtue with a desire to use instruments of taxation in a practical way to achieve a wide range of social goals, only one of which was the advancement of capitalism. The chapter also reflects on the reactions of the rich to progressive policies that have singled them out for heavy taxation. From World War I through World War II, when progressive assaults were most ambitious and threatening, the rich generally reacted not by shrugging and going "on strike," as Ayn Rand (1957) proposed. Instead, they stayed in both the economic and political marketplaces and struggled to turn back the assaults. By the late 1940s they had largely succeeded in removing the redistributional fangs from the movement for progressive taxation (see Blum 1959, 327–37).

THE EARLY REPUBLIC

During the constitutional crisis of the late eighteenth century, Americans began to wrestle with the problem of how to tax the richest members of society. In these formative years, governments—federal, state, and local—saw the question of how to tax the rich as part of the central social issue of determining the exact role that privilege ought to have in a republic.

Amid the formation of the early republic, Americans came to understand their society as a res publica, or a commonwealth. Government's central responsibility was, in the words of Oscar and Mary Handlin (1975, 59), "to protect and advance the common wealth." Stated somewhat differently, the political language advanced by the constitutional crisis of the American Revolution embraced an idealism that went far beyond a Lockean liberalism, with its emphasis on private rights. The idealism of the Revolution also asserted a classical republicanism, or a civic humanism, that stressed communal responsibilities. These ideas trumpeted, on the one hand, the need to foster public virtue and, on the other, the threat of corruption and commercialism to public order. The founders, and even Adam Smith, held these ideas of classical republicanism in tension with those of liberalism.[4]

In implementing republican ideals, governments treated privilege with skepticism. They granted privileges to individuals or groups in limited and well-defined forms, and then only when such privileges would clearly advance the collective interest of the commonwealth. Moreover, the governments of the new republic established special taxes on recipients of privilege, such as individuals who received corporate charters by special legislation. But as such special grants of privilege became more limited and the grants themselves less common, legislatures often reduced or abolished the special taxes. Similarly, state governments grew reluctant to use taxation as a means for granting privilege. Instead, they increasingly used taxation to affirm communal responsibilities, deepen citizenship, and demonstrate the fiscal virtues of a republican citizenry.

The ideal of a harmonious republic of citizens equal before the law embraced the notion that taxpaying was one of the normal obligations of a citizenry bound together in a republic by ties of affection and respect. This communal thinking went further, emphasizing the direct relationship between wealth and the responsibility to support government and public order. It embraced enlightened self-interest and included "ability to pay" as a criterion in determining patterns of taxation. It was in that spirit that Adam Smith declared, in his first canon of taxation in *The Wealth of Nations* (1937, 777), that "the subjects of every state ought to contribute towards the support of the government, as nearly as possible, in proportion to their respective abilities."

American governments shared Smith's enthusiasm for "ability to pay" and, like Smith, regarded the property tax—in particular, the taxation of property according to its value—as the tax that offered the greatest potential for taxing according to ability to pay. They were aware, as was Smith, that the rich of their day spent more of their income on housing than did the poor and that a flat, ad valorem property levy was therefore progressive. Smith (1937, 794) was cautious in advancing the desirability of progressive taxation, but he wrote that "it is not very unreasonable that the rich should contribute to the public expense, not only in proportion to their revenue, but something more than in proportion."[5]

Even in the colonial period, property taxation was the mainstay of local government, and after 1775 state governments employed it extensively. Then the democratic forces unleashed by the American Revolution fueled movements to reform state taxation by expanding property taxation. These movements focused on abandoning deeply unpopular poll taxes and shifting taxes to wealth as measured by the value of property holdings. The explicit goal of the expansion of property taxation was the enhancement of the commonwealth, and the practical import was to increase the taxes on all citizens with property and to subject the wealthiest citizens to the highest rates of increase.

The accomplishments of these reform movements varied widely across the new states. But support continued to grow, even during the hard deflation of the 1780s. Proponents of tax reform worried that the new national government might preempt the use of property taxation by state and local governments. Consequently, in the new Constitution, through article I, section 9, they severely limited the national government's ability to levy property taxes. The clause specified: "No capitation, or other direct tax shall be laid, unless in proportion to the census."[6]

The restriction imposed by article I, section 9, along with the requirement imposed by article I, section 8, that "all duties, imposts, and excises shall be uniform throughout the United States," reflected not only enthusiasm for state and local property taxation but also the fact that American republicans thought about taxation in the context of the corruption of the British Parliament and the monarchy. They sought to prevent similar abuse by the new federal government. The federal government, they feared, could become too far removed from the people or captured by a powerful faction. The consequence might be abuses of power in taxation. They saw the property tax in particular as well suited to the purposes of discriminatory federal taxation. The national government might single out particular regions or groups and then apply discriminatory taxes to their property holdings. The framers who were associated with a particular industry or section of the country often worried that the federal government might identify their industry or section as one that deserved higher property taxation. Slave-owners, for example, worried about federal property taxation that would single out slave property. Representatives of rural districts worried about taxation that might favor town dwellers over farmers. An example of such taxation was the taxation of property holdings on the basis of their acreage rather than their value. Urban commercial interests worried about the reverse—federal taxation of property holdings on the basis of their value.

Such fears, in turn, fueled the fear of factionalism that James Madison, perhaps the new republic's foremost civic humanist, expressed in *Federalist* No. 10. He predicted that "the most common and durable source of factions" would be "the various and unequal distribution of property." He concluded that the issue of taxation, more than any other, created an opportunity and temptation for "a predominant party" in the new government "to trample on the rules of justice." Madison regarded the large scale of the republic as the fundamental protection against factionalism, but he valued article I, section 9, for the way in which it provided additional security.

The Constitution restrained the federal government from undertaking experiments in class-based taxation aimed at the rich. Until the Civil War, the federal government depended primarily on revenues from regressive tariffs and rarely singled out wealthy individuals through taxation. There were exceptions to the general pattern. Hamilton experimented with excises on goods and services consumed almost exclusively by the affluent. These taxes included a kind of luxury tax on carriages, a stamp tax on legal transactions, and a tax on snuff. But the taxes were never important revenue raisers, and Hamilton supported them not so much to tax the rich as to exercise the constitutional powers of the federal government without arousing the kind of democratic opposition represented by the Whiskey Rebellion. Similarly, in 1798 the Federalists adopted a progressive property tax to help finance the naval buildup against France. Under this tax legislation, Congress assigned revenue goals to the states on the basis of population but required that each state, in raising its share of revenue, tax houses at rates that increased as the value of the houses increased.

None of the Federalist experiments with progressive taxes worked well. Moreover, these taxes contributed to Federalist political defeats in 1798 and 1800. Subsequently, in 1802 the Jefferson administration, despite its more democratic proclivities, led in the abolition of all excise and direct taxation by the federal government.

As the federal government removed itself from the realm of direct taxation, state and local governments forged ahead in developing revenue systems that relied on property taxes. Most dramatic was the use of property taxation by state governments. Two fundamental forces—the democratization of politics and the industrialization of the economy—accelerated the property tax movement. Jacksonian democracy, with its successful assault on the property qualifications for voting, and the Industrial Revolution gathered force during the 1820s and 1830s. At the same time, Jacksonian reformers extended the scope of property taxation, trying to tax new and rapidly growing forms of wealth.

By the Civil War, in most states, reformers had created the elements of a general property tax designed to reach all property—intangible (personal property such as cash, credits, notes, stocks, bonds, and mortgages) as well as tangible property (tools, equipment, and furnishings, as well as real estate). Some states simply expanded the statutory definitions of what constituted property for tax purposes. Other states added to their constitutions provisions for uniformity (requiring that properties of equal value be taxed at the same rate) and for universality (requiring that all property be taxed). For example, Ohio's 1851 constitution provided that "laws shall be passed taxing by a uniform rule all moneys, credits, investments in bonds, stocks, joint-stock companies or otherwise; and also all real and personal property, according to its true value in money" (article 12, section 2). Ohio had launched general property tax reform as early as 1825 and had garnered sustained increases in taxes on personal property. But in only two years, the state, empowered by its 1851 constitution, doubled its assessment of personal property—to about two-thirds the value of real property. In the same two-year period state and local tax collections each nearly doubled.

By the 1860s, in much of the nation, property taxation had become the dominant source of state and local revenues, and the movement for general property taxation had significantly increased the relative contribution of the wealthiest Americans to government. As a consequence of the apparent success of property taxation for meeting state and local revenue needs, state and local political leaders became increasingly vigilant in watching for possible federal incursions into their property tax base. This vigilance helped keep the taxation of the rich almost exclusively a matter for state and local government.[7]

THE CIVIL WAR

The Civil War crisis compelled the federal government to reconsider taxing the rich. The very first taxes the Civil War administration of Abraham Lincoln imposed were regressive consumption taxes—high tariffs and excises on an enormous range of consumer goods and services. But Republican leaders worried that new, regressive taxes could undermine confidence in the Republican Party and the war effort, particularly in western and border states. Consequently, they looked for a supplementary tax that bore a closer relationship to "ability to pay" than did the tariffs and excises. The goals of such a tax would be to raise additional revenue, thus easing inflationary pressures, to convince taxpayers that the wartime fiscal system was fair, and to persuade the public that it was embarked on more than a "rich man's war and a poor man's fight."

The Republican leadership had very few options. In light of the rudimentary accounting practiced by homes, farms, and businesses, the most practical method to raise huge amounts of revenue quickly was the one they had already chosen: taxing goods at the point of importation or sale. Even this approach required the swift development of a large administrative apparatus for the collection of excises.

Less practical, but perhaps feasible, was co-opting the administrative systems that state and local governments had developed for property taxation. Secretary of the Treasury Salmon P. Chase and Thaddeus Stevens, chair of the House Ways and Means Committee, favored this approach at first, and they proposed an emergency property tax modeled after one that the federal government had adopted as an emergency measure during the War of 1812. The federal government allocated this direct tax according to the restrictions on "direct" taxation established by article I, section 8, of the Constitution. Thus, the federal government allocated the tax to the states according to population. Under the law, however, states, in turn, allocated the tax to counties according to assessed value of property in each county. During the Civil War, members of Congress from western states (including the Great Lakes states), border states, and poorer northeastern states complained that such a tax would result in a higher rate of taxation on property in their states. They also complained that the tax, as initially drafted during the Civil War, would not tax the rich. It would focus on real estate and would not reach real estate improvements and "intangibles" such as stocks, bonds, mortgages, and cash. Congressman Schuyler Colfax of Indiana declared, "I cannot go home and tell my constituents that I voted for a bill that would allow a man, a millionaire, who has put his entire property into stock, to be exempt from taxation, while a farmer who lives by his side must pay a tax." (*Congressional Globe* 1861, 248).

In response to the complaints, the leadership took note of how the British Liberals had used income taxation in financing the Crimean War as a substitute for heavier taxation of property. Justin S. Morrill of Vermont, who chaired the Ways and Means Subcommittee on Taxation and was a staunch proponent of high tariffs, introduced a proposal for a new and very different tax—the first federal tax levied against personal income. Congressional leaders viewed the tax as an indirect tax because it did not directly tax property values.[8]

The first income tax of the Civil War was ungraduated, imposing a basic rate of 3 percent on incomes above a personal exemption of $800. (The federal government had no scientific way to measure personal income, but Congress came surprisingly close to setting the exemption close to average annual family income, which was about $900 in 1870 [U.S. Bureau of the Census 1975, 41, 240]). Amendments in subsequent war years reduced the exemption and introduced graduation. In 1865 the tax imposed a 5 percent rate on incomes between $600 and $5,000 and 10 percent on incomes over $5,000. The rates may seem low by twentieth-century standards, but they imposed significantly higher taxes on the wealthy—perhaps twice as high—than the wealthy were used to paying under the general property tax. Moreover, this was the first time that the federal government had discriminated among taxpayers by virtue of their income.[9]

The tax reached well into the affluent upper-middle classes of the nation's commercial and industrial centers. By the end of the war, more than 10 percent of all Union households were paying an income tax, and the rate of taxpaying probably reached 15 percent in the northeastern states, where the federal government collected three-fourths of its income tax revenues. These households probably constituted roughly the slice of society that economic historians have estimated as owning 70 percent or more of the nation's wealth in 1860. By the end of the war, most of the richest 1 percent of the nation's families—as measured by their Civil War tax returns—paid income taxes at the marginal rate of 10 percent.[10]

The administrative machinery created by the Commissioner of Internal Revenue relied heavily on the cooperation of taxpayers. Compliance was high, at least during the war, because of patriotic support for the Union cause and because of the partial enactment of British "stoppage at the source"—that is, collection at the source, or the withholding of taxes by corporations and others who made payments of income. The Commissioner of Internal Revenue lacked the administrative capacity to obtain earnings reports or collect taxes from farms and small businesses, where most Americans earned their income. But the law did require corporations—railroads, banks, and insurance companies primarily—to collect taxes on dividends and interest, forms of income that constituted a large share of the income of the affluent citizens Congress wanted to tax. Also, the law required agencies of the federal government to collect taxes on salaries, which grew substantially during the wartime mobilization.

The Civil War decade was probably the high-water mark in nineteenth-century America for the taxation of the rich. After the war the tax rates paid by wealthy citizens almost certainly declined, by virtually any measure, and did so at every level of government.

After the Civil War, Republican Congresses responded to the complaints of the affluent citizens who had accepted the income tax only as an emergency measure. In fact, little organized political support had emerged for permanent income taxation, and only a minority of the party's congressional leadership thought about the tax as a shield to protect regressive tariffs. Fewer still actually liked the distributional effects of the tax. Republican leaders found it relatively easy to eradicate the income tax because, during the late 1860s and early 1870s, they were phasing out most of the excise taxes, which the general public resented in peacetime and blamed for postwar increases in the cost of living. Beginning in 1867, the Republican leadership increased the income tax exemptions and lowered the rates. In 1870 Congress—mistakenly fearing a deficit—extended the tax but then allowed it to expire in 1872.

TOWARD PROGRESSIVE INCOME TAXATION

Introduction of the general property tax had offered the promise of taxing all wealth at the same rate and taxing rich families, who received more of their income from personal property, at progressive rates. But after the Civil War, in most urban areas, that egalitarian promise vanished. The swiftly growing desire of city governments to build modern infrastructure (parks, schools, hospitals, transit systems, waterworks, and sewers) drove up tax rates to levels at which wealthy urbanites were unwilling to pay. They responded by underreporting the value of their intangible personal property (cash, credits, notes, stocks, bonds, and mortgages), and urban governments lacked the administrative machinery to expose and assess such property. State governments, meanwhile, were at the mercy of local governments in the assessment of property values for state property taxation. Consequently, state and local governments began to abandon general property taxation and to develop in its place a property tax that was less burdensome on the wealthy: the modern property tax, with its standardized assessment practices and its focus on real estate.[11]

The easing of the relative tax burden on the rich, especially during the hard depression of the mid-1890s, stimulated Populists in the West and the South and champions of Henry George's "single tax," who were scattered throughout urban America, to promote social justice through tax reform. The Populists championed a progressive tax on the profits of corporations and the incomes of the wealthy, and single-taxers often supported it at the federal level while they sought radical reform of the property tax at the state and local levels.[12]

The Populist and single-tax movements each harkened back to classical republicanism by highlighting the responsibility of government to punish and discourage special privilege. Central to the appeal of a highly progressive income tax during the 1890s was the claim that the tax would reallocate fiscal burdens according to both ability to pay and the distribution of government benefits in the form of special privilege. The tax, therefore, would help restore a virtuous republic free of concentrations of economic power. Part of the attack focused on the protective tariff, which tax reformers claimed had become in itself a source of special privilege, encouraging the growth of corporate monopolies.

The reform rhetoric was, in a fundamental sense, conservative; it directed attention to the values of the early republic. What was potentially radical about the movement for progressive income taxation was its content: the goal of raising the government's revenues primarily or even entirely from the largest incomes and corporate profits. The radical advocates for income taxation regarded such incomes and profits as the consequence of monopoly power and unfair advantages. They argued that their tax would not touch the wages and salaries of ordinary people but rather would attack unearned profits and incomes. The tax, its proponents claimed, would redress the wealth and power maldistribution that was responsible for the evils of industrialization. Those who believed they had faced expropriation now wanted to do the expropriating.

Thus, support for a radical progressive income tax had far more to do with the search for social justice in an industrializing nation than with the quest for an elastic source of revenue. The progressive income tax became an integral part of democratic statism—a radical program of invoking instruments of government power to create a more democratic social order by redistributing wealth. Democratic statism represented a new kind of liberalism—the adaptation to industrial conditions of classic nineteenth-century liberalism and the commonwealth tradition of early republicanism, which had included a distrust of commerce. Democratic statists like the Populists and the single-taxers regarded themselves as applying the ideals of the American Revolution to the new conditions of industrial society. Although the strategy remained one of liberating individual energies by providing a social order of abundant opportunity, the tactics had changed. To these new liberals, the state had become a necessary instrument and ally, not an enemy. They designed their tax program to restructure the machinery for distributing income and wealth.[13]

The new grassroots pressure changed the politics of federal taxation. During the Civil War, the Republican leadership had exercised a great deal of discretion in crafting the income tax. To be sure, they had developed the tax in anticipation of sectional and class resistance to a federal property tax. But they had designed the tax without any group's insistence that they do so. After the war, they set their own timetable for its demise. In contrast, when Congress began to reconsider income taxation during the early 1890s, it did so primarily in response to popular pressure. Moreover, Congress then faced numerous proposals for a high degree of progression, and the proposers' arguments had a sharp, radical edge.

The pressures for progressive tax reform from western and southern Populists became strong enough to force a shift in the position of the leaders of the Democratic Party. A contributing factor was the decline of foreign trade and tariff revenues during the depression of 1893 to 1897. This enabled the Democrats to embrace a proposal for a new tax while still calling for the shrinkage of swollen Republican programs of public works, pensions, and military expenditures. Democrats took control of both houses of Congress in 1893, and their leaders in the House from the South and the West, including Benton McMillin of Tennessee, who chaired the Ways and Means Subcommittee on Internal Revenue, enacted an income tax in 1894 as part of the Wilson-Gorman tariff. They sensed an opportunity to use tax issues for a major realignment of the two political parties along sectional and class lines, and they debated the income tax with unprecedented agrarian ferocity.[14]

Hostility from northeastern Democrats, as well as the opposition of most Republicans (including leaders like Senators John Sherman of Ohio and Justin Morrill of Vermont, who had supported the Civil War income tax), limited the progressivity of the tax. Within both parties, leaders recalled how effective the Civil War income tax had been in reaching the incomes of the nation's wealthy families. Congress reproduced many of the technical features of the Civil War income tax and set a somewhat lower rate on incomes (2 percent). But Congress also introduced several changes that reflected rising popular enthusiasm for taxing the rich. It established a much higher personal exemption ($4,000), thus focusing the tax more directly on very wealthy individuals. Congress also defined as taxable income any personal property acquired by gift or inheritance. Finally, Congress applied the 2 percent tax to the income of business corporations (defined as revenues above operating expenses, including interest on indebtedness). This tax embodied the assumption that the federal government ought to tax corporations according to a "benefit" theory of taxation as well as the principle of ability to pay. Americans had begun to regard corporate taxation as an especially important vehicle for both taxing the rich and assaulting special privilege.[15]

The 1894 tax was short-lived. In 1895 the Supreme Court, in *Pollock v. Farmers' Loan and Trust Company*, declared that the income tax of the Wilson-Gorman tariff was unconstitutional. The *Pollock* decision raised a significant institutional barrier to progressive taxation, but it also stimulated popular support for income taxation. Populists and Democrats from the South and the West now attacked the Court and found that their audiences responded enthusiastically. Democrats began to introduce constitutional amendments that would permit income taxation, and in

1896 the Democratic Party formally endorsed income taxation. This was the first time a major party had done so.[16]

The Democrats, however, went down to a decisive defeat in 1896, and the victorious Republicans felt no urgency in adopting progressive tax reform, especially when economic recovery took hold during the late 1890s. By the time Republicans had to face the problem of financing the Spanish-American War, they had recovered the power to neutralize the Democratic thrust for income taxation. Republicans were willing to accept, however, a progressive but modest tax on estates. That tax, which Congress repealed in 1902, helped finance not only the Spanish-American War but also the suppression of the Huks and the intervention in the Boxer Rebellion.[17]

During the first decade of the new century, support for income taxation resumed its growth. The gains were most marked across rural America but especially strong in the Midwest and the West. Republican leaders like Robert M. LaFollette Jr. of Wisconsin discovered that income taxation was one of the reform issues that attracted and held voters to the alignment the party had crafted in 1896. Presidents Theodore Roosevelt and William Howard Taft both recognized this support and made vague gestures on behalf of a graduated income tax (in 1906 and 1908, respectively). But popular backing for income taxation grew too in the urban Northeast. There, both Republican and Democratic leaders found that the tax had begun to appeal to their constituents.

An important new element in the growing support for federal income taxation was the formation of an urban-rural alignment of middle-class citizens who favored state and local tax reform. The economic depression of the 1890s, followed by accelerating demands for services from state and local governments, accentuated the flaws in general property taxation. Both farmers and middle-class property owners in towns and cities resented the growth in their tax burdens as a consequence of the inability of local and state governments to use general property taxation to reach intangible personal property. And these groups became interested in the adoption of new taxes such as income, inheritance, and corporate taxes. Small property owners, both rural and urban, assumed that they would not have to pay the new taxes, and that those new taxes would replace state property taxes. In effect, the proponents of the new taxes believed that they would help restore the progressiveness lost in the administrative collapse of the Jacksonian general property tax under industrial conditions. Richard T. Ely (1888, 140, 288), the economist who most vigorously championed reform of state general property taxation, captured the essence of the new reform program. In the 1880s he wrote that "some way must be contrived to make owners of . . . new kinds of property, *who include most of our wealthiest citizens* [emphasis mine], pay their due share of taxes." His solution was for states to adopt the income tax, "the fairest tax every devised."[18]

But states were very slow to adopt the new, alternative taxes. No state enacted a modern income tax until 1911, when Wisconsin did so. The Wisconsin tax pioneers finessed the administrative problems by collecting most of the revenues from corporations, which faced a stringently administered 6 percent tax on their profits. Manufacturers accounted for about two-thirds of the corporate burden. But the tax slowed the pace of industrial investment in Wisconsin by increasing the cost of capital to Wisconsin manufacturers significantly above the levels faced by their competitors located elsewhere in the Great Lakes states.

Political leaders in the other Great Lakes states and in industrial states elsewhere regarded the damage to industry in Wisconsin as a cautionary tale. Massachusetts and New York did not adopt income taxes until they faced the fiscal problems imposed by World War I, and not until they were confident that they could build the administrative machinery required to assess and collect a tax based primarily on individual incomes rather than corporate profits. Most industrial states did not enact income taxes until the revenue crisis created by the Great Depression (Brownlee 1970, 1974).[19]

Nonetheless, the debates prompted by the Wisconsin experience promoted widespread interest in all measures, including adoption of income taxes, that might rebalance the equity of the tax system. In addition, the sluggish progress of income taxation at the state level increasingly convinced middle-class citizens that it would be desirable to enact the tax at the federal level.

During the ferment over tax issues at the state and local levels, some defenders of the wealthiest property owners joined the movement for federal income taxation. They concluded that the tax might help take the wind out of the sails of more radical tax measures at the state and local levels. The most influential among these conservatives was a group of urban economists and attorneys who were tax experts. The economists Edwin R. A. Seligman of Columbia University and Charles J. Bullock of Harvard University led them in promoting income taxation, on the one hand, and in moderating the rhetoric used to justify the tax, on the other. As early as 1894 Seligman had argued that the point of the tax was to "round out the existing tax system in the direction of greater justice" (610). Such language helped shift the discourse over taxation from a focus on the salvation of industrial America to an emphasis on a moderate redistribution of the tax burden.

Conservative support for moderate income taxation might be described as expressing a kind of "corporate liberalism," or "progressive capitalism." More generally, this vision, developing in tension with democratic statism, influenced not only the development of income taxation but also the ideas of the so-called progressive movement. Reformers of this more conservative persuasion wanted to bring a greater degree of order to industrial society and to strengthen national institutions, just as did the democratic statists. In contrast with democratic statists, however, "progressive capitalists" or "corporate liberals" admired the efficiency of the modern corporation. Government regulation, including taxation, was desirable only if it served to protect the investment system.[20]

By 1909 there were enough insurgent Republicans in Congress who supported a graduated income tax to force action. A diverse group of representatives and senators from both parties supported the immediate enactment of such a tax. Congressman Cordell Hull (1948, 49), a first-term Democrat who represented the same Populist-leaning Tennessee district as had Benton McMillin, noted changes in the composition of the Supreme Court and found it "inconceivable" that the nation "had a Constitution that would shelter the chief portion of the wealth of the country from the only effective method of reaching it for its fair share of taxes."

A bipartisan group hammered out a proposal, but they had to limit the progressiveness of the tax in order to generate enough support in Congress. Senator Nelson Aldrich of Rhode Island, the chair of the Senate Finance Committee, proved resourceful in both preserving Republican Party union and blunting the thrust toward income taxation. He worked closely with President Taft to persuade the insurgents to accept a modest tax, described as "a special excise tax," of 2 percent on corporate incomes. He also worked to submit the Sixteenth Amendment, legalizing a federal income tax, to the states for ratification. Aldrich and the northeastern Republicans recognized the growing popular support for income taxation but hoped that the measure would fail.

Ratification prevailed in 1913, much to the surprise and consternation of standpat conservatives. The process of ratification succeeded in part because of two sets of political campaigns.[21]

One set consisted of revivals of the single-tax movement. Beginning in 1909, the soap magnate Joseph Fels, who had converted to Henry George's faith in the single tax, began to finance campaigns for constitutional reforms permitting classification of property for the purpose of taxation (and thus high rates of taxation on the "site value" of land) and local option in taxation (see Dudden 1971, 199–245; Young 1916, 163–83). Although the campaigns won no significant electoral victories except one in Oregon in 1910, they awakened the interest of the urban middle class in using the income tax to redistribute wealth and further popularized Henry George's ideal of allocating taxes according to the distribution of special privilege. The campaigns also convinced more wealthy property owners that they needed moderate reform as a defensive measure, and their support was important to the crucial victory of ratification in New York in 1911.

The second set of political campaigns were those of the presidential candidates in the election of 1912. As a consequence of the campaigns of Woodrow Wilson, Theodore Roosevelt, and Eugene Debs, popular enthusiasm for federal attacks on monopoly power reached an all-time high. Many Americans entertained vague ideas that federal income taxation would provide a means either for assaulting monopoly power or for recouping some of its ill-gotten gains for the benefit of the republic.

In 1913 bipartisan support for income taxation was broad, and the Democrats controlled Congress. Nonetheless, the income tax measure they enacted was modest. To some extent this happened because the leaders of both parties were cautious and wanted to maximize support for income taxation within the Northeast, where they feared the tax would be unpopular, and thus maintain party unity. To a greater extent, however, the 1913 tax measure was limited in scope because the nation's political leaders, as well as the general public, were unsure of how much redistribution they wanted the new tax instrument to accomplish. On September 4, Woodrow Wilson urged caution on Furnifold M. Simmons of North Carolina, chair of the Senate Finance Committee. "Individual judgments will naturally differ," Wilson wrote, "with regard to the burden it is fair to lay upon incomes which run above the usual levels" (Link 1978, 254). Moreover, the supporters of income taxation were themselves uncertain how income ought to be defined or how the income tax would work administratively.

Finally, in 1913 virtually none of the income tax proponents within the government believed that the income tax would become a major, let alone the dominant, permanent source of revenue within the consumption-based federal tax system. Certainly the advocates of income taxation who were hostile to the protective tariff hoped that the tax would help reduce tariffs, but they doubted that the new revenues would be substantial. And the idea that the tax would enable the federal government to grow significantly was far from the minds of the drafters of the 1913 legislation.

To be sure, Congressman Hull, the primary author of the 1913 legislation, wanted to ensure that the federal government would have access to the income tax in wartime; he believed that the federal government could make the tax, as an emergency measure, even more productive than it had been during the Civil War. But for Hull, as well as for the other income tax enthusiasts, the revenue goals of the tax were far less important than the desire to use the tax to advance economic justice.[22]

Consequently, the Underwood-Simmons Tariff Act of 1913 was less progressive and less ambitious in its revenue goals than the Civil War legislation or even the legislation of 1894. The new tax established the "normal" rate of 1 percent on both individual and corporate incomes, with a high exemption ($3,000 for single taxpayers) that excused virtually all middle-class Americans from the tax. The tax also established a graduated surtax of up to 6 percent on personal income. The wealthiest 1 percent of American families paid marginal rates ranging between 1 and 7 percent—rates that were substantially lower than those they had faced during the Civil War. The act also exempted dividends up to $20,000 from the personal income tax. Thus, the act attempted a partial integration of corporate and personal taxes, limiting the double taxation of corporate earnings to the portion of those earnings received as dividends by the richest Americans.

In the first several years of the income tax, only about 2 percent of American households paid taxes. Meanwhile, the tariff and taxation of tobacco and alcohol remained the most productive sources of revenue. The tariff, in fact, became even more productive when the 1913 reduction of tariff rates by the Wilson administration stimulated trade and increased revenues. If it had not been for World War I mobilization, the major consequence of the passage of the income tax in 1913 might have been the protection of the regime of consumption taxation inherited from the Civil War.

As it turned out, the great wars of the twentieth century made all the difference. Income taxation, especially of the "soak the rich" variety, enacted during World War I caused the role of income tax revenues to grow swiftly between 1913 and the 1920s (see table 2.1). Because the Great Depression shrank the income tax base, the relative importance of income tax revenues declined during the 1930s. But those revenues soared during World War II and then continued to grow, although at a reduced rate, until the 1980s.

The heavy reliance on income taxation that resulted distinguished the tax system of the United States from that of most industrial nations. Even by the late 1980s, the United States relied more heavily on income taxation than did the other major industrial nations, except for Canada and Japan, which employed a highly productive corporate income tax (see table 2.2). In contrast, the other industrial nations,

Table 2.1   Distribution of Revenues by Type of Tax

Year	Income Taxes	Sales Taxes	Property Taxes	Miscellaneous
1902	0%	37.5%	51.4%	11.1%
1913	1.5	29.5	58.7	10.3
1927	24.3	16.5	50.0	9.2
1932	14.5	18.6	56.2	10.7
1936	15.8	32.0	38.7	14.2
1940	19.4	32.4	34.9	13.3
1950	54.1	25.4	14.4	6.1
1960	58.2	21.6	14.5	5.7
1970	59.2	20.9	14.6	5.3
1980	63.4	19.5	11.9	5.2
1983	59.3	20.4	13.4	6.9
1990	56.7	21.1	11.6	10.6

Sources: U.S. Department of the Treasury (1985, 47–49); U.S. Department of Commerce (1992, 10).

with the exception of Japan, made far greater use of sales taxes, particularly national value-added taxes.

"SOAK-THE-RICH" TAXATION AND WORLD WAR I

Between 1913 and American entry into World War I in 1917, the forces of industrialization pressed the federal government and the states to play a greater role in humanizing the conditions of industrial life. Following the enactment of the 1913 income tax, there was a decided increase in the concentration of incomes earned by the best-paid individuals. In fact, during these years the concentration of income reached its zenith in the United States. Workers, small farmers, and small businessmen enjoyed significant income gains in the expansive economy of 1915 and 1916, but they could observe the far more dramatic gains of the very wealthy.[23] Redistributional energies acquired a special edge and focused increasingly on using the tax system on behalf of redistribution.

Table 2.2   Contributions of Various Taxes to Total Tax Revenues, 1987

	Personal Income Tax	Corporate Income Tax	Goods and Services Taxes
United States	36.2%	8.1%	16.7%
Canada	38.7	8.0	29.8
France	12.7	5.2	29.3
Germany	29.0	5.0	25.4
Japan	24.0	22.9	12.9
Netherlands	19.7	7.7	26.0
Sweden	37.2	4.1	24.1
Switzerland	34.0	6.2	19.1
United Kingdom	26.6	10.6	31.4

Source: OECD (1990).

In addition, during these years the organization of financial and managerial capitalism matured through the blossoming of corporations that were multidivisional, hierarchical, and national in scope.[24] Middle- and lower-class Americans intensified their interest in curbing monopoly power through taxation and, in particular, through national-level taxation that could effectively reach the income and assets of large corporations. At the same time, the development of modern corporations and of sophisticated financial intermediaries created much of the organizational capability necessary for assessing and collecting direct taxes on the incomes of corporations and wealthy individuals.

To maintain social order—even if the war and its stresses had not intervened—the federal government had to play a major, and expanding, role of mediation between a variety of social groups and the new corporations. But without the intervention of the United States in World War I and the management of that intervention by the leadership of the Democratic Party, the federal government would have been slow to adopt income taxation, and federal taxation would have developed with a much greater reliance on the taxation of consumption.[25]

The war effort made mediation on behalf of social order more difficult for the federal government because it had to acquire the resources for a massively expensive war effort. As it mobilized for the war, the administration could not escape addressing the raw distributional issue of how the huge costs of war would be allocated, or "who should pay." The Democratic administration of Woodrow Wilson concluded that the issue created political and social opportunities rather than problems. The result was the creation of a democratic-statist tax regime. That regime, with its highly progressive tax rates and its tax base consisting of the incomes of corporations and wealthy individuals, provided the core of wartime finance.

The tax reform process began in 1916 when President Wilson and Secretary of the Treasury William G. McAdoo made the single most important financial decision of the war. In arranging wartime financing, they chose to collaborate with a group of insurgent, largely southern congressional Democrats who harbored Populist hostilities to northeastern capitalists. Led by Congressman Claude Kitchin of North Carolina, who chaired the House Ways and Means Committee, the insurgent Democrats attacked concentrations of wealth, special privilege, and public corruption. Kitchin exploited the influence of the Ways and Means Committee. The Democratic insurgents were able to insist that if military preparedness, and later the war effort, was to move forward, it would do so only on their financial terms. They embraced taxation as an important means to achieve social justice according to the humanistic ideals of the early republic; taxation would be a tool for asserting community values over the interests of "Wall Street" and the wealthy elites of the Northeast. For southerners in particular sectionalism reinforced the class-based populism represented by Claude Kitchin. For the Wilson administration, highly progressive taxation then became a major element of its program for steering between socialism and unmediated capitalism.[26]

The war provided an opportunity for Democratic progressives to focus the debate over taxation on one of the most fundamental and sensitive social issues in modern America: What stake does society have in corporate profits? More specifically, the question became one of whether the modern corporation was the central engine of productivity, which tax policy should reinforce, or whether it was an economic predator, which tax policy could and should tame. The outcome of the debate was that the nation embraced a new tax system: "soak the rich" income taxation.[27]

Thus, during the period of crisis, one in which the pressure of fighting a modern war coincided with powerful demands to break the hold of corporate privilege, Wilson and the Democratic Party turned Republican fiscal policy on its head. They embraced a tax policy that they claimed—just as the Republicans had claimed for their tariff system—would sustain a powerful state and economic prosperity. But the new tax policy of the Democrats was one that assaulted, rather than protected, the privileges associated with corporate wealth.[28]

The Democratic tax program, implemented in the Revenue Act of 1916 and the wartime revenue acts that followed, transformed the experimental, rather tentative income tax into the foremost instrument of federal taxation. The Revenue Act of 1916 imposed the first significant tax on personal incomes, doubled (to 2 percent) the tax on corporate incomes, and introduced an excess profits tax of 12.5 percent on munitions makers. It rejected a broadly based personal income tax—one falling most heavily on wages and salaries—and focused on the taxation of the wealthiest families. Among the provisions of the 1916 legislation was the elimination of the personal exemption for dividends. Thus, the act deliberately introduced the double taxation of corporate earnings distributed as dividends. In effect, the 1916 legislation embraced the concept of using the corporate and personal income taxes as two different means of taxing the rich. The architects of the Revenue Act of 1916 intended to implement, on the one hand, through the personal income tax an ability-to-pay philosophy and, on the other hand, through corporate taxation, a benefit theory of taxation. The Democratic tax program of 1916 also introduced federal estate taxation. Estates larger than $50,000 paid a progressive tax that increased from a minimum of 1 percent to a maximum of 10 percent (on estates over $5 million) (Brownlee 1985).[29]

In 1918 only about 15 percent of American families had to pay personal income taxes, and the tax payments of the wealthiest 1 percent of American families accounted for about 80 percent of the revenues from the personal income tax. In 1918, even without taking into account the incidence of the corporate income tax on the rich, this wealthiest 1 percent paid marginal tax rates that ranged from 15 to 77 percent, and effective rates that averaged 15 percent, having increased from 3 percent in 1916 (see table 2.3).[30] Similarly, the richest Americans accounted for almost all of the estate taxes paid. Wartime legislation raised the maximum estate tax rates to 25 percent (on estates larger than $10 million) but did not lower the exemption or increase the minimum tax rate. Consequently, only slightly more than 1 percent of decedents paid any estate taxes.[31]

Finally, the Democratic program of finance embraced the concept of taxing corporate "excess profits." The Revenue Act of 1917 increased the tax on corporate incomes to 6 percent and expanded the excess profits tax on munitions makers to a graduated tax on all business profits above a "normal" rate of return. Rates of taxation were graduated by rates of return on invested capital. In 1917, the taxes ranged from 20 percent on profits less than 15 percent over the "normal" rate of return to 60

Table 2.3   Personal Income Tax Rates on the Richest 1 Percent of Households, 1916 to 1929

Year	Marginal Rates	Effective Rates[a]
1916	2 to 12%	3.0%
1917	5 to 67	9.2
1918	13 to 77	15.0
1919	9 to 73	13.1
1920	11 to 73	15.8
1921	9 to 73	9.9
1922	9 to 58	9.8
1923	9 to 58	7.8
1924	10 to 46	9.3
1925	10 to 25	7.5
1926	6 to 25	7.4
1927	6 to 25	7.8
1928	6 to 25	8.9
1929	5 to 25	8.1

Sources: U.S. Department of the Treasury (1916 to 1929); U.S. Bureau of the Census (1975, 41–43).
Note: The richest 1 percent of households in a given year is taken as the aggregation of the highest-income taxpayers equalling 1 percent of the households in the nation.

percent on profits more than 33 percent over the "normal" rate of return. The Revenue Act of 1918 doubled the basic corporate income tax, to 12 percent, and further increased excess profits taxation. The act reduced the number of tax rates from six to two but increased the lowest rate to 30 percent and the top rate to 65 percent (on profits earned by more than a 20 percent rate of return). The excess profits tax accounted for about two-thirds of all federal tax revenues during World War I and added to the tax burden that the personal income tax imposed on the rich. Only the United States and Canada among the belligerents taxed excess profits in this way, and only the United States placed excess profits taxation at the center of wartime finance.[32]

The designers of the new corporate taxes made two key assumptions about the incidence and effects of the taxes. First, they assumed that corporations would not be able to pass them on to others. They were certain that the new taxes would not operate as disguised sales taxes. Because progressives assumed that corporations were already maximizing profits, having pushed prices as high as possible and kept wages as low as possible, they concluded that corporations would have to pay their taxes out of those profits. Thus, the assumptions of progressives about the shifting and incidence of taxes on corporate profits were remarkably similar to those made fifty years later by neoclassical analysts.

Second, they assumed that taxing the rich, particularly through the corporation tax, would in fact stimulate the accumulation of private capital and the advance of economic growth. Excess profits taxation would, they assumed, break the hold of monopoly power on the stimulating forces of competition. Claude Kitchin and his allies also hoped that this system of taxation, which included a large Treasury bureaucracy devoted to studying and determining appropriate rates of return for each American industry, would survive the war and become a permanent part of American governance.[33]

The complex and ambitious new public finance regime required a vast expansion of the Treasury's administrative capacity. A major arm of the Treasury was the Bureau of Internal Revenue (BIR), the forerunner to the Internal Revenue Service; its personnel increased from 4,000 to 15,800 between 1913 and 1920 as it underwent a reorganization along multifunctional lines, with clear specifications of responsibilities and chains of command. One of the most demanding chores of the bureau was the administration of the excess profits tax. In the process of interpreting, selling, explaining, and assessing the new business tax, the Treasury created a modern staff of experts—accountants, lawyers, and economists. Much of this bureaucracy also implemented the new individual income tax by processing the huge volume of information on individual taxpayers. This flow of information resulted from an "information at the source" provision in the Revenue Act of 1916, which required corporations to report on salaries, dividends, and interest payments. In short, the Treasury built a class of mediators—defining themselves as experts—whose task was to reconcile the goals of corporations and affluent individuals with the needs of the state. But under Secretary McAdoo's leadership, the Treasury undertook far more than a "broker-state" balancing of contesting interest groups; it enhanced the power of the state to advance economic justice and the war.

The income tax with excess profits taxation at its core enraged business leaders—for good reason. Redistributional taxation, along with the wartime strengthening of the Treasury, posed a long-term strategic threat to the nation's corporations. Those most severely threatened were the largest corporations, which believed their financial autonomy to be in jeopardy. In addition, the new tax system empowered the federal government, as never before, to implement egalitarian ideals. No other single issue aroused as much hostility to the Wilson administration among corporate leaders and America's richest families as did the financing of the war. Even Wilson's longtime supporters within the business community, among them Bernard Baruch, Jacob Schiff, and Clarence Dodge, bitterly attacked his tax program within the administration and often quietly supported Republican critics. The conflict between advocates of democratic-statist, soak-the-rich taxation, on the one hand, and business leaders, on the other hand, would rage for more than two decades.

Despite the damage to business confidence, the Wilson administration and congressional Democratic leaders paid almost no attention to the complaints of Baruch and other business critics, in part because they shared Kitchin's ideal of using taxation to restructure the economy according to nineteenth-century liberal ideals. They presumed that the largest corporations exercised inordinate control over wealth and that a "money trust" dominated the allocation of capital. For Wilson and McAdoo, the tax program, with its promise to tax monopoly power and break monopoly's hold on America's entrepreneurial energy, added an attractive new dimension to Wilson's "New Freedom" approach to the "emancipation of business." Thus, wartime public finance was based on the taxation of assets that democratic statists regarded as ill gotten and socially hurtful, comparable to the rents from land monopolies that Henry George and his followers had wanted to tax. In fact, both Wilson and McAdoo entertained explicit single-tax ideas as they developed their tax reform program.[34]

Party government also played a crucial role in the decision of the Wilson administration to go after the rich and the corporations. Wilson and McAdoo knew they could have easily engineered passage of a much less progressive tax system—one relying more heavily on consumption taxes and taxation of middle-class incomes—in cooperation with Republicans and a minority of conservative Democrats. They were confident in their ability to administer such broad-based taxes effectively. But they regarded mass-based taxation as a betrayal of the principles of their party. After all, the Democratic Party had strong traditions of representing the disadvantaged, of hostility to a strong central government as the instrument of special privilege, of opposition to the taxation of consumption, and of support for policies designed to widen access to economic opportunity. A failure to adopt a highly progressive and "reconstructive" tax program would have had serious political consequences for Wilson and McAdoo. It would have bitterly divided the Democratic Party, and they would have spoiled their opportunities for attracting Republican progressives to their party. Moreover, they would have destroyed their strong partnership with congressional Democrats—a partnership that both leaders regarded as necessary for the effective advancement of national administration.[35]

As the war neared its end, corporate leaders and Republicans mounted an effective counterattack against democratic statism. They found an opening in 1918 when President Wilson tried to make a case for doubling taxes. In the congressional elections, the Republicans used vigorous antitax, antigovernment campaigns throughout the nation and antisouthern campaigns in the West. There they argued that Claude Kitchin and the southerners in the Wilson administration had imposed discriminatory taxation on the rest of the nation. The appeals worked: Republicans gained control of Congress. Then, in 1920, they rode to a presidential victory during the postwar economic depression. At the conclusion of the war, the Democratic Party of Woodrow Wilson had failed to do what the Republican Party of Abraham Lincoln had done—establish long-term control of the federal government through a party realignment.

REPUBLICAN REFORMS OF THE WORLD WAR I REGIME

The Republicans who assumed control of both the presidency and the Congress in 1921 saw tax reform as a means to roll back democratic statism. Under the leadership of Secretary of the Treasury Andrew Mellon, one of the wealthiest men in America, the Republicans blocked new soak-the-rich legislation and attacked the most redistributional parts of the wartime tax system.[36]

In the process, the Republicans granted substantial, across-the-board tax reductions to corporations and the rich—the nation's wealthiest individuals. In 1921 they abolished the excess profits tax, dashing Claude Kitchin's hopes that the tax would become permanent. In addition, they made the nominal rate structure of the personal income tax less progressive. The primary goal was to make that tax less burdensome on the rich. In 1921 the Republicans cut the top marginal rate on the rich by one-third, reducing it from 73 to 58 percent. They reduced it further in 1926 and 1928, so that in 1928 the top marginal rate fell to 25 percent (see table 2.3). Finally, Republicans attacked the estate tax. They were unable to eradicate it, as Andrew Mellon had hoped to do, but in 1926 they did succeed in reducing the top rate from 25 to 20 percent and increasing the exemption from $50,000 to $100,000. As a consequence, by 1928 the percentage of decedents paying federal estate taxes had shrunk by half, to about 0.5 percent (Shammas et al. 1987).

At the same time, the Republicans were busy opening new loopholes. Beginning in 1921, in response to intense lobbying, they installed a wide range of special tax exemptions and deductions, which the highly progressive rate structure of the income tax made valuable to wealthy taxpayers. The Revenue Act of 1921 introduced the preferential taxation of capital gains at a rate of 12.5 percent for assets held longer than two years. (This rate held until 1934.) That act also introduced a variety of deductions, such as oil- and gas-depletion allowances, that favored particular industries. The effect of these provisions on the taxation of the rich was to cut their effective rates nearly in half. By 1923 the effective rate on the richest 1 percent of American families had fallen to less than 8 percent, and it remained at this general level through the rest of the decade. It would have fallen even further if the economic growth of the 1920s had not pushed the less-rich households within the top 1 percent into higher tax brackets (see table 2.3).

Mellon argued that these tax reductions, especially on wealthy Americans and corporations, were necessary to stimulate economic expansion and restore prosperity. He argued, in effect, that rich Americans responded to high taxes in three different ways (all of which damaged the nation's economic health): those who paid the taxes might become discouraged and reduce their entrepreneurial effort; those who were able to pass on the taxes to consumers raised the general cost of living; and those who avoided taxes by, for example, investing in tax-exempt bonds moved their capital into less productive avenues. Slashing the highest marginal tax rates would, Mellon claimed, encourage the rich to invest at higher rates, and in more productive enterprises, thereby enhancing economic efficiency. In short, Mellon declared that there was a trade-off between progressivity and equity and recommended sacrificing progressivity on behalf of growth.[37]

On one occasion, Mellon's interest in promoting growth led him to try to close off a significant loophole in the tax code. The loophole was the complete or partial exemption from personal income taxation of interest payments from the government bonds issued during four wartime Liberty Loans and the postwar Victory Loan. Mellon proposed a constitutional amendment removing the tax deductibility of all government securities. He was concerned that the deductibility encouraged wealthy taxpayers to invest in tax-exempt government bonds, thereby drawing capital away from investments that would be more stimulative of economic growth. Congress, however, under great pressure from the beneficiaries of this loophole, did not follow Mellon's recommendation.

Along with the regime of highly progressive taxes created by World War I came enhanced power for the tax-writing committees of Congress. During the 1920s, legislators on these committees discovered how much influence they wielded through the incremental, relatively invisible consideration of valuable loopholes. Although they did not use the term, they had discovered the political appeal of "tax expenditures." They could establish what amounted to new expenditure programs by creating pockets of privilege within the tax code. In turn, they won or maintained the support of powerful, wealthy groups or individuals while avoiding the political costs associated with raising taxes. Just like the system of protective tariffs before it, the federal income tax had become an instrument to advance special privilege.

To exert and reinforce their new power, the committees won approval in the Revenue Act of 1926 for creating the Joint Committee on Internal Revenue Taxation (JCIRT), which would become the Joint Committee on Taxation (JCT) in 1976. Congress originally charged the JCIRT with investigating ways to simplify the law and with improving its administration, and the professional staff of the JCIRT did increase the technical capabilities of the tax-writing committees. But the JCIRT immediately became primarily a vehicle for enhancing the influence of the senior members of the tax-writing committees.[38]

The Republicans were tempted to go even further in their tax reforms. But Secretary Mellon moderated the reactionary assault by leading a struggle within the Republican Party to protect income taxation from those who wanted to replace it with a national sales tax. Mellon helped persuade corporations and the wealthiest individuals to accept *some* progressive taxation and the principle of ability to pay. This approach would, Mellon told them, demonstrate their civic responsibility and defuse radical attacks on capital by recognizing the popular support that soak-the-rich taxation had gathered. Thus, while shrinking the state, Republican leaders took care to preserve progressive estate and personal income taxes. Also, Republican leaders supported retaining the basic corporation income tax; they held it at the World War I rate of about 12 percent. Mellon (1924, 56–57) went so far as to advocate providing a greater reduction in taxes on "earned" than on "unearned" income, and the Revenue Act of 1924 included such a provision. "The fairness of taxing more lightly incomes from wages, salaries, or from investments is beyond question," Mellon asserted. As he explained: "In the first case, the income is uncertain and limited in duration; sickness or death destroys it and old age diminishes it; in the other, the source of income continues; the income may be disposed of during a man's life and it descends to his heirs." Thus, Mellon helped to preserve a revenue system that, even in its weakened form, advanced social justice.

Mellon's strategy was what might be described as the pursuit of enlightened self-interest—as corporate liberalism, in contrast with Woodrow Wilson's democratic statism. Mellon received crucial support for his approach from the tax-writing committees of Congress. They wanted to preserve the political influence they found they could exert under a progressive system of income taxation.

At the same time, Mellon attempted to strengthen the Treasury by transforming it into a "nonpartisan" agency. In his 1924 book *Taxation: The People's Business* (written largely by his expert assistant secretaries), he explained, "Tax revision should never be made the football either of partisan or class politics but should be worked out by those who have made a careful study of the subject in its larger aspects and are prepared to recommend the course which, in the end, will prove for the country's best interest" (10–11).

Mellon was interested in more than scientific policymaking. His main goal was to insulate the Treasury from pressure from Democratic Congresses. He wanted to ensure that the Treasury operated within the confines of conservative assumptions about the state and corporate power and within a political framework that advanced the Republican Party. Consequently, when Mellon approached tax cutting during the postwar reconversion and downsizing of government, he rejected the advice of the Yale economist Thomas S. Adams, who was the primary tax adviser in the Mellon Treasury.

Adams had a powerful concern with growing administrative burdens and tax complexity, and this concern led him to agree with Mellon on the need to eliminate the excess-profits tax. Adams still approved of the tax in principle, but had concluded that "No federal administration . . . is capable during the next five or six years of carrying with even moderate success two such burdens as the income tax and the excess profits tax" (Adams 1921, 370). That same concern prompted Adams to advise Mellon against expanding exemptions and deductions within the income tax. In fact, Adams began to entertain the idea of replacing the income tax with a progressive spendings tax, one that would tax "unnecessary or surplus comsumption." Rather than follow Adams's lead, Mellon chose to promote tax complexity. He recommended tax-cutting that created privileged groups and industries while providing protection to Republican administrations and Congresses against the charge that they favored the abolition of progressive taxation.[39]

The Republican administrations and Congresses of the 1920s had shifted ground within the World War I tax regime. Soak-the-rich taxation remained, but only at reduced rates containing major loopholes and with its sharp anticorporate edge dulled. As a consequence of the path-dependent nature of the development of the tax regime initiated by American involvement in World War I, the income tax conveyed very mixed messages about the nature of wealth and civic responsibility in the United States. Without the wartime crisis, the growth of the federal government almost certainly would have been slower and dependent on some combination of tariff revenues, sales taxes, and low-rate taxation of personal and corporate incomes or spending. That system might have been just as riddled with inconsistencies, departures from horizontal equity, and theoretical confusion as the highly progressive tax system that emerged during and after the World War I crisis. In contrast with the system that probably would have emerged from a more incremental process, however, the system for financing World War I involved a substantial raising of the stakes of conflict over tax policy. Along with highly progressive taxation came opportunities both for undertaking massive assaults on wealth and corporate power and for carving out lucrative enclaves of special privilege within the tax code. These high stakes helped keep taxation at the center stage of politics through the Great Depression and World War II.

THE NEW DEAL IN TAXATION

The New Deal of Franklin D. Roosevelt introduced a new tax regime that once again focused attention on the rich. Roosevelt personally favored soak-the-rich taxation and recognized the large constituency that the Depression had created for the sort of tax reform—redistributional and anticorporate—undertaken by the Wilson administration. But Roosevelt moved slowly against the rich.

One reason for his delay was the repeal of Prohibition, which produced significant increases in federal revenue. Another reason was the Revenue Act of 1932, signed into law by President Herbert Hoover. That act had already produced a sharp increase in the rates of personal income taxation. In fact, the act represented a resumption of soak-the-rich taxation. It raised the top marginal rate from 25 percent to 63 percent and thus nearly restored it to World War I levels. In addition, the 1932 act dramatically increased estate taxes by cutting the exemption in half (down to $50,000) and more than doubling the maximum rate (to 45 percent). In 1934, as a consequence of the 1932 act, some economic recovery in 1933 and 1934, and loophole closing in the Revenue Act of 1934, the effective income tax rate on the rich rose to about 11 percent, which was higher than at any time during the years of Republican "normalcy" (see table 2.4).[40]

Another reason Roosevelt moved slowly was his fear, which a Democratic Congress shared, that a democratic-statist tax policy, if accompanied by a failure of economic recovery, would arouse business opposition and pave the way for a counterattack on the New Deal. The Democrats remembered well how the economic troubles of 1918 to 1920 had fueled the Republican backlash against Wilson. Also important in slowing the pace of tax reform was the institutional legacy of twelve years of Republican leadership at the Department of Treasury. The Treasury staff that Roosevelt inherited was unenthusiastic about undertaking the work of devising new progressive taxes. Roosevelt's long-term secretary of the Treasury, Henry Morgenthau Jr., did not assume office until January 1934, and his immediate deputies needed about six months to rebuild a capability within the department for advancing democratic-statist reform.

In 1935 Roosevelt decided that political and economic conditions favored a resumption of a democratic-statist tax policy. Most important, the growing "Thunder on the Left," particularly Huey Long's "Share Our Wealth" movement, opened

Table 2.4   Personal Income Tax Rates on the Richest 1 Percent of Households, 1930 to 1940

Year	Marginal Rates	Effective Rates
1930	6 to 25%	6.6%
1931	3 to 25	3.4
1932	8 to 63	6.8
1933	8 to 63	8.1
1934	5 to 63	10.7
1935	9 to 63	11.3
1936	10 to 79	16.4
1937	10 to 79	15.7
1938	10 to 79	14.8
1939	10 to 79	15.1
1940	14 to 79	21.6

Sources: U.S. Department of the Treasury (1930 to 1940); U.S Bureau of the Census (1975, 41–43).

the way for vigorous redistributional taxation designed to remedy flaws in the nation's economic structure.[41]

Morgenthau's staff now contained a group of law professors, including Herman Oliphant and Roswell Magill as general counsel. Magill, a tax expert from Columbia University, directed a comprehensive survey of the federal tax system in preparation for a reform initiative. The monetary economist Jacob Viner also advised Morgenthau on tax issues, and Carl S. Shoup, Roy Blough, and Lawrence H. Seltzer—all economists who specialized in public finance—worked closely with Magill. Central to their efforts was an intensified effort to study the distributional effects of taxation at all levels of government.[42]

At the end of the summer of 1934, Magill and his colleagues in the Treasury had presented Morgenthau with recommendations designed to raise new revenues and attack concentrations of wealth; by December, Morgenthau had forwarded the proposals to the White House. In developing a tax proposal for Congress, Roosevelt drew assistance from his close adviser Felix Frankfurter, who had been urging the president to use the taxing power to attack bigness in business. Roosevelt and Frankfurter used the Treasury recommendations to craft an ambitious program of radical tax reform, which Roosevelt presented to Congress in June. He told Secretary of the Interior Harold Ickes that the speech was "the best thing he had done as President."[43]

Roosevelt proposed a graduated tax on corporations to check the growth of monopoly, a tax on the dividends that holding companies received from corporations they controlled, surtaxes to raise the maximum income tax rate on individuals from 63 to 79 percent, and an inheritance tax, to be imposed in addition to federal estate taxation. In his message to Congress (see Schlesinger 1960, 328; and Lambert 1970, 259–60), he explained that accumulations of wealth meant "great and undesirable concentration of control in relatively few individuals over the employment and welfare of many, many others." Moreover, "whether it be wealth achieved through the cooperation of the entire community or riches gained by speculation—in either case the ownership of such wealth or riches represents a great public interest and a great ability to pay." But Roosevelt's goal was not a simplistic redistribution of wealth and power. Later that year he explained to a newspaper publisher that his purpose was "not to destroy wealth, but to create a broader range of opportunity, to restrain the growth of unwholesome and sterile accumulations and to lay the burdens of Government where they can best be carried." Thus, he justified his tax reform program in terms of both its inherent equity and its ability to liberate the energies of individuals and small corporations, thereby advancing recovery. There was no trade-off, Roosevelt believed, between growth and vertical equity.

During his 1935 initiatives, and throughout the peacetime New Deal, Roosevelt was able to count on the support of Robert Doughton, who served as chair of the House Ways and Means Committee from 1933 until 1947. (Counting a second term, from 1949 to 1953, he was the longest-serving chair of the committee in its history.) Doughton's support was often crucial in mobilizing Senator Pat Harrison of Mississippi, chair of the Senate Finance Committee, and other southern Democrats behind New Deal tax reform. Doughton at times had his doubts about the more sophisticated New Deal tax proposals and resisted large tax increases of any kind. He complained privately in 1935, "We have had too many theories in key places under this administration." But he believed in the justice of shifting the distribution of taxes away from the "poor, weak, and humble," who, he was certain, paid a higher percentage of their incomes in taxes than did the wealthy (Lambert 1970, 297, 226).[44]

Doughton and many of his southern colleagues may have had reservations about big government, but for them taxing the rich became an effective expression of community values. Even one of the most conservative among the southerners, John Rankin of Mississippi, supported taxing the rich. In 1932 he told a group of disabled World War I veterans that he was for "taxing profits of the last war in order to take care of the deficit, care for our disabled veterans, redistribute the wealth of the nation, and lift the burden of taxation from those least able to bear it." He then invoked the symbolism of Andrew Mellon. "I am told," Rankin declared, that "[he] has an income of $30 million a year. If I had my way we would put a wound stripe [the World War I equivalent of a purple heart] on his purse big enough to be seen from Pittsburgh to Philadelphia" (U.S. Congress 1932 , 16).[45]

Led by Doughton, Congress gave Roosevelt much of the tax reform he wanted. The Revenue Act of 1935, joined with economic recovery, pushed households into higher tax brackets and raised effective rates on the rich by nearly 50 percent. In 1936 the effective rate paid by the rich increased to 16.4 percent, higher than during any year of World War I, and in fact the highest level it had ever reached. It remained roughly at that level until 1940, when economic recovery pushed enough taxpayers into higher marginal rates to increase the effective rate even further, to more than 20 percent (see table 2.4). The Revenue Act of 1935 also pushed up the maximum rate of estate taxation to 70 percent. By 1938 this change, along with the 1932 amendments to the estate tax, returned the share of decedents paying federal estate taxes to the level (1.2 percent) that had been reached in 1925 and raised the average tax per estate (in constant dollars) to more than triple the level of 1925 (Shammas et al. 1987, 128).

Roosevelt believed that the Revenue Act of 1935 would generate enough revenue so that he would not have to request any further tax increases until after the presidential election of 1936. But in early 1936 the Supreme Court invalidated the processing tax of the Agricultural Adjustment Act, and Congress overrode Roosevelt's veto of a bonus bill for World War I veterans. Both events threatened a substantial increase in the federal deficit.

In response, Morgenthau recommended an undistributed profits tax, a measure that Roosevelt had previously ignored as a major revenue-raiser. Morgenthau's proposal was to eliminate the tax on corporate income along with the minor taxes on capital stock and corporate excess profits and replace them all with a tax on retained earnings—the profits that corporations did not distribute to their stockholders.[46] The new tax would be graduated according to the proportion of the profits that were undistributed.[47]

Morgenthau and his Treasury staff held the view that the measure would fight tax avoidance. Corporations, they were convinced, deliberately retained profits to avoid the taxation of dividends under the personal income tax. They noted that the Revenue Act of 1932 had restored the marginal rates of taxation on the wealthiest

1 percent of the nation's families almost to World War I levels. They believed that an undistributed profits tax was necessary to make these rates effective (U.S. Department of the Treasury 1937).

Further, the Treasury staff believed that the measure would fight the concentration of corporate power. They were convinced that the largest corporations had the power to retain shares of surpluses greater than those retained by small companies. The surpluses, they were certain, gave large corporations an unfair competitive advantage by reducing the need to borrow new capital. Moreover, the Treasury claimed that the tax would promote recovery. Oliphant and Morgenthau believed that large corporations saved excessively or reinvested their surpluses unwisely. The undistributed profits tax would provide a powerful incentive for such corporations to distribute their profits to their shareholders. Those shareholders, in turn, as Oliphant and Federal Reserve Board Chairman Marriner Eccles stressed, would spend some portion of their dividends and thus stimulate the economy.

Roosevelt endorsed the undistributed profits tax in a message to Congress in March and received support, in principle, from the Ways and Means Committee. But the administration faced the hostility of the Senate Finance Committee and its staffs, which feared revenue loss and preferred retaining the existing corporate income taxes while adding a small flat tax on undistributed earnings. In June 1936, Congress passed a graduated tax on undistributed profits, despite heavy business lobbying against Roosevelt's proposal and intense wrangling over widely divergent revenue estimates. Morgenthau personally intervened in the negotiations between the House and the Senate and had much to do with the outcome. Because of Senate objections, the graduation was less severe than the Treasury had proposed, but Congress retained the basic corporate income tax. The new tax had five steps, rising from 7 percent to a maximum of 27 percent, on undistributed earnings.

The new corporate tax posed the greatest threat to the autonomy of corporate finance since the passage of the excess profits tax during World War I. In July, Secretary of the Interior Ickes talked privately with Harry F. Guggenheim and concluded, "The fundamental policy issue today is taxation." The increases in the higher brackets, "taxing surpluses in corporation treasuries, and fear of further increases," Ickes commented in his diary, had made "a bitter enemy out of practically everyone" among the "very rich."[48]

The threat to the rich from new legislation was all the more acute because Morgenthau and Roosevelt vigorously prosecuted tax evaders and tried to close loopholes used by tax avoiders. They launched their most spectacular crusade in 1934, when the Treasury prosecuted its former secretary, Andrew Mellon, for tax evasion. The Treasury claimed Mellon owed more than $3 million in back taxes and penalties. They chose Mellon as their special target because he seemed to represent the power of financial capitalism, its ability to shape national policy in its interest, the transmogrification of the tax system into an agency of special privilege, and the abuses of Republican government during the 1920s. Morgenthau told the government prosecutor, "I consider that Mr. Mellon is not on trial but Democracy and the privileged rich and I want to see who will win" (Blum 1959, 324–35).

Mellon won in court; a grand jury refused to indict, and in 1937 the Board of Tax Appeals (BTA) found him innocent of tax evasion. But Mellon lost the public relations battle. The BTA also said he had made errors that happened to be in his favor and added that he owed $400,000 in back taxes. The BTA went further, using the Mellon case to publicize the loopholes in the tax code. The commissioner of the BIR pointed out that as secretary of the Treasury, Mellon had solicited from the bureau "a memorandum setting forth the various ways by which an individual may legally avoid tax" (Blum 1959, 324–35). It turned out that Mellon had used five of the ten methods detailed in the memorandum, as well as some others that he had devised on his own.

In the spring of 1937, the outcome of the Mellon case, coupled with a $600 million shortfall in tax revenues—a deficit that Treasury analysts blamed on tax avoidance—led Morgenthau and Roosevelt to seek remedial legislation. At the same time that the Treasury systematically investigated tax avoidance, Roosevelt won the support of the chairs of the tax-writing committees for creating the Joint Committee on Tax Evasion and Avoidance (JCTEA), with power to acquire the names of tax avoiders from the Treasury. With staff assistance from Thurman Arnold, whom the Treasury borrowed from the Department of Justice, Treasury witnesses inventoried loopholes and, under the pressure of congressional questioning, identified sixty-seven "large, wealthy taxpayers" who had used the device of incorporation to reduce their taxes. The press zeroed in on Alfred P. Sloan, the president of General Motors, who had incorporated his yacht. Sloan explained, "While no one should desire to avoid payment of his share [of taxes] . . . neither should anyone be expected to pay more than is lawfully required" (Blum 1959, 335).

Until the investigation by the JCTEA, the public had only rarely had access to information about individual income tax returns. Virtually the only period of such access had been between 1923 and 1926, when congressional progressives like George Norris and Robert LaFollette had succeeded in making public the amount paid by the nation's wealthiest taxpayers. In 1937, before the creation of the JCTEA, Roosevelt wanted to call out the identities of very wealthy individuals who avoided taxes through loopholes. Morgenthau tried to convince him that doing so might be illegal, but he nonetheless provided his boss with names and data. When he settled on the idea of establishing the JCTEA, Roosevelt finally gave up the idea of using his office to publicize data from the tax returns of the rich. Nonetheless, he passed on some information to administration figures Jim Farley and Homer Cummings, perhaps hoping that they would leak them to the press (Blum 1959, 327–37).

The disclosures by the joint committee persuaded Congress to pass, unanimously, the Revenue Act of 1937. The measure increased taxation of personal holding companies, limited deductions for corporate yachts and country estates, restricted deductions for losses from sales or exchanges of property, reduced incentives for the creation of multiple trusts, and eliminated favors for nonresident taxpayers.

The economic recovery, which had cut the rate of unemployment in half by 1937, encouraged Roosevelt to plan an even more intense reform program in 1938. He intended to increase the undistributed profits tax, to establish a graduated tax on capital gains, and to tax the income from federal, state, and local bonds.

These ambitious plans, more than any other dimension of the New Deal, aroused fear and hostility on the part of large corporations. They correctly viewed Roosevelt's tax program as a threat to their profits, their control over capital, and their latitude for financial planning. The tax program, along with other New Deal measures, may well have contributed significantly to the exceptionally low level of private investment during the 1930s, and even, by depressing business expectations, to the severity of the recession of 1937 to 1938. Antimonopolist New Dealers like Harold Ickes went so far as to charge that capitalists had conspired and gone "on strike" in response to New Deal taxes.[49] There is no evidence of such a conspiracy, but the possibility may have inspired Ayn Rand, in her novel *Atlas Shrugged* (1957), to embed at its core a strike of capital—a "moratorium on brains"—against oppressive statism.[50]

In *Atlas Shrugged,* the conspirators withdrew from society into a capitalist Shangri-la, "The Utopia of Greed." In the real world of the late 1930s, however, business leaders did what American business leaders had generally done when they felt threatened by tax initiatives that were radical and popular. They entered the political arena and searched for support outside the business community. In 1938 they found Roosevelt vulnerable, weakened by two major errors: reinforcing the recession of 1937 to 1938 and opening in 1937 the disastrous fight to restructure the Supreme Court. Some northeastern Democrats, led by Bernard Baruch and Joseph P. Kennedy, broke with the president and argued that tax cuts were necessary to restore business confidence. They agreed with Senator Pat Harrison, who declared in December 1937 that Roosevelt's tax program had "retarded progress and contributed to the unemployment situation" (Lambert 1970, 422).[51]

In 1938 a coalition of Republicans and pro-business Democrats, working through the tax-writing committees, took advantage of Roosevelt's mistakes to try to block further New Deal tax reforms. Roosevelt fought back, but the new bipartisan coalition had gathered enough strength to prevail. It pushed through Congress, over the opposition of Ways and Means Chair Doughton, a measure that gutted the tax on undistributed profits and discarded the graduated corporate income tax. Roosevelt, respecting the strength of the opposition, decided not to veto the bill. Instead, he allowed the Revenue Act of 1938 to become law without his signature and denounced the owners of "closely-held corporations making large profits" for wanting "to avoid legitimate income taxes." The Revenue Act would allow them to renew this practice," he said, and it therefore represented the "abandonment of an important principle of American taxation"—taxation according to ability to pay (Roosevelt 1941, 362, 364). In 1939 Congress wiped out the undistributed profits tax.

Roosevelt's defeats in 1938 and 1939 signaled a reassertion of congressional power over the shape of revenue legislation. From that time until the end of World War II, the tax-writing committees of Congress carefully maintained their control over the initiation of tax policy. The influence of Morgenthau and his Treasury advisers had waned; they were able to influence Congress decisively only when Roosevelt was able to mobilize public opinion.

The New Deal's most radical program of tax reform ended in the late 1930s, but Roosevelt and Congress had already ushered in a new tax regime, which featured a strengthened soak-the-rich component. And Roosevelt's program of reform of income taxation had conditioned Americans to expect that any significant tax increases would take place through increasing taxes on the rich and on corporations. To Roosevelt and some of his advisers, it seemed that intervention in another world war—an intervention managed once again by a Democratic administration—would be the occasion for renewed victories for democratic statism.

ANOTHER WARTIME REGIME

World War II, like the great national emergencies before it, created opportunities for public finance reforms that had clear social intent and organizational coherence. As had been the case during World War I and the Great Depression, decisive presidential leadership contributed significantly to the creation of a new tax regime. Motivated by a concern for social justice as well as by the threat to the nation's security, the wartime administration of President Franklin D. Roosevelt shaped the new tax regime and then used the media to persuade Americans to accept it. The new regime proved even more resilient after the war than the World War I regime had been during the 1920s. In fact, ever since, the World War II tax system has remained at the core of federal finance.

President Roosevelt and Secretary of the Treasury Morgenthau began to prepare for financing mobilization as early as 1939. Like Wilson and McAdoo in 1916 and 1917, they set out to finance a large fraction of the costs of war with taxation and to use taxes that bore heavily on corporations and upper-income groups. Roosevelt focused more on the issue of tax structure than on the level of taxation. He talked extensively about the need for an excess profits tax; in the summer of 1940 he proposed such a tax, to be steeply graduated, on both individuals and corporations. Roosevelt, the Treasury, the Ways and Means Committee, and Senate liberals such as Robert LaFollette favored a World War I–style tax on profits above a minimum rate of return. Pat Harrison and some other conservative Democrats, however, opposed this. In the Second Revenue Act of 1940, passed in October, they established a graduated tax on excess profits, reaching a maximum of 50 percent, but provided a generous credit based on prewar profits. Secretary of the Interior Ickes complained that this was "abandoning advanced New Deal ground with a vengeance," but Roosevelt decided not to challenge the power of Congress by accusing it of having sold out to big business.[52]

In 1941, following the passage of the Lend-Lease Act, the Roosevelt administration faced growing inflationary pressures. In response to those pressures, as well as to the need for new revenues, Roosevelt and Morgenthau decided to support reducing the exemptions from personal income as a way to restrain consumption. But they did not abandon reform. Morgenthau proposed taxing away all corporate profits above a 6 percent rate of return, as well as increasing surtaxes on personal income and increasing the base for gift and estate taxes. Roosevelt made it clear that he favored a massive elimination of personal income tax deductions by switching to the taxation of gross income. But in the Revenue Act of 1941, Congress once again rejected most of the reform measures. The act's major provisions consisted of lower exemptions and higher tax rates on upper-middle-class families.

After Pearl Harbor, Morgenthau and Roosevelt resumed their bid for public support of redistributional tax reform. "In time of this grave national danger, when all excess income should go to win the war," Roosevelt told a joint session of Congress in 1942, "no American citizen ought to have a net income, after he has paid his taxes, of more than $25,000" (Congressional Record 1942, 4448).

Roosevelt faced stiff opposition, however, from strategic planners who believed that only a mass-based system of taxation would both adequately fund the war and mitigate economic strains, and from congressional Democrats who feared that a redistributional tax program would weaken the postwar economy. Morgenthau complained that his opponents had forgotten about the "people in the lower one-third." He noted, "I can get all my New Dealers in the bathtub now" (Blum 1967, 35).

In the summer of 1942, Morgenthau, on the recommendation of Randolph Paul and Roy Blough, tried to bridge the gap between the administration and Congress by proposing the adoption of a sharply graduated spendings tax designed to raise large revenues and restrain consumption while increasing progressiveness.[53] Adoption of such a tax would have been by far the most radical departure in American tax policy since 1916. But the tax-writing committees regarded this proposal as too radical economically and too threatening to the influence they enjoyed as gate-keepers for the complex exemptions and deductions in the income tax. Roosevelt recognized the power of the committees and regarded the spendings tax as a bargaining tool for defeating a general sales tax and for making the income tax more progressive. The president decided not to support Morgenthau, explaining to him that "I always have to have a couple of whipping boys" (Blum 1967, 48).[54]

In October, Congress finally agreed to a few progressive concessions and settled on the income tax as the centerpiece of war finance. One of the concessions was increasing the rate of excess profits taxation to 90 percent, but Congress rejected the World War I method of determining excess profits, made the tax explicitly a temporary measure, and taxed only incorporated businesses. The committees also protected major loopholes favoring the wealthy and provided less than half the revenues that Roosevelt had requested.

The Revenue Act of 1942 represented agreement between Congress and Roosevelt on what became the core of a new tax regime—a personal income tax that was both broadly based and progressive. The act made major reductions in personal exemptions, establishing the means for the federal government to acquire huge revenues from the taxation of middle-class wages and salaries. At the same time, the imposition of a surtax that was graduated from 13 percent on the first $2,000 to 82 percent on taxable income over $200,000 raised the marginal rates of taxation on personal incomes higher than at any other time in the history of the income tax in the United States.

The highly progressive income tax, coupled with the defeat of general sales taxation, was the major payoff from Roosevelt's earlier tax reform campaigns, which had established widespread expectations that any significant new taxes would be progressive. At the same time, Roosevelt and many New Deal legislators hoped to be able to distribute much of the new revenues in progressive fashion. They believed that a mass-based income tax would be the best way to ensure a permanent flow of revenues to support federal programs of social justice.

Roosevelt continued his fight to make the income tax even more progressive, to tax corporations more heavily, and to shift revenue raising from borrowing to taxation, but he suffered two major defeats in 1943. The first was over the introduction of withholding. Roosevelt and the Treasury wanted taxpayers, after the introduction of withholding, to pay both their 1942 and their 1943 obligations during the calendar year 1943. Roosevelt told the chair of the Ways and Means Committee, "I cannot acquiesce in the elimination of a whole year's tax burden on the upper income groups during a war period when I must call for an increase in taxes . . . from the mass of people" (Blum 1967, 63). But Beardsley Ruml, chairman of the New York Federal Reserve Bank and treasurer of R. H. Macy and Company, led a radio and press campaign that persuaded Congress to adopt the Ruml plan in the Current Tax Payment Act of 1943.

The second defeat for Roosevelt's wartime tax program occurred in the Revenue Act of 1943. In that legislation, Congress provided for only modest tax increases ($2.3 billion versus the $10.5 billion requested by the Treasury) while creating a host of new tax favors for business, especially the mining, timber, and steel industries. Roosevelt denounced the bill as "not a tax bill but a tax relief bill, providing relief not for the needy but for the greedy" (U.S. Congressional Record 1943, 1958–1959). He vetoed the bill, but for the first time in history, Congress overrode a presidential veto of a revenue act. Alben Barkley, the Democratic majority leader in the Senate, described Roosevelt's veto message as a "calculated and deliberate assault upon the legislative integrity of every member of Congress" (Blum 1967, 76). Secretary of the Interior Harold Ickes hoped that Roosevelt would go "to the people with his case against the Congress" for enacting "a vicious bill designed to protect the rich at the expense of the poor."[55] But the humiliating defeat convinced Roosevelt that he had to accept the structure of the income taxation without further complaint.

Despite the focus on the development of mass-based income taxation and the congressional defeats of Roosevelt's efforts to make the new income tax system more progressive, the wartime legislation did increase dramatically the rates of taxation of America's rich through the personal income tax. Wartime revenue acts increased the marginal rates of taxation to levels ranging from 50 to over 90 percent throughout the war. The substantially higher marginal rates, coupled with wartime inflation, produced effective rates that, from 1942 through 1945, were more than 40 percent, or roughly twice the effective rate achieved in 1940. In 1944 the effective rate on the rich reached an all-time high of nearly 60 percent, or almost four times the highest level achieved during World War I (see table 2.5). The rates were high enough so that, even with the broad base of taxation, in 1945 the richest 1 percent of households produced 32 percent of the revenue yield of the personal income tax (U.S. Department of the Treasury 1951, 71).

Roosevelt's defeats in 1943 essentially ended the conflict, which had begun during World War I, between business and progressive advocates over soak-the-rich income taxation. The winning of World War II and a postwar surge of economic prosperity, following so closely on the heels of the Great Depression, all helped produce a popular, bipartisan consensus of support for sustaining the basic policy shifts, including the adoption of mass-based income taxation, undertaken during the Roosevelt administration. In the realm of tax policy, the World War II emergency institutionalized a new tax regime. It had three elements: a progressive but mass-based

Table 2.5   Personal Income Tax Rates on the Richest 1 Percent of Households, 1940 to 1946

Year	Marginal Rates	Effective Rates
1940	14 to 79%	21.6%
1941	29 to 81	30.1
1942	42 to 88	43.6
1943	46 to 88	43.9
1944	50 to 94	58.6
1945	50 to 94	42.1
1946	47 to 91	37.6

Sources: U.S. Department of the Treasury (1940 to 1946); U.S. Bureau of the Census (1975, 41–43).

income taxation for general revenues; a flat-rate tax on corporate income, also for general revenues; and a regressive payroll tax for social insurance.

BIPARTISAN MANAGEMENT OF THE NEW REGIME

After World War II, some important differences between the two major political parties remained, but both parties insisted on maintaining the central characteristics of the World War II revenue system and eschewing both progressive assaults on corporate financial structures and the regressive taxation of consumption. For the first time since the early nineteenth century, the two political parties agreed on the essential elements of the nation's fiscal policy.

The general decline of partisanship after World War II no doubt contributed to the convergence of the two parties on fiscal policy. The convergence on tax policy involved acceptance by the Republican Party of levels of taxation of large incomes and corporate profits that were substantially higher than before World War II. These were levels that the rich and the business community had regarded as unconscionable at the time World War II ended. In the immediate postwar years, Republicans accepted marginal rates of personal income taxation on the rich that were as high as during World War II (see table 2.6). The postwar tax on corporate incomes reached a peak of 52 percent, which held until 1964; thereafter, until 1986, it was usually either 46 percent or 48 percent.

The convergence of the two parties, however, was more the product of a shift in direction by the Democratic Party. In the postwar era, Democrats largely abandoned taxation as an instrument to mobilize class interests. Southern Democrats, who had constituted a significant force within the Democratic Party on behalf of soak-the-rich taxation, fell under the sway of neoclassical economics and its approach to tax policy. During the 1950s and 1960s, it was the fiscal conservatism of Wilbur Mills of Arkansas, rather than the populism of Claude Kitchin and Robert Doughton, that guided the southern Democrats who shaped tax policy in Congress.[56] Northeastern Democratic leaders, including those with close ties to organized labor, also abandoned "soak-the-rich" taxation. The Democratic tax politics that Joseph P. Kennedy and Bernard Baruch had pioneered during the 1930s now prevailed. Given the buoyancy of revenues under the World War II tax regime,

Table 2.6   Personal Income Tax Rates on the Richest 1 Percent of Households, 1952 to 1988

Year	Marginal Rates	Effective Rates
1952	—	32.2%
1961	38 to 91%	—
1963	—	24.6
1967	—	26.3
1969	46 to 77	—
1972	—	26.1
1974	45 to 70	—
1977	—	27.8
1979	59 to 70	—
1981	—	28.9
1984	45 to 50	—
1986	—	22.1
1988	28	

Sources: Bakija and Steuerle (1991, 474–475), for the marginal rates; Pechman (1989, 22), for the effective rates. Pechman, who relied on Treasury Department *Statistics of Income* data, found consistently higher effective income tax rates than did Richard Kasten et al. (1994, 18), who relied on Congressional Budget Office data.

Democrats had no need to consider significant tax increases and thus had no need to justify them by calls to "soak the rich." If their commitment to vertical equity was ever in question, they could point to the highly progressive tax system they had implemented during World War II and preserved after the war.

During the 1950s the Democratic congressional leadership accepted revisions of the personal income tax that reduced the effective rates of taxation on the rich to roughly 25 percent. Such rates were high by pre–World War II standards, but about half the peak rates of effective taxation during the war. Presidents John F. Kennedy and Lyndon B. Johnson continued to support tax reforms, such as the taxation of capital gains at death, but they were careful not to push too hard for the reforms for fear of seeming to threaten increasing the cost of living or to put expansion at risk. Moreover, they advocated a variety of selective tax cuts that favored the wealthy. The Kennedy-Johnson administrations did so by hawking the "supply-side" benefits, much as Andrew Mellon had done during the 1920s. In 1964 Congress responded to Johnson's call for a tax cut "to increase our national income and Federal revenues" by slashing taxes in the face of large deficits (Public Papers of the Presidents of the United States 1965, 9–10). The Council of Economic Advisers, also committed to "growthmanship," actively supported the 1964 cuts, which reduced capital gains taxes and allowed more generous depreciation allowances. Most liberals regarded the 1964 tax cuts as a victory for aggressive countercyclical stimulation of demand; they also embraced a supply-side rationale for the cuts, particularly those that reduced the marginal rates on the rich (see table 2.6).

In effect, Democrats assisted the Republican Party in finishing the job it had begun during the 1920s: taking both the partisan sting and the redistributional threat out of taxation. The shift in the tax policy favored by the Democratic Party was part of its more general shift—one begun after 1937, accelerated during World War II, and completed in the Kennedy-Johnson era—away from democratic statism and toward corporate liberalism. This line of thinking had expanded its intellectual ambit, and its political potency, by incorporating Keynesian countercyclical policies. Presidents Kennedy and Johnson invoked Keynesian ideas as part of a strategy for winning business support for their tax reform program.[57]

Democrats and Republicans generally reached agreement as well over the need for support of effective income tax administration and kept issues surrounding tax administration out of politics. During the presidency of Harry Truman, both Democratic and Republican leaders saw withholding as crucial to the success of the income tax. Both parties supported ensuring adequate funding for the Bureau of Internal Revenue, including its efforts to punish employers who refused to withhold taxes.

The Truman administration shifted enforcement emphasis from the tax dodges of established fortunes to the "tax chiseling" of those who had profited during wartime and the period of prosperity following the war. In a 1947 *Collier's* article, Undersecretary of the Treasury A. L. M. Wiggins described how the BIR had sent 128 revenue agents to a farming community in Minnesota to examine bank accounts, store accounts, government payments, crop yields, and the records of grain and cattle buyers. Wiggins reported that the BIR had collected over $5 million in additional taxes and penalties from farmers in that community. The Treasury and the BIR did not reveal that, although they were increasing their efforts to audit individuals, efforts such as the Minnesota investigation were unusual. They wanted those tax dodgers who were, in Commissioner of Internal Revenue George Schoeneman's (1949, 129) words, "a tragic group of otherwise respectable individuals" to fear apprehension and punishment.

To that end, Wiggins and Schoeneman exaggerated the efficiency of the BIR. In 1949 Schoeneman told the readers of *American Magazine*, "You see, it's almost impossible to deceive our investigators, because most of them are generally familiar with every type of dodge ever attempted, and if they run across what appears to be a new one, they can look into the files and find it's been tried before." The Treasury that had used propaganda to stress patriotic values during World War II used the mass media to deliver its threats during the postwar era. Fear of the Bureau of Internal Revenue (renamed the Internal Revenue Service in 1953), combined with the political popularity of the individual income tax, led to what was, by worldwide standards, an unusually high level of taxpayer compliance.[58]

The bipartisan consensus on taxation ushered in an era of buoyant public finance that lasted until the 1980s. Usually well removed from the contested turf of partisan politics, the tax policies and political actions that produced the era were nearly invisible. Persistent inflation, as well as economic growth, helped to extend the life of the World War II tax regime. Inflation, which was most intense in the late 1940s and then during the period from the late 1960s throughout the 1970s, produced larger revenues through "bracket creep," or the push of increasing numbers of families into higher tax brackets faster than their real incomes increased.[59] In effect, the structure of income tax rates became substantially more progressive.

Although the Kennedy-Johnson tax cuts had reduced the marginal rates of personal income taxation of the rich, and these rates remained relatively stable until the 1980s, the effective rates of taxation paid by the rich edged up during the 1970s. The rates reached nearly 30 percent, or roughly those that had prevailed immediately before and after World War II (see tables 2.5 and 2.6). Meanwhile, the corporate income tax, with a flat rate and hence no bracket creep, became a less dynamic source of revenue. In 1950 individual and corporate income tax revenues were roughly equal; by 1980 individual income tax revenues were nearly four times as large as corporate revenues.[60]

The inflation-driven increases in revenues permitted new "tax expenditures"—special preferences offered under the tax code in the form of exclusions, deductions, and credits. Tax expenditures had accompanied the introduction and expansion of mass-based income taxation during the 1940s and 1950s. Some of these benefited broad categories of middle-class Americans.[61] Others, like the introduction of accelerated depreciation in 1954, favored the wealthy.[62] During the 1960s and 1970s tax expenditures became even more popular, and both old and new forms grew relative to conventional expenditures. Politicians became attracted to tax expenditures as a way to accomplish social goals, including reducing the tax burden on the rich. In other words, many Democratic and Republican members of Congress found self-serving political benefits in hiding tax programs from public scrutiny. Also contributing to the movement were taxpaying groups that aggressively sought preferential treatment within the tax code in order to offset the effects of bracket creep. In turn, the taxpayers and legislators who benefited from the tax expenditures developed a vested interest in increasing the complexity of the process of tax legislation.[63]

The decline of inflation during the 1970s, along with the weakening productivity that had ensued, undermined the fiscal capacity of the progressive, mass-based income tax, but it was the tax reforms undertaken during the administration of Ronald Reagan that ended the "era of easy finance" and significantly reduced the taxation of the rich. The Economic Recovery Tax Act of 1981 (ERTA) indexed tax rates for inflation and slashed the marginal rates on the rich. The result was a decline in the effective rates of taxation to the levels that had prevailed during the early 1960s (see table 2.6). The Tax Reform Act of 1986 broadened the base of income taxation and may have thereby restored some progressivity to the federal income tax system as a whole, but the measure reduced further the marginal rates of taxation on the rich and confirmed ERTA's reductions in the effective rates paid by the rich.[64]

TOWARD FUNDAMENTAL REFORM?

The years since the Tax Reform Act of 1986 have been disappointing to reformers who hoped to see further broadening of the income tax base or further reductions in the taxation of the rich. The administrations of both George Bush and Bill Clinton resumed an interest in enlarging tax expenditures, and the Clinton administration has focused on increasing taxes on the wealthy while offering tax cuts to the middle class. Meanwhile, proposals for a "flat tax" or a national sales tax have made little headway through the thicket of pluralistic government.

The lack of reform along the lines pioneered in 1986 is hardly surprising, however, when placed within the long history of American taxation. The nation has never embraced a new tax regime outside of a national emergency. And when the United States has launched a new regime, it has always sought middle-class support by including far more "vertical equity" than the current flat tax or national sales tax proposals provide. The lesson of virtually every major episode of regime creation is that reformers must honor American ideals of republicanism. They therefore must seek an increase in progressiveness at the same time as they strive to stimulate investment, productivity, and economic growth.

NOTES

1. In this essay, when I refer to "the rich," I follow Joel Slemrod's (1994, 179) suggestion of focusing on "households whose income is in the top 1 percent of all household . . . units."

2. For a provocative discussion of the international comparisons, see Steinmo (1993, 35–40).

3. By a "tax regime" I mean a system of taxation with its own characteristic tax bases, rate structures, administrative apparatus, and social intentions. For a survey of the history of taxation organized around the tax regimes created during national emergencies, see Brownlee (1996).

4. See Handlin and Handlin (1975, 57–81) for a useful overview of the history of government in the new republic. An excellent introduction to the modern intellectual history of the revolutionary era is found in the essays in Greene (1987). For important suggestions as to the long-run influence of civic humanism, see Ross (1979). On Adam Smith as a civic humanist, see Winch (1978).

5. For discussion of Smith's point, see Groves (1974, 19–20).

6. The complicated story of tax reform during the American Revolution is ably told by Becker (1980).

7. For overviews of the antebellum reform movement for general property taxation, see Benson (1965) and Ely (1888). On Ohio's property tax experience, see Ely (1888, 146–59, 456). The major exceptions in the increasing reliance by state governments on property taxation were in the South, where the waxing movement to protect slavery increasingly shielded slaves from state taxation. In North Carolina, for example, during the 1840s and 1850s the state government relied on investment income from banks and railroads and on borrowing to reduce its reliance on property taxes (see Sylla 1986). Another valuable study for understanding nineteenth-century public finance in the South is Wallenstein (1987).

8. The most informative scholarship detailing the development of income tax legislation between the Civil War and World War I remains Blakey and Blakey (1940, 1–103), Ratner (1942, 13–340), and Seligman (1914). Robert Stanley (1993) has revised this scholarship, emphasizing the conservative forces behind the development of the federal income tax through 1913. In explaining the adoption of the first federal income tax, he emphasizes the Republican desire to provide political protection for the consumption-based tax regime. For a description of direct taxation by the federal government during the early republic, see Adams (1884, 50–60).

9. On the point that propertied New Yorkers paid substantially higher income taxes than property taxes, see Seligman (1914, 473–75).

10. The estimates of the percentages of Union households paying income taxes are based on the well-known data on taxpayers developed by the Commissioner of Internal Revenue for 1866. By contrast with my emphasis, Robert Stanley (1993, 39–40, 263–64), citing a figure of only 1.3 percent of the American people paying income taxes, claims that the tax did not reach the middle class. Stanley seriously understates the social reach of the income tax by including the Confederate population and by using "people" rather than taxpaying households for his denominator. On estimates

regarding the distribution of income and wealth between 1790 and 1860, see Brownlee (1979, 134–36). On the distribution of taxpayers by income groups, see U.S. Government (1873, vi).

11. On the complex difficulties with the general property tax, see Yearley (1970, 3–95, 137–65).

12. Traditional "progressive" scholarship placed a great deal of emphasis on the importance of such grassroots pressure by farmers in shaping the inception of the federal income tax. See, for example, Ellis (1940), and Ratner (1942, passim).

13. For a discussion of the meaning of democratic statism and its relationship to progressive income taxation, see Brownlee (1990).

14. On the realignment strategy, see Stewart (1980). Stewart (1974) has also described the way in which political parties, in building consensus, moderated the content and rhetorical tone of income tax proposals after 1896.

15. Nearly a century later, average Americans still favored levying additional taxes on corporations (see Sheffrin 1994, 321–24).

16. Modern scholarship has modified an older "progressive" interpretation of the *Pollock* decision as a conspiratorial act of judicial fiat. For that view, see McCloskey (1960, 140–41) and Ratner (1942, 193–214), among others. The best current discussion of the role of the Court is Stanley (1993, 136–75), who argues that the Court was engaged in a kind of Jacksonian attack on the dominant role of Congress in "statist capitalism." Consistent with his interpretation is Morton Horwitz's (1992, 19–27) argument that the *Pollock* decision was a logical culmination of a process that established an "anti-redistributive principle" as "part of the very essence of the constitutional law of a neutral state."

17. For suggestions of the influence on tax policy of what political scientists call "critical elections" (like 1896), see Hansen (1983). On the estate tax enacted during the Spanish-American war, see Ratner (1942, 234–50).

18. For discussions of the urban interest groups that developed a taste for tax reform, see Thelen (1972, 202–22), Yearley (1970, 193–250), Buenker (1973, esp. 103–17), and Keller (1990, 208–15).

19. For challenges to my views, see Stark (1987, 1991) and Buenker (1998, 510–11, 551–54, 689–90).

20. Exemplary discussions of corporate liberalism are Furner (1990, 241–86) and Sklar (1988).

21. The standard source on the ratification movement is Buenker (1985).

22. Jordan A. Schwartz (1993, 14) has cited Cordell Hull's emergency-revenue argument in claiming that "anticipation of war made the income tax a war tax." There is no evidence, however, that Hull expected war in 1910, when he made the cited comment, and there is much evidence that Hull was then primarily interested in a redistribution of the tax burden. For Hull's own description of his important role in federal tax reform before World War I, see Hull (1948, 45–74). Between 1894 and 1913, when champions of income taxation referred to the possible need to levy it in wartime, they were usually buttressing their legal arguments for the constitutionality of the federal tax. See, for example, the dissenting opinion of Justice John Marshall Harlan in *Pollock v. Farmers' Loan and Trust Company,* 158 US 601, 15 SCt 673, 39 LEd 1108 (1895), and the essay "The Proposed Sixteenth Amendment to the Constitution" in Seligman (1914, 627–28). (Seligman first published this part of the essay in 1910.) Historians have only rarely claimed that the architects of the Sixteenth Amendment or the 1913 legislation expected the tax to produce major additions to federal revenue. The leading examples are Ben Baack and Edward J. Ray (1985,135), who claim that the passage of the 1913 income tax "signaled voters that the federal government had the wherewithal to provide something for everybody."

23. On the increasing concentration of incomes between 1913 and 1916, see Williamson and Lindert (1980, 81–82), who identify 1916 as the year of peak income concentration in American history. They attribute the income wave of 1913 to 1916 not to monopoly power, however, but to sharply rising food prices.

24. Alfred D. Chandler Jr. (1977, 345) finds that the modern integration of American industry was complete by World War I. "By the second decade of the century," Chandler concludes, "the shakedown period following the merger movement was over." The result was that "modern business enterprises dominated major American industries, and most of these same firms continued to dominate their industries for decades."

25. For an appreciation of the impact of World War I on the nature of the income tax, see Bartlett (1993).

26. Some political science scholarship has stressed the crippling effect of post–Civil War southern sectionalism, and the associated hostility toward the federal government, on the development of a modern state. But this scholarship does not discuss progressive federal income taxation, which this sectionalism (expressed, for example, in the careers of Claude Kitchin and Cordell Hull) promoted (see Bensel 1984, 1990; Quadrango 1988). Historians are well aware of the general significance of the many southerners who were in the Wilson administration or among his supporters in Congress, but no one has systematically examined their ideas on government. The best analyses are Link (1950–51, 314–24) and Tindall (1967, 1–60).

27. By World War I the description of highly progressive taxation as "soak-the-rich" taxation was common in both the United States and England. The term had emerged in the United States in the late 1890s, accompanied by the introduction of a new meaning of *soak:* "to impose upon by an extortionate charge or price" (Simpson and Weiner 1989, 892–93; see also Partridge 1984, 1108; and Wentworth and Flexner 1967, 498–99).

28. A contrasting view of the importance of redistributional impulses is that of John Witte (1985, 81–82), who, in explaining the crucial Revenue Act of 1916, stresses the "dictates of war" and asserts that "there is little evidence of an independent interest in redistributing income through the tax system."

29. On the sympathy of leading figures in the Wilson administration for benefit approaches to taxation, see Brownlee (1993).

30. Because they ignore the incidence of corporate income taxation on the rich, these estimates seriously understate the effective rates. Richard Kasten, Frank Sammartino, and Eric Toder (1994, 21) estimated that in 1980, for example, the corporate income tax might have increased the effective rate of all federal taxes on the top 1 percent of households from 28.7 percent (assuming that all of the corporate tax fell on labor income) to 34.9 percent (assuming that all of the corporate tax fell on capital income).

31. For the percentages of decedents who were over twenty-five years of age and whose estates paid estate taxes between 1922 and 1977, see Shammas et al. (1987, 128–29).

32. Excess profits taxation turned out to be responsible for most of the tax revenues raised by the federal government during the war. Taxes accounted for a larger share of total revenues in the United States than in any of the other belligerent nations, despite the fact that by the end of 1918 the daily average of war expenditures in the United States was almost double that in Great Britain and far greater than that in any other combatant nation. The best accounting of American war costs remains Seligman (1921, 748–82).

33. For an influential example of the latter assumption, see Jorgenson (1965).

34. Wilson, however, was much more suspicious of the administrative state than was McAdoo. In 1916, because of that suspicion, Wilson may well have been attracted to using taxation, rather than administrative regulation, to tackle "the monopoly problem." As the war wore on and he was unable to resist the growing influence of business within the wartime bureaucracy, Wilson became even more attracted to the antimonopoly potential of excess profits taxation. But no scholar has fully explored the linkages between Wilson's approach to the taxation of business and his overall relations with business. The best study of Wilson and business during the war is Cuff (1973).

35. For a discussion of the sustained hostility toward special privilege within the Democratic Party, see Kelley (1969).

36. In 1924 Andrew Mellon paid more income tax ($1.9 million) than all but three other Americans (John D. Rockefeller Jr., Henry Ford, and Edsel Ford). Mellon was a relative newcomer to the ranks of the nation's super-rich. Only a decade earlier, he (and the Fords as well) had not been counted among the nation's wealthiest fifty citizens (Lebergott 1976, 169–71). For a discussion of the largest income tax payers in 1923 and 1924, as made public by a provision in the Revenue Act of 1923, see Atwood (1926, 253–56).

37. For Andrew Mellon's pro-growth arguments, see Mellon (1924, esp. 93–107, 127–38). For a discussion of the significance of Mellon's policies, see King (1983; 1993, 104–11). King argues that Mellon invoked a "hegemonic tax logic" that was finally victorious in the Kennedy-Johnson tax cuts of 1964. No one has ever demonstrated that the Mellon tax cuts actually stimulated economic growth, but two economists (Smiley and Keehn 1995) have argued persuasively that the postwar lowering of the marginal rates at the top reduced tax avoidance through the purchase of tax-exempt securities.

38. On the formation of the JCIRT, see Blakey and Blakey (1940, 542–43, 546–48); see also Kennon and Rogers (1989, 330–33) and Reese (1980, 61–88).

39. For a discussion of Adams's analysis, see Brownlee (1990, 430–31).

40. Among the congressional efforts at loophole closing was a request that the Treasury establish systematic procedures for corporations to calculate their depreciation deductions. The Treasury responded by requiring straight-line depreciation for income-producing property. See Hogan (1967, 7–8); see also note 62, this chapter. The 1934 act retained the preferential taxation of capital gains but increased the tax rate and made it progressive. For example, the act taxed gains from assets held between two and five years at 60 percent of the personal tax rates, or at marginal rates that ranged between 3 and 36 percent, rather than the previous flat rate of 12.5 percent (see Blakey and Blakey 1940, 586–88). This approach to taxing capital gains remained in place through World War II, although the Revenue Act of 1938 cut the percentage of long-term capital gains subject to personal income taxation from 60 to 50 percent, see Bureau of Internal Revenue (1952, 50–56, 420–23).

41. Roosevelt was as interested in the substance as in the symbols of soak-the-rich tax reform. But for a very different view of Roosevelt's tax program than the one presented here, see the work of the historian Mark Leff (1984), who argues that Franklin D. Roosevelt looked only for symbolic victories in tax reform. For a critique of Leff, see Brownlee (1986). The following account of the making of tax policy within the Roosevelt administration through World War II draws on Blum (1959, 297–337, 439–51; 1965, 22–30, 278–318; 1967, 33–78). Blum's work still stands as the best general treatment of this subject. Also valuable is Blakey and Blakey (1940, 301–577) and Paul (1954, 168–406). See also Lambert (1970) for excellent details on the relationship between the Roosevelt administration and Congress. Lambert found no evidence that Roosevelt favored a radical distribution of tax burdens, but he did find a deep ethical commitment to the principle of ability to pay.

42. The most important study of tax incidence undertaken during the 1930s was the unpublished analysis of the economist Louis Shere (1934). For an excellent survey of the modern measurement of tax burden in the United States, see Atrostic and Nunns (1990).

43. On the significance of Frankfurter's interest in this tax legislation, see Hawley (1966, 344–59). Hawley concludes, however, that the revenue acts of 1935 and 1936 were "relatively innocuous" (359). Harold Ickes's discussion of the 1935 tax measure is in the June 19, 1935, entry in his diaries (Harold L. Ickes Papers, Library of Congress).

44. For suggestions as to the significance to the New Deal of Doughton and other southern congressmen, see Tindall (1967, 607–49) and Freidel (1965). Pat Harrison was less energetic than Doughton, and also less of a Populist on tax matters. In 1935 he opposed Roosevelt's proposal for the taxation of inheritances.

45. On Rankin, see Freidel (1965, 80–81). For a stimulating analysis of conservative support for various aspects of the New Deal, including taxation, see Lowi (1995, 130–35).

46. In 1933, to help finance public works, the National Industrial Recovery Act had included, as a modest experimental measure, a temporary set of taxes on capital stock and excess profits. The key tax was a levy of 0.1 percent on the declared value of a company's stock. As an incentive for full valuation of stock, the act also included a tax of 5 percent on all corporate profits over 12.5 percent of declared value (see Hawley 1966, 31; Bryan 1934).

47. Magill's team of experts had discovered this idea when digging into the Treasury archives for inspiration. They had discovered a 1919 proposal by the Treasury adviser Thomas S. Adams for an undistributed profits tax, which he had favored as a replacement for excess profits taxation. For evidence of Adams's influence, see Louis Shere to Robert M. Haig, March 6, 1936, Robert Murray Haig Papers, Butler Library, Columbia University.

48. See the July 27, 1936, entry in his diaries (Harold L. Ickes Papers, Library of Congress).

49. On the causes of the recession of 1937 to 1938, see Roose (1954, esp. 10–12, 209–16), who discusses the effects of the undistributed profits tax. Schumpeter (1939, 1038–40) also stresses the role of that tax. On the conspiracy charges, see Leff (1984, 212–13).

50. The novel did not appear in print until 1957, but Ayn Rand began writing it at least a decade earlier, and she formulated her political assessment of the New Deal during the late 1930s. She saw the political issues of the 1930s in stark, black-and-white terms. In 1940, for example, she plunged vigorously into Wendell Willkie's presidential campaign but wound up condemning him for "abandoning his moral stand for capitalism" (see Branden 1986, 158–231; Rand 1957).

51. Harrison was one of the southern Democrats who broke with Roosevelt during the court-packing episode. The break had more to do with the New Deal's threat to traditional race relations than its challenge to economic elites (see Tindall 1967, 625ff.).

52. In June, Roosevelt had favored a graduated tax on all profits in excess of 4 percent (Harold Ickes Diaries, entries of June 9 and August 10, 1940, Harold L. Ickes Papers, Library of Congress).

53. As noted earlier, immediately in the wake of World War I, the Treasury adviser Thomas S. Adams had suggested a spendings tax. Subsequently, the economist Irving Fisher's advocacy of the tax had kept the idea before his profession (see Fisher and Fisher 1942).

54. A series of memoranda drafted in the Treasury's Division of Tax Research describes the proposed tax (see, for example, U.S. Department of the Treasury 1942). William Vickrey, a Ph.D. student of Irving Fisher, served in the Division of Tax Research and may have been the author of this memorandum. For an analysis of Vickrey's views on spendings tax, see Groves (1974, 110–13). The best survey of the development of Vickrey's views on taxation is Arnott et al. (1994, 99–185).

55. Entry of February 26, 1944, Harold Ickes Diaries, Harold L. Ickes Papers, Library of Congress.

56. For an analysis of Wilbur Mills's career that emphasizes his commitment to neoclassical analysis of taxation, see Zelizer (1998). On the underlying transformation of southern society, see Black and Black (1987, 3–72).

57. The scholarly literature on the Kennedy-Johnson tax programs has become impressive in depth and scope. See, for example, King (1993, 151–319), Martin (1991,1996), Stein (1969, 372–453), Witte (1985, 155–75), and Zelizer (1996).

58. On the wartime propaganda and the postwar enforcement efforts, see Jones (1996). We do not have a scholarly history of the Internal Revenue Service and the BIR, but for a very useful reference work, see Davis (1992).

59. Because of unanticipated inflation, the revenue system proved to be far more elastic after World War II than experts had predicted. Economists at the Committee for Economic Development (CED), for example, had believed that after the war federal tax receipts as a share of gross domestic product would fall from the wartime peak of 22 percent to somewhere between 10 and 15 percent. In fact, the tax share of national product dipped below 15 percent only briefly, in 1950. By 1952 it was approaching 20 percent and ever since has remained close to, or slightly above, 20 percent. Herbert Stein (personal communication, June 20, 1994) provided the author with the information regarding the CED estimates at the end of World War II.

60. For a summary of the operation of postwar individual income tax, including the trends in progressiveness, see Bakija and Steuerle (1991).

61. After World War II, and the ebbing of patriotism as a factor in income tax compliance, Congress relied increasingly on tax expenditures and other measures—including the introduction of the income-splitting joint return for husbands and wives and the acceptance of community property status—to enhance the legitimacy of the new tax regime. However, a deduction that had been in the tax code since 1913—the deduction for mortgage interest—was the most expensive of the tax expenditures. On the joint return and community property status, see Jones (1996).

62. For a discussion of how accelerated depreciation for income-producing structures helped turn real estate development into a rewarding tax shelter and may have contributed to an explosion in shopping center construction, see Hanchett (1996).

63. The leading analysis of the bureaucratic complexity of making tax policy, especially within Congress, during the 1960s and 1970s is Reese (1980).

64. For excellent histories of the Tax Reform Act of 1986, see Birnbaum and Murray (1987), Conlan, Wrightson, and Beam (1990), and Steuerle (1992, 71–162).

REFERENCES

Adams, Henry Carter. 1884. *Taxation in the United States, 1789–1816*. Baltimore: Johns Hopkins University Press.

Adams, Thompson S. 1921. "Should the Excess Profits Tax Be Repealed." *Quarterly Journal of Economics* 35(May): 363–93.

Arnott, Richard, et al., eds. 1994. *Public Economics: Selected Papers by William Vickrey*. Cambridge: Cambridge University Press.

Atrostic, B. K., and James R. Nunns. 1990. "Measuring Tax Burden: A Historical Perspective." In *Fifty Years of Economic Measurement: The Jubilee of the Conference on Research in Income and Wealth*, National Bureau of Economic Research Studies in Income and Wealth, vol. 54, edited by Ernest R. Berndt and Jack E. Triplett. Chicago: University of Chicago Press.

Atwood, Albert W. 1926. *The Mind of the Millionaire*. New York: Harper & Brothers.

Baack, Ben, and Edward J. Ray. 1985. "The Political Economy of the Origin and Development of the Federal Income Tax." In *Emergence of the Modern Political Economy: Research in Economic History*, supp. 4, edited by Robert Higgs. Greenwich, Conn.: JAI Press.

Bakija, Jon, and Eugene Steuerle. 1991. "Individual Income Taxation Since 1948." *National Tax Journal* 44(December).

Bartlett, Bruce. 1993. "The Futility of Raising Tax Rates." *Policy Analysis* 192(April 8): 9–10.

Becker, Robert A. 1980. *Revolution, Reform, and the Politics of American Taxation, 1763–1783*. Baton Rouge: Louisiana State University Press.

Bensel, Richard. 1984. *Sectionalism and American Political Development, 1880–1980*. Madison: University of Wisconsin Press.

———. 1990. *Yankee Leviathan: The Origins of Central State Authority in America, 1859–1877*. New York: Cambridge University Press.

Benson, Sumner. 1965. "A History of the General Property Tax." In *The American Property Tax: Its History, Administration, and Economic Impact*, edited by George C. S. Benson, et al. Claremont, Calif.: Claremont Men's College.

Birnbaum, Jeffrey H., and Alan S. Murray. 1987. *Showdown at Gucci Gulch: Lawmakers, Lobbyists, and the Unlikely Triumph of Tax Reform*. New York: Random House.

Black, Earl, and Merle Black. 1987. *Politics and Society in the South*. Cambridge, Mass.: Harvard University Press.

Blakey, Roy G., and Gladys C. Blakey. 1940. *The Federal Income Tax*. London: Longmans, Green.

Blum, John Morton. 1959. *From the Morgenthau Diaries: Years of Crisis, 1928–1938*. Boston: Houghton Mifflin.

———. 1965. *From the Morgenthau Diaries: Years of Urgency, 1938–1941*. Boston: Houghton Mifflin.

———. 1967. *From the Morgenthau Diaries: Years of War, 1941–1945*. Boston, Houghton Mifflin.

Branden, Barbara. 1986. *The Passion of Ayn Rand.* Garden City, N.Y.: Doubleday.

Brownlee, W. Elliot. 1970. "Income Taxation and Capital Formation in Wisconsin, 1911–1929." *Explorations in Economic History* 8(September): 77–102.

———. 1974. *Progressivism and Economic Growth: The Wisconsin Income Tax, 1911–1929.* Port Washington, N.Y.: Kennikat Press.

———. 1979. *Dynamics of Ascent: A History of the American Economy.* New York: Alfred A. Knopf.

———. 1985. "Wilson and Financing the Modern State: The Revenue Act of 1916." *Proceedings of the American Philosophical Society* 129: 173–210.

———. 1986. "Taxation as an X-ray." *Reviews in American History* 14(March): 121–26.

———. 1990. "Economists and the Formation of the Modern Tax System in the United States: The World War I Crisis." In *The State and Economic Knowledge: The American and British Experience,* edited by Mary O. Furner and Barry E. Supple. Cambridge: Cambridge University Press.

———. 1993. "Social Investigation and Political Learning in the Financing of World War I." In *The State and Social Investigation in Britain and the United States,* edited by Michael J. Lacey and Mary O. Furner. Cambridge: Cambridge University/Woodrow Wilson Center.

———. 1996. *Federal Taxation in America: A Short History.* Cambridge: Cambridge University/Woodrow Wilson Center.

Bryan, Malcolm H. 1934. "The Excess Profits Tax" (September 20). In U.S. Department of Treasury, Office of Tax Analysis, National Archives, Washington, D.C.

Buenker, John D. 1973. *Urban Liberalism and Progressive Reform.* New York: W. W. Norton.

———. 1985. *The Income Tax and the Progressive Era.* New York: Garland.

———. 1998. *The History of Wisconsin,* vol. 4, *The Progressive Era, 1893–1914.* Madison: State Historical Society of Wisconsin.

Chandler, Alfred D., Jr. 1977. *The Visible Hand.* Cambridge, Mass.: Harvard University Press.

Congressional Globe. 1861. 37th Congress, First Session. Washington, D.C.: U.S. Government Printing Office.

Conlan, Timothy J., Margaret T. Wrightson, and David R. Beam. 1990. *Taxing Choices: The Politics of Tax Reform.* Washington, D.C.: Congressional Quarterly Press.

Cuff, Robert D. 1973. *The War Industries Board: Business-Government Relations During World War I.* Baltimore: Johns Hopkins University Press.

Davis, Shelley L. 1992. *IRS Historical Fact Book: A Chronology, 1646–1992.* Washington, D.C.: U.S. Department of the Treasury, Internal Revenue Service.

Dudden, Arthur P. 1971. *Joseph Fels and the Single-Tax Movement.* Philadelphia: Temple University Press.

Ellis, Elmer. 1940. "Public Opinion and the Income Tax, 1860–1900." *Mississippi Valley Historical Review* 27(September): 225–42.

Ely, Richard T. 1888. *Taxation in American States and Cities.* New York: Thomas Y. Crowell.

Fisher, Irving, and Herbert W. Fisher. 1942. *Constructive Income Taxation.* New York: Harper.

Freidel, Frank. 1965. *FDR and the South.* Baton Rouge: Louisiana State University Press.

Furner, Mary. 1990. "Knowing Capitalism: Public Investigation and the Labor Question in the Long Progressive Era." In *The State and Economic Knowledge: The American and British Experience,* edited by Mary O. Furner and Barry E. Supple. Cambridge: Cambridge University Press.

Greene, Jack P., ed. 1987. *The American Revolution: Its Character and Limits.* New York: New York University Press.

Groves, Harold M. 1974. *Tax Philosophers: Two Hundred Years of Thought in Great Britain and the United States.* Edited by Donald J. Curran. Madison: University of Wisconsin Press.

Handlin, Oscar, and Mary F. Handlin. 1975. *The Wealth of the American People: A History of American Affluence.* New York: McGraw-Hill.

Hanchett, Thomas W. 1996. "U.S. Tax Policy and the Shopping-Center Boom of the 1950s and 1960s." *American Historical Review* 101(October): 1082–1100.

Hansen, Susan B. 1983. *The Politics of Taxation: Revenue Without Representation.* New York: Praeger.

Hawley, Ellis. 1966. *The New Deal and the Problem of Monopoly: Study in Economic Ambivalence.* Princeton, N.J.: Princeton University Press.

Hogan, William T. 1967. *Depreciation Policies and Resultant Problems.* New York: Fordham University Press.

Horwitz, Morton J. 1992. *The Transformation of American Law, 1870–1960: The Crisis of Legal Orthodoxy.* New York: Oxford University Press.

Hull, Cordell. 1948. *The Memoirs of Cordell Hull.* Vol. 1. New York: Macmillan.

Jones, Carolyn C. 1996. "Mass-Based Income Taxation: Creating a Taxpaying Culture, 1940–1952." In *Funding the Modern American State, 1941–1995: The Rise and Fall of the Era of Easy Finance,* edited by W. Elliot Brownlee. Cambridge: Cambridge University Press.

Jorgenson, Dale W. 1965. "Anticipations and Investment Behavior." In *The Brookings Quarterly Econometric Model of the United States,* edited by James S. Duesenberry. Chicago: Rand McNally.

Kasten, Richard, Frank Sammartino, and Eric Toder. 1994. "Trends in Federal Tax Progressivity, 1980–1993." In *Tax Progressivity and Income Inequality,* edited by Joel Slemrod. Cambridge: Cambridge University Press.

Keller, Morton. 1990. *Regulating a New Economy: Public Policy and Economic Change in America, 1900–1933.* Cambridge, Mass.: Harvard University Press.

Kelley, Robert E. 1969. *The Transatlantic Persuasion: The Liberal-Democratic Mind in the Age of Gladstone.* New York: Alfred A. Knopf.

Kennon, Donald R., and Rebecca M. Rogers. 1989. *The Committee on Ways and Means: A Bicentennial History, 1789–1989.* Washington, D.C.: U.S. Government Printing Office.

King, Ronald Frederick. 1983. "From Redistributive to Hegemonic Logic: The Transformation of American Tax Politics, 1894–1963." *Politics and Society* 12(1): 1–52.

———. 1993. *Money, Time, and Politics: Investment Tax Subsidies in American Democracy.* New Haven, Conn.: Yale University Press.

Lambert, Walter K. 1970. "New Deal Revenue Acts: The Politics of Taxation." Ph.D. diss., University of Texas at Austin.

Lebergott, Stanley. 1976. *The American Economy: Income, Wealth, and Want.* Princeton, N.J.: Princeton University Press.

Leff, Mark. 1984. *The Limits of Symbolic Reform: The New Deal and Taxation.* New York: Cambridge University Press.

Link, Arthur S. 1950–51. "The South and the 'New Freedom': An Interpretation." *American Scholar* 20: 314–24.

———, ed. 1978. *The Papers of Woodrow Wilson.* Vol. 28. Princeton, N.J.: Princeton University Press.

Lowi, Theodore J. 1995. *The End of the Republican Era.* Norman: University of Oklahoma Press.

Martin, Cathie Jo. 1991. *Shifting the Burden: The Struggle over Growth and Corporate Taxation.* Chicago: University of Chicago Press.

———. 1996. "American Business and the Taxing State: Alliances for Growth in the Postwar Period." In *Funding the Modern American State, 1941–1995: The Rise and Fall of the Era of Easy Finance,* edited by W. Elliot Brownlee. Cambridge: Cambridge University Press.

McCloskey, Robert G. 1960. *The American Supreme Court.* Chicago: University of Chicago Press.

Mellon, Andrew W. 1924. *Taxation: The People's Business.* New York: Macmillan.

Organization for Economic Cooperation and Development (OEDC). 1990. *OECD Statistics on the Member Countries in Figures.* Supplement to the *OECD Observer* 164. Paris: OECD (June-July).

Partridge, Eric. 1984. *A Dictionary of Slang and Unconventional English,* edited by Paul Beale. London: Routledge and Kegan Paul.

Paul, Randolph. 1954. *Taxation in the United States.* Boston: Little, Brown.

Pechman, Joseph. 1989. *Tax Reform: The Rich and the Poor.* Washington, D.C.: Brookings Institution.

Public Papers of the Presidents of the United States. 1965. *Lyndon B. Johnson, 1963–1964,* book I. Washington, D.C.: 1965.

Quadrango, Jill. 1988. *The Transformation of Old-Age Security: Class and Politics in the American Welfare State.* Chicago: University of Chicago Press.

Rand, Ayn. 1957. *Atlas Shrugged.* New York: Random House.

Ratner, Sidney. 1942. *American Taxation: Its History as a Social Force in Democracy.* New York: W. W. Norton.

Reese, Thomas J. 1980. *The Politics of Taxation.* Westport, Conn.: Quorum Books.

Roose, Kenneth D. 1954. *The Economics of Recession and Revival: An Interpretation of 1937–1938.* New Haven, Conn.: Yale University Press.

Roosevelt, Franklin Delano. 1941. *The Public Papers and Addresses of FranklinD. Roosevelt, 1938 Vol.* New York: Macmillan.

Ross, Dorothy. 1979. "The Liberal Tradition Revisited and the Republican Tradition Addressed." In *New Directions in American Intellectual History*, edited by John Higham and Paul K. Conkin. Baltimore: Johns Hopkins University Press.

Schlesinger, Arthur M., Jr. 1960. *The Age of Roosevelt: The Politics of Upheaval.* Boston: Houghton Mifflin.

Schoeneman, George. 1949. "Tax Cheaters Beware!" *American Magazine* (February).

Schumpeter, Joseph A. 1939. *Business Cycles.* New York: McGraw-Hill.

Schwartz, Jordan A. 1993. *The New Dealers: Power Politics in the Age of Roosevelt.* New York: Alfred A. Knopf.

Seligman, Edwin R. A. 1894. "The Income Tax." *Political Science Quarterly IX:* 610.

———. 1914. *The Income Tax: A Study of the History, Theory, and Practice of Income Taxation at Home and Abroad.* New York: Macmillan.

———. 1921. *Essays in Taxation.* New York: Macmillan.

Shammas, Carole, et al. 1987. *Inheritance in America: From Colonial Times to the Present.* New Brunswick, N.J.: Rutgers University Press.

Sheffrin, Steven M. 1994. "Perceptions of Fairness in the Crucible of Tax Policy." In *Tax Progressivity and Income Inequality*, edited by Joel Slemrod. Cambridge: Cambridge University Press.

Shere, Louis. 1934. "The Burden of Taxation." Unpublished memorandum. U.S. Department of the Treasury, Division of Research and Taxation.

Simpson, J. A., and E. S. C. Weiner. 1989. *The Oxford English Dictionary.* Oxford: Clarendon.

Sklar, Martin J. 1988. *The Corporate Reconstruction of American Capitalism, 1890–1916.* Cambridge: Cambridge University Press.

Slemrod, Joel. 1994. "On the High-Income Laffer Curve." In *Tax Progressivity and Income Inequality*, edited by Joel Slemrod. Cambridge: Cambridge University Press.

Smiley, Gene, and Richard H. Keehn. 1995. "Federal Personal Income Policy in the 1920s." *Journal of Economic History* 55(June): 285–303.

Smith, Adam. 1937. *An Inquiry into the Nature and Causes of the Wealth of Nations.* New York: Modern Library.

Stanley, Robert. 1993. *Dimensions of Law in the Service of Order: Origins of the Federal Income Tax, 1861–1913.* New York: Oxford University Press.

Stark, John O. 1987. "The Establishment of Wisconsin's Income Tax." *Wisconsin Magazine of History* 71(Autumn): 27–45.

———. 1991. "Harold M. Groves and Wisconsin Taxes." *Wisconsin Magazine of History* 74(Spring): 196–214.

Stein, Herbert. 1969. *The Fiscal Revolution in America.* Chicago: University of Chicago Press.

Steinmo, Sven. 1993. *Taxation and Democracy: Swedish, British, and American Approaches to Financing the Modern State.* New Haven, Conn.: Yale University Press.

Steuerle, C. Eugene. 1992. *The Tax Decade.* Washington, D.C.: Urban Institute Press.

Stewart, Charles V. 1974. "The Formation of Tax Policy in America, 1893–1913." Ph.D. diss., University of North Carolina at Chapel Hill.

———. 1980. "The Federal Income Tax and the Realignment of the 1890s." In *Realignment in American Politics: Toward a Theory*, edited by Bruce A. Campbell and Richard J. Trilling. Austin: University of Texas Press.

Sylla, Richard. 1986. "Long-term Trends in State and Local Finance: Sources and Uses of Funds in North Carolina, 1800–1977." In *Long-term Factors in American Economic Growth*, edited by Stanley L. Engerman and Robert Gallman. National Bureau of Economic Research Studies in Income and Wealth, vol. 51. Chicago: University of Chicago Press.

Thelan, David P. 1972. *The New Citizenship: Origins of Progressivism in Wisconsin, 1885–1900.* Columbia: University of Missouri Press.

Tindall, George B. 1967. *The Emergence of the New South, 1913–1945.* Baton Rouge: Louisiana State University Press.

U.S. Bureau of the Census. 1975. *Historical Statistics of the United States: Colonial Times to 1970.* Washington, D.C.: U.S. Government Printing Office.

U.S. Congress. 1942a. *Congressional Record*. 78th Congress, 1st sess., Vol. 89 (1942). Washington, D.C.: U.S. Government Printing Office.

———. 1942b. *Congressional Record*. 78th Congress, 2d sess., Vol. 90 (1942). Washington, D.C.: U.S. Government Printing Office.

———. 1932. *Proceedings of Eleventh National Convention of Disabled American Veterans of the World War*, House Doc. 50, 72d Cong., 1st sess (1932). Washington, D.C.: U.S. Government Printing Office.

U.S. Department of Commerce. 1992. *Survey of Current Business* 72 (March).

U.S. Department of the Treasury, Bureau of Internal Revenue. 1916–1946. *Statistics of Income*. Washington, D.C.: U.S. Government Printing Office.

———. 1951. *Statistics of Income for 1945, Part I*. Washington, D.C.: U.S. Government Printing Office.

———. 1952. *Statistics of Income for 1946, Part I*. Washington, D.C.: U.S. Government Printing Office.

U.S. Department of the Treasury, Office of Tax Analysis. 1937. "Tax Revision Studies, 1937," vol. 4, "Undistributed Profits Tax." National Archives.

———. 1942. Proposal for a "Consumption Expenditure Tax." Memorandum (July 9). National Archives.

U.S. Department of the Treasury, Office of State and Local Finance. 1985. *Federal-State-Local Relations* (September).

U.S. Government. 1873. *Annual Report of the Commissioner of Internal Revenue for the Year 1872*. Washington, D.C.: U.S. Government Printing Office.

Wallenstein, Peter. 1987. *From Slave South to New South: Public Policy in Nineteenth-Century Georgia*. Chapel Hill: University of North Carolina Press.

Wentworth, Harold, and Stuart Berg Flexner. 1967. *Dictionary of American Slang*. New York: Crowell.

Wiggins, A. L. M. 1947. "They Can't Fool the Internal Revenue Man." *Collier's* (September).

Williamson, Jeffrey G., and Peter H. Lindert. 1980. *American Inequality: A Macroeconomic History*. New York: Academic Press.

Winch, Donald. 1978. *Adam Smith's Politics: An Essay in Historiographic Revision*. Cambridge: Cambridge University Press.

Witte, John. 1985. *The Politics and Development of the Federal Income Tax*. Madison: University of Wisconsin Press.

Yearley, Clifton K. 1970. *The Money Machines: The Breakdown and Reform of Governmental and Party Finance in the North, 1860–1920*. Albany: State University of New York Press.

Young, Arthur N. 1916. *The Single-Tax Movement in the United States*. Princeton, N.J.: Princeton University Press.

Zelizer, Julian E. 1996. "Learning the Ways and Means: Wilbur Mills and a Fiscal Community, 1954–1964." In *Funding the Modern American State, 1941–1995: The Rise and Fall of the Era of Easy Finance*, edited by W. Elliot Brownlee. Cambridge: Cambridge University/Woodrow Wilson Center.

———. 1998. *Taxing America: Wilbur D. Mills, Congress, and the State, 1945–1975*. Cambridge: Cambridge University Press.

3

Who Are the Rich? A Demographic Profile of High-Income and High-Wealth Americans

Edward N. Wolff

Two issues are addressed in this chapter: How do the characteristics of the rich differ from those of the general population? And have there been any notable changes in these characteristics over the period from 1983 to 1992?

In many ways, this chapter follows up the work of Joel Slemrod (1994), who explored these questions for the period from 1962 to 1983. However, his analysis was confined to the characteristics of the high-income population, whereas this chapter investigates both the high-income and high-wealth groups.

Several questions are of particular interest. First, with the substantial increase of inequality over this period, and especially with the record-high salaries recorded on Wall Street and among professional workers in general, has there been a shift in the composition of the rich away from the classic "coupon-clippers" toward entrepreneurs? Second, along with this trend, has there been a shift toward finance and professional services as the main sources of employment of the rich? Third, a related issue is whether there has been a corresponding change in the composition of the rich toward younger families and away from middle-aged and older groups. Fourth, with the large incomes recorded in the entertainment and sports industries, do we find an increasing proportion of black Americans in the ranks of the rich? Fifth, given the rising premium on education observed over the decade of the 1980s, has there been a notable shift in the composition of the rich toward college-educated workers? Sixth, with the strong correlation observed between health and wealth, are the rich healthier in 1992 in comparison to 1983?

The first section provides a short discussion on data sources and methods. The next section looks at broad trends in household wealth over the period from 1983 to 1992. The characteristics of high-wealth households in the two years are analyzed in the third section, and the fourth performs a similar analysis for high-income households.

DATA SOURCES AND METHODS

The data sources used for this study are the 1983 and 1992 Survey of Consumer Finances (SCF) conducted by the Federal Reserve Board. Both surveys consist of a core representative sample combined with a high-income supplement. The supplement is drawn from the Internal Revenue Service's Statistics of Income (SOI) data file. For the 1983 SCF, for example, an income cutoff of $100,000 of adjusted gross income is used as the criterion for inclusion in the supplemental sample. Individuals were randomly selected for the sample within predesignated income strata. The advantage of the high-income supplement is that it provides a much "richer" sample of high income and therefore potentially very wealthy families. However, the presence of a high-income supplement creates some complications, because weights must be constructed to meld the high-income supplement with the core representative sample.[1]

The SCF also supplies alternative sets of weights. For the 1983 SCF, I have used the so-called Full Sample 1983 Composite Weights because this set of weights provides the closest correspondence between the national balance sheet totals derived from the sample and those in the Federal Reserve Board Flow of Funds. For the 1992 SCF, I chose the Designed-Base Weights, for the same reason. However, this set produced major anomalies in the size distribution of income for 1991. As a result, I have modified the weights somewhat to conform to the size distribution of income as reported in the Internal Revenue Service's Statistics of Income.[2]

The Federal Reserve Board imputes information for missing items in the SCF. However, despite this procedure, there still remains a notable discrepancy for several assets between the total balance sheet value computed from the survey sample and the Flow of Funds data. As a result, the results presented later in this chapter are based on my adjustments to the original asset and liability values in the surveys. This takes the form of the alignment of asset and liability totals from the survey data to the corresponding national balance sheet totals. In most cases, this entails a proportional adjustment of reported values of balance sheet items in the survey data (for details, see Wolff 1987, 1994, 1996).[3] It should be noted that the alignment has very little effect on the measurement of wealth inequality—both the Gini coefficient and the quantile shares. However, it is important to make these adjustments when comparing changes in mean wealth both overall and by asset type.

In this study, I use marketable wealth (or net worth), which is defined as the current value of all marketable or fungible assets less the current value of debts. Net worth is thus the difference in value between total assets and total liabilities or debt. Total assets are defined as the sum of: the gross value of owner-occupied housing; other real estate owned by the household; the gross value of vehicles; cash and demand deposits; time and savings deposits, certificates of deposit, and money market accounts; government bonds, corporate bonds, foreign bonds, and other financial securities; the cash surrender value of life insurance plans; the cash surrender value of pension plans, including IRAs and Keogh plans; corporate stock, including mutual funds; net equity in unincorporated businesses; and equity in trust funds. Total liabilities are the sum of: mortgage debt; consumer debt, including auto loans; and other debt.[4]

I also introduce the concept of "financial wealth." This is defined as net worth minus net equity in owner-occupied housing and automobiles. Financial wealth is a more "liquid" concept than marketable wealth, since one's home and automobiles are difficult to convert into cash in the short term. It thus reflects the resources that may be immediately available for consumption or various forms of investments.

TRENDS IN HOUSEHOLD WEALTH AND INCOME, 1983 TO 1992

I begin the analysis by examining overall trends in wealth and income from 1983 to 1992. Table 3.1 shows changes in median and mean net worth. Mean wealth is

Table 3.1   Mean and Median Wealth and Income, 1983 and 1992 (1992 Dollars)

	1983	1992	Percentage Change 1989 to 1992
Net worth			
Median	$53,680	$50,895	−5.2
Mean	189,938	212,488	11.9
Financial wealth			
Median	10,151	10,051	−1.0
Mean	132,793	155,370	17.0
Income[a]			
Median	28,521	28,952	1.5
Mean	40,405	42,793	5.9
Number of households (thousands)	83,893	95,463	13.8
Sample size	4,263	3,906	—
Memo			
CPS household income[b]			
Median	$29,602	$31,033	4.8
Mean	35,675	39,064	9.5

Sources: Author's own computations from the 1983 and 1992 SCF. The 1983 and 1992 asset and liability entries are aligned to national balance sheet totals. See Wolff (1994, 1996) for details on the alignment. For CPS household income, U.S. Bureau of the Census (1993, table B-2).
[a.] The figures are for 1982 and 1991, respectively.
[b.] The figures are for 1982 and 1991, respectively.

much higher than the median—$212,488 versus $50,895 in 1992 (all figures are in 1992 dollars). This means that the vast bulk of household wealth was concentrated in the richest families. Median wealth fell by 5 percent between 1983 and 1992, from $53,680 to $50,895. In contrast, mean wealth grew by 12 percent, from $189,938 in 1983 to $212,488 in 1992. Median wealth thus declined while mean wealth holdings rose. Median financial wealth was a bare $10,051 in 1992, in comparison to a mean value of $155,370, and in fact fell by 1 percent from 1983 to 1992. In contrast, mean financial wealth increased by 17 percent over the same period, from $132,793 to $155,370.

According to the SCF data, median household income increased slightly between 1982 and 1992, from $28,521 to $28,952. Mean household income grew by 6 percent over the same period, from $40,405 to $42,793. A comparison is also shown with household income data from the Current Population Survey (CPS). The CPS data show higher median values for income and lower mean values. The latter result is likely due to the fact that the SCF has a high income supplement and, as a result, provides better coverage of property income. The higher medians in the CPS might be attributable to the difference in sampling frame and to better coverage of transfer income. It is interesting that the CPS data show higher growth in both median and mean income between 1982 and 1991.

The finding that mean wealth and income increased faster than the corresponding medians between 1983 and 1992 is an indicator of rising inequality over the period. This is confirmed in table 3.2. The share of net worth held by the top 1 percent rose by 3.3 percentage points between 1983 and 1992, from 32.6 to 35.9 percent. The share of the next 4 percent also increased somewhat, while the shares of all other groups, particularly the second decile and the second quintile, fell. The Gini coefficient increased from 0.78 to 0.80.

Inequality of financial wealth also grew. The share of the top 1 percent rose by 3.3 percentage points, from 42.9 to 45.6 percent, the share of the next 4 percent remained unchanged, and the shares of all other groups, particularly the second decile and the second quintile again, fell. The Gini coefficient also showed an increase, from 0.893 to 0.903.

Income inequality showed an even more substantial rise. The share of the top 1 percent went up by 2.9 percentage points, from 12.8 to 15.7 percent, the share of the next 4 percent gained by 1.5 percentage points, and that of the second decile by 0.3 percentage points, while the bottom four quintiles, particularly the middle, all lost. The Gini coefficient showed a large increase, from 0.480 to 0.528.

These calculations show an extreme concentration of wealth in 1992. The top 1 percent of families (as ranked by marketable wealth) owned 36 percent of total household wealth, and the top 20 percent of households held 84 percent. Financial wealth was even more concentrated, with the richest 1 percent (as ranked by financial wealth) owning 46 percent of total household financial wealth and the top 20 percent owing 92 percent. The top 1 percent of families (as ranked by income) earned 16 percent of total household income in 1991, and the top 20 percent accounted for 58 percent—large figures but still considerably lower than the corresponding net worth and financial wealth shares.

The second panel of table 3.2 shows average wealth in 1992 dollars by wealth quantile for 1983 and 1992. Over the period from 1983 to 1992, the largest gains in relative terms were made by the wealthiest households. The top 1 percent saw their average wealth (in 1992 dollars) rise by $1.4 million, or by 23.0 percent, the next 4 percent by 14.6 percent, and the next 5 percent by 8.2 percent. The mean wealth of the second decile increased by only 2.7 percent, and that of the second quintile by 2.8 percent, while the average wealth of the third quintile fell by 3.8 percent and that of the bottom two quintiles by, collectively, 19.3 percent.

The pattern of results is quite similar for financial wealth. The largest gains were made by the top percentile at 24.4 percent, followed by the next 4 percent at 16.4 percent, the next five percent at 9.8 percent, the second decile at 8.0 percent, and the second quintile at 8.7 percent. The third quintile held its own, while the bottom two saw their net financial wealth decline.

A similar calculation using income data reveals that the only groups to enjoy positive gains in real income over the period from 1983 to 1992 were households in the top 20 percent of the income distribution. Within this group, gains were greatest for the top 1 percent of households (29.5 percent), followed sequentially by the next 4 percent (18.1 percent), the next 5 percent (9.0 percent), and the next 10 percent (4.8 percent). The greatest losses were sustained by the bottom two quintiles, followed by the third quintile and then the second quintile. Indeed, while the top per-

Table 3.2 Size Distribution of Wealth and Income, 1983 and 1992

Year	Gini Coefficient	Top 1 Percent	Next 4 Percent	Next 5 Percent	Next 10 Percent	Second Quintile	Third Quintile	Fourth Quintile	Fifth Quintile	All	All but Top 1 Percent
					Percentage Share of Wealth or Income Held by Each Quantile						
Net worth											
1983	0.779	32.6	21.8	12.0	13.1	13.0	5.7	1.7	0.0	100.0	67.4
1992	0.802	35.9	22.4	11.6	12.1	11.9	4.9	1.4	-0.2	100.0	64.1
Financial wealth											
1983	0.893	42.9	25.1	12.3	11.0	7.9	1.7	0.2	-1.0	100.0	57.1
1992	0.903	45.6	25.0	11.5	10.2	7.3	1.5	0.1	-1.1	100.0	54.4
Income											
1982	0.480	12.8	13.3	10.3	15.5	21.6	14.1	8.6	3.7	100.0	87.2
1991	0.528	15.7	14.8	10.6	15.3	20.4	12.8	7.5	3.0	100.0	84.3
					Mean Wealth and Income by Quantile (in Thousands, 1992 Dollars)						
Net worth											
1983		6,198	1,036	457.4	249.8	123.4	54.3		[7.8]	189.9	129.3
1992		7,624	1,187	495.1	256.5	126.9	52.3		[6.3]	212.5	137.6
Percent change		23.0	14.6	8.2	2.7	2.8	-3.8		[-19.3]	11.9	6.5
Financial wealth											
1983		5,695	833.9	325.9	146.1	52.5	11.3		[-2.9]	132.8	76.6
1992		7,085	970.7	357.7	157.7	57.0	11.3		[-4.1]	155.4	85.4
Percent change		24.4	16.4	9.8	8.0	8.7	0.5		[—]	17.0	11.4
Income											
1982		518.8	134.0	83.2	62.5	43.7	28.6		[12.5]	40.4	35.6
1991		671.8	158.3	90.7	65.5	43.6	27.4		[11.2]	42.8	36.4
Percent change		29.5	18.1	9.0	4.8	-0.2	-4.2		[-9.9]	5.9	2.4

Source: Author's own computations from the 1983 and 1992 SCF. The 1983 and 1992 asset and liability entries are aligned to national balance sheet totals.
Note: For the computation of percentile shares of net worth, households are ranked according to their net worth; for the computation of percentile shares of financial wealth, households are ranked according to their financial wealth; and for the computation of percentile shares of income, households are ranked according to their income.

centile saw its average income increase by 30 percent over this period, the average income of the remaining households grew by only 2.4 percent.

CHARACTERISTICS OF THE RICHEST 1 PERCENT OF HOUSEHOLDS, AS RANKED BY WEALTH

Are the rich really different from the rest of us? Table 3.3 provides some information on the demographic characteristics of the top 1 percent of households as ranked by net worth, in comparison to that of all households in both 1983 and 1992. Panel A (as well as figure 3.1) shows the age distribution in both years. In 1983 the rich were considerably older, on average, than other households. Whereas the mean age of household heads in the top 1 percent was 57.3 and their median age 56.0, the mean age of all household heads in that year was 46.8 and the median was 44.0. Although 8 percent of all household heads were under the age of twenty-five, 23 percent aged twenty-five to thirty-four, and 20 percent aged thirty-five to forty-four, none of the rich were under twenty-five, only 0.7 percent were twenty-five to thirty-four, and only 9 percent were thirty-five to forty-four. In contrast, 43 percent of all household heads were between forty-five and seventy-four, but 84 percent of the rich were in this age group. The fraction of the rich aged seventy-five or older was slightly lower than for all households—5.9 versus 7.1 percent.

Between 1983 and 1992, the general population aged somewhat, with the mean age of household heads rising from 46.8 to 48.4 and the median age from forty-four to forty-five. However, despite this trend, the proportion of the top 1 percent under age thirty-five increased from 0.7 percent in 1983 to 2.2 percent in 1992, and the proportion aged thirty-five to forty-four from 9.2 to 12.8 percent. This result is consistent with the observation that the huge salaries generated on Wall Street, in the entertainment business, and in other professions created a whole new class of young wealthy individuals.

The proportion of the top 1 percent aged forty-five to fifty-four fell sharply, from 32.9 to 24.6 percent, and the percentage aged sixty-five to seventy-four declined substantially relative to the overall demographic trends. Interestingly, however, the percentage of the rich aged fifty-five to sixty-four increased somewhat, from 29.4 to 31.3 percent, though this seems to be a cohort effect since that group was highly represented in the top 1 percent in 1983 (then aged forty-five to fifty-four). This group consists of individuals born during the Great Depression (1928 to 1937). Moreover, those seventy-five or older also gained as a share of the very rich, from 5.9 to 9.8 percent, and also relative to overall demographic trends.

The rich are also much more highly educated than the overall population (panel B and figure 3.2). In 1983, while 21 percent of household heads were college graduates (or had advanced degrees), 76 percent of the top 1 percent had graduated from college or attended graduate school. While 29 percent of household heads overall had failed to graduate from high school in 1983, less than 3 percent of the very rich fell into this category.

Between 1983 and 1992, overall educational attainment increased in the general population. The percentage of household heads who had graduated from high school increased from 71 to 79 percent, and the percentage who had graduated from

Table 3.3   Demographic and Work-Related Characteristics of the Top 1 Percent of Wealth-Holders and All Households, 1983 and 1992 (Percentages Except for Mean and Median Values)

	1983			1992		
	Top 1 Percent	All	Difference	Top 1 Percent	All	Difference
A. Age of head						
Less than twenty-five	0.0	8.0	-8.0	0.2	5.2	-5.0
Twenty-five to thirty-four	0.7	22.6	-21.8	2.0	20.4	-18.4
Thirty-five to forty-four	9.2	19.5	-10.3	12.8	22.7	-9.9
Forty-five to fifty-four	32.9	15.6	17.2	24.6	16.4	8.2
Fifty-five to sixty-four	29.4	15.1	14.4	31.3	13.4	17.9
Sixty-five to seventy-four	21.8	12.1	9.7	19.3	12.7	6.6
Seventy-five and over	5.9	7.1	-1.2	9.8	9.2	0.6
All age groups	100.0	100.0	0.0	100.0	100.0	-0.0
Mean age	57.3	46.8	10.5	58.1	48.4	9.8
Median age	56.0	44.0	12.0	58.0	45.0	13.0
B. Education of head						
Eleven years or less	2.7	29.0	-26.3	1.8	21.1	-19.3
High school graduate	10.0	30.2	-20.1	9.2	28.9	-19.7
One to three years of college	11.6	19.6	-8.1	15.6	21.0	-5.4
College graduate	40.0	10.6	29.4	32.9	16.5	16.3
Some graduate school	35.7	10.6	25.1	40.6	12.5	28.1
All educational groups	100.0	100.0	0.0	100.0	100.0	-0.0
Mean education	15.5	12.2	3.3	15.6	12.9	2.7
Median education	16.0	12.0	4.0	16.0	13.0	3.0
C. Race						
White (non-Hispanic)	97.9	80.9	17.0	94.2	75.3	18.9
Black (non-Hispanic)	0.5	12.7	-12.2	0.1	12.6	-12.5
Hispanic	0.0	3.5	-3.5	0.9	7.6	-6.6
Asian and others	1.6	2.8	-1.2	4.8	4.6	0.2
All racial groups	100.0	100.0	0.0	100.0	100.0	-0.0

Table 3.3 *Continued*

	1983			1992		
	Top 1 Percent	All	Difference	Top 1 Percent	All	Difference
D. Marital status						
Married, spouse present[a]	88.1	60.8	27.3	83.4	57.6	25.7
Male, separated, divorced, or widowed	3.2	6.8	-3.6	7.0	8.6	-1.5
Male, never married	1.3	6.3	-5.0	2.3	6.5	-4.2
Female, separated, divorced, or widowed	7.4	19.9	-12.5	7.3	19.4	-12.1
Female, never married	0.0	6.2	-6.2	0.0	7.9	-7.9
All marital groups	100.0	100.0	0.0	100.0	100.0	0.0
E. Employment status of head (less than sixty-five only)						
Full-time	86.4	75.8	10.6	76.7	74.9	1.9
Part-time	4.6	4.0	0.6	8.6	4.5	4.1
Unemployed or temporarily laid off	0.0	8.8	-8.8	1.4	7.1	-5.7
Retired	3.6	7.3	-3.7	9.7	3.8	5.9
Not in labor force	5.4	4.1	1.3	3.6	9.8	-6.1
All under age sixty-five	100.0	100.0	0.0	100.0	100.0	0.0
F. Industry of employment of head (employed persons only)						
Agriculture	9.2	3.9	5.3	1.4	2.7	-1.3
Mining	5.1	1.4	3.7	[4.7]	[7.4]	[-2.7]
Construction	6.4	7.5	-1.1			
Manufacturing	19.5	23.7	-4.2	[21.8]	[28.3]	[-6.5]
Transportation, communications, or utilities	0.6	8.9	-8.4			
Trade (wholesale and retail)	11.3	15.5	-4.2	13.3	14.9	-1.5
Finance, insurance, or real estate	21.9	5.3	16.6	35.8	13.8	22.0
Business or professional services	24.9	23.1	1.8	[22.5]	[25.5]	[-3.0]
Personal services	1.0	3.4	-2.3			

(*Table continues on p. 84.*)

Table 3.3 *Continued*

	1983			1992		
	Top 1 Percent	All	Difference	Top 1 Percent	All	Difference
Public administration	0.0	7.2	-7.2	0.4	7.4	-7.0
All employed persons	100.0	100.0	0.0	100.0	100.0	0.0
G. Occupation of head (employed persons only)						
Self-employed[b]	37.5	15.4	22.1	68.9	17.2	51.7
Professionals[c]	6.4	15.0	-8.6	[26.5]	[25.5]	[0.9]
Managers and administrators	55.2	13.9	41.3			
Sales and clerical workers[d]	1.0	13.0	-12.1	2.8	22.4	-19.6
Craft workers[e]	0.0	16.9	-16.9	1.8	10.6	-8.8
Other blue-collar workers[f]	0.0	25.8	-25.8	0.0	24.3	-24.3
All employed persons	100.0	100.0	0.0	100.0	100.0	0.0
H. Health of head of household						
Excellent	61.2	37.9	23.3	55.9	34.6	21.3
Good	32.1	39.6	-7.5	31.8	40.9	-9.1
Fair	5.9	15.4	-9.6	7.8	17.5	-9.7
Poor	0.8	7.1	-6.2	4.5	7.0	-2.5
All	100.0	100.0	0.0	100.0	100.0	0.0
I. Inheritances received						
Percentage receiving inheritances	—	—	—	48.8	20.6	28.2
Average value of inheritances[g]	—	—	—	$782,056	$96,140	$685,916

Source: Author's own computations from the 1983 and 1992 Surveys of Consumer Finances.

Note: The asset and liability entries are aligned to national balance sheet totals. The top 1 percent is defined as households with net worth in excess of $1.55 million in 1983 and in excess of $2.42 million in 1992. All computations are for heads of household unless otherwise indicated. Please note that geographical information is not available for the high-income supplement in 1983.

a. Includes "partners" in 1992.
b. Self-employed of any occupation are classified separately in this category.
c. Includes technical workers in 1983.
d. Includes technical workers in 1992.
e. Includes protective service workers in 1983.
f. Includes operatives (both machine and transportation equipment), laborers, service workers (except protective services in 1983), and farm workers.
g. Inheritance recipients only. Present value as of 1992, using a 3 percent real interest rate.

Figure 3.1   Age Distribution of All Households and Top 1 Percent of Wealth-Holders, 1983 and 1992

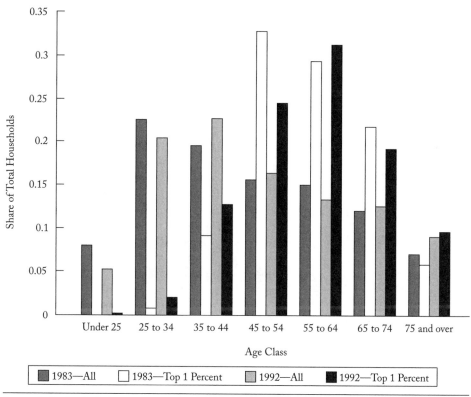

Source: Author's calculations.

college from 21 to 29. Mean educational attainment rose from 12.2 to 12.9 years, and median education from 12 to 13 years. Somewhat surprisingly, the proportion of the rich who had graduated from college actually fell from 76 to 73 percent, though of this group the proportion who had done some graduate work increased. There was a particularly large increase in the percentage of college "dropouts" (one to three years of college) among the rich, from 11.6 percent in 1983 to 15.6 percent in 1992—perhaps the "Bill Gates" phenomenon. In any case, there is no clear evidence that more education paid off in terms of entry into the ranks of the top 1 percent of wealth-holders over the period 1983 to 1992.

The racial composition of the very rich also differs significantly from that of the general population (panel C and figure 3.3). Whereas 81 percent of households in 1983 were non-Hispanic whites, 98 percent of the rich fell into this category. While 16.2 percent of households classified themselves as black or Hispanic, only 0.5 percent of the top 1 percent were in this group.

Between 1983 and 1992, the overall racial composition of households shifted rather significantly, with non-Hispanic whites falling from 81 to 75 percent, non-Hispanic blacks remaining at about 12.6 percent, Hispanics increasing from 3.5 to 7.6 percent, and Asians and others from 2.8 to 4.6 percent. The proportion of white

Figure 3.2   Educational Distribution of All Households and Top 1 Percent of Wealth-Holders,
1983 and 1992

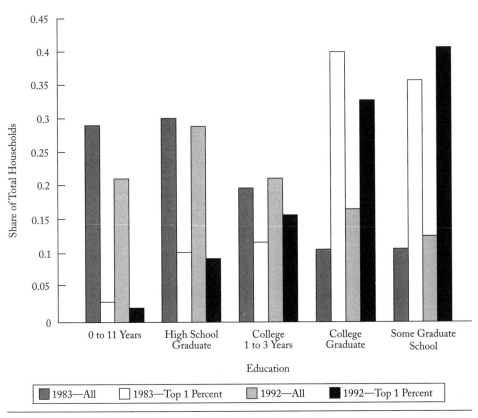

Source: Author's calculations.

household heads among the top 1 percent did fall somewhat over this period, from
97.9 to 94.2 percent. However, the proportion of non-Hispanic blacks also fell,
from 0.5 to 0.1 percent, while the proportion of Hispanics increased somewhat,
from 0.0 to 0.9 percent. The largest growth was in the share of Asians and other
races among the top 1 percent of wealth-holders, from 1.6 to 4.8 percent.

Panel D shows the marital status of the two groups. In 1983 the very wealthy
were much more apt to be married than the general population (88 versus 61 percent). Unmarried males made up 4.5 percent of the very rich (in contrast to a population share of 13.1 percent); formerly married women (separated, divorced, or
widowed) constituted 7.4 percent of the wealthy (in comparison to a population
share of 19.9 percent); and there were no women who had never married in the
ranks of the top 1 percent (compared to an overall proportion of 6.2 percent).

Between 1983 and 1992, the proportion of married families in the top 1 percent
of wealth-holders fell from 88 to 83 percent, and this change was almost exactly offset by the increase in the percentage of unmarried males in this group, from 4.5 to
9.3 percent. The share of formerly married women in the top percentile remained

Figure 3.3   Racial Composition of All Households and Top 1 Percent of Wealth-Holders, 1983 and
1992

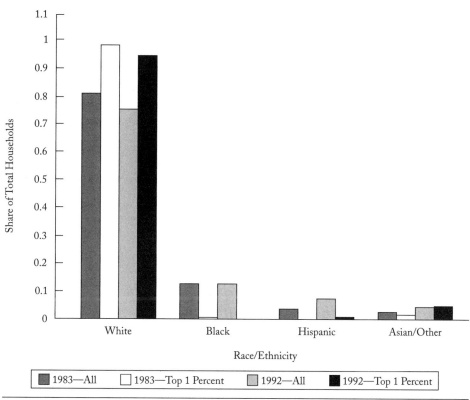

Source: Author's calculations.

almost unchanged, and there were again no women who had not married among
the rich.

The next three panels provide employment statistics for the very wealthy. As
shown in panel E, the percentage of non-elderly households whose head worked
full-time in 1983 was much higher among the rich than in the general population
(86 versus 76). In contrast, none of the wealthy reported that they were unemployed
or temporarily laid off, compared to 8.8 percent of all non-elderly households. Only
3.6 percent of the (non-elderly) wealthy reported that they were retired in 1983, in
contrast to 7.3 percent of the general population.

Between 1983 and 1992, the proportion of full-time workers in the ranks of the
non-elderly wealthy fell precipitously, from 86 to 77 percent. This change was offset by big increases in the share of part-time workers in this group, from 4.6 to 8.6
percent, and in the share of retirees, from 3.6 to 9.7 percent. These results indicate
that the very rich, defined in terms of wealth, cut back rather dramatically on their
work effort over this period.

In 1983, 22 percent of rich families reported working in finance, insurance, or
real estate, compared to only 5 percent of all workers (panel F). Farmers and min-

ing employees were also overrepresented in the ranks of the rich (14.3 compared to 5.3 percent of all workers), and those providing business and professional services were slightly overrepresented (24.9 versus 23.1 percent). In contrast, workers in manufacturing, transportation, communications, utilities, trade, and personal services were underrepresented among the rich. Moreover, there were no government employees in the ranks of the very rich in 1983 (compared to 7.2 percent of all workers).

The most notable change between 1983 and 1992 was, as speculated, a huge gain in the share of finance, insurance, and real estate employees in the ranks of the rich, from 22 to 36 percent (and also a large increase relative to the employment share of all workers, from a difference of 16.6 to 22.0 percent). The proportion of farmers in the ranks of the very rich fell precipitously, from 9.2 to 1.4 percent, as did the proportion employed in mining and construction, from 11.5 to 4.7 percent. Interestingly, the proportion of the rich working in business and professional or personal services also declined in both absolute terms (from 25.9 to 22.5 percent) and in relative terms (from a difference of −0.5 to −3.0 percent).

In terms of occupational composition, as shown in panel G, the results show that the self-employed were substantially overrepresented in the ranks of the rich in 1983—38 percent versus 14 percent of all workers. The same was true for managers and administrators—55 percent compared to 14 percent of all persons in the labor force. In contrast, only 6.4 percent of the rich classified themselves as professional workers, compared to a 15.0 percent share of all workers. Moreover, there were virtually no sales, clerical, craft, or other blue-collar workers found among the top 1 percent of wealth-holders in 1983.

Between 1983 and 1992, the most notable change was a huge increase in the share of the self-employed among the top 1 percent—almost doubling from 38 to 69 percent—in contrast to a modest gain among all workers, from 15.4 to 17.2 percent.[5] This result tends to confirm our speculation about increased entrepreneurial activity among the ranks of the rich. Correspondingly, the proportion of professional, managerial, and administrative workers declined sharply, from 62 to 29 percent.[6] There were modest gains in sales, clerical, and craft workers among the top 1 percent, from 1.0 to 4.6 percent.

Panel H shows statistics on health. This is a self-reported category, so that there is a large subjective element involved in the classification. However, the results suggest rather strongly that the rich are healthier than the average population. In 1983, 61 percent of the rich classified themselves as having excellent health, compared to 38 percent of the overall population. Only 6.7 percent of the top 1 percent indicated that their health was fair or poor, in comparison to 22.5 percent of all respondents.

Between 1983 and 1992, there appears to have been a slight deterioration in the health of the rich and the overall population. In the general population, the proportion reporting excellent health fell from 37.9 to 34.6 percent, while the percentage reporting fair or poor health increased from 22.5 to 24.5 percent. Among the very wealthy, the share with excellent health fell from 61 to 56 percent, whereas the share with fair health grew from 5.9 to 7.8 percent, and the share with poor health from 0.8 to 4.5 percent.

The last panel shows some statistics on inheritances received in 1992. These results are based on respondent recall—the individual was asked to indicate both the amount and the date that any bequests were received. Despite the difficulties with "recall" variables, the results clearly indicate that the very rich were more apt to receive inheritances than the general population (49 versus 21 percent), and the present value (in 1992) of the inheritances received (among inheritors only) was much greater—more than eight times as great among the very wealthy than in the general population.

Table 3.4 shows the composition of the gross assets of the top 1 percent of households as ranked by net worth, in comparison to that of all other households in 1983 (see also figure 3.4). It is at once apparent that the rich hold their wealth in forms very different from those held by other households. Compared to the average portfolio of the bottom 99 percent of households, the top percentile had a higher proportion of their gross assets in the form of non-home real estate (19.5 versus 12.3 percent), stocks and mutual funds (17.0 versus 5.3 percent), business equity (32.1 versus 12.4 percent), and trust funds (6.9 versus 0.7 percent); and lower proportions in their principal residence (8.1 versus 38.0 percent), savings and time deposits, CDs, and money market funds (6.3 versus 14.8 percent), and vehicles (0.3 versus 4.4 percent). The richest 1 percent also had a lower debt-equity ratio—5.7 versus 18.9 percent. Moreover, whereas the top percentile accounted for 32.6 percent of total net worth, they held 40.0 percent of non-home real estate, 57.5 percent of stocks and mutual funds, 41.9 percent of financial securities, 52.1 percent of business equity, and 80.0 percent of trust fund equity.

Table 3.5 shows the corresponding statistics for 1992. The most notable shift in the overall household portfolio between 1983 and 1992 has been a sharp drop in the share of gross assets held in the form of savings and time deposits, CDs, and money market funds (from 12.3 to 7.7 percent) and a corresponding rise in the share held in the form of pension accounts (from 1.4 to 7.0 percent). This is a clear indication of the substitution of nontaxable for taxable assets. The debt-equity ratio also rose substantially, from 14.6 to 17.9 percent.

Among the richest 1 percent of households (who may be different in the two years), the major change has been a fall in the share of gross assets held in stocks and mutual funds (from 17.0 to 12.1 percent) and in trust funds (from 6.9 to 4.6 percent) and corresponding increases in the share held in financial securities (from 5.7 to 9.9 percent) and pension accounts (0.9 to 3.0 percent). The substitution of financial securities for stocks is a bit of a surprise, given the robust performance of the stock market over these years; the switch to pension accounts is probably due to their preferred tax status. Interestingly, the share of total assets held in both investment real estate and business equity remained virtually unchanged over this period, suggesting very little burst of entrepreneurship among the very rich, at least according to this dimension. While the share of total net worth held by the top 1 percent increased from 32.6 to 35.9 percent between 1983 and 1992, their share of non-home real estate increased from 40.0 to 45.7 percent, their share of financial securities from 41.9 to 65.5 percent, and their share of net business equity from 52.1 to 62.0 percent. In contrast, their share of total stocks and mutual funds fell from 57.5 to 50.1 percent, and their share of trust fund equity from 80.0 to 56.5 percent.

Table 3.4 Composition of Gross Assets of the Top 1 Percent and Bottom 99 Percent of Wealth-Holders and All Households, 1983 (Billions of Current, 1983 Dollars)

| | Top 1 Percent | | All Households | | Bottom 99 Percent | Holdings of Top 1 |
	Total Value	Percentage of Gross Assets	Total Value	Percentage of Gross Assets	Percentage of Gross Assets	Percent as Percentage of Total Value
Net worth	3,691.1	—	11,312.1	—	—	32.6
Gross asset values	3,838.4	100.0	12,958.8	100.0	100.0	29.6
Principal residence	311.3	8.1	3,777.8	29.2	38.0	8.2
Other real estate	747.9	19.5	1,871.1	14.4	12.3	40.0
Stocks and mutual funds	651.9	17.0	1,134.4	8.8	5.3	57.5
Financial securities[a]	220.4	5.7	525.8	4.1	3.3	41.9
Checking accounts	55.1	1.4	327.0	2.5	3.0	16.8
Savings and time deposits, CDs, and money market funds	242.4	6.3	1,590.4	12.3	14.8	15.2
Net business equity[b]	1,232.0	32.1	2,364.1	18.2	12.4	52.1
Life insurance cash surrender value	29.2	0.8	270.5	2.1	2.6	10.8
Pension accounts[c]	32.9	0.9	184.2	1.4	1.7	17.9
Net equity in personal trusts	264.8	6.9	331.2	2.6	0.7	80.0
Vehicles	12.5	0.3	413.9	3.2	4.4	3.0
Miscellaneous assets[d]	38.2	1.0	168.0	1.3	1.4	22.7

Liabilities	208.5	5.4	1,646.7	12.7	15.8	12.7
Debt on principal residence	25.5	0.7	789.2	6.1	8.4	3.2
Debt on other real estate	8.9	0.2	93.8	0.7	0.9	9.5
All other debt[e]	174.2	4.5	763.7	5.9	6.5	22.8
Memo						
Net home equity[f]	285.8	7.4	2,988.6	23.1	29.6	9.6
Debt-equity ratio	—	5.7	—	14.6	18.9	—

Source: Author's own computations from the 1983 Survey of Consumer Finances.

Note: The 1983 asset and liability entries are aligned to national balance sheet totals. The top 1 percent is defined as households with net worth in excess of $1.55 million.

a. Includes corporate bonds, government bonds, including U.S. savings bonds, open-market paper, and notes.

b. Includes net equity in unincorporated farm and nonfarm businesses and closely held corporations.

c. Includes IRAs, Keogh plans, 401(k) plans, the accumulated value of defined contribution pension plans, and other retirement accounts.

d. Includes gold and other precious metals, royalties, jewelry, antiques, furs, loans to friends and relatives, future contracts, and miscellaneous assets.

e. Includes mortgage, installment, consumer, and other debt.

f. Gross value of principal residence less mortgage on principal residence.

Figure 3.4   Composition of Assets of All Households and Top 1 Percent of Wealth-Holders, 1983 and 1992

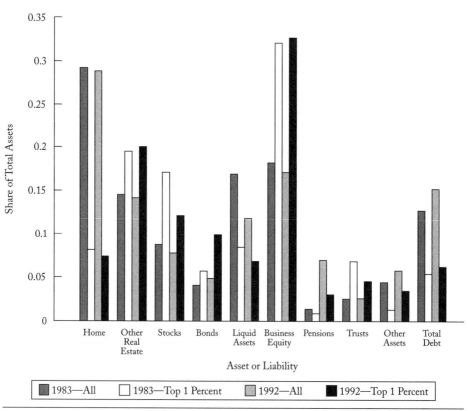

Source: Author's calculations.

Table 3.6 shows the composition of total household income in 1983 of all households and of the richest 1 percent of households ranked in terms of net worth (see also figure 3.5). Among all households, the primary source of income was wages and salaries, which made up 63 percent of total income. Self-employment or proprietary income, including partnership and net profit from unincorporated businesses, ranked second, constituted 12 percent of all income. Together, labor income constituted three-quarters of all income. Retirement income, including social security and pension benefits, comprised 8.2 percent of total personal income. The only other significant entry is interest income, 5.3 percent of total income.

Among the richest 1 percent of households, the primary source of income was proprietary income, which amounted to 27.4 percent of their total income. This was followed by wages and salaries, at 23.6 percent. Interest income made up 12.7 percent of their income, dividends another 12.0 percent, capital gains 13.2 percent, and rental, royalty, and trust income 7.8 percent. The other components were all very small. All told, the top 1 percent of households earned over half of all dividends and capital gains, 22 percent of proprietary income, 25 percent of all interest, and 31 percent of rental, royalty, and trust income.

Table 3.5 Composition of Gross Assets of the Top 1 Percent and Bottom 99 Percent of Wealth–Holders and All Households, 1992 (Billions of Current, 1992 Dollars)

	Top 1 Percent		All Households		Bottom 99 Percent	Holdings of Top 1
	Total Value	Percentage of Gross Assets	Total Value	Percentage of Gross Assets	Percentage of Gross Assets	Percent as Percentage of Total Value
Net worth	7,278.2	—	20,284.8	—	35.9	—
Gross asset values	7,770.6	100.0	23,903.5	100.0	100.0	32.5
Principal residence	581.2	7.5	6,885.7	28.8	39.0	8.4
Other real estate	1,550.2	19.9	3,388.7	14.2	11.4	45.7
Stocks and mutual funds	939.7	12.1	1,874.0	7.8	5.8	50.1
Financial securities	770.0	9.9	1,174.7	4.9	2.5	65.5
Checking accounts	137.9	1.8	563.7	2.4	2.6	24.5
Savings and time deposits, CDs, and money market funds	353.8	4.6	1,835.2	7.7	9.2	19.3
Net business equity	2,533.2	32.6	4,083.8	17.1	9.6	62.0
Life insurance cash surrender value	41.7	0.5	417.1	1.7	2.3	10.0
Pension accounts	235.6	3.0	1,671.9	7.0	8.9	14.1
Net equity in personal trusts	355.6	4.6	629.6	2.6	1.7	56.5
Vehicles	54.6	0.7	832.8	3.5	4.8	6.6
Miscellaneous assets	217.1	2.8	569.8	2.4	2.2	38.1
Liabilities	492.4	6.3	3,629.2	15.2	19.4	13.6
Debt on principal residence	95.9	1.2	2,249.7	9.4	13.3	4.3
Debt on other real estate	305.5	3.9	785.3	3.3	3.0	38.9
All other debt	90.9	1.2	594.2	2.5	3.1	15.3
Memo						
Net home equity	485.3	6.2	4,636.0	19.4	25.7	10.5
Debt-equity ratio	—	6.8	—	17.9	24.1	—

Source: Author's own computations from the 1992 Survey of Consumer Finances.
Note: The 1992 asset and liability entries are aligned to national balance sheet totals. The top 1 percent is defined as households with net worth in excess of $2.42 million. See notes to table 3.4 for technical details.

Table 3.6   Composition of Total Household Income of Top 1 Percent of Wealth-Holders and All
Households, 1983 (Billions of Current, 1983 Dollars)

	Top 1 Percent		All Households		Holdings of Top 1 Percent as Percentage of Total Income Type
	Total Value	Percentage of Total Income	Total Value	Percentage of Total Income	
Total income[a]	235.8	100.0	2,326.5	100.0	10.1
Wages and salaries	55.7	23.6	1,464.4	62.9	3.8
Self-employment income[b]	64.7	27.4	288.8	12.4	22.4
Total interest	30.0	12.7	122.4	5.3	24.5
Dividends	28.3	12.0	52.5	2.3	53.9
Capital gains	31.1	13.2	61.1	2.6	50.9
Rental, royalty and trust income	18.5	7.8	60.1	2.6	30.8
Unemployment and worker compensation	0.0	0.0	20.9	0.9	0.0
Alimony payments[c]	0.7	0.3	35.4	1.5	1.9
Public assistance[d]	0.0	0.0	23.1	1.0	0.0
Retirement income[e]	5.8	2.5	191.2	8.2	3.0
Other income	1.0	0.4	6.7	0.3	15.0

Source: Author's own computations from the 1983 Survey of Consumer Finances.
Note: The top 1 percent is defined as households with net worth in excess of $1.55 million.
[a] Defined as the sum of income components.
[b] Includes partnership and net profit from unincorporated businesses.
[c] Includes child support payments.
[d] Includes AFDC, food stamps, SSI, and other welfare benefits.
[e] Includes Social Security and pension benefits, annuities, disability payments, and other forms of retirement income.

Between 1983 and 1992, the biggest change in the overall composition of personal income was that the share of wages and salaries fell from 62.9 to 58.5 percent (see table 3.7). This was compensated to some extent by self-employment income, which rose from 12.4 to 13.8 percent. However, retirement income also appears to have fallen as a share of total income, from 8.2 to 6.6 percent, though this was offset by a huge increase in the "other income" category, from 0.3 to 8.0 percent. (I suspect that this results from a misclassification of a large portion of retirement income, such as proceeds from defined contribution benefit plans like 401[k] plans.) The changes in the other components of personal income were relatively small.

Among the richest 1 percent of households, the most significant development is that proprietary income rose from 27.4 percent of their total income in 1983 to 39.5 percent in 1992. This accords with the results reported in table 3.3, which shows a huge increase of self-employed household heads in the ranks of the top wealth percentile. Moreover, wages and salaries increased from 23.6 to 29.6 percent (see table 3.7). Altogether, labor earnings rose from 51 to 69 percent. Property forms of income—particularly interest, dividends, and capital gains—all declined as a pro-

Figure 3.5   Composition of Income of All Households and Top 1 Percent of Wealth-Holders, 1983 and 1992

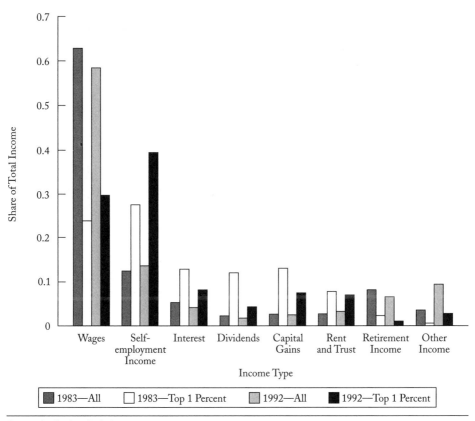

Source: Author's calculations.

portion of their total proceeds, from 46 percent to 27 percent. In 1992 the richest 1 percent earned 6.4 percent of all wage and salary income (up from 3.8 percent in 1983), 36.2 percent of all self-employment income (up from 22.4 percent), and 26 percent of all interest income (about the same share as in 1983). However, their share of total dividends and capital gains both fell sharply, and their share of total rental, royalty, and trust income was also down. On the surface at least, the evidence does seem to support the presumption that the rich in 1992 were more entrepreneurial and less apt to depend on property wealth for their support.[7] Moreover, they were also more apt to depend on wage and salary earnings.

CHARACTERISTICS OF THE RICHEST 1 PERCENT OF HOUSEHOLDS, AS RANKED BY INCOME

The next group of tables shows a similar set of statistics, except that the rich here are defined as households in the top 1 percent of the income distribution. One important difference from the preceding tables based on wealth holdings as the def-

Table 3.7   Composition of Total Household Income of Top 1 Percent of Wealth-Holders and All
Households, 1992 (Billions of Current, 1992 Dollars)

	Top 1 Percent		All Households		Holdings of Top 1 Percent as Percentage of Total Income Type
	Total Value	Percentage of Total Income	Total Value	Percentage of Total Income	
Total income	524.4	100.0	4,145.8	100.0	12.6
Wages and salaries	155.4	29.6	2,424.7	58.5	6.4
Self-employment income	206.9	39.5	571.1	13.8	36.2
Total interest	43.1	8.2	168.0	4.1	25.6
Dividends	22.7	4.3	71.7	1.7	31.7
Capital gains	38.6	7.4	99.8	2.4	38.7
Rental, royalty, and trust income	36.8	7.0	141.3	3.4	26.0
Unemployment and worker compensation	0.0	0.0	19.2	0.5	0.0
Alimony payments	0.0	0.0	16.4	0.4	0.0
Public assistance	0.0	0.0	25.6	0.6	0.1
Retirement income	6.0	1.1	275.5	6.6	2.2
Other income	14.9	2.8	332.4	8.0	4.5

Source: Author's own computations from the 1992 Survey of Consumer Finances.
Note: The top 1 percent is defined as households with net worth in excess of $2.42 million. See notes to table 3.6 for technical details.

inition of being rich is that there are fewer elderly in this grouping, since the vast majority of the elderly are retired and therefore have little or no labor income. However, the elderly, as we saw earlier, have amassed a considerable amount of wealth holdings.

Table 3.8 illustrates these differences by presenting the joint distribution of income and wealth in the two years, 1983 and 1992. The joint distribution is surprisingly diffuse. For example, households in the sixth decile of the income distribution (centiles 50 to 60) are found in all wealth centiles except the top wealth percentile, and the distribution appears almost uniform from wealth deciles 1 through 9. There is a concentration of households at the top of both distributions. For example, households in the top percentile of the income distribution are found exclusively in the top five percentiles of the wealth distribution in both 1983 and 1992, and households in the top percentile of the wealth distribution are found only in the top decile of the income distribution in 1983 and the top two deciles in 1992. However, the overall correlation between household income and wealth (computed from the original sample microdata) is surprisingly low—0.61 in 1983 and 0.64 in 1992.

Despite this low correlation, the new results based on the top income recipients are qualitatively very similar to those based on the top 1 percent of wealth-holders. Table 3.9 shows the demographic characteristics of the richest 1 percent of households as ranked by income. As shown in panel A, only 1.6 percent of all households ranked in the top 1 percent by income in 1983 had a head under the age of thirty-five,

Table 3.8 The Joint Distribution of Income and Wealth by Centile, 1983 and 1992 (Percentages)

Income Centile	Wealth Centile												
	0 to 10	10 to 20	20 to 30	30 to 40	40 to 50	50 to 60	60 to 70	70 to 80	80 to 90	90 to 95	95 to 99	99 to 100	Total
A. 1983													
0 to 10	3.2	2.0	1.3	1.2	0.8	0.7	0.3	0.3	0.1	0.1	0.0	0.0	10.0
10 to 20	2.3	1.8	1.4	1.2	0.8	0.8	0.8	0.5	0.2	0.1	0.0	0.0	10.0
20 to 30	1.4	1.9	1.3	1.0	1.0	0.9	1.1	0.6	0.6	0.1	0.1	0.0	10.0
30 to 40	1.3	1.3	1.2	1.2	0.9	1.0	1.1	0.9	0.8	0.3	0.1	0.0	10.0
40 to 50	0.7	1.0	1.5	1.4	1.3	1.3	0.9	0.8	0.7	0.3	0.1	0.0	10.0
50 to 60	0.6	1.1	1.1	1.2	1.1	1.5	1.1	0.7	1.0	0.4	0.2	0.0	10.0
60 to 70	0.2	0.5	1.1	1.2	1.4	1.2	1.4	1.2	1.0	0.5	0.3	0.0	10.0
70 to 80	0.2	0.2	0.6	1.1	1.4	1.5	1.3	1.5	1.5	0.5	0.4	0.0	10.0
80 to 90	0.0	0.2	0.4	0.3	1.1	0.8	1.4	2.2	1.9	1.2	0.6	0.0	10.0
90 to 95	0.1	0.0	0.0	0.1	0.2	0.3	0.6	0.8	1.2	0.9	0.7	0.1	5.0
95 to 99	0.0	0.0	0.0	0.0	0.1	0.1	0.1	0.5	1.1	0.6	1.2	0.2	4.0
99 to 100	0.0	0.0	0.0	0.0	0.0	0.0	0.0	0.0	0.0	0.0	0.3	0.6	1.0
Total	10.0	10.0	10.0	10.0	10.0	10.0	10.0	10.0	10.0	5.0	4.0	1.0	100.0

Overall correlation coefficient: 0.610

Income Centile	0 to 10	10 to 20	20 to 30	30 to 40	40 to 50	50 to 60	60 to 70	70 to 80	80 to 90	90 to 95	95 to 99	99 to 100	Total
B. 1992													
0 to 10	3.1	2.3	1.1	1.1	1.2	0.7	0.3	0.2	0.1	0.1	0.0	0.0	10.0
10 to 20	2.2	2.0	1.3	1.0	1.0	0.9	0.7	0.6	0.3	0.1	0.0	0.0	10.0
20 to 30	1.2	1.7	1.3	1.0	1.1	1.1	0.9	0.9	0.6	0.1	0.0	0.0	10.0
30 to 40	0.8	1.4	1.4	1.1	1.0	1.1	1.3	0.8	0.8	0.2	0.1	0.0	10.0
40 to 50	0.9	1.2	1.7	1.0	1.2	1.0	0.9	0.7	1.1	0.3	0.1	0.0	10.0
50 to 60	0.6	0.6	1.3	1.3	1.0	1.1	1.1	1.1	1.2	0.4	0.2	0.0	10.0
60 to 70	0.7	0.4	0.9	1.5	1.2	1.2	1.4	0.8	1.1	0.6	0.2	0.0	10.0
70 to 80	0.3	0.2	0.5	1.1	1.2	1.6	1.4	1.6	1.4	0.6	0.2	0.0	10.0
80 to 90	0.1	0.1	0.3	0.7	1.0	1.0	1.5	2.1	1.5	1.0	0.6	0.1	10.0
90 to 95	0.1	0.0	0.1	0.0	0.2	0.4	0.5	0.9	1.0	0.9	0.8	0.1	5.0
95 to 99	0.0	0.0	0.0	0.0	0.0	0.0	0.2	0.2	0.9	0.8	1.5	0.3	4.0
99 to 100	0.0	0.0	0.0	0.0	0.0	0.0	0.0	0.1	0.0	0.0	0.4	0.5	1.0
Total	10.0	10.0	10.0	10.0	10.0	10.0	10.0	10.0	10.0	5.0	4.0	1.0	100.0

Overall correlation coefficient: 0.639

Source: Author's own computations from the 1983 and 1992 Surveys of Consumer Finances.

Table 3.9   Demographic and Work-Related Characteristics of the Top One Percent of Households, as Ranked by Income and All Households, 1983 and 1992 (Percentages Except for Mean and Median Values)

	1983			1992		
	Top 1 Percent	All	Difference	Top 1 Percent	All	Difference
A. Age of head						
Less than twenty-five	0.0	8.0	−8.0	0.5	5.2	−4.7
Twenty-five to thirty-four	1.6	22.6	−21.0	5.2	20.4	−15.2
Thirty-five to forty-four	16.3	19.5	−3.2	25.5	22.7	2.8
Forty-five to fifty-four	28.6	15.6	13.0	25.8	16.4	9.4
Fifty-five to sixty-four	33.8	15.1	18.8	29.1	13.4	15.7
Sixty-five to seventy-four	16.8	12.1	4.6	10.1	12.7	−2.5
Seventy-five and over	2.9	7.1	−4.3	3.7	9.2	−5.5
All age groups	100.0	100.0	0.0	100.0	100.0	0.0
Mean age	55.3	46.8	8.5	51.9	48.4	3.5
Median age	56.0	44.0	12.0	51.0	45.0	6.0
B. Education of head						
Eleven years or less	0.1	29.0	−28.9	0.7	21.1	−20.4
High school graduate	3.8	30.2	−26.4	4.6	28.9	−24.3
One to three years college	10.4	19.6	−9.3	11.5	21.0	−9.5
College graduate	33.6	10.6	22.9	32.7	16.5	16.2
Some graduate school	52.1	10.6	41.5	50.5	12.5	38.0
All educational groups	100.0	100.0	0.0	100.0	100.0	0.0
Mean education	16.1	12.2	3.9	16.0	12.9	3.1
Median education	16.0	12.0	4.0	16.0	13.0	3.0
C. Race						
White (non-Hispanic)	97.0	80.9	16.1	94.1	75.3	18.8
Black (non-Hispanic)	1.2	12.7	−11.5	0.1	12.6	−12.5
Hispanic	0.0	3.5	−3.5	0.0	7.6	−7.6
Asian and others	1.8	2.8	−1.0	5.8	4.6	1.2
All racial groups	100.0	100.0	0.0	100.0	100.0	0.0
D. Marital status						
Married, spouse present[a]	91.9	60.8	31.1	87.6	57.6	30.0
Male, separated, divorced, or widowed	6.1	6.8	−0.7	6.7	8.6	−1.9
Male, never married	2.0	6.3	−4.3	1.5	6.5	−5.0
Female, separated, divorced, or widowed	0.1	19.9	−19.8	2.1	19.4	−17.3
Female, never married	0.0	6.2	−6.2	2.1	7.9	−5.8
All marital groups	100.0	100.0	0.0	100.0	100.0	0.0
E. Employment status of head (less than sixty-five only)						
Full-time	92.1	75.8	16.3	87.4	74.9	12.6
Part-time	3.1	4.0	−1.0	7.4	4.5	2.9
Unemployed or temporarily laid off	0.0	8.8	−8.8	2.2	7.1	−5.0
Retired	4.8	7.3	−2.4	1.8	3.8	−2.0
Not in labor force	0.0	4.1	−4.1	1.3	9.8	−8.4
All under age sixty-five	100.0	100.0	0.0	100.0	100.0	0.0

Table 3.9   *Continued*

	1983			1992		
	Top 1 Percent	All	Difference	Top 1 Percent	All	Difference
F. Industry of employment of head (employed persons only)						
Agriculture	0.6	3.9	−3.3	1.1	2.7	−1.7
Mining	5.3	1.4	3.9	⎡ 5.8	7.4	−1.5 ⎤
Construction	3.8	7.5	−3.7	⎣		⎦
Manufacturing	20.0	23.7	−3.8	⎡ 13.3	28.3	−15.1 ⎤
Transportation, communications, or utilities	1.1	8.9	−7.8	⎣		⎦
Trade (wholesale and retail)	8.3	15.5	−7.2	5.3	14.9	−9.6
Finance, insurance, or real estate	26.1	5.3	20.8	26.5	13.8	12.7
Business or professional services	32.9	23.1	9.8	⎡ 47.4	25.5	21.9 ⎤
Personal services	1.8	3.4	−1.5	⎣		⎦
Public administration	0.0	7.2	−7.2	0.6	7.4	−6.8
All employed persons	100.0	100.0	0.0	100.0	100.0	0.0
G. Occupation of head (employed persons only)						
Self-employed[b]	26.6	15.4	11.3	63.7	17.2	46.5
Professionals[c]	12.0	15.0	−3.0	⎡ 34.1	25.5	8.6 ⎤
Managers and administrators	58.1	13.9	44.1	⎣		⎦
Sales and clerical workers[d]	3.2	13.0	−9.8	2.2	22.4	−20.1
Craft workers[e]	0.0	16.9	−16.9	0.0	10.6	−10.6
Other blue-collar workers[f]	0.0	25.8	−25.8	0.0	24.3	−24.3
All employed persons	100.0	100.0	0.0	100.0	100.0	0.0
H. Health of head of household						
Excellent	63.1	37.9	25.2	64.3	34.6	29.7
Good	33.1	39.6	−6.5	32.5	40.9	−8.4
Fair	2.9	15.4	−12.5	3.1	17.5	−14.4
Poor	0.8	7.1	−6.3	0.1	7.0	−6.9
Total	100.0	100.0	0.0	100.0	100.0	0.0
I. Inheritances received						
Percentage receiving inheritances	—	—	—	35.9	20.6	15.3
Average value of inheritances[g]				$696,651	$96,140	$600,511

Source: Author's own computations from the 1983 and 1992 Surveys of Consumer Finances.
Note: Top 1 percent is defined as households with income in excess of $170,000 in 1983 and in excess of $285,000 in 1992. All computations are for heads of household unless otherwise indicated. Note that geographical information is not available for the high-income supplement in 1983.
[a.] Includes "partners" in 1992.
[b.] Self-employed of any occupation are classified separately in this category.
[c.] Includes technical workers in 1983.
[d.] Includes technical workers in 1992.
[e.] Includes protective service workers in 1983.
[f.] Includes operatives (both machine and transportation equipment), laborers, service workers (except protective services in 1983), and farm workers.
[g.] Inheritance recipients only. Present value as of 1992, using a 3 percent real interest rate.

compared to 30.6 percent of all households in that age range (see also figure 3.6). Moreover, while 19.5 percent of all household heads were aged thirty-five to forty-four, only 16.3 percent of the top 1 percent were in that age group. In contrast, the age groups forty-five to fifty-four, sixty-five to seventy-four, and especially fifty-five to sixty-four were overrepresented in the ranks of the very rich.

However, between 1983 and 1992, the share of all rich household heads in the top 1 percent under the age of thirty-five increased from 1.6 to 5.7 percent, even as their share of the total population fell. The proportion aged thirty-five to forty-four also increased very sharply, from 16.3 to 25.5 percent (and increased relative to the size of their overall population share). The percentage of the top 1 percent in the next three older age groups all fell, both as a fraction of all households in the top 1 percent and relative to changes in overall population shares by age group. On net, the mean age of the very rich declined by 3.4 years, as the overall population aged, and their median age declined by 5 years. This "youthening" of the rich continues a trend noted by Slemrod (1994) for the period 1977 to 1983.

A comparison of tables 3.3 and 3.9 indicates that the households that were rich in terms of income tended to be younger than those rich in terms of wealth. This

Figure 3.6   Age Distribution of All Households and Top 1 Percent Ranked by Income, 1983 and 1992

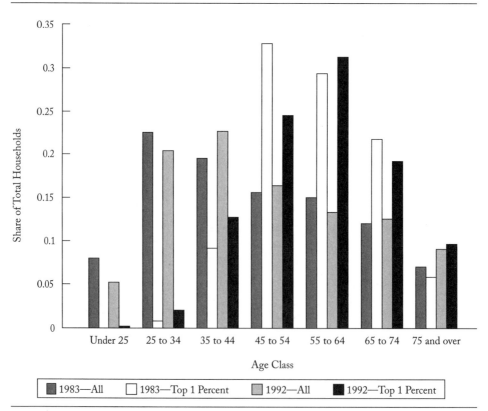

Source: Author's calculations.

was true in both 1983 and 1992, though especially in the later year. For example, in 1992, whereas 15 percent of the top percentile in terms of wealth were under the age of forty-five, 31 percent of the top income percentile were in this age group. Conversely, while 29 percent of household heads in the top wealth percentile were sixty-five or over, only 14 percent of the top income percentile were in this age bracket.

In 1983 over half of the top 1 percent of income-earners had engaged in graduate work, and 86 percent of this group were college graduates or better, compared to 21 percent of the general population (see panel B and figure 3.7). Indeed, only 4 percent of this group had not attended college, compared to 59 percent of all household heads. However, here too, despite the general rise in educational attainment in population between 1983 and 1992, there was a slight decline in the educational attainment of the top 1 percent. The fraction with some graduate school fell from 52.1 to 50.5 percent, the fraction who were college graduates or better fell from 86 to 83 percent, and the fraction who had never attended college rose from 3.9 to 5.3

Figure 3.7   Education Distribution of All Households and Top 1 Percent Ranked by Income, 1983 and 1992

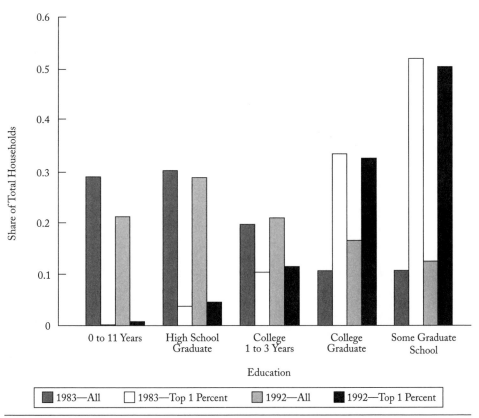

Source: Author's calculations.

percent. There was also a moderate increase in the fraction of the rich who were college dropouts. The "income rich" were also somewhat better educated than those who were rich in terms of wealth. For example, whereas over half of the top income percentile had attended graduate school in both 1983 and 1992, the corresponding percentages for the top wealth percentile were 36 and 41 percent, respectively.

In 1983, 97 percent of the household heads in the top 1 percent according to income were non-Hispanic whites, compared to a population share of 81 percent (see panel C and figure 3.8). Non-Hispanic blacks made up only 1.2 percent of the top 1 percent of household heads (compared to a 12.7 percent population share), Hispanics 0.0 percent (compared to a 3.5 percent population share), and Asians and other races 1.8 percent. Between 1983 and 1992, while the share of non-Hispanic white household heads in the general population fell by 5.6 percentage points, their proportion of the top 1 percent fell by only 2.9 percentage points. Non-Hispanic black families constituted only 0.1 percent of the top 1 percent, down from 1.2 percent in 1983, while Hispanic families remained at 0.0 percent of the top 1 percent, despite the fact that their population share more than doubled. However, Asians

Figure 3.8   Racial Composition of All Households and Top 1 Percent Ranked by Income, 1983 and 1992

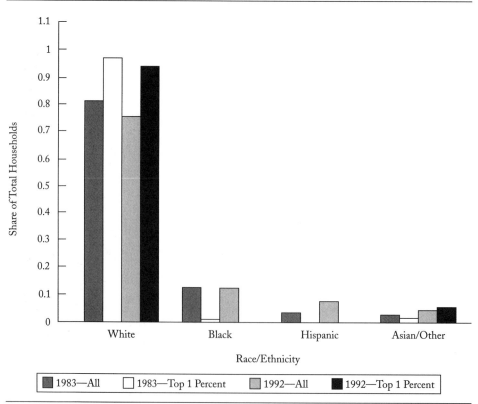

and other races increased as a share of the top 1 percent from 1.8 to 5.8 percent. The racial composition of the top income percentile was almost identical to that of the top wealth percentile in each of the two years.

As shown in panel D, in 1983, 92 percent of the very rich in terms of income were found in households with a married couple (compared to 61 percent of the general population); 8.1 percent were headed by unmarried men, and virtually none by unmarried women (compared to 26.1 percent of the overall population). Between 1983 and 1992, while the proportion of married families among the top 1 percent of income-earners fell from 92 to 88 percent, the proportion of households headed by an unmarried women increased from 0.1 to 4.2 percent and the share of households headed by an unmarried male remained almost unchanged. The major difference between the top percentile of income-earners and wealth-holders was the greater presence of separated, divorced, or widowed women in the ranks of the latter.

In 1983, 92 percent of non-elderly rich households were headed by a full-time worker (compared to 76 percent of all non-elderly households), 3 percent by a part-time worker, and 5 percent by a retiree (see panel E). The most striking change between 1983 and 1992 is that the proportion of very rich households headed by a full-time worker declined from 92 to 87 percent; this was almost exactly offset by a corresponding rise in the percentage headed by a part-time worker, from 3.1 to 7.4 percent. The share of retirees in the ranks of the top percentile also fell, from 4.8 to 1.8 percent, but this was compensated by a corresponding rise in the proportion who were either unemployed (from 0.0 to 2.2 percent) or not in the labor force (from 0.0 to 1.3 percent). These results also seem to suggest a reduction in work effort among the non-elderly rich, in this case as defined in terms of income. However, not surprisingly, there was a greater percentage of full-time workers in the ranks of the top income percentile than in the top wealth percentile (even for household heads under age sixty-five) and a smaller percentage of retirees, at least in 1992.

In 1983, 26 percent of the top percentile headed by someone at work reported working in finance, insurance, or real estate, compared to only 5 percent of all workers, and 33 percent reported working in business and professional services, in contrast to 23 percent of all workers (panel F). The most dramatic change between 1983 and 1992 was a huge increase in the share of workers employed in business, professional, and personal services in the ranks of the very rich, from 35 to 47 percent (and also a large increase relative to the employment share of all workers, from a difference of 8.3 to 21.9 percent). The share of finance, insurance, and real estate workers in the ranks of the very rich remained almost unchanged over this period, despite a large increase in the percentage of all workers employed in this sector. However, together, these two sectors accounted for almost three-quarters of all rich households headed by someone at work in 1992. In contrast, the shares of workers in the top percentile employed in goods-producing industries, transportation, communications, utilities, and trade all fell in both absolute and relative terms.

The major differences between the industry composition of the top income and wealth percentiles were the much larger proportion of the former who were employed in business and professional services, particularly in 1992 (47 versus 23 percent), and the correspondingly smaller share employed in the financial sector (27 versus 36 percent in 1992) and in manufacturing, transportation, communications, utilities, and trade (19 versus 35 percent). One explanation for these differences may be that current wealth reflects, to a large extent, incomes in the past. Thus, the results suggest that manufacturing, transportation, communications, utilities, and trade have diminished over time (probably since the 1950s) as major sources of large incomes, whereas finance, business, and professional services have increased in importance. Moreover, the greater importance of business and professional services over finance as a source of very high earnings in 1992 (in comparison to high wealth holdings) probably reflects the stock market downturn of 1989, the recession of 1991 to 1992, and the ensuing shrinkage of the finance sector. It is likely that finance has now overtaken business and professional services as the major source of very large earnings.

Self-employed workers were substantially overrepresented in the ranks of the top percentile of households in terms of income in 1983—27 percent versus 15 percent of all workers—as were managers and administrators, at 58 versus 14 percent (see panel G). However, only 12 percent of the very rich classified themselves as professionals, in contrast to 15 percent of all workers. These results are very similar to those of table 3.3. Moreover, as we saw before, there was a striking growth in the share of the self-employed among the top 1 percent—in this case, from 27 to 64 percent. In contrast, the proportion of professional, managerial, and administrative workers who were not self-employed fell precipitously, from 70 to 34 percent.

As we also saw in table 3.3, the rich (in terms of income here) appear to be much healthier than the average population. In 1983, 63 percent of the rich said that their health was excellent, compared to 38 percent of the overall population (see panel H). Only 3.7 percent of the top 1 percent indicated that their health was fair or poor, in comparison to 22.5 percent of all respondents. While the overall health of the population appears to have deteriorated somewhat between 1983 and 1992, the health of the very rich, as defined by income, seems to have improved slightly, with the proportion reporting excellent health rising by 1.2 percentage points and the proportion reporting fair or poor health falling by 0.6 percentage points.

The very rich in terms of income were more apt to receive a bequest than the general population in 1992—36 versus 21 percent (see panel I). Moreover, the value of these inheritances was much greater among households in the top percentile than in the general population (a sevenfold difference). However, as to be expected, the proportion of the top income percentile who had received bequests was smaller than the share of the top wealth percentile (36 versus 49 percent).

As shown in table 3.10 and figure 3.9, in 1983 the top 1 percent of households as ranked in terms of income had a higher share of their wealth in the form of non-home real estate than did other households in the population (19.1 versus 12.8 percent for the bottom 99 percent of households), stocks and mutual funds (17.9 versus 5.6 percent), business equity (27.8 versus 14.9 percent), and trust funds (7.8 versus 0.7 percent); and lower proportions in their principal residence (8.9 versus 36.2 percent), savings and time deposits, CDs, and money market funds (7.0 versus 14.1 percent), and vehicles (0.4 versus 4.2 percent). The richest 1 percent in terms of income also had a lower debt-equity ratio—6.8 versus 17.5 percent. Moreover, whereas the top income percentile accounted for 27.6 percent of total net worth, they owned 33.9 percent of non-home real estate, 52.6 percent of stocks and

Table 3.10   Composition of Net Worth of the Top One Percent of Households as Ranked by Income and All Households, 1983 (Billions of Current, 1983 Dollars)

| | Top 1 Percent | | All Households | | Bottom 99 Percent | Holdings of Top 1 |
	Total Value	Percentage of Gross Assets	Total Value	Percentage of Gross Assets	Percentage of Gross Assets	Percent as Percentage of Total Value
Net worth	3,117.4	—	11,312.1	—		27.6
Gross asset values	3,330.6	100.0	12,958.8	100.0	100.0	25.7
Principal residence	296.8	8.9	3,777.8	29.2	36.2	7.9
Other real estate	634.7	19.1	1,871.1	14.4	12.8	33.9
Stocks and mutual funds	597.2	17.9	1,134.4	8.8	5.6	52.6
Financial securities	203.4	6.1	525.8	4.1	3.3	38.7
Checking accounts	51.7	1.6	327.0	2.5	2.9	15.8
Savings and time deposits CDs, and money market funds	233.0	7.0	1,590.4	12.3	14.1	14.7
Net business equity	926.8	27.8	2,364.1	18.2	14.9	39.2
Life insurance cash surrender value	27.7	0.8	270.5	2.1	2.5	10.2
Pension accounts	42.7	1.3	184.2	1.4	1.5	23.2
Net equity in personal trusts	259.1	7.8	331.2	2.6	0.7	78.2
Vehicles	13.2	0.4	413.9	3.2	4.2	3.2
Miscellaneous assets	44.2	1.3	168.0	1.3	1.3	26.3
Liabilities	213.2	6.4	1,646.7	12.7	14.9	12.9
Debt on principal residence	36.3	1.1	789.2	6.1	7.8	4.6
Debt on other real estate	11.6	0.3	93.8	0.7	0.9	12.4
All other debt	165.3	5.0	763.7	5.9	6.2	21.6
Memo						
Net home equity	260.5	7.8	2,988.6	23.1	28.3	8.7
Debt-equity ratio		6.8		14.6	17.5	

Source: Author's own computations from the 1983 Survey of Consumer Finances.
Note: The 1983 asset and liability entries are aligned to national balance sheet totals. The top 1 percent is defined as households with income in excess of $170,000. See notes to table 3.4 for technical details.

Figure 3.9   Composition of Assets of All Households and Top 1 Percent by Income, 1983 and 1992

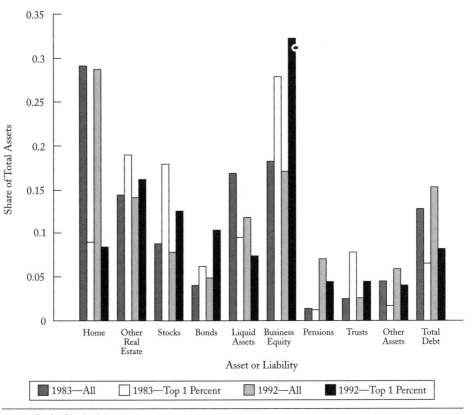

Source: Author's calculations.

mutual funds, 38.7 percent of financial securities, 39.2 percent of business equity, and 78.2 percent of trust fund equity. These results closely resemble those presented in table 3.4 concerning the top wealth percentile.

Among the richest 1 percent of households, the major change between 1983 and 1992 (see table 3.11) has been a fall in the share of gross assets held in stocks and mutual funds (from 17.9 to 12.6 percent), in investment real estate (from 19.1 to 16.3 percent), and in trust funds (from 7.8 to 4.4 percent) and corresponding increases in the share held in business equity (27.8 to 32.2 percent), financial securities (from 6.1 to 10.3 percent) and pension accounts (1.3 to 4.5 percent). While the share of total net worth held by the top 1 percent of income recipients remained unchanged at 27.6 percent between 1983 and 1992, their share of business equity increased sharply from 39.2 to 48.0 percent and their share of financial securities from 38.7 to 53.4 percent. In contrast, their share of non-home real estate fell from 33.9 to 29.2 percent, their share of total stocks and mutual funds from 52.6 to 40.8 percent, their share of trust fund equity from 78.2 to 42.8 percent, and their share of pension assets from 23.2 to 16.2 percent.

Table 3.11 Composition of Net Worth of the Top 1 Percent of Households as Ranked by Income and All Households, 1992 (Billions of Current, 1992 Dollars)

	Top 1 Percent		All Households		Bottom 99 Percent	Holdings of Top 1
	Total Value	Percentage of Gross Assets	Total Value	Percentage of Gross Assets	Percentage of Gross Assets	Percent as Percentage of Total Value
Net worth	5,605.9	—	20,284.8	—	—	27.6
Gross asset values	6,095.4	100.0	23,903.5	100.0	100.0	25.5
Principal residence	507.9	8.3	6,885.7	28.8	35.7	7.4
Other real estate	990.5	16.3	3,388.7	14.2	13.4	29.2
Stocks and mutual funds	763.9	12.6	1,874.0	7.8	6.2	40.8
Financial securities	627.9	10.3	1,174.7	4.9	3.1	53.4
Checking accounts	110.8	1.8	563.7	2.4	2.5	19.7
Savings and time deposits CDs, and money market funds	294.2	4.8	1,835.2	7.7	8.6	16.0
Net business equity	1,962.0	32.2	4,083.8	17.1	11.9	48.0
Life insurance cash surrender value	41.6	0.7	417.1	1.7	2.1	10.0
Pension accounts	271.7	4.5	1,671.9	7.0	7.8	16.2
Net equity in personal trusts	269.5	4.4	629.6	2.6	2.0	42.8
Vehicles	54.2	0.9	832.8	3.5	4.4	6.5
Miscellaneous assets	191.9	3.2	569.8	2.4	2.1	33.7
Liabilities	493.1	8.1	3,629.2	15.2	17.6	13.6
Debt on principal residence	131.9	2.2	2,249.7	9.4	11.9	5.9
Debt on other real estate	273.2	4.5	785.3	3.3	2.9	34.8
All other debt	88.1	1.4	594.2	2.5	2.8	14.8
Memo						
Net home equity	376.0	6.2	4,636.0	19.4	23.9	8.1
Debt equity ratio	—	8.8	—	17.9	21.4	—

Source: Author's own computations from the 1992 Survey of Consumer Finances.
Note: The 1992 asset and liability entries are aligned to national balance sheet totals. The top 1 percent is defined as households with income in excess of $285,000. See notes to table 3.4 for technical details.

These results do suggest increased entrepreneurial activity among the very rich, at least as classified by income. However, the results are mixed when the rich are classified by wealth. The share of total wealth held in the form of business assets by the top wealth percentile remained virtually unchanged between 1983 and 1992, but the share of total business equity held by the top 1 percent of wealth-holders increased from 52 to 62 percent.

In 1983 the primary source of income among the richest 1 percent of households ranked in terms of income was wages and salaries, at 34.5 percent of their total income (see table 3.12 and figure 3.10). Proprietary income was second, at 25.9 percent, followed by capital gains at 11.7 percent, interest at 10.2 percent, and dividends at 9.4 percent. The top 1 percent of households accounted for over half of all dividends and capital gains, and about one-quarter of proprietary income, interest, and rental, royalty, and trust income. They also accounted for 11.5 percent of all alimony payments!

Between 1983 and 1992, the most substantial change is that wages and salaries increased from 34.5 to 44.1 percent of the total income of the top 1 percent (see table 3.13). Although all labor earnings rose from 60 to 68 percent, proprietary income fell somewhat, from 25.9 to 23.5 percent. Property income, including interest, dividends, capital gains, rents, royalties, and trust income, declined as a proportion of their total proceeds, from 36 to 30 percent.

In 1992 the richest 1 percent earned 11.8 percent of all wage and salary income (up from 7.0 percent in 1983), 26.7 percent of all self-employment income (the same as in 1983), and 32 percent of all interest income (up from 25 percent in 1983).

Table 3.12   Composition of Total Household Income of Top 1 Percent of Households, as Ranked by Income and All Households, 1983 (Billions of Current, 1983 Dollars)

	Top 1 Percent		All Households		Holdings of Top 1 Percent as Percentage of Total Income Type
	Total Value	Percentage of Total Income	Total Value	Percentage of Total Income	
Total income	298.5	100.0	2,326.5	100.0	12.8
Wages and salaries	103.1	34.5	1,464.4	62.9	7.0
Self-employment income	77.3	25.9	288.8	12.4	26.7
Total interest	30.3	10.2	122.4	5.3	24.8
Dividends	28.2	9.4	52.5	2.3	53.7
Capital gains	35.0	11.7	61.1	2.6	57.3
Rental, royalty, and trust income	15.1	5.0	60.1	2.6	25.1
Unemployment and worker compensation	0.0	0.0	20.9	0.9	0.1
Alimony payments	4.1	1.4	35.4	1.5	11.5
Public assistance	0.0	0.0	23.1	1.0	0.0
Retirement income	5.1	1.7	191.2	8.2	2.6
Other income	0.4	0.1	6.7	0.3	6.3

Source: Author's own computations from the 1983 Survey of Consumer Finances.
Note: The top 1 percent is defined as households with income in excess of $170,000. See notes to table 3.6 for technical details.

Figure 3.10   Composition of Income of All Households and Top 1 Percent by Income, 1983 and 1992

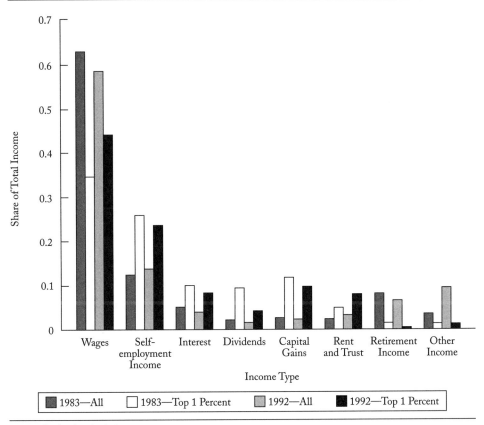

Source: Author's calculations.

However, while their share of total dividends fell sharply, their share of capital gains actually increased somewhat and their share of total rental, royalty, and trust income was also up sharply.

When classified by wealth holdings, the rich also show a substitution of earned income for property income over the same period. Among the top percentile of wealth-holders, the share of total income received in the form of labor earnings grew from 51 percent in 1983 to 69 percent in 1992—though this was primarily a result of a sharp increase in self-employment income—whereas property income declined from 46 percent of their total income to 27 percent. Moreover, whereas the share of total wage and salary income and of proprietary income received by the top wealth percentile both increased, their share of total property income fell.

CONCLUDING REMARKS

The results do show some striking differences between the characteristics of the very rich and those of the general population, but some important changes in the composition of the very rich over the period 1983 to 1992. First, the rich are, on aver-

Table 3.13   Composition of Total Household Income of Top 1 Percent of Households, as Ranked by Income and All Households, 1992 (Billions of Current, 1992 Dollars)

	Top 1 Percent		All Households		Holdings of Top 1 Percent as Percentage of Total Income Type
	Total Value	Percentage of Total Income	Total Value	Percentage of Total Income	
Total income	650.9	100.0	4,145.8	100.0	15.7
Wages and salaries	286.9	44.1	2,424.7	58.5	11.8
Self-employment income	152.7	23.5	571.1	13.8	26.7
Total interest	53.9	8.3	168.0	4.1	32.1
Dividends	28.0	4.3	71.7	1.7	39.1
Capital gains	63.3	9.7	99.8	2.4	63.4
Rental, royalty, and trust income	52.0	8.0	141.3	3.4	36.8
Unemployment and worker compensation	0.1	0.0	19.2	0.5	0.5
Alimony payments	0.3	0.1	16.4	0.4	2.0
Public assistance	0.0	0.0	25.6	0.6	0.1
Retirement income	4.9	0.7	275.5	6.6	1.8
Other income	8.7	1.3	332.4	8.0	2.6

Source: Author's own computations from the 1992 Survey of Consumer Finances.
Note: The top 1 percent is defined as households with income in excess of $285,000. See notes to table 3.6 for technical details.

age, older than the population at large. However, there were notable increases in the number of young families in the ranks of the very rich. Between 1983 and 1992, the fraction of household heads in the top 1 percent of wealth-holders under the age of forty-five rose from 10 to 15 percent. Moreover, the percentage of the top 1 percent of income-earners under the age of thirty-five increased from 2 to 6 percent, the percentage aged thirty-five to forty-four went up very sharply, from 16 to 26 percent, and their median age dropped from fifty-six to fifty-one.

Second, the very rich are much better educated than the overall population. However, despite significant growth in the overall educational attainment of the population between 1983 and 1992, there was no corresponding increase in the educational attainment of the top percentile as ranked by both wealth and income— indeed, the fraction of these two groups that had graduated college actually declined.

Third, the very rich remain almost exclusively non-Hispanic whites. The proportion of non-Hispanic black households and Hispanic households among the very rich, as defined by both wealth and income, stayed largely unchanged between 1983 and 1992. However, Asian Americans (and other races) did show large advances, relative to their population share, into the ranks of the rich over this period.

The very rich, both in terms of income and wealth, were composed predominantly of married couples, particularly in comparison to the population at large. Moreover, in 1983, 99.9 percent of households in the top percentile of income-earners were headed by men (either married or unmarried). However, unmarried women (both never and formerly married) made some modest inroads into the ranks of the top income percentile between 1983 and 1992.

The household heads of both the top income and wealth percentiles also appear to be much healthier than the general population. However, while the (self-reported) health of the heads of households in the top income percentile improved somewhat between 1983 and 1992, a slight deterioration occurred in the health of the top wealth percentile.

There were some interesting changes in both the labor-force participation and employment patterns of the very rich. First, in both 1983 and 1992, the vast majority of household heads under sixty-five in both the top wealth and the top income percentiles were full-time workers. However, in both cases the share of full-time workers in the ranks of the very rich declined over this period. In the case of the high-income-earners, this shift was almost completely offset by a corresponding rise in the proportion of part-time workers. Among the high-wealth-holders, this change was made up for by increases in the share of both part-time workers and retirees in their ranks.

Yet, despite this apparent reduction in labor-force effort among the very rich, the income statistics show a greater reliance on labor income than other forms of income among the very rich. Between 1983 and 1992, labor earnings (both wages and salary and self-employment income) as a share of the total income of the top wealth percentile jumped from 51 to 69 percent, and that of the top income percentile from 60 to 68 percent. This apparent contradiction can be explained by two factors. First, the number of non-elderly households as a fraction of all households increased from 73 to 81 percent among the top wealth percentile, and from 80 to 86 percent among the top income percentile. Second, there was a substantial increase in the number of working wives in very rich households. Indeed, the number of two-earner families as a share of all non-elderly married families grew from 36 to 40 percent among the top wealth percentile, and from 40 to 48 percent among the top income percentile.

Second, there is also evidence that entrepreneurial activity played much more of a role in gaining entry to the ranks of the very rich. A huge increase occurred in the number of self-employed persons in the ranks of the very rich, both in terms of income and wealth, and the number of salaried managers and professionals declined correspondingly. (There are almost no sales, clerical, or blue-collar workers among the top wealth or income percentile.) The number of self-employed household heads as a share of the total number of employed household heads in the top wealth percentile almost doubled between 1983 and 1992, from 38 to 69 percent, and the corresponding proportion in the top income percentile more than doubled, from 27 to 64 percent.

There is also some corroborating evidence from the household income statements and balance sheets. Among the richest 1 percent of households ranked in terms of wealth, the share of proprietary income, from self-employment, partnerships, and unincorporated business ownership, in their total income rose sharply, from 27 to 40 percent. Moreover, while the proportion of the total wealth of the top wealth percentile held in the form of business equity remained unchanged between 1983 and 1992, their share of the total value of business equity among all households increased substantially, from 52 to 62 percent. Among the richest 1 percent of households as ranked by income, the proportion of their wealth held in the form of business equity increased from 28 to 32 percent, and their share of the total value of business equity surged from 39 to 48 percent. However, proprietary income fell somewhat as a share of their total income, from 26 to 24 percent.

These results have to be interpreted with some caution, since, as Slemrod (1996) argues, tax law changes stemming from the 1986 Tax Reform Act have given regular corporations a strong incentive to convert to subchapter S corporations and partnerships, which are categorized as unincorporated business enterprises (and the corresponding income as self-employment income). These conversions may also be responsible for the rising importance of business equity in the portfolios of the very rich and the corresponding declines in corporate stock holdings.

Third, whatever the rationale behind the increased importance of self-employment income and unincorporated business equity among the rich, they appear to be relying less and less on property income. In particular, property income of all forms, such as interest, dividends, capital gains, rental, royalty, and trust income, declined sharply, from 46 to 27 percent of the total income of the top wealth percentile, and from 36 to 30 percent for the top income percentile. Moreover, the percentage of the total wealth of the rich, classified by both dimensions, held in the form of stocks, mutual funds, and trust funds fell sharply over this period, as did their share of the total outstanding value of these assets. However, this was in part compensated by sharply increased holdings of financial securities, both as a percentage of the total assets of the top 1 percent and as a share of the total amount of financial securities held by all households.

Fourth, the traditional sources of large fortunes in this country—notably, agriculture, mining, construction, manufacturing, transportation, communications, utilities, and trade—appear to have diminished in importance and to have been supplanted by the financial sectors, as well as by business and professional services. The former group of industries accounted for 52 percent of the employment of heads of households in the top wealth percentile in 1983 and only 41 percent in 1992, whereas the share employed in finance, business, and professional services rose from 47 to 58 percent. The results are even more dramatic for the top income percentile, among whom the share of total employment in these traditional industries fell from 39 to 26 percent and correspondingly rose from 59 to 74 percent in the latter group of industries.

In sum, this study indicates that the wealthy are apt to be healthier, wiser (at least better educated), and older than the general population, but they did not appear to become healthier or wiser from 1983 to 1992, though they did become younger. Moreover, the rich are more apt to be self-employed and to work in finance, business, and professional services than the overall population, and over this period they have relied more on labor income and less on property income as sources of their fortunes.

NOTES

1. The construction of the weights is further complicated by differential response rates among families in the high-income supplement and the cross-section sample. According to Curtin, Juster, and Morgan (1989), only 9 percent of the families chosen for the high-income supplement for

the 1983 SCF agreed to be interviewed. However, of this group, the response rate was 95 percent, compared to 71 percent for the families in the cross-section sample. Two major studies conducted by the Federal Reserve Board—Kennickell and Woodburn (1992) for the 1989 SCF and Kennickell, McManus, and Woodburn (1996) for the 1992 SCF—discuss the problems associated with developing these weights and propose alternative sets of weights as solutions.

2. It should be noted at the outset that there appears to be a substantial change in the sampling frame used in the new 1992 SCF in comparison to the 1989 SCF. For consistency with the earlier results, I have adjusted the weights used in the 1992 SCF. The problem can be seen most easily in the following table:

Comparison of SOI and SCF Size Distributions

Adjusted Gross Income or Household Income (Current $)	SCF Distribution Percentage of All Households		SOI Distribution Percentage of All Tax Returns	
	1989	1992	1989	1992
Under $100,000	95.7	94.9	97.4	96.7
$100,000–199,999	3.107	3.948	1.864	2.474
$200,000–499,999	0.895	0.892	0.546	0.657
$500,000–999,999	0.187	0.182	0.103	0.124
$1,000,000 or more	0.073	0.040	0.051	0.059
Of which				
$1,000,000–3,999,999	0.0550	0.0293		
$4,000,000–6,999,999	0.0128	0.0021		
$7,000,000 or more	0.0049	0.0002		

Sources: For SCF distributions, own computations from the 1989 and 1992 SCF. For SOI distributions, U.S. Department of the Treasury (1993–1994, 179–80; 1994–1995, 180–81).

A comparison of weights used in the 1989 and 1992 SCF shows a very sharp attenuation in the weights at the top of the income distribution. According to these figures, the percentage of households with incomes between $1 million and $4 million declined from 0.055 to 0.029, or by almost half; the percentage in the income range $4 million to $7 million fell from 0.013 to 0.002, or by over 80 percent; and the percentage with incomes of $7 million or more decreased from 0.0049 to 0.0002, or by over 95 percent. These changes are highly implausible—particularly in light of results from the Current Population Survey (CPS) (available on the Internet), which show a slightly rising degree of income inequality over this period. (The Gini coefficient increases from 0.427 to 0.428.)

The table also compares the size distribution of income computed from the IRS SOI in 1989 and 1992 with that from the two SCF files. The SOI figures are based on actual tax returns filed in the two years. There are three major differences between the two data sources. First, the SOI data use the tax return as the unit of observation, whereas the SCF figures are based on the household unit. Second, individuals who do not file tax returns are excluded from the SOI tabulations. Third, the size distribution for the SOI data is based on adjusted gross income (AGI), whereas the SCF distributions are based on total household income.

Despite the differences in concept and measurement, trends in the size distribution of AGI can give a rough approximation to actual changes in the size distribution of household (census) income. What is most striking is that the SOI figures show a slight increase in the percentage of units in the income class $1 million and more, from 0.051 in 1989 to 0.059 percent in 1992, whereas the SCF figures show a sharp decline, from 0.073 to 0.040 percent.

Results from the SOI data fail to provide any independent corroboration for the sharp decline in the number of households with incomes of $1 million or more between 1989 and 1992. Accordingly, I adjusted the 1992 weights to conform to the 1989 weighting scheme. The adjustment factors for the 1992 weights are given by the inverse of the normalized ratio of weights between 1992 and 1989, shown in the last column of the preceding table.

Income in 1989 Dollars	Adjustment Factors for 1992 Weights
Under $200,000	0.992
$200,000–999,999	1.459
$1,000,000–3,999,999	1.877
$4,000,000–6,999,999	4.844
$7,000,000 or more	12.258

The resulting size distribution of income for 1989 and 1992 is as follows:

Income Shares (Percentages)	1989 SCF Using Original Weights	1992 SCF Using Adjusted Weights
Share of the top 1 percent	16.4	15.7
Share of the top 5 percent	29.7	30.5
Share of the top 10 percent	40.1	41.1
Share of the top 20 percent	55.3	56.4
Gini coefficient:	0.521	0.528

The calculations show a slight increase in overall income inequality, as measured by the Gini coefficient, a result that is consistent with both the SOI and the CPS data.

3. The adjustment factors by asset type and year are as follows:

	1983 SCF	1992 SCF
Checking accounts	1.68	
Savings and time deposits	1.50	
All deposits		1.32
Financial securities	1.20	
Stocks and mutual funds	1.06	
Trusts		1.41
Nonmortgage debt	1.16	

Note: Other asset and debt components required no adjustment.

4. It should be noted that my definition of net worth includes the value of vehicles. As a consequence, these results differ from those reported in Wolff (1987, 1994, 1996), which exclude vehicles in the definition of net worth.

5. Though there are some problems with the "self-employed" category in the 1992 SCF data, I have tried to make the definition as consistent as possible with the 1983 SCF concept. The fact that the overall share of self-employed shows only a modest increase between the two years suggests that the definitions are roughly comparable in the two years.

6. There was no separate category for professional workers in the 1992 SCF.

7. On the other hand, Slemrod (1996) argues that a large part of the increase in reported self-employment income over this period was due to the conversion of corporations to subchapter S corporations and partnerships for tax reasons. In particular, the 1986 Tax Reform Act caused the top marginal tax rate on personal income to fall below that on corporate earnings. Since income from S corporations and partnerships is treated as personal rather than corporate income, many corporations converted to S corporations. In this case, the purported rise in entrepreneurship might simply be due to a reclassification of income. I return to this issue in the conclusion.

REFERENCES

Curtin, Richard T., F. Thomas Juster, and James N. Morgan. 1989. "Survey Estimates of Wealth: An Assessment of Quality." In *The Measurement of Saving, Investment, and Wealth*, edited by Robert E. Lipsey and Helen Stone Tice. Studies of Income and Wealth, vol. 52. Chicago: University of Chicago Press.

Kennickell, Arthur B., Douglas A. McManus, and R. Louise Woodburn. 1996. "Weighting Design for the 1992 Survey of Consumer Finances." Unpublished paper. Federal Reserve Board (March).

Kennickell, Arthur B., and R. Louise Woodburn. 1992. "Estimation of Household Net Worth Using Model-Based and Design-Based Weights: Evidence from the 1989 Survey of Consumer Finances." Unpublished paper. Federal Reserve Board (April).

Slemrod, Joel. 1994. "On the High-Income Laffer Curve." In *Empirical Foundations of Household Taxation*, edited by Martin Feldstein and James Poterba. Chicago/Cambridge, Mass.: University of Chicago Press/National Bureau of Economic Research.

———. 1996. "High-Income Families and the Tax Changes of the 1980s: The Anatomy of Behavioral Responses." In *Tax Progressivity and Income Inequality*, edited by Joel B. Slemrod. Cambridge: Cambridge University Press.

U.S. Bureau of the Census. 1993. *Money Income of Households, Families, and Persons in the United States: 1992. Current Population Reports* series P60–184. Washington, D.C.: U.S. Government Printing Office.

U.S. Department of the Treasury, Internal Revenue Service. 1993–94. "Selected Historical and Other Data." *Statistics of Income Bulletin* 13(4, Winter).

———. 1994–95. "Selected Historical and Other Data." *Statistics of Income Bulletin* 15(3, Winter).

Wolff, Edward N. 1987. "Estimates of Household Wealth Inequality in the United States, 1962–1983." *Review of Income and Wealth* series 33 (September): 231–56.

———. 1994. "Trends in Household Wealth in the United States, 1962–1983 and 1983–1989." *Review of Income and Wealth* series 40 (2, June): 143–74.

———. 1996. "Trends in Household Wealth, 1983–1992." Report submitted to the Department of Labor (July).

4

The Tax Environment Facing the Wealthy

Douglas A. Shackelford

This chapter analyzes the effect of income and transfer (gift and estate) taxes on the sources and uses of wealth in order to estimate the real tax burden on working and saving and the relative prices of certain forms of consumption. The principal question addressed is: If laborers faced only a tax on wages (that is, if returns to capital were exempt and transfer taxes were abolished), what tax rate would leave them indifferent compared with the current tax system?

To address this question, I develop a model that attempts to capture the individual income and transfer-tax incentives facing wealthy individuals. The model is used to estimate the marginal tax rates arising in the absence of tax planning. It also provides comparisons of different forms of consumption, including inter vivos gifts versus bequests for spouses, children, and charities.

I find that the wage tax rate that would leave laborers indifferent depends critically on two factors. First, can the laborer transform wages into a return of capital for tax purposes? Marginal tax rates on labor income fall if the wages are paid in a form that qualifies for capital treatment, for example, employer equity. Second, how will the laborer dispose of the wealth generated by his labor? Wealth dispositions are taxed differently, causing the marginal tax rate on labor income to vary with the intended disposition. For example, charitable contributions are deductible. Thus, labor income that is contributed to charities faces a zero marginal tax rate. Conversely, labor income that is bequeathed to children is reduced by a wage tax, the returns to investment of the remaining wages are subject to capital taxes, and the bequest faces estate tax rates ranging up to 55 percent. Under the most tax-disadvantaged conditions analyzed in this chapter, laborers who bequeath the wealth from their labor to their children are indifferent between a single wage tax of 91 percent and the current tax system.

Not surprisingly, taxpayers, facing such potentially exorbitant marginal tax rates, create a demand for tax plans that supports a vast tax-avoidance industry composed of attorneys, accountants, bankers, insurers, and appraisers. To assess the potential effect of tax planning on marginal tax rates, I outline several income and transfer-tax plans currently employed by wealthy individuals.

Income tax plans generally attempt to skirt the realization principle, enabling consumption and diversification without income taxation. The realization principle triggers taxation when the legal ownership of the property changes. For example, the payment of dividends generates income taxation to the recipient (and sometimes to the payor) because dividends shift the ownership of the distributed assets from the corporation to the shareholders. Taxation arises even though shareholder wealth does not change on the dividend payment date (except for taxes) because the dividend decreases the value of the company by the same amount that it increases the shareholder's cash. In other words, dividends are taxed even though shareholder value is unchanged.

Income tax avoidance opportunities arise because income recognition is determined by legal rather than economic changes in ownership. By designing income tax plans that permit economic changes, such as reinvestment, without changing the legal form of ownership, planners can lower wealthy individuals' marginal tax rates without deleterious effects on their lifestyles. For example, wealthy individuals might borrow against appreciated property rather than sell the property and trigger income taxation.

Transfer-tax plans generally exploit inherent difficulties in determining valuations, enabling justification of below-market values. Transfer taxes are levied on the fair market values of gifts annually and on the fair market value of decedents' net assets. Gifts and bequests to spouses and charities are exempt from transfer taxes. Every donor also can exempt from the transfer tax $10,000 per donee annually.[1] In addition, a $192,800 credit allows each individual to transfer his first $600,000 of gifts and bequests tax-free.[2] The $600,000 includes neither $10,000 annual exclusions nor spousal or charitable transfers. Transfer taxes, whether arising from lifetime gifts or at death, are assessed on the cumulative transfer-tax base. For example, suppose an individual dies with a $2 million estate, has no spousal or charitable bequests, and has made taxable gifts of $1 million during his life (excluding $10,000 annual exclusions). The transfer tax is computed on a $3 million base (a tax of $1,025,800 using 1997 rates) and reduced by the current tax on a $1 million base ($248,300) leaving the estate with a tax of $777,500, which is reduced by the credit of $192,800, to produce an estate tax liability of $584,700.[3]

Gift and estate tax plans that successfully undervalue assets enable more property to be transferred tax-free under the annual exclusions and the lifetime credit and reduce the taxes due on amounts exceeding these de minimis provisions. For example, a wealthy couple who intend to leave their home to their children after their deaths could give their children a future interest in their home today through a trust. The transfer would be valued at the present value of the future interest in the home, which is substantially less than its value after the death of the couple. As a result, by gifting the less valuable future interest rather than bequeathing a complete interest, the transfer taxes are reduced without affecting the eventual owners of the house.

The income and transfer-tax plans detailed in this study include a diverse set of transactions (for example, shorting-against-the-box and like-kind exchanges), products (such as derivatives and life insurance) and organizational structures (for example, family partnerships and investment companies). Customized to individuals' specific tax needs, the plans are capable of lowering the actual marginal tax rates faced by wealthy individuals enough that marginal tax rates approaching zero are not implausible.

The next section derives a model for evaluating the effects of income and transfer taxes and estimates various marginal tax rates in the absence of tax planning. The third section describes current income tax plans. The section that follows details current transfer-tax plans. I then revisit the marginal tax rate estimates in light of

the tax plans. The final section provides concluding remarks, including policy recommendations.

MODEL
Derivation

Individuals can accumulate wealth from four sources: wages, which generally are
taxed at ordinary rates on receipt; returns to capital, whose tax character (capital versus ordinary) and tax timing (present versus future) are sufficiently determined by
the legal form of the earnings process (that is, the realization principle) that taxpayers have some discretion over their tax treatment; gifts, which are tax-exempt to
the donee but carry the donor's tax basis; and bequests, which are tax-exempt to the
heir and have tax basis equal to fair market value. During her life an individual can
consume personally, give her wealth to her spouse, charities, or other individuals or
enterprises (hereafter called "children"), pay income taxes, or purchase tax-avoidance
plans. At death, the remaining wealth is bequeathed to her spouse, children, or
charities or forfeited in transfer taxes.

The model assumes the individual is work-averse but values her own consumption and the wealth of her spouse, children, and charities at her death, as described
in the following utility function:[4]

$$\text{Max } U(L, C, S, K, D),$$

subject to a budget constraint:

$$w(1 - L)(1 - t_p) + G = C + S_0 + K_0(1 + e_0) + D_0(1 - t_p) + A(1 - t_p) + (S_n + K_n + D_n/[(1 + R_p)^n(1 - t_p) + t_p b_p]$$

where

w = wage rate,
L = leisure (time endowment = 1),
t = income tax rate,
$\quad = \tau_y{}^{\gamma_y} A_y,$
G = gifts and bequests received,
C = individual's consumption,
S = spouse's consumption,
$\quad = S_0[(1 + R_s)^n(1 - t_s) + t_s b_s] + S_n,$
K = children's consumption
$\quad = K_0[(1 + R_k)^n(1 - t_k) + t_k b_k] + K_n(1 - e_n),$
e = transfer-tax rate,
$\quad = \tau_e{}^{\gamma_e} A_e,$
D = charity's consumption
$\quad = D_0(1 + R_d)^n + D_n,$
A = tax-avoidance expenditures,
$\quad = \alpha(A_y + A_e),$

R = the savings rate of return before considering income and transfer taxes,
n = years remaining in individual's life,
b = tax basis as a percentage of fair market value,
τ_i = statutory tax rate i,

and subscripts p, s, k, and d refer to the individual, spouse, children, and charities, respectively; subscripts 0 and n refer to inter vivos gifts and bequests, respectively; subscripts y and e refer to income taxes and transfer taxes, respectively; L, C, Si, Ki, D_i, and A, where i = 0, n, are non-negative, $\gamma > 0$ and $\alpha > 1$.

The budget constraint equates the individual's initial sources of wealth (labor income and gifts and bequests received) with the uses of wealth (her and her donees' consumption plus tax-avoidance fees), adjusted for the individual's returns to capital from investing the retained wealth. The individual can transfer wealth to her spouse, children, and charities during her lifetime and at her death. The donor is assumed to be indifferent to the timing of the consumption of those she cares about and seeks only to maximize the present value of the transfers. Obviously, the donor can consume only during her lifetime.

The form of the model's savings vehicles, used for both donor and donees, $[(1 + R)^n(1 - t) + tb]$, presents tax-favored business returns. The model adopts these tax-favored savings vehicles to ensure that the taxes analyzed in the chapter are focused on individual income and transfer-tax planning, not business tax planning (unless it affects the taxes of interest). Therefore, any value from tax planning identified in this chapter can be linked specifically to personal income and transfer taxes.

Specifically, the savings vehicles assume that business returns grow tax-exempt. This assumption probably understates the tax burden facing wealthy individuals. If savings are invested in C corporations, and corporate taxes arise or taxable dividends are distributed, the returns to the investor are overstated and the total tax burden of the wealthy is understated. Similarly, if savings are invested in "flow-through" business entities, such as partnerships, limited liability corporations, and S corporations, and investors recognize annual taxes from their pro rata share of the enterprise's profits, the returns to the investor are overstated and the tax burden is understated. On the other hand, the savings vehicles provide accurate accumulations for investors in businesses that do not generate taxable income and that realize all appreciation at the end of the investment period. For example, if a start-up company pays no taxes or dividends and yet appreciates in value, its investors can sell their stock in the company and realize all of the gains to the investment as modeled with the savings vehicles used in this chapter. To assess the sensitivity of this restriction, this assumption is relaxed, enabling consideration of less tax-favored business returns later in the chapter.

The wealthy are assumed to purchase tax avoidance until the tax savings associated with tax plans equal the costs of tax avoidance, including planners' fees, implicit taxes, opportunity costs, tax-motivated restructuring that would be suboptimal without taxes (Scholes and Wolfson 1992), and the increase in expected costs associated with an audit as a result of engaging in tax-avoidance activities (as captured by α in the model).[5] However, to assess the importance of individual income and transfer-tax planning, I initially analyze the model assuming no tax plans are purchased (A = 0). Two questions are addressed under this assumption. First, should wealthy individuals accelerate transfers to donees through inter vivos gifts or defer transfers until death? A general tax preference for accelerating transfers is noted. The second question is: What is the marginal tax rate facing labor income? The findings show that taxpayers can face marginal tax rates on wages from zero to over 90 percent, depending on whether wages are treated for tax purposes as returns to labor or capital and on the desired disposition of the wealth arising from the labor. The wide range of marginal tax rate estimates implies variation in the demand for tax avoidance and the nearly insatiable need for tax planning by certain taxpayers.

Transfers to Spouses

Analysis of the model indicates that inter vivos spousal gifts dominate bequests when the spouse can earn at a higher after-tax rate of return than the donor $[(1 + R_s)^n(1 - t_s) + t_s b_s > (1 + R_p)^n(1 - t_p) + t_p b_p]$. Transfer taxes are irrelevant to this decision because spousal transfers are subject to neither gift nor estate taxes. Thus, individuals wishing to maximize their spouses' wealth should direct their avoidance energies to income taxes. Because the decedent's tax bases are adjusted to fair market value at death, appreciated (depreciated) properties bequeathed to the spouse face a lower (higher) tax when sold by the spouse than if the properties had been transferred to the spouse during the transferor's life. Thus, the spouse's wealth is maximized if the donor transfers depreciated properties during life and bequeaths appreciated properties.

Transfers to Children

Inter vivos gifts to children dominate bequests when the children's after-income tax earnings on the gift exceed the parent's after-income tax earnings on the gift and the avoided gift tax, less estate taxes $[(1 + R_k)^n (1 - t_k) + t_k b_k > (1 + e_0)[(1 + R_p)^n(1 - t_p) + t_p b_p](1 - e_n)]$. Assuming time-invariant transfer-tax rates ($e_0 = e_n$) and identical after-tax returns for child and parent ($R_k = R_p$, $t_k = t_p$, $b_k = b_p$), bequests produce only $1 - e^2$ percent (70 percent, using the current maximum transfer-tax rate) of the wealth that lifetime gifts do, evaluated at the parent's death.

The preference for inter vivos gifts is counterintuitive because gifts accelerate the transfer taxes that could have been deferred until death. However, the tax-favored status of lifetime gifts arises because the transfer-tax base excludes gift taxes but not estate taxes.[6] In other words, the estate tax is tax-inclusive (the base includes the tax) and the gift tax is tax-exclusive (the base excludes the tax). Thus, if the estate tax rate is e, then the gift tax rate is $e/(e + 1)$. Consequently, at the current maximum transfer-tax rate of 55 percent, the estate tax rate is 55 percent but the effective gift tax rate is only 35 percent (0.55/1.55).

This analysis assumes that the after-tax earnings rates of parents and children are equal, but that assumption may be inappropriate for at least two reasons. First, step-up in the tax basis to fair market value at death enables parents to earn at before-tax rates. If $t_p = 0$, $R_k = R_p$, and $e_0 = e_n$, the tax disadvantage of bequests (stated as a percentage of the wealth created by gifts) shrinks to $(1 - e^2)/[(1 - t_k) + (t_k b_k)/(1 + R)^n]$.

If the tax basis of the transferred property is zero ($b_k = 0$) or $(1 + R)^n_{\to\infty}$, the parent is indifferent between gifts and bequests when $e^2 = t_k$. Applying current maximum statutory tax rates (55 percent transfer and 20 percent capital gains—reduced from 28 percent by the recent Taxpayer Relief Act of 1997 [TRA97]), bequests' yields approach 87 percent of lifetime gifts, retaining some bias toward acceleration.

A second reason parents' returns could exceed their children's returns is differences in financial experience, maturity, or savvy. If $t_k = t_p$, $b_k = b_p = 0$, and $e_0 = e_n$, $1 - e^2 = [(1 + R_k)^n]/[(1 + R_p)^n]$. Using the current maximum transfer-tax rate, the parent is indifferent between inter vivos gifts and bequests if his before-tax accumulations are 143 percent of his children's. Such accumulation differences are not implausible. Indifference occurs after ten (twenty) years if the parent earns 10 percent annually before tax and the child earns 6 (8) percent.

As an aside, if a couple wishes to defer transfer of wealth to their child until they both die, the child may receive a smaller bequest than if a partial transfer is made at the death of the first parent. The couple's combined estate taxes increase because the surviving spouse cannot use her late husband's credits at her death. In other words, the transfer-tax credit cannot be bequeathed; each individual can use only one credit.

Transfers to Charities

The optimal timing of philanthropy is relatively straightforward. The model shows that inter vivos donations dominate bequests if the charity's tax-exempt earnings, augmented by the individual's income tax deduction for inter vivos charitable contributions, exceed the individual's after-tax earnings rate $[(1 + R_d)^n/(1 - t_p) > (1 + R_p)^n(1 - t_p) + t_p b_p]$. Relative to charitable gifts, charitable bequests are tax-disadvantaged because they forfeit income tax deductions and forgo the charity's opportunity to earn at the before-tax rate of return.

Although acceleration usually dominates deferral in charitable settings, two factors can shift the balance toward bequests. First, the step-up in the tax basis at death enables the donor to earn at the before-tax rate of return on assets held at death, reducing the tax advantages of inter vivos gifts. Second, to the extent that charities restrict their investment opportunity set (for example, to avoid political costs), their donors' before-tax returns may exceed the charities' returns.

On a final note, depreciated properties should be neither gifted nor bequeathed to charities. Instead, they should be sold before death, generating a tax deduction for the donor, and the proceeds donated, because charities cannot avail themselves of deductions imbedded in tax bases; moreover, the step-up in the tax basis at death prevents usage of the tax basis in excess of fair market value for any party.

Children Versus Charities

Among transferees, charities are the most tax-advantaged recipients and children are the most tax-disadvantaged. Comparing inter vivos gifts, the charity's accumulations exceed the child's accumulations (at the death of the donor) if the charity's before-tax yields, augmented by the donor's income tax deduction, exceed the child's after-tax returns, diminished by the gift tax: $(1 + R_d)^n/(1 - t_p) > [(1 + R_k)^n (1 - t_k) + t_k b_k]/(1 + e_0)$. Applying current maximum statutory rates ($t_p = t_k = 39.6$ percent and $e_0 = 55$ percent) and letting $R_d = R_k$ and $b_k = 0$, gifts to children accumulate only 24 percent of the amount that gifts to charities accumulate. Similarly, charitable bequests are exempt from estate tax, while children's bequests are taxed. Thus, at the current maximum statutory estate tax rate of 55 percent, children's bequests are 45 percent of charitable bequests, after payment of estate taxes. As a result of the differential taxation, we can infer from observing transfers to children by taxpayers in the highest tax brackets that the utility those donors derive from enhancing their children's wealth far exceeds the utility they derive from philanthropic activities.

Implied Tax Burden on Labor-Sourced Dispositions

This section attempts to estimate the tax burden assessed on wealth derived from wages and transferred in the most tax-disadvantaged manner, children's bequests. Assume a laborer invests his after-income tax wages in a savings account that provides his children with $(1 - t_p)[(1 + R_p)^n(1 - t_p) + t_p b_p](1 - e_n)$ dollars for every dollar of wages. As discussed earlier, this savings account permits tax-free accumulation until immediately before death, when all returns from capital are subjected to income taxation.

Let t^* equal the tax rate on labor that would produce the same bequest if no other income or transfer taxes were levied:

$$(1 - t_p)[(1 + R_p)^n(1 - t_p) + t_p b_p](1 - e_n) = (1 - t^*)(1 + R_p)^n$$

As

$$(1 + R_p)^n, \; t^* \; [1 - (1 - t_p)^2(1 - e_n)]$$

Using current maximum statutory rates ($t_p = 39.6$ percent and $e_n = 55$ percent), $t^* = 0.84$.[7] In other words, if 84 percent of wages were extracted in taxes and returns to capital and transfers were tax-exempt, heirs would inherit the same wealth as they would under current law. If the returns to capital are subject to more favorable capital gains taxes ($t_p = 20$ percent), $t^* = 0.71$ as $(1 + R_p)^n_{\to\infty}$.

If the returns to capital avoid income taxation by being held until death and receiving step-up in the tax basis (that is, $[1 + R_p]^n[1 - t_p] + t_p b_p = [1 + R_p]^n$), then $t^* = [1 - (1 - t_p)(1 - e_n)]$. Applying current estate and ordinary income tax rates, $t^* = 0.73$. In other words, exempting capital from labor income taxation lowers the tax rate from 0.84 to 0.73. Similarly, if the laborer dies immediately following the performance of services, each dollar of labor income provides $(1 - t_p)(1 - e_n)$ dollars to the laborer's children, or a labor tax rate of 73 percent.

Even higher marginal tax rates on wages are possible if less tax-favored savings vehicles are employed. Recall that the model assumes that business returns in the savings vehicles accumulate tax-free. Alternatively, if the investment is made through a flow-through entity and all returns to capital are taxed immediately at ordinary rates (for example, $[1 + R_p(1 - t_p)]^n - t_p[1 - b_p]$), assumptions are needed for R_p and n to estimate t^*. Assuming that before-tax returns to capital are 10 percent for twenty years, current tax rates apply, and the tax basis equaled fair market value at the time of the investment (that is, $b_p = 1$), $t^* = 0.87$.

If the investment is made through a more tax-disadvantaged savings vehicle (a C corporation), the total implied tax rate on labor income soars even higher. Suppose that no dividends are paid but that all returns are subject annually to corporate taxes, $[1 + R_p(1 - t_c)]^n(1 - t_p) + t_p b_p$, where t_c is the corporate tax rate. Using current maximum corporate tax rates of 35 percent and the same assumptions as in the preceding paragraph, $t^* = 0.90$. If all returns are distributed annually in taxable dividends (for example, $[1 + R_p(1 - t_c)(1 - t_p)]^n - t_p[1 - b_p]$), $t^* = 0.91$.

The substitution of inter vivos gifts for bequests lowers the implied labor tax. Analyzing the original model (tax-exempt business returns) for the effects of the gift tax, $t^*[1 - (1 - t_p)^2(1 + e_0)]$ or 0.76 as $(1 + R)^n_{\to\infty}$ (assuming parents' and children's after-tax earnings rates are equal). This is eight percentage points lower than the 0.84 estimate for children's bequests.

Furthermore, using the same analysis, the implied labor tax on inter vivos philanthropic donations is zero because the charitable contribution creates a tax deduction offsetting the tax on labor and the charity's returns to capital are tax-exempt. Charitable bequests are less tax-favored because the returns to both labor and capital, which create the wealth that is bequeathed to the charity, are taxed. Only the estate tax is avoided. Thus, for philanthropic bequests, $t^*(1 - t_p)^2$ or 0.64 as $(1 + R)^n_{\to\infty}$. This marginal tax rate is the same rate facing the laborer on wealth, whether consumed immediately preceding his death or given or bequeathed to his spouse (assuming identical after-tax earnings by husband and wife).

In summary, the marginal tax rate on wages varies widely depending on the disposition option and the taxation accorded the returns to capital. The marginal tax rate for labor income could range from zero (inter vivos philanthropy) to 91 percent (bequests to children employing tax-disfavored savings vehicles) depending largely on the disposition option.

Finally, each laborer's marginal tax rate is a blend of the rates associated with his preference for each option. For example, an individual who desires to donate half of his labor earnings to charity during his life and bequeath the remainder to his children using tax-disfavored investment options would face a 45.5 percent (the mean of zero and 91 percent) marginal tax rate on each dollar of wages.

INCOME TAX AVOIDANCE PLANS

The preceding section shows that, in the absence of tax planning, large percentages of wealth (particularly labor-sourced and children-bequeathed) can flow to the government through income and transfer taxes. Predictably, taxpayers facing these arguably confiscatory levels of tax demand tax avoidance and are satiated only when the costs of tax plans exceed the reduction in tax payments.

This section and the following section illustrate the tax plans currently employed to meet the demand for lower tax burdens. The half-life of these plans is short. They become obsolete as the law changes and as tax innovators, unaided by patents and copyrights, are forced to recover their investments quickly and develop superior avoidance techniques. Perhaps the pertinence of this discussion in understanding the avoidance industry, however, will outlast the usefulness of the plans. The analysis begins with specific examples of the effect of the source of the wealth (capital versus labor) on the appropriate income tax plan.

Capitalists usually face lower marginal tax rates and have more control over when their income is taxed than do laborers. Thus, capitalists typically implement tax plans that enable them to manage their portfolio while avoiding or timing income tax recognition. Laborers strive to gain the tax-favored status of capitalists by implementing tax plans that convert wages into a form of payment that qualifies for capital tax treatment, including increased discretion over the timing of the tax payment and the possibility of favorable capital gains tax rates. As a result of lowering the maximum individual capital gains tax rate from 28 to 20 percent, TRA97 increases the demand for tax plans that can convert ordinary income into capital gains income. Conversion nearly halves the tax burden for taxpayers in the upper tax bracket, from 39.6 to 20 percent. Unfortunately for laborers, they face relatively few options to camouflage their wages as returns to capital unless they hold equity in their employers.

Capital

Reinvestment Without Taxation   Highly appreciated securities and real estate typically mark the portfolio of individuals who derive their wealth from capital.[8] A principal tax objective for a wealthy capitalist is to avoid capital gains taxes without interfering with his pattern of consumption or the diversification and redeployment of his capital to its most appropriate investment. A common thread in most capitalist income tax plans is that they enable investors to manage their portfolio and consumption without generating taxable income.

A major tax impediment to portfolio management is that selling or exchanging property typically causes the recognition of taxable income for the excess of the property's fair market value over its tax basis. For some transactions, the statutes provide an exception to the recognition of taxable income at the time of realization (for example, real estate exchanges). However, realization is an inherently flawed trigger for determining the transfer of ownership (and consequently income tax recognition) because realization generally relies on a shift in legal ownership, rather than economic ownership, to determine whether a sale has occurred. This flaw facilitates tax avoidance and spawns endless tax plans designed to enable reinvestment without taxation.

Perhaps the simplest form of reinvestment without taxation is borrowing against appreciated property. Issuing debt secured by highly appreciated assets does not trigger taxation of the assets. Moreover, the interest expense arising from the leverage is deductible to the extent of investment income. Collateralization is an efficient means of reinvestment without taxation because the legal owner of the property retains all rights to the underlying income streams. This provides the owner with an inexpensive option to redeploy his capital in the original investment (by repaying the loan). Although collateralization can provide some diversification (by creating additional income flows), it alone cannot provide complete divestiture because the owner remains the residual claimant of the securitized property.

To divest fully of the investment and still avoid tax realization, alternate tax plans are needed. One option is statutory exemption from tax realization. For example, the tax law permits divestiture of real estate without taxation if the properties are exchanged for other real estate. These like-kind exchanges are common and permit unlimited diversification and reinvestment within the real estate sector. For example, a developer can exchange an appreciated shopping mall for undeveloped land without incurring gain for the mall's appreciation, and the land can be used for any business purpose. Recycling real estate through like-kind exchanges enables investors to earn at the before-tax rate of return indefinitely, including step-up in the tax basis if the property is held until death. If reinvestment is desired outside the real estate market, then the new real estate holdings (obtained without triggering income taxation on the appreciation) can be collateralized and the cash reinvested in non-real estate properties.

Similarly, the statutes permit the appreciated stock of closely held companies to be sold to employee stock ownership plans (ESOPs) tax-free if the proceeds from the sale are reinvested in domestic corporate securities.[9] The shareholder's basis in the closely held company is allocated to the new securities, deferring taxation until sale of the diversified portfolio.

The statutes do not provide similar deferral for holders of appreciated publicly traded securities. However, creative tax planners developed transactions and synthetic products that achieved similar ends. "Shorting-against-the-box" (borrowing and selling short shares identical to those held long) merged collateralization with divestiture. For many years shorting-against-the-box enabled investors to convert securities to cash, maintain the appreciation in the security, and postpone taxation. Tax deferral was achieved because the investor did not transfer legal ownership of the long shares even though all risk associated with the shares was eliminated. If the shorted shares were repaid by selling the long shares, gain was recognized when the long shares were sold. If the shorted shares were repaid by buying additional shares or the individual died before repayment was required, the deferral of the gain on the long shares continued. Creative financial maneuvers, such as shorting-against-the-box, were not inexpensive. Tax planners tell me that bankers typically charged individuals between 100 and 150 basic basis points annually to short-against-the-box.

Shorting-against-the-box required borrowable shares and access to an actively traded capital market. Increasingly specialized financial products are providing the benefits of shorting-against-the-box in markets where such transactions have been infeasible. An example of these products is Salomon Smith Barney's DECS (debt exchangeable for common stock). With DECS, the holder of the appreciated securities issues notes secured by the appreciated stock. At maturity, the issuer has the option to repay the note with either the securities or cash. If the issuer repays the note with cash there is no taxable event.[10] Alternatively, if the issuer repays the note with the stock, it triggers taxation for the difference between the stock's tax basis and the face value of the note. In this case, the proceeds from the sale are accelerated, the taxation on the sale is deferred, and the stock price decline is averted.

In recent years another derivative product, equity swaps, provided tax-free diversification. In an equity swap, the shareholder paid a financial intermediary a fee, plus any dividends received on her stock, plus (or minus) any appreciation (depreciation) in the stock during a fixed period. In exchange, the shareholder received the returns from a diversified portfolio (for example, Standard & Poors 500 index). Taxation was avoided because the shareholder retained legal ownership of the security, even though the shareholder's returns were unrelated to the security during the contract period.[11] According to *Tax Notes* on October 17, 1994, Bankers Trust, a leading developer of equity swaps, reportedly represented orally that it charged 150 basis points annually to effect an equity swap (270).

Finally, controlling shareholders can defer taxation on appreciated stock by selling their company in a form that qualifies as a tax-deferred reorganization. For example, an individual can sell his wholly owned company and avoid any current taxation if he is willing to accept the buyer's stock. The tax basis in the original company carries over to the buyer's equity. Again the investor has reinvested without taxation.

The Taxpayer Relief Act of 1997

TRA97 eliminated the usefulness of the relatively pristine forms of shorting-against-the-box and equity swaps by treating such transactions as constructive sales and subjecting their appreciated financial positions to immediate taxation. However, tax planners seem confident that alternatives to shorting and equity swaps will be developed that permit reinvestment without triggering constructive sale treatment. The long-term effect of TRA97 will probably be to slow, not halt, the exploitation of the realization principle through financial engineering.

The legislation is too new to understand fully its effects on reinvestment with taxation. The Treasury is instructed to promulgate regulations that delineate precisely between transactions subject to immediate taxation and those that maintain deferral. In its guidance to the regulators, the Senate committee report hints at potential areas for renewed tax-avoidance planning. For example, it states that constructive sale treatment should be limited to transactions that substantially eliminate *both* opportunities for gain and loss. Products that provide asymmetric risk elimination presumably retain tax deferral for the underlying investment.

The TRA97 changes will probably spur the development of tax-avoidance options. Combinations of puts and calls already are used to mitigate risk when risk elimination is neither desired nor prohibitively expensive. Similarly, these products would seem ideally situated to retain sufficient risk of gain or loss for the taxpayer to avoid income taxation, but to reduce risk enough to remain attractive to investors. Examples of partial risk retention instruments are "collars," which are common in many derivative products, such as interest rate swaps. With a collar, the investor eliminates the risk associated with extreme price changes while retaining the risk of smaller changes. Tax planners tell me that the annual cost of these customized products is about 200 basis points.

The future usefulness of established financial tax-avoidance products, such as shorting and equity swaps, and relatively recent developments, such as collars, depends critically on how broadly the Treasury attempts to define constructive sale.

For example, how dissimilar must a shorted security be from the security held in a long position to avoid a tax-generating short sale? Similarly, what percentage of risk must the investor retain following implementation of a risk reduction product, such as a collar, to effect constructive sale?

Definitive answers to these questions may be years in coming; however, incomplete information is not preventing the development of creative financial instruments that enable taxpayers to reinvest without facing income taxation. Tax advisers tell me that the avoidance industry assumes, in the absence of regulations, that if the investor retains the risk of a 10 percent increase or a 10 percent decrease in value, a collar will not trigger constructive sale. For example, if a stock is currently worth $100, the holder of an appreciated stock can construct a collar by buying a put exercisable at $90 and buying a call exercisable at $110. This transaction is not believed to constitute constructive sale; however, it achieves similar effects to shorting-against-the-box.

State Income Taxes

Although the computations in this chapter ignore them, state income taxes can amount to as much as one-quarter of the income tax burden faced by wealthy individuals. A special Delaware state tax exemption may provide an incentive for wealthy individuals to manage any financial assets trapped in a C corporation through a Delaware investment company. As long as a Delaware-domiciled investment company maintains minimal activities in Delaware, such as board of directors' meetings, it may not be subject to state taxation in any state. Thus, by transferring their intangible properties (tax-free) to a Delaware-domiciled investment company, individuals may avoid all state income taxes on interest, dividend, rents, and royalties.

The downside of any C corporation, including a Delaware investment company, is that it can produce two levels of taxation (corporate and individual). However, the corporation can limit double federal taxation by restricting distributions. Special federal tax assessments for excessive retention within the corporation (for example, accumulated earnings and personal holding company taxes) can be mitigated through: deductible payments to shareholder-employees, such as compensation and fringe benefits such as corporate aircraft; interest expense from collateralized properties; and active management of publicly traded companies controlled by the Delaware investment company. Moreover, if assets are retained in the corporate form, the investment company shelters the income from higher personal income tax rates.

Labor

Converting Labor Income into Capital Income   Compared to wealthy capitalists, highly compensated laborers, such as corporate executives and entertainers, face few tax-avoidance options. Before the Tax Reform Act of 1986 (TRA86), nonlabor (passive) deductions and losses could shelter labor income. Since 1986, such losses have not been permitted to offset labor income, dramatically limiting tax-avoidance opportunities for laborers. The effect of this separation has been to increase the long-standing incentive to transform compensation received for services rendered into a payment that is treated for tax purposes as capital income.

One way to transform labor income into capital income is to give employees equity. This enables employers to repackage wages as capital income. An example of repackaged wages is stock options. With incentive stock options, employees are taxed at the favorable capital gains tax rate on the difference between the sales proceeds and the strike price when the stock is sold. With nonqualified stock options, employees are taxed at the ordinary income tax rate on the difference between fair market value and the strike price when the option is exercised. Later, when the stock received from the option is sold, the capital gains tax rate is applied to the difference between sales proceeds and the fair market value at exercise.[12]

Similarly, a partnership can compensate an employee by providing an interest in the partnership's profits. The value of this claim on the partnership's profits is directly related to the value of the partnership. If the partnership is sold, the compensation to the holder of an interest in the partnership's profits is taxed as a capital asset at the favorable capital gains tax rates. As with the stock options, wages are transformed into a capital asset that qualifies for capital gains treatment.

Labor income, which cannot be converted into capital income, can be deferred and then taxed when received. From the employee's perspective, deferred compensation is tax-favored compared with current wages if the employee's marginal tax rate is expected to decrease or be less than the employer's tax rate during the deferral period (Scholes and Wolfson 1992). Unfortunately for employees, deferred compensation obligations are unsecured, leaving them as general creditors in bankruptcy. Protection against bankruptcy usually triggers immediate income taxation. Thus, tax and bankruptcy considerations must be jointly evaluated.

Anecdotal evidence suggests that deferred compensation is widely used, at least by the largest corporations. Reportedly, Coca-Cola's late CEO, Roberto Goizueta, accumulated more than $1 billion in deferred compensation, mostly in highly appreciated company stock with forfeiture restrictions, and according to the *New York Times* (October 13, 1996), several other executives defer in excess of $1 million annually. Besides the potential tax savings, executive-deferred compensation is popular because it is not governed by the Employees Retirement Income Security Act of 1974 (ERISA), which limits the amount of qualified plan contributions for high-income taxpayers and imposes substantial administrative costs.

Finally, fringe benefits can transform labor income into tax-exempt earnings. Besides the standard fringes available to many employees, such as health insurance, wealthy laborers may assign value to the use of corporate aircraft, limousines, luxurious offices, exotic travel, admission to selective social gatherings, and the like. Not only may recipients avoid income taxes for receiving these perquisites, but employers may be able to deduct them. Moreover, the wealthy may use them to avoid taxation on capital income as well as labor income because fringes are so tax-favored. For example, a family-owned business may employ shareholders and compensate them with fringe benefits.

A downside of each plan detailed here is that, although it lowers the employee's tax burden, it increases his capital concentration in the source of his labor income. A fundamental weakness of labor income tax plans is that taxes are avoided at the costs of reduced diversification. Thus, laborers whose compensation derives largely from company-specific skills must balance diversification and tax avoidance. Consequently, employees' marginal tax rates on labor income should be increasing in employers' risk because the need for diversification increases with employers' risk and, at some point, diversification dominates income tax avoidance.

Entrepreneurs   Entrepreneurs constitute a special group of wealth producers whose human and financial capitals are typically invested in a nondiversified portfolio, such as a single company. It is easier for them to extract labor income as capital income than it is for corporate executives and other highly compensated laborers because their equity investment constitutes a larger component of their total investment in the enterprise. In particular, by assuming a major equity stake at business formation and limiting cash wages, the entrepreneur's wealth grows within the business and is extracted at favorable capital gains tax rates.

Summary

The common thread woven into the income tax plans typically used by wealthy capitalists is exploitation of the realization concept. With the ability to determine the timing, character, and amount of taxable income, the capitalist can transform the income tax into a somewhat voluntary assessment. The distinct advantage of the wealthy in this regard is their ability to forgo taxable income under tax-disadvantaged circumstances. This tax management is possible because the wealthy can consume from sources that do not generate taxable income. However, their ability to reinvest without generating capital gains on appreciated property raises important policy questions about the efficacy of employing a tax that can so easily be avoided. On the other hand, the income tax on labor is much more difficult to avoid. Laborers' primary planning technique is devising schemes that transform labor income into capital income, enabling them to mimic the tax-favored condition of capitalists.

TRANSFER-TAX AVOIDANCE PLANS
Undervaluation of the Transfer-Tax Base

While income tax plans exploit realization, transfer-tax plans exploit valuation.[13] Transfer taxes are levied on the fair market value of gifts and estates for donees other than spouses and charities (such as children). Thus, taxpayers with such donative intentions have incentives to undervalue their properties. With up to fifty-five cents of tax associated with every dollar of valuation, taxpayers and taxing authorities predictably disagree about property values. Understatement is facilitated by the law's reliance on arm's-length fair market values to determine the transfer-tax base. This link to prices between unrelated parties leads to many avoidance opportunities because the appropriate valuations between distrustful independent parties often are economically inappropriate for transfers between related parties, who are often members of the same family.[14]

Discount Partnerships   One example of a popular transfer-tax plan that exploits valuation is a family partnership. Suppose that parents own a portfolio of assets they wish to leave for their children following their deaths. Instead of giving the assets to the children (through bequests or inter vivos gifts) and paying transfer taxes on their fair market value, they contribute them (tax-free) to a partnership. Retaining control of the partnership, they then give their children minority interests in the partnership that are taxable gifts. However, that gift typically is valued at substantially less than the fair market value of the child's pro rata share of the investment's market prices because the child does not control the partnership.

The discount varies with the restrictions on the interest and the nature of the partnership assets. Michael Allen (1987) states that discounts range from 30 to 70 percent. William Zabel (1995) terms 30 percent the "quite usual discount" but notes that discounts can range up to 60 percent. For example, if the partnership's net assets are $100, a gift of a one-tenth interest in the partnership may be discounted from $10 ($100 × 1/10) to perhaps as little as $3 using a 70 percent discount. Discounts are permitted because unrelated third parties (the basis for determining fair market values) would not pay as much for partnership assets, over which they had no control, as they would pay for the same assets if they held a controlling interest. Thus, partnership minority interests avoid transfer taxes because they enable donors to discount valuations as though the agency problems between independent parties depress the price regardless of whether the family partnership is impeded by such agency concerns.

Equity Interests   Entrepreneurs can exploit valuation by giving capital interests in start-ups or out-of-the-money stock options to their children. The fair market value of the new venture interests or stock options have little value at assignment and are discounted (much as they are with family partnerships) because the children have no control over the enterprise. If the company prospers, significant portions of the owner's wealth are transferred to the children at little tax cost. If the company fails, the owner has forgone only the relatively insignificant gift tax associated with the transfer of the equity interests. If the wealthy individual has many investments, there may be little value in any single option, but a portfolio of capital interests probably includes a few that will increase substantially. The valuation exploitation with these interests is that the taxpayer is likely to be able to substantiate a tiny allocation of value to any single interest.

Personal Residences   Another common transfer-tax avoidance scheme involves personal residences. Suppose a parent wants her children to own her home after she dies. If she bequeaths the house, her taxable estate will include its fair market value. Alternatively, she can place the house in a qualified personal residence trust for the benefit of the children, conditional on her rent-free occupancy for a set period of years. At the end of the period, ownership of the house transfers tax-free from the trust to the children. The value of the taxable gift is the present value of a residual interest in a house, subject to rent-free occupancy by a tenant whose lease cannot be terminated. The taxable gift of the residual interest is assigned a heavily discounted value because of the unfavorable terms of the lease from an unrelated landlord's perspective. For family members, the residual interest becomes a tax-favored means of reducing the transfer tax without changing the eventual owners.

Life Insurance   The value of life insurance can be transferred across generations without transfer taxation if the wealth used to buy the policy and the proceeds received at death are structured to escape transfer taxes. One life insurance option involves placing a policy in an irrevocable trust and removing all ownership rights and control from the insured individual. The insured pays the premiums (often without triggering transfer taxes), and the proceeds from the life insurance policy pass tax-free to the beneficiaries of the trust.

For closely held businesses, split-dollar life insurance can be a particularly attractive means of transfer-tax avoidance. With split-dollar, the company purchases a policy for its executive. At death, the company recovers its payments on the policy and the remaining benefits are paid to the executive's estate and are subject to transfer taxes. However, if the executive contributes the policy to an irrevocable trust, the benefits pass directly to the beneficiaries, escaping estate taxes. Transfer taxes are avoided because the gift taxes, if any, from placing the policy in the irrevocable trust are less than the estate taxes incurred if the policy is not placed in a trust. This occurs because the gift taxes are assessed on a fraction of the premiums paid by the company, not on all premiums paid. The base for transfer (and income) tax purposes is the cost of a one-year term life insurance policy (known as PS 58 costs), as determined using IRS tables.

Zabel (1995) describes a transfer-tax plan using split-dollar and irrevocable trusts that he evaluated for a client. The company considered purchasing a $50 million life insurance policy for an executive by paying $2 million per year for ten years. Using the IRS tables, the PS 58 cost in the first year of the policy would have been $76,000, and subject to income taxes and gift taxes (reduced by annual exclusions if available). The valuation exploitation is that annual gift taxes are assessed on only $76,000, although at death the proceeds in excess of the premiums (at least $30 million) transfer tax-free to the beneficiaries of the trust.

Income and Transfer-Tax Avoidance Philanthropy

Recall that charitable contributions reduce both income and transfer taxes, enabling the wealthy to fulfill tax-advantaged philanthropic goals. Charitable remainder trusts are one of the more popular structures for tax-avoidance philanthropy. They provide fixed or variable returns to noncharitable beneficiaries during the life of the grantor. At the grantor's death, the trust assets are distributed to charitable organizations.[15]

The tax advantages of charitable remainder trusts are threefold. First, the trusts permit appreciated properties to be sold tax-free. Grantors can contribute appreciated properties to the trusts; then the trusts sell the properties and the capital gains escape taxation.[16] Second, when the property is contributed to the trust, the grantor receives an income tax deduction based on the fair market value of the property. The amount of the deduction depends on the grantor's life expectancy and the expected distributions from the trust during the life of the grantor. The younger the grantor, the lower the assessed value of the gift. Finally, because the trust's assets are distributed to charities, no transfer tax is assessed at death. The tax savings can be large enough that by reinvesting the combined income and transfer taxes avoided in life insurance, the noncharitable heirs' inheritance may be restored to the level that would have occurred without the charitable remainder trust. Tax planners tell me that the annual fees for charitable remainder trusts are approximately 200 basis points.

The latest development in charitable trusts is a NIM-CRUT (net income with makeup charitable remainder unitrust), which provides a further tax benefit by enabling beneficiaries to shift distributions to years when their marginal income tax rates are relatively low. Charitable remainder trusts are required to distribute a minimum amount of assets each year to trust beneficiaries. A charitable remainder unitrust (CRUT) may distribute the lesser of a statutory percentage of assets (increased from 5 to 10 percent by TRA97) or net income. A NIM-CRUT invests in non-income-producing assets (for example, deferred annuities) when the beneficiary faces high marginal tax rates and shifts to high-income-producing assets (for example, utility equities) when the beneficiary's marginal tax rates fall (during retirement, for instance). The NIM-CRUT makes up for the forgone distributions, which occurred when no taxable income was produced in the high-tax-bracket early years, with excess distributions in the high-income, low-tax-bracket later years. Recent creative uses of NIM-CRUT include joint use with family partnerships. The purported tax benefits and abuses of NIM-CRUT have not gone unnoticed by the Internal Revenue Service. Recently it has been strongly opposed to the most abusive forms of NIM-CRUT, creating uncertainty about their future viability.

TAX PLANS AND MARGINAL TAX RATES
Income Tax Plans

Ignoring tax planning, the second section of this chapter estimated that marginal tax rates on labor income range up to 91 percent depending on the manner in which the wealth is disposed. The next two sections described numerous income and transfer-tax plans, each designed to reduce the tax burdens of the wealthy. This section reestimates the marginal tax rates on labor income, considering tax-avoidance opportunities.

The taxes levied on labor-sourced income can be trichotomized into: the wage taxes levied at the time when services are performed; the taxes on returns from investments of after-tax wages; and the transfer taxes at disposition. Suppose that the laborer intends to bequeath any wealth from an additional dollar of labor income, after income and transfer taxes, to his children. If the tax on savings is deferred until immediately prior to death, the bequest can be expressed as: $(1 - t_p)$ $[(1 + R_p)^n(1 - t_p) + t_p b_p](1 - e_n)$.

As discussed earlier, laborers have few options for tax mitigation unless they can reclassify wages as returns to capital, such as through equity interests. For example, professional basketball players cannot hold equity positions in their NBA teams.

Consequently, the high wages enjoyed by professional basketball players are probably subject to immediate taxation at the highest statutory tax rate. The only apparent avoidance option is deferred compensation, which can shift their cash flow and tax realization to future years when their marginal tax rates may be lower. The likelihood of achieving tax savings from income shifting for professional athletes and other laborers with particularly short periods of labor productivity is greater than for laborers whose labor income is less concentrated in time. However, substantive tax reduction is probably difficult. All in all, professional athletes and other laborers who cannot obtain equity interests in their employers (such as government and not-for-profit employees) have few options for substantially lowering the marginal tax rates on their labor income below the rates estimated earlier.

Conversely, laborers who can obtain equity interests in their employers may lower the tax burden on wages substantially. Suppose an entrepreneur establishes a wholly owned company with zero tax basis and never draws a salary. He withdraws the same amount from the company as he would through a salary except in a manner, such as collateralization, that does not trigger income tax realization.[17] Immediately preceding his death, the company is sold and he pays taxes on the appreciation in the company at the capital gains tax rate. The proceeds are bequeathed to his children and equal $(1 + R_p)^n(1 - t_p)(1 - e_n)$. Setting the bequest equal to $(1 - t^*)(1 + R_p)^n$ and solving for t^*, using current maximum statutory rates ($t_p = 0.20$ and $e_n = 0.55$), the implied tax burden on labor, t^*, is 0.64. In other words, the children inherit 36 percent of the value of the business, as measured immediately preceding the sale and death. This 0.64 marginal tax rate estimate compares favorably with the earlier estimate of 0.71 for t^* when the laborer invests after-income tax wages in the same business. The sole difference between the two estimates is the wage tax avoidance.[18] In other words, the entrepreneur who derives his wealth from his business through capital appreciation or other payments that avoid personal income tax realization eliminates the first tax on labor (the direct wage tax).

If the business is not sold but passes to the children at death with a step-up in the tax basis, then all income taxes are eliminated and only the transfer tax applies. Thus, $t^* = 0.55$ and 45 percent of the business can be bequeathed to the children. This compares to the earlier t^* estimate of 0.73. Again the difference is attributable to the entrepreneur's ability to avoid wage taxes. Identical income-tax-exempt returns are possible from using some of the tax plans, detailed earlier, such as like-kind exchanges for real estate, selling closely held stock to ESOPs, and disposing of equity through derivative products.

Transfer-Tax Plans

The preceding discussion shows that tax planners can mitigate income tax burdens for laborers if wages can be transformed into capital without triggering tax realization. Unless a wealthy individual desires to transfer his wealth to his children, there is no additional demand for tax planning. However, to the extent that transfers to children matter, even if the income tax plans successfully eliminate income taxes, the wealthy still risk forfeiting over half of their wealth to the government at death unless transfer taxes can be reduced.

The simplest and most effective transfer-tax plan is maximum utilization of each person's annual $10,000 exclusion per donee. Assuming 10 percent annual returns, a wealthy couple could transfer tax-free $2.8 million (in future value) to each child with forty years of $20,000 gifts. Without the gifts, if they live forty years, up to 55 percent ($1.5 million) could be paid in estate taxes at their deaths. If the couple have ten children and grandchildren and the maximum annual gifts are made, the transfer taxes avoided grow to $15.2 million. If they also make gifts to their descendents' spouses, the tax savings double to over $30 million. Consequently, annual gifts may be sufficient for a taxpayer's transfer-tax planning.

If more wealth is involved, larger gifts are the optimal tax strategy. As noted earlier, even though a common transfer-tax rate schedule is used for gifts and bequests, because gift taxes are tax-exclusive levies, inter vivos gifts are effectively subject to a maximum 35 percent tax rate, as opposed to the 55 percent tax rate facing bequests. Thus, one-fifth of estates can be salvaged and passed tax-free to children by shifting bequests into inter vivos gifts. The limited data concerning taxable inter vivos gifts suggest that the wealthy are passing nontrivial amounts to their children through relatively tax-favored gifts. Edward McCaffery (1994) notes that in 1990, $2 billion of the $11.5 billion paid in transfer taxes arose from inter vivos gifts, concentrated among the wealthiest taxpayers. He estimates that these taxable gifts enabled approximately $7 billion to avoid the higher estate tax rates.

However, the 35 percent favorable gift tax rate probably overstates the percentage of wealth captured by transfer taxes. In the last section, I argued that undervaluing wealth is the principal component of more sophisticated transfer-tax plans. For example, property gifted to children through discount partnerships are subject to a transfer tax of $1 - e(1 - \delta)$, where δ is the discount applied to the partnership minority interest. Using the maximum gift tax rate of 35 percent and a 30 percent discount, the family partnership can reduce the transfer-tax rate to 25 percent, permitting three-quarters of the parent's wealth to pass transfer tax-free to her children. Using more aggressive discounts enables even greater reductions in the marginal tax rate. If the discount is 70 percent, the transfer-tax rate falls to 11 percent.

The remaining transfer-tax plans discussed in the previous section can largely eliminate the transfer tax for parts of the estates of the wealthy. For example, giving equity interests to children permits them to gain a toehold on possible future wealth with little, if any, immediate gift tax. To the extent that parents can pass these interests to their children, future appreciation largely escapes transfer taxes. Gifting personal residences through qualified trusts transfers the wealth in houses at a minimal transfer-tax cost. Similarly, life insurance trusts enable the wealthy to avoid the estate tax on death benefits.

In summary, annual tax-free gifts, substitution of inter vivos gifts for bequests, and transfer of selective properties through tax-advantaged structures emasculate the transfer tax. The 55 percent marginal tax rate for bequests to children probably is relegated to wealthy individuals with limited philanthropic goals who invest little in tax planning, perhaps because they die unexpectedly. In other words, the transfer tax largely becomes a voluntary assessment that the wealthy can pay in full to the government or in part to tax planners.

Tax Avoidance and Wealth

To summarize, the marginal tax rates estimated earlier justify investment by the wealthy in tax avoidance. This section concludes that current tax plans significantly reduce the actual marginal tax rate faced by wealthy individuals. The estimates in this chapter suggest that the heaviest personal income tax burdens fall on laborers who cannot avoid the wage tax, and that the heaviest transfer tax burdens fall on the wealthy whose bequests to their children are subject to the estate tax.

The remainder of this section focuses on how marginal tax rates change as the tax base (income or transfer) increases. The model presented in the second section indicates that effective tax rates are decreasing, at a diminishing rate, in tax-avoidance expenditures. I now posit that the demand for tax avoidance causes the functional form linking taxes to the tax base to assume a relation similar to the logistic model. Specifically, taxes are always increasing in income. For low levels of income, the second derivative is positive. For high levels of income, the second derivative is negative. Restated, marginal tax rates are increasing in lower levels of income and decreasing in higher levels of income.

The reason for declining marginal tax rates for taxpayers with the largest tax bases lies in the tax planner's production function. The relation between the tax planner's fees (Fee) and the costs of producing a tax plan can be expressed as:

$$\text{Fee} = f(\text{Profit, Fixed Cost}, r_1X_1, r_2X_2, r_3X_3, \ldots, r_kX_k)$$

where Profit is the equilibrium profit on the plan, Fixed Cost is the fixed cost of constructing the plan, r_k is the factor input price associated with the kth variable factor input, and X_k is the kth factor input. Fixed costs are probably a major component of planners' costs. Human capital becomes obsolete with every legislative change, judicial ruling, and administrative regulation, requiring continual reinvestment in professional education that cannot be assigned to a specific client's tax plan.

Taxpayers purchase a tax plan if the costs of the plan are less than the taxes it saves. Otherwise, the taxpayer pays the taxes and avoids the costlier avoidance option. To the extent that the planner's costs are fixed, individuals with tax bases below a certain level do not purchase tax plans while taxpayers with larger bases purchase the plan and avoid the taxes. Thus, taxpayers with smaller tax bases (from a lower income, for instance) face higher marginal tax rates than taxpayers with larger tax bases (from a higher income) because the latter group can amortize the planner's fixed costs across a larger tax base.

At least three of the tax plans described in this chapter illustrate this separating equilibrium. These plans are restricted to the wealthiest of taxpayers because the implementation fees are so large that the income or transfer taxes saved must be enormous to justify purchasing the tax plan. For example, in June 1996, Eli Broad became the first individual taxpayer to use a DECS. His plan reportedly saved $54 million in income taxes on the sale of some of his SunAmerica stock (*New York Times*, December 28, 1996). A generic version of the plan that Broad used to avoid taxes on his equity holdings could benefit many taxpayers holding appreciated securities; however, the costs of Broad's plan are prohibitively expensive for smaller equity holdings. Note that Broad's net savings were the reduced taxes less the tax planners' fees.

Similarly, establishing and maintaining a Delaware investment company involves substantial legal and tax costs, regardless of the state income tax savings. Thus, Delaware investment companies are limited to the wealthiest taxpayers. Consequently, the marginal tax rates on state income taxes are lower for the highest-income taxpayers than for other taxpayers, who cannot afford to purchase state tax relief. As with Broad's DECS, the cost of state income taxes to the wealthiest sector is not zero; rather, it is the tax consultant's fee.

Likewise, family discount partnerships provide a mechanism for understating wealth and avoiding transfer taxes. If the present value of avoided transfer taxes, provided through a discount partnership, exceeds the planner's fee, the plan is purchased, the partnership is formed, and the marginal tax rate on every additional dollar of wealth is reduced. If not, the plan is not purchased and transfer taxes are paid in full.

To summarize, high-income (wealth) individuals may face lower marginal income (transfer) tax rates than persons of more moderate income (wealth) because larger tax bases enable them to acquire tax plans that are too expensive for taxpayers with smaller bases. These marginal tax rate differences are attributable to fixed costs in planners' fee structures.

CLOSING REMARKS

The tax environment for the wealthy is a complex composite of income and transfer-tax incentives that vary with the source and use of wealth. Without tax planning, many wealthy individuals face heavy tax burdens. Tax planners have responded with an array of products that successfully mitigate income and transfer-tax payments. Thus, wealthy individuals exchange large tax levies for smaller tax-avoidance fees.

One area of continuing policy interest about which this chapter may provide some insight is the appropriate level for capital gains tax rates. To the extent that capitalists avoid the taxes levied on their returns, favorable capital gains tax rates seem redundant. However, if avoidance opportunities are limited to the wealthiest taxpayers, then lower capital gains tax rates may equalize the capital gains tax burdens across different levels of wealth. The recent TRA97's reduction in the capital gains tax rate (as with any tax reduction) also reduces the demand for tax avoidance for assets subject to capital gains taxes. However, by reducing capital gains tax rates, the new law increases the demand for tax plans that transform ordinary income into an asset subject to the more favorable capital gains tax rate.

Having concluded that tax planning is a successful response by taxpayers to potentially confiscatory tax burdens, the remainder of the chapter proposes two modifications to the current tax system that could reduce substantially the demand for tax planning. Such reduction is warranted because the current levels of investment in tax avoidance substantially reduce government revenue, erode public support of the current taxation systems, and employ too many bright minds. To curtail tax-avoidance investments, I recommend the elimination of both transfer taxes and the step-up of the tax basis to fair market value at death.[19]

Abolishing transfer taxes would eliminate the demand for transfer-tax avoidance and redeploy a sizable sector of the tax-avoidance industry to more productive tasks without substantial government revenue loss.[20] It also would eliminate administrative and compliance costs plus suboptimal structuring of family wealth (in the absence of transfer taxes). If transfer taxes were eliminated, the primary losers, besides transfer-tax planners, would be the charities that enjoy financial windfalls from a tax system that encourages philanthropy. An assessment of the efficiency of the current transfer-tax system in funding charities would be a useful exercise. The primary winner would be the wealthy who would avoid transfer taxes, planning fees, and tax-induced dispositions to charity.

Eliminating step-up at death would mitigate the increased wealth concentration from abolishing transfer taxes by removing a key weapon from the income tax planners' arsenal. Step-up at death provides the ultimate deferral incentive, exemption, and creates an inefficient lock-in effect for older taxpayers. Its elimination would restore to the income tax base property appreciation that currently escapes taxation at death. By providing a carryover basis to heirs, income taxation could be deferred until reinvestment ended. Although continued deferral would provide a windfall to the wealthy, it also would eliminate the necessity for cash-constrained closely held businesses to acquire extensive life insurance coverage for their major shareholders or risk forced liquidation to pay taxes at death.

The effect of these proposals on the timing of intergenerational transfers is unclear. To the extent that current inter vivos gifts are motivated by estate tax avoidance, gifts might decline. On the other hand, without step-up, the elderly would have fewer incentives to retain assets until death.

Finally, eliminating step-up at death only partly addresses the income tax system's fundamental realization flaw. Without step-up, taxpayers could still reinvest without taxation by borrowing against appreciated properties or using related, more complex financial options, such as puts and calls. Abandonment of income as a tax base and movement to alternative tax systems—for example, consumption taxes—probably are the only realistic means of remedying the avoidance opportunities provided by income tax realization. Retaining the income tax system and treating loan proceeds as income and principal repayments as deductions is too farfetched to warrant further consideration. Moreover, taxing debt issues and deducting debt repayments would introduce frictions into the capital markets that might be socially counterproductive, even if they improved the comprehensiveness of the tax system. In summary, any tax system built on income has inherent avoidance opportunities depending on the triggering device for determining income. To my knowledge, no policy changes could eliminate fully the current income tax avoidance opportunities available from exploitation of the realization principle.

This chapter has benefited greatly from comments from Mary Margaret Myers, Joel Slemrod, Steve Slezak, Herman Spence, and participants in the 1997 spring conference of the University of Michigan Business School's Office of Tax Policy Research.

NOTES

1. Additional tax-free transfers are possible to cover medical and educational needs.

2. The Taxpayer Relief Act of 1997 (TRA97) increases the exempt gifts and bequests to $625,000 in 1998 and continues increasing the exemption total until it reaches $1 million in 2006. It adds a new estate tax exclusion for certain closely held businesses that can enable up to $1.3 million in total exempt gifts and bequests, effective 1998.

3. For purposes of determining the estate tax, the credit for previous gift taxes paid is the gift tax that would have been paid if the current transfer-tax rates had applied when the gifts were made, not the actual gift taxes paid.

4. For simplicity, and because conclusions are not qualitatively affected, the model ignores the transfer-tax credit and annual $10,000 exclusions. The relative importance of both provisions decreases in wealth. The credit excludes de minimis bequests to children, and the exclusions permit tax-free de minimis annual transfers to children. However, it should not be inferred from the exclusion of these provisions from the model that they are irrelevant for planning purposes. In fact, exploitation of both of these de minimis provisions is the initial component of transfer-tax avoidance and may constitute the entire transfer-tax avoidance strategy for smaller estates. Also for simplicity, the model assumes that the individual predeceases his spouse and children. The model's implications hold if this expectation is not met; however, the introduction of uncertainty about life expectancy adds a probabilistic component to the analysis.

5. Anecdotal evidence suggests that the opportunity costs that taxpayers assign to tax planning vary greatly. Some taxpayers enjoy tax avoidance, while others have little tolerance for any planning. This heterogeneity enables tax planners who have developed a keen understanding of their clients' "tax taste functions" to compete against competitors with dominant tax plans but less client-specific knowledge. The importance of this client-specific information also may explain the willingness of tax planners to underprice initial products in a new client relationship in exchange for a better understanding of the client's specific tax interests.

6. To maintain the transfer-tax base as death approaches, gift taxes arising during the last three years of life are included in the estate tax base.

7. The income tax rates on wages, used throughout the chapter, understate the tax burden on labor because they exclude FICA and in particular the 2.9 percent Medicare charge, which, unlike other FICA payments, applies to all labor income levels. Other taxes also are understated because they exclude state and local assessments.

8. Appreciation historically has marked the properties of the wealthy because capital appreciation is a means of becoming wealthy, income taxes provide an incentive to sell depreciated properties, and tax bases are not adjusted for inflation. In recent years the U.S. equity bull market has greatly enhanced the appreciated financial assets held by the wealthy.

9. ESOPs are defined contribution retirement plans. Besides the tax advantages to shareholders noted in the text, they are unique because they must invest primarily in the stock of the sponsoring employer and can borrow to purchase plan assets. See Shackelford (1991) and Scholes and Wolfson (1992) for more details.

10. TRA97 reduces the attractiveness of DECS and related products by disallowing the deductibility of interest on debt that can be repaid with common stock of a related party.

11. Bankers Trust markets equity swaps with claims such as, "Is your wealth too concentrated in one stock? Here's how to diversify, reduce risk, and enhance income—while retaining ownership and avoiding tax liability"; see *Tax Notes* (October 17, 1994), 267.

12. The appropriate type of option from a tax perspective depends on both the employer's and the employee's tax positions. Although incentive stock options are tax-favored from the employee's perspective compared with nonqualified stock options, they are tax-disadvantaged from the employer's perspective. Incentive stock options never create a corporate tax deduction. Nonqualified stock options provide a corporate tax deduction equal to the employee's ordinary income at the time of exercise. See Matsunaga, Shevlin, and Shores (1992) for more analysis.

13. For a more complete discussion of transfer-tax avoidance, see Zabel (1995) and Scholes and Wolfson (1992).

14. Taxpayer advantages arising from related-party transactions pervade the tax system and account for much of its complexity. Examples include transfer pricing between commonly owned businesses located in different jurisdictions, the capital structure of closely held businesses, and interest-free loans between related parties.

15. Charitable lead trusts offer similar tax-advantaged philanthropic opportunities. Lead trusts are distinguished from remainder trusts in that they create charitable gifts during the grantor's life and noncharitable contributions at death, whereas remainder trusts create charitable gifts at death and noncharitable distributions during the grantor's life.

16. TRA97 restricts the most aggressive forms of charitable remainder trusts by requiring that at the time of contribution the remainder interest be at least 10 percent of the net fair market value of the property transferred.

17. To ensure that the marginal tax rates estimated here are comparable to those estimated earlier, the value of the business (after considering any business tax effects) must decrease by the same amount regardless of whether the owner is compensated through salary, which is taxable to the owner, or with other payments that are not taxable to the owner. Also, this analysis ignores business taxes. To the extent that the form of payment (for example, salary versus collateralization) affects the company's tax payments, the analysis becomes more complex. In general, if the employer's marginal tax rate exceeds the employee's marginal tax rate, the corporate deduction for salary exceeds the laborer's taxable income. If so, salary becomes a more attractive vehicle for extracting cash from the business.

18. To prove: $(1 - t_p)(1 - 0.64) = 0.29$, which yields the earlier tax estimate of 0.71.

19. Bruce Bartlett (1997) advances similar policy recommendations.

20. In 1990 transfer-tax collections accounted for $11.5 billion, or 1.12 percent of federal revenue (McCaffery 1994).

REFERENCES

Allen, Michael. 1987. *The Founding Fortunes: A New Anatomy of the Super-Rich Families in America.* New York: E. P. Dutton.

Bartlett, Bruce. 1997. "The End of the Estate Tax?" *Tax Notes,* July 7: 105–10.

McCaffery, Edward. 1994. "The Uneasy Case for Wealth Transfer Taxation." *Yale Law Journal* 104: 283–365.

Matsunaga, Steve, Terry Shevlin, and D. Shores. 1992. "Disqualifying Dispositions of Incentive Stock Options: Tax Benefits Versus Financial Reporting Costs." *Journal of Accounting Research* 30 (supplement): 37–76.

Scholes, Myron, and Mark Wolfson. 1992. *Taxes and Business Strategy: A Planning Approach.* Englewood Cliffs, N.J.: Prentice-Hall.

Shackelford, Douglas. 1991. "The Market for Tax Benefits: Evidence from Leveraged ESOPs." *Journal of Accounting and Economics* 14(2, June): 117–45.

Zabel, William. 1995. *The Rich Die Richer and You Can Too.* New York: Wiley.

Part II
New Empirical Evidence on Behavioral Response

5

It's Not About the Money: Why Natural Experiments Don't Work on the Rich

Austan Goolsbee

One of the liveliest areas of debate in public economics over the last twenty years has been the argument about the behavioral effects of marginal tax rate changes. Whereas an early literature based on conventional measures of labor supply found very small effects of tax rates on hours worked, a new literature looking at total taxable income and using a more subtle "natural experiments" approach has usually found large elasticities of taxable income with respect to the net of tax share. Because of such findings, this literature has emphasized the futility of tax progressivity and the benefits of reducing marginal rates on high-income people.

The methodological approach in what I term the new tax responsiveness (NTR) literature is to control for the unobserved determinants of taxable income by using natural experiments—in other words, by comparing different income groups and assuming that unobserved variables are identical for individuals in those groups. If true, changes to the progressivity of the rate structure can be used to identify the effect of taxation. The NTR literature simply compares the changes in taxable income of the different groups to the changes in the tax rates of the groups to determine what is commonly referred to as the "difference in differences" estimate of the elasticity of taxable income. Although many of the papers simply compare the groups without using statistical estimation, the same assumptions are required to identify regression estimates of the elasticity of taxable income.

The influence of the NTR literature, such as Lawrence Lindsey (1987) and Martin Feldstein (1995a), is undeniable and, if correct, has profound implications for tax policy and revenue estimation. The backbone of the NTR approach, however, is the assumption that lower-income people are a valid control group for higher-income people—that the change in income of the two groups would have been identical had there been no change in taxes. If this assumption is false, existing estimates may have significant biases. Little is known about the natural experiment assumption, however, because the NTR literature has been based on tax return data that contain little information about individuals and whether they differ in important ways.

In this chapter, I examine the natural experiment assumption by looking at other data to see whether there are differences between the very rich and the "somewhat" rich and, if so, how much bias such differences may create for the NTR literature. I do this by examining data on prominent high-income people, primarily panel data on thousands of high-income executives from the detailed compensation data reported by companies in proxy statements and 10-Ks and compiled for all companies in the Standard & Poors 500, Standard & Poors Mid-Cap 400, and Standard &

Poors Small-Cap 600 from 1991 to 1995, but also general data on prominent high-income people like professional athletes. The results from these data raise serious concerns with natural experiment methods that compare the very rich even to the somewhat rich. These publicly identified rich individuals may not be representative of other high-income people, but if they are, existing elasticities in the NTR literature may be overstated by 75 percent or more.

Three differences between the very rich and other groups in these data account for the bias. First, the cash compensation of very-high-income people relative to even moderately-high-income people has risen substantially, creating a spurious correlation between tax cuts and the relative income growth of the wealthy. As an example, subtracting out these income trends could cut the elasticity estimated from TRA86 in half or even by three-quarters.

Second, the compensation of very-high-income people is much more responsive to demand conditions than the compensation of other individuals, and the state of the business cycle during the tax bills of the last two decades may have biased the estimated elasticities upward—20 to 25 percent for TRA86, for example. For executives, this is true based just on cash compensation. The increasing importance of stock options and other types of capital income makes this responsiveness even more pronounced.

Third, the share of income in a form whose timing can be shifted in the short run (for example, bonuses, options, and long-term incentive payouts) rises dramatically with income in these data. Thus, natural experiments, especially those based on the tax increase of 1993, may detect large temporary changes in the timing of transactions but classify them as behavioral responses. The true long-run responses are small. The increasing use of stock options at the high end has also generated a substantial mean reverting component of income, which makes the choice of sample problematic in NTR studies since they use tax return data.

By documenting these three facts and exploring the biases they create, this chapter provides quantitative evidence against the NTR natural experiments approach when applied to very rich people. The very rich really are different. The results presented here are in the tradition of papers such as Richard Blundell, Alan Duncan, and Costas Meghir (1995) and James Heckman (1996), which criticize the difference-in-differences methodology, but the results are specifically directed toward the top of the income distribution. For each of the objections presented, the chapter also presents methods that could be used at least to improve the estimates in existing NTR research, even when tax return data are the only data available.

The current sample of several thousand very-high-income people is substantially larger and more detailed than almost all samples in the previous literature but may not be representative of the full universe of high-income people, especially given the high salary income of executives.[1] I do not examine in this chapter the interest income or portfolio decisions of the rich, only wages and salaries. The theory implicit in the NTR literature, however, is concerned with individuals' decisions about how to take their salary income, not with when they choose to realize capital gains, so, if anything, these executives are of *greater* interest to tax policy research than is the average rich person. For example, these executives make up only a small fraction of the very rich (1 percent or less) but account, as I have shown elsewhere (Goolsbee

2000), for up to 20 percent of the total wage and salary decline of the top one million taxpayers in response to the tax increase of 1993.

The first section outlines the NTR literature and its findings. The next section presents an overview of the new data on the rich. That discussion is followed by a section that presents three empirical facts from the data and explains how they may bias conventional NTR estimates and what could be done about them.

THE NEW TAX RESPONSIVENESS LITERATURE

The NTR literature arose in response to the literature on taxes and labor supply. In the conventional literature (see Pencavel 1986; Heckman 1993; Moffitt and Wilhelm, this volume), tax responsiveness was measured as tax-induced changes to hours worked. Supporting the general notion that labor supply is close to zero, this literature found that taxes seemed to have little impact, especially for men (see Eissa 1996).[2]

The NTR literature looks at changes to total taxable income rather than hours worked. Individuals can control not just their hours of work but also how much of their income they take in nontaxable form or report at all. Tax increases can reduce taxable income dramatically even if individuals work the same number of hours. Between the two, it is taxable income that revenue authorities should care about when calculating deadweight loss or making revenue forecasts, and therefore when calculating the optimal size of the government (see Feldstein 1995b; Slemrod and Yitzhaki 1996).

The founder of the NTR literature is really Lawrence Lindsey (1987), who showed that the tax cuts of the early 1980s at the high end of the income distribution corresponded to a large increase in the share of total taxable income going to high-income people. In essence, he compared high-income people to people in other brackets over the period from 1982 to 1984, used the tax cut as a natural experiment, and found substantial implied elasticities. This work was based on cross-sectional tax return data, as was the later work of Daniel Feenberg and James Poterba (1993), which looked at the share of total income going to very-high-income people over time and found an important increase around TRA86. In response to criticism of cross-sectional data and the potential for "rank-reversal" problems (see Slemrod 1992), later efforts turned to data on panels of tax returns.

Feldstein's (1995a) exploration of the tax cuts of TRA86 with panel data is the canonical NTR paper. It explicitly described TRA86 as a natural experiment and used a difference-in-differences methodology to identify the taxable income elasticity. By assuming that people in the 49 to 50 percent brackets, 42 to 45 percent brackets, and 22 to 38 percent brackets would have had the same income growth but for the tax changes, Feldstein compared the relative income changes of the various tax bracket groups with their relative tax changes and found that the incomes of the very rich rose the most and that they were also the group with the biggest tax cut. The resulting elasticities of taxable income exceeded 1.

So that I can revisit these estimates later in the chapter, I present his exact calculation in the first table 5.1. The first three rows in the first panel list the change in the net of tax share and adjusted taxable income plus gross loss for each of the

Table 5.1   Difference-in-Differences Estimates Based on TRA86

| Taxpayer Group (by 1985 Rate) | Percent Change 1985 to 1988 | | |
	Net of Tax Rate	Adjusted Taxable Income Minus Gross Loss	Elasticity
Medium (22 to 38 percent)	12.2	6.4	
High (42 to 45 percent)	25.6	20.3	
Highest (49 to 50 percent)	42.2	44.8	
Difference-in-differences			
High minus medium	13.4	13.9	1.04
Highest minus high	16.6	24.5	1.48
Highest minus medium	30.0	38.4	1.25
with income trends			
Medium (0.5 percent annual)	12.2	4.9	
High (3.4 percent annual)	25.6	9.7	
Highest (8.9 percent annual)	42.2	15.7	
Difference-in-differences			
High minus medium	13.4	4.8	.36
Highest minus high	16.6	6.0	.36
Highest minus medium	30.0	10.8	.36
with income trends			
Medium (1.3 percent annual)	12.2	2.4	
High (3.4 percent annual)	25.6	9.7	
Highest (7.7 percent annual)	42.2	24.9	
Difference-in-differences			
High minus medium	13.4	7.3	.54
Highest minus high	16.6	15.2	.92
Highest minus medium	30.0	22.5	.75

Notes: The first panel comes from the calculations in Feldstein (1995a). The first three rows list the percent change in net of tax share and of adjusted taxable income minus gross loss (as calculated by Feldstein). The next three rows show a difference-in-differences calculation comparing the three groups. The next two panels repeat the same procedure but subtract out from the income growth the three-year time trends for each group whose annual rate is given in parentheses. This yields the pure effect of the tax.

three groups as calculated on a panel of tax returns. The second three rows show the difference-in-differences for various combinations of the three groups. The implied elasticities are then listed in the last column of the second three rows. They are all greater than 1, indicating substantial shifts of taxable income in response to rate changes, shifts possibly large enough to trigger what Joel Slemrod (1994a) has called the high-income Laffer curve where cutting taxes on the rich would actually raise revenue.

Feldstein's findings were criticized (see Slemrod 1995) for using only a small number of observations at the high end (fifty-seven in the top two brackets), and for not using statistical methods that could indicate the precision of the estimates. Gerald Auten and Robert Carroll (forthcoming), however, using an internal Treasury sample of thousands of high-income tax returns and a regression methodology, were again able to find significant elasticities, though smaller than those in Feldstein. From this dataset that is not publicly available they also had information on occupation and other nontax factors as reported on the tax returns, and they found that the controls for other factors and the weighting of the sample did make some difference to the results. Their best estimate of the elasticity was around two-thirds.

One lingering question in the NTR literature has remained the critique of Slemrod (1992, 1994a, 1995) that the elasticities estimated in these natural experiments are not behavioral elasticities at all, nor even permanent changes to the form of compensation, but rather simply changes to the timing of transactions in the short run. This timing issue returned to the forefront when Clinton raised taxes on the rich in 1993. Feldstein and Feenberg (1996), doing a preliminary analysis of the increase with cross-sectional tax return data, find that incomes of approximately the one million richest taxpayers fell significantly from the period 1992 to 1993, when taxes rose, while incomes of lower-income groups rose. Their calculations indicate a large elasticity. Others have responded that the change was temporary (Parcell 1996).

As the discussion later in the chapter indicates, the tax increase of 1992–1993 is extremely important for evaluating the NTR literature, and the debate over its effect has resisted resolution with tax return data.[3] Using the detailed compensation data on high-income executives, however, I have shown (Goolsbee 2000) that more than 20 percent of the total wage and salary decline of the top one million taxpayers may be accounted for by around ten thousand executives, and that this change was almost entirely temporary, driven by a dramatic rise in the exercise of options in late 1992 in anticipation of higher rates. In these data, the long-run elasticity of taxable salary income is at most .4, and probably close to zero.

In summary, the NTR literature consistently makes the natural experiment assumption, uses tax return data to estimate effects, and usually finds a large elasticity. There are serious questions, however, whether tax changes are indeed natural experiments. Do the rich and the moderately rich differ only because of taxes, or is the difference about more than money? With tax return data, it is difficult to know. To whatever extent the groups differ systematically in a way that is correlated with tax changes, the existing estimates are biased. Data with more information on the rich and their money are required to compare these groups.

INDEPENDENT DATA ON HIGH-INCOME PEOPLE

For an independent source of data that allows for tests of the natural experiment assumption, I primarily use in this chapter information on the individual corporate executives of fifteen hundred companies from 1991 to 1995. By law, all publicly traded firms are required to report the total compensation in a variety of forms for their top five highest-paid employees in various Securities and Exchange Commission (SEC) documents like 10-Ks and proxy statements. Standard & Poors compiles the information for all companies in the Standard & Poors 500, the Standard & Poors Mid-Cap 400, and the Standard & Poors Small Cap 600 in its EXECUCOMP database. These are the same data used in Goolsbee (2000, forthcoming). This chapter also uses data on the incomes of other prominent high-income people, such as professional athletes.

The data on executive pay are much more detailed in their description of income variables than are the data from a tax return. In addition to total compensation, the executive compensation data follow the same individuals over time and separately report their income from salaries, bonuses, long-term incentive plan (LTIP) pay-outs, options exercised, "other" income, and the Black-Scholes value of the options granted. The executive compensation data also include information on the finan-cial and accounting performance of the executive's firm as well as other informa-tion on the individual. I restrict the sample to people with data in at least four years and whose firms have fiscal years ending in December so as to coincide with the tax year. The number of years executives were in the sample made no difference to the results.

A summary of data about these executives is listed in table 5.2. Clearly these are very-high-income people. The average total income in taxable forms for these exec-utives in 1992 dollars is $877,000 per year, and the median is $490,000. Salary and bonus make up the predominant share of taxable compensation (about two-thirds). Additional forms of income not currently taxable, such as options granted and "other" compensation, are also important. Because the choice of companies does not restrict the sample to large firms, and because the data are not restricted to CEOs, about 20 percent of the executives have relatively low incomes of less than $250,000.

One major advantage of using non-tax-return data on income is that there is no need to worry about making income comparable across years with different tax laws, as is necessary for taxable income. The meaning of each of the categories is unam-biguous. One disadvantage of using independent income data, however, is that no information is available about income not coming from the firm, such as interest income. Slemrod (1994) has shown that among high-income taxpayers, the share of income coming from wages and salaries is highly bimodal, with modes at 90 to 100 percent from wages and at 0 to 10 percent from wages. An examination of these executives obviously picks up one side of the distribution, so nonfirm income may be relatively less important for them, but there is still little evidence on the matter.

Table 5.2   Descriptive Statistics for Executive Income, 1991 to 1995

Type of Income	Average Value (in 1992 Dollars)
Salary	$320,000
Bonus	219,000
LTIP payout	59,000
Options exercised	279,000
Total taxable compensation	877,000
Median total taxable compensation	490,000
Options granted	364,000
Total "other" compensation	41,000
Executive years of data	17,240
Number of executives	4,231

Source: Author's calculations based on data described in the text.
Notes: The total number of nonmissing observations differs by type of income. The number listed is based on total taxable income.

I define an individual's taxable income as the sum of salary, bonus, options exercised in the year, and LTIP payments. LTIP payouts are predominantly, but not always, cash. Because they are sometimes shares and therefore not taxable in the current year, the results tend to be biased toward finding no response of this form of compensation to tax rates. A similar problem exists for bonus income in that some firms report bonuses for the current year but technically pay the bonus in an adjoining calendar year. This should not affect the estimates of long-run elasticities but tends to bias downward any temporary responses.

I classify exercised options as taxable wage income because this is the tax treatment of the most common type of option, the non-qualified option (NQO). At exercise, the difference between the stock price and the option strike price is treated as wage income to the individual and is deductible for the firm. The incentive stock option (ISO) is not treated as income until the shares are actually sold, at which time the income is treated as capital gains and is not deductible for the firm. NQOs are by far the most common, however, and are generally the overall tax-advantaged form (see Scholes and Wolfson 1992; and the data in Conference Board 1992), so this assumption is fairly accurate.

Nontaxed forms of compensation are reported as "other compensation," which is anything not included in the other categories. Although this is not entirely non-taxable income, in practice it includes mainly perquisites, other personal benefits, and premiums paid for split-dollar life insurance policies. By law, firms are required to report perquisites that total more than $50,000 or 10 percent of the executive's annual base salary. The compensation data, starting in 1992, also include the Black-Scholes value of options granted, which is not reported on a tax return.

To separate people into income groups, the NTR literature usually takes incomes in the year before the tax change and divides individuals by tax bracket using that income. As the results presented here indicate, mean reversion has increasingly made this a poor way to divide an income sample. Instead, I use a measure of permanent income to divide the groups. This permanent income is the average sum of salary, bonus, LTIP payouts, the Black-Scholes value of options by individual, and the value of "other" compensation. This is, in some sense, the average amount of money the individual receives in a given year regardless of whether the income is reported on the tax return. This is obviously unavailable with data from tax returns because individuals do not have to report any nontaxable income they receive, such as the value of options granted but not exercised or the value of nontaxed perquisites. I use different cutoff values in different circumstances, but previous work has shown that the choice of income cutoffs does not matter in these data (Goolsbee 2000).

ARE THE RICH SYSTEMATICALLY DIFFERENT?

The NTR assumption that the taxable income of different groups grows at the same rate except for the changes in tax rate may be violated for many reasons, and most of these reasons can lead to bias in the estimated tax price elasticities. The data on executives show that three differences in particular may be important.

Relative Incomes of the Very Rich Increased Greatly in the Period

Rising wage inequality in the 1980s has been well documented in the labor literature and explained by a variety of nontax factors (see Katz and Murphy 1992; Levy
and Murnane 1992). Obviously, a tax cut for the rich when the incomes at the top
are growing faster than those lower down creates a bias in the natural experiment.
All the relative increase in the income of the rich is incorrectly attributed to the tax
change. This is potentially quite important for evaluating the 1980s tax cuts, which
were largest for the highest group, and this critique of such work has been made
from the beginning. In fact, Slemrod (1996) shows that including a simple measure
of inequality removes all evidence that taxes matter for the incomes of the very rich
from 1954 to 1985. He regresses the data of Feenberg and Poterba (1993) listing
the share of total income going to the top 0.25 percent of the distribution on marginal rates, but he controls for wage inequality trends by including the log difference of the ninetieth and tenth percentiles of male weekly wages. The results show
virtually no effect of tax rates. Taxes matter only in the years around TRA86. Goolsbee (1999) shows that elasticities estimated with tax return data in earlier periods
(where income trends differed) are quite different than in most of the NTR literature.

Some of the literature has argued that the inequality trend itself is the result of
falling marginal rates (see discussions in Feenberg and Poterba 1993; Slemrod 1994;
Auten and Carroll, forthcoming). The argument is summarized by Slemrod using
figure 1 from Feenberg and Poterba (1993) (see figure 5.1), which shows the share
of wages received by the top 0.25 percent of the adult population. The trend begins
at around the time when high marginal rates started a monotonic fall through the
1970s and 1980s, suggesting a tax-based source.

Several observations, however, cast serious doubt that taxes are the source of the
rise in inequality. (As indicated in note 5, the doubts remain looking at AGI rather
than just wages.) First, by far the largest increase in U.S. history of the net of tax share
at the high end of the income distribution was the reduction in the top marginal rate
from 91 to 70 percent following the 1964 Revenue Act. The net of tax share more
than tripled—a vastly larger tax cut even relative to other income groups than anything that occurred in the 1980s. There is, however, no evidence of an increase in
the wage share at the high end.[4] Second, the income trend at the high end remains
almost exactly constant from the mid-1970s to the mid-1980s despite major tax cuts
in the early 1980s and no tax cuts in the late 1970s or the mid-1980s up to TRA86.[5]
Third, as the data presented here demonstrate, the relative incomes of the very rich
have continued to rise through the 1990s despite rising marginal rates.

The trend in figure 5.1 is precisely the type of bias that will lead the NTR literature to overstate the elasticities using tax cuts as a natural experiment. The NTR
literature attributes the entire increase in the share going to the rich in figure 5.1 to
taxes when it should attribute only the amount going to the rich over and above the
trend line. The latter is obviously much more modest. (This is a graphical demonstration of the results in Slemrod [1996] showing that, except for TRA86, taxes
have little effect.)

The most common response of NTR practitioners to this critique has been to
tighten the natural experiment and argue that comparing the rich to the moderately
rich should eliminate most of the inequality trend bias because high-income groups

Figure 5.1   Share of Wages Received by Top .25 Percent of Adults

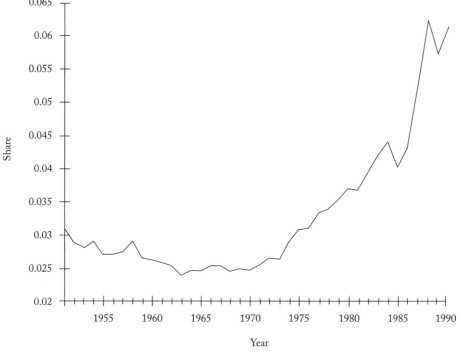

Source: Feenberg and Poterba (1993). Reprinted with permission by the MIT press.

are similar. The idea is that someone in the top 1 percent of the distribution may face a very different environment or income trend than someone at the median but probably the same environment as someone in the top 10 percent. Thus, comparing those two with a natural experiment avoids the problem. The data on corporate executives, however, show that even this natural experiment assumption is not true and that correcting it can reduce the estimated elasticities greatly.

To estimate the true effect of tax rates, any analysis must subtract out the non-tax-related trends in income for each group. Table 5.3 presents the average growth rate of salary and bonus from 1991 to 1995 for various income classes. The early 1990s is a period with no tax cuts, so tax-induced growth is not an issue. I take as a group comparable to the "highest" group in Feldstein (1995) people with permanent income greater than $177,000 in 1985 dollars, and as comparable to the "high" group executives with income below $177,000.[6] There are not enough executives with incomes substantially below $100,000, so I do not calculate a growth rate for the "medium" group.

It is very clear that the growth rates differ substantially by income class. The incomes of individuals in the highest group grew at 9.1 percent annually, and in the high group at 2.4 percent. This may be seem like an extreme case, but the trends are similar to those cited in Hall and Liebman (1997) for other high-income people from 1982 to 1994. They find that average incomes in high-income occupations (CEOs, National Basketball Association [NBA] players, Major League Baseball

Table 5.3   Growth Rates of Cash Income of Executives with Permanent Income

Group/Occupation	Average Income (Start of Period)	Average Annual Growth
From 1991 to 1995		
Greater than $177,000	$514,000	9.1%
$177,000 or less	154,000	2.4
From 1982 to 1994		
CEOs	945,110	7.7
MLB players	376,300	9.0
NBA players	325,600	12.8
Top 0.5 percent AGI	180,900	3.4
Professors	40,700	1.3
Average workers	30,400	0.5

Source: The first two rows of data are based on the author's calculations using the data described in the text. The other data come from Hall and Liebman (1997).

[MLB] players) rose between 7.7 and 12.5 percent per year, while the income cut-off to claim a place in the top 0.5 percent of AGI (which had a starting income in Feldstein's high group) rose 3.4 percent per year. They also cite a growth rate for professors and average workers (who are around Feldstein's medium group) of between 0.5 and 1.3 percent.

Any growth rates of these magnitudes can easily explain the majority of the estimated elasticities of taxable income in natural experiments even if restricted to the relatively rich. To see the potential importance, the bottom panels of table 5.1 redo the difference-in-differences calculation of Feldstein (1995a) but subtract out, using various income growth rates, the amount that income would have risen *without any tax effect whatsoever.* With growth rates of 8.9 percent, 3.4 percent, and 0.5 percent for the three groups, as in the middle panel, the actual elasticity of taxable income is not in the one to one and a half range originally estimated but instead falls to slightly over one-third. Presumably these estimates would be even smaller using the data in Auten and Carroll (forthcoming), whose sample is longer and whose estimated elasticities were not as large to begin with.

The relative trends actually observed in the data are even larger than the trends subtracted from the middle panel, as are trends in the income of the other rich people. Even taking the lowest growth rate for the highest group (7.7 percent annually) and the highest rates for the other groups (3.4 percent and 1.3 percent), as in the bottom panel of table 5.1, the elasticities are still cut by 40 to 50 percent.

These results suggest that inequality trends may account for much of the estimated income response of the wealthy to the tax cuts of the 1980s. Future work may establish that the differences in trend rates are not as large as they are among these individuals, but at the very least the data here indicate that there is a clear difference between the very rich and other groups in this attribute and that this difference biases the work of the NTR. These same trends should work the opposite way for tax *increases* on the rich; the Omnibus Budget Reconciliation Act of 1993 (OBRA93) will thus be a key piece of evidence for evaluating the elasticities in the NTR (for evidence on the topic, see Goolsbee 2000).

The results also suggest that NTR work should allow for income trends that vary by income class. They cannot evaluate tax changes with a before-after comparison of two individual years of data. With multiple years of data, regression methods could control for differing trends by income class and still identify the tax effect, even if only tax return data are available.

The Income of the Very Rich Is More Sensitive to Demand Conditions

The NTR literature has used, almost exclusively, tax return data to analyze income elasticities, but it is important to note how little information is provided on a tax return. The individual's economic environment is not known. Auten and Carroll (forthcoming), using their nonpublic tax return samples, have done careful work using occupation, age, region, and other controls available on the returns and find that these factors are important for income growth. We know painfully little, however, about how the pay of different groups responds to economic conditions and firm performance.[7] The natural experiment approach is simply to assume that the responses are the same for the rich as for the somewhat rich and to conclude that the unobserved factors therefore do not bias the results. Unfortunately, the data on executives indicate that this assumption is false.

Without even looking at stock options, which are taken up in the next section, table 5.4 presents a regression of the log of cash compensation (salary, bonus, and LTIP) from 1991 to 1995 with individual fixed effects and separate trends but allows different coefficients by income class on the log of the market value of the individual's firm, the ratio of earnings to the book value of capital for the firm, and the growth rate of GDP. The coefficients show that the income of the rich group is about twice as responsive to real market value and to aggregate economic growth, and 50 percent more responsive to earnings, than is the income of the lower group.

This makes theoretical sense if one believes that the leaders of firms are more responsible for performance. It is possible, of course, that the differences are greater

Table 5.4   Sensitivity of Cash Income to Economic Conditions

Variations	(1)
Ln (market value) × [high income]	.275 (.008)
Ln (market value) × [moderate income]	.146 (.017)
Earnings to capital ratio [high income]	.334 (.033)
Earnings to capital ratio [moderate income]	.217 (.090)
GDP growth rate [high income]	1.625 (.212)
GDP growth rate [moderate income]	.836 (.561)
Controls	individually fixed effects
	time trends by income class
n	18618
R^2	.90

Notes: The dependent variable is the log of real cash compensation as defined in the text. Standard errors are in parentheses. The sample covers executives with four or more years of data and December fiscal years from 1991 to 1995.

among executives than among other high-income people. It is likely, however, that the same effects are at work among other groups, such as doctors, lawyers, athletes, and investment bankers—in other words, in any field in which the highest-paid individuals are more responsible for firm performance.

The tax bills of the last two decades have been enacted at particular points in the business cycle that make this issue relevant for the NTR literature. The most famous NTR papers, Lindsey (1987) and Feldstein (1995a), look across samples (1982 to 1984 for Lindsey and 1985 to 1988 for Feldstein) in which the stock market increased dramatically, corporate profits rose, and GDP growth increased. The regression of table 5.4 suggests that these conditions tend to increase the incomes of the rich more than those of the moderately rich even without tax changes.

To illustrate its importance, I reexamined TRA86 but subtracted out the effect of stock prices, GDP growth, and corporate profits on pay and recalculated the elasticity. To do so, I made the simplifying assumption that all firms had increases in real market value equal to the increase in real market value of the Standard & Poors market index and increases in earnings-to-capital ratios equal to the increase in the profits-before-taxes-to-shareholder-equity ratio for manufacturing, both of which, as well as the real GDP growth rate, came from the Economic Report of the President. Owing to these economic conditions, the highest group's income should have risen by 12.2 percent and that of the high group by 6.7 percent without any tax changes. Taking these growth rates out and recalculating the tax response reduces the estimated elasticity by about 25 percent. These market effects are also potentially important when analyzing the tax increases of 1993 and 1994 because of the high variability of the stock market and the business cycle from 1991 to 1995.

Unfortunately for the NTR, truly correcting for this bias is impossible using tax return data because returns lack any information about firm performance. But even with tax return data, gains could be made by including more than just two years of data and allowing national economic conditions like unemployment or GDP growth to vary by income class as a control. With the detailed tax return data, industry performance could also be used.

The Share of Time-Shiftable Compensation Rises Dramatically with Income

Slemrod (1992, 1994, 1995, forthcoming) has consistently remarked that we must be careful not to interpret short-run changes to the timing of transactions as long-run elasticities. NTR practitioners such as Feldstein and Feenberg (1996) have argued that natural experiments comparing the very rich to the somewhat rich probably do not suffer from this problem because there must be differences in the timing sensitivity of pay between the rich and very rich for the natural experiment to be biased. Evidence of precisely such a difference is the final important element found in the data on executive compensation.

Certain forms of income are much easier to retime than others (exercising stock options or receiving bonuses in December rather than January, for example). The data suggest that the share of income in these shiftable forms may be much higher for the very rich. Figure 5.2 presents a nonparametric kernel regression of the share of total compensation coming as bonus or LTIP payout by income level.[8] These

Figure 5.2   Bonus as a Share of Total Compensation by Income Level

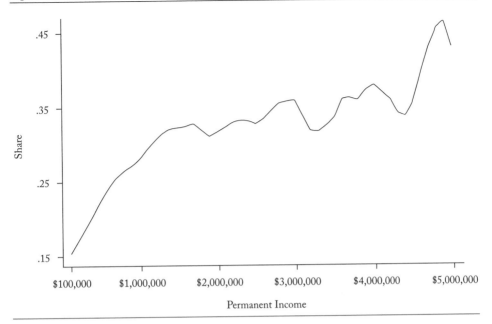

Source: Author's calculations.

payments are usually made in lump sums, often at the end of the year or quarter, and so retiming these payouts is a relatively easy way to shift income in the short run from one year to another. The figure clearly shows that the share of income in shiftable form rises dramatically with permanent income, more than doubling when income rises from $100,000 to $1,000,000. Figure 5.3 presents a similar kernel regression, but for the share of compensation coming as stock options (valued by the Black-Scholes formula). There is, again, a dramatic rise in the share as income rises. The share almost triples when income rises from $100,000 to $1,000,000. Note that this is not the value of options *exercised* (which would usually appear on a tax return as wage income) but the value of options *granted* (which does not appear anywhere on a tax return). As such, these regressions show that the *potential* for short-run shifting is much greater for the very rich than for the moderately rich. Since NTR papers do not separate long- and short-run effects, the natural experiments tend to confuse the two and to overestimate the long-run elasticities.

The increasing use of options and the large outstanding stock of unexercised options have also created a large mean reverting component to the income of many of the very rich. Any sampling strategy, such as the common NTR one of dividing up individuals based on their income in a year before a tax change, tend, at least in the 1990s, to choose disproportionately precisely those people who are cashing in their stock options and whose income will fall in the future back to a more "normal" level.[9] There is positive serial correlation in salary compensation for individuals in this sample, but very strong negative serial correlation in exercised option income. Since exercised options are largely included only as part of wages and salaries on a

Figure 5.3 Options Granted as a Share of Total Compensation by Income Level

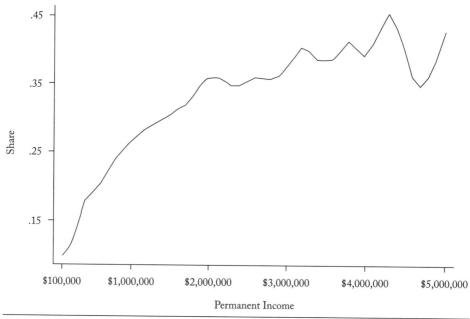

Source: Author's calculations.

tax return, it means that, again, tax return data are becoming less useful over time. At the very least, it is imperative to get some measure of permanent income when breaking up groups for a natural experiment.

To see the importance of temporary shifts versus long-run changes, table 5.5 conducts a simple difference-in-differences analysis of these executives using short-run data from the period 1992 to 1993 and then longer-run data from 1992 to 1995 to see whether there is a difference in responsiveness.[10] The short-run analysis is

Table 5.5   Short- Versus Long-Run Elasticity of Taxable Income in the 1990s

	Net of Tax Rate	Taxable Compensation	Elasticity
Short run (1992 to 1993)			
High	7.2	6.9	
Very high	12.5	−11.8	
Difference-in-differences			
Very high minus high	5.2	18.7	3.6
Long run (1992 to 1995)			
High	11.5	16.5	
Very high	16.7	14.6	
Difference-in-differences			
Very high minus high	5.2	1.9	0.4

Source: Author's calculations based on executive compensation data described in the text. The "high" income group is defined as executives with permanent income of less than $275,000, and "very high" as executives with more than $275,000.

basically a counterpart of the work of Feldstein and Feenberg (1996), who look at the 1992 to 1993 change and find a large elasticity, although the same issues would apply in a regression framework.

In the first panel we see that high-income people had a 12.5 percent reduction in their net of tax share from 1992 to 1993, while the next group had a decrease of 7.2 percent. (Below $140,000 per year there was no change, but this is a small fraction of the sample.) The real incomes for the panel of individuals with data in all of the years from 1991 to 1995 fall by 11.8 percent for executives in the highest group but rise by 6.9 percent for the lower group. This indicates an elasticity of taxable income of 3.6(!).

The second panel, however, looks at the longer-run change from 1992 to 1995 for the same people. Now we see that the change in the net of tax shares for the two groups (counting the change to the payroll tax in 1994) is 5.2 percent, but their income growth differs by only 1.9 percent. The elasticity is slightly less than .4 and almost ten times smaller than the short-run response. Even the longer-run elasticity of .4 is biased upward by the fact that income in the base year of 1992 is artificially high, owing to timing shifts. In other words, the incomes of the rich and the very rich responded very differently in the short run but very similarly over the longer run—a response that is totally consistent with a simple retiming story. Another fact drives this point home. In 1991, 27 percent of the total taxable compensation to executives came as options exercised; in 1992 this rose to 42 percent, and in 1993 it returned to 27 percent.

For the 1993 tax increase at least, timing issues seem to be quite important, and they may also be important for other tax changes. This problem would be easy to address in future NTR work given sufficient data. In the tradition of the work on permanent versus transitory tax effects in other contexts found in Gerald Auten and Charles Clotfelter (1982), Leonard Burman and William Randolph (1994), and Randolph (1995), regression-based methods could simply include future tax rates as well as current rates to separate out anticipatory and transitory reactions from permanent responses. By doing so, however, the conclusions of the NTR might be changed substantially. In the more detailed regression-based analyses found in Goolsbee (2000, forthcoming), including future tax, the terms show large short-run responses to taxation but more permanent responses as much as twenty times smaller. With the true elasticity of taxable income between 0 and .4, the deadweight loss from the Clinton tax increase, for example, rather than being almost 200 percent of the revenue collected, as claimed in Feldstein and Feenberg (1996), is more like 20 to 25 percent.

CONCLUSION

After ten years of finding large elasticities of taxable income with respect to the net of tax share by using tax changes as natural experiments, the NTR literature has had a great impact on the conventional wisdom regarding progressivity and the efficiency loss of high marginal tax rates. I argue, however, that the results from these papers are based on the faulty assumption that the very rich differ from other income groups only in having different tax rates. Independent data on several thousand high-income executives, as well as on other prominent rich people, show that even the moderately rich are not a valid control group. Three facts lead to problems.

First, secular trends in income inequality that are not related to taxation dramatically alter estimated elasticities from the 1980s. The executive data, confirming other data in the literature, show that income for individuals in the highest income class grew significantly faster than for those in lower income classes. Correcting for this trend could reduce the elasticities based on TRA86, for example, from between 1 and 1.5 to around one-half or one-third.

Second, the pay of the very rich is about twice as responsive to demand conditions and firm performance as the pay of the moderately rich. There is little information available on a tax return to correct for this problem, and the natural experiments in the NTR literature, particularly of the tax cuts of the 1980s, examine years when this was specifically problematic. For TRA86, accounting for these factors may reduce the estimated elasticity by a further 20 to 25 percent.

Finally, the very rich have a much greater share of income in forms whose timing can be shifted, thus making their relative responsiveness in a natural experiment much higher in the short run than in the long run. Much larger fractions of the income of higher-income classes come as stock options, bonuses, or LTIP payouts. In the 1990s this difference has become even more important. The higher share means that at least part of the relative response to taxation picked up in a natural experiment is likely to be temporary. Looking at the executives following the tax increase of 1993, the short-run elasticity is almost ten times larger than the long-run elasticity.

Taken together, these three facts suggest that the elasticities of the NTR literature may be significantly overstated. Future research may find more areas in which the rich differ from other income classes, but it is clear from these data that, as they say, the rich really are different, and not just because they have more money. It is possible, as suggested in this chapter, for the NTR to correct at least partially for these problems using regression methods on more years of data and including more controls, but the results here suggest that the conclusions from such an exercise might change substantially.

For some of the problems raised, however, tax return data will never be able to provide the information necessary to estimate the tax responsiveness correctly. Perhaps the most accurate conclusion is that we need more data sources on the rich that include information allowing us to correct and control for the types of issues raised here, data such as information on executive compensation. Only these types of data will allow us to estimate the true behavioral response to taxation.

I wish to thank Steve Levitt, Maggie Newman, James Poterba, Terry Shevlin, and Joel Slemrod for helpful comments, and the University of Chicago Graduate School of Business for financial support.

NOTES

1. The only sample of comparable size is the internal (not publicly available) U.S. Treasury sample in Auten and Carroll (1995, forthcoming), which has about the same number of high-bracket individuals as the current sample but much less information about forms of compensation or the individual's economic environment.

2. This has always been less true for women; see Eissa (1996).

3. The debate continues with contemporaneous work by Frank Sammartino and David Weiner (1997) arguing that the long-run elasticity is small and Robert Carroll (1997) arguing that it is large. The results depend critically on how the sample of high-income people is chosen and whether the "control" groups are actually comparable to the "treatment" groups for high-income people.

4. There is evidence that incomes rose for very-high-income people in Lindsey (1990), and it is repeated in Feenberg (this volume), but a simple natural experiment on these data comparing the relative income changes of the rich to their relative tax rates changes implies an elasticity of taxable income of only about 0.2 or less.

5. Feenberg and Poterba (1993) also look at the share of total AGI going to high income and find that the rise starts around 1981. Again, however, there is no rise in income around the massive tax cut of 1964. In addition, once they take out capital gains income, there is very little evidence of any increasing share in the 1980s until TRA86. Slemrod (1996) found that the trend removed all influence of tax rates from 1954 to 1985 for both wages and AGI.

6. This is the average salary in the lowest bracket of Feldstein's "highest" group, but the exact cutoff was unimportant.

7. There is a related macroeconomic literature on the effect of business cycle fluctuations on income distribution; for a discussion, see Blinder and Esaki (1978) and Cutler and Katz (1991).

8. A kernel regression is just a type of local averaging. The most important choices to be made in such methods are the weighting scheme for the averaging (the choice of kernel) and the size of the local window over which to average (bandwidth selection). The regressions here use an Epanichnekov kernel with a bandwidth chosen according to the plug-in method of Silverman (1986). Details on nonparametric regression can be found in Hardle (1990).

9. This is probably less of a problem for the work on the 1980s, when stock options were less common.

10. To be conservative, the cutoff between groups is set at permanent income of $275,000 per year even though the cutoff for the tax increase was $250,000. Here too the cutoff point does not change the conclusions at all.

REFERENCES

Auten, Gerald, and Robert Carroll. Forthcoming. "The Effect of Income Taxes on Household Behavior." *Review of Economics and Statistics.*

Auten, Gerald, and Charles Clotfelter. 1982. "Permanent Versus Transitory Tax Effects and the Realization of Capital Gains." *Quarterly Journal of Economics* 97(4): 613–32.

Blinder, Alan, and Howard Esaki. 1978. "Macroeconomic Activity and Income Distribution in the Postwar United States." *Review of Economics and Statistics* 60: 604–9.

Blundell, Richard, Alan Duncan, and Costas Meghir. 1995. "Estimating Labor Supply Responses Using Tax Reforms." *Econometrica* 66(July,4): 827–61.

Burman, Leonard, and William Randolph. 1994. "Measuring Permanent Responses to Capital-Gains Tax Changes in Panel Data." *American Economic Review* 84(4): 794–809.

Carroll, Robert. 1997. "Taxes and Household Behavior: New Evidence from the 1993 Tax Act." Unpublished paper. U.S. Department of the Treasury, Office of Tax Analysis.

Conference Board. Various years. *Top Executive Compensation.*

Cutler, David, and Lawrence Katz. 1991. "Macroeconomic Performance and the Disadvantaged." *Brookings Papers on Economic Activity* 2: 1–74.

Eissa, Nada. 1996. "Tax Reforms and Labor Supply." In *Tax Policy and the Economy,* edited by James Poterba, vol. 10. Cambridge, Mass.: MIT Press.

Feenberg, Daniel, and James Poterba. 1993. "Income Inequality and the Incomes of Very-High-Income Taxpayers." In *Tax Policy and the Economy,* edited by James Poterba, vol. 7. Cambridge, Mass.: MIT Press.

Feldstein, Martin. 1995a. "The Effect of Marginal Tax Rates on Taxable Income: A Panel Study of the 1986 Tax Reform Act." *Journal of Political Economy* 103 (3, June): 551–72.

———. 1995b. "Tax Avoidance and the Deadweight Loss of the Income Tax." Working paper 5055. Cambridge, Mass.: National Bureau of Economic Research.

———. Forthcoming. "Tax Avoidance and the Deadweight Loss of the Income Tax." *Review of Economics and Statistics.*

Feldstein, Martin, and Daniel Feenberg. 1996. "The Effect of Increased Tax Rates on Taxable Income and Economic Efficiency: A Preliminary Analysis of the 1993 Tax Rate Increases." In *Tax Policy and the Economy,* edited by James Poterba, vol. 10. Cambridge, Mass.: MIT Press.

Goolsbee, Austan. 1999. "Evidence on the High-Income Laffer Curve from Six Decades of Tax Reform." *Brookings Papers on Economic Activity* (2): 1–47.

———. 2000. "What Happens When You Tax the Rich? Evidence from Executive Compensation." *Journal of Political Economy* 108(2, April): 352–78.

———. Forthcoming. "Taxes, High-Income Executives, and the Perils of Revenue Estimation in the New Economy." *American Economic Review Paper and Proceedings.*

Hall, Brian, and Jeffrey Liebman. 1997. "Are CEOs Really Paid Like Bureaucrats?" *Quarterly Journal of Economics* 113(3, August): 653–91.

Hardle, Wolfgang. 1990. *Applied Nonparametric Regression.* Cambridge: Cambridge University Press.

Heckman, James. 1993. "What Has Been Learned About Labor Supply in the Past Twenty Years?" *American Economic Review* 83(2): 116–21.

———. 1996. "Comment on Eissa." In *Empirical Foundations of Household Taxation,* edited by Martin Feldstein and James Poterba. Chicago: University of Chicago Press.

Katz, Lawrence, and Kevin Murphy. 1992. "Changes in Relative Wages, 1963–1987: Supply and Demand Factors." *Quarterly Journal of Economics* 107(1): 35–78.

Levy, Frank, and Richard Murnane. 1992. "U.S. Earnings Levels and Earnings Inequality: A Review of Recent Trends and Proposed Explanations." *Journal of Economic Literature* 30: 1333–81.

Lindsey, Lawrence. 1987. "Individual Taxpayer Response to Tax Cuts, 1982–1984, with Implications for the Revenue Maximizing Tax Rate." *Journal of Public Economics* 33: 173–206.

———. 1990. *The Growth Experiment.* New York: Basic Books.

Parcell, Ann. 1996. "Income Shifting in Response to Higher Tax Rates: The Effects of OBRA93." U.S. Department of the Treasury, Office of Tax Analysis. Paper presented at the Allied Social Sciences meetings, San Francisco (January).

Pencavel, John. 1986. "Labor Supply of Men: A Survey." In *Handbook of Labor Economics,* edited by Orley Ashenfelter and Richard Layard, vol. 2. Amsterdam: Elsevier.

Randolph, William. 1995. "Dynamic Income, Progressive Taxes, and the Timing of Charitable Contributions." *Journal of Political Economy* 103(4): 709–38.

Sammartino, Frank, and David Weiner. 1997. "Recent Evidence on Taxpayers' Response to the Rate Increases of the 1990s." *National Tax Journal* 50(3, September): 683–705.

Scholes, Myron, and Mark Wolfson. 1992. *Taxes and Business Strategy.* Englewood Cliffs, N.J.: Prentice-Hall.

Silverman, Benjamin. 1986. *Density Estimation for Statistics and Data Analysis.* London: Chapman and Hall.

Slemrod, Joel. 1992. "Do Taxes Matter? Lessons from the 1980s." *American Economic Review* 82(2): 250–56.

———. 1994. "On the High-Income Laffer Curve." In *Tax Progressivity and Income Inequality,* edited by Joel Slemrod. Cambridge: Cambridge University Press.

———. 1995. "Income Creation or Income Shifting? Behavioral Responses to the Tax Reform Act of 1986." *American Economic Review* 85(2): 175–80.

———. 1996. "High-Income Families and the Tax Changes of the 1980s." In *Empirical Foundations of Household Taxation,* edited by Martin Feldstein and James Poterba. Chicago: University of Chicago Press.

———. Forthcoming. "A General Model of the Behavioral Response to Taxation." *International Tax and Public Finance.*

Slemrod, Joel, and Shlomo Yitzhaki. 1996. "The Cost of Taxation and the Marginal Efficiency Cost of Funds." *IMF Staff Papers* 43(1, March): 172–98.

Commentary on Chapter 5

Terry Shevlin

Austin Goolsbee's chapter provides evidence on the effects of three specific problems on estimated elasticities for wealthy individuals derived from the natural experiments approach (as employed by, for example, Lindsey [1987] and Feldstein [1995]). Although some of these problems have been noted in prior literature (as pointed out by Goolsbee), he employs a new data set (top executive compensation) to provide direct estimates of the effects of these problems on estimated elasticities. I believe Goolsbee's chapter makes an important contribution to the tax responsiveness literature and reminds us of the difficulties in conducting empirical tests based on archival data (in contrast to data generated under controlled experimental conditions). The remainder of my discussion contains some background comments on the general topic of income elasticities, then presents a brief discussion of the difference-in-differences approach, a critique of Goolsbee's critiques, and finally some closing comments.

BACKGROUND COMMENTS

The underlying topic of Goolsbee's chapter is an estimation of the elasticity of taxable income of the "rich" with respect to statutory marginal tax rate changes. Feldstein (1995, 551) comments on the importance of this topic: "Changes in marginal tax rates induce taxpayers to alter their behavior in ways that affect taxable income and therefore tax revenue. The magnitude of this response is of critical importance in the formulation of appropriate tax and budget policies."

There are two major points here. First, if tax rule makers (for example, Congress) are using taxes as a tool to achieve some policy objective (such as to redistribute income, stimulate the economy, or raise revenue), then as researchers we want to be able to quantify predicted outcomes of tax rule changes. Presumably, we can hope, a more informed decisionmaker leads to better decisions being made. The second point is closely related to the first: given current law, and the supposed revenue-neutrality of proposed tax law changes, the tax rule makers need to have estimates of the revenue effects. These revenue effects very much depend on the predicted responses of affected taxpayers.

For those not familiar with the literature—and I would have counted myself in that number prior to this conference—an example might illustrate the issue. Suppose the elasticity for the rich is 1.25 (extracted from table 5.1), and Congress enacts an increase in the top marginal tax rate from 31 to 39.6 percent on incomes over $250,000. (My example ignores the removal of the Medicare ceiling and the interim increase to 36 percent for incomes between $140,000 and $250,000.) For a taxpayer with a $300,000 taxable income, if we assume no behavorial response, then we predict the tax rate increase will increase tax receipts to the Treasury by $4,300 (calculated as .086 × $50,000 = $4,300).

Contrast this predicted tax revenue increase with the increase we can expect if we assume a behavioral response by the taxpayer. In this literature, the elasticity is with respect to the net of tax share. The tax rate increase represents a 14 percent decrease in the net of tax share = $[(1 - .31)/(1 - .396) = 1.142]$. With an elasticity of 1.25, this implies a decrease in taxable income of $1.25 × .14 = .175$, or $52,500. The predicted post-tax-rate-change taxable income is $247,500, and tax revenue is predicted to decline by more than $16,000 (.31 × $52,500). Thus, this elasticity estimate is important.[1]

THE DIFFERENCE-IN-DIFFERENCES APPROACH

Goolsbee's chapter addresses three problems in the natural experiments approach, which he labels the New Tax Responsiveness, or NTR, approach, a nomenclature I also adopt. The NTR approach uses a difference-in-differences approach:

$$(\%\Delta TI_1 - \%\Delta TI_2)/(\%\Delta\text{'tax'}_1 - \%\Delta\text{'tax'}_2) \tag{5C.1}$$

where TI denotes taxable income, Δ denotes change, 'tax' is the net of tax share calculated earlier, and the subscript refers to group. Recall that elasticity is defined as

$$(\%\Delta TI_1/\%\Delta\text{'tax'}_1) \tag{5C.2}$$

From table 5.1, this would imply for the highest marginal tax rate group an elasticity of 44.8/42.2 = 1.05. The difference-in-differences approach, however, adds a second group to the calculation. In general terms, the problem is an interrupted time series test, and in theory the threats to this type of test are well known. One way to mitigate the threats to external validity is to add a control group, with the added assumption that the only difference between the treatment and control groups is the treatment. In terms of a regression framework,

$$\%\Delta TI_1 = a_1 + b_1 \%\Delta\text{'tax'}_1$$

$$\%\Delta TI_2 = a_2 + b_2 \%\Delta\text{'tax'}_2$$

Differencing gives

$$\%\Delta TI_1 - \%\Delta TI_2 = a_1 - a_2 + b_1 \%\Delta\text{'tax'}_1 - b_2 \%\Delta\text{'tax'}_2 \tag{5C.3}$$

It is argued (see, for example, Feldstein 1995, 565) that differencing eliminates the common constant term and provides an estimate of the slope term.

$$\%\Delta TI_1 - \%\Delta TI_2 = b(\%\Delta\text{'tax'}_1 - \%\Delta\text{'tax'}_2) \tag{5C.4}$$

But note that the idea of individual constant terms is to allow for differences between the treatment and control groups. Further, the estimated slope coefficient (b in [5.4]) is only meaningful if $b_1 = b_2$, but this is the point of the calculation. Thus, I am somewhat confused by the application of the difference-in-differences approach. A more powerful approach consistent with the underlying objective is the following regression model:

$$\%\Delta TI = b_0 + b_1\, GP2 + b_2\, \%\Delta\text{'tax'} + b_3\, \%\Delta\text{'tax'}GP2 + e \qquad (5C.5)$$

where GP2 is a dummy variable set equal to 1 if the firm is a member of the treatment group (the high-income group) and 0 for the control group. This approach allows for different intercept terms; does not constrain $b_1 = b_2$; and highlights that in fact the elasticity estimate is an incremental estimate, not an absolute estimate for the treatment group. Although I suspect this is well known to the researchers employing the difference-in-differences approach, care needs to be taken by the researcher and readers not to interpret the result as an estimate of the absolute elasticity.[2] That is, the elasticity of 1.25 used in the earlier example is really an incremental elasticity measure. Of course, if there is no change in the tax rates for the control group, then the estimate represents both an incremental and an absolute elasticity.

CRITICISMS OF THE DIFFERENCE-IN-DIFFERENCES APPROACH
Relative Incomes of the Very Rich Increase Greatly over Time

As noted earlier, differencing is assumed to control for any differences between the two groups. But what if the incomes of the two groups are growing at fundamentally different rates? Goolsbee notes that differences in growth rates have been pointed out as a possible problem, but his contribution here is to provide evidence on the magnitude of any bias arising from differences in growth rates.[3]

Table 5.2 presents estimates of growth rates and table 5.1 recalculates the elasticities after adjusting the change in taxable income for differential growth rates. The adjustment involves simply subtracting the mean growth rate for a particular group from that group's change in taxable income over the test period. This adjustment results in elasticity estimates in the range of .33 to .50 (depending on the income growth rates used). An alternative approach consistent with the regression framework outlined earlier is simply to add the growth variable to the regression model in equation (5C.5).

$$\%\Delta TI = b_0 + b_1\, GP2 + b_2\, \%\Delta\text{'tax'} + b_3\, \%\Delta\text{'tax'}GP2 + b_4\, \text{Growth} + e \qquad (5C.6)$$

One issue that might be debatable among economists is whether the differential growth rates are caused by tax rate changes and differential elasticities. To the extent that this is the case, controlling for differential growth rates "throws the baby out with the bathwater;" that is, the elasticity estimates are downward biased. (If the differential growth rates are not caused by tax rate changes, failure to control for them can lead to upwardly biased elasticity estimates. This arises because even though the growth rates are not correlated with the tax rate changes, they are correlated with the group membership.)

The Income of the Very Rich Is More Sensitive to Demand Conditions

The criticism here is that the incomes of the very rich are more sensitive to economic conditions—both micro and macro conditions. Specifically, since Goolsbee is using data on corporate executives, the income of higher-income individuals is argued to be more sensitive to firm size and firm performance.[4] The regressions reported by Goolsbee in table 5.4 indicate that higher-paid executives exhibit a higher pay-for-performance sensitivity, although strictly speaking, the regression model estimated by Goolsbee does not test for significant differences in the two groups. (Given the standard errors on some variables, it might not be possible to reject the null of no difference; see, for example, the earnings-to-capital ratio estimates). But taken at face value, and as noted by Goolsbee, these differences are not surprising given the agency literature (higher sensitivities for those individuals who have the greatest ability to affect firm performance), provided we make the assumption that the higher-paid executives in the EXECUCOMP database are the CEOs.

Given these differences in pay-for-performance sensitivities, it is necessary in an interrupted time series test to control for changes in firm performance and in macroeconomic conditions. Otherwise, we could falsely ascribe increases in CEO income to tax rate decreases. In controlling for macroeconomic conditions, the approach controls for variations in the growth in income around the trend line, which was the focus of the first adjustment.

Goolsbee does some simple adjustments using macro series to estimate the size of any bias. These adjustments result in reducing the elasticity estimate by approximately 25 percent. Somewhat surprisingly since he has firm-specific data, Goolsbee does not adjust for firm-specific performance but rather simply for the change in the manufacturing-sector profitability. (As noted by Goolsbee, these same macro adjustments can be made using tax return data.) These adjustments could easily be incorporated into the regression approach by adding to equation (5C.6) as follows:

$$\%\Delta TI = b_0 + b_1\, GP2 + b_2\, \%\Delta\text{'tax'} + b_3\, \%\Delta\text{'tax'}GP2 + b_4\, \text{Growth} + b_5\, \text{Firm perfor-}$$
$$\text{mance} + b_6\, \text{Firm size} + b_7\, \%\Delta GDP + e \qquad (5C.7)$$

The Share of Time-Shiftable Compensation Rises Dramatically with Income

Goolsbee conjectures, and I concur, that bonuses and stock options for corporate executives allow them to time realization more than is possible for lower-level employees. Disney executives provide a good example of the acceleration of stock option exercises into December 1992, before the higher statutory rates took effect in 1993. (For an excellent analysis of this issue, see Huddart 1997).[5] The implication here is that we need to beware of interpreting short-run responses (for example, shifting income into 1992 from 1993) as longer-run responses.

Thus, Goolsbee compares the change in executives' taxable income from 1992 to 1993, which results in an estimate of the short-run response, with changes from 1992 to 1995, which results in an estimate of the longer-run response. The estimated longer-run elasticity is more than ten times smaller. Goolsbee also makes the excellent point that the existence of taxable option gains in a particular year leads to spikes (mean reversion) in reported taxable income, making it difficult to form groups based on their income in a given year. That is, some members of the highest income group (say in 1992) are there because of the acceleration of option exercise, so that in 1993 their income falls, resulting in a negative change in taxable income.

Again, we can think about this problem in a regression framework. Goolsbee refers to some of his own work, which includes future tax rate variables to control for short-run shifting incentives. Thus, we can add future tax rate variables to equation (5C.7):

$$\%\Delta TI = b_0 + b_1 \, GP2 + b_2 \, \%\Delta\text{'tax'} + b_3 \, \%\Delta\text{'tax'}GP2 + b_4 \, \text{Growth} + b_5 \, \text{Firm performance} + b_6 \, \text{Firm size} + b_7 \, \%\Delta GDP + b_8 \, \text{Future tax rates} + e \qquad (5C.8)$$

One reason for presenting this final model is to make the point that it would be interesting, and a further contribution, if all three criticisms and adjustments suggested by Goolsbee were combined to estimate a final elasticity for, say, the period from 1992 to 1995. As currently presented, we have some idea of the reduction in elasticities of the individual adjustments, but not the net effects of all three combined.

One point that confounds the analysis and estimation of the elasticities in response to the 1993 tax rate changes is that President Clinton and others were pushing for denial of corporate tax deduction for excessive executive pay.[6] This also encouraged executives to accelerate income into 1992, yet this is unrelated to a change in statutory tax rates for individuals. Thus, the short-run response is biased up by this factor. More generally, in an interrupted time series test one has to consider carefully the assumption of ceterus paribus. I am somewhat surprised that more caveats are not associated with the elasticities estimated around TRA86 given the widespread changes in that act.

Finally in this section, note that by quite correctly focusing on the reported taxable income of the executives, Goolsbee addresses the gain on option exercises over the test period. However, a longer-term joint response by firms and top executives to the change in statutory tax rates for both individuals and corporations and to section 162(m) could very well be substitution among differentially taxed compensation components—and we do not know very much about firms' option-granting strategies (for a start, however, see Yermack 1995, 1997).

CONCLUDING COMMENTS

Overall, this is an interesting paper exploiting a new database to highlight and address problems in the new tax responsiveness difference-in-differences approach to estimating tax rate elasticities for the very rich. Goolsbee is to be commended both for quantifying the effect on estimated elasticities using the executive compensation database and for suggesting ways in which other researchers using tax return data can incorporate adjustments to control for these problems.

NOTES

1. As the example illustrates, an elasticity of greater than 1 indicates that a tax rate increase could result in a decline in tax revenues. An elasticity of 0 indicates no behavioral response, and an elasticity of between 0 and 1 indicates that a tax rate increase will lead to an increase in tax revenues.

2. For example, suppose in table 5.1 that both the high and highest marginal tax rate groups had a net of tax rate change of 40 percent and a change in taxable income of 45 percent; then the difference-in-differences approach implies an elasticity of 0 for the highest income group. (Whereas for policymaking purposes I would suggest that an elasticity of .45/.40 = 1.125 is more relevant, in addition to being a large difference in the estimate!

3. Note that Feldstein (1995) calculates his change in taxable income assuming an across-the-board 17.5 percent increase in taxable income from 1985 to 1988 but does not allow for differences in the growth rate across groups. In note 20 he also mentions that John Navratil examined income growth rates between 1983 and 1985 and found no difference across groups. Goolsbee also refers to a study by Slemrod (1996) that provides some evidence on the magnitude of the effects of differences in income growth rates.

4. Note that it is well known in the corporate finance literature that cross-sectional regressions of salary on firm performance are misspecified if firm size is omitted (see, for example, Murphy 1985). Further, there is a long literature in accounting and finance on the determinants of executive pay and on the pay-for-performance sensitivity.

5. Note that for this acceleration to be tax-motivated either the options exercised in 1992 had to be NQOs in which the gain was taxed as ordinary income to the option-holder at that time or, if they were incentive stock options, the stock acquired had to be sold immediately, subjecting the gains to immediate taxation.

6. Subsequently, section 162(m) of the Tax Code was added to deal with this issue.

REFERENCES

Blundell, Richard, Alan Duncan, and Costas Meghir. 1995. "Estimating Labour Supply Responses Using Tax Reforms." Mimeo. Institute for Fiscal Studies.

Feldstein, Martin. 1995. "The Effect of Marginal Tax Rates on Taxable Income: A Panel Study of the 1986 Tax Reform Act." *Journal of Political Economy* 103: 551–72.

Huddart, Steven. 1997. "Patterns of Stock Option Exercise in the United States." Working paper. Durham, N.C.: Duke University.

Lindsey, Lawrence. 1987. "Individual Taxpayer Response to Tax Cuts, 1982–1984, with Implications for the Revenue Maximizing Tax Rate." *Journal of Public Economics* 33: 173–206.

Murphy, Kevin, J. 1985. "Corporate Performance and Managerial Remuneration: An Empirical Analysis." *Journal of Accounting and Economics* 7: 11–42.

Slemrod, Joel. 1996. "High-Income Families and the Tax Changes of the 1980s." In *Empirical Foundations of Household Taxation,* edited by Martin Feldstein and James Poterba. Chicago: University of Chicago Press.

Yermack, David. 1995. "Do Corporations Award CEO Stock Options Effectively?" *Journal of Financial Economics* 39: 237–69.

———. 1997. "Good Timing: CEO Stock Option Awards and Company News Announcements." *Journal of Finance* 52: 449–76.

6

Are the Rich Different?

James Alm and Sally Wallace

> Let me tell you about the very rich. They are different from you and me. . . . They think, deep in their hearts, that they are better than we are. . . . They are different.
> —F. Scott Fitzgerald

> The rich and the poor are differentiated by their incomes and nothing else, and the average millionaire is only the average dishwasher dressed in a new suit.
> —George Orwell

There is little doubt that the rich are in fact different from the rest of us. There is the obvious and significant dimension that they have more income than the average person. However, there are numerous other dimensions that are also important to explore. Aside from their level of income, do the rich differ from the rest of us in the composition of their income? How have these levels and compositions of income changed, both for the rich and for others, in the last decade, a period in which there have been several major changes in tax policies? There is also the possibility that there is much heterogeneity within the rich themselves; that is, are the rich different not only from the rest of us but also from each other?

A particularly important dimension is that of behavioral responses of the rich: Are the rich more or less responsive to changes in taxes than other groups of individuals? Recently the behavioral responses of the very rich have received increasing attention, especially their decisions on how much income to report on their tax returns. The magnitude of these responses is a central issue in debates about the effects of income taxation, especially the impact of changes in marginal tax rates on the level of tax revenues. Evidence from several studies suggests that high-income taxpayers are particularly sensitive to changes in marginal tax rates (Feenberg and Poterba 1992; Slemrod 1994; Feenberg and Feldstein 1995), even if the average taxpayer is not especially responsive; that is, these studies suggest that the rich are different from the rest of us, at least in how they respond in their reporting decisions to taxes.[1]

In this chapter we attempt to answer these and other questions about the rich by examining a wide range of taxpayer reporting decisions over the last decade. In particular, we examine the reporting behaviors of individuals in the top 1 percent and the top 0.5 percent of the distribution of income (what we term the "very rich") and compare these behaviors to that at the population mean (the "average" taxpayer). Our analyses are based on the 1984, 1989, and 1994 Individual Tax Model Files (ITMFs) from the Internal Revenue Service Statistics of Income. These ITMFs are microlevel data sets that contain detailed information on individual observations from a stratified random sample of U.S. taxpayers. They have information on federal individual income tax reporting decisions prior to the enactment of the Tax Reform Act of 1986 (the 1984 ITMF), after the reform was fully phased in (the 1989 ITMF), and after the enactment of the Omnibus Reconciliation Acts of 1990 and 1993 (the 1994 ITMF). For each of the three years, we select from each return the levels of numerous types of reported income (for example, wages and salaries, interest, dividend, capital gains, schedules C and E incomes and losses, passive and nonpassive incomes and losses, adjusted gross income [AGI], and a calculated measure of comprehensive income); we also select the major forms of itemized deductions (for example, charitable contributions, mortgage interest deductions, and state and local tax deductions) and various other items. We examine the level, composition, and trends of these reporting decisions that individuals at different income levels made in 1984, 1989, and 1994. We also attempt to explain the reasons for changes in these decisions over time by applying a method of analysis that exploits the natural experiment aspect of tax changes, called the difference-in-difference approach. Each of the various tax changes in the last decade constituted a significant break from previous tax policy. If we can control for the major influences on reporting behavior that reflect such factors as the growth in income over time and changes in the definition of the tax base, then any differences in reported decisions that we observe over time must be largely due to modifications in individual behavior in response to tax policies.

Our results indicate that taxes matter in the reporting decisions of most individuals. However, there are significant differences in the reporting responses across (and within) income levels, across income types, and even across tax regimes. In short, our analyses suggest that the rich are different from the rest of us, that the rich are different from each other, and that the rich are different now compared to what they were a decade ago.

In the next section we briefly discuss the major tax changes in the last decade. In the following two sections we present the data and methods employed and then consider the results.

TAX POLICIES IN THE LAST DECADE

There have been at least three major tax changes since 1986.[2] The first was the Tax Reform Act of 1986 (TRA86). Also signed into law over the last decade were the Omnibus Budget Reconciliation Act of 1990 (OBRA90) and of 1993 (OBRA93). This section highlights the major features of these tax bills.

TRA86 was arguably the most comprehensive federal income tax reform in the last fifty years. Signed into law by President Reagan in October 1986, its basic features are well known. First, it sharply reduced marginal tax rates on nearly all taxpayers. The top individual income tax rate was reduced from 50 percent to 28 percent, and marginal tax rates for other brackets were also substantially reduced. Fourteen marginal tax brackets ranging from 11 to 50 percent were reduced for the years after 1987 to two (15 and 28 percent); however, the top marginal tax rate was actually 31 percent, owing to a provision that phased out the tax benefits of exemptions and deductions for certain high-income taxpayers. Overall, individual income rates fell by an average of 7 percent. Second, TRA86 changed a number of features in the definition of income, most of which had the effect of greatly expanding the tax base. For example, eligibility for tax savings from individual retirement accounts (IRAs) was restricted, the dividend exclusion was eliminated, and various itemized deductions (such as medical expenses, interest expenses, state and local sales taxes, business expenses, and the two-earner deduction) were also limited or eliminated. In addition, preferential tax treatment of realized capital gains was eliminated, and the ability to use passive investment losses as an offset to other forms of income was sharply curtailed. The standard deduction and personal exemptions were also increased.[3]

The intent of TRA86 was, at least in part, to encourage individuals (and firms) to devote more of their efforts to productive activities. The reduction in marginal tax rates allowed individuals to keep more of each dollar of earned income and reduced incentives to engage in activities whose only purpose was to save taxes. The expansion of the tax base reduced their ability to engage in tax shelter and arbitrage activities. However, the actual magnitudes of the individual responses to these massive federal and state changes in the income remain controversial.

OBRA90 reversed the downward trend in marginal tax rates that had begun in the 1980s. In exchange for a congressional promise to restrain spending growth, President Bush reversed his campaign pledge of "no new taxes" and agreed to raise income taxes. The top statutory marginal tax rate was increased from 28 to 31 percent, so that there were now three tax brackets (15, 28, and 31 percent), although the top rate on realized capital gains remained at 28 percent. Again, some high-income taxpayers faced effective marginal tax rates in excess of 31 percent, owing to limits on deductions and exemptions; for taxpayers with adjusted gross income above $100,000, total itemized deductions (excluding medical expenses, casualty and theft losses, and investment interest) were reduced by 3 percent of the amount of AGI in excess of $100,000. OBRA90 also increased the earned income tax credit (EITC) and its phaseout percentage, and it increased the alternative minimum tax (AMT) tax rate from 21 to 24 percent.

OBRA93 was enacted in President Clinton's first year in office, and it continued the upward movement in marginal tax rates begun in 1990. The top tax rate was increased to 36 percent for couples with taxable income above $140,000, and couples with income above $250,000 were also subject to a 10 percent surcharge that raised their marginal tax rate to 39.6 percent (or 36 percent plus 3.6 percent). Consequently, the three tax brackets under previous law were replaced with five (15, 28, 31, 36, and 39.6 percent), although realized capital gains continued to be taxed at a top rate of 28 percent. OBRA93 also expanded the income tax base, by limiting various itemized deductions (such as business meals and entertainment expenses, club dues, and moving expenses) and by increasing the portion of Social Security benefits subject to the income tax. It also increased the AMT rates and exemption amounts, and it raised the EITC for lower-income families.

Each of these bills represented a major change in the tax environment facing all taxpayers. The next section discusses our approach to analyzing the ways in which individuals responded to these changes.

DATA AND METHODS
Data

Our analyses are based on the 1984, 1989, and 1994 Individual Tax Model Files from the Statistics of Income (SOI) of the Internal Revenue Service. These ITMFs are microlevel data sets that contain detailed information on individual observations from a stratified random sample of U.S. taxpayers.[4] The 1984 ITMF contains 79,556 individual records drawn from a population total of approximately 110 million tax return records; the 1989 file contains 96,588 records from a population of more than 112 million records; and the 1994 ITMF contains 96,385 records from a population of 115.9 million records. In all years, high-income tax returns, or those for taxpayers with AGI above $200,000, are significantly oversampled, so that these ITMFs contain perhaps the most detailed and comprehensive information available for high-income taxpayers. For example, the 1994 ITMF contains 29,260 high-income returns, which represent 30.3 percent of the total ITMF sample of records and 2.6 percent of the total population of high-income returns. Similarly, the 1984 and 1989 ITMFs contain 21,675 and 28,402 returns for taxpayers with AGI above $200,000.

Each individual record of an ITMF contains roughly two hundred variables that represent information coded from the actual federal individual income tax return. The taxpayer name, Social Security number, and other identifying information (other than the primary state of residence) are excluded from the file. We include returns filed by married couples filing jointly and separately and those filed by single individuals; we exclude returns filed by heads of households and by dependents.[5]

The main advantages of the ITMFs are the incredibly rich information they contain on items reported on the tax returns and the very large numbers of observations they make available on individuals at all points in the income distribution, especially those at higher income levels. However, there are several problems with these data. One limitation of the ITMFs is the relative lack of demographic information. Although the ITMFs contain virtually all reported tax items, the tax returns contain little information on individual characteristics. Nevertheless, we are able to extract a limited amount of demographic information from items reported on the returns. For example, we infer the age of individuals based on their use of the elderly exemption, the marital status from the filing form, and the number of children from the child exemptions that are claimed on the return.

Another limitation of the ITMFs is that each is a cross-section of different individuals at a point in time, so that the same individuals are not included in each of the two years. Ideally, we would like to examine the responses of the same individuals over time, as in Martin Feldstein (1995) and Gerald Auten and Robert Carroll (1997), something that is not possible with separate cross-sections. Nevertheless, we have examined various aspects of the individuals in the two years, and their characteristics in such dimensions as proportions that are elderly or married are generally similar over time. In addition, the estimation approach used here can be viewed as transforming unrelated cross-sections over time into something like panel data; this estimation method is discussed in more detail later. It is important to note that, as with any time series data (separate cross-sections or even panel data), the individuals in the top 1 percent in 1984 are not necessarily the same as those in the top 1 percent in 1989 or 1994. This is because the classification of taxpayers in the top 1 and 0.5 percent is based on income, so that, if individuals experience a decrease in any component of income from one year to the next, they could fall to a lower ranking. This issue of rank reversal has been discussed in depth elsewhere (Slemrod 1994).

For each of the three years we select from each return the levels of numerous reported income types, such as wages and salaries, interest, dividend, capital gains, schedules C and E incomes and losses, passive and nonpassive incomes and losses, and AGI. We supplement these measures of reported income by calculating a measure of total, or "comprehensive," income as the sum of AGI, Social Security income not included in AGI, dividends not reported in AGI, pension income not reported in AGI, capital gains not reported in AGI, retirement contributions, and self-employed health insurance deductions; this definition of total income captures as much of an individual's income as can be measured using tax return information and also gives a consistent definition of total income over time.[6] We also select the major forms of itemized deductions (such as charitable contributions, mortgage interest deductions, and state and local tax deductions), as well as several other reported items of interest. Our intent is to compare the levels of these various items that individuals report in 1984, 1989, and 1994 holding constant as many factors as possible that might affect these decisions. To do this, we must consider such things as structural changes in the definition of the income tax base and secular trends in nominal income over the period 1984 to 1994.

Accordingly, we make several adjustments in the reported information to control for these types of changes. First, for dividend and capital gains incomes we add back the portion of each that is not included in AGI so that our measure represents the true level of each income type actually received. Second, all nominal amounts (except interest income) are adjusted to 1994 levels by the rate of inflation over the entire period. Any remaining changes in incomes are, we believe, largely due to changes in reporting behavior as people respond to the different tax regimes.

Tables 6.1 to 6.7 contain a variety of information on the composition of income, the distribution of various tax return items, demographic information, and the growth in incomes for 1984, 1989, and 1994 for high-income earners as well as for the general tax filing population. These tables are discussed in detail later in the chapter.[7]

Methods

The trends shown in the tables are of interest on their own merits, and we spend some time discussing them later. In addition, we use these files to estimate the responses of individuals in their reporting behavior to changes in individual income taxation arising from TRA86, OBRA90, and OBRA93. We focus here on the responses of individuals in their reporting of wages and salaries, interest income, capital gains income, dividend income, AGI, and total income, as well as in their reporting of various itemized deductions.

It should be emphasized that the reporting response of, say, wages and salaries is not the same as, say, a simple labor supply response. Although reporting behavior is certainly influenced by any changes in hours worked or in labor-force participation rates that may occur in response to tax reform, the reporting decision is a far broader decision. It is affected also by behavioral changes in such dimensions as employee compensation, itemized deductions, the realization of incomes, tax compliance, and the like.[8] Similar comments apply to other reporting decisions.

Importantly, it should also be emphasized that this reporting response is likely to vary for individuals at different levels of income and with different forms of income, and it may also vary over different tax regimes. As implied earlier, the magnitude of the change in incentives faced by, say, higher-income individuals is significantly different from that faced by lower-income individuals. Also, the ability to vary the reporting of, say, wages and salaries is not likely to be the same as that for capital gains.

We use several approaches in our estimation of the reporting responses of the rich. The starting point is a basic ordinary least squares (OLS) specification for each form of reporting behavior, or

$$Y = \beta X + \varepsilon \qquad\qquad (6.1)$$

where Y is some reported item, β is a vector of parameters (including a constant), X is a vector of individual characteristics, and ε is an error term. By estimating separate equations for different reported items, we are able to measure differential responses across these various items.

Individual characteristics include: a dummy variable for *marital status*, equal to 1 if married and 0 otherwise; the number of *children*, as reported through dependent exemptions; a dummy variable for the receipt of *unemployment compensation*, equal to 1 if unemployment compensation is reported and 0 otherwise; a dummy variable for *elderly* status, equal to 1 if the elderly deduction is claimed and 0 otherwise; a dummy variable for *itemization* status, equal to 1 if the individual itemizes deductions on the federal tax return and 0 otherwise; a dummy variable for the use of *schedule C* (for reporting income from a business or a profession operated as a sole proprietor), equal to 1 if the individual files a schedule C form and 0 otherwise; and a dummy variable for the use of *schedule E* (for reporting income from rental real estate, royalties, partnerships, S corporations, estates, and trusts), equal to 1 if the individual files a schedule E form and 0 otherwise.

We modify equation (6.1) to incorporate the impact of taxpayer reporting behavior stemming from the major changes in taxation represented by TRA86, OBRA90, and OBRA93. In particular, we apply a method of estimation that has sometimes been called the differences approach and has been increasingly employed in the analysis of, for instance, labor supply decisions (Angrist 1991; Eissa and Liebman 1996), minimum wages (Card 1992), and health insurance (Gruber 1994; Gruber and Poterba 1994). TRA86, OBRA90, and OBRA93 each constituted a significant break from previous tax policy. If we can control for the major influences on reporting behavior that reflect factors such as the growth in income over time and changes in the definition of the tax base, then any differences in reported incomes that we observe between 1984 and 1989 will be largely due to modifications in individual behavior in response to TRA86, and any differences in reported incomes that we observe between 1989 and 1994 will be largely due to modifications in individual behavior in response to OBRA90 and OBRA93.

The basic notion underlying the differences approach is to use the momentous changes in tax policy stemming from TRA86, OBRA90, and OBRA93 as a natural experiment, comparable to controlled experiments in the natural sciences. Suppose that we assume that a tax innovation like TRA86 (the natural experiment) affects one group of taxpayers (the treatment group) but not another group (the control group). If we measure the change in response of each group (the group difference), then the difference between these responses is the "difference-in-difference" estimate of the impact of taxation.

It should be noted that the use of the differences approach is not without some difficulties. As emphasized by James Heckman (1996) and Leonard Burman (1997), the differences approach assumes that the experiment affected only the treatment group and that other events over the period affected both groups equally, even though it is difficult to know this. In particular, if there is a difference in the trend growth of income for the treatment and the control groups, and if this difference is independent of any tax changes, then the differences approach will mistakenly attribute this change in behavior to tax changes. In fact, Austan Goolsbee (this volume) argues that recent trends in the compensation of higher-income individuals versus lower-income individuals are quite different; that is, the relative income of the rich has increased significantly in recent years, independently of any tax changes, so that a difference-in-difference estimator overstates the marginal tax rate responses of the rich. The approach also often attributes the difference-in-difference estimate to a specific feature of the experiment, such as changes in marginal tax rates, even though there are numerous other tax provisions that are also changed by major tax bills like TRA86, OBRA90, and OBRA93. We discuss the relevance of these issues for our estimation results later.

The crucial issue in the differences approach is how to determine the sources of identifying variation. As discussed in more detail in the next section, we use several sources of identification. The most obvious source is a time-specific factor (for example, pre- versus post-TRA86, or pre- versus post-OBRA90 or -OBRA93). We also use an individual-specific factor (such as individuals who are high-income versus those who are low-income). These variables are introduced as separate dummy variables and as interacted variables.

To illustrate the differences approach, consider the information on, say, wages and salaries pre- and post-TRA86 in table 6.2. The simplest comparison of the effect of TRA86 on the reporting decisions of individuals is between the 1984 and 1989 levels. This time-specific comparison shows that the reporting of wage income increased on average by $177 (or $25,447 to $25,270) over this period, controlling for nominal changes in income over time, and this is one measure of the effect of tax reform on reporting behavior. When expressed as a percentage change (or 0.7 percent) by the use of the difference in the natural logarithms, and then divided by the percentage change in marginal tax rates (or −7.2 percent), this "difference" (D) estimator is one measure (or −0.1) of the marginal tax rate elasticity of wages and salaries.

However, it may be inappropriate to attribute this change in wages entirely to TRA86, since individual-specific factors may also be responsible, and it may also be necessary to allow for differential responses by income class. Another comparison, a difference-in-difference (DID) estimator, introduces such individual-specific factors with the time-specific factors and also allows us to identify the differential responsiveness of high-income individuals. Suppose that it is assumed that high-income individuals (say, those in the top 1 percent of the income distribution) behave differently than all other individuals, before and after TRA86. The difference in the average amount of wages and salaries reported by the top 1 percent between 1984 and 1989 is $49,209, while the difference for all other individuals is $–318; these are denoted the time differences within the high-and low-income groups in wages between 1984 and 1989. The difference between the two income groups in 1984 is $132,452, and $181,979 for 1989; these are denoted the individual differences at a point in time. This difference-in-difference in wages and salaries is therefore $49,527, equal either to ($49,209 to $–318) or to ($181,979 to $132,452); it can be expressed as a percentage, and when divided by a similar calculation for the difference-in-difference in marginal tax rates, it can be converted to a marginal tax rate elasticity for wages and salaries. This estimator equals –1.2.

The efficiency of the differences approach can be increased by controlling for other factors that may affect taxpayer decisions. In a regression context, this suggests that we estimate a variant on equation (6.1). If the only source of identification is time-specific (say, a dummy variable TRA86, equal to 1 for 1989 observations and 0 for 1984 observations), then we can estimate

$$Y = \beta X + \phi_1 \, TRA86 + \varepsilon \qquad (6.2)$$

where Y, X, β, and ε are defined as in equation (6.1). The coefficient on TRA86, or ϕ_1, represents the difference estimator for the effects of tax reform on reporting behavior and measures the difference in reporting of, say, wages and salaries, before versus after the enactment of TRA86. If we introduce individual-specific variation with time-specific variation, then we estimate

$$Y = \beta X + \phi_1 \, TRA86 + \phi_2 \, High\ Income + \phi_3 \, TRA86 \times High\ Income + \varepsilon \qquad (6.3)$$

where High Income is a dummy variable equal to 1 for individuals in the top 1 percent of income recipients and 0 otherwise. Now it is the coefficient on TRA86 × High Income, or ϕ_3, that represents the difference-in-difference estimator for the effects of tax reform on reporting behavior. More precisely, ϕ_3 measures the difference in reporting of wages and salaries of high-income individuals relative to low-income individuals after the enactment of TRA86; it measures whether the reporting of high-income individuals changed more after the tax reform than did the reporting of low-income individuals. This framework is easily modified to incorporate the other tax bills or various demographic variables.

We apply this basic differences approach to the entire sample and to the high-income subsamples (the top 1 percent and the top 0.5 percent) for the two separate periods 1984 to 1989 and 1989 to 1994. Also, by estimating for the two periods, we examine separately any taxpayer differential responses to TRA86 and to OBRA90 and OBRA93. We have also estimated a wide range of alternative specifications, with relatively little impact on our results. In some specifications we have used the shares of the income types as the dependent variables. We have used different definitions for the top income earners in the construction of the individual-specific dummy variable High Income. We have also estimated all specifications using both unweighted and weighted ITMF data.[9] All of these results are available on request.

RESULTS
Who Are the Rich?

Table 6.1 reports some limited demographic information on the rich, as well as on all taxpayers, generated from the ITMFs. This information reveals that the rich are different from us, but not that different from each other. For example, in 1984 nearly 38 percent of all returns reported some dependents, but over one-half of the two top earner groups reported dependents. Further, in 1984 the very rich were significantly more likely than the average taxpayer to claim the elderly deduction, to be married, and to be self-employed. Similar demographic characteristics occurred in 1994, with one notable exception: the rich are no longer more likely to report an elderly deduction. This latter result is consistent with other information that shows a growth in the number of "new millionaires," or those relatively young individuals who made their incomes as entrepreneurs in the 1980s and 1990s.

The Composition of Income

Table 6.2 shows the composition of comprehensive income for the top income holders, as well as for the entire taxpaying population. The pre-TRA86 composition of income is heavily weighted toward nonwage forms of income for both the top 1 percent and top 0.5 percent of the taxpaying population. In 1984 wages and salaries amounted to 44 and 38 percent, respectively, of the reported comprehensive income of the top 1 percent and the top 0.5 percent of filers. The entire population received about twice as much of their income in wages and salaries (79 per-

Table 6.1   Demographic Characteristics, 1984 and 1994

Characteristic	Percentage of Top 1 Percent	Percentage of Top 0.5 Percent	Percentage of All Returns
1984			
Dependents	53.41	50.88	37.97
Elderly	20.92	25.28	11.96
Married	86.83	85.89	48.62
Self-employed	26.93	28.30	11.30
1994			
Dependents	50.62	47.81	36.20
Elderly	13.93	14.30	12.00
Married	88.37	88.47	44.23
Self-employed	29.77	28.44	13.64

Source: Authors' calculations from ITMFs, various years.

Table 6.2   Composition of Comprehensive Income, 1984, 1989, and 1994

Income Type	1984			1989			1994		
	Top 1 Percent	Top 0.5 Percent	All	Top 1 Percent	Top 0.5 Percent	All	Top 1 Percent	Top 0.5 Percent	All
Wages and salaries	44.03%	38.08%	79.30%	41.12%	37.09%	73.07%	47.02%	42.83%	73.89%
Interest	5.71	5.70	5.57	7.61	7.98	5.60	5.19	5.73	3.16
Dividends	4.26	4.42	2.21	5.67	5.97	2.42	4.44	4.82	1.99
Net capital gains	34.92	40.70	5.69	19.26	22.05	4.29	15.17	17.68	3.34
Schedule C net income	4.54	3.50	3.12	5.37	4.32	3.95	5.67	4.69	4.07
Schedule E net income	3.83	4.53	-0.13	13.55	15.18	2.04	19.22	21.60	3.35
Social Security benefits	0.44	0.32	1.64	0.39	0.28	2.35	0.48	0.33	2.81

Source: Authors' calculations from ITMFs, various years.

cent) for the same period. For the high-income earners, capital gains income played an especially important role in 1984, when it accounted for over one-third of total comprehensive income for the upper income earners. At the same time the general population earned less than 6 percent of their income in the form of capital gains.

In 1989 the composition of income changed somewhat, at least partially in response to TRA86. Net capital gains income dropped significantly for the top income earners. Also, schedule E income as a share grew the most of any one item, probably owing to a combination of the reduction in passive losses allowed by law and to the transfer of C corporations to S corporations stemming from the relative reduction in individual versus corporate income tax rates. Although there were similar patterns of change in the composition of income for the entire population, this schedule E shift was much greater for high-income earners. Other changes in the composition of income between 1984 and 1989 were relatively minor.

From 1989 to 1994 there was a movement away from capital income (or interest, dividend, and capital gains income) as a share of total comprehensive income and toward wages and salaries income. Recall that in 1993 there was a significant increase in the top marginal tax rate on taxable income. If capital income is somewhat more movable than other forms of income, then it is not surprising to see evidence of this shift in the composition of income for high-income earners.

Levels of Reported Items

Table 6.3 shows the mean levels of various tax return items for the top 1 percent of tax filers, and the mean of all tax filers (in italics in parentheses), for the years 1984, 1989, and 1994; also shown in table 6.3 is the coefficient of variation for the top group (in parentheses). Table 6.4 presents similar information for the top 0.5 percent of tax filers. Recall that all amounts are adjusted for changes in prices and are in constant dollars; also, the individual income item entries are adjusted for changes in tax base definitions over the period.

Over the period 1984 to 1989 most mean real reported entries grew significantly at all income levels, especially the various types of reported incomes. For example, average real wages and salaries of the top 1 percent of filers increased on average by 28 percent, interest by 83 percent, dividends by 83 percent, and pensions by 34 percent (table 6.3). Mean schedule C net income (or income from sole proprietorships) and especially schedule E net income (or income from real estate, royalties, partnerships, S corporations, estates, and trusts) rose enormously, by 62 and 386 percent, respectively. Overall mean real AGI of the top 1 percent grew from $269,000 to more than $467,000, an average increase of 77 percent; our measure of mean comprehensive income rose by 38 percent, from $383,000 to nearly $500,000. The increase in schedule E net income is particularly striking and is probably due in large part to the increased incentive, stemming from TRA86, for the use by individuals of S corporations rather than C corporations. Note, however, that average capital gains fell significantly from 1984 to 1989, from $129,000 to $96,000, as preferential treatment of realized gains was eliminated by TRA86.

It is also worth noting that mean real levels of itemized deductions rose significantly for the top 1 percent of tax filers. State and local income taxes, mortgage interest, and charitable contributions all increased from 1984 to 1989.

Table 6.3 Means and Coefficients of Variation for Top 1 Percent of Tax Filers, Tax Years 1984, 1989, and 1994, in Constant Dollars (*Population Means*)

	Means (Coefficient of Variation)		
Variable	1994	1989	1984
Comprehensive income	455,768 (1,618)	499,991 (1,913)	383,416 (1,839)
	(34,432)	*(34,824)*	*(31,864)*
Adjusted gross income (AGI)	451,248 (1,644)	467,152 (2,156)	268,986 (1,886)
	(32,889)	*(33,462)*	*(29,201)*
Wages and salaries	214,305 (1,138)	205,606 (1,248)	156,397 (903)
	(25,443)	*(25,447)*	*(25,270)*
Interest	23,634 (6,381)	38,048 (3,548)	21,439 (2,786)
	(1,088)	*(1,948)*	*(1,774)*
Dividends	20,228 (5,431)	28,353 (7,799)	22,908 (4,566)
	(687)	*(841)*	*(705)*
Schedule C net income/(loss)	25,823 (3,780)	26,861 (4,038)	15,815 (4,498)
	(1,402)	*(1,375)*	*(996)*
Net capital gains/(loss)	69,169 (7,298)	96,306 (7,347)	127,992 (4,835)
	(1,152)	*(1,492)*	*(1,815)*
Schedule E net income/(loss)	87,591 (3,968)	67,747 (4,820)	13,169 (14,208)
	(1,153)	*(710)*	*(−40)*
Social Security benefits	2,203 (1,912)	1,973 (1,757)	1,969 (1,717)
	(969)	*(818)*	*(521)*
State and local income taxes	24,324 (2,174)	24,361 (2,620)	15,773 (2,102)
	(885)	*(837)*	*(828)*
Home mortgage interest	12,304 (773)	13,330 (913)	6,599 (1,024)
	(1,546)	*(1,508)*	*(1,027)*
Total contributions	14,626 (6,723)	13,192 (11,082)	11,905 (5,155)
	(594)	*(576)*	*(589)*
Total income tax	126,600 (1,734)	111,952 (2,118)	89,768 (2,111)
	(4,493)	*(4,493)*	*(4,221)*

Source: Authors' calculations from ITMFs, various years.

As shown in table 6.4, the reported incomes of the top 0.5 percent of tax filers show a similar pattern for the years 1984 to 1989, with, if anything, slightly larger percentage increases. Specific forms of income (for example, wages and salaries, interest, dividends, schedules C and E incomes, pensions) rose enormously. Mean AGI and comprehensive income also rose by slightly greater percentage amounts than experienced by the top 1 percent of filers. Again, capital gains income fell for the top 0.5 percent group, from $226,000 to $168,000, and itemized deductions all increased.

Compared to these two top groups, the average tax filer did not fare nearly so well over the period from 1984 to 1989. Although most forms of income rose, the increases were generally quite modest. For example, average real wages and salaries grew by only $177, AGI by $4,261, and comprehensive income by $2,960. Like the two top groups, however, the schedules C and E incomes of the average taxpayer rose, and mean capital gains fell. There are no consistent patterns in itemized deductions.

Table 6.4   Means and Coefficients of Variation for Top 0.5 Percent of Tax Filers, Tax Years 1984, 1989, and 1994 in Constant Dollars (*Population Means*)

Variable	Means (Coefficient of Variation)		
	1994	1989	1984
Comprehensive income	671,179 (1,419)	760,264 (1,346)	580,493 (1,284)
	(34,432)	*(34,824)*	*(31,864)*
Adjusted gross income (AGI)	666,832 (1,165)	709,204 (1,476)	388,319 (1,362)
	(32,889)	*(33,462)*	*(29,201)*
Wages and salaries	287,447 (874)	281,945 (925)	201,185 (695)
	(25,443)	*(25,447)*	*(25,270)*
Interest	38,469 (4,164)	60,695 (2,336)	32,626 (2,786)
	(1,088)	*(1,948)*	*(1,774)*
Dividends	32,326 (3,601)	45,357 (5,152)	37,159 (2,996)
	(687)	*(841)*	*(703)*
Schedule C net income (loss)	31,458 (3,187)	32,877 (4,038)	17,787 (3,947)
	(1,402)	*(1,375)*	*(966)*
Net capital gains/(loss)	118,659 (4,522)	167,670 (4,440)	226,049 (2,901)
	(1,152)	*(1,492)*	*(1,815)*
Schedule E net income/(loss)	144,965 (2,530)	115,377 (2,947)	23,747 (838)
	(1,153)	*(710)*	*(−40)*
Social Security benefits	2,191 (1,492)	2,098 (1,295)	8,717 (1,302)
	(969)	*(818)*	*(521)*
State and local income taxes	36,489 (1,524)	38,146 (1,739)	23,978 (1442)
	(885)	*(837)*	*(848)*
Home mortgage interest	13,559 (629)	14,998 (732)	6,833 (862)
	(1,546)	*(1,508)*	*(1,027)*
Total contributions	22,975 (4,554)	20,985 (7,319)	19,069 (3,417)
	(594)	*(576)*	*(589)*
Total income tax	196,948 (1,162)	173,354 (1,418)	141,686 (1,399)
	(4,493)	*(4,493)*	*(4,221)*

Source: Authors' calculations from ITMFs, various years.

The experiences of the different groups of individuals for the period from 1989 to 1994 were substantially different. Although mean real wages and salaries continued to rise modestly for the top two groups of filers, most other forms of their income tended to fall. For example, mean real AGI of the top 1 percent (top 0.5 percent) fell by 4 percent (6 percent), and mean real comprehensive income of the top 1 percent (top 0.5 percent) dropped by 9 percent (12 percent). AGI and comprehensive income also fell for the average taxpayer, but these drops (2 and 3 percent, respectively) were slightly smaller than those experienced by the top groups.

It should be noted that many of the entries in tables 6.3 and 6.4 are simple averages of reported items for the two top income groups. These averages mask considerable—and sometimes enormous—variation in some specific reported items, as measured by the coefficient of variation (CV), calculated as the standard deviation of an entry divided by its mean. Although there is relatively little variation in broad-based measures of income like AGI or comprehensive income for the top income groups, the component parts of income often vary enormously. For example, the

CVs for taxable interest, dividends, schedule C income, capital gains, and schedule E income typically exceeded three thousand for the top 1 percent in 1984, 1989, and 1994, and some specific entries, such as passive or nonpassive losses, have CVs well in excess of ten thousand. The CVs for the top 0.5 percent also often vary enormously. These results suggest that the rich are a very diverse group when it comes to the source of their incomes.

Shares in Income of the Rich

The wealthy obviously hold a significant amount of the reported income of the tax filers in our samples. Table 6.5 shows the percentage of various income items received by the top 1 percent and top 0.5 percent of the tax-filing population for each year, 1984, 1989, and 1994. As shown in these data, the top income earners received over 11 percent of total comprehensive income in 1984. The greatest concentration of any one income type was in the form of capital gains income in 1984, when the affluent held over 70 percent of reported capital gains. The difference between the concentration of income for the top 1 percent and the top 0.5 percent is quite subtle. For example, the 0.5 percent group held about 75 percent of all comprehensive income held by the top 1 percent group, 64 percent of the wages held by the top 1 percent, and 88 percent of the capital gains income held by the top 1 percent in 1984.

By 1989 there was an increase in this concentration of all income in the top groups. The top 1 percent increased their holdings of comprehensive income by about three percentage points over 1984. In virtually all categories the top earners' shares increased (with the exception of capital gains, pension, and Social Security income). This general growth did not, however, change the relative concentration between the top 1 percent group and the top 0.5 percent group. For example, in 1989 the top 0.5 percent held 76 percent of the total comprehensive income of the top 1 percent group. As discussed earlier, this was the period of the explosion in schedule E income.

Table 6.5   Distribution of Income (as Percentage of Total)

	1984		1989		1994	
Income Type	Top 1 Percent	Top 0.5 Percent	Top 1 Percent	Top 0.5 Percent	Top 1 Percent	Top 0.5 Percent
Comprehensive income	11.78%	8.92%	14.39%	10.96%	13.73%	10.47%
Wages and salaries	6.19	3.98	8.10	5.56	8.73	6.07
Interest	12.08	9.19	19.56	15.63	22.52	18.99
Dividends	32.47	26.33	33.75	27.05	30.53	25.27
Net capital gains	70.52	62.27	64.46	56.04	62.25	55.33
Schedule C net income	15.88	8.93	19.57	12.00	19.09	12.05
Schedule E net income[a]	−326.21	−294.12	95.59	81.56	78.73	67.49
Social Security benefits	3.77	2.27	2.42	1.29	2.36	1.21

Source: Authors' calculations from ITMFs, various years.

[a] The total amount of schedule E net income is negative in 1984, while the amounts received by the top 1 percent and the top 0.5 percent are positive.

The trend from 1989 to 1994 differed from that of 1984 to 1989. The top income groups saw a slight decrease in their holdings of total comprehensive income, from 14.4 percent of the total to 13.7 percent. During this period the top income earners increased their share of wage and salary income slightly over the earlier period, while their share of capital income fell. As explained later in the chapter, these trends are consistent with expected responses (true behavioral or timing) to the tax changes that occurred during these periods.

Growth in Incomes

Table 6.6 shows the indexed percentage growth in each individual income item for the top income filers, as well as for the entire filing population, from 1984 to 1989. Over this period there was a substantial growth in income for the top earners. The patterns of income growth for the top two income groups are again somewhat similar, but the patterns for the top groups are very different from those for the entire population. The rich filers saw a larger increase in every income item except for capital gains, schedule E income, and pension and Social Security income. The relative growth in comprehensive income was almost twice as large for the high-income earners as for the entire population. Capital income (except capital gains) soared for these top income groups—again, relative to the entire population.

The second period tells a much different story (see table 6.7). The relatively large growth in income items in the period from 1984 to 1989 was followed by a slight decrease in total indexed comprehensive income for the top income groups, while the overall population witnessed a small increase in comprehensive income. For the top groups, gains came from wages and salaries (much less so for the entire population) and from other, smaller forms of income. Capital income growth was negative for all filers. This is again roughly consistent with some expectations associated with tax law changes.

Another way to investigate these changes is by allocating the total growth in various income amounts to the top income groups. For example, total comprehensive income grew for all taxpayers by over $671 billion from 1984 to 1989. Of this total,

Table 6.6   Total Indexed Growth, 1984 to 1989

Income Type	Top 1 Percent		Top 0.5 Percent		All	
	Total	Mean	Total	Mean	Total	Mean
Comprehensive income	47.48%	30.40%	48.43%	30.97%	20.74%	7.01%
Wages and salaries	48.68	31.46	58.82	40.14	13.63	0.70
Interest	100.70	77.47	110.82	86.03	23.97	9.81
Dividends	39.97	23.75	38.33	22.06	34.69	19.43
Net capital gains	−13.26	−24.76	−14.89	−25.83	−5.43	−17.75
Schedule C net income	92.08	69.85	109.47	84.43	55.85	38.05
Schedule E net income	481.83	414.44	450.61	385.86	2085.70	1875.00
Social Security benefits	13.39	0.20	0.25	0.03	77.08	57.01
AGI	96.41	73.67	106.98	82.63	26.17	11.82

Source: Authors' calculations from ITMFs, various years.

Table 6.7   Total Indexed Growth, 1989 to 1994

Income Type	Top 1 Percent		Top 0.5 Percent		All	
	Total	Mean	Total	Mean	Total	Mean
Comprehensive income	−1.80%	−3.78%	−3.01%	−4.81%	−0.22%	−1.91%
Wages and salaries	8.29	6.51	9.14	7.55	1.28	−0.83
Interest	−55.83	−58.86	−54.24	−56.93	−67.09	−70.58
Dividends	−36.90	−39.56	−37.85	−40.25	−18.69	−21.33
Net capital gains	−31.46	−31.94	−28.74	−29.37	−21.60	−21.90
Schedule C net income	3.97	2.10	2.21	0.51	0.89	−1.18
Schedule E net income	11.72	10.00	9.28	7.70	27.79	26.27
Social Security benefits	10.63	8.95	8.94	7.33	18.29	16.53
AGI	−4.57	−6.61	−5.60	−7.44	−0.81	−2.96

Source: Authors' calculations from ITMFs, various years.

the top 1 percent of tax filers claimed about 27 percent of the growth, and the top 0.5 percent claimed 21 percent. This result holds for most types of capital income, general pension income, and income from schedules C and E. While the top income earners' total comprehensive income decreased for the period 1989 to 1994, their shares of wages and salaries, interest income, and dividend income grew substantially.

Estimation Results

Tables 6.8 and 6.9 report some selected results from the difference-in-difference estimations for charitable donations, wages and salaries, AGI, and comprehensive income, for the two periods 1984 to 1989 and 1989 to 1994. The results for other forms of itemized deductions (for example, mortgage interest deductions and state and local income taxes), as well as for the different forms of capital income (such as interest, dividend, and capital gains incomes), are more variable but generally show similar patterns.

Recall that it is the coefficient of the interaction term (for example, TRA86 × High Income in table 6.8) that represents the difference-in-difference estimator for the effects of tax reform on the reporting behavior of the affluent. More precisely, this coefficient, denoted ϕ_3 in equation (6.3), measures the difference in reporting of, say, wages and salaries of high-income individuals relative to low-income individuals before versus after the enactment of tax reform; it measures whether the reporting of high-income individuals changed more after the tax reform than did the reporting of low-income individuals. The comparable coefficient in table 6.9 is on the term OBRA × High Income, where OBRA is a dummy variable equal to 1 for 1994 observations and 0 for the 1989 observations and High Income is defined as in table 6.8. Note that we present two sets of results in each table. In the first set the data include all tax filers, while in the second set we limit our observations to the top 1 percent of tax filers in order to focus on the reporting behavior of this group of individuals. For these latter results, High Income is defined as a dummy variable equal to 1 for individuals in the top 0.5 percent of all tax filers and 0 otherwise. Other variable definitions were discussed earlier.

Table 6.8   OLS Estimation Results, 1984 to 1989

| | All Tax Filers | | | | Top 1 Percent of Tax Filers | | | |
| | Dependent Variable | | | | Dependent Variable | | | |
Independent Variable	Charitable Donations	Wages and Salaries	AGI	Comprehensive Income	Charitable Donations	Wages and Salaries	AGI	Comprehensive Income
Constant	−173*	11,248***	9,408***	10,458***	−10,647*	47,835***	−138,605***	85,970*
Marital status	55	15,059***	14,371***	15,873***	−3,541	46,072***	5,099	−10,778
Children	8	1,523***	496	261	−349	10,602***	−10,072*	−9,270
Unemployment	−127	−3,586***	−3,061*	−2,761*	−4,598	−31,245*	−106,937*	−75,945
Elderly	375**	−22,694***	−4,535***	−1,309	13,386***	−126,764***	21,397	28,681
Itemization	1,352***	22,351***	28,013***	27,085***	13,323***	−67,507***	262,763***	62,671*
Schedule C	166	−12,391***	−4,676***	−2,925***	4,402**	67,528***	7,219	46,878***
Schedule E	435**	2,563***	7,249***	10,550***	4,145*	−657	77,979***	90,165***
TRA86	102	2,591***	5,421***	4,125***	427	87	43,955**	10,548
High Income[a]	12,261***	128,952***	251,142***	381,556***	16,487***	116,675***	275,785***	472,756**
TRA86 × High Income	−2,126**	18,062***	114,039***	9,156	−4,381*	17,766***	129,751***	31,015
R^2	0.010	0.266	0.068	0.093	0.003	0.075	0.027	0.030
DID marginal tax rate elasticity	0.8	−0.7	−1.7	—	0.6	−1.2	−2.4	—

[a]. For regressions using all tax filers, High Income is a dummy variable equal to 1 for individual in the top 1 percent of tax filers and 0 otherwise. For regressions using the top 1 percent of tax filers, High Income is a dummy variable equal to 1 for individuals in the top 0.5 percent of tax filers and 0 otherwise.

***:$P \le .001$; **:$P \le .01$; *:$P \le .05$

Table 6.9 OLS Estimation Results, 1989 to 1994

| | All Tax Filers | | | | Top 1 Percent of Tax Filers | | | |
| | Dependent Variable | | | | Dependent Variable | | | |
Independent Variable	Charitable Donations	Wages and Salaries	AGI	Comprehensive Income	Charitable Donations	Wages and Salaries	AGI	Comprehensive Income
Constant	-123	13,138***	13,003***	13,304***	-15,858***	83,563***	-26,249	131,994***
Marital status	36	15,564***	15,804***	17,065***	-1,310	47,801***	-17,454	-11,573
Children	10	1,773***	718	381	-634	8,198***	-9,800*	-15,491**
Unemployment	-136	-3,883***	-3,421*	-3,294**	-6,217	-94,577***	-210,868***	-111,145***
Elderly	428**	-22,461***	-3,905***	-274	16,474***	-137,627***	21,400	30,800*
Itemization	1,573***	24,349***	31,267***	29,514***	16,807***	57,692***	208,348***	55,363*
Schedule C	111	-12,050***	-4,739***	-3,378***	2,476	-72,461***	4,742	12,997
Schedule E	464**	-3,883***	10,164***	12,424***	5,690**	-20,477***	113,351***	107,291***
OBRA	4	206	-116	-43	1,512	3,154	13,670	14,702
High-Income	11,424***	161,746***	408,433***	439,353***	13,667***	151,873***	448,659***	488,530***
OBRA* High-Income	866*	449	-40,311***	-31,034***	3,088*	-2,846*	-34,662*	-32,783*
R^2	0.006	0.249	0.077	0.112	0.003	0.066	0.028	0.034
DID marginal tax rate elasticity	0.6	—	-0.8	-0.6	0.6	-0.5	-0.9	-0.8

[a.] For regressions using all tax filers, High Income is a dummy variable equal to 1 for individual in the top 1 percent of tax filers and 0 otherwise. For regressions using the top 1 percent of tax filers, High Income is a dummy variable equal to 1 for individuals in the top 0.5 percent of tax filers and 0 otherwise.

***:P ≤ .001; **:P ≤ .01; *:P ≤ .05

As shown in table 6.8 by the coefficient on TRA86, tax reform by itself had a consistently positive impact on the income-reporting decisions of all tax filers, as well as on the charitable donations of these individuals. Not surprisingly, high-income individuals also reported much greater amounts of income and donated significantly greater amounts to charities than did low-income individuals, as shown by the coefficient on High Income. Of most importance, the coefficient on the interaction term, or ϕ_3, demonstrates that the reporting decisions of high-income individuals increased relative to those of low-income individuals after the enactment of tax reform; that is, the reporting of high-income individuals changed more after the tax reform than did the reporting of low-income individuals. This difference is $18,062 for wages and $114,039 for AGI; the coefficient is not statistically significant for comprehensive income. This coefficient varies considerably across income type, with a much larger magnitude for AGI than for wages and salaries. Charitable donations responded as expected to the decline in marginal tax rates, as indicated by the negative coefficient of $-2,126 on the interaction term.[10]

It would be convenient to attribute all of these changes in reporting directly to the changes in taxation represented by TRA86. However, it should be recognized that ϕ_3 may also measure nontax factors that increased the relative incomes of high-income individuals, factors such as technological change, international trade, the returns to education, and the like.[11] Also, as noted earlier, there are good reasons for cautious interpretation of the results from the differences method.

Despite these concerns, we find a similar pattern when we use different definitions of High Income. When High Income is defined as a dummy variable equal to 1 for individuals in the top half of all tax filers and 0 otherwise, the sign on the interaction term remains positive and significant for most forms of reported income in the period from 1984 to 1989, while this coefficient is not significant for the period from 1989 to 1994. Not surprisingly, however, the magnitude of the coefficient drops significantly, since the coefficient is now measuring the relative difference in reporting of groups of individuals whose incomes are much closer in size (for example, the top half versus the bottom half rather than the top 1 percent versus the bottom 99 percent). For example, the impact of TRA86 on reported wages changes from $18,062 in table 6.8 to $3,522, and its impact on AGI changes from $114,039 to $10,481.

We find similar results even when the sample includes only the top 1 percent of tax filers, or a sample in which nontax factors should operate in broadly similar ways on all individuals. As shown in table 6.8, ϕ_3 is large, positive, and statistically significant for wages and AGI, and it is negative and significant for charitable donations.[12] The coefficient ϕ_3 also tends to be larger when the sample is limited to the top 1 percent of income earners. These results suggest that there is a difference in reporting behavior even among the very rich.

Importantly, our results are quite similar when we apply the differences approach to the tax changes of the 1990s, a period in which there is little evidence of different trends in the income growth of high- versus low-income groups. These results are reported in table 6.9. When the sample includes all taxpayers, the coefficient on the interaction term is consistently negative and significant (except for wages and salaries), so that the amounts of income reported by the rich tended to fall more than those of other individuals; when the sample includes only the top 1 percent of tax filers, a similar pattern is found.[13] As for charitable donations, ϕ_3 is positive and significant for both samples. Given that TRA86 substantially reduced marginal tax rates while OBRA90 and OBRA93 raised rates, the results in table 6.9 are broadly consistent with those in table 6.8, in that both tend to show that income reporting and marginal tax rates are negatively related, while itemized deductions and marginal tax rates are positively related.

These DID estimates can be converted to marginal tax rate elasticities, as reported in tables 6.8 and 6.9.[14] In general, the income-reporting elasticities vary substantially, between −0.5 and −2.4 with a clustering around −1.0; the charitable donations elasticities are consistently less than 1. There is also a clear tendency for all of the elasticities to be higher in the earlier than in the later period, as well as for the income-reporting elasticities to vary across both the type of income and the nature of the sample. These reporting elasticities are similar to those estimated by Feldstein (1995) and Auten and Carroll (1997).[15]

The signs on the control variables are generally consistent with expectations. When the sample includes all tax filers, married individuals, couples with children, and individuals who itemize or who have schedule E income tend to have higher forms of all reported incomes. In contrast, individuals who receive unemployment compensation, who are elderly, and who report schedule C income typically have lower reported incomes. When the sample includes only the top 1 percent of tax filers, these results change somewhat. For example, when the elderly report lower levels of wage income, they sometimes have higher levels of other reported incomes (for example, capital gains, dividends, and interest). Not surprisingly, the receipt of schedule E income among the top groups is associated with lower levels of wages but higher levels of AGI and comprehensive income.

CONCLUSIONS

So, are the rich different? Our results indicate clearly that the answer is yes. The rich differ from the average taxpayer in terms of their demographics, their income composition, and their income changes. There is also some evidence that they differ from the average population in their responses to tax changes. And our results suggest that the rich are different from each other, at least in terms of the magnitudes of their responses to tax law changes. It seems likely that these differential responses are due largely to the greater control and flexibility of the rich in overall financial matters, especially in the forms of their compensation.

Nevertheless, these results must be tempered by the difficulties inherent in any empirical work. There is little doubt that data on the behavior of the rich are limited and flawed in important ways; in particular, the data do not allow for a complete examination of timing versus accounting versus real responses of the rich. There is also little doubt that the estimation method used here is subject to some criticism, even though we believe that the limitations of the differences approach do not negate our main results. Until—if ever—these issues are resolved, our conclusions must remain suggestive.

We are grateful for helpful comments from preconference and conference participants, especially Dan Feenberg.

NOTES

1. Also, the reporting decisions of all taxpayers have been examined. For example, Lawrence Lindsey (1987) uses information from 1979 and 1982 samples of individual tax returns to estimate reporting changes from the Economic Recovery Tax Act of 1981, and Martin Feldstein (1995) and Gerry Auten and Robert Carroll (1997) use panel data from individual tax returns to estimate reporting changes arising from the Tax Reform Act of 1986. All of these studies have found that the individual reporting responses can be substantial. For general discussions of behavioral responses to taxation, see Aaron and Pechman (1981), Slemrod (1992), and Auerbach and Slemrod (1997).

2. An especially informative guide to tax policies of the 1980s is Steuerle (1992).

3. In part because of changes in the federal income tax, many states also altered their state income taxes. Among states that relied heavily on the definition of the income tax base in the federal income tax, a typical state action was to reduce marginal tax rates in the state individual income tax in order to avoid a major income tax increase on state citizens. For a similar reason, another common action was to modify in some way the federal base definition. In some states that changed neither their rates nor their definition of the tax base state income taxes rose significantly. For a detailed discussion of state and local responses to TRA86, see Bahl (1987), Courant and Rubinfeld (1987), Courant and Gramlich (1992), and Metcalf (1993).

4. For more detailed information on these data sets, see Internal Revenue Service (1984, 1989, 1994).

5. We exclude dependent returns because of the significant change in tax treatment of such returns between 1984 and 1989.

6. Note that total income does not include such items as nonretirement transfer payments, fringe benefits, unrealized capital gains, and underreported income, items about which there is no information on the individual tax return; it also does not include income that is mistakenly or purposely underreported or that is not reported at all on tax returns. See Erard and Ho (1995) for an analysis of the factors that determine nonfiling.

7. See Levy and Murname (1992), Papadimitriou and Wolff (1993), and Danziger and Gottschalk (1995) for detailed discussions of studies that detail the distributional changes in the last several decades.

8. Lindsey (1987), Feldstein (1995), and Auten and Carroll (1997) make a similar point.

9. The use of weighted versus unweighted observations is discussed by DuMouchel and Duncan (1983).

10. Note also that the coefficient on the interaction term is not significant in regressions for dividend income, that it is positive and significant for interest income, and that it is negative and significant for capital gains income.

11. Again, see Levy and Murname (1992), Papadimitriou and Wolff (1993), and Danziger and Gottschalk (1995) for a discussion of these factors and their contributions to increasing inequality.

12. The coefficient and the interaction term for the top 1 percent of tax filers is positive and significant for interest income, negative and significant for capital gains income, and insignificant for dividend income.

13. The coefficient for ϕ_3 for the estimations of the period from 1989 to 1994 is consistently negative and significant for all other forms of income (such as dividend, interest, and capital gains income).

14. The elasticity based on equation (6.3), with TRA86 and High Income, is calculated as

$$([\ln(Y_{1989, \text{ High Income}}) - \ln(Y_{1989, \text{ Low Income}})] - [\ln(Y_{1984, \text{ High Income}}) - \ln(Y_{1984, \text{ Low Income}})])/$$
$$([\ln(\text{MTR}_{1989, \text{ High Income}}) - \ln(\text{MTR}_{1989, \text{ Low Income}})] - [\ln(\text{MTR}_{1984, \text{ High Income}}) - \ln(\text{MTR}_{1984, \text{ Low Income}})])$$

where $Y_{1989,\text{High Income}}$ is some type of reported income for high-income taxpayers in 1989, $MTR_{1989,\text{High Income}}$ is the combined federal-state marginal tax rate for high-income taxpayers in 1989, and so on. Other elasticities are calculated in a comparable manner.

15. Feldstein (1995) and Auten and Carroll (1997) report tax price elasticities rather than the marginal tax rate elasticities used here; that is, their elasticities equal $(\partial Y/\partial[1 - MTR])([1 - MTR]/Y)$, where Y is some form of reported income and MTR is the marginal tax rate. The elasticities reported here equal $(\partial Y/\partial[MTR])(MTR/Y)$. It is straightforward to convert one elasticity to the other.

REFERENCES

Aaron, Henry J., and Joseph A. Pechman, eds. 1981. *How Taxes Affect Economic Behavior.* Washington, D.C.: Brookings Institution.

Angrist, Joshua. 1991. "Grouped-Data Estimation and Testing in Simple Labor Supply Models." *Journal of Econometrics* 47(2): 243–66.

Auerbach, Alan J., and Joel Slemrod. 1997. "The Economic Effects of the Tax Reform Act of 1986." *Journal of Economic Literature* 35(2): 589–632.

Auten, Gerald, and Robert Carroll. 1997. "Behavior of the Affluent and the 1986 Tax Reform Act." Unpublished manuscript.

Bahl, Roy. 1987. "Urban Government Finance and Federal Income Tax Reform." *National Tax Journal* 40(1): 1–18.

Burman, Leonard. 1997. "Review of *Empirical Foundations of Household Taxation.*" *National Tax Journal* 50(2): 381–95.

Card, David. 1992. "The Effects of Minimum Wage Legislation: A Case Study of California." *Industrial and Labor Relations Review* 44(1): 38–54.

Courant, Paul N., and Edward M. Gramlich. 1992. "The Impact of the Tax Reform Act of 1986 on State and Local Fiscal Behavior." In *Do Taxes Matter?: The Impact of the Tax Reform Act of 1986,* edited by Joel Slemrod. Cambridge, Mass.: MIT Press.

Courant, Paul N., and Daniel R. Rubinfeld. 1987. "Tax Reform: Implications for the State-Local Public Sector." *Journal of Economic Perspectives* 1(1): 87–100.

Danziger, Sheldon, and Peter Gottschalk. 1995. *American Unequal.* Cambridge, Mass.: Harvard University Press.

DuMouchel, William H., and Greg J. Duncan. 1983. "Using Sample Survey Weights in Multiple Regression Analyses of Stratified Samples." *Journal of the American Statistical Association* 78(383): 535–43.

Eissa, Nada, and Jeffrey B. Liebman. 1996. "Labor Supply Response to the Earned Income Tax Credit." *Quarterly Journal of Economics* 111(2): 605–37.

Erard, Brian, and Chih-Chin Ho. 1995. "Searching for Ghosts: Who Are the Nonfilers and How Much Tax Do They Owe?" Unpublished manuscript. Carleton University, Northfield, Minn.

Feenberg, Daniel, and Martin Feldstein. 1995. "The Effect of Increased Tax Rates on Taxable Income and Economic Efficiency: A Preliminary Analysis of the 1993 Tax Rate Increases." Working Paper 5370. Cambridge, Mass.: National Bureau of Economic Research.

Feenberg, Daniel R., and James M. Poterba. 1992. "Income Inequality and the Incomes of Very-High-Income Taxpayers." In *Tax Policy and the Economy,* edited by James M. Poterba. Cambridge, Mass.: MIT Press.

Feldstein, Martin. 1995. "The Effect of Marginal Tax Rates on Taxable Income: A Panel Study of the 1986 Tax Reform Act." *Journal of Political Economy* 103(2): 551–76.

Gruber, Jonathan. 1994. "The Incidence of Mandated Maternity Benefits." *American Economic Review* 84(3): 622–41.

Gruber, Jonathan, and James M. Poterba. 1994. "Tax Incentives and the Decision to Purchase Health Insurance: Evidence from the Self-employed." *Quarterly Journal of Economics* 109(4): 701–33.

Heckman, James J. 1996. "Comment." In *Empirical Foundations of Household Taxation,* edited by Martin Feldstein and James M. Poterba. Chicago: National Bureau of Economic Research/University of Chicago Press.

Internal Revenue Service. 1984. *1984 Individual Tax Model File*. Washington, D.C.: Internal Revenue Service, Statistics of Income Division.

———. 1989. *1989 Individual Tax Model File*. Washington, D.C.: Internal Revenue Service, Statistics of Income Division.

———. 1994. *1994 Individual Tax Model File*. Washington, D.C.: Internal Revenue Service, Statistics of Income Division.

Levy, Frank, and Richard J. Murname. 1992. "U.S. Earnings Levels and Earnings Inequality: A Review of Recent Trends and Proposed Explanations." *Journal of Economic Literature* 30(3): 1333–81.

Lindsey, Lawrence. 1987. "Individual Taxpayer Response to Tax Cuts: 1982–1984." *Journal of Public Economics* 33: 173–206.

Metcalf, Gilbert. 1993. "Tax Exporting, Federal Deductibility, and State Tax Structure." *Journal of Policy Analysis and Management* 12 (Winter): 109–26.

Papadimitriou, Dimitri B., and Edward N. Wolff, eds. 1993. *Poverty and Prosperity in the USA at the End of the Twentieth Century*. New York: St. Martin's Press.

Parcell, Ann D. 1996. "Income Shifting in Response to Higher Tax Rates: The Effects of OBRA93." U.S. Department of Treasury, Office of Tax Analysis. Paper prepared for the Allied Social Science Association meetings, San Francisco (January).

Slemrod, Joel, ed. 1992. *Do Taxes Matter?: The Impact of the Tax Reform Act of 1986*. Cambridge, Mass.: MIT Press.

———. 1994. "On the High-Income Laffer Curve." In *Tax Progressivity and Income Inequality*, edited by Joel Slemrod. Cambridge: Cambridge University Press.

———. 1995. "Income Creation or Income Shifting?: Behavioral Responses to the Tax Reform Act of 1986." *American Economic Review Papers and Proceedings* 85(2): 175–80.

Steuerle, C. Eugene. 1992. *The Tax Decade: How Taxes Came to Dominate the Public Agenda*. Washington, D.C.: Urban Institute Press.

Commentary on Chapter 6

Daniel Feenberg

James Alm and Sally Wallace use difference-in-differences techniques to examine the effects of changes in the tax law from 1986 to 1992 on high-income taxpayers. They find strong effects of marginal rates on income reporting, consistent with earlier work by Lawrence Lindsey (1987) and Daniel Feenberg and James Poterba (1992). The work of Alm and Wallace is chiefly distinguished by the use of individual-level data with additional control variables; earlier work based on pooled cross-sections has not had controls for any individual characteristics. This is a welcome improvement, if only for the presence of standard errors.

Austan Goolsbee (this volume) has artfully dubbed this the "new tax responsiveness" (NPR) literature, but he and others in this volume have raised questions about the validity of differences methods in this context. I want to examine these criticisms in detail.

CHANGES IN CORPORATE DISTRIBUTIONS

Roger Gordon and Joel Slemrod (this volume) suggest that changes in the income reported on personal income tax returns may merely reflect changes in corporate distributions stimulated by changes in the relative taxes paid by individuals and corporations. Before the Economic Recovery Tax Act of 1981 (ERTA) the 46 percent corporate rate could be used as a shelter against the 70 percent maximum personal rate. So tax planners would minimize payouts. After ERTA the top personal rate is less than the corporate rate, suggesting that planners should increase payouts, but by 1992 that rate had climbed to 39.6 percent, 5.6 points above the corporate rate, again reversing the incentives. If increases in personal income are mirrored by reductions in corporate profits, the changes in personal tax revenue might not be an accurate description of the total revenue effect.

Of course, just increasing the dividend is not a very helpful way to shelter corporate profits. Because the dividend is not deductible at the corporate level, increasing it just adds the personal tax to the corporate tax. However, many closely held firms engage in a variety of transactions with their owners and could transfer income to owners as wages, rents, royalties, and so on. Although the IRS attempts to regulate such transactions, there must be a wide gray area where taxpayer decisions are unquestioned. Gordon and Slemrod provide regression evidence that this is sensitive to relative tax rates. If this effect were sufficiently large, it could entirely vitiate Alm and Wallace's results, because the tax revenue effects they observe on the personal tax could be offset by opposite effects on the corporate side.

Could retained earnings have fallen sufficiently to explain a substantial share of Alm and Wallace's result? Table 6C.1 shows corporate retained earnings for the

Table 6C.1   Retained Earnings for Selected Years

Year	Retained Earnings
1981	$33 billion
1985	$92 billion
1989	$76 billion
1994	$123 billion

Source: Economic Report of the President for 1997.

years before and after the major tax reforms of the recent era. Changes in retained earnings are more relevant than changes in profits, because dividends are not a shelter. We can see that after the 1981 tax act, retained earnings increased by $59 billion, during a period when the non-gain personal income of the richest 0.5 percent of taxpayers also increased by $15 billion (Feenberg and Poterba 1992). It seems exceedingly unlikely that in the absence of ERTA retained earnings would have fallen to *negative* $18 billion, so that changes in corporate distributions cannot explain the 1981 experience. The relative changes in personal and corporate tax rates in 1986 and the period 1990 to 1992 are much smaller, suggesting even less potential for explaining away the Alm and Wallace results in those years. From table 6.8 we see that from 1985 to 1989 the OBRA dummy adds about $131 billion to high-income AGI, but about one-third of that comes from capital gains. Retained earnings increased by $11 billion. Again, to account for the increase in personal income, retained earnings would have to be reduced to about zero. From 1991 to 1994 corporate rates again exceeded the personal rate, suggesting that retained earnings should decrease, but we see an increase of $39 billion. However, the 1992 tax change was smaller than the preceding ones, and given the economic recovery, it is not obvious that this could not have been higher but for the effect that Gordon and Slemrod document.

Nor does the simple lesson of table 6C.1 contradict anything in the Gordon and Slemrod chapter. As they point out, "the forecasted response of personal incomes is an order of magnitude larger than the forecasted response of corporate income." In other words, only one-tenth of the additional personal income came at the expense of corporate tax revenues.

ARE ALM AND WALLACE OVERINTERPRETING A TREND?

Goolsbee points out that the period 1981 to 1988 corresponds to a period of rapid growth in inequality of incomes, and that Alm and Wallace and other participants in the NTR literature are confusing the effects of marginal tax rate reductions with an unrelated trend.

He dates the start of this trend to about 1968, citing a figure in Feenberg and Poterba (1992) showing the share of wage income to high (top 0.5 percent) AGI taxpayers. But it is hardly clear why the ordinary interpretation of that figure—that it shows a response to the maximum tax on earned income—should be rejected.

Other, more relevant measures, such as the share of AGI, or AGI less capital gains, are quite flat until 1981 (see figure 6C.1).

Goolsbee believes the trend to increasing inequality continues at least through the end of his data in 1995. His evidence for this is a data set covering the period 1991 through 1995 with the compensation information for each of the top five executives at firms required to file 10-K reports with the Securities and Exchange Commission (SEC). He finds a continuing and sharp increase in inequality within this select group. But there is no evidence in the aggregate data for any increase in inequality after 1988, as figure 6C.1 makes clear. Although the executives may be an important fraction of the total of high-income taxpayers, their experience is not sufficiently typical of top AGI recipients to show up in the aggregate data.

Since the trend to increasing inequality seems to overlap exactly the period of marginal rate relief and ends in the period of increasing marginal rates, the plausibility of a relationship is enhanced.

In the sample of executives, compensation is highly sensitive to the stock market. Since the periods studied by Alm and Wallace were all periods of rapid stock price increases, the observed increase in personal incomes might be caused by the

Figure 6C.1   Share of Income to the Top 0.5 Percent of Taxpayers, 1960 to 1995.

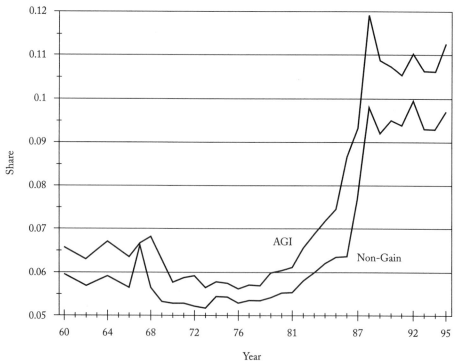

Source: Author's calculations.

market. However, if the apparent effects of ERTA and TRA86 are really due to the stock market, what about the 1990 and 1992 acts? Taken literally, Goolsbee's explanation for the earlier years would suggest a dramatic rise in the share of incomes to the top AGI recipients over the period from 1990 to 1993, but nothing like that occurred. Indeed Slemrod (1994) fails to find any positive relationship of stock values to inequality for the period from 1954 to 1990. I therefore think it is unlikely that Alm and Wallace's results are artifacts of a buoyant stock market.

WHAT ABOUT 1964?

Goolsbee offers the experience of 1964 as a counterexample to the NTR literature. However, Lindsey (1990) has examined that experience and found that the reduction from a maximum rate of 90 percent to 70 percent raised the share of income to the over-$500,000 AGI taxpayers by 47 percent. Although this is not a large elasticity, it is impressive as a one-year change in incomes. There are a number of reasons the 1964 experience may not be precisely comparable to the later tax reforms. The top rate in 1964 was levied at an income level far higher than the top rate in 1980, and the use of corporate shelters kept the practical top rate at 52 percent for many taxpayers. A thorough study would be of great interest, but please do not look for signs of the Lindsey number in figure 6C.1—the AGI breakpoint to be in the top 0.5 percent of taxpayers in 1964 was only $37,000.

WHAT ABOUT HOURS WORKED?

Robert Moffitt and Mark Wilhelm (this volume) show that hours worked among the affluent are not much influenced by tax rates. I do not find this surprising, nor do I believe it contradicts Alm and Wallace. There are many margins on which taxpayers can adjust their behavior, and reported hours worked are likely to be among the least adjustable for many taxpayers. For high-income taxpayers, work and recreation are likely to be conflated, and it is hardly clear how any survey respondent would classify time spent socializing with clients or employees. Intensity of effort, timing of realizations, and tax-deductible consumption are more likely sources of response.

WOULD A PANEL BE PREFERABLE?

With pooled cross-sections, Alm and Wallace can show that the inequality of income changes substantially over the brief periods around changes in the tax treatment of the wealthy. With TRA86 (as with ERTA earlier in the decade) marginal rates declined for the wealthy and the share of pretax income to the top 0.5 percent or 1 percent increased quite sharply. Alm and Wallace suggest that the former caused the latter, but the logical connection would be stronger if they could show that the increase occurred exactly among the taxpayers whose marginal rates declined. That is the intent of panel analysis (see Feldstein 1995; Auten and Carroll 1997). But panels present their own difficulty. Since the marginal rate is endogenous, the change in the rate has to be instrumented. The obvious instrument is the change in the marginal rate evaluated at the initial income. However, some high-income taxpayers in the initial year are transient residents of that stratum. So in the panel data one would expect a strong reduction in the share of high-income taxpayers with high initial marginal rates, even with no change in tax rates, and no change in the overall income distribution. This is regression-to-the-mean bias. When tax rates are declining, it lowers the estimated elasticity of income with respect to tax rates, but for tax increases it raises the estimated elasticity. In any case, the pooled cross-sections do not suffer from this bias, an important advantage for Alm and Wallace.

Repeated cross-sections are a problem for Alm and Wallace when they discuss the composition of income among the high-income. An across-the-board increase in capital gains will have a disproportionate effect on the observed incomes of high-income taxpayers, because taxpayers with larger gains will displace other taxpayers from the high-income group. This may merely exaggerate the quantitative result, but it is still something to be concerned about. Slemrod (1994) has an extensive discussion of this point.

SUMMARY

None of the points raised against Alm and Wallace in this volume turn out to be quantitatively decisive, so the conclusions they draw must be seen as unrefuted.

REFERENCES

Auten, Gerald, and Robert Carroll. 1997. "Behavior of the Affluent and the 1986 Tax Reform Act." Unpublished paper. U.S. Department of the Treasury, Office of Tax Analysis.

Feenberg, Daniel, and James M. Poterba. 1992. "Income Inequality and the Incomes of Very-High-Income Taxpayers." In *Tax Policy and the Economy*, edited by James M. Poterba, vol. 7. Cambridge, Mass.: MIT Press.

Feldstein, Martin S. 1995. "The Effect of Marginal Tax Rates on Taxable Income: A Panel Study of the 1986 Tax Reform Act." *Journal of Political Economy* 103(2): 551–76.

Lindsey, Lawrence B. 1987. "Individual Taxpayer Response to Tax Cuts: 1982–1984." *Journal of Public Economics* 33: 173–206.

———. 1990. *The Growth Experiment*. New York: Basic Books.

Slemrod, Joel. 1994. "On the High-Income Laffer Curve." In *Tax Progressivity and Income Inequality*, edited by Joel Slemrod. Cambridge: Cambridge University Press.

7

Taxation and the Labor Supply
Decisions of the Affluent

Robert A. Moffitt and Mark O. Wilhelm

Research on the labor supply effects of taxation has a long history (Hausman 1985), but very little research has been directly concerned with high-income taxpayers. This is a serious deficiency in the literature, owing to the widespread assumption that high-income taxpayers may be more responsive to tax rate changes than other income groups, both because their marginal tax rates are very high and because they have more opportunities for altering their behavior. In part this neglect has been the result of data difficulties, for relatively few data sets have contained labor supply information on a sufficient number of high-income taxpayers (for example, hours of work). The most widely used data sets for tax analysis of high-income taxpayers have contained information from IRS tax returns (see, for example, Feldstein 1995a), but these data sets contain no direct information on labor supply other than whether family earnings are positive. We address this data difficulty by using the Survey of Consumer Finances (SCF), a data set that oversampled high-income taxpayers and was conducted at several points during the 1980s and 1990s. We use the SCF to analyze the effects of the 1986 Tax Reform Act on the labor supply decisions of the affluent.

A number of methodological issues must be addressed in any study of the labor supply effects of income taxation, and several special issues must be addressed in a study of the affluent. Among the general issues are those concerning how to obtain cross-sectional variation in changes in marginal tax rates, for the same federal tax law, in essence, applies to everyone. Another, separate issue concerns the nonlinearity of the tax schedule when a nonproportional tax schedule is in force. Because of its special importance, we address the first issue in detail here. The latter issue receives only cursory attention.

The first section reviews prior work in evaluating the effects on high-income taxpayers. The second section outlines our approach to estimation, and the next section presents our data and results.

PRIOR WORK ON TAXATION AND LABOR SUPPLY

The empirical work on the effect of taxation on labor supply through the early 1980s is reviewed by Jerry Hausman (1985). By and large those studies suggested that male labor supply is rather insensitive to tax rates, but that female labor supply, at least that of married women, is considerably more sensitive.[1] Studies of the effects of 1981 and 1986 tax legislation have found generally consistent results, with responses larger for women than for men and small, if not zero, effects for the latter (Bosworth and Burtless 1992; Eissa 1995, 1996a, 1996b; Mariger 1995; Ziliak and Kniesner 1996). With the exception of two recent studies of high-income physicians, lawyers, and managers (Showalter 1997; Showalter and Thurston 1997), these studies have not had large numbers of observations of high-income taxpayers.[2]

Because IRS data have many more such observations, there have been more studies of the effects of the 1981 and 1986 legislation on incomes as reported to the IRS. These studies have generally revealed quite significant responses to tax rates, although the magnitude of the effect differs considerably across studies (Auten and Carroll 1999; Feenberg and Poterba 1993; Feldstein 1995a; Feldstein and Feenberg 1996; Lindsey 1987).[3]

The methodological issue that has preoccupied much of the recent literature has concerned how to identify the effects of the federal income tax on either labor supply or income, given that individuals with the same characteristics face the same tax schedule at a given point in time. If the social and economic characteristics that cause tax schedules to differ across individuals (marital status, family size, forms of nonlabor income, and so on) have independent effects on behavior, there is no remaining variation in tax rates to permit the identification of tax responsiveness once these variables are controlled for. Although many of the earlier studies reviewed in Hausman (1985) made the assumption that some of those characteristics did not in fact affect behavior independently, the studies since that time have eschewed that variation in favor of other forms of identification. Cross-sectionally, a few studies have used state variation in taxes for identification (Auten and Carroll 1999; Showalter and Thurston 1997), but these studies ignore migration and income shifting across states. The more common methods of identification have used the "difference-in-differences" method, which uses variation over time in tax schedules for different individuals to identify tax effects (for U.S. studies, see Eissa 1995, 1996a, 1996b; for a U.K. study using this method, see Blundell, Duncan, and Meghir 1998).

We devote the next section to a discussion of this method and its underlying assumptions. We show that the most relevant form of the difference-in-differences method for tax response estimation is a form of instrumental-variables estimation that requires exclusion restrictions for identification. We then proceed with our empirical work and apply that method to the effect of the 1986 tax act on the labor supply of high-income men, using the SCF data.

MODELING THE LABOR SUPPLY EFFECTS OF TAXATION

As just noted, a major problem in estimating the effects of nationwide tax systems is that they provide no variation on which to base estimation, at least holding constant individual characteristics. The methodology of "difference-in-differences," or fixed effects, which is employed in some of the recent studies, makes use of panel data or repeated cross-section data to address these problems. This methodology can be applied in a simple tabular fashion but can also be applied in a regression context. We begin by discussing this method in general and show that, when put into a regression framework, the method can be seen to rely for identification on exclusion restrictions of a particular kind and that a leading case of the methodology is equivalent to instrumental-variables estimation with panel data. We then briefly discuss the issues raised by using repeated cross-section data and by the non-linearity of the budget constraint.[4]

Difference-in-Differences (Fixed Effects) with Panel Data

The difference-in-differences methodology can be viewed within the context of the treatment-effects literature (for example, Heckman and Robb 1985), in which interest centers on the effect of some treatment d (usually defined as a dummy variable) on some outcome variable y, possibly conditional on a vector of other regressors x, which we take to be individual socioeconomic characteristics (possibly including income amounts). However, the models with which we are concerned differ in an important respect from the standard model in the treatment-effects literature, for here it is assumed that d has no cross-sectional variation conditional on x. The federal income tax is of this type because all individuals with the same characteristics face the same schedule, and all individuals with the same characteristics and income components and amounts face the same marginal tax rate.

The fact that the tax schedule does vary with individual characteristics and income implies that the stimulus induced by the tax system is a function of x, and this is what furnishes variation that can be used for identification. In the case of tax systems, the tax formula dictates that marginal tax rates differ for individuals with different characteristics (marital status, number of dependents, income, homeownership, and other variables). Letting p denote the time period, our starting point is a linear model of the form

$$y_p = \alpha_p + \beta d_p(x_p) + \gamma_p x_p + \varepsilon_p \qquad (7.1)$$

where $d_p(x_p)$ is the treatment variable of interest, which is often the marginal tax rate faced by the individual.[5] For a particular choice of tax variable $d_p(x_p)$, the parameter of interest is the effect of that variable, which is β. For the most part, we assume that $d_p(x_p)$ is a known parametric function because the tax formula is known and hence x_p are the variables that go into the tax formula. However, all of our important conclusions apply as well to the case in which d_p is an observed variable, x_p are instruments, and $d_p(x_p)$ is a function to be estimated (for example, in a first-stage regression); in this interpretation, the identification problem arises if there are no instruments that do not appear independently in the equation.

We assume that equation (7.1) is derived from theory and hence is the "true" equation, or at least that it can be formally derived as an approximation to that theory. That is, we assume that the theory puts no other restrictions on the equation that might furnish sources of identification. This is an issue in the labor supply case, where one element of x_p (the wage rate) interacts with $d_p(x_p)$ (the marginal tax rate) according to most theories. We address this issue later; for now we restrict ourselves to the class of theories, whether a large or small class, that generate equations of the form of equation (7.1).

To illustrate the problem most simply, we assume in equation (7.1) that the set of x that enters the tax formula is equivalent to the set that appears independently in equation (7.1); in practice, the former is likely to be a subset of the latter, but this merely would mean that we should add another set of variables into equation (7.1).[6] Adding such a set does not affect the identification problem, so we do not do so. All variables and parameters in equation (7.1) are assumed to vary over time except β, which is not allowed to vary because it is the main parameter of interest and it is generally desired to estimate only a single time-invariant response effect, at least over a short period of time.

As it stands, with a single cross-section of data, β is identifiable from nonlinearities in the $d_p(x_p)$ function because x_p appears linearly in the equation. But this source of identification is weak because sufficient relaxations of linearity would result in a loss of identification.[7] If instead variables can be found that affect marginal tax rates but do not affect y_p directly, the effect of $d_p(x_p)$ on y_p would be nonparametrically identified (at least over the range of the data) and the problem would be solved. We assume throughout, however, that such variables are not available.

The critical vector of variables in this model is x_p, and a number of different cases can be distinguished depending on the nature of that vector. One major distinction is whether it is time-invariant or varies over time; another is whether it is endogenous (that is, correlated with ε_p) or exogenous. For an income tax application, the relevant case is clearly endogenous, time-varying x, because x includes income, which varies over time and is endogenous because y, if labor supply, is one determinant of income. However, we build up to that case by first considering exogenous time-invariant x and then exogenous time-variant x_p; we then consider endogenous x and x_p.[8]

The case that serves as the prototype for all the others is the case of a time-invariant exogenous x. In the tax case, filing status, if taken as exogenous and time-invariant in the short term, is one example. Assuming that panel data on a set of individuals are available for two periods (we consider later the case of more than two waves of data), and that the law changes between the periods, we have

$$y_{p+1} - y_p = (\alpha_{p+1} - \alpha_p) + \beta[d_{p+1}(x) - d_p(x)] + (\gamma_{p+1} - \gamma_p)x + (\varepsilon_{p+1} - \varepsilon_p) \qquad (7.2)$$

With this first-differenced equation, β is identifiable (apart from nonlinearities in $d_p[(x)]$ if $\gamma_{p+1} = \gamma_p$, in which case x drops out of equation (7.2) as an independent determinant of the change in y. In other words, it must be assumed that there is no trend in the independent effect of x on y. This is the assumption that has figured in much of the difference-in-differences analysis of tax effects (see, for example, Eissa 1995, 1996a, 1996b; Feldstein 1995a; Blundell et al. 1998; Carroll et al. 1998; for a challenge to the method, see Goolsbee, this volume). Thus, at least one variable must be found that affects how individuals react to the program but whose independent effect is stationary; that is, an exclusion restriction is necessary for equation (7.2). This is the critical assumption in all the models to be discussed. Note that the model is equivalent to a fixed-effects model where x is the fixed effect that differences out.[9]

The assumption $\gamma_{p+1} = \gamma_p$ is a nontestable, just-identifying assumption in the model as stated because estimates of β cannot be obtained if it is relaxed. However, if data on additional periods prior to p are available, the assumption can be relaxed to some degree because a time pattern of γ_p can be estimated and it can thereby be determined whether γ_p contains a time trend. Although it can never be known for certain whether the independent effect of x on y would have changed from p to p + 1 in the absence of a change in the d (this is the usual problem of the missing counterfactual in treatment-effects models), more history on y and x can at least assist in establishing priors on whether the effect changed between p and p + 1.[10]

If x is a time-varying exogenous variable (for example, number of dependents, if taken as exogenous), a differenced equation (7.1) is

$$y_{p+1} - y_p = (\alpha_{p+1} - \alpha_p) + \beta[d_{p+1}(x_{p+1}) - d_p(x_p)] + \gamma_{p+1}x_{p+1} - \gamma_p x_p + \varepsilon_{p+1} - \varepsilon_p \quad (7.3)$$

where the effect of taxes is again unidentified if the linearity assumptions in equation (7.3) are sufficiently relaxed. Here the problem is not solved if $\gamma_{p+1} = \gamma_p$ (again, if linearities are relaxed). But a simple way of dealing with this issue is to select the subsample for which $x_{p+1} = x_p$; for that subsample, $\gamma_{p+1} = \gamma_p$ again is a sufficient condition for identification. Because both x_{p+1} and x_p are exogenous, this selection introduces no bias.

Many of the more important applications of the difference-in-differences, fixed-effects approach are cases where the excluded variable in first differences is instead endogenous. To keep this case notationally separate from the previous ones, we use z to denote the variable instead of x, where now it is assumed that z and ε_p are not independent. Here the difference between time-invariant z and time-varying z is more important, and most of the interesting cases arise when z is time-varying. But time-invariant z is an important case as well, although examples are more difficult to imagine in practice. In the tax case where y is labor supply, selecting a subsample for whom marital status is unchanged from p to p + 1 is one such z if marital status is considered to be jointly determined with labor supply.

The application of the methodology in this case can be most easily rationalized by the assumption of the panel data random-effects model. Hence, we assume

$$y_p = \alpha_p + \beta d_p(z) + \mu + \nu_p \quad (7.4)$$

where μ is a time-invariant individual effect. In equation (7.4), z is not included as a separate regressor because it is assumed to be an endogenous variable jointly determined with y and hence not to have an independent structural effect on y. The endogeneity of z can arise either from a relation to μ or to ν_p or both, but it is the former that can be addressed by first differencing. Because μ and z are both time-invariant, it follows that $E(\mu|z)$ is constant over time and therefore that the "types" (μ) of individuals associated with different values of z do not change. Hence

$$y_{p+1} - y_p = (\alpha_{p+1} - \alpha_p) + \beta[d_{p+1}(z) - d_p(z)] + (\nu_{p+1} - \nu_p) \quad (7.5)$$

The assumption needed in this model for consistent estimation of β is that z is uncorrelated with $(\nu_{p+1} - \nu_p)$, the trend in the unobservables in the equation (or more precisely, that the function $[d_{p+1}(z) - d_p(z)]$ is uncorrelated with $[\nu_{p+1} - \nu_p]$).[11] This case is thus once again equivalent to a simple fixed-effects model. The assumption that $\gamma_p = \gamma_{p+1}$ in prior models is equivalent in this model to the assumption that there is no time-varying coefficient on μ.[12]

If z is a time-varying endogenous variable, we have, again assuming the presence of an individual effect,

$$y_p = \alpha_p + \beta d_p(z_p) + \mu + v_p \tag{7.6}$$

$$y_{p+1} = \alpha_{p+1} + \beta d_{p+1}(z_{p+1}) + \mu + v_{p+1} \tag{7.7}$$

and, first-differencing,

$$y_{p+1} - y_p = (\alpha_{p+1} - \alpha_p) + \beta[d_{p+1}(z_{p+1}) - d_p(z_p)] + (v_{p+1} - v_p) \tag{7.8}$$

The leading case in the tax application is that in which income or some function of income, which determines the individual marginal tax bracket, is used for z. Thus, consistent estimation of β again requires that $[d_{p+1}(z_{p+1}) - d_p(z_p)]$ and $(v_{p+1} - v_p)$ be uncorrelated. This is a much stronger assumption than has been needed thus far because if z is jointly determined with y (as income and labor supply are, for example), then z_{p+1} is likely to be correlated with v_{p+1}, and z_p with v_p. Hence, the fundamental exclusion restriction necessary for the difference-in-differences approach is in jeopardy.[13]

The conventional solution to problems of endogenous regressors is to seek correlates of those regressors that satisfy exclusion and other restrictions for identification. Instrumental-variables (IV) is one method, among others, for consistent estimation subject to those restrictions. In the IV case, we seek an instrument that is asymptotically correlated with $[d_{p+1}(z_{p+1}) - d_p(z_p)]$, but not with $(v_{p+1} - v_p)$ and is excluded from equation (7.8). The classes of instruments that can be sought for this purpose are precisely the three we have already discussed—time-invariant and exogenous x, time-variant and exogenous x_p, and time-invariant but endogenous z—in each case again requiring that the exclusion and orthogonality restrictions in the first-differenced equations we have already discussed for these three classes of variables be satisfied. With $d_p(x)$, $d_p(x_p)$, and $d_p(z)$ now reinterpreted as to-be-estimated functions of instruments, all of the above analysis applies. Thus, the analysis at this point comes full circle back to the original three cases, with time-invariant exogenous variables x with stationary coefficients constituting presumably the strongest instruments.

In our empirical discussion later, we are more specific about the types of instruments in the labor-supply-tax application that might satisfy these conditions. However, here we discuss an approach used in a number of prior applications, namely, the use of the period-p value of z_p as an instrument (see, for example, Feldstein 1995a). The variable z_p is an endogenous but time-invariant variable (if it is held constant through $p + 1$, that is) and hence, assuming it is both correlated with the change in the tax variable and independent of $(v_{p+1} - v_p)$, it is a candidate instrument. In the two-stage-least-squares version of its application, $[d_{p+1}(z_{p+1}) - d_p(z_p)]$ is regressed on z_p, and its predicted value replaces the actual value in equation (7.8). In an alternative version, one linearizes the tax schedule with the approximation

$$d_{p+1}(z_{p+1}) = \theta_0 + \theta_1 d_{p+1}(z_p) + \eta \tag{7.9}$$

and uses predicted values from estimates of this equation in place of actual d_{p+1} (z_{p+1}) in equation (7.8). Consistent estimation requires in either case that the predicted values be asymptotically uncorrelated with $(v_{p+1} - v_p)$.[14]

The difficulty with this instrument is that z_p is unlikely to be correlated to the same degree with v_p and v_{p+1} and hence is likely to be correlated with the difference $v_{p+1} - v_p$. Because z_p and y_p are jointly determined—either because z_p is equal to y_p (that is, if the lagged dependent variable is used) or is a direct function of y_p (as income is of labor supply)—the transitory error v_p has a direct effect on z_p. This covariance translates into a dependence of z_p on the differenced error, $v_{p+1} - v_p$ because z_p is almost certainly not related to v_{p+1} in the same way that it is related to v_p. For example, if v_{p+1} and v_p are independent, there is no relation between z_p and v_{p+1}), and the resulting bias takes the form of regression to the mean.

The influence of v_p could be accounted for by entering z_p directly and independently into equation (7.8), but then identification of β would be lost because the change in d would have no variation independent of z_p; in this sense the issue is an identification problem more than a regression-to-the-mean problem. But if z_p is entered independently in the regression, some other instrument is needed to address the initial endogeneity problem, and there one again returns to the need for one of the classes of instruments, discussed previously, that satisfies the same set of conditions. In addition, adding a lagged dependent variable changes the model and the interpretation of β, which makes the estimate noncomparable to estimates without the lag.[15]

A variant of this procedure that has apparently not been reported in the published literature is the use of z_{p+1} as the instrument.[16] That instrument qualifies under the same conditions as z_p; equation (7.8) is perfectly symmetrical with respect to periods p and p + 1, and the fact that period p + 1 is after the tax law change has no direct bearing on the validity of z_{p+1} as an instrument. To the contrary, there is little a priori reason to suppose that the correlation between z_{p+1} and v_{p+1} differs from that between z_p and v_p. Unfortunately, if both are tested as instruments and the estimates of β are the same, this can arise either because there is no bias or because the bias is the same for both. If the estimates differ, it is likely that they are biased in opposite directions, and this can indicate the presence of serial correlation in the errors. In the simple case where the instrument is y_p or y_{p+1}, which contain v_p and v_{p+1}, respectively, the covariances between the error term in equation (7.8) and these two instruments are $[\text{Cov}(v_p, v_{p+1}) - \text{Var}(v_p)]$ and $[\text{Var}(v_{p+1}) - \text{Cov}(v_p, v_{p+1})]$. Assuming the variances are the same in the two periods, the estimated β using y_p as the instrument is higher (lower) than the estimated β using y_{p+1} as the instrument if serial correlation is positive (negative).

Repeated Cross-Sections

Because our empirical work uses panel data, we do not discuss the application of the principles just outlined to data consisting of a series of repeated cross-sections. However, we provide in the appendix a summary of the issues that arise in that case. As the analysis there shows, the models discussed here that rely on time-invariant x or z for identification can be applied to repeated-cross-section data with only small modification, and consistent estimates of β obtained under the same conditions. However, models using time-variant x require additional assumptions for identification, and models using time-variant z are very difficult, if not impossible, to use with repeated cross-section data without the imposition of implausible restrictions.

Piecewise-Linear Tax Schedules

The federal income tax creates a piecewise-linear budget constraint from which individuals can choose labor supply locations. The econometrics of this problem have been analyzed extensively in past work (Hausman 1985; Moffitt 1986, 1990; MaCurdy, Green, and Paarsch 1990; Blundell and MaCurdy 1999). The implication of this body of literature for present purposes is that the interpretation of the coefficient on the marginal tax rate variables that we estimate, and that other investigators have estimated using similar methods, must be made with caution.

The object of interest in the piecewise-linear-constraint literature has generally been the estimation of the parameters of a static utility function U(H,C)—where H is hours of work and C is consumption. If the labor supply function is linear, those parameters are the coefficients in the equation for H if utility maximization occurs on segment s of the constraint:

$$H = \alpha + \beta W[1 - t_s(x)] + \delta \tilde{N}_s(x) + \gamma x + \varepsilon \tag{7.10}$$

where W is the hourly wage rate, $t_s(x)$ is the marginal tax rate on segment s for an individual with characteristics x, and $\tilde{N}_s$ is virtual nonlabor income for segment s. Aside from the interaction between W and the marginal tax rate, $t_s(x)$, and the presence of the virtual income variable, equation (7.10) fits into the framework of equation (7.1) that formed the basis for the earlier econometric analysis.

Unfortunately, as shown in the appendix, the values of H observed in a cross-sectional data set to be located on a segment s are not generated by equation (7.10), for segment classification error implies that the observed segment s is not the true segment s generating H. Such error is necessarily present if the variance of ε is nonzero; consequently, assuming away such classification error is inconsistent with the existence of ε. Instead, H observed along a segment s is determined by a weighted average of marginal tax rates on all other segments of the constraint. Further, first-differencing in the manner of the difference-in-differences, fixed-effects model does not lessen this problem.

In light of these issues, estimates of the effect of $t_s(x)$, or of $W[(1 - t_s(x)]$ on H, where s is the observed segment in the data, cannot be interpreted as representing estimates of β in equation (7.10). Instead, those estimates must be interpreted as the net effect of a change in the marginal tax rate in one segment on H, including those effects arising from correlated changes in the marginal tax rates of other segments. This is the interpretation we give to our parameter estimates.

We should also note at this point that the static labor supply theory clearly implies that an income term should be included in the equation and that the wage rate should be interacted with the marginal tax rate, regardless of nonlinear constraint issues. We test an income term in our models, and we also test interactions of W with the marginal tax rate in our empirical work. However, we do not use the theoretically implied interaction between W and the marginal tax rate as a source of identifying variation (for example, we enter W separately as well) on the presumption that the effects of the two variables may be different for a variety of reasons.[17]

Applying the Methodology

In the labor-supply-tax case, we study the federal income tax and its effect on hours of work. There are many variables in the federal income tax code that affect the individual's marginal tax rate and are thus candidates for x or z. These variables include adjusted gross income (AGI); deductions, exemptions, and filing status, which determine taxable income; and various tax credits and adjustments for other taxes. Each of these categories includes subcategories as well. However, few of these variables are direct candidates for x or x_p, for most are likely to be endogenous because they are related too closely to income and hence labor supply. Earned income is clearly in this category, but unearned income in its many forms is as well, for the majority of that income arises from investment decisions that are probably jointly made with labor supply decisions. As for the remaining variables that go into the tax formula, we are constrained by our data, which are household survey in nature (see discussion later in the chapter), to those obtained in the questionnaire. The only two major non-income-tax-formula variables in our data are marital status, which is highly correlated with filing status, and family size, which is correlated with the number of exemptions. We test both of these variables as instruments.

When instruments for the endogenous earned and unearned income variables are considered, a larger number of instruments might seem to be available. Any instruments that can be thought of as determinants of permanent income or wages are candidates, because they should be correlated with contemporaneous income and hence tax rates, but uncorrelated with the transitory income components that are probably correlated with the change in labor supply. In this category we consider education and broad-category occupation, which are both roughly constant over short periods of time.[18] We also test as instruments various forms of assets that are moderately illiquid in form, such as the value of a house or the value of life insurance. Because these assets are fairly illiquid and do not generate cash income flows, they should not be directly correlated with contemporaneous income but should be correlated with permanent income.[19]

As noted previously, because the static labor supply model implies that W is interacted with $(1 - t)$, we also test interactions of our instrumented tax variable with the wage rate and with its predictors (such as education). We also test specifications that directly incorporate income effects.

We will also test the use of z_p (the pre-law-change value of income or AGI or hours of work) as an instrument, as well as various transforms of z_p. Of the transforms, the one we use most heavily is the period-p value of the marginal tax rate, $t_p(z_p)$. This is the instrument used by Feldstein (1995a). We also test including z_p as an independent regressor and using the other instruments we have described to identify the model; this controls for regression-to-the-mean and other serial correlation effects.

The major focus of our empirical work is specifically on the labor supply response of the rich. To maintain this focus we test instruments that stratify the population into groups that separate individuals in the upper tail of the distribution from the rest of the population. Thus, our instruments are variously formulated as those with very high period-p income, period-p marginal tax rates, very high education or high-earning occupations, and very high asset levels.

As we have stressed in our earlier analysis, the major condition needed for validity of the instruments is that their effects on labor supply be constant over time. Obtaining evidence on this question is not possible with only a two-period, before-and-after panel such as the one we use, but indirect evidence can be obtained from other data sets. The Current Population Survey (CPS) contains information on income, earnings, and labor supply for a number of years, as well as on education, occupation, marital status, and family size. Figures 7.1 through 7.4 provide information on the a priori validity of education and occupation in this respect. Figure 7.1 shows trends in annual hours of work for prime-age men in high-earning occupations (professionals and managers) and all others, while figure 7.2 shows such trends for those with high education (college degree or more) and all others.[20] Interestingly, the figures demonstrate relatively little trend in the hours-worked gap prior to 1986 for either variable, suggesting that they might be suitable as instruments.[21] The figures also show little evidence of a widening of the gap after 1986, but this has no bearing on the validity of the variables as instruments, because the true effect of the law affects the post-1986 trends. These results do not extend to family income and male earnings; those variables significantly widened prior to 1986, between both the two education groups and the two occupation groups (figures not shown).

Figure 7.1   Annual Hours of Work by Occupational Category: Male Heads

Source: Authors' calculations.

Figure 7.2 Annual Hours of Work by Educational Category: Male Heads

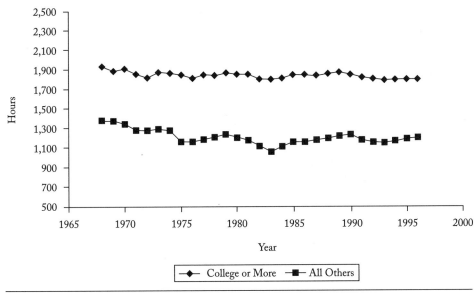

Source: Authors' calculations.

Figure 7.3   Family Income by Occupational Category: Male Heads

Source: Authors' calculations.

Figure 7.4   Individual Earnings by Occupational Group: Male Heads

Source: Authors' calculations.

DATA AND RESULTS
The Survey of Consumer Finances

The Survey of Consumer Finances (SCF) is a household survey conducted to gather financial information from a nationally representative sample of American households (Kennickell and Shack-Marquez 1992). Since 1983 the SCF has been fielded triennially, and in 1983 and 1989 the surveys had a panel feature for which a subsample of households appeared in both. The primary focus of the survey is on wealth information, and considerable detail is devoted to the composition of financial and nonfinancial assets and various types of debt. Because wealth holdings are very concentrated at the top of the wealth distribution, the SCF oversamples high-income households. The relatively large size of the affluent sample in the SCF has been used for estimating aggregate wealth and studying trends in wealth inequality (see, for example, Wolff 1994, 1995). We use this oversample feature of the SCF to analyze the labor supply of the rich.[22]

We use only the 1983 and 1989 waves of the SCF and the panel of individuals who appeared in both. The 1986 Tax Reform Act took effect midway between these years, but not close enough to either to warrant concern about contamination due to timing responses. The fortuitous fielding of the SCF before and after the act makes it particularly useful both for purposes of reexamining the effect of the tax changes on adjusted gross income with data other than those available from tax returns and for investigating the response of labor supply to the act. An additional advantage of the SCF is that it contains data that enable us to examine the sensitivity of our results—and by extension the previous results of others—to the use of a fairly wide array of alternative instruments. Importantly, many of these instruments are not based on income, or some function of income, from the first period.

The SCF obtained AGI information using different methods in 1983 and 1989. In 1989 respondents were queried directly about 1988 AGI in a section of the survey dealing with their federal income taxes.[23] In 1983 there was no direct query about AGI, but rather the SCF constructed two measures of respondent AGI from the responses to questions in the sections on income and household characteristics. One measure was designed to be current-law (1982) AGI, and the other was constructed to include full capital gains and the dividend exclusion (unlike 1982 law). When the weighted 1983 cross-section SCF is used to generate aggregate 1982 AGI, the first measure underestimates the published IRS totals for 1982 AGI by $200 billion, or 11 percent (Internal Revenue Service 1984), but the second measure (adjusted to current 1982 law by subtracting 60 percent of capital gains and the dividend exclusion) differs from the IRS totals by only $1 billion.[24] Hence, we use the second measure. Because it already includes full capital gains and the dividend exclusion, it is comparable in definition to 1989 (tax law 1988); hence, when we use the change in AGI from 1983 to 1989 as the dependent variable, it is relatively free of definitional changes.

We use several criteria to select a sample for analysis. Table 7A.1 provides a summary of these criteria as well as their effects on sample size. We analyze male heads of households aged twenty-five to fifty-four in 1983. The age restriction implies that the oldest men were no more than sixty in the second period of the panel and, for the most part, were probably not considering retirement decisions. We select men for whom there was no ambiguity in linking 1983 data from the household record to the data from 1989. Lastly, we analyze men who had positive AGI and positive wage rates and who worked more than two hundred hours in both years; we also exclude the few observations whose labor hours were imputed in the 1989 survey. Our final sample consists of 490 men.

We calculate a marginal tax rate (MTR) for each observation in each year from the data available on the SCF, using tax rules applicable in 1982 and 1988. To calculate an estimate of taxable income, actual AGI (in 1982 AGI is reduced by 60 percent of capital gains and the dividend exclusion) is reduced by the number of household members times the exemption amount and by an estimate of average deductions of those with similar AGI based on published IRS tables (Internal Revenue Service 1984, 1991).[25] This estimate of taxable income is then used with the tax tables to determine the MTR as well as the value of the tax payment. For 1983 the MTR is reduced by 5 percent if the deduction for a second worker was effective (that is, the man's earnings had to have been under $30,000 and less than his wife's).

Table 7.1 shows the means and standard deviations of the major variables in the analysis in 1983 and 1989. The sample for this table includes only 406 men with 1983 MTR greater than 0.20, for reasons we discuss later (this is the sample closest to that used by Feldstein [1995a]); means for the entire sample of 490 observations, as well as for those with lower 1983 MTR values, are presented in Table 7A.2. The last four columns in table 7.1 subdivide the sample into groups with midrange 1983 MTR values (from 0.20 to 0.44) and high 1983 MTR values (over 0.44).

Table 7.1 Means and Standard Deviations in the 1983 and 1989 SCF Panel (Men, Twenty-Five to Fifty-Four in 1983)

Variable	Midrange or High 1983 MTR		Midrange 1983 MTR		High 1983 MTR	
	1983	1989	1983	1989	1983	1989
Adjusted gross income (AGI)	49,720	61,913	44,723	52,470	168,899	287,115
	(49,475)	(128,805)	(16,117)	(41,861)	(199,575)	(563,590)
Annual hours worked	2,340	2,380	2,336	2,375	2,434	2,501
	(617)	(546)	(611)	(536)	(745)	(726)
Total income	55,723	69,773	49,213	58,850	210,967	330,285
	(60,118)	(154,809)	(21,364)	(38,337)	(231,976)	(699,832)
Wage and salary income	40,945	53,409	39,107	50,519	84,808	122,342
	(25,715)	(43,663)	(18,008)	(28,461)	(81,810)	(152,001)
Wage and salary and business income	49,857	63,138	44,909	55,053	167,861	255,021
	(39,190)	(114,499)	(17,726)	(32,208)	(127,126)	(512,512)
Net-of-tax rate (NTR = 1 – t)	0.692	0.776	0.700	0.778	0.506	0.709
	(0.074)	(0.064)	(0.065)	(0.064)	(0.006)	(0.038)
Hourly wage rate (W)	17.60	21.81	15.79	18.98	60.78	89.44
	(16.34)	(45.44)	(8.92)	(21.58)	(52.81)	(188.28)
W × NTR	11.57	16.42	10.77	14.44	30.66	63.53
	(8.33)	(32.60)	(5.21)	(15.51)	(26.45)	(135.50)
Tax payment	8,480	9,690	6,861	7,389	47,099	64,577
	(13,802)	(29,360)	(3,975)	(10132)	(52,940)	(125,829)
Married	0.849	0.846	0.846	0.846	0.930	0.845
	(0.358)	(0.361)	(0.361)	(0.361)	(0.254)	(0.362)
Percentage with no change in marital status	—	0.828	—	0.828	—	0.848
	—	(0.377)	—	(0.378)	—	(0.359)
Household size	3.207	3.089	3.198	3.096	3.407	2.918
	(1.424)	(1.300)	(1.426)	(1.299)	(1.373)	(1.319)
Percentage with no change in household size	—	0.473	—	0.476	—	0.421
	—	(0.499)	—	(0.499)	—	(0.494)

Age thirty to thirty-four	0.226	—	0.232	—	0.063	—
	(0.418)		(0.422)		(0.243)	
Age thirty-five to thirty-nine	0.180	—	0.180	—	0.168	—
	(0.384)		(0.384)		(0.374)	
Age forty to forty-four	0.133	—	0.128	—	0.244	—
	(0.339)		(0.334)		(0.430)	
Age forty-five to forty-nine	0.186	—	0.181	—	0.304	—
	(0.389)		(0.385)		(0.460)	
Age fifty to fifty-four	0.101	—	0.096	—	0.206	—
	(0.301)		(0.295)		(0.404)	
Distribution of 1983 MTR						
0.20 < t ≤ 0.22	0.191	—	0.199	—	0.000	—
	(0.393)		(0.393)		(0.000)	
0.22 < t ≤ 0.25	0.160	—	0.166	—	0.000	—
	(0.366)		(0.366)		(0.000)	
0.25 < t ≤ 0.29	0.188	—	0.196	—	0.000	—
	(0.391)		(0.391)		(0.000)	
0.29 < t ≤ 0.33	0.193	—	0.201	—	0.000	—
	(0.395)		(0.395)		(0.000)	
0.33 < t ≤ 0.40	0.162	—	0.169	—	0.000	—
	(0.369)		(0.369)		(0.000)	
0.40 < t ≤ 0.44	0.066	—	0.069	—	0.000	—
	(0.249)		(0.249)		(0.000)	
0.44 < t ≤ 0.50	0.040	—	0.000	—	1.000	—
	(0.197)		(0.000)		(0.000)	

(Table continues on p. 208.)

Table 7.1 *Continued*

Variable	Midrange or High 1983 MTR		Midrange 1983 MTR		High 1983 MTR	
	1983	1989	1983	1989	1983	1989
High 1983 income (rich dummy)	0.075	—	0.038	—	0.914	—
	(0.260)		(0.190)		(0.281)	
Postcollege	0.175	—	0.153	—	0.705	—
	(0.380)		(0.360)		(0.456)	
Professional–manager	0.453	—	0.434	—	0.887	—
	(0.498)		(0.496)		(0.317)	
Log 1983 house value	8.618	—	8.497	—	11.485	—
	(4.891)		(4.915)		(3.092)	
Zero 1983 house value (dummy)	0.241	—	0.249	—	0.064	—
	(0.428)		(0.432)		(0.245)	
Log 1983 life insurance value	10.268	—	10.181	—	12.344	—
	(3.095)		(3.111)		(1.668)	
Zero 1983 life insurance (dummy)	0.073	—	0.076	—	0.010	—
	(0.260)		(0.265)		(0.010)	
High 1983 house value or life insurance value (dummy)	0.123	—	0.104	—	0.578	—
	(0.328)		(0.305)		(0.494)	
Observations (unweighted)	406	406	277	277	129	129

Source: Authors' calculations.

Notes: All values are weighted. Midrange 1983 MTR values are those greater than 0.20 and less than or equal to 0.44, and high 1983 MTR values are those greater than 0.44 and less than or equal to 0.50. All monetary amounts are in 1988 dollars. Standard deviations appear in parentheses.

Approximately 68 percent of the sample is in the former group, and 32 percent (but only 4 percent of the weighted population) is in the latter group; thus, the latter is our "high-income" sample.

The first several rows in table 7.1 show mean 1983 and 1989 AGI, hours of work, and other outcome variables of interest.[26] Although AGI grew for midrange-MTR men, it grew more in both absolute and percentage terms for high-MTR men. Annual hours worked (calculated from the product of normal weekly hours and normal annual weeks worked) increased for both MTR groups, but by approximately the same amount.[27] Total income, wage and salary income, and the latter combined with business income also increased for all men, but more for those with high 1983 MTR values.[28]

A key variable in the table is the net-of-tax rate (NTR), equal to 1 minus the marginal tax rate. Between 1983 and 1988 the NTR increased much more for those with high initial MTR values than for those with lower values, consistent with many prior calculations of the effect of the 1986 Tax Reform Act (see, for example, Hausman and Poterba 1987). It is this differential effect that forms the basis for all the difference-in-differences, fixed-effects estimates in this chapter and in much recent work. The table also shows that both gross and net hourly wage rates increased over the period, but more for the high-initial-MTR group.

The rest of the variables in table 7.1 are used in the subsequent analysis as control variables (particularly marital status, household size, and age) or as instruments for the change in the NTR. In all cases, only the 1983 value of the variable is used. In addition to the distribution of the observations across seven (rather than two) 1983 MTR groups, the table shows the means of several additional variables. These include a high-income ("rich") dummy, equal to 1 if 1983 total income exceeded $100,000; a dummy for educational experience after college; a dummy for those in professional or managerial occupations; variables for the value of a house and of life insurance plans, as well as a dummy for those either owning an expensive house (greater than $200,000 in value) or holding a large amount of life insurance (greater than $300,000).

Results

Although our major focus is on hours of work, we initially benchmark our results against those of Feldstein (1995a), both to determine whether our data give similar results to his for AGI and to illustrate the use of alternative instruments. We find results for AGI in our data quite similar to those of Feldstein, although we also find the magnitude to be somewhat sensitive to the use of alternative instruments.

AGI Results   Table 7.2 shows the estimates of effects of the 1986 tax act on AGI using a tabular methodology similar to that of Feldstein, and table 7.3 shows those estimates using a regression methodology. The instrument used in the Feldstein model is the initial-period level of the MTR grouped into categories. We construct three groups—low (less than or equal to 0.20), midrange (0.20 to 0.44) and high (0.44 to 0.50)—that differ slightly from a four-group categorization used by Feldstein.[29] Feldstein omits the first group, those with low MTRs, from the sample, so we also omit that group for our initial analysis (though we subsequently add that

Table 7.2   Difference-in-Differences Estimates of the Effect of NTR on AGI

Variable	1989–1983 Differences by 1983 MTR Group		Difference of Differences	Implied Elasticity
	High 1983 MTR	Midrange 1983 MTR		
AGI				
Average linear difference	118,000	7,747	110,000	1.992[a]
Percentage change in average	0.700	0.173	0.527	1.828
Average of percentage changes	0.706	0.213	0.494	1.757
NTR				
Average linear difference	0.203	0.079	0.124	
Percentage change in average	0.401	0.113	0.288	
Average of percentage changes	0.401	0.120	0.281	

Source: Authors' calculations.

[a] The absolute difference-in-differences estimate is 890,000 [=(118,000 – 7,747)/(0.203 – 0.079)]. We convert to an arc elasticity by multiplying by [(0.203 + 0.079)/(118,000 + 7,747). N = 406.

subsample back in). In table 7.2 the first two columns show changes in AGI and in the NTR for the midrange- and high-MTR groups. For linear differences (ΔAGI and ΔNTR), it can be readily seen that the high-MTR group experienced greater increases both in AGI and in the NTR. The magnitudes imply that a 0.01 increase in the change-in-NTR is associated with a large absolute increase of $8,900 of annual AGI (1988 dollars). Converted to an elasticity at the means of the data, this yields a sizable elasticity of 1.992. Feldstein estimated elasticities in the range (1.10,3.05) for a taxable-income-related concept and (0.26,0.88) for an AGI-related concept.[30] Although the latter is closer in concept to our income definition than the former, our estimates are closer to the former range. Given the marked differences in the way income information is obtained in the two data sets, our estimates should be judged to be reasonably consistent with those of Feldstein.

Feldstein calculates his elasticities somewhat differently, however, by first calculating mean AGI and NTR for each group, then calculating the percentage change in that mean between the years and using the difference in the differences of these percentages for his calculations. As shown in table 7.2, when we apply this method to our data, we obtain an elasticity estimate of 1.828, quite close to the linear-difference calculation and again reasonably consistent with the Feldstein elasticities. We also show in table 7.2 a third possible means of calculating an elasticity: computing percentage changes in AGI and NTR at the individual level and then computing an elasticity from the means of these percentage changes. This yields an elasticity of 1.757, which is close to our estimates from the other methods.

Of the three methods of calculating elasticities reported in table 7.2, only the first and third—not the second, which is the precise method used by Feldstein—can be formulated in regression terms. We do this in table 7.3, where we show IV estimates of two types of equations, one for which the linear change in AGI is the dependent variable and one for which the percentage change in AGI (for the individual observation) is the dependent variable. In both cases there is a single regressor, which is either the linear change in the NTR or the percentage change in NTR.

Table 7.3 Regressions to Generate Difference-in-Differences Estimates of NTR on AGI

	Linear Differences			Individual Percentage Changes		
	AGI (Reduced-Form)	NTR (First Stage)	AGI (2SLS)	AGI (Reduced-Form)	NTR (First Stage)	AGI (2SLS)
Midrange 1983 MTR group dummy	7,747 (5,934)	0.079*** (0.004)	—	0.213*** (0.044)	0.120*** (0.006)	—
High 1983 MTR group dummy	0.118*** (0.029)	0.203*** (0.018)	—	0.706*** (0.216)	0.401*** (0.029)	—
Change in NTR	—	—	890,000*** (289,000)	—	—	1.757** (0.882)
Constant	—	—	-62,464** (25,250)	—	—	0.002 (0.126)

Source: Authors' calculations.

Notes: In columns 1 and 3 the dependent variable is the linear change in AGI; in column 2 the dependent variable is the linear change in the NTR; in columns 4 and 6 the dependent variable is the percentage change in AGI; in column 5 the dependent variable is the percentage change in the NTR. All regressions are weighted. Standard errors appear in parentheses. $N = 406$.

*Significant at .10 level; **significant at .05 level; ***significant at .01 level

Instrumental-variables is applied by using a single dummy, in effect—whether the 1983 MTR is in the high category—as the instrument.[31] Table 7.3 shows, for both methods, the reduced forms as well as the first-stage regressions, whose coefficients are identical to the entries in table 7.2. The second-stage IV coefficient on the change in NTR is 890,000 in the linear model and 1.757 in the percentage-change model, thus replicating the estimates in table 7.2; the former must be converted to an elasticity, which we showed to be 1.992 in table 7.2. Table 7.3 shows standard errors on the estimates that are far below the coefficient magnitudes and hence imply highly significant effects.

Table 7.4 shows the effect of adding additional independent variables to the model as well as, more importantly, the effect of using alternative instruments, on the second-stage estimated coefficient on the linear change in NTR in regressions for the linear change in AGI. The first row shows the coefficient that results when a number of additional regressors are included (in both the first and second stages)—family size, marital status, and age. This addition has little effect on the coefficient. The second half of the table shows the F-statistic on the instruments,

Table 7.4   2SLS Estimates of the Effect of NTR on AGI with Alternative Instruments

| | Second-Stage Equation[a] | | First-Stage Equation | | |
| | Coefficient on | Standard | | | |
Instrument(s)	Change in NTR	Error	F-Statistic	P-Value	R^2
Two 1983 MTR groups	0.969***	0.320	38.578	0.000	0.126
Seven 1983 MTR groups	0.162	0.126	42.742	0.000	0.420
High 1983 income dummy	0.839***	0.297	41.756	0.000	0.132
Log 1983 AGI	0.345***	0.140	202.16	0.000	0.365
1983 marital status (married dummy)	0.123	1.343	0.672	0.328	0.065
1983 household size	−0.152	1.128	0.683	0.317	0.075
Postcollege	0.341	0.435	14.336	0.000	0.074
Professional-manager	1.974	2.714	0.662	0.338	0.043
Log 1983 house value and log 1983 life insurance value[b]	0.649**	0.289	9.824	0.000	0.128
High 1983 house value or life insurance value (dummy)	0.660**	0.327	30.465	0.000	0.109

Source: Authors' calculations.
Notes: Sample of men with midrange and high 1983 MTR ($N = 406$). All regressions are weighted two-stage least squares, using linear differences in AGI and NTR in second and first stages, respectively. Each line in table shows results from a different model with a different set of instruments. The F-statistics test zero restrictions on the instruments in the first stage and the p-values associated with those statistics are shown along with the R^2 from the first-stage regression. Each model contains in both the first and second stages a constant term and independent variables for 1983 age, marital status (dummy for whether married), and household size; the estimates on these control variables are presented in table 7A.3 for two of the models. When marital status and household size are used as instruments, these variables are omitted from the second stage. When these two instruments are used, only those with no change in marital status or household size are included.
[a.] Coefficients and standard errors divided by 10^6.
[b.] Instruments also include dummies for zero house value and life insurance.
*Significant at .10 level; **significant at .05 level; ***signficant at .01 level

the p-value for that statistic, and the R-squared of the first-stage regression; the high F-statistic on the instrument (that is, the MTR dummy) shows this instrument to be strong.

The second row shows the effect of using seven separate 1983 MTR groups as instruments instead of the two used heretofore. (See table 7.1 for group definitions; the highest of the groups is the same as the 0.44-and-over group.) Interestingly, the NTR coefficient loses significance in this specification. The source of the difference is illustrated in figure 7.5, which shows the change in AGI between the time periods for the different MTR groups. The figure includes the less-than-or-equal-to-0.20 MTR group, so it shows three and eight MTR groups instead of two and seven, respectively.[32] For all of the eight MTR groups except the highest (MTR between 0.44 and 0.50), the relationship between initial-period MTR (and hence the change in NTR) is flat or negative, but the highest-MTR group has a very large increase in AGI. Thus, it appears that it is the highest-MTR group that is responsible for the positive elasticities being estimated.[33]

Because initial-period MTR is primarily a function of initial-period AGI, we examine whether using AGI itself as the instrument would alter any of these conclusions. The third and fourth rows of table 7.4 show that it would not. Using a dummy for high 1983 income, a positive and significant elasticity is obtained in the same range as that obtained by using the two-MTR groups. But when the log of AGI is used—thereby not making a special distinction between the highest-AGI group and the rest of the population—the estimated coefficient is significant but drastically reduced in magnitude.

That initial-period AGI is the implicit instrument in this approach, even if MTR groups are used, brings the two issues described earlier into consideration.

Figure 7.5   Change in AGI by Change in NTR

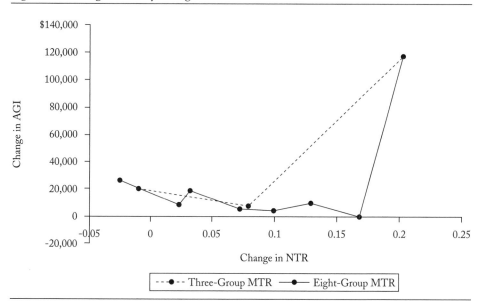

Source: Authors' calculations.

Regression-to-the-mean effects in AGI—or more generally, serially correlated errors—bias estimates that use AGI as an instrument. In addition, even if a measure of permanent income or AGI were used (that is, one purged of serially correlated transitory components), the more fundamental issue arises of whether its coefficient has been changing over time. For these reasons, we test several alternative instruments shown in table 7.4. First, we test the 1983 values of marital status and household size, because these both enter the tax formula independently of AGI.[34] However, as the table indicates, they are extremely weak instruments—they do not discriminate well between different change-in-NTR values—and yield insignificant results. Inasmuch as the results using AGI and MTR instruments have indicated that positive tax effects are arising only from the very top of the distribution, the fact that marital status and household size do not discriminate well between that upper group and the rest of the population makes their insignificance not unexpected.[35]

We next test education and occupation as instruments. To discriminate to the greatest extent possible between the upper tail of the distribution and the rest of the population, we construct a dummy for whether an individual has postcollege educational experience and a dummy for whether an individual is in a professional or managerial occupation, the highest-paid occupations. As table 7.4 shows, the occupational dummy is a very weak instrument, but the education dummy is not (perhaps because the occupational dummy has a mean of only 0.45); nevertheless, even the latter yields an insignificant tax response estimate. However, the tax response estimate when education is used is still positive and sizable in economic terms, even though its standard error is also quite large, indicating imprecision in the estimate.

We test in the last two rows two measures of assets that are available in our data—the value of an owned house and the value of life insurance. These variables, while financial in nature, are sufficiently loosely connected to current income flows as to increase their likelihood of exogeneity and, similarly, are less likely to be affected by regression-to-the-mean effects than AGI. In addition, assets are less equally distributed than income or the other instruments we have tested and hence have a better chance of discriminating between the top earners and those below. However, asset values are subject to the trending-coefficient problem, because asset inequality has been growing (Wolff 1994, 1995).

We test a set of instruments that include the log of house value, log of life insurance value, and dummies for those with zero house value and life insurance; and a dummy for whether either is high (see discussion of table 7.1 for exact definitions). As the results in the table show, these instruments are strong in the first stage and also yield significant estimated tax response coefficients, albeit only about two-thirds the magnitude of those using the two-MTR or top-AGI-group instruments.

Finally, we show in table 7.5 the effects of adding the low-MTR group back into the sample (which we have continued to exclude, for comparability with the Feldstein analysis), as well as tests for the importance of regression-to-the-mean effects. Adding the low-MTR group into the sample lowers the estimated tax effect arising when the small-MTR-group instruments are used.[36] We also show results from using the asset instruments, because they not only are strong instruments but yielded significant results in table 7.4; the estimated coefficient falls slightly when the low-MTR group is added as well (from 0.649 in table 7.4 to

Table 7.5   2SLS Estimates of the Effect of NTR on AGI Using Alternative Instruments and Samples and Controls for Regression to Mean

	Instrument Set				
	Two 1983 MTR Groups	Log 1983 House Value Log 1983 Life Insurance			High 1983 House Value or Life Insurance Value
Change in NTR[a]	0.815***	0.552**	0.885**	1.006**	0.977**
	(0.255)	(0.224)	(0.430)	(0.443)	(0.510)
1983 AGI	—	—	−0.414*	−0.694**	−0.674**
	—	—	(0.249)	(0.329)	(0.371)
Low 1983 MTR group included?	y	y	n	y	y
First stage:					
F-statistic	44.408	12.036	5.201	4.432	13.033
p-value	0.000	0.000	0.000	0.002	0.000
R^2	0.128	0.135	0.173	0.211	0.204
Observations (unweighted)	490	490	406	490	490

Source: Authors' calculations.
Notes: All regressions are weighted two-stage least squares using linear differences in AGI. Standard errors appear in parentheses.
[a] Coefficients and standard errors divided by 10^6.
*Significant at .10 level; **significant at .05 level; ***significant at .01 level

0.552 in table 7.5, for example, for the log asset instrument). With these instruments, we can also test for regression-to-the-mean effects by entering AGI into both the first- and second-stage equations.[37] As table 7.5 shows, controlling for AGI in this way increases the estimated tax response coefficient. This should be expected, because pure regression-to-the-mean effects would tend to bias the coefficient in a negative direction. (Those with positive 1983 transitory errors should experience declines in AGI over time.)

We thus have replicated the sizable tax elasticities for AGI found by Feldstein (1995a) and have shown that those elasticities arise from behavior of the extreme upper tail of the income distribution that is quite discontinuous with that of the rest of the population. Instruments that are successful in discriminating between that top group and the balance of the population, even if they are instruments not strictly AGI-based (for example, asset instruments), yield similarly sizable tax elasticities even if regression-to-the-mean effects are accounted for.

Results for Hours Worked

Having tested instruments for AGI, we now turn to hours of work and apply the same strategy and test the same set of instruments. Figure 7.6 shows the distribution of 1983 annual hours worked by the three 1983 MTR groups we used for the AGI analysis. The distribution is remarkably different for the high-MTR group and the rest of the population, with about 60 percent of the high-MTR group working more than 2,500 hours per year and almost 30 percent working more than 3,000 hours per

Figure 7.6   Annual Hours Worked by Marginal Tax Rate, 1983

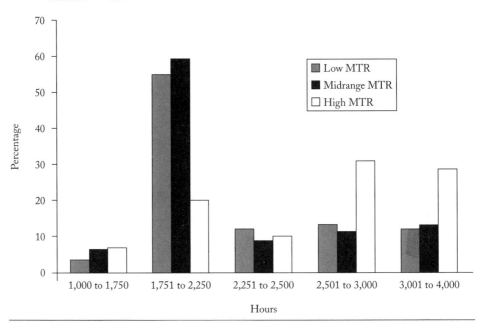

Source: Authors' calculations.

year. For the rest of the population the mode is typically in the range of 1,751 to 2,250 hours. Given these high hours of work, there is at least some prima facie question of whether there is much opportunity for additional work among the rich.[38]

Table 7.6 shows IV estimates of the effect of NTR on annual hours worked, using the same methodology as in table 7.4—with the exact same specification and sample for each equation but with a different dependent variable. As the table indicates, none of the effects are significant except that for the high-asset group, and that effect is negative. The strength of the estimates, shown in the latter columns of the table, is necessarily the same as in table 7.4; thus, the insignificance of the estimated effects cannot be ascribed to the weakness of the instruments.

Figure 7.7 shows the pattern of changes in hours worked over the period by 1983 MTR group, in analogy to figure 7.5. The relative hours changes for the midrange- and high-MTR groups are slightly positive but small in magnitude; the coefficient in table 7.6 is negative because of the addition of the other independent variables, but it is still insignificant.

Even if the lack of hours response of the upper tail of the distribution can be ascribed to hours that are already near their maximum, this is not true for the rest of the population. Indeed, the very high hours worked of the upper tail is incontrovertible evidence that hours of work are fundamentally flexible upward in the U.S. labor market for those who are working "only" two thousand hours per year (that is, year-round full-time). Yet figure 7.7 does not show any particular positive relationship between initial MTR (and hence the change in NTR) and the change in hours worked. Nor do the instruments in table 7.6 that treat all parts of the pop-

Table 7.6   Estimates of the Effect of NTR on Annual Hours Worked with Alternative Instruments

Instrument(s)	Second-Stage Equation[a]		First-Stage Equation		
	Coefficient on Change in NTR	Standard Error	F-Statistic	P-Value	R^2
Two 1983 MTR groups	−0.010	0.135	38.578	0.000	0.126
Seven 1983 MTR groups	−0.013	0.063	42.742	0.000	0.420
High 1983 income dummy	−0.246	0.135	41.756	0.000	0.132
Log 1983 AGI	−0.038	0.069	202.16	0.000	0.365
1983 marital status (married dummy)	−2.011	2.211	0.672	0.328	0.065
1983 household size	0.936	1.088	0.683	0.317	0.075
Postcollege	−0.320	0.229	14.336	0.000	0.074
Professional-manager	−1.369	1.627	0.662	0.338	0.043
Log 1983 house value and log 1983 life insurance value[b]	0.072	0.134	9.824	0.000	0.128
High 1983 house value or life insurance value (dummy)	−0.488***	0.173	30.465	0.000	0.109

Source: Authors' calculations.
Notes: Sample of men with midrange and high 1983 MTR. All regressions are weighted two-stage least squares, using linear differences in AGI and NTR in second and first stages, respectively. Each line in table shows results from a different model with a different set of instruments. The F-statistics test zero restrictions on the instruments in the first stage and the p-values associated with those statistics are shown along with the R^2 from the first-stage regression. Each model contains in both the first and second stages a constant term and independent variables for 1983 age, marital status (dummy for whether married), and household size; the estimates on these control variables are presented in table 7A.3 for two of the models. When marital status and household size are used as instruments, these variables are omitted from the second stage. When these two instruments are used, only those with no change in marital status or household size are included.
[a] Coefficients and standard errors divided by 10^4.
[b] Instruments also include dummies for zero house value and life insurance.
*Significant at .10 level; **significant at .05 level; ***significant at .01 level

ulation distribution equally show any more positive responses than those that focus on the upper tail. Consequently, the evidence in these data is that hours of work are, as found in much previous work, inelastic for prime-age males in the United States.

Table 7.7 provides several additional specifications to test alternative hypotheses for the effects of hours worked. Adding the low-MTR group into the sample has no effect on the significance of the tax effects, nor does controlling for regression-to-the-mean effects in hours of work. We also show in the last two columns of table 7.7 a specification that includes the change in tax payment as well as the change in the NTR. This specification approximates more closely the neoclassical labor supply function by accounting for income effects.[39] The results show insignificant income effects and do not change the insignificance of the NTR effects. The house value and life insurance variables are extremely weak instruments for the change in tax payment that could, in principle, be responsible for this result.

We turn in table 7.8 to test whether NTR effects might be significant on hours of work for some subportions of the distribution. The theoretically appropriate price of

Figure 7.7   Change in Hours Worked by Change in NTR

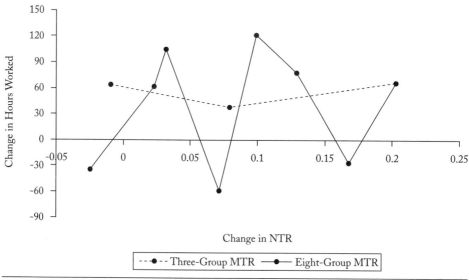

Source: Authors' calculations.

leisure is $W(1 - t)$, which, unless it affects hours of work in simple logarithmic form, implies that the percentage effect of a change in NTR should vary with the value of the wage rate. For completeness, we also test such interactions for AGI as a dependent variable. We test the same sets of samples and instruments shown in table 7.7.

The results in table 7.8 show no effects of this type to be present in the data for hours of work. When the NTR change is interacted with our postcollege dummy (a predictor of the wage), the interaction coefficients are insignificant in all cases save one where the coefficient is a counterintuitive negative. When the net wage itself is treated as the endogenous variable of interest and is instrumented accordingly, the same pattern results.

Interestingly, several positive and significant education interaction effects are found when AGI is the outcome of interest. Indeed, for some specifications the AGI effects are insignificant for the population without postcollege experience. These results are consistent with the hypothesis that higher-wage taxpayers respond more heavily to changes in their marginal tax rates than those with lower wages. However, these results are sensitive to adjustment for regression to the mean. As table 7.8 shows, when such adjustment is made the AGI results disappear for the high-educated group but are stronger for the rest of the population; interestingly, hours of work effects appear for the latter as well.

Income Decomposition   To explore the mechanism by which the AGI tax response occurs, we briefly decompose income into three major constituent parts—wage and salary income, business income, and other income—and apply our same methodology to estimating tax responses for these three variables. We should note

Table 7.7   2SLS Estimates of the Effect of NTR on Annual Hours Worked Using Alternative Instruments and Controls for Regression to Mean

	Two 1983 MTR Groups	High House Value or Life Insurance Value		Log 1983 House Value Log 1983 Life Insurance		
Change in NTR[a]	0.025	−0.044	0.164	−0.024	−0.015	0.129
	(0.127)	(0.117)	(0.111)	(0.122)	(0.300)	(0.231)
Change in tax payment	—	—	—	—	−0.001	−0.001
	—	—	—	—	(0.030)	(0.024)
1983 hours worked	—	−0.609***	−0.609***	—	—	−0.613***
	—	(0.041)	(0.042)	—	—	(0.075)
Low 1983 MTR group included?	y	n	n	y	y	y
First-stage NTR equation						
F-statistic	44.408	32.329	9.824	12.036	12.036	12.536
p-value	0.000	0.000	0.000	0.000	0.000	0.000
R^2	0.128	0.113	0.128	0.135	0.135	0.140
First-stage tax payment equation						
F-statistic	—	—	—	—	0.747	1.241
p-value	—	—	—	—	0.253	0.293
R^2	—	—	—	—	0.012	0.014
Observations (unweighted)	490	406	406	490	490	490

Source: Authors' calculations.
Notes: All regressions are weighted two-stage least squares using linear differences. Standard errors appear in parentheses.
[a] Coefficients and standard errors divided by 10^4.
*Significant at .10 level; **significant at .05 level; ***significant at .01 level

that the sum of these three components, or total income, is not the same as AGI in our data set. Total income is the sum of all forms of income reported on the survey; not only is AGI not from tax records, but it is the response to a specific question on the survey.

Table 7.9 shows the results of this exercise. The first column shows the results of applying the Feldstein methodology to total income, wage and salary income, and the sum of wage and salary income and business income. Business income is included with wage and salary because it is zero for most of the sample; business income responses are necessarily equal to the difference in the coefficients in the second and third rows of the table. The coefficients for other income are also obtainable by subtracting the third row from the first. The Feldstein methodology shows significant tax effects on wage and salary income and its sum with business income, and the larger coefficient when business income is included indicates that business income is the largest source of the response. However, this result does not

Table 7.8   Estimates of the Effects of NTR on AGI and Annual Hours Worked with Education and Wage Interactions Using Alternative Instruments and Samples and Controls for Regression to Mean

	Instrument Set					
	Two 1983 MTR Groups		Log 1983 House Value Log 1983 Life Insurance		High 1983 House Value or Life Insurance Value	
Hours worked: I						
NTR	−0.077	0.272	0.042	0.356***	0.236**	0.274*
	(0.260)	(0.169)	(0.155)	(0.135)	(0.122)	(0.156)
NTR × (postcollege)	0.186	−0.528	−0.063	−0.263	−0.033	−0.407*
	(0.294)	(0.358)	(0.348)	(0.287)	(0.278)	(0.246)
Hours worked: II						
NTR × W	−4.344	−3.996	−3.752	−3.908	−2.860	−7.311*
	(4.042)	(3.395)	(3.746)	(2.684)	(3.012)	(4.405)
AGI: I						
NTR	1.202**	0.452	0.393	0.823*	1.047***	0.972**
	(0.499)	(0.328)	(0.250)	(0.427)	(0.398)	(0.475)
NTR × (postcollege)	−0.149	1.448**	1.298**	0.645	0.423	0.167
	(0.565)	(0.694)	(0.560)	(0.484)	(0.328)	(0.315)
AGI: II						
NTR × W	2,215.6***	1,606.0**	1,679.7***	1,753.0***	1,963.9***	947.1
	(655.2)	(559.7)	(519.2)	(679.8)	(633.3)	(986.4)
Low 1983 MTR group included?	n	n	y	n	y	y
Control for regression to mean?	n	n	n	y	y	y
Observations (unweighted)	406	406	490	406	490	490

Source: Authors' calculations.

Notes: All regressions are weighted two-stage least squares using linear differences, and all include the aforementioned control variables in both stages. The regression-to-the-mean specifications include the 1983 value of the respective dependent variables. The coefficients in the AGI models are divided by 10^6, and those in the hours worked models are divided by 10^4.

* Significant at .10 level; **significant at .05 level; ***significant at .01 level

hold up when asset instruments are used and regression-to-the-mean effects are allowed, as the remaining columns show. The major change occurs when regression-to-the-mean effects are permitted, thus wiping out the business income effect. (In fact, it turns negative.) This result implies that serial correlation in business income between 1983 and 1988 was positive, not negative; those with above-average (below-average) business income in 1983 had even greater (lesser) business income in 1988. Thus, the implication of the table is that the large business income responses shown in the first column are incorrectly assigning differential growth rates of such income to the tax law change.

Table 7.9   2SLS Estimates of the Effect of NTR on Other Dependent Variables Using Alternative Instruments and Samples and Controls for Regression to Mean

	Instrument Set					
Dependant Variable	Two 1983 MTR Groups		Log 1983 House Value Log 1983 Life Insurance			High 1983 House Value or Life Insurance Value
Total income	0.983***	0.583*	0.504**	0.475	0.500	0.249
	(0.347)	(0.316)	(0.243)	(0.432)	(0.398)	(0.486)
Wage/Salary	0.230**	0.293***	0.287***	0.494***	0.608***	0.398***
	(0.106)	(0.110)	(0.092)	(0.153)	(0.174)	(0.124)
Wage/salary and business income	0.701***	0.452*	0.377**	0.153	0.137	−0.145
	(0.256)	(0.235)	(0.180)	(0.367)	(0.396)	(0.481)
Low 1983 MTR group included?	n	n	y	n	y	y
Lagged dependent variable included?	n	n	n	y	y	y
Observations (unweighted)	406	406	490	406	490	490

Source: Authors' calculations.

Notes: All regressions are weighted two-stage least squares using linear differences. Each row shows the NTR coefficients for a different dependent variable. All models include a constant term and independent variables for age, marital status, and household number in 1983 in both stages.

[a.] Coefficients and standard errors are divided by 10^6.

* Significant at .10 level; **significant at .05 level; ***significant at .01 level

The tax response does remain for wage and salary income, however, and it is therefore this form of income that we conclude constitutes the major source of adjustment to the act. Because we have found no hours-of-work response, we therefore have found implicitly that the entire response to the Tax Reform Act of 1986 for men occurred in hourly wage rates.

CONCLUSIONS

A long-standing issue in the effects of taxation on individual behavior concerns whether labor supply, most commonly measured by hours of work, responds to taxation. We have examined whether high-income men—the rich—so respond. High-income taxpayers are often thought to have more opportunities to respond to tax law changes and to have a greater incentive to do so because of their high marginal tax rates. Our analysis of changes in the hours of work of such men between 1983 and 1989, in response to the marginal tax rate reductions legislated in the 1986 Tax Reform Act, find essentially no evidence of any such response. We speculate that this is partly a result of the fact that such men are already working long hours (often more than three thousand per year) that there is little remaining opportunity for response.

The major limitation of our study for learning about the behavior of the rich in response to taxation arises from the limitations of the data in yielding information about other aspects of the labor-force behavior of the rich. Incentives to work as self-employed and incentives to work in jobs in which compensation is deferred or otherwise tax-sheltered are just two examples. Better data on these behaviors of the rich are required before further progress can be made in investigating them.

APPENDIX: MODELING ISSUES IN THE USE OF REPEATED CROSS-SECTIONS AND IMPLICATIONS OF PIECEWISE-LINEAR TAX SCHEDULES
Repeated Cross-Sections

Here we discuss the application of the difference-in-differences, fixed-effects method of estimation with repeated cross-section (RCS) data instead of panel data. We assume we have two independent cross-sections of the population with information on y and x or z, but that the individuals in the two are different.[40] Estimation of the models with time-invariant x or z is not difficult because the invariance of x and z implies that individuals in the two cross-sections can be matched to one another using common values of x and z; although they are not the same individuals, they are drawn from the same strata of the population. This also implies that all time-invariant error terms (like μ) will have the same mean for individuals with the same value of z in both populations. In the case of time-invariant x, equation (7.1) can be pooled across periods to estimate

$$y_t = \alpha_p + [\Delta\alpha_p]D_t + \beta[d_{p+1}(x) - d_p(x)]D_t + \beta d_p(x) + \gamma x + \varepsilon_t \qquad (7A.1)$$

$$(t = p, p+1)$$

where D_t equals 1 if $t = p + 1$ and 0 otherwise. The coefficient on the change in law shown in brackets is identified (apart from nonlinearities) by virtue of the assumption that γ does not vary with p; if it did, then an extra term $D_t x$ would be required and the effects of the two x variables would be confounded with the effect of the change in law. Note that the separate $d_p(x)$ variable could either be allowed to have a different coefficient than that on the law-change variable, or it could be folded into it.

In the case of time-invariant z, equation (7.4) can be pooled across periods to give

$$y_t = \alpha_p + [\Delta\alpha_p]D_t + \beta[d_{p+1}(z) - d_p(z)]D_t + \beta d_p(z) + \mu + \varepsilon_t \qquad (7A.2)$$

$$(t = p, p+1)$$

In this case, the coefficient on $d_p(z)$ is a biased estimate of β because z and μ are not independent, but the coefficient on the change in d is asymptotically unbiased because that variable is independent of μ conditional on $d_p(z)$.[41]

Time-varying x and z raise more difficult issues because the populations with the same values of x and z from which the two cross-sections are drawn are not composed of the same individuals. However, at least if the variable is exogenous (the "x" case), those with the same value of x in the two cross-sections will have the same mean y in the absence of an effect of the law. Consequently, in this case equation (7.1) can be pooled across periods to obtain an estimating equation analogous to equation (7A.2), namely,

$$y_t = \alpha_p + [\Delta\alpha_p]D_t + \beta[d_{p+1}(x_{p+1}) - d_p(x_p)]D_t + \beta d_p(x_p) + \gamma[x_p(1 - D_t) + x_{p+1}D_t] + \varepsilon_t$$
$$\text{(7A.3)}$$

$$(t = p, p + 1)$$

As in equation (7A.2), the separate term for $d_p(x_p)$ could be used to obtain a separate estimate of β or be included in the first term in brackets for a single β estimate.[42] On the other hand, if time-varying, endogenous z is the variable used for identification, using RCS data is more problematic. Pooling equations (7.6) and (7.7) across periods, we have:

$$y_t = \alpha_p + [\Delta\alpha_p]D_t + \beta[d_{p+1}(z_{p+1}) - d_p(z_p)]D_t + \beta d_p(z_p) + \mu + \varepsilon_t \qquad \text{(7A.4)}$$
$$(t = p, p + 1)$$

Once again, the issue is whether z_p is independent of ε_p, and z_{p+1} of ε_{p+1}. It is difficult to generalize across all applications because the degree of jointness of y (and therefore of ε) and z depends on the particular variables in question, but in many cases such independence is unlikely to hold.

If the independence condition fails, the distribution of individuals with different values of z will change between the periods, as will the mean of y among individuals with fixed values of z. Thus, the implicit groups formed by different values of z will be endogenous, thus biasing the estimated effects. The availability of lagged z_p in panel data made possible an approach that used z_p as an instrument (albeit with the regression-to-the-mean problems noted there), but this approach is not possible with RCS data.[43]

Piecewise-Linear Tax Schedules

The common approach to estimation of labor supply choice in the face of a bracket income tax system has been to specify the "marginal" labor supply function along a segment of the budget constraint—that is, labor supply as a function of the "local" marginal tax rate (or net wage rate) and "virtual" nonlabor income (see references to this literature given in the text). Assume that the marginal tax rate in bracket s is t_s (s = 1, . . . S) and that the value of income (or a transform of income, like AGI) at the beginning of bracket s is $a_s(x)$, where x is a set of socioeconomic characteristics that affect the individual's tax position (that is, variables affecting AGI or affecting which schedule is applied, such as filing status). These 2S parameters characterize the tax system completely for a taxpayer with characteristics x. Maximizing a utility function U(H,Y − T;x) along segment s, where H is hours of work, Y is gross income, T is the amount of the tax payment, and x is a vector of exogenous socioeconomic characteristics that affect preferences for work, gives the "marginal" labor supply function

$$H = g\{W[1 − t_s(x)],\tilde{N}_s(x);x\} + \varepsilon = \alpha + \beta W[1 − t_s(x)] + \delta\tilde{N}_s(x) + \gamma x + \varepsilon \qquad (7A.5)$$

as given in equation (7.10) and with variables as defined there.

If individuals observed to locate on only one segment in a cross-section are used for estimation of equation (7A.5), the model is identified only under the same conditions described for equation (7.1).[44] Thus, the basic identification problem posed in the text is present here as well. Variation in the net wage and virtual nonlabor income can instead be obtained by pooling the data across segments, because different individuals with the same x will usually choose a variety of segments. However, this variation is endogenous, because the segment upon which an individual is observed is a function of ε, an error term that includes heterogeneity of preferences, measurement error, and "optimization" error (that is, deviations from optimal choice arising from the cost of fine-tuning labor supply location relative to the brackets). Further, this endogeneity cannot be eliminated for the same reason already discussed, namely, that there are no exclusion restrictions that, apart from nonlinearities in functional form, could be used to identify the model.

Formally, let D_s be a dummy variable equal to 1 if the individual is observed on segment s and equal to 0 otherwise. Then implicitly all variables in equation (7A.5) are multiplied by D_s. Denote by V the set of variables W, N, all 2S parameters of the tax schedule, and x. Then $D_s = f(V,\varepsilon)$. If instrumental variables estimation is used to address the endogeneity, then identification is not achievable (apart from nonlinearities) because all variables in V are already in equation (7A.5) and there is no variation in the tax parameters in V independent of W,N, and x.[45] Thus, obtaining variation by pooling across segments does not solve the identification problem.

With it therefore established that the fundamental identification problem discussed in the text applies as well to the model when the piecewise-linear nature of the budget constraint is accounted for, it may be asked whether the use of first-differencing and the existence of a variable in x with stationary effects on H may permit identification here as well. In a fundamental sense, the answer is affirmative, because the effect of tax rates is nonparametrically identified under those conditions and hence must be here as well. If $E(H_p|x) = f[T_p(x),x]$, where T_p is the 2S vector of tax parameters that change with time (p), then the existence of an x with stationary effects is equivalent to the assumption that p does not enter the function f independently or, equivalently, that the function f is not indexed by p. Two waves of a panel thus identify the effect of $T_p(x)$ on $E(H_p|x)$.

The question instead is what parameters are identified by this strategy, and here the answer is that no simple function of the parameters in equation (7A.5) are identified. This is easy to see if we consider the mean of equation (7A.5) conditional on being on segment s:

$$E(H|V,D_s = 1) = \alpha + \beta W[1 − t_s(x)] + \delta\tilde{N}_s(x) + \gamma x + E(\varepsilon|V,D_s = 1) \qquad (7A.6)$$

from which it is clear that the residual term $E(\varepsilon|V,D_s = 1)$ is not constant over time if the tax schedule changes and hence does not cancel out in first-differencing, even if γx does. An additional complication, which is more fundamental, is that equation (7A.5) is not consistent with a nonzero variance of ε in the first place because of the problem of segment classification error. Given the presence of measurement error and optimization error in ε, a sufficiently large positive or negative value of ε moves the individual to a segment other than s. Thus, the H of some individuals observed on segment s is not generated by the net wage and virtual nonlabor income on that segment, and hence $E(H|V,D_s = 1)$ is not equal to $g\{W[1 - t_s(x)],\tilde{N}_s(x);x\}$ + $E(\varepsilon|V,D_s = 1)$ in general, where s is the observed (rather than true) segment. Thus, the regressors are misspecified. The mean H of those observed to be on segment s is consequently not the mean of equation (7A.5) but is rather

$$E(H|V,D_s = 1) = \sum_{s'=1}^{S} Q_{ss'}(V) \ E(H|V,D_{s'}^* = 1) + \sum_{k=1}^{S} R_{sk}(V) \ E(H|V,D_k^* = 1) \quad (7A.7)$$

where D_s^*, is a dummy variable equal to 1 if the true segment (defined as that implied by utility maximization with no optimization costs) is segment s'; $Q_{ss'}(V)$ is the probability that an individual observed on s is optimizing on s'; D_k^* is a dummy variable equal to 1 if the true optimizing point is at the kink at the beginning of segment k; and $R_{sk}(V)$ is the probability that an individual observed on segment s is optimizing at kink k.[46] Thus, observed H is a weighted average of the net wage rates and virtual nonlabor incomes on all segments, for these are the determinants of H on each segment. The fact that D_s^* and D_k^* are not observed implies that the conditional means in equation (7A.7) cannot be directly estimated.[47]

Equation (7A.7) thus represents the function whose mean can be thought to be approximated by the local net wage and virtual income. A linear projection of equation (7A.7) onto those two local variables, and x, yields as coefficients nonlinear functions of the other parameters and variables in the model, including the other tax parameters. It is the coefficient on the net tax rate in such a projection that is the "β" estimated by the models reported in the text tables 7.6,7.7,7.8, and related tables for AGI.

APPENDIX

Table 7A.1   Sample Inclusion Criteria and Sample Size

Inclusion Criteria	Sample Size Remaining
Full SCF panel 1983 to 1989	1,479
Including only . . .	
Male heads of households	1,214
Aged twenty-five to fifty-four in 1983	695
No ambiguity in tracing individuals between 1983 and 1989	628
AGI in both 1983 and 1989 greater than zero	563
Wages in both 1983 and 1989 greater than zero	498
Annual hours worked in both 1983 and 1989 greater than or equal to 200	496
1989 hours worked not imputed	490

Source: Authors' calculations.

Table 7A.2 Means and Standard Deviations in the 1983 and 1989 SCF Panel (Men Twenty-Five to Fifty-Four in 1983): All Men and Men with Low 1983 Marginal Tax Rates

Variable	All Men		Men with Low 1983 Marginal Tax Rates	
	1983	1989	1983	1989
Adjusted gross income (AGI)	43,129	57,082	20,084	40,193
	(45,408)	(115,515)	(5,450)	(40,294)
Annual hours worked	2,325	2,371	2,272	2,337
	(621)	(584)	(631)	(702)
Total income	48,995	63,285	25,470	40,602
	(54,645)	(138,570)	(8,839)	(43,383)
Wage and salary income	35,390	48,342	15,964	30,625
	(25,383)	(41,926)	(9,981)	(28,881)
Wage and salary and business income	44,000	57,474	23,524	37,669
	(36,468)	(102,962)	(8,407)	(36,405)
Net-of-tax rate (NTR = 1 − t)	0.723	0.786	0.832	0.823
	(0.088)	(0.065)	(0.024)	(0.051)
Hourly wage rate (W)	15.75	19.82	9.31	12.86
	(14.91)	(40.62)	(3.67)	(11.62)
W × NTR	10.71	15.07	7.71	10.36
	(7.65)	(29.12)	(2.96)	(8.27)
Tax payment	6,898.	8,587.	1,365.	4,727.
	(12,529.)	(26,377.)	(694.)	(9,758.)
Married	0.867	0.858	0.926	0.899
	(0.340)	(0.349)	(0.261)	(0.301)
Percentage with no change in marital status	—	0.861	—	0.973
	—	(0.346)	—	(0.162)
Household size	3.405	3.255	4.100	3.833
	(1.492)	(1.374)	(1.515)	(1.467)
Percentage with no change in household size	—	0.471	—	0.461
	—	(0.499)	—	(0.499)
Age thirty to thirty-four	0.213	—	0.168	—
	(0.409)	—	(0.374)	—
Age thirty-five to thirty-nine	0.175	—	0.160	—
	(0.380)	—	(0.367)	—
Age forty to forty-four	0.140	—	0.165	—
	(0.347)	—	(0.370)	—
Age forty-five to forty-nine	0.183	—	0.172	—
	(0.387)	—	(0.378)	—
Age fifty to fifty-four	0.093	—	0.066	—
	(0.290)	—	(0.247)	—
Distribution of 1983 MTR				
0.00 ≤ t ≤ 0.20	0.222	—	1.000	—
	(0.416)	—	(0.000)	—
0.20 < t ≤ 0.22	0.148	—	0.000	—
	(0.356)	—	(0.000)	—
0.22 < t ≤ 0.25	0.124	—	0.000	—
	(0.330)	—	(0.000)	—

(Table continues on p. 227.)

Table 7A.2   *Continued*

Variable	All Men		Men with Low 1983 Marginal Tax Rates	
	1983	1989	1983	1989
0.25 < t ≤ 0.29	0.146	—	0.000	—
	(0.353)	—	(0.000)	—
0.29 < t ≤0.33	0.150	—	0.000	—
	(0.357)	—	(0.000)	—
0.33 < t ≤ 0.40	0.126	—	0.000	—
	(0.332)	—	(0.000)	—
0.40 < t ≤ 0.44	0.051	—	0.000	—
	(0.221)	—	(0.000)	—
0.44 < t ≤ 0.50	0.031	—	0.000	—
	(0.174)	—	(0.000)	—
Postcollege	0.150	—	0.062	—
	(0.357)	—	(0.241)	—
Professional-manager	0.413	—	0.273	—
	(0.492)	—	(0.445)	—
Log 1983 house value	8.279	—	7.096	—
	(5.010)	—	(5.236)	—
Zero 1983 house value (dummy)	0.266	—	0.351	—
	(0.442)	—	(0.478)	—
Log 1983 life insurance value	10.103	—	9.527	—
	(3.158)	—	(3.306)	—
Zero 1983 life insurance (dummy)	0.079	—	0.100	—
	(0.270)	—	(0.300)	—
High 1983 house value or life insurance value (dummy)	0.101	—	0.026	—
	(0.302)	—	(0.158)	—
Observations (unweighted)	490	490	84	84

Source: Authors' calculations.
Notes: All values are weighted. Low 1983 MTRs are those less than or equal to 0.20. All monetary amounts are in 1988 dollars. Standard deviations appear in parentheses.

Table 7A.3   2SLS Estimates of the Effect of NTR on AGI and Annual Hours Worked Using Alternative Instruments: Complete Model Estimates.

Dependent Variable	Change in AGI		Change in Hours	
Instrument	Two 1983 MTR Groups	Log 1983 House Value and Life Insurance Value	Two 1983 MTR Groups	Log 1983 House Value and Life Insurance Value
NTR	0.969***	0.649**	−0.010	0.072
	(0.320)	(0.289)	(0.135)	(0.134)
Age thirty to thirty-four	−0.064	−0.044	0.202**	0.197*
	(0.245)	(0.224)	(0.103)	(0.104)
Age thirty-five to thirty-nine	−0.331	−0.223	0.255**	0.227*
	(0.282)	(0.257)	(0.119)	(0.119)
Age forty to forty-four	−0.329	−0.206	0.499***	0.467***
	(0.312)	(0.284)	(0.131)	(0.132)
Age forty-five to forty-nine	−0.334	−0.216	0.161	0.130
	(0.284)	(0.259)	(0.120)	(0.120)
Age fifty to fifty-four	−0.282	−0.169	0.223*	0.194
	(0.318)	(0.290)	(0.134)	(0.134)
Married	−0.070	−0.077	−0.413***	−0.411***
	(0.264)	(0.242)	(0.111)	(0.112)
Household size	0.015	0.012	0.056*	0.056*
	(0.069)	(0.063)	(0.029)	(0.029)
Constant	−47,155.	−26,065.	11.014	−43.281
	(30,180.)	(27,430.)	(127.0)	(127.1)
Observations (unweighted)	406	406	406	406

Source: Authors' calculations.

Notes: All regressions are weighted two-stage least squares using linear differences. The coefficients and standard errors in the AGI models are divided by 10^6 and those in the hours-worked models are divided by 10^4.

*Significant at .10 level; **significant at .05 level; ***significant at .01 level

The authors would like to thank Gerhard Fries, Jerry Hausman, Arthur Kennickell, Lillian Mills, Joel Slemrod, Christopher Taber, James Ziliak, and other participants at the conference for suggestions and comments, as well as seminar participants at several universities and research organizations. Cristian de Ritis provided excellent research assistance.

NOTES

1. We consider here only the uncompensated elasticity. If income elasticities are sufficiently large, compensated elasticities can be nontrivial. See Hausman (1981) for an example.

2. There is also a literature on the effects of the earned income tax credit (EITC) on labor supply. Because that tax feature is aimed at low-income families, and we are concerned with high-income families, we do not review those studies.

3. We note that a major issue in these studies is whether the changes in income reported to the IRS reflect real changes in behavior or only changes in the form of income as a means of tax avoidance

(Slemrod 1996, forthcoming). However, Slemrod (1998) has pointed out that deadweight losses occur even in the latter case.

4. See Blundell and MaCurdy (1999) for another econometric discussion of the difference-in-dif-ferences method, and Meyer (1995) for an earlier discussion with references to applications of the method in areas other than taxes and labor supply.

5. We leave aside for the moment exactly what feature of the tax formula is of interest, including the issue of which marginal tax rate is of interest if the tax system is nonlinear. We discuss this issue in the next section.

6. If $d_p(x_p)$ is the exact tax function, then necessarily x_p includes endogenous variables like income. In that case, those variables generally do not appear on the righthand side of equation (7.1), but their variation nevertheless does not identify β because they will be correlated with ε_p.

7. If $d(x)$ is linear in x, identification would clearly be lost (p subscripts, which are irrelevant in a sin-gle cross-section, are ignored). If $d(x)$ is nonlinear in x, identification is generally lost if equation (7.1) is generalized to $y = \alpha+h[d(x)] + g(x) + \varepsilon$, where g and h are arbitrarily nonlinear functions with unknown parameters. (Recall that $d[x]$ is a known parametric function.) A qualification to this statement is that some portions of $g(x)$ can be identified if x is a vector rather than a scalar because multiple points in the support of x yield identical values of $d(x)$. We ignore this source of identification.

8. Under the interpretation of x_p in equation (7.1) as instruments, these cases correspond to the use of different types of instruments. The discussion is thus relevant to a different, but perhaps larger class of applications than the tax example.

9. With x defined as a vector of individual or area-specific dummy variables, the model fits into the standard individual-level or state-level fixed effects models.

   As in all fixed-effect and difference-in-differences models, an issue is the degree to which the lin-earity and additivity in the model can be relaxed and identification retained. Replacing the addi-tive linear γx by an additive nonlinear $g(x)$ requires for identification only the restriction that the function g be constant over time. Relaxing additivity and permitting interactions between x and $d_p(x)$ is also possible. If we let $y_p = \alpha_p + h[d_p(x),x]$, where h is of unknown form, a nonparametric regression of the change in y on x identifies differences in response across different values of x. The fundamental restriction is that h is not indexed by p and that all non-law-related changes over time appear in an additive term (the intercept). Thus, there is still a substantive difference-in-differences restriction even when additivity and nonlinearity is considerably reduced.

10. See Bosworth and Burtless (1992) and Eissa (1996a) for two labor supply studies that sought to establish longer-term time trends and to determine whether there have been deviations from trends. These types of tests are common in models that permit not only fixed effects in levels but also fixed effects in trends, for example. Note too that this method is made more complicated if the law has been changing in past periods (for example, prior changes in tax law), which may make it difficult to establish the existence of a trend.

11. This is a case of a "balanced" bias analogous to that in randomized trials based on the endoge-nously selected populations discussed by Heckman (1996b).

12. If $[d_{p+1}(Z)-d_p(Z)]$ interacts with μ, however, identification problems ensue.

13. Note that the issue of whether z_{p+1} is affected by the change in law is irrelevant. The issue is instead whether the values of y_{p+1} and z_{p+1} are chosen together, in which case there will be a dependence between them that is independent of the law change and hence could introduce a spurious relation between $d_{p+1}(z_{p+1})$ and y_{p+1}. Of course, in many cases one would expect the law change also to affect z_{p+1}, but this is not necessary for bias to occur.

14. In one case it is z_p, and in the other it is $d_p(z_p)$, that must be uncorrelated with $(v_{p+1} - v_p)$.

15. Auten and Carroll (1999) entered the period-p value of income as a control. Identification rested in their case on other variables (state-level tax rates, composition of income, and so on).

Another approach to the problem would be to utilize data for additional periods in the past. Assuming that tax rates had not changed over those periods, and that the regression-to-the-mean effect is stationary, that effect could be estimated from past periods' data and then "subtracted" off of the effect estimated from period p to p + 1. The additional restriction needed for identification is that the autocorrelation is of order one, and hence there is no direct additional regression-to-the-mean effect from periods prior to p.

16. We thank Joel Slemrod and Lillian Mills for pointing this out to us.

17. One reason is that there may be omitted variables correlated with the wage rate that would bias its coefficient; another is that the theory is potentially misspecified and that some behaviorally important differences in individual responses to wage rates and tax rates are left out of the model. Reasons for, and tests of, the hypothesis that wage and tax effects are different were discussed many years ago in the negative-income-tax experiment and related literatures. See Moffitt (1979, 480), Moffitt and Kehrer (1981, 106, 123), and Rosen (1976).

18. Eissa (1996a) and Blundell et al. (1998) both used education as a instrument. (Both allowed education to affect labor supply in levels but assumed that it disappeared in differences.) Note that we do not test the wage rate itself as an instrument, partly because it should appear explicitly in the labor supply equation, but also because we regard it as a choice variable and one that may respond to changes in tax law, as emphasized by Feldstein (1995b).

19. We reemphasize that eliminating serial-correlation and regression-to-the-mean effects, by using instruments orthogonal to transitory errors, is necessary but not sufficient for consistent estimation; it is also required that the coefficient on the instrument (for example, permanent income or its predictors) not change over time.

20. The figures use all working men between the ages of twenty-five and fifty-four in the year in question in the CPS.

21. We confirmed this with simple regression tests, which yielded insignificant coefficients for the difference in trends for the two groups prior to 1986.

22. Because of this oversampling, we use the SCF-supplied weights for all our analyses.

23. Aggregate AGI estimated from these responses exceeds published IRS totals by $400 billion, or 13 percent (Internal Revenue Service 1991).

24. This correspondence is in large part a result of the weight we use (called the "panel weight" in the SCF), whose construction was partially based on poststratification to match IRS tables on AGI with full capital gains and the dividend exclusion. There is another weight on the SCF that conducts further stratification, but we do not use it; our results appear not to be sensitive to which weight we utilize.

25. Thus, we take deductions as exogenous; see Triest (1992) and Feldstein (1999) for a discussion of this assumption. The IRS publishes the percentage of returns that itemized deductions and the average amount of those deductions by AGI category. We calculate a weighted average of the standard deduction and itemized deductions, using the percentage itemizing and the amount of deductions if itemizing. For filing status, we use a direct question on the 1989 SCF, but because no direct question was asked in 1983, we treat all married couples as filing jointly and all single men as filing singly in that year.

26. All monetary values in our chapter are in 1988 dollars using the personal consumption expenditure deflator. We continue to refer to "1983" and "1989" AGI even though the SCF follows the usual survey practice of obtaining this and all other income data for the year preceding the survey.

27. We investigated SCF measures of other measures of work effort and labor market behavior and compensation—such as self-employment and executive and deferred compensation. Unfortunately, either these measures were not well defined at all in the SCF or their definitions changed between 1983 and 1989 (as in the case of self-employment).

28. The income questions in the survey are separate from those for AGI and hence provide an independent measure of income. The total income measure includes wage and salary income, busi-

ness income, interest and dividends, capital gains, rents, pension income, transfers, and all other sources of income in the household.

29. His four MTR groups were those less than 0.22, 0.22 to 0.38, 0.42 to 0.45, and 0.49 to 0.50. The major difference is that we collapse his upper two groups into one for sample size reasons.

30. The first range of elasticities is taken from Feldstein (1995a, table 2), and the second range has been calculated by the authors from the figures in Feldstein (1995a, table 1).

31. We say "in effect" because, for illustration purposes in table 7.3, we omit the constant term in both the reduced form and first-stage regressions and include both a high- and midrange-MTR dummy. This generates coefficients that are comparable to the figures in table 7.2. In the remainder of the chapter, we include the constant and only the high-MTR dummy.

32. The figures for the lowest-MTR groups in the three- and eight-MTR plots are not precisely equal because the former is 0 to 0.20 and the latter is 0 to 0.19.

33. There are five or ten very large AGI gains and losses (over $1 million in absolute value) in the data in the upper group. Deleting these extreme values reduces the magnitude of the coefficient, but it remains statistically and economically significant.

34. These instruments are time-varying but exogenous (by assumption) and hence are the type of instruments for which we recommended earlier that only those with no change be included. Hence, our estimates for these instruments include only those with no change in marital status or household size from 1983 to 1989.

35. We also tested the 1989 MTR group and the log of 1989 AGI as instruments, as discussed earlier. The estimated tax response coefficient becomes, surprisingly, negative and significant in this specification. However, when a dummy for high 1989 AGI (the top 4 percent of the distribution) is used, the coefficient becomes positive and significant once again. A plot analogous to figure 7.5, but using seven 1989 AGI groups, shows the 1989 response to occur only in the top part of the distribution. Thus, the two years are consistent with each other at the top end. The top 1989 MTR group does not yield a positive response coefficient, because the top bracket in that year includes almost 30 percent of the population (unlike the top 1983 MTR group).

36. When adding the low-MTR group into the sample, we retain only one instrument, a dummy for being in the high-MTR group.

37. We could also have tested AGI in the MTR-based instruments, but the inference would be weak because identification would rely entirely on nonlinearities in AGI effects.

38. Some of the high hours figures may be a result of overreporting of hours worked per week. For evidence on such overreporting, see Robinson and Bostrom (1994).

39. The tax payment in both years is evaluated at the actual AGI in those years. Use of this income variable rather than nonwage income converts the coefficient on the NTR variable to compensated form (Ashenfelter and Heckman 1973, 1974).

40. As usual in these models, it must be assumed that there is no significant entry or exit from the population over time through immigration, birth, or mortality. See Deaton (1985) and Moffitt (1993) for more general discussions of estimation of models with RCS data, and see Heckman and Robb (1985) for a discussion of estimation of the impact of interventions with RCS data.

41. This can be shown formally. The variable $[d_{p+1}(z) - d_p(z)]$ is a deterministic (though nonlinear) function of $d_p(z)$, while the variable D_t is independent of μ by the assumption of the time-invariance of μ.

42. As in the panel data case, identification issues arise if sufficient nonlinearities are introduced that confound the effects of an independent change in x from a change in x working through tax law effects. A weakness of RCS data shows up in this case because, unlike the case of panel data, the sample cannot be subselected down to those with no change in x.

43. See the comment of Heckman (1996a) on Eissa (1996b).

44. Equation (7A.5) has the wage interacted with the marginal tax; this is sufficient, however, for identification without any additional nonlinearities. We ignore this source of identification of equation (7A.5) (for example, assume that W and Wt have different coefficients). The nonidentification still holds nonparametrically if an analysis pointwise in W is undertaken. See Blomquist and Newey (1996) for a nonparametric analysis.

45. Indeed, IV is not appropriate in this model in any case because x, in addition to net wage and virtual nonlabor income, is correlated with the error term and hence should, in principle, be instrumented. The mean of ε conditional on $D_s = 1$ is a function of all variables in V, and therefore of x.

46. Although utility maximization implies that some individuals invariably locate at kinks, assuming smoothness of preferences, the presence of measurement and optimization error implies that no observations are precisely located at kinks. In addition, if the variance of ε is sufficiently large, there will be no clustering around kinks as well.

47. The classification problem can be eliminated by assumption if ε is taken to represent only heterogeneity of preferences and not measurement or optimization error. In that case, observed segment location equals optimized location. But that assumption requires that some observations be clustered at kinks. In addition to the fact that significant clustering is rarely observed, it implies that the model is misspecified if all observations are assigned to segments.

REFERENCES

Ashenfelter, Orley, and James Heckman. 1973. "Estimating Labor Supply Functions." In *Income Maintenance and Labor Supply,* edited by Glen Cain and Harold Watts. Chicago: Markham.

———. 1974. "The Estimation of Income and Substitution Effects in a Model of Family Labor Supply." *Econometrica* 42(January): 73–85.

Auten, Gerard, and Robert Carroll. 1999. "The Effect of Income Taxes on Household Income." *Review of Economics and Statistics* 81(November): 681–93.

Blomquist, Soren, and W. Newey. 1996. "Taxation and Labor Supply." Unpublished paper. Department of Economics, Uppsala University, Sweden.

Blundell, Richard, Alan Duncan, and Costas Meghir. 1998. "Estimating Labor Supply Responses Using Tax Reforms." *Econometrica* 87(November): 115–43.

Blundell, Richard, and Thomas MaCurdy. 1999. "Labor Supply: A Review of Alternative Approaches." In *Handbook of Labor Economics,* edited by Orley Ashenfelter and David Card, vol. 3A. New York: Elsevier Science.

Bosworth, Barry, and Gary Burtless. 1992. "Effects of Tax Reform on Labor Supply, Investment and Saving." *Journal of Economic Perspectives* 6: 3–26.

Carroll, Robert, Douglas Holtz-Eakin, Mark Rider, and Harvey Rosen. 1998. "Income Taxes and Entrepreneurs' Use of Labor." Working paper 6578. Cambridge, Mass.: National Bureau of Economic Research (May).

Deaton, Angus. 1985. "Panel Data from Time Series of Cross-Sections." *Journal of Econometrics* 30: 109–26.

Eissa, Nada. 1995. "Taxation and the Labor Supply of Married Women: The Tax Reform Act of 1986 as a Natural Experiment." Working paper 5023. Cambridge, Mass.: National Bureau of Economic Research (February).

———. 1996a. "Tax Reforms and Labor Supply." In *Tax Policy and the Economy,* edited by James Poterba, vol. 10. Cambridge, Mass.: MIT Press.

———. 1996b. "Labor Supply and the Economic Recovery Act of 1981." In *Empirical Foundations of Household Taxation,* edited by Martin Feldstein and James Poterba. Chicago: University of Chicago Press.

Feenberg, Daniel, and James Poterba. 1993. "Income Inequality and the Incomes of Very High-Income Taxpayers." In *Tax Policy and the Economy,* edited by James Poterba, vol. 7. Cambridge, Mass.: MIT Press.

Feldstein, Martin. 1995a. "The Effect of Marginal Tax Rates on Taxable Income: A Study of the 1986 Tax Reform Act." *Journal of Political Economy* 103(June): 551–72.

———. 1995b. "Behavioral Responses to Tax Rates: Evidence from the Tax Reform Act of 1986." *American Economic Review* 85(May): 170–74.

———. 1999. "Tax Avoidance and the Deadweight Loss of the Income Tax." *Review of Economics and Statistics* 81(November): 674–80.

Feldstein, Martin, and Daniel Feenberg. 1996. "The Effect of Increased Tax Rates on Taxable Income and Economic Efficiency: A Preliminary Analysis of the 1993 Tax Rate Increases." In *Tax Policy and the Economy,* edited by James Poterba, vol. 10. Cambridge, Mass.: MIT Press.

Hausman, Jerry A. 1981. "Labor Supply." In *How Taxes Affect Economic Behavior,* edited by Henry Aaron and James Pechman. Washington, D.C.: Brookings Institution.

———. 1985. "Taxes and Labor Supply." In *Handbook of Public Economics,* edited by Alan Auerbach and Martin Feldstein. Amsterdam: North-Holland.

Hausman, Jerry, and James Poterba. 1987. "Household Behavior and the Tax Reform Act of 1986." *Journal of Economic Perspectives* 1(Summer): 101–19.

Heckman, James. 1996a. "Comment." In *Empirical Foundations of Household Taxation,* edited by Martin Feldstein and James Poterba. Chicago: University of Chicago Press.

———. 1996b."Randomization as an Instrumental Variable." *Review of Economics and Statistics* 78(May): 336–41.

Heckman, James, and Richard R. Robb. 1985. "Alternative Methods for Evaluating the Impact of Interventions." In *Longitudinal Analysis of Labor Market Data,* edited by James Heckman and Burton B. Singer. Cambridge: Cambridge University Press.

Internal Revenue Service. 1984. "Individual Income Tax Returns." *Statistics of Income: 1982.* Washington, D.C.: U.S. Government Printing Office.

———. 1991. "Individual Income Tax Returns." *Statistics of Income: 1988.* Washington, D.C.: U.S. Government Printing Office.

Kennickell, Arthur, and Janice Shack-Marquez. 1992. "Changes in Family Finances from 1983 to 1989: Evidence from the Survey of Consumer Finances." *Federal Reserve Bulletin* (January): 1–18.

Lindsey, Lawrence. 1987. "Estimating the Behavioral Responses of Taxpayers to Changes in Tax Rates: 1982–1984." *Journal of Public Economics* (July): 173–206.

MaCurdy, Thomas, David Green, and Harry Paarsch. 1990. "Assessing Empirical Approaches for Analyzing Taxes and Labor Supply." *Journal of Human Resources* 25(Summer): 415–90.

Mariger, Randall. 1995. "Labor Supply and the Tax Reform Act of 1986: Evidence from Panel Data." Discussion Paper 95–34. Washington, D.C.: Federal Reserve Board.

Meyer, Bruce. 1995. "Natural and Quasi-Experiments in Economics." *Journal of Business and Economic Statistics* 13(April): 151–61.

Moffitt, Robert. 1979. "The Labor Supply Response to the Gary Experiment." *Journal of Human Resources* 14(Fall): 477–87.

———. 1986. "The Econometrics of Piecewise-Linear Budget Constraints." *Journal of Business and Economic Statistics* 4(July): 317–28.

———. 1990. "The Econometrics of Kinked Budget Constraints." *Journal of Economic Perspectives* 4(Spring): 119–39.

———. 1993. "Identification and Estimation of Dynamic Models with a Time Series of Repeated Cross-Sections." *Journal of Econometrics* 59: 99–123.

Moffitt, Robert, and Kenneth Kehrer. 1981. "The Effect of Tax and Transfer Programs on Labor Supply: The Evidence from the Income Maintenance Experiments." In *Research in Labor Economics,* edited by Ronald Ehrenberg, vol. 4. Greenwich, Conn.: JAI Press.

Robinson, John, and Ann Bostrom. 1994. "The Overestimated Workweek: What Time Diary Estimates Suggest." *Monthly Labor Review* 117(August): 11–23.

Rosen, Harvey. 1976. "Tax Illusion and the Labor Supply of Married Women." *Review of Economics and Statistics* 58(May): 167–72.

Showalter, Mark. 1997. "An Investigation of the Labor Supply Response of High-Income Individuals to the Tax Changes of the 1980s." Unpublished paper. Brigham Young University, Salt Lake City.

Showalter, Mark, and Nunmar Thurston. 1997. "Taxes and Labor Supply of High-Income Physicians." *Journal of Public Economics* 66(October): 73–97.

Slemrod, Joel. 1996. "High-Income Families and the Tax Changes of the 1980s: The Anatomy of Behavioral Response." In *Empirical Foundations of Household Taxation*, edited by Martin Feldstein and James Poterba. Chicago: University of Chicago Press.

————. 1998. "Methodological Issues in Measuring and Interpreting Taxable Income Elasticities." *National Tax Journal* 51(December): 773–88.

————. Forthcoming. "A General Model of the Behavioral Response to Taxation." *International Tax and Public Finance*.

Triest, Robert. 1992. "The Effect of Income Taxation on Labor Supply When Deductions Are Endogenous." *Review of Economics and Statistics* 74(February): 91–99.

Wolff, Edward. 1994. "Trends in Household Wealth in the United States, 1962–83 and 1983–89." *Review of Income and Wealth* (June): 143–74.

————. 1995. *Top Heavy: A Study of the Increasing Inequality of Wealth in America*. New York: Twentieth Century Fund Press.

Ziliak, James, and Thomas Kniesner. 1996. "Estimating Life Cycle Labor Supply Tax Effects." Unpublished paper. University of Oregon, Eugene (November).

Commentary on Chapter 7

Christopher R. Taber

Robert Moffitt and Mark Wilhelm's chapter is one in a large literature on the effects of taxes on hours of labor supplied, and it can also be included in a newer literature on the effects of taxation on taxable income. Much of the previous work that looks at the effects of tax changes on hours of work by prime-age males finds very small effects. The newer literature looks at the effects of tax changes on taxable income, which is argued to be a much better indicator of tax avoidance (Feldstein 1995a). Much of this work shows large effects of tax changes on taxable income. This chapter combines the two literatures by using exactly the same data and methods to look at the effects of tax changes on hours of work and on taxable income. I think this leads to three important empirical contributions:

1. It extends the analysis of Feldstein (1995a) by using additional exclusion restrictions and by estimating on survey data. Moffitt and Wilhelm obtain results similar to Feldstein's under these conditions.

2. Using exactly the same methodology and data, they then demonstrate that there is virtually no effect of tax changes on labor supply.

3. Finally, they decompose the earnings gain and show that it can be explained at least in part by an increase in wage and salary income.

The first result is important, since Feldstein (1995a) uses tax return data that are collected in a totally different manner than survey data. Since these data sources are substantially different, it is nice to see that the results are so close. Given the previous work on hours of work by prime-age men, the second result is not surprising. However, it is important to document that we have small elasticities for very wealthy men and to demonstrate that hours of work was not an important factor leading to the effect on taxable income. The third result is also interesting in that it rules out some explanations of the effects of tax changes on taxable income. Gaining an understanding about precisely how these effects operate is an important area for future research.

The chapter also makes a substantial methodological contribution. In the first section, Moffitt and Wilhelm do an excellent job of laying out precisely which assumptions are needed to identify the parameter of interest in a number of different environments. These results are then related to methods that are commonly used. The identification problem for the tax case is related to the literature on program evaluation, and the differences between this case and others (for example, nonlinear tax schedules) are clearly laid out. The chapter demonstrates that Feldstein's difference-in-differences approach essentially uses the initial tax rate as an instrumental variable.

There has been a lot of discussion about estimation of tax effects using instrumental variables in recent years, so much of what I say here simply amplifies points made in previous work, including Feldstein (1995a, 1995b), Blundell, Duncan, and Meghir (1998), Heckman (1996), Slemrod (1996), and Goolsbee (this volume). I first discuss an interpretation of the results, then the econometric issues involved in estimation, and finally I make some comments on the empirical work and methodology.

Feldstein (1995a, 1995b) argues that the proper way to evaluate the effects of taxes on behavior is to look at taxable income. The point is that people may react to tax changes in a number of different ways—changing their work habits, form of compensation, form of investment, or form of consumption. One can account for all of these possibilities only through analyzing total taxable income. Given that the subject of this chapter is labor supply, I want to expand on a particular point that Feldstein (1995a) makes. He emphasizes that there are multiple aspects of labor supply beyond hours worked and that high-skilled workers may have more discretion about these types of decisions. To formalize this idea, imagine that each worker can choose to spend his time performing different tasks. Let T be a large vector denoting different tasks, and let L be the vector denoting the fraction of time devoted to each task.[1] Each task has a separate payoff, which I denote by the vector W.[2] A worker's total earnings are thus $W'L$. Assuming a flat tax τ and no nonlabor income, a worker consumes $(1 - \tau)W'L$. I allow utility to depend on consumption and time spent in each task $U(C,L)$. Let U_i denote the marginal utility with respect to time spent working on task i, L_i, and U_c denote the marginal utility of consumption. Then for any two tasks i and j, assuming an interior solution, we obtain the first-order condition

$$U_i + U_c(1 - \tau)W_i = U_j + U_c(1 - \tau)W_j.$$

On the margin, if consumption is compensated, decreases in the tax rate cause workers to substitute away from tasks that are relatively more enjoyable (higher U_i) to tasks that pay more (higher W_i).

This framework is meant to be very general in order to allow us to consider a broad range of types of tasks. Leisure can be incorporated as a task with zero market wage. We can also think of different tasks as representing different levels of effort on the job. For example if the same job can be performed quickly or take longer, the slower rate may give less disutility ($U_s > U_q$) but pay at a lower rate ($W_q > W_s$). The tasks may also represent career choice where there are compensating differentials for unpleasant careers. Even within a job, workers may choose different projects to work on. This is clearly important for academics, who may be induced by a tax decrease to work on a project that is likely to lead to an outside offer rather than a project that is more enjoyable. Although most workers do not have this amount of discretion about how to spend their time at work, the very rich probably have a substantial amount. It may be the case that individually the magnitude of each of these effects for any task is very small, but that the aggregate effect is substantial. This explanation is consistent with the finding that tax cuts lead to a rise in labor income as increasing labor supply on more highly paid tasks leads to an increase in W'L. Furthermore, if high-wage workers have more discretion over this type of behavior, it can also explain why the positive effects on wages are found only for the highest-income group.

I discuss next some of the issues involved in estimation of the model. As Moffitt and Wilhelm show, identification of the tax effects can be seen from their equation (7.5),

$$y_{p+1} - y_p = (\alpha_{p+1} - \alpha_p) + \beta(d_{p+1}(z_{p+1}) - d_p(z_p)) + v_{p+1} - v_p$$

The key to identification is finding a variable that is correlated with $[d_{p+1}(z_{p+1}) - d_p(z_p)]$ but uncorrelated with $v_{p+1} - v_p$. They show that Feldstein essentially uses $d_p(z_p)$ as an instrumental variable, and they expand his analysis to include some additional instruments.

In constructing instrumental variables and interpreting the results in this context, there are at least two important factors to keep in mind. The first is that we need to worry about time effects. This is particularly important in examining the effect of tax rates on earnings, as Joel Slemrod (1996) and Austan Goolsbee (this volume) have pointed out. During the 1980s there were huge increases in the return to skill (Katz and Murphy 1992), so anything correlated with skill levels typically would not be a valid instrument. To illustrate this, I extend Moffitt and Wilhelm's notation so that $v_p = \gamma_p \mu + \varepsilon_p$, where μ represents unobserved skill and γ_p is the payoff to unobserved skill at time p, which is increasing over time. Then $v_{p+1} - v_p = (\gamma_{p+1} - \gamma_p) \mu + \varepsilon_{p+1} - \varepsilon_p$, so anything correlated with μ is almost surely correlated with $v_{p+1} - v_p$. This leads one to question the use of $d_p(z_p)$ as an instrumental variable, since we would generally expect income to be correlated with ability.

I am puzzled as to why this is not more of a problem. The previous work on the changing wage structure typically uses data sets in which there is no oversampling of the very rich, so it is surprising that we seem to pick up the effects only for the very rich. We also know that there was a huge increase in returns to schooling over this time period, so one would expect the effect on taxable income to be biased upward when postcollege is used as an instrumental variable. However, the effect is insignificant in this case (although the standard error is large). This seems to indicate that there is no evidence of an increase in returns to schooling in this data set.

When looking at labor supply, the changes in the wage structure should be much less of a problem and may actually aid identification of the elasticities. Typically the changes in the wage structure are taken to be demand-driven (see Katz and Murphy 1992). Thus, if one views these changes as exogenous to labor supply, then the changes in the wage structure itself provide additional identifying information, as Heckman (1996) and Blundell, Duncan, and Meghir (1998) point out. Even if there were no changes in the tax system, initial AGI would still be a strong instrument for changes in tax rates. However, this does not help solve the problem that an instrumental variable may be correlated with $v_{p+1} - v_p$.

The second important factor to keep in mind in constructing instrumental variables for this problem is life-cycle effects. Potential problems arise because the data are longitudinal. Moffitt and Wilhelm look at the same individuals in 1983 and in 1989, when they are six years older. Thus, the error term $v_{p+1} - v_p$ embodies not only time effects but life-cycle effects as well. This is potentially important for both labor supply effects and wage effects. The labor-force patterns across the life cycles of both of these variables have been well documented. Since these patterns are non-linear, it is not obvious why variables related to the levels of these variables should not be related to life-cycle changes in them. Since all of the potential instruments used here are correlated with the initial values of ATI and hours, it is not clear to me why we would expect them not to be correlated with the life-cycle growth of these variables. This can be true only under strong functional form assumptions. For example, if the argument is that the growth in logs should be unrelated to the variable, then it would not be a valid instrument when we look at growth in levels.

I also have a fairly minor comment related to the use of z_{p+1} as an instrumental variable. Although it may be possible to construct examples in which the problem is completely symmetric, if there is uncertainty in the model it typically is not possible to construct such examples. In particular, if the workers do not get to observe the variable v_p until time p, then the value of v_p may influence the choice of z_{p+1} directly, but the value of v_{p+1} cannot influence the choice of z_p directly. Even though z_p may be correlated with v_p in the same way as z_{p+1} is correlated with v_{p+1}, in general the joint distribution of z_p and v_{p+1} is different from the joint distribution of z_{p+1} and v_p. For example, under these conditions, if v_p is a random walk with independent increments, then z_p is a valid instrument, since it is uncorrelated with $v_{p+1} - v_p$, but z_{p+1} is not.

In summary, I think this is a nice paper. It shows that even though there is evidence that the tax change of 1986 had an effect on taxable income, there is no evidence that it had an effect on hours worked for high-income prime-age males. This result is not surprising given previous work in the area, but the change in taxable income is so large that it is important to document that it does not arise from changes in hours worked. I echo the author's desire for better data that would allow us to determine the margins on which workers are adjusting to the change in tax laws.

NOTES

1. Thus, the elements of L must sum to 1.

2. I am assuming that there are no diminishing returns to working in any task, but that time spent on each task is elastically demanded at a given rate.

REFERENCES

Blundell, Richard, Alan Duncan, and Costas Meghir. 1998. "Estimating Labor Supply Responses Using Tax Reforms." *Econometrica* 66: 827–51.

Feldstein, Martin. 1995a. "The Effect of Marginal Tax Rates on Taxable Income: A Study of the 1986 Tax Reform Act." *Journal of Political Economy* 103(June): 551–72.

———. 1995b. "Tax Avoidance and the Deadweight Loss of the Income Tax." Working Paper 5055. Cambridge, Mass.: National Bureau of Economic Research.

Heckman, James. 1996. "Comment on Nada Eissa, 'Labor Supply and the Economic Recovery Tax Act of 1981.'" In *Empirical Foundations of Household Taxation*, edited by Martin Feldstein and James Poterba. Chicago: University of Chicago Press.

Katz, Lawrence, and Kevin Murphy. 1992. "Changes in Relative Wages, 1963–87: Supply and Demand Factors." *Quarterly Journal of Economics* 107: 35–78.

Slemrod, Joel. 1996. "High-Income Families and the Tax Changes of the 1980s: The Anatomy of Behavioral Response." In *Empirical Foundations of Household Taxation*, edited by Martin Feldstein and James Poterba. Chicago: University of Chicago Press.

8

Are "Real" Responses to Taxes Simply Income Shifting Between Corporate and Personal Tax Bases?

Roger H. Gordon and Joel B. Slemrod

Tax changes frequently generate large apparent changes in the behavior of high-income individuals. For example, Lawrence Lindsey (1987) finds that the U.S. tax cuts enacted between 1981 and 1983 led to a substantial jump in the reported income of the richest individuals. Similarly, Martin Feldstein (1995) estimates that the increase in reported taxable income among high-income taxpayers after the Tax Reform Act of 1986 (TRA86) more than compensated for the drop in their tax rates. Feldstein and Daniel Feenberg (1996) report that the tax increase in 1993 (affecting mainly the richest individuals) caused a sufficient drop in their reported income that on net little or no extra revenue was collected. Under normal circumstances, the revenue change corresponding to these behavioral responses measures the efficiency gain (loss) from a tax cut (increase).[1]

However, there is an explanation for these changes in reported personal income with radically different policy implications: a shift by taxpayers of their reported income between the personal and the corporate tax bases to take advantage of the difference between personal and corporate tax rates. When personal tax rates were reduced relative to the corporate tax rate in the early 1980s, individuals and firms faced a sharply increased incentive to shift taxable income out of the corporate sector. This shifting could be accomplished in any number of ways. For example, increasing the use of corporate debt finance causes an increase in interest deductions for firms and an equivalent increase in interest income for individuals. Alternatively, shifting assets or activity from corporate to noncorporate firms shifts taxable income between the two tax bases. Finally, income can be shifted by changing forms of compensation for executives or other workers, moving to greater use of wage compensation and away from stock options.[2]

The possibility of such income shifting has many implications. For one, it forces a reexamination of the efficiency effects of tax changes. If an increase in reported personal income following a tax cut simply represents a shift of taxable income from the corporate to the personal tax base, then corporate tax revenue and perhaps even total tax revenue has fallen as a result of this behavioral response.[3] If so, efficiency has declined rather than increased. This possibility is particularly intriguing in light of Alan Auerbach and James Poterba's (1987) finding that reported corporate rates of return fell during the first half of the 1980s.

Income shifting also forces a reexamination of existing statistics on the distribution of income. If the big jump in the reported income of the richest individuals following the tax cuts in the early 1980s simply reflects a shift in the form of compensation—for example, away from accruing capital gains on stock options and toward cash wages—then their true income may not in fact have changed much. The further reduction in personal relative to corporate tax rates in 1986 would have reinforced this incentive to shift to observed rather than unobserved forms of compensation.[4] Thus, the observed growth in the income of the richest individuals relative to the rest of the population may, at least in part, be a fiction, reflecting simply a shift in their form of compensation.

Similarly, income shifting can make the level of and changes over time in corporate rates of return misleading. Estimating corporate rates of return based on the ratio of reported income to the replacement cost of the capital stock presumes that the reported income represents the return accruing to capital owners. This ignores, however, the existence of various forms of compensation that, unlike wage payments, do not generate a deduction from reported corporate income. Observed real rates of return in the corporate sector, as calculated, for example, in Feldstein and Summers (1977), have been on the order of 10 percent per year even though real interest rates have been close to zero. Perhaps the explanation for this puzzling gap is simply that the observed corporate income includes a substantial amount of labor income that is shifted into the corporate tax base to avoid high personal tax rates. As already suggested, income shifting could explain the otherwise puzzling fall in corporate rates of return during the 1980s reported by Auerbach and Poterba (1987). It could also undermine any attempt to use differences in corporate rates of return to measure cross-sectional differences in market power and would even make comparison of price-earnings ratios over time more difficult to interpret.

All in all, income shifting plays havoc with the usual interpretation of many kinds of data, because it blurs the return to capital and the return to labor. This phenomenon is likely to be especially important for affluent taxpayers, who have relatively easy access to income-shifting opportunities.[5] For this reason, income shifting is a promising explanation of the extraordinary sensitivity of the taxable income of affluent taxpayers. This is especially true because alternative explanations apparently do not apply; for example, Robert Moffitt and Mark Wilhelm (this volume) find no evidence of increased labor supply of high-income individuals in response to the tax cuts of TRA86, and Charles Christian (1994) finds no evidence that tax evasion of the affluent decreased over this period.

The objective of this chapter is to assess quantitatively the extent of income shifting in response to recent tax changes. In the next section, we lay out the means by which income shifting can occur, and the economic consequences of such income shifting. We then examine closely how the incentives to engage in income shifting have changed over time and differ across taxpayers. That section is followed by a review of earlier work on income shifting. The next section then makes use of various sources of evidence from U.S. tax returns to investigate the magnitude and nature of income shifting in response to past tax incentives.

INCOME SHIFTING
Theoretical Possibilities

Much of the past work analyzing how taxes affect individual and firm behavior has entirely ignored the various possibilities for income shifting. The principal focus when analyzing individual income taxes has been on their impact on labor supply and savings behavior, while the principal focus for corporate taxes has been on implications for real investment behavior. A separate literature has analyzed the effects of tax rates on tax evasion, but even here the primary evasion considered involves nonreporting rather than a shift in reporting between one tax base and another.[6]

To be sure, certain forms of income shifting have been studied intensively, a key example being the use of debt finance by corporations. Through the use of debt finance, corporate taxable income is reduced through interest deductions while the resulting interest income would normally accrue to some individual taxpayer. A large literature has examined to what extent the use of debt finance depends on the difference between the corporate tax rate (plus any personal taxes due on corporate income) and some representative personal tax rate on interest income.[7] The empirical studies of corporate use of debt finance, however, have at best found only limited and indirect evidence of behavioral responses to tax distortions, leading to the development of a newer literature focusing on nontax explanations for the use of debt.[8]

More recently, stimulated by Gravelle and Kotlikoff (1989, 1993),[9] a line of research has begun to investigate the possibility of firms changing between corporate and noncorporate status in response to tax incentives; this required a break from the conventional assumption, embodied, for example, in Harberger (1962), that nontax factors dominate in this decision, so that certain industries are necessarily corporate and others necessarily noncorporate. When a firm chooses to be corporate, its income is taxed at the corporate rate (and is subject to some further personal taxes). If instead it chooses to be noncorporate, the resulting profits are taxable personal income for each of the owners of the firm. Thus, the incentive to choose one form of organization over another depends in part on the difference between the corporate and personal tax rates.[10] This implies that the drop in personal relative to corporate tax rates as a result of the tax reform of 1986 made it more attractive for any firm with positive income to shift from corporate to noncorporate status. In fact, Jeffrey MacKie-Mason and Roger Gordon (1997) do report a striking increase in the amount of noncorporate activity following the tax change.

The incentives faced when choosing an organizational form depend on the particular tax rates faced by the owners of each firm. In general, some firm owners have marginal personal tax rates higher than the corporate rate, while others have lower personal tax rates. Firms with tax losses would gain by being noncorporate only when they are owned by individuals who face personal rates above the corporate rate, and conversely for firms with positive income. During the early 1980s many firms had tax losses, in part because of the deep recession at the time, and in part because of the accelerated-depreciation deductions introduced as part of the Economic Recovery Tax Act of 1981. In addition, certain types of capital, such as real estate, tended to generate tax losses given the depreciation provisions and the typical use of debt finance for those types of capital. As a result, during this period there was a substantial shift in ownership of such capital, largely real estate and oil and gas drilling equipment, from corporations to individuals in high tax brackets. The shift was large enough that the partnership sector had aggregate tax losses on net during the early 1980s.

As noted in MacKie-Mason and Gordon (1997), the observed shift in *assets* between corporate and noncorporate status was much less dramatic than the shift in *taxable income*. In part this may simply reflect sorting by type of capital: assets generating tax losses shift in one direction while assets generating taxable profits shift in the other direction. Little net change in assets may result even though a substantial shift in net income occurs. The much larger income shifting than asset shifting, however, probably also reflects changes in other forms of income shifting that are undertaken by firms that remain corporate.

It has not been much noted in the past literature that one way this shift may have occurred is through changes in the form of compensation of employees in the firm. Tax incentives encourage some employees to report earnings as personal income, and other employees to report earnings as corporate income. To report earnings as personal income simply involves paying compensation in the form of wages and bonuses and avoiding other forms of compensation such as stock options. In fact, most compensation takes the form of wages and salary, pension contributions, or royalty payments, all of which are taxable income to the employee and deductible expenditures for the firm.[11]

In practice, however, the tax law has tried to limit the available opportunities to shift reported earnings into the corporate tax base. Opportunities for this kind of income shifting, however, do remain. At one extreme, consider the situation of a small family-owned corporation. The family has virtually full flexibility to shift income between the personal and corporate tax bases. Although it can still pay itself wages, it can easily retain profits within the firm instead. Retaining earnings implies extra corporate taxable income and less personal taxable income in the short term, though it also probably implies larger realized capital gains when and if the firm is sold.

For closely held corporations with a broader set of owners, income shifting becomes somewhat more complicated, because extra retained earnings generate accruing capital gains to all owners, not just to owner-employees. If all owners are also employees, then wages can be adjusted to keep total compensation as desired; the only issue is reconciling perhaps conflicting tax incentives regarding wage versus nonwage compensation. When some owners are not employees, then the firm can issue new shares to those wishing nonwage compensation. In principle, these new shares should generate taxable income for the employees based on their market value, as well as an equivalent tax deduction for the firm, and thus be equivalent to wage payments for tax purposes. In practice, however, the market value is difficult to ascertain, allowing considerable flexibility for undervaluation and thus creating extra corporate and less personal taxable income.

For publicly traded firms, compensation in the form of new share issues can easily be valued based on market prices, thus eliminating any effective means to shift taxable income between the firm and employees. Under U.S. tax law, however, qualified stock options provide an effective mechanism to achieve income shifting. When an individual receives compensation in the form of qualified[12] stock options, the corporation receives no deduction for this payment, and the individual receives no taxable income, until the shares obtained through the option are sold, at which time the gain (sale price minus strike price) is taxed at the (often preferential) long-term capital gains rate.[13] However, there is a maximum of $100,000 that can be exercised in any one year by any one employee. Firms can also provide "deferred" compensation in the form of nonqualified stock options. With these options, the employee receives taxable income, and the firm receives a tax deduction, not when the option is paid as compensation to the employee but when the option is exercised, possibly as much as ten years later. This deferral is particularly valuable if there is some prospect that personal tax rates will fall in the interim relative to corporate rates.

The fact that income shifting is easier in a closely held firm implies that individuals have a tax incentive to work in a closely held firm during periods when income shifting is particularly valuable. These firms almost always are much smaller than publicly traded firms because it is difficult to raise substantial amounts of outside capital without shares being publicly traded. This suggests that there should be more smaller corporations when the incentives to engage in income shifting are larger. In addition, given that these firms can more readily engage in income shifting, we forecast, and later empirically test, that their reported rates of return will be more responsive to relative tax rates than those for larger, generally publicly traded firms.

Even in a closely held firm, employees may be reluctant to accept too much equity from the firm as compensation, in part because of the fear that the firm's insiders will favor equity compensation particularly at those times when they know that the firm is doing badly. Insiders in the firm, in contrast, face no such problems with asymmetric information. Therefore, when incentives to engage in income shifting are high, individuals have an incentive to become insiders in some firm. This is another reason to expect the formation of additional smaller corporations when taxes encourage income shifting, as a mechanism to allow more people to become insiders.[14]

At any given time, of course, tax incentives differ across individuals. Most individuals face personal tax rates below the corporate tax rate, so that the combined tax liabilities of the employee and the firm are minimized if compensation takes the form of wages and salaries. However, in most years at least some high-income taxpayers face marginal personal tax rates above the corporate rate. These are the individuals whose behavior is likely to vary most in response to tax reforms. In the data analysis later in the chapter, we focus particularly on the behavior of these individuals in higher tax brackets.

In judging the relative size of the effective tax rate on regular compensation versus income retained within a corporation, for simplicity we have compared the personal tax rate on wage and salary income with the corporate tax rate due on any extra income that accrues when compensation takes a nondeductible form. In fact, income subject to corporate tax may also eventually be subject to further personal taxes, either when profits are paid out in the form of dividends or else when shares are sold. For closely held firms, owners have sufficient flexibility that they should be able to avoid the double taxation of dividend income. Moreover, the effective capital gains tax rate is likely to be very low, because not only do owners benefit from the deferral of taxes due on capital gains until the gains are realized, but they also benefit from the lower statutory rate that has normally applied to capital gains realized during a person's life and from the write-up of the tax basis at death to the current market value, implying full exemption of these gains from personal taxes. Our presumption is that many of the firms that most aggressively engage in income shifting are small, closely held corporations that are able to avoid most, if not all, personal taxes due on corporate income; thus, in the empirical work that follows, we take the difference between the personal and the corporate tax rates as the measure of the reward to income shifting.

Implications of Income Shifting

Misleading Distributional Statistics   Income shifting can complicate any attempt to measure changes over time in the income distribution as well as changes in the relative tax burdens across income groups. Given inherent data limitations, estimates of the income distribution necessarily must omit actual accruing but unrealized capital gains income, although imputations can be made. If the relative importance of accruing capital gains relative to observed sources of income is stable within each income bracket, then at least changes in the income distribution over time are informative. But tax changes can have major effects on the relative importance of accruing capital gains. When corporate tax rates are relatively low, firms make less use of debt finance, implying larger accruing profits and therefore larger capital gains and less interest income for individuals. In addition, in response to a lower corporate tax rate, employees in higher tax brackets attempt to shift away from wage compensation toward other forms of compensation that generate corporate rather than personal taxable income, in the process reducing observed personal incomes but increasing accruing capital gains. As mentioned earlier, the jump in the observed income of the high-income individuals during the 1980s could in part reflect the effects of a reduction in income shifting and an increased use of wage compensation in response to the drop in personal tax rates relative to corporate rates that occurred from 1981 to 1983 and again during the period 1987 to 1988.[15] Only a close examination of changes in taxable income for any given firm and its employees can document convincingly to what degree the observed changes reflect income shifting. Because such information is not available, we examine more indirect evidence later in the chapter.

Calculations of relative tax rates across taxpayers are also misleading to the extent that individuals engage in income shifting. When individuals engage in income shifting into corporations, personal tax payments fall and corporate tax payments rise. The resulting effects on measured relative tax rates then depend on how the increased corporate tax payments and increased corporate income are allocated across taxpayers. The problem here is the lack of consensus about the incidence of the corporation income tax—that is, which individuals are ultimately worse off because of the revenue it collects.

As an example, consider the tax incidence methodology of the U.S. Treasury, as explained in Nunns (1995). It recognizes that the income of households that own corporate stock is understated if only dividends are included in income, because of the failure to consider the undistributed profits of corporations; there is a procedure that imputes each household's share of pre-tax undistributed profits based on dividends received. The burden of the corporate tax is assumed to be shared among households in proportion to their total capital income, not just their income from corporate stock ownership.

How should the tax incidence methodology deal with an individual who shifts from wage compensation to compensation in the form of, say, qualified stock options? Other shareholders are left indifferent to the change, assuming that the extra resulting corporate income is simply offset by the drop in the fraction of the firm owned by these other shareholders. For distributional purposes, the extra corporate tax payments, as well as the extra corporate income resulting from the use of options instead of wage compensation, should therefore be attributed to the employee who receives the extra nonwage compensation. In contrast, the Treasury procedure allocates the extra tax payments and the extra income across all individuals in proportion to their capital income.

What difference does this choice make for the Treasury calculation of the effective tax rates in different income brackets? Because the representative individual engaging in income shifting probably has much higher income than the representative capital income recipient,[16] the Treasury procedure allocates corporate income and corporate taxes to a less affluent subgroup of the population than would be appropriate given income shifting. The allocation of income and tax payments to any individual raises (lowers) their calculated effective tax rate to the extent that the average corporate tax rate is above (below) their average personal tax rate. Because almost all individuals face an average personal tax rate below the average corporate tax rate, the Treasury procedure overestimates the effective tax rate paid by capital owners and underestimates the effective tax rate paid by corporate executives engaging in income shifting. As a result, it underestimates the progressivity of the existing tax system, particularly during periods when income shifting is more important. This implies, for example, that the true drop in the progressivity of the tax system during the 1980s would be larger than when measured using the Treasury procedure.

Another implication of income shifting is that observed rates of pay for those working in small versus large firms, and for the self-employed versus other workers, may be misleading. Because those working in small firms should be able to engage in income shifting more easily, they should have lower observed rates of pay; that forcast is consistent with the evidence.[17] In addition, the self-employed should be more able to engage in income shifting, assuming they have incorporated their firm, because as insiders they do not face problems with asymmetric information when accepting equity compensation. The data consistently show that the self-employed earn less than others, controlling for standard factors.[18]

Misleading Corporate Rates of Return   Observed corporate profit rates have long puzzled researchers. How can the equilibrium rate of profit earned on corporate capital have been as high as 10 percent at least through the mid-1970s, as found by Feldstein and Summers (1977), given that the real interest rate during this period was around zero? Why did this rate of return fall during the 1980s, as reported by Auerbach and Poterba (1987)?

One possible explanation is that the higher return is simply a premium for the extra risk in the return on corporate capital. However, while Feldstein and Summers (1977) do find that the rate of return to corporate capital fluctuates over time, the *minimum* reported rate of return during their sample period is still far higher than the *maximum* real rate of return to bonds. The return to corporate capital appears to stochastically dominate the return to bonds, so that risk cannot easily explain why the average rates of return are so different.

Another proposed explanation for the difference in rates of return is taxes: although the pre-tax returns are very different on corporate capital and bonds, the after-tax returns could be comparable if the effective tax rate on corporate capital is high enough relative to that on bonds. Under closer examination, this explanation also seems unlikely, because for bonds the resulting nominal income is fully taxable, while for corporate capital taxable income substantially underestimates the firm's real income. Gordon and Slemrod (1988), Shoven (1991), and Kalambokidis (1992) all find that existing deductions under the corporate tax were more generous than would have existed with expensing for new investment in all the years they examined (1975 to 1987).[19] Yet, with expensing, there is no tax at the margin on new investment. Of course, corporate income is subject to further personal taxes. But Gordon and Slemrod (1988) find that all the personal taxes on the return to capital in 1983 were still not quite sufficient to offset the revenue loss from the excess deductions relative to expensing that have existed under the corporate tax. Therefore, at best the evidence suggests a very low effective tax rate on corporate capital.

Income shifting provides an alternative explanation for the high observed corporate rate of return. To put the apparently high corporate rate-of-return figures in perspective, Gordon and MacKie-Mason (1994) note that the comparable rate-of-return figures for noncorporate firms are even higher. For example, they found that the average annual rate of return in the noncorporate service sector was 165 percent! The obvious explanation for such anomalous "rates of return" is simply that the reported noncorporate income reflects largely the labor income of the partners working in the firm that was not paid out in the form of deductible wages.[20] For the same reason, reported corporate income includes labor as well as capital income to the extent that some employees engage in income shifting. Thus, income shifting could to some degree reconcile the corporate rates of return with observed real returns on bonds.

If income shifting is important, then changes in observed corporate rates of return over time can reflect changes in the extent of income shifting as well as changes in rates of return to corporate capital. For example, the 1981 tax reform should have caused a reduction in the extent of income shifting as personal tax rates fell relative to corporate rates. Auerbach and Poterba (1987) do observe a fall in corporate profit rates in the 1980s, and the explanation may simply be that the level of income shifting in corporations fell.

Efficiency Consequences   The possibility of income shifting also has important implications for the estimation of the marginal excess burden resulting from any tax change. The logic used in any calculation of the excess burden from a marginal tax change proceeds from the observation that the (dollar-equivalent) burden to each individual is equal to the extra tax payments the individual would have made in the absence of any behavioral response.[21] The *excess* burden from a marginal tax change equals the dollar-equivalent loss, minus the resulting increase in government revenue. The key step in any excess burden measure is thus to calculate the impact of a marginal tax change on government revenue. If individual behavior does not change, then the gain in revenue to the government exactly equals the sum of the dollar-equivalent losses to individuals, and the excess burden is zero. In general, of course, behavior does change, and the changes affect tax revenue in various ways. The excess burden equals the change in tax revenue resulting from these behavioral responses.

When income shifting is ignored, it is convenient to assume that changes in individual behavior affect revenues from the personal income tax but do not affect corporate tax payments, and conversely for changes in firm behavior. The studies by Lindsey (1987) and Feldstein (1995), for example, estimate the implications of individual behavioral responses from the 1981 and 1986 tax changes for tax revenue and argue that any resulting increase in tax revenue measures the drop in the excess burden. But if income shifting was occurring, then the estimates for the change in revenue must also take into account the effects of changes in individual behavior on corporate tax payments, and the effects of changes in firm behavior on individual tax payments.[22]

For example, following the cuts in personal tax rates in 1981, individuals would no longer have faced as strong an incentive to leave funds within the firm. The resulting drop in income shifting would increase reported individual taxable income and decrease reported corporate earnings. The net effect on tax revenue of the drop in income shifting depends on the difference in the average marginal tax rate of the individuals involved and the average marginal corporate tax rate. It is likely that the average effective individual tax rate was a bit lower than the corporate (plus personal) tax rate on corporate income, implying an efficiency loss on net.

As argued in Slemrod (1992), income shifting is generally much more responsive to tax incentives than such aspects of real behavior as labor supply and savings. In the current context, income shifting simply involves a change in the *form* of compensation rather than a change in its level. If so, then there are strong reasons on efficiency grounds to keep corporate rates no lower than the top personal tax rate. In particular, if the corporate rate were reduced below the top personal tax rate, then at least some individuals gain from income shifting. Their income shifting results in a loss in tax revenue and so a loss in efficiency. The corporate income tax is in effect serving as a backstop to the personal income tax on labor income, to prevent avoidance of the personal tax through use of nonwage forms of compensation.[23]

One key simplifying assumption in this discussion is that any marginal change in one individual's behavior has no effect on the welfare of other individuals—that is, there are no externalities. In the context of income shifting, this assumption can easily be questioned. For example, income shifting in publicly traded corporations may occur largely through the use of qualified stock options, and any tax incentive favoring income shifting encourages further use of stock options. Stock options also play an important role in aligning the incentives faced by employees with the interests of the owners of the firm. The use of stock options is limited, however, because of problems of asymmetric information between the insiders and other employees within any firm. If the firm is interested in making heavy use of stock options, then employees may rightly fear that the firm owners know, based on inside information, that the stock is overvalued. The breakdown in the use of stock options resulting from the "lemons" problem implies that any increase in the use of stock options induced by marginal tax incentives favoring income shifting is an efficiency gain.[24]

Similarly, closely held firms often respond to their difficulties in raising capital from outside investors by relying on equity rather than wage compensation of employees. Both outside investors and employees are reluctant to provide financing, fearing that the insiders most anxious to reduce their ownership share are those who know that their firm is overvalued. Perhaps the information asymmetries between insiders and employees is less than between insiders and outside investors, so that extra financing first comes from employees. The same arguments used earlier, however, still imply that at least a marginal increase in financing provided by employees in response to tax incentives creates an efficiency gain.[25]

When new entry is encouraged by the tax law, as individuals try to become insiders in firms to facilitate income shifting, other types of externalities may arise. New firms almost by necessity must try out some new product or new service, or at least a new location, in order to develop a market niche. Any attempt to try out a new activity involves risk and learning, and the resulting information is often readily available to other potential entrants. If the firm succeeds, these other potential entrants discover a new profitable activity to pursue; if it fails, they know what to avoid. These externalities suggest that, on efficiency grounds, there may be too little entry of new firms. However, new entrants can also gain at the expense of previous entrants by copying the ideas they used in order to get started. In this case, the entrant imposes a negative externality on the earlier entrant, perhaps more than offsetting any benefits to consumers through a drop in the product price brought on by competition. Whether additional entry generates positive or negative externalities on net is therefore unclear.

Whether these complications arising from asymmetric information are important enough to justify serious revision of any calculations of the excess burden of tax changes can be debated. The point is simply that, in the context of income shifting, these externalities and potential market failures are pervasive.

A HISTORY OF THE RECENT U.S. TAX RATE STRUCTURE AND ITS IMPLICATIONS FOR INCOME SHIFTING

The previous discussion suggests that, via many avenues, the extent to which income appears as corporate taxable income or individual taxable income will be influenced by the differential between the corporate tax rate (τ) and an individual's personal tax rate (θ_i). Given the variation in θ_i across taxpayers under a progressive rate schedule, tax incentives certainly differ by individual. Moreover, the corporate tax also has a progressive rate schedule. Many firms are subject to the lower rates of tax, although most corporate income is subject to the top rate.

To give a sense of the strength of the tax incentives faced by individuals to convert personal into corporate income in the United States, table 8.1 provides time series information on U.S. tax rates. Column 1 reports the top personal tax rate on earned income θ_{max}, column 2 the top corporate tax rate τ_{max}, and column 3 the difference between the two rates, labeled Δ. As can be seen in the table, the difference exceeded 30 percent until the early 1960s and remained high until the early 1970s.

Table 8.1   U.S. Corporate and Personal Tax Rates, 1955 to 1993

Year	θ_{max} (1)	τ_{max} (2)	Δ (3)	$\theta > \tau_{max}$ if Y > (4)	τ_{min} (5)	$\theta > \tau_{min}$ if Y > (6)	Y^{med} (7)
1955	87%	52%	35%	$36,000	30%	16,000	$4,919
1956	87	52	35	36,000	30	16,000	5,319
1957	87	52	35	36,000	30	16,000	5,488
1958	87	52	35	36,000	30	16,000	5,685
1959	87	52	35	36,000	30	16,000	6,070
1960	87	52	35	36,000	30	16,000	6,295
1961	87	52	35	36,000	30	16,000	6,437
1962	87	52	35	36,000	30	16,000	6,756
1963	87	52	35	36,000	30	16,000	7,138
1964	77	50	27	40,000	22	8,000	7,488
1965	70	48	22	40,000	22	12,000	7,800
1966	70	48	22	40,000	22	12,000	8,341
1967	70	48	22	40,000	22	12,000	8,994
1968	75.25	52.8	22.45	44,000	24.2	12,000	9,834
1969	77	52.8	24.2	40,000	24.2	12,000	10,623
1970	71.75	49.2	22.55	40,000	22.55	12,000	11,167
1971	60	48	12	40,000	22	12,000	11,626
1972	50	48	2	40,000	22	12,000	12,808
1973	50	48	2	40,000	22	12,000	13,710
1974	50	48	2	40,000	22	12,000	14,969
1975	50	48	2	40,000	20	12,000	15,848
1976	50	48	2	40,000	20	12,000	17,315
1977	50	48	2	40,000	20	12,000	18,723
1978	50	48	2	40,000	20	12,000	20,428
1979	50	46	4	45,800	17	7,600	22,512
1980	50	46	4	45,800	17	7,600	24,332
1981	50	46	4	45,800	17	7,600	26,274
1982	50	46	4	60,000	16	11,900	27,619
1983	50	46	4	85,000	15	11,900	29,181
1984	50	46	4	109,000	15	11,900	31,097
1985	50	46	4	113,800	15	12,390	32,777
1986	50	46	4	118,050	15	12,840	34,716
1987	38.5	40	−1.5	N/A	15	28,000	37,086
1988	28	34	−6	N/A	15	29,750	39,051
1989	28	34	−6	N/A	15	29,750	40,763
1990	28	34	−6	N/A	15	32,450	41,451
1991	31	34	−3	N/A	15	34,000	43,056
1992	31	34	−3	N/A	15	35,800	44,251
1993	39.6	35	4.6	140,000	15	36,900	45,161

Source: Pechman (1987) and authors' calculations for tax information. For median household income, 1955 to 1988, U.S. Bureau of the Census, Current Population Reports, Series P-60, no. 167, *Trends in Income by Selected Characteristics: 1947 to 1988*; for 1989 to 1993, U.S. Bureau of the Census website: www.census.gov/hhes/income/4person.

Notes: θ_{max} (τ_{max}) represents the personal (corporate) tax rate in the top tax bracket, while τ_{min} is the corporate tax rate in the lowest tax bracket. Δ equals $t_{max} - \tau_{max}$. Y represents personal taxable income. Y^{med} is median income for four-person families in current dollars. For the period 1971 to 1980, for θ_{max} we report here the statutory maximum tax rate on earned income.

For the earlier years this measure actually understates the tax incentive faced by individuals in the top tax bracket, since before 1975 individuals setting up a business could divide it into many separate corporations for tax purposes.[26] If the cost of doing this were zero, then the effective marginal corporate tax rate would be the corporate tax rate on the first dollar of income, denoted τ_{min} in column 5 of table 8.1.

In some years very few individuals normally face the top personal tax rate. However, all individuals with a personal tax rate above the corporate rate face some incentive to engage in income shifting. Column 4 of table 8.1 gives the minimum taxable income level at which the marginal personal tax rate for married couples filing jointly exceeds the maximum corporate tax rate, and column 6 gives the minimum income level at which the personal rate exceeds the minimum corporate tax rate. Column 7 lists the median income of four-person families as a benchmark. These income levels are low enough that many people would face incentives to shift income into the firm. The figures also grow less quickly over time than median income until the early 1980s, implying that a growing fraction of individuals faced at least some tax incentive to shift income into a corporation. In contrast, individuals in lower tax brackets faced tax incentives to shift money out of the firm. For example, tax incentives would discourage the use of stock incentive schemes as a form of compensation for these individuals, even if the incentives were otherwise valuable.

Tables 8.2 and 8.3 present more information on changes in the personal tax rate schedule over time. Table 8.2 presents the tax rate schedules for a married couple fil-

Table 8.2   Marginal Tax Rates for Married Taxpayers Filing Jointly, at Constant Dollar Incomes: 1962, 1977, 1982, and 1988

Adjusted Gross Income	Marginal Tax Rates (%)			
(1988 Dollars)	1962	1977	1982	1988
$5,000	0	0	0	0
10,000	18	0	14	15
20,000	18	17	19	15
35,000	20	25	29	15
50,000	26	32	39	28
75,000	34	42	44	28
100,000	43	50	49	33
150,000	53	55 (50)	50	33
250,000	62	64 (50)	50	28
500,000	78	70 (50)	50	28
1,000,000	89	70 (50)	50	28
2,000,000	91	70 (50)	50	28

Source: Slemrod (1994), table 3, and authors' calculations.
Note: Calculations assume that the couple does not itemize, that they claim two exemptions (for themselves), and that they do not receive the earned income tax credit or use the alternative minimum tax. Note that in 1962, despite statutory rates that exceeded 87 percent, the average rate was capped at that figure. Figures in parentheses for 1977 reflect the maximum statutory rate on earned income.

Table 8.3   Marginal Tax Rates at the 99.0, 99.5, and 99.9 Percentile of the Tax Rate Distribution, 1964 to 1993 (Excluding 1965)

Year	99.0 Percentile	99.5 Percentile	99.9 Percentile
1964	37.5%	44.5%	58.5%
1966	39	46	58
1967	39	48	60
1968	42	50	60
1969	42	50	60
1970	42	50	60
1971	42	50	60
1972	42	50	62
1973	45	52	62
1974	45	53	62
1975	48	53	64
1976	50	55	64
1977	50	55	66
1978	53	58	67
1979	54	55	68
1980	54	59	68
1981	53.325	58.2625	67.15
1982	49	50	50
1983	45	50	50
1984	45	49	50
1985	45	49	50
1986	45	49	50
1987	38.5	38.5	38.5
1988	33	35	35
1989	33	35	35
1990	33	35	35
1991	31	31	31
1992	31	31	31
1993	36	36	39.6

Source: Authors' calculations using public-use personal income tax return data files.

ing jointly for 1962, 1977, 1982, and 1988 (all the income brackets are expressed in 1988 dollars). Note first that the notoriously high top marginal taxes of 1962 applied only to very high real-income levels. For example, the top marginal tax rate of 91 percent applied only to incomes above about $1.5 million (in 1988 dollars). At the real-income level where the 70 percent rate began in 1977, in 1962 the marginal tax rate was 78 percent—higher, but not that much higher. Note, however, that the maximum tax on *earned* income in 1977 was, in principle, capped at 50 percent.

Table 8.3 shows the marginal personal tax rates at the 99.0, 99.5, and 99.9 percentiles of the tax rate distribution. It supports the notion that most of the income of the affluent was taxed at rates below the top rate. It also shows that "bracket creep" was responsible for a gradual increase in marginal tax rates between 1966 and

1980. Over that period the marginal rate for the 99.0, 99.5 and 99.9 percentiles increased by fifteen (from 39 to 54 percent), thirteen (from 46 to 59 percent), and ten (from 58 to 68 percent) percentage points, respectively.

The changing rate structure seen in the tables reflects in part the gradual drift due to inflation and a fixed nominal tax schedule—namely, "bracket creep." In addition, however, several major statutory tax changes were enacted during this period. We next examine each of the major tax regimes over this period.

Tax Law Pre-1969

Although the Revenue Act of 1964 reduced the top rate from 91 percent to 70 percent (effective in 1965), prior to 1971 the top personal tax rate was much higher than the top corporate tax rate, creating a strong incentive for individuals in the top tax brackets to engage in income shifting. This incentive was duly noted by tax planners and others. The influential text on taxation and management decisions by Sommerfeld (1981, 82) noted that, prior to 1970, "the owners of small and medium-sized businesses tended to accumulate all their business income beyond personal consumption needs within the corporations formed to take advantage of the lower corporate rates." A 1952 *Fortune* magazine article on the "new rich" reported the impact of the tax structure:

> Most spectacular of all was the effect of income taxes on top corporation personnel. . . . When the rates rose to a point where the tax on salaries of $150,000 to $200,000 was almost three times the capital-gains rate, the implication could no longer be ignored: men of ability could make more money by building up a business of their own, and then selling it, than they could by working as a salaried official of a big corporation. (62)

As noted earlier, one other important aspect of the tax law until 1975 was that business owners had substantial flexibility to divide their business into multiple units, so that each unit could take advantage of the initial brackets in the corporate tax rate schedule. Sommerfeld (1981, 51) remarks that the "practical consequence [of the tax advantage of business splitting] was that literally thousands of small corporations were formed, where fewer would otherwise have sufficed, primarily to achieve the substantial tax benefits that were available."

The 1969 Tax Reform Act

The 1969 Tax Reform Act made several important changes. First, it provided that, after December 31, 1974, controlled groups of corporations (defined to encompass both brother-sister and parent-subsidiary ownership arrangements) would be treated as if they were a single taxable entity; this reduced the value of corporate status because it eliminated the tax advantage of "business splitting."

Second, the 1969 tax act increased the tax rate on individual long-term capital gains. Before 1969 the maximum rate on long-term capital gains was 25 percent, but after the act this maximum rate applied to only $50,000 per year in long-term gains. Alternatively, the taxpayer could elect to have half (reduced to 40 percent as of 1978) of long-term gains included as ordinary income. Thus, in 1969 there was an increase in the tax penalty incurred when the owner sold the capital stock of a corporation that had appreciated in value because of retentions.

Another important element of the 1969 act was the establishment of a "maximum tax on earned income": the maximum marginal tax rate on earned income under the individual income tax was set at 50 percent, even while the maximum tax rate on other sources of income remained equal to 70 percent.[27] In particular, it allowed a qualifying taxpayer to subtract from the ordinary tax liability the difference between the ordinary tax liability on "earned taxable income" and what that liability would have been if the top tax rate were 50 percent.

For this purpose, earned income referred to compensation for the rendering of personal services rather than income derived from property. In most small businesses, the income of the owners is attributable jointly to their labor effort (personal service) and a return to capital they provide; it is no easy matter to identify them separately. Before 1980 the law allowed no more than 30 percent of the income of an unincorporated business to be characterized as earned income. No such statutory rule applied to corporations, however, thus providing, as Sommerfeld (1981, 79) notes, an incentive to incorporate, distribute the corporation's income as a salary to the owner-employee, and thus have it taxed as earned income, which was subject to a maximum 50 percent rate.

The upshot of these two changes in 1969 was that corporate taxable income over $50,000 was taxed at 48 percent, compared to an intended maximum individual tax rate of wage and salary income of 50 percent. As a result, Sommerfeld (1981, 82) notes, between 1969 and 1978 many business people decided to distribute nearly all their corporation's income as salary: "In exchange for the penalty of only two percentage points in taxes, the owner could be immediately free to consume or invest the additional income as he or she desired."

However, the maximum tax on earned income did not literally impose a maximum marginal tax rate of 50 percent. In fact, the effective marginal tax rate on earned income became $0.50 + t_0 - \alpha t_E$, where t_0 is the marginal tax rate on all income, t_E is the (hypothetical) marginal tax rate if there is no unearned income, and α is the fraction of earned income treated as earned taxable income (where the difference is the amount of deductions that had to be apportioned to earned income).[28] Nevertheless, although the maximum tax did not impose a ceiling of 50 percent, it did significantly reduce the marginal tax rate on earned income for high-income taxpayers. For example, Lindsey (1981) calculated that taxpayers whose marginal tax rate in the absence of the maximum tax would have been between 65 percent and 70 percent faced an average marginal tax rate of 58.6 percent with it.

Between 1971 and 1976 the maximum tax also had an indirect "poisoning" effect on the marginal tax rate on capital gains, because in some cases additional capital gains reduced the amount of earned income eligible for the maximum-tax preference. Moreover, there was an absolute limit on the amount of income eligible for the maximum tax; this limit was equal to taxable income minus the included portion of capital gains. For some individuals, the effective capital gains tax rate was also raised by an "add-on" minimum tax of 10 percent on a set of "preference" items, including the excluded part of long-term capital gains; the rate was increased to 15 percent by the Tax Reform Act of 1976.

On net, the tax changes in 1969 resulted in an increase in the effective marginal corporate tax rate faced by smaller businesses, owing to the consolidation of returns from corporations with common control and an increase in the effective capital gains tax rate. In addition, the act decreased the personal tax rate that individuals in the top tax brackets faced on their wage and salary income. These changes together should have reduced substantially the incentives faced by individuals in the top tax brackets to engage in income shifting, resulting in an increase in their reported personal income and a drop in corporate income, particularly of small corporations.

Tax Reforms of 1981 to 1983

The second major tax change was the Economic Recovery Tax Act (ERTA), passed in 1981 and phased in by 1983. Under ERTA, the top personal tax rate was reduced immediately to 50 percent, and all other personal tax rates were gradually reduced.[29] Statutory corporate tax rates, in contrast, remained unaffected. These changes reduced the incentive to shift income into corporations for individuals in all tax brackets. As a result, corporate income should have fallen and personal income should have risen. Plausibly, the rise in personal income should have been concentrated in the top brackets, where any previous income shifting was presumably most concentrated.

In addition, ERTA substantially accelerated business depreciation deductions, and businesses with tax losses could more readily transfer these tax losses to other firms. As a result, many more forms of business activity started to generate tax losses, causing a rapid growth in the tax shelter industry. These businesses were most valuable to owners who were in the highest tax bracket. This growth resulted in partnerships owned by individuals in the top tax brackets who would lease many types of capital to corporations, particularly buildings and oil drilling equipment.

The Tax Reform Act of 1986

The third major tax change of this era was the Tax Reform Act of 1986 (TRA86), which was phased in during 1987 and 1988. In exchange for some base broadening, marginal personal tax rates were reduced substantially, with the top rate falling from 50 percent to 28 percent. Although the maximum corporate tax rate was also reduced, 1988 marks the first time in our sample period when the maximum statutory corporate rate exceeded even the maximum personal tax rate. Reinforcing this change, long-term capital gains became fully taxable under the personal income tax, whereas previously only 40 percent of such gains were taxable. In the post-TRA86 era it would appear that all taxpayers faced tax incentives discouraging income shifting, reversing the historic tax-planning calculus. Witness Sommerfeld and Jones (1991, 72): "Under prior laws tax advisors were often concerned about justifying the retention of earnings within the closely-held corporation; now they will be equally concerned about the details of getting money out of the same corporation with only a single income tax being applicable to the amounts withdrawn." This could be accomplished by increasing the salary paid to the owner-employee. Alternatively, it could be accomplished by having the corporation rent property from its sole share-holder and pay a reasonable rent for the use of that property, have the corporation pay interest on money borrowed, or have the corporation pay a royalty for the corporation's use of the owner's talent or copyright.

In addition, TRA86 reduced depreciation rates, implying that fewer firms would have tax losses. In addition, it phased in restrictions preventing individuals from deducting losses from nonbusiness income resulting from their financial invest-ments in noncorporate firms. These changes effectively wiped out the tax shelter industry. In any case, the fact that corporate rates exceeded even the maximum per-sonal rate implied that any firms that continued to generate tax losses would be more valuable if they were corporate and thus could deduct losses subject to corporate rather than personal tax rates.

Soon after TRA86, the historical relationship between the top personal and cor-porate rates was restored. First, in 1991, the top personal rate was increased from 28 percent to 31 percent. Then, in 1993, it was increased to 39.6 percent, again higher than the top corporate rate, which was also raised, but just by one point, to 35 percent.

EVIDENCE ON INCOME SHIFTING

As discussed earlier, income shifting can be accomplished in a variety of ways. Some ways, such as the use of debt finance and changes in organizational form, have been studied at some length. Other ways, primarily changes in forms of compensation, have received little attention in the past. We first summarize the findings from past work on the use of debt finance and changes in organizational form and then turn to our analysis of new evidence on other mechanisms of income shifting.

Debt-Equity Ratios

The most studied form of income shifting is the use of corporate debt to reduce cor-porate taxable income and increase personal taxable income. The realization that taxes can create an incentive for corporations to increase their use of debt finance dates back to Miller and Modigliani (1961). Empirical estimation of the effects of taxes on corporate financial policy has been hampered by the very limited variation, until recently, of relative tax rates. Jeffrey MacKie-Mason (1990) and Alan Auer-bach (1985) provide evidence that firms with tax loss carry-forwards tend to have less debt, as would be expected on tax grounds because these firms cannot save on corporate taxes through extra interest deductions (except through the possible use of loss carry-forwards at some point in the future). This evidence is somewhat hard to interpret, however, since firms have tax losses in part because of substantial inter-est deductions arising from past borrowing, and the existence of current losses makes further borrowing more difficult; thus, taxes and the use of debt finance may be correlated for reasons other than the incentives created by a tax differential between the corporate and personal rates.

Another indirect approach to estimating the effects of taxes on the corporate use of debt was tried in Gordon (1982). That paper started with the observation that the tax savings from an extra dollar of debt depend on the product of any difference between corporate and personal tax rates and nominal interest rates. Although relative tax rates had not varied much during the time period available for that study, nominal interest rates had varied substantially. The paper did find that the use of debt was noticeably higher when nominal interest rates were higher. Based on the resulting estimates, Gordon and MacKie-Mason (1990) forecast that TRA86 will increase corporate debt-equity ratios by 0.155, a substantial change. In fact, however, the use of debt increased only modestly after 1986.

The lack of evidence confirming any appreciable effect of taxes on the use of debt, which led Stewart Myers (1984, 588) to argue that "I know of no study clearly demonstrating that a firm's tax status has predictable material effects on its debt policy," is not evidence to the contrary, given the minimal pre-1986 variation in relative tax rates. However, the more recent tax changes may well provide the needed variation in relative tax rates essential to estimating the role of taxes in corporations' choice of debt finance. Valerie Amerkhail, Gillian Spooner, and Emil Sunley (1988), for example, calculate that net interest payments relative to profits before interest deductions equaled only 4.7 percent from 1960 to 1969, but rose to 17.1 percent from 1970 to 1979, and 29.9 percent from 1980 to 1987. As noted earlier, during this period each major tax change resulted in a fall in personal tax rates relative to corporate rates, raising the incentive to use debt finance.

Organizational-Form Choices

As emphasized by Jane Gravelle and Larry Kotlikoff (1989, 1993), differences between personal and corporate tax rates can also affect a firm's choice of whether to incorporate. Based on tax considerations alone, it should incorporate only if the resulting corporate (plus some personal) tax liabilities are less than the personal tax that would be owed if the firm were noncorporate. The two forms of organization differ on nontax grounds as well, however, since only corporations have limited liability by default, and only corporations can have publicly traded shares and infinite life.[30]

The empirical question is the degree to which tax differences are strong enough to more than outweigh these nontax considerations and induce firms to change organizational form. Gordon and MacKie-Mason (1994), MacKie-Mason and Gordon (1997), and Goolsbee (1998) all report evidence indicating some statistically significant responsiveness to tax incentives. Roughly, their results suggest that a cut of 10 percent in the corporate rate, holding personal rates fixed, would result in a shift of about half a percent of total business assets into the corporate sector. However, the estimates also imply that such a tax change would result in a shift of about 5 percent of aggregate business profits into the corporate sector, as well as a shift of 5 percent of aggregate losses into the noncorporate sector. These shifts would be large enough to have noticeable effects on reported corporate and noncorporate tax revenue.

In fact, MacKie-Mason and Gordon (1997) find that they underestimated the extent to which income shifted into the noncorporate sector following the 1986 Tax

Reform Act, perhaps because they were unable to capture the effects of the base broadening and the restrictions on nonbusiness interest deductions that were important components of this tax reform. The relative share of total business net income (less deficit) accounted for by C corporations fell quite dramatically, from 78.3 percent to 59.4 percent between 1980 and 1992. Put in a more striking way, the fraction of net business income accounted for by pass-through entities nearly doubled over this period, increasing from 21.7 to 40.6 percent.

NEW EVIDENCE ON INCOME SHIFTING
Reported Corporate Rates of Return

There is little evidence for income shifting other than through shifts of assets between corporate and noncorporate firms, or through changes in the corporate use of debt finance. One partial exception is evidence in Wilkie, Young, and Nutter (1996), reproduced here in table 8.4. This table reports the size of the sum of corporate deductions for rent, interest payments, and officers' compensation as a fraction of "distributable income" (defined as net income plus these deductions). In the table, we find that this ratio jumped substantially after TRA86 among smaller firms, but not for larger firms. If the jump reflects changes in the use of debt finance, then this may represent clearer evidence for tax effects on the use of debt than has appeared in the past literature. It is unlikely that we are seeing an increase in deductions for rent after 1986; designed to kill off real estate tax shelters, TRA86 should have caused a shift in ownership of buildings back into the corporate sector. The one other possible explanation for the observed increase in deductions is an increase in officers' compensation. Such an increase could represent a change in the forms of compensation for these officers. However, such an interpretation is clouded by the fact that the data sources report compensation for at most five officers per firm. To begin with, this means that changes in the income shifting undertaken by other employees is unreported. In addition, however, the reported figures reflect changes in the number of firms as well as changes in the reported compensation per officer. TRA86 should have reduced the incentive to set up small firms to engage in income shifting, thus leading to a drop in the number of firms. If officers' compensation went up in spite of this expected drop in the number of firms, this suggests that the true change in income shifting was even larger.

In this section, we examine aggregated corporate tax return data to search for evidence of changes in the amount of income shifting with respect to tax incentives, other than through changes in the use of debt finance or shifts in assets between corporate and noncorporate firms. To the extent that income shifting is occurring, reported corporate income will be higher than otherwise. We focus on income relative to corporate assets to control for any changes in income simply resulting from a shift in assets. In addition, we look at income *before* interest deductions to eliminate from the analysis the effects of changing uses of debt finance. With these procedures, any resulting evidence of income shifting would suggest that firms are using some income-shifting mechanism in addition to debt finance and shifts in assets between corporate and noncorporate firms.

Table 8.4   Deductible Dividends of C Corporations as a Percentage of Distributable Income, by Size of Total Assets, Tax Years 1984 to 1990

Tax Year	All Returns	Under $100,000	$100,001 to $250,000	$250,001 to $500,000	Size of Total Assets $500,001 to $1,000,000	$1,000,001 to $5,000,000	$5,000,001 to $10,000,000	More than $10,000,000
1984	72.11	105.47	85.39	92.01	89.69	85.96	81.81	61.95
1985	75.20	106.21	86.33	93.53	92.85	88.81	87.38	65.61
1986	77.98	105.76	86.39	93.16	93.09	88.74	86.52	69.58
1987	71.93	107.60	87.30	93.99	94.19	90.10	86.60	61.95
1988	66.70	112.52	101.00	98.18	94.69	91.88	87.83	56.97
1989	71.78	113.68	103.29	103.01	96.96	96.58	91.56	63.89
1990	73.77	118.87	105.21	101.59	99.75	100.48	97.45	66.10

Source: Wilkie, Young, and Nutter (1996, figure K).

Notes: Deductible dividends equals the sum of rental expense, interest expense, and officers' compensation. Distributable income equals deductible dividends plus net income (less deficit).

Table 8.5 reports, for various asset size ranges, the ratio of corporate income before interest deductions to corporate assets, measured as a percentage.[31] As seen in the table, rates of return for all firms have been somewhat more stable over time than those for smaller firms. Reported rates of return for smaller firms fell following the 1986 tax reforms. There is also a clear growth in reported rates of return during the 1970s, in spite of the attempt to cap the top personal tax rate on wages and salaries to 50 percent.[32]

Table 8.5   The Ratio of Corporate Income Before Interest Deductions to Corporate Assets for Various Size Firms, 1964 to 1993

	Asset Size				
Year	Under $1 Million (A)	$5 Million to $10 Million (B)	All (C)	A-C	B-C
1964	6.71	5.25	5.24	1.47	0.01
1965	7.12	5.76	5.60	1.52	0.16
1966	7.15	6.13	5.91	1.24	0.22
1967	7.54	5.72	5.57	1.97	0.15
1968	7.49	4.74	5.40	2.09	-0.64
1969	7.34	5.92	5.38	1.96	0.54
1970	7.09	5.72	5.05	2.04	0.67
1971	7.28	6.06	5.08	2.20	0.98
1972	7.49	6.26	5.11	2.38	1.15
1973	7.98	7.05	5.83	2.15	1.22
1974	8.76	7.77	6.82	1.94	0.95
1975	8.29	7.99	6.37	1.92	1.62
1976	8.24	8.04	6.67	1.57	1.37
1977	8.80	8.14	6.77	2.03	1.37
1978	9.70	9.02	7.07	2.63	1.95
1979	9.95	9.41	7.74	2.11	1.67
1980	9.95	9.44	7.52	2.43	1.92
1981	10.12	9.88	8.02	2.10	1.86
1982	9.94	8.73	7.37	2.57	1.36
1983	9.11	7.98	6.61	2.50	1.37
1984	9.62	8.09	6.85	2.77	1.24
1985	9.44	7.49	6.25	3.19	1.24
1986	9.52	7.13	5.69	3.83	1.44
1987	8.17	6.30	5.57	2.60	0.73
1988	7.31	6.18	6.03	1.28	0.15
1989	7.27	6.38	6.34	0.93	0.04
1990	6.83	5.90	6.15	0.68	-0.25
1991	6.36	5.49	5.43	0.93	0.06
1992	5.92	4.93	4.67	1.25	0.26
1993	5.62	4.77	4.33	1.29	0.44

Source: Authors' calculations based on data from *Statistics of Income* publications on corporation income tax returns.

As indicators of the extent of income shifting, these figures suffer from various weaknesses. The definition of taxable income changed several times during the sample period (for example, because of the acceleration of depreciation following the 1981 tax reform and the deceleration enacted in 1986), resulting in changes in reported profit rates without any behavioral change. In addition, the measure of income is not neutral to the inflation rate, given the use of historic cost figures for depreciation and inventory deductions; during the sample period the inflation rate fluctuated substantially. Third, business cycle effects can be important. Finally, profit rates can differ between small and large firms because successful firms grow and unsuccessful firms shrink, implying that the small firms tend to be the "losers."

To address these problems, we next report on a series of regression analyses that seek to explain the reported rate of return from 1965 to 1993, before interest deductions, of firms of various size over time. In recognition of the fact that over time many factors are changing that could affect rates of return, in most specifications we include time dummies. As long as inflation, business cycles, and changes in depreciation rates affect equally the profitability of all firms, then these time dummies capture the effects of these factors. As a result, however, in these specifications we can estimate the effects of tax changes only to the extent to which they affect different firms differently, owing either to the differential marginal corporate tax rates that apply or to differential responsiveness by size of firm.

Another obvious issue is that the available data, by firm size, divides firms into asset categories based on the *nominal* value of a firm's assets in each year; table 8.5 is an example. Because rates of return can differ by firm size for nontax reasons, it is important to define "large" and "small" in a consistent way across years and not to allow the data to be contaminated by "bracket creep." Our approach is to set up a flexible functional form linking the observed rate of return for firms in year t that have nominal assets below some nominal cutoff value A_t^i to the value of $a_{it} \equiv A_t^i/GDP_t$, where GDP_t is nominal gross domestic product in year t.[33] The intuition here is that when the economy is larger, the (nominal) size distribution of firms shifts out as well.[34] In particular, and ignoring for the moment the tax incentive terms, we investigate piecewise linear functions of the following form:

$$R_t(A_t^i) = \alpha_0 + \alpha_1 \min(a_{it}, .5) + \alpha_2 \min(.5, \max(a_{it} - .5, 0))$$
$$+ \alpha_3 \min(4, \max(a_{it} - 1, 0)) + \alpha_4 \max(a_{it} - 5, 0) + \sum_t \beta_t d_t + \epsilon_{it}, \qquad (8.1)$$

where $R_t(A_t^i)$ equals the average rate of return for all firms in year t with nominal assets below (A_t^i), where the d_t are time dummies, and where the numbers 0.5, 1, 4, and 5 refer to millions of 1992 dollars. The number of nominal brackets i for any given year varies from year to year.

Equation (8.1) represents the rate of return of a given-size firm as a piecewise-linear function of its asset size relative to the nominal GDP of that year. If small firms on average report a lower rate of return (because they are more likely to be either new entrants or failing firms), then the estimates of the α_1 through α_4 coefficients should be positive. In fact, when equation (8.1) is estimated, they all turn out to be negative, implying that the smallest firms reported earning 3.0 percent *more* per year, as a fraction of assets, than large firms (those with $1 million in assets).[35] This finding is suggestive of income shifting, because the smallest firms are in the best position to take advantage of its benefits, and for most of the sample period the richest individuals had clear tax incentives to reclassify their earnings as corporate income.

Testing explicitly to what degree reported rates of return respond to tax changes requires an estimate of the difference between marginal corporate and personal tax rates for each group of firms, for each year. We faced several issues in coming up with such estimates. To begin with, the marginal corporate tax rate varies not only over time but also across firms, owing to the progressive rate structure under the U.S. corporate income tax. We proceed as follows. Based on the observed average taxable income per firm for any asset category i in year t, we calculate the marginal corporate tax rate based on the corporate tax schedule in that year.[36] However, this estimate of the marginal tax rate depends on some of the same data used to construct the dependent variable, so it may be endogenous. To deal with this, we constructed an instrument by recalculating the marginal corporate tax rate for observation i in year t using an estimate of average taxable income per firm, equal to average assets per firm in asset category it, multiplied by the ratio of aggregate taxable income to aggregate assets among *all* firms in year t. We then determined the marginal corporate tax rate at that income level from the tax schedules and used this figure as an instrument. By this procedure, the reported rate of return within a particular asset category is not used to calculate the appropriate corporate tax rate. Note that this procedure implies that the corporate tax rate varies across firm-size categories within a year, allowing the tax incentive effect to be identified in the presence of time dummies.

A second issue is how best to capture the incentive effects of the personal income tax, given that individuals in different brackets face different incentives. To capture some of the flavor of these diverse incentives, we investigate two different measures of tax incentives, one for those individuals in tax brackets above the corporate rate and a second for those in brackets below the corporate rate. The first (second) variable equals the appropriate corporate tax rate minus the weighted average marginal personal tax rate for those in tax brackets above (below) the appropriate corporate rate,[37] multiplied by the fraction of labor income subject to a tax rate above (below) the corporate rate. We denote these two variables by T_a and T_b, respectively.[38]

Table 8.6, column 2, shows the results of estimating equation (8.1) with T_a and T_b added, using the instruments discussed earlier. The coefficients on T_a and T_b are −.153 (.025) and −.037 (.011), respectively, with standard errors in parentheses. These coefficients have the signs and relative sizes that were expected and are strongly significant statistically. They are fairly modest, however, in terms of magnitude. Since on average only 23.6 percent of labor compensation is received by those with personal tax rates above the corporate rate, the regression implies that a one-point increase in the corporate tax rate lowers the reported corporate rate of return by just .064 (.236 × 153 + .764 × .037) percentage points.

As a sensitivity test, we tried decomposing both T_a and T_b. Each of these variables equals an average difference between the corporate and personal tax rates for

Table 8.6   Regression Results for Reported Corporate Rates of Return

Equation Number	1	2	3	4	5	6
Asset / GDP 1	−2.226	−4.568	−4.677	−4.396	−4.493	−4.675
	(1.352)	(0.552)	(0.557)	(0.563)	(0.565)	(0.552)
Asset / GDP 2	−0.205	−0.634	−0.582	−0.087	−0.639	−0.618
	(0.800)	(0.329)	(0.331)	(0.533)	(0.333)	(0.327)
Asset / GDP 3	0.157	0.118	−0.043	0.094	0.132	0.088
	(0.096)	(0.055)	(0.076)	(0.062)	(0.065)	(0.059)
Asset / GDP 4	−0.0008	−0.0006	−0.0004	−0.0006	−0.0005	−0.0006
	(0.0003)	(0.0001)	(0.0001)	(0.0001)	(0.0001)	(0.0001)
T_a	−0.312	−0.153	—	—	—	−0.238
	(0.047)	(0.025)				(0.052)
T_b	−0.002	−0.037	—	—	—	−0.039
	(0.022)	(0.011)				(0.011)
$(\tau-\theta_a)$	—		−0.109	—	—	—
			(0.029)			
$(\tau-\theta_b)$	—		−0.035	—	—	—
			(0.009)			
wgt_a	—		0.313	—	—	−1.277
			(0.634)			(0.747)
$\tau \times Wgt_a$	—		—		−0.479	—
					(0.078)	
$\tau \times Wgt_b$	—		—		−0.061	—
					(0.014)	
$\theta \times Wgt_a$	—	—	—	—	0.319	—
					(0.084)	
$\theta \times Wgt_b$	—	—	—	—	0.058	—
					(0.079)	
Small $\times T_a$	—	—	—	−0.168	—	—
				(0.047)		
Small $\times T_b$	—	—	—	−0.251	—	—
				(0.170)		
Large $\times T_a$	—	—	—	−0.094	—	—
				(0.035)		
Large $\times T_b$	—	—	—	−0.046	—	—
				(0.011)		
Small	—	—	—	0.553	—	—
				(0.764)		
Year dummy	n	y	y	y	y	y
Adjusted R^2	0.329	0.890	0.890	0.895	0.887	0.892
Number of observations	295	295	295	295	295	295

Source: Authors' calculations.
Note: Dependent variable is the average rate of return.

a subset of individuals times the share of labor income represented by each subset. In column 3 we report the results of including in the regression separately the average difference in marginal tax rates for each group, and the fraction of the population in the richest group.[39] The coefficients on the two tax terms were now −.109

(.029) and −.035 (.009). Given that the tax variables are no longer weighted by the fraction of the population in each group, the measured effects of tax changes are a bit larger—a one-point increase in the corporate tax rate is now forecast to lower corporate rates of return by .144 (.109 + .035) percentage points, holding constant the fraction of people facing a personal tax rate above the corporate rate.

In addition, we tried decomposing T_a and T_b each into two separate terms: one equal to τ times the appropriate fraction of the population, and the other equal to θ times that fraction of the population. This decomposition allows us to investigate the separate effects of τ and θ. If income shifting is important, we expect a negative coefficient on τ and a positive coefficient of equal absolute value on θ. Finding an effect of θ would be strong evidence of income shifting, since it is difficult otherwise to explain its effects on corporate rates of return. In addition, a negative effect of τ on rates of return would be inconsistent with the traditional notion that taxes discourage investment, that any fall in investment raises rates of return both because less capital would raise the average product of the remaining capital and because of a fall in the front-loaded tax deductions for new investments. As column 5 reports, when T_a is decomposed, the coefficients on the τ and θ components become, respectively, −.479 (.078) and .319 (.084). Similarly, the coefficients on the two components of T_b become −.061 (.014) and .058 (.079). These results are consistent with an income-shifting story, and inconsistent with the normal focus on real behavioral responses.

We also tested to see whether the reactions of small firms to income-shifting incentives are different from those of larger firms. To do so, we included T_a and T_b separately for small firms (firms with "real" assets in 1992 dollars of less than $1 million) and for other firms; the results are reported in column 4. For small firms, the two coefficients were −.168 (.047) and −.251 (.170), whereas for the remaining firms the coefficients were −.094 (.035) and −.046 (.011). All coefficients are of the expected sign, and all but one are strongly statistically significant. As expected, small firms are more responsive to tax incentives. This appears to be particularly the case with respect to the tax incentives faced by individuals facing personal tax rates below the corporate rate. Perhaps these lower-paid employees in a small firm are much more likely to be compensated in the form of equity in the firm for nontax reasons (compared to lower-paid employees in larger firms), implying that they have more flexibility to respond to tax incentives.

Because in our specification there are time dummies, the estimated effect of taxes is identified entirely via the within-year variation of $\tau-\theta$, which arises because different size firms can face different marginal corporate tax rates. This procedure ignores as a source of information the large changes over time in tax rates, but sidesteps the problem that over time many factors affecting rates of return change; because we cannot hope to control adequately for these factors, there is a problem of spuriously attributing to taxation the influence of other time-varying factors. Column 1 displays the results of eliminating the time dummies in the basic specification. The results remain consistent with the theory—the coefficients on both T_a and T_b are negative, but only the former is significantly different from zero. In addition, the estimated coefficient on T_a is about twice its magnitude in the specification with time dummies. Thus, ignoring the possibility of spurious correlation with time-varying omitted factors, the evidence suggests that it is predominantly income shifting by high-income taxpayers that affects the reported corporate rate of return.

In figures 8.1 and 8.2, we illustrate the estimated impact of income shifting on the reported rates of return of two size categories of firms. Figure 8.1 reports our estimates for the rate of return over time, with and without taxes, for firms with assets below $1 million in 1992 dollars. Figure 8.2 reports the same two rates of return for firms with assets below $100 million in 1992 dollars.[40] Since small firms faced very low corporate tax rates, most employees gained by shifting income into the corporation, whereas the higher marginal corporate rate faced by larger firms implied that employees on net shifted money out of the firm. The inflationary bracket creep in the 1970s shows up clearly in the graphs, as do the relative cuts in personal tax rates during the period 1981 to 1983 and the period 1987 to 1988.

Figures 8.3 and 8.4 provide a different perspective on the same figures. Figure 8.3 reports the forecasted rates of return without taxes for the two different size categories of firms. Here we find, as expected, that larger (and presumably more successful) firms are forecasted to have a slightly higher rate of return, ignoring tax incentives. In figure 8.4, however, we find that tax incentives reverse the relative rates of return, causing the forecasted rate of return to jump for smaller firms, owing to their much lower marginal corporate tax rate.

How much excess burden from income shifting do these estimates of behavioral response imply? If we ignore the kinds of externality problems discussed earlier, we

Figure 8.1   Predicted Rate of Return, With and Without Tax-Induced Income Shifting, 1964 to 1993, for Firms With Assets Less than $1 Million (in 1992 Dollars)

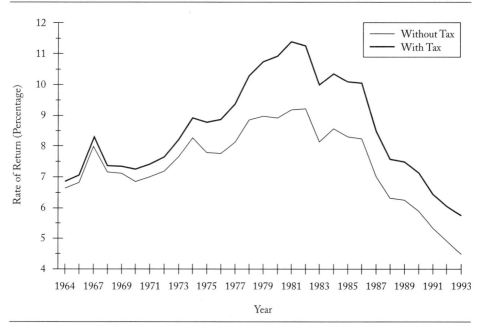

Source: Authors' calculations.

Figure 8.2   Predicted Rate of Return, With and Without Tax-Induced Income Shifting, 1964 to 1993, for Firms With Assets Less than $100 Million (in 1992 Dollars)

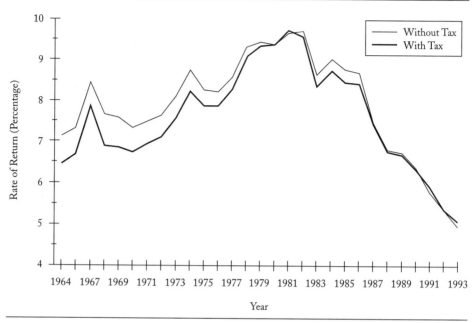

Source: Authors' calculations.

can proceed by using the following simple approximation of the excess burden arising from any individual's behavioral response:

$$L_i \approx 0.5 t_i^2 \frac{\Delta X_i}{\Delta t_i} \tag{8.2}$$

where t_i is the relevant tax wedge for individual i and $\Delta X_i/\Delta t_i$ is the (compensated) change in the tax base due to the behavioral responses of individual i. In this case the tax wedge is $\tau - \theta_i$, and ΔX_i refers to the amount of income shifted from one tax base to the other.

In the base case of column 1 and 2 in table 8.6, our estimated response, denoted $\hat{\alpha}_a$ or $\hat{\alpha}_b$ for the coefficients of T_a or T_b, respectively, is defined to equal the change in the *rate of return* with respect to either T_a or T_b. Here the rate of return equals taxable income divided by corporate assets A, and T_a equals $\tau - \theta_a$ times the fraction of labor income, L_a/L, received by workers in group a, and similarly for T_b. Therefore, $\Delta X_i/\Delta t_i = \hat{\alpha}_a A(L_i/L)$.

One complication is that τ varies by potential employer. We therefore take a weighted average of the above expression, using the appropriate value of τ_f for each reported size category of firm, and weighting each expression by the fraction of corporate assets A_f/A used by firms in that size category.[41]

Figure 8.3   Predicted Rate of Return, Without Tax-Induced Income Shifting, 1964 to 1993, for Firms With Assets Under $1 Million and Under $100 Million (in 1992 Dollars)

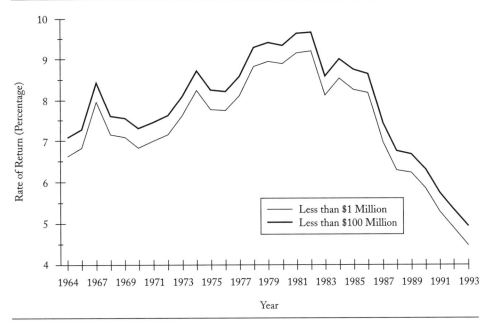

Source: Authors' calculations.

Our measure of the excess burden from individual i therefore equals

$$\sum_{f} 0.5\left(\tau_f - \theta_i\right)^2\left(\delta_a\hat{\alpha}_a + \left(1 - \delta_a\right)\hat{\alpha}_b\right)w_iA_f, \tag{8.3}$$

where δ_a is equal to 1 if $\theta_i > \tau_f$, and 0 otherwise, and where w_i is the individual's share in total labor income. The aggregate excess burden is the sum of these expressions over all individuals.

We graph the resulting estimates for the excess burden, as a percentage of GDP, in figure 8.5. To capture the sensitivity of these figures to the particular estimates for α_a and α_b, we graph results using coefficient estimates from columns 1, 2 and 5 from table 8.6. In order to understand the differing time patterns of the three curves in the graph, it is important to remember that these curves capture the effects of income shifting not only by high-paid employees (those with $\theta > \tau$) who shift income *into* the firm but also by lower-paid employees who forgo stock incentives in order to shift income *out* of the firm. According to the coefficient estimates from column 1, only high-paid employees respond to tax incentives. Therefore, the inflationary bracket creep during the 1970s led to a sharp rise in income shifting into firms, and therefore in the excess burden. In contrast, the results based on the coefficient estimates from columns 2 and 5 are affected much more heavily by the

Figure 8.4   Predicted Rate of Return, With Tax-Induced Income Shifting, 1964 to 1993, for Firms
With Assets Under $1 million and Under $100 Million (in 1992 Dollars)

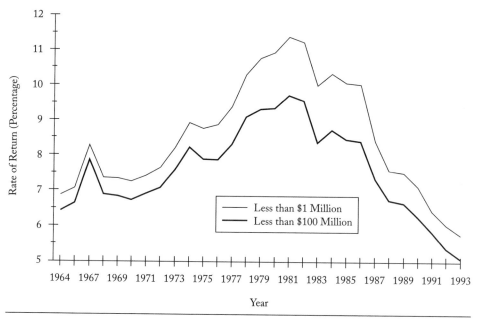

Source: Authors' calculations.

income shifting by lower-paid employees, who far outnumber the high-paid
employees. As a result, the corporate tax surcharge during 1968 to 1969 increased
the tax incentive to shift income out of the firm, raising the excess burden. Similarly,
the bracket creep during the 1970s reduced the tax distortion faced by these lower-
paid employees. All three figures, though, show that the compression in relative tax
rates during the two tax reforms in the 1980s reduced excess burdens, and that the
increase in the top tax rates in 1993 caused a slight increase in burdens.

Overall the excess burden generated by income shifting is modest. In contrast to
Harberger's estimate that the corporate tax-generated efficiency losses are equal to
half a percent of GDP, we find that the efficiency losses from income shifting were
at most one-fifth of a percent of GDP in the beginning of the time period, and at
most one-twentieth of a percent of GDP in more recent years.

Increased Personal Income Inequality

A number of recent papers have explored the potential impact of tax law changes
on changes in reported personal income over time. Lindsey (1981) was among the
first to point out that the 1981 tax cut in the top tax rate from 70 percent to 50 percent coincided with a very large increase in the share of income reported by the top
1 percent of the income distribution to the Internal Revenue Service. Lindsey's

Figure 8.5   Estimates of the Excess Burden from Income Shifting, 1964 to 1993

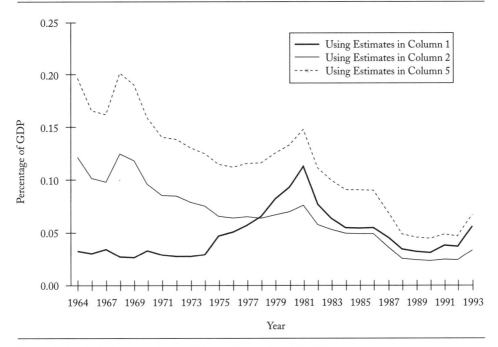

Source: Authors' calculations, using coefficient estimates from table 8.6.

methodology did not enable him to distinguish his tax causality hypothesis from an obvious alternative—that, for nontax reasons, pre-tax income inequality was growing rapidly between the two years he studied, 1981 and 1985. In fact, as Karoly (1993) documents, data from the Census Bureau reveal that inequality among families, after reaching a postwar low in the period 1967 to 1968, began to increase during the 1970s and continued to rise through the 1980s.

That pre-tax income inequality began to increase about 1970 is quite consistent with a tax causality hypothesis. Recall that 1970 marked the introduction of the maximum tax on earned income, which reduced the top marginal tax rate on labor income to 50 percent (or slightly more). Therefore, the richest individuals had more incentive to report personal income starting in the early 1970s, consistent with the observed growth.

Summary measures of income inequality based on tax data show the same patterns—increasing inequality since 1972 of all income, and also of wages and salaries by themselves. Feenberg and Poterba (1993) report the share of adjusted gross income (AGI) received by the top 0.5 percent of households arranged by income, after being approximately flat at about 6.0 percent from 1970 to 1981, began in 1982 to increase continuously to 7.7 percent in 1985, and then jumped sharply in 1986 to 9.2 percent. There was a slight increase in 1987 to 9.5 percent, then another sharp increase in 1988 to 12.1 percent; after 1988 there was a decline to 11.2 percent in 1989, and to 10.9 percent in 1990.[42]

Feenberg and Poterba (1993, 163, 170) argue that the surge of inequality in the period 1986 to 1988 "reflect[s] . . . factors including a tax-induced change in the incentives that high-income households face for reporting taxable income." They add that, with their data, "it is impossible to determine how much of the increase in reported income was due to changes in tax avoidance behavior; how much was due to changes in real behavior such as labor supply; and how much was due to changing returns to the factors, labor and capital, that high-income taxpayers own." We would add to this list of potential causes a drop in income shifting into corporations.

All of the evidence discussed so far is based on a comparison of consecutive cross-sectional samples. The well-known potential hazards of inferring behavioral response from comparing the behavior of two distinct groups of taxpayers can be mitigated by analyzing longitudinal, or panel, data on an unchanging set of taxpayers. This has been done in the work of Feldstein (1995) and Auten and Carroll (1999).

Feldstein (1995) investigates the high-income response to the TRA86 by making use of the Ernst & Young University of Michigan tax return panel data, which follow the same set of taxpayers from 1979 to 1988. Feldstein analyzed married couples for whom both 1985 and 1988 tax returns were available. After making several adjustments to the data, he concludes that the percentage increase from 1985 to 1988 in various measures of income, particularly taxable income excluding capital gains, was much higher, compared to the rest of the population, for those high-income groups whose marginal tax rate was reduced the most. Based on this finding, he estimates that the elasticity of taxable income with respect to the marginal tax rate is very high, and he suggests that an increase in the top marginal tax rate would raise little, if any, revenue. In this data set, however, the top income class, on which Feldstein focuses most of his attention (nonelderly couples in the 49 to 50 percent tax brackets in 1985), contains only fifty-seven observations. Generalizing from such a small sample is problematic.

Auten and Carroll (1999) make use of a much larger longitudinal data set, consisting of over fifteen thousand tax returns for the same set of taxpayers for 1985 and 1989. Because the sample observations are stratified so that high-income taxpayers are oversampled, there are over four thousand taxpayers in the 49 to 50 percent tax rate brackets in 1985. They regress the change in AGI between 1985 and 1989 against the change in marginal tax rate and, in some specifications, some demographic variables. They also control for occupation, as a proxy for demand-side (nontax) factors that might have affected the change in compensation over this period. They conclude that changes in tax rates appear to be an important determinant of the income growth of the late 1980s, and they estimate a base-case elasticity of taxable income to the net-of-tax rate of 0.569.

Finally, Slemrod (1996) investigated the role of tax and nontax effects in explaining the trends in the high-income shares from 1954 to 1990. He concludes that, for the period 1950 to 1985, changes in the high-income share can be largely explained by nontax factors, because they are highly correlated with changes in wage inequality for the rest of the population. However, the surge between 1985 and 1990 cannot be so explained, because overall inequality actually fell. Thus, he concludes, the surge was probably tax-driven; he leaves open, however, the question of to what extent the surge was caused by income shifting or income "creation."

These changes in reported income can occur for many reasons: the definition of taxable income has changed over time, business cycle effects can matter, work effort and savings rates can change, and the extent of tax avoidance and evasion can change. We are attempting to focus on yet another reason for changes in reported personal income: changes in income shifting between the personal and the corporate tax bases via the flexibility in forms of compensation. Although compensation normally takes the form of wages, salaries, and perhaps royalty payments, all of which generate personal taxable income and tax deductions for the firm, other forms of compensation (such as qualified stock options) avoid generating personal taxable income at the price of not providing a tax deduction to the firm. Tax returns provide no direct means of detecting compensation in these forms, since no personal taxable income is generated until the shares are sold, perhaps many years after being granted, and at that point the resulting capital gains cannot be distinguished from other capital gains coming from passive investments.

We instead investigate changes over time in taxable labor compensation, as a function of changes in personal relative to corporate tax rates. The data come from the public-use files of individual tax returns, covering the year 1964 and the years from 1966 to 1993. Taxable labor compensation certainly includes wages and salaries plus royalty income; less clear is how to treat income from proprietorships, partnerships, and subchapter S corporations. Some of this income undoubtedly reflects a return to capital investments, but much of it should reflect a return to labor effort. We follow Cutler and Katz (1992) and adopt the ad hoc assumption that in each year two-thirds of reported noncorporate business income represents labor income.[43]

We confine our attention to individual returns in the top half of the income distribution in each year (based on the above measure of labor compensation) on the presumption that other individuals in practice engaged in little or no income shifting during the sample period. Our starting assumption is that, taxes aside, the shape of the distribution of labor compensation should remain unchanged over time. We proceed by dividing the sample population in each year into twenty-three fractiles based on the distribution of labor compensation.[44] Let ω_{it} equal the average labor compensation for individuals in fractile i in year t. We begin by assuming that, in the absence of tax effects,

$$\ln(\omega_{it}) = \alpha_i + \beta_t + \varepsilon_{it} \tag{8.4}$$

where the time dummies, β_t, capture business cycle effects and changes in the price level, as well as real (proportional) growth in incomes over time, and α_i captures the baseline distribution of labor compensation.[45]

The next step is to add to equation (8.4) measures of the tax incentives to engage in income shifting, which should depend on the difference between personal and corporate tax rates, $\tau_t - \theta_{it}$. The personal rate, θ_{it}, was set equal to the average marginal personal tax rate for individuals in each fractile. We then add $\tau_t - \theta_{it}$ to the above specification, so that the presence of income shifting would be indicated by a positive coefficient on the tax incentive term. As column 1 of table 8.7 reveals, in this form the estimated coefficient on the tax incentive term was 0.029, with a standard error of only 0.001. This coefficient implies that a one-percentage-point increase in $\tau_t - \theta_{it}$ is associated with a 2.9 percent increase in reported labor income.

A potential econometric problem with this approach is that the dependent variable (labor income) is used in the calculation of θ_{it}, making the resulting tax rate endogenous. To deal with this endogeneity, we construct an instrument using the average personal tax rate in each fractile calculated using the estimate $\alpha_i + \beta_t$ from equation (8.4) instead of actual labor compensation for each individual.[46] The estimation is then done using instrumental-variable techniques. Column 2 shows that the coefficient of $\tau_t - \theta_{it}$ rises to 0.034, again with a standard error of 0.001, implying even stronger income shifting than found with OLS.[47]

Note that these estimates assume that all individuals respond equally to tax incentives that affect income shifting. Yet we might presume that the rich would be much more responsive at the margin to tax incentives—many of the less rich individuals would simply be at a corner solution in which all their compensation takes the form of wages and salaries. To test for this, we estimated separate coefficients on $\tau_t - \theta_{it}$ for individuals in the top 1 percent of the income distribution versus others in the top half of the income distribution. The estimated differences turned out to be fairly small: the coefficient on the tax variable for the top 1 percent of the population is .0364 (.002), while for the rest of the population it is .0327 (.001).

Of course, taxes affect not just income shifting but also real behavior. In particular, the personal tax rate θ_{it} can affect ω_{it} through changes in individual labor supply as well as through changes in income shifting. The most compelling explanation for any effect of τ_t on labor income, however, is income shifting.[48] To test for this, we included τ_t and θ_{it} separately, again allowing for different effects for the top 1 percent of the income distribution versus the rest of the (top half of the) population. However, given that τ_t varies only across time and that we continue to include time dummies,

Table 8.7   Regression Results for Personal Income

$\tau - \theta$	0.0295	0.0339	—	—
	(0.0010)	(0.0011)		
$(\tau - \theta) \times D$	—	—	0.0364	—
			(0.0017)	
$(\tau - \theta) \times (1 - D)$	—	—	0.0327	—
			(0.0012)	
$\tau \times D$	—	—	—	-0.010
				(0.002)
$\theta \times D$	—	—	—	-0.028
				(0.002)
$\theta \times (1 - D)$	—	—	—	-0.016
				(0.002)
IV?	n	y	y	y
Number of observations	667	667	667	667

Source: Authors' calculations.
Note: Dependent variable is the log of labor income. Fractile and year dummies are included in all regressions but not reported in the table. The dummy variable D equals one for observations in the top 1 percent of the income distribution, and equals zero otherwise.

the most we can do is estimate the degree to which any variation in τ_t has a stronger effect on the top 1 percent of the income distribution compared with its effects on the rest of the population. As column 3 details, we find that a 1 percent increase in τ_t in fact lowers the relative income of the richest individuals by 1.0 percent, with a standard error of 0.2 percent. In contrast, a 1 percent increase in θ_{it} lowers the income of the top 1 percent by 2.8 percent (standard error of 0.2 percent), compared with a 1.6 percent (standard error of 0.2 percent) drop for the rest of the sample population. Changes in θ_{it} therefore appear to have stronger effects on the richest individuals, whereas changes in τ_t have stronger effects on the less rich. We therefore forecast an increase in the relative income of the top 1 percent following the drop in τ_t after 1986, even though the drop in τ_t should encourage more income shifting into corporations, particularly by the rich. This coefficient estimate may simply be capturing any increases in income inequality after 1986 that occurred for other reasons.

The key weakness of our methodology is that the specification does not allow for any source of variation in the distribution of labor compensation over time other than the changes in relative tax rates. Undoubtedly, though, the shape of the distribution has changed owing to other factors as well, such as changes in technology or trade barriers, and these changes can be correlated with relative tax rates. The problem is that there are no obvious measures of the timing of these nontax changes. To provide an indirect test of whether the tax variable is in fact capturing a causal role of taxes, we also examine the effects of introducing the tax variable with various leads or lags to find the lead-lag pattern that best explains the observed variation in the dependent variable. If taxes are in fact *causing* the observed changes, then the most powerful choice should be close to contemporaneous.[49] To test for this, we tried replacing $\tau_t - \theta_{it}$ with its value at either $t - 2$, $t - 1$, $t + 1$ or $t + 2$. To maintain a consistent sample period, we restricted the sample to 1967 through 1991 for all runs. The maximum coefficient, .0328 (.0011), was found with the value at $t - 1$; other terms were monotonically smaller as the date differed from $t - 1$.[50] A one-period lag for tax effects is very plausible, so the coefficients are consistent with the variable having a causal effect and not simply serving as a proxy for some other underlying trend that affects relative wage rates.

If income shifting is behind these responses, then the dollar size of the increase in personal income in response to a rise in the corporate tax rate should be equal in absolute value to the implied fall in corporate income in response to the same tax change. Using the above figures, however, the forecasted response of personal incomes is an order of magnitude larger than the forecasted response of corporate income. We also do not find, as we expected, a stronger effect of a rise in the corporate tax rate on the personal incomes of richer relative to less rich individuals. However, the effects of taxes other than from income shifting, and omitted effects of nontax factors on relative labor incomes, could well explain these anomalous findings.

CONCLUSIONS

Much of the past work in public finance has suggested that higher personal tax rates reduce reported labor income, and that higher corporate tax rates reduce reported corporate income. This chapter explores the hypothesis that these explanations are incomplete because they ignore income shifting between the corporate and personal tax bases, whereby individuals seek to have their earnings taxed at whichever rate is more attractive. Under this hypothesis, for example, an increase in the corporate tax rate raises reported personal income at the same time that it lowers reported corporate income. Similarly, an increase in personal tax rates should result in an increase in reported corporate income as well as a drop in reported personal income. If income shifting is in fact a major factor in previously reported effects of tax changes, then the efficiency consequences of observed behavioral responses can be dramatically different.

It has long been recognized that corporations can vary their use of debt finance in order to take advantage of differences between corporate and personal tax rates. Recent evidence suggests that firms are in fact responding to these incentives. In addition, firms can change from corporate to noncorporate tax status when the corporate tax rate rises relative to personal rates. A substantial amount of such income shifting through changes in organizational form occurred, for example, following the Tax Reform Act of 1986.

In this chapter we present evidence that a substantial amount of income shifting can occur in other ways, such as where compensation to labor is reported and therefore taxed. We find that an increase in corporate tax rates relative to personal tax rates results in an increase in reported personal income and a drop in reported corporate income, even after controlling for the use of debt finance and for the amount of corporate assets. Our results imply, for example, that a one-point increase in the tax differential raises reported personal labor income by 3.2 percent and results in a fall in the reported corporate rate of return of 0.147 percent. Both effects are in the expected direction and highly significant statistically.

The potential importance of income shifting that our evidence suggests requires a reinterpretation of both the efficiency and the distributional consequences of changes in the tax structure. We caution, though, that this evidence suggesting the presence of income shifting is only indirect. The only way to capture definitively the presence of income shifting is to examine changes within a firm following a tax change and to match this with data about employees' income receipts. Unfortunately, for confidentiality reasons such data are not readily available.

DATA APPENDIX

Corporate Rate of Return (R_{it})   Taxable income plus interest payments, divided by total assets. For all but 1993 the three variables are taken from the *SOI Corporation Income* publications; for 1993 they are taken from the *Source Book: Statistics of Income*. For 1966 and 1967 taxable income is unavailable; we impute values by first calculating the average ratio of taxable income to net income less the deficit for 1965 and 1968, and then multiplying this figure by the known 1966 and 1967 value of net income less deficit.

Corporate Statutory Tax Rates (τ^{max} and τ^{min})   Taken from either Pechman (1987) or *SOI Corporation Income* publications. The value of τ^{min} is the first positive rate applied, and the τ^{max} is the rate applied to the top, open-ended bracket. In years when, owing to phaseouts, a higher marginal rate applied to an intermediate bracket of income, we do not use this higher marginal rate.

In the corporate rate-of-return regressions, we make use of asset size (and year) for specific marginal corporate tax rates, τ^m. We calculate this value by first determining the average taxable income per firm in each asset class and applying the appropriate marginal rate at that level of income. To get a value for a cumulative class spanning several asset classes, we take the asset-weighted average.

In the regression analyses we utilize instruments for that potentially endogenous value. To get average taxable income for each asset class, we first find the average level of firm assets and then multiply that value by the overall average rate of return for all firms; that yields an estimate of average taxable income within each asset class. The subsequent steps are identical to those described earlier.

Tax Incentive Indicators $(T_a, T_b, wgt_a, \tau \times wgt_a, \theta \times wgt_a)$

$$T_a = \left[\tau^m - \frac{\displaystyle\sum_{\theta > \tau^m} \theta_i L_i}{\displaystyle\sum_{\theta > \tau^m} L_i} \right]\left[\frac{\displaystyle\sum_{\theta > \tau^m} L_i}{\displaystyle\sum_{all} L_i} \right]$$

$$T_b = \left[\tau^m - \frac{\displaystyle\sum_{\theta < \tau^m} \theta_i L_i}{\displaystyle\sum_{\theta < \tau^m} L_i} \right]\left[\frac{\displaystyle\sum_{\theta < \tau^m} L_i}{\displaystyle\sum_{all} L_i} \right]$$

$$wgt_a = \frac{\displaystyle\sum_{\theta > \tau^m} L_i}{\displaystyle\sum_{all} L_i}$$

$$\tau \times wgt_a = \tau^m - \frac{\displaystyle\sum_{\theta > \tau^m} \theta_i L_i}{\displaystyle\sum_{all} L_i(\ )}$$

$$\theta \times wgt_a = \left[\frac{\displaystyle\sum_{\theta > \tau^m} \theta_i L_i}{\displaystyle\sum_{\theta > \tau^m} L_i} \right]\left[\frac{\displaystyle\sum_{\theta > \tau^m} L_i}{\displaystyle\sum_{all} L_i} \right]$$

where θ_i is the marginal personal tax rate of individual i, as defined later, and L_i is individual i's labor compensation, also defined later. We calculate θ_{it} using information in the tax return files on taxable income and marital status.

Marginal Personal Tax Rates on Labor Income (θ_i)   In years when it is available, the marginal personal rate is taken from the appropriate field in the public-use tax return data file released by the Statistics of Income Division of the IRS, known as the Individual Tax Model File (ITMF). In years when this field is not available (1960, 1962, 1964, 1966, 1967 through 1970, 1972, and 1978), we calculate θ_i using information in the tax return files on taxable income and marital status.

For the period 1971 to 1980 the marginal tax rates were adjusted to take account of the maximum tax on earned income. For 1971 the tax rate was subject to a maximum of 60 percent. For 1972 through 1980 we transferred the ITMF rates into θ_i by applying the mapping presented in Lindsey (1981, table 1).

For 1981 the marginal tax rate variables from the ITMF data for all but the top rate of 50 percent were multiplied by 0.9875 to take account of the 1.25 percent rate reduction.

Labor Compensation (L_i)   Taken from public-use tax return files. Defined as wages plus royalties plus 0.66 times business income, where business income is the sum of income from schedule C and partnership and S corporation income from schedule E.

We are grateful to David Adelson and especially Young Lee for outstanding research assistance, and to David Bradford for very helpful comments on an earlier draft. The first author would like to acknowledge financial support from NSF Grant SBR-9422589 during the writing of this chapter.

NOTES

1. At the margin, individuals should be indifferent to any change in their behavior. But these changes affect government revenue, generating social gains or losses as a consequence.

2. As described later in the chapter, the firm does not get a deduction for compensation paid in the form of qualified stock options and has to defer any deduction when it uses nonqualified stock options.

3. Tax revenue falls if the resulting taxable personal income faces a lower tax rate than would be faced on reported corporate income.

4. Feenberg and Poterba (1993) and Slemrod (1996) report a jump in the reported personal income of the richest individuals following the 1986 tax change.

5. Taxes create an incentive for lower-paid workers to prefer cash wages and higher-paid workers to prefer stock options. If cash wages are preferable based on nontax considerations alone, then lower-paid workers are at a corner solution with only cash wages, so their behavior is unresponsive to marginal tax changes. The behavior of higher-paid workers, in contrast, can be very sensitive to relative tax rates.

6. The analysis of transfer pricing is one clear exception. Here, though, the form of income shifting is between a multinational corporation's units in different countries rather than between the personal and corporate tax bases.

7. See, for example, Gordon and Malkiel (1981) for a description of such a theoretical model of this phenomenon.

8. See, for example, Myers and Majluf (1984).

9. For an earlier examination of these issues, see Ebrill and Hartman (1983).

10. Unless otherwise noted, references to corporations have to do with subchapter C corporations, not pass-through entities such as subchapter S corporations.

11. In the case of pension contributions, the firm can deduct the expenditures immediately, but the employee owes tax on the income only when it is received during retirement. Pension income

avoids any tax on the return to savings but faces a lower tax on the earnings only to the extent that the individual's tax rate is lower during retirement than while employed.

12. Qualification entails meeting several timing and definitional requirements.

13. Under U.S. law, if the shares are held until death, as the evidence in Bhatia (1970) suggests is the norm, then the capital gains are never taxed.

14. Note, though, that new firms normally start out in noncorporate form and then incorporate only when the firm is well established. One reason is that new firms typically generate tax losses during their first few years, given the substantial setup costs they face and the time lags in developing a market niche, and owners of a noncorporate firm can deduct any such business losses against other income. In contrast, owners of a corporation can only carry these losses forward in time and deduct them against future profits. Therefore, when individuals face incentives to set up new corporations, one might also observe higher noncorporate business formations as well.

15. Slemrod (1996) examines this issue.

16. For example, pension plans, which now own a substantial fraction of wealth, are broadly dispersed in the population.

17. This should be true mainly for the most skilled workers in small firms, however, yet Brown and Medoff (1989) suggest that workers in all occupations in small firms earn less than those in the same occupations in large firms.

18. Of course, tax evasion may also be more important for the self-employed, another possible explanation for their lower reported pre-tax earnings.

19. Inflation creates many offsetting biases in the measurement of real corporate incomes, but these studies found that the gain to the firm from being able to deduct nominal rather than real interest payments more than offset the losses from the effects of inflation on depreciation and inventory deductions. As noted by Auerbach and Hines (1988), in practice depreciation schedules have been adjusted to largely offset the effects of inflation.

20. In a partnership, paying wages has no effect on the income tax liabilities of the partners.

21. For simplicity, we ignore here the effects of changes in market prices that may occur in equilibrium. For any increase in price, buyers are worse off and sellers are better off. These effects exactly offset each other in any excess burden calculation. We also ignore initially any externalities, assuming that marginal changes in the behavior of one individual have no effect on the utilities of other individuals.

22. The calculation should also consider the present value of revenue and thus also take account of the retiming of tax payments, for example, deferral of taxes due to greater investment in IRAs.

23. For a formal analysis, see Gordon and MacKie-Mason (1995).

24. See, for example, Arnott and Stiglitz (1986) for a formal demonstration.

25. Corporate use of debt finance can also be limited by asymmetric information problems, as emphasized by Myers and Majluf (1984). Here again, tax incentives that encourage the use of debt finance can at the margin generate efficiency gains.

26. It also ignores personal taxes due on dividends and capital gains income received on income shifted into the firm.

27. This provision was phased in beginning in tax year 1971 and was fully effective in 1972.

28. This was pointed out by Sunley (1974) and Lindsey (1981); see their papers for further discussion, including a definition of the concept of earned taxable income.

29. Since, as discussed, the effective maximum tax rate on earned income following the 1969 act remained above 50 percent, the 1981 tax changes reduced the top effective rate on labor as well as on capital income.

30. See MacKie-Mason and Gordon (1997) for further discussion of the degree to which a firm must incorporate to take advantage of these provisions, and the degree to which they in fact are an advantage to the firm.

31. Data sources and definitions for this table and all subsequent analysis are detailed in a data appendix. Although the theory of income shifting applies to subchapter C corporations, the data disaggregated by asset size over time is available only for *all* corporations, thus adding in subchapter S corporations, which are pass-through entities. This muddies the interpretation of the results, although it is likely to be an important factor only in the data subsequent to 1986.

32. Bracket creep, which put more individuals into top tax brackets, may have more than offset this cap on the top tax rate.

33. In particular, we normalize GDP_t so that it equals 1 in 1992.

34. As an alternative, we compared the observed rate of return to the value of A^t_i/CPI. The fit was not quite as good.

35. This regression, with no tax terms, is not reported in table 8.6.

36. Of course, the marginal corporate tax rate at the average income is not identical to the average marginal tax rate. Since the errors from this approximation are probably of the second order, we ignored it.

37. The weights equal the total labor income of individuals subject to each marginal tax rate. Using as weights the number of people with rates above (below) the corporate tax rate led to very similar results.

38. As an example, consider a year in which the corporate tax was 35 percent for firms of all sizes, and where 90 percent of labor income was received by people with a personal tax rate of 15 percent, and 10 percent was received by people with a 50 percent personal tax rate. In this case, $T_a = -.015$ and $T_b = .18$.

39. Given the presence of time dummies, we cannot identify the effects of the remaining fraction of the population.

40. In each case, the return with taxes is simply the forecasted value for the rate of return based on the coefficient estimates reported in column 2 of table 8.6 and actual tax distortions. The return without taxes is the forecast if T_a and T_b are both set to zero.

41. We implicitly assume here that the fraction of *employees* in each size category equals the fraction of assets in that size category.

42. Slemrod (1992) shows that Feenberg and Poterba's use of a concurrent definition of AGI overstates the increase in inequality around 1986. Using a consistent definition does not change the impression that the measured concentration of AGI increased sharply between 1981 and 1990; the magnitude of the increase, however, is smaller than what one would estimate using concurrent income definitions.

43. If we observed business assets, we might be able to do better. Unfortunately, this information is not collected as part of the tax return data.

44. These fractiles were: individuals between the 50th and 55th percentiles, in the intervals (55,60), (60,65), (65,70), (70,75), (75,80), (80,85), (85,90), (90,91), (91,92), (92,93), (93,94), (94,95), (95,96), (96,97), (97,98), (98,99), (99.0,99.2), (99.2,99.4), (99.4,99.6), (99.6,99.8), (99.8,99.9), (99.9,100).

45. We took into account that the number of observations in each fractile differs by weighting each observation by $\sqrt{s_i}$, where s_i is the sample size in the i'th fractile.

46. We continue to use each individual's actual marital status and actual reported nonlabor income in the calculations.

47. All subsequent reported results continue to make use of this instrumental-variables technique.

48. There could still be indirect effects of the corporate tax through changes in the capital stock. These general equilibrium effects affect our estimates only to the degree to which they affect *relative* wages, owing to the inclusion of time dummies.

49. Taxpayers may on occasion anticipate a future tax change and more frequently respond with a lag to past tax changes. Given the ease with which financial transactions can be adjusted, however, the largest changes should occur around the date of the tax change.

50. We also conducted tests with a sample period 1966 to 1992 with a one-period lead or lag, and with a sample period 1968 to 1990 with up to three-period leads or lags. In the first case the maximum coefficient was again at a one-period lag. In the latter case the contemporaneous tax variable had the maximum coefficient.

REFERENCES

Amerkhail, Valerie L., Gillian M. Spooner, and Emil L. Sunley. 1988. "The Fall and Rise of the U.S. Corporate Tax Burden." *National Tax Journal* 41: 273–84.

Arnott, Richard, and Joseph Stiglitz. 1986. "Moral Hazard and Optimal Commodity Taxation." *Journal of Public Economics* 29: 1–24.

Auerbach, Alan. 1985. "Real Determinants of Corporate Leverage." In *Corporate Capital Structures in the United States,* edited by Benjamin Friedman. Chicago: University of Chicago Press.

Auerbach, Alan, and James R. Hines Jr. 1988. "Investment Tax Increases and Frequent Tax Reforms." *American Economic Review* 78: 211–16.

Auerbach, Alan, and James Poterba. 1987. "Why Have Corporate Tax Revenues Declined?" In *Tax Policy and the Economy,* edited by Lawrence Summers, vol. 1. Cambridge, Mass.: MIT Press.

Auten, Gerald, and Robert Carroll. 1999. "The Effect of Income Taxes on Household Income." *Review of Economics and Statistics* 81(4): 681–93.

Bhatia, Kul. 1970. "Accrued Capital Gains, Personal Income, and Savings in the United States, 1948–1964." *Review of Income and Wealth*: 363–78.

Brown, Charles, and James Medoff. 1989. "The Employer Size-Wage Effect." *Journal of Political Economy* 97: 1027–59.

Christian, Charles. 1994. "Voluntary Compliance with the Individual Income Tax: Results from the 1988 TCMP Study." *IRS Research Bulletin* (1993–94), publication 1500 (revised September 1994). Washington, D.C.: Internal Revenue Service.

Cutler, David, and Lawrence Katz. 1992. "Rising Inequality?: Changes in the Distribution of Income and Consumption in the 1980s." *American Economic Review* 82: 546–51.

Ebrill, Liam, and David Hartman. 1983. "The Corporate Income Tax, Entrepreneurship, and the Noncorporate Sector." *Public Finance Quarterly* 11: 419–36.

Feenberg, Daniel, and James Poterba. 1993. "Income Inequality and the Incomes of Very-High-Income Taxpayers." In *Tax Policy and the Economy,* edited by James Poterba, vol. 7. Cambridge, Mass.: MIT Press.

Feldstein, Martin. 1995. "The Effect of Marginal Tax Rates on Taxable Income: A Panel Study of the 1986 Tax Reform Act." *Journal of Political Economy* 103: 551–72.

Feldstein, Martin, and Daniel Feenberg. 1996. "The Effect of Increased Tax Rates on Taxable Income and Economic Efficiency: A Preliminary Analysis of the 1993 Tax Rate Increases." In *Tax Policy and the Economy,* edited by James Poterba, vol. 10. Cambridge, Mass.: MIT Press.

Feldstein, Martin, and Lawrence Summers. 1977. "Is the Rate of Profit Falling?" *Brookings Papers on Economic Activity* 1: 211–27.

Fortune. 1952 (January). "The New Rich." Pp. 60–65.

Goolsbee, Austan. 1998. "Taxes, Organizational Form, and the Deadweight Loss of the Corporate Income Tax." *Journal of Public Economics* 69: 143–52.

Gordon, Roger. 1982. "Interest Rates, Inflation, and Corporate Financial Policy," *Brookings Papers on Economic Activity* 2: 61–88.

Gordon, Roger, and Jeffrey MacKie-Mason. 1990. "Effects of the Tax Reform Act of 1986 on Corporate Financial Policy and Organizational Form." In *Do Taxes Matter? The Impact of the Tax Reform Act of 1986,* edited by Joel Slemrod. Cambridge, Mass.: MIT Press.

———. 1994. "Tax Distortions to the Choice of Organizational Form." *Journal of Public Economics* 55: 297–306.

———. Forthcoming. "Why Is There Corporate Taxation in a Small Open Economy?: The Role of Transfer Pricing and Income Shifting." In *Issues in International Taxation*, edited by Martin S. Feldstein and James R. Hines Jr. Chicago: University of Chicago Press.

Gordon, Roger, and Burton Malkiel. 1981. "Corporation Finance." In *How Taxes Affect Economic Behavior*, edited by Henry Aaron and Joseph Pechman. Washington, D.C.: Brookings Institution.

Gordon, Roger, and Joel Slemrod. 1988. "Do We Collect Any Revenue from Taxing Capital Income?" In *Tax Policy and the Economy*, edited by Lawrence Summers, vol. 2. Cambridge, Mass.: National Bureau of Economic Research.

Gravelle, Jane, and Larry Kotlikoff. 1989. "The Incidence and Efficiency Costs of Corporate Taxation When Corporate and Noncorporate Firms Produce the Same Goods." *Journal of Political Economy* 97: 749–81.

———. 1993. "Corporate Tax Incidence and Inefficiency When Corporate and Noncorporate Goods Are Close Substitutes." *Economic Inquiry* 31: 501–16.

Harberger, Arnold. 1962. "The Incidence of the Corporation Income Tax." *Journal of Political Economy* 70: 215–40.

Kalambokidis, Laura. 1992. "What Is Being Taxed?: A Test for the Existence of Excess Profit in the Corporate Income Tax Base." Ph.D. diss., University of Michigan.

Karoly, Lynn. 1993. "The Trend in Inequality Among Families, Individuals, and Workers in the United States: A Twenty-five-Year Perspective." In *Uneven Tides: Rising Inequality in America*, edited by Sheldon Danziger and Peter Gottschalk. New York: Russell Sage Foundation.

Lindsey, Lawrence. 1981. "Is the Maximum Tax on Earned Income Effective?" *National Tax Journal* 34: 349–55.

———. 1987. "Individual Taxpayer Response to Tax Cuts, 1982–1984, with Implications for Revenue Maximizing Tax Rate." *Journal of Public Economics* 33: 173–200.

MacKie-Mason, Jeffrey. 1990. "Do Taxes Affect Corporate Financing Decisions?" *Journal of Finance* 45: 1471–93.

MacKie-Mason, Jeffrey, and Roger Gordon. 1997. "How Much Do Taxes Discourage Incorporation?" *Journal of Finance* 52: 477–505.

Miller, Merton, and Franco Modigliani. 1961. "Dividend Policy, Growth, and the Valuation of Shares." *Journal of Business* 34: 411–33.

Myers, Stewart. 1984. "The Capital Structure Puzzle." *Journal of Finance* 39: 575–92.

Myers, Stewart, and Nicholas Majluf. 1984. "Corporate Financing and Investment Decisions When Firms Have Information That Investors Do Not Have." *Journal of Financial Economics* 13: 187–221.

Nunns, James R. 1995. "Distributional Analysis at the Office of Tax Analysis." In *Distributional Analysis of Tax Policy*, edited by David D. Bradford. Washington, D.C.: AEI Press.

Pechman, Joseph A. 1987. *Federal Tax Policy*. 5th ed. Washington, D.C.: Brookings Institution.

Shoven, John. 1991. "Using the Corporate Cash Flow Tax to Integrate Corporate and Personal Taxes." *Proceedings of the Eighty-third Annual Conference of the National Tax Association* 83: 19–26.

Slemrod, Joel. 1992. "Do Taxes Matter?: Lessons from the 1980s." *American Economic Review* 82: 250–56.

———. 1994. "On the High-Income Latter Curve." In *Tax Progressivity and Income Inequality*, edited by Joel Slemrod. Cambridge: Cambridge Unversity Press.

———. 1996. "High-Income Families and the Tax Changes of the 1980s: The Anatomy of Behavioral Response." In *Empirical Foundations of Household Taxation*, edited by Martin Feldstein and James Poterba. Chicago: University of Chicago Press/National Bureau of Economic Research.

Sommerfeld, Ray M. 1981. *Federal Taxes and Management Decisions*. 3d ed. Homewood, Ill.: Richard D. Irwin.

Sommerfeld, Ray M., and Sally M. Jones. 1991. *Federal Taxes and Management Decisions*. 1991–1992 ed. Homewood, Ill.: Richard D. Irwin.

Sunley, Emil. 1974. "The Maximum Tax on Earned Income." *National Tax Journal* 27: 543–52.

Wilkie, Patrick J., James C. Young, and Sarah E. Nutter. 1996. "Corporate Business Activity Before and After the Tax Reform Act of 1986." *Statistics of Income Bulletin* 16: 32–45.

Commentary on Chapter 8

David F. Bradford

Roger Gordon and Joel Slemrod's chapter explores the determinants of the split observed in the data between corporations and individual income recipients. As the exposition makes clear, the subject is much more complex than some might have thought. My comments are addressed to three aspects of the research: the adequacy of the conceptual framework, the nature of income shifting between corporations and individuals, and the empirical models.

CONCEPTUAL FRAMEWORK

Although I am sure the authors understand the fallacy, I think there lurks in the background of their discussion of income shifting what I might call a "hydraulic" view of income. Under this view, there is in any given year a definite quantum of income in the aggregate that is directed through various conduits to income recipients. Income recipients include corporations and individuals. By changing the settings on valves, the flow can be directed more toward one or the other recipient. Income shifting refers to such changes in the routing. The thesis of the chapter is that the setting on the valves tends to be manipulated by taxpayers toward recipients with the lower tax rates. (An aside: I found somewhat frustrating the lack of a sign convention. The statement that income shifting "increases" in response to a change in some tax parameter might mean more income reported at the corporate level, or the opposite. Perhaps it would help to introduce jargon such as in-shifting and out-shifting.)

The hydraulic model is, however, a poor representation of reality. Just how it relates to reality depends on the income definition. To illustrate, consider how things would work out in the case of a Schanz-Haig-Simons (hereafter SHS) income definition: a person's income consists of the amount he consumes during the year plus the increase in his net worth at market value between the beginning and end of the year. Although making operational sense of this idea requires a great deal of interpretation (What kind of wealth counts as net worth? Anticipated future payments under an employment contract? Anticipated retirement benefits? Anticipated inheritances?), an economist is not likely to turn to statutory or common law convention for help.

It has to be otherwise if we seek to understand the notion of corporation income, since a corporation is a quintessentially legal construct. In its "definitions" chapter, the federal income tax statute states simply, "The term 'corporation' includes associations, joint-stock companies, and insurance companies." The fifth edition of Bittker and Eustice's magisterial casebook observes, in chapter 2 (1987, 2-1): "Although this 'definition' leaves much to be desired in the way of precision, the issue of whether a business organization constitutes a 'corporation' for federal tax purposes is not often encountered in practice."[1] Already in chapter 1 the authors have eliminated from their field of coverage regulated investment companies (such as mutual funds, which are taxed only on undistributed income), real estate investment trusts (somewhat like mutual funds), real estate mortgage investment conduits (income is taxed at the receiving end of the conduit), small business investment companies, banks and trust companies (subject to special rules), insurance companies (subject to special rules), cooperatives (patronage dividends are deducted from income and taxed to the recipient), and tax-exempt corporations (such as universities and churches). It becomes clear upon further reading in chapter 2 that even if the problem is not often encountered in practice, distinguishing corporations from other forms of organization for purposes of taxation is far from straightforward.

An important distinction for the present purposes is between subchapter C corporations, which are subject to the classic double taxation familiar to tax analysis, and other associations, including subchapter S corporations, the economic accounts of which are effectively integrated with those of their owners for tax purposes. Contrary to the impression one might take from Gordon and Slemrod's chapter, even though they recognize the distinction between C and S corporations, the financial characteristics of a corporation, including especially limited liability, are available without the tax advantages or disadvantages of the separate corporation income tax through the S corporation or limited liability company legal form. Such an entity is taxed like a partnership of its stockholders, with all tax accounting attributes flowing through to the shareholder level. For a business organized as an S corporation, shifting cannot be much of an issue, since the accounts are integrated.[2] The shifting that is the focus of this chapter is between C corporations and individuals.

Without further elaboration, let us, therefore assume a C corporation. A corporation can own things and have creditors. I suppose the analogue of SHS individual income is the sum of the increase of a corporation's net worth at market value and amounts distributed to its shareholders during the year. (I ignore niceties such as intrayear timing and the treatment of claimants like holders of preferred stock.)

The hydraulic model fails in this case because the income of corporations is *added to* that of individuals in a given year. Contrary to what one might think, the amount in a given time period is independent of the distributions by the corporations to owners. A dollar distributed has to go somewhere on the stockholder's balance sheet or into the shareholder's consumption, but it comes out of the corporation's balance sheet. There is thus no effect on the income of either the corporation or its owners.

The SHS income concept is not actually used in the tax law, so it would not be productive to pursue the inquiry about income shifting in a SHS world very far. One property of the SHS story does, however, carry over pretty generally: to reduce "double counting," get assets out of the relevant corporate form (which, in the present context, would be subchapter C form).

The actual income concept (I will call it "tax income," not to be confused with "taxable income") is defined in terms of realization accounting based on past and present transactions rather than market values. As far as the split between corporations and individuals is concerned, like the SHS concept, tax income does not have the hydraulic property. Generalization is difficult, however, because so much depends on the behavioral choices that result in realization.

To illustrate, suppose a corporation generates an extra dollar of tax income (sells a product for more than the cost of goods sold, for example). If the corporation makes no distribution to shareholders, this increment to corporate profit may result in no extra income to shareholders. On the other hand, if the increment to corporate profit gives rise to an equal increase in market value, and if the shareholders sell their shares to others during the year, then the "same income" shows up twice in the aggregate. Similarly, if the corporation distributes the extra dollar to the shareholders, there is double counting of the income unless, again, the distribution reduces the value of the stock and this in turn is reflected in reduced realized income at the shareholder level. Matters are even worse for the hydraulic model than this example suggests, since there is no particularly tight connection between tax income and market value changes and since the determinants of realization behavior are so complex.[3]

VARIETIES OF INCOME SHIFTING

Gordon and Slemrod are by and large careful to identify their subject as "reported" income (thereby focusing on the accounting concepts) and to focus on the behavior by companies and their owners and employees that might change reported amounts on various accounts. The notion that reported amounts can be "shifted" smacks, however, of the constant-sum hydraulic view.

As I think the authors accept, when it comes to explaining the amounts reported on the accounts of C corporations versus amounts reported on individual tax accounts, the most important factors must be the choice of financial structure and organizational form. The focus of their empirical work, however, is on the varieties of transactions between C corporations and their owners and employees.

The broad general topic is the question of how people should organize their business activity in view of the tax rules. In the present context, how in particular would we expect variations in the rules to affect the reporting of "income" on individual and C corporation tax returns according to the different relationships between individuals and companies?

I think it is helpful to consider separately the delivery of rewards to suppliers of services (including, especially, "labor") and to owners (who may also be suppliers of services). When we do this, we find an amazing array of incentives that affect whether income shows up on business (C corporation) or individual returns, and when.

How Can Corporate Owners Reward the Non-Owner Supplier of Personal Services?

The joint problem for the employer corporation and employee (I use this term as the generic label for a non-owner provider of services) is to deliver any given after-tax result to the employee at minimum after-tax cost to the employer. The starting point is the payment of ordinary wages and salaries. Any amount paid is simultaneously deductible by the corporation and includible by the employee.

Some forms of compensation are deductible by the employer corporation and never included by the employee. Examples include health benefits and employee amenities such as a comfortable office. These forms of compensation are generally self-limiting in that one can take only so much health care. Compensation paid in this form reduces corporation income with no offsetting increase in employee income. We would expect the extent of fringe benefits to be positively related to the employee's tax rate and independent of the employer's tax rate. (Elaborate "non-discrimination" rules apply to some of these forms of compensation, introducing an interesting dependence of the incentive to use fringe benefits such as health insurance on the whole composition of an employer's workforce.)

Some forms of compensation are deductible to the paying corporation but includible only later by the recipient, with advantageous treatment of the accruing gain in the meantime. This is the treatment of pre-funded or defined-contribution pensions. The employee may be able, to some extent, to engage in arbitrage with other forms of saving or even borrowing to exploit this tax differential. (For example, an employee unambiguously gains by shifting a dollar of pay into retirement saving if he can draw down other forms of saving.) The payoff is a function of the distance into the future at which the employee will draw down the compensation flow, the nominal rates of return, and the employee's income tax rate—the higher the tax rate, the greater the incentive. If the corporation's tax rate is constant, the incentive does not vary with the level of that tax rate. Intertemporal variation of the employer's tax rate might, however, introduce some incentives to move the deductions and receipts around in time.

Compensation in the form of qualified stock options is unusual in that it never gives rise to a deduction by the corporation and is includible by the employee only later and at a favorable capital gains rate. There are no direct tax consequences for the corporation associated with the qualified stock option transaction. For the employee, there is income only after the options have been exercised and the underlying stock has been sold. At that time the employee pays tax at the capital gains rate on the difference between sales price and the strike price on the options (normally the value of the company's stock at the time the options are issued). As far as the tax aspects are concerned, this would seem an attractive form of compensation when the company's tax rate is very low (for example, zero), so that the difference between capital gain rates and the employee's ordinary income rates can compensate for the loss of deduction by the employer.

This treatment may be contrasted with that of a "nonqualified" option. As with a qualified option, there are typically no tax consequences to either issuer or employee at the time of issue. When the employee exercises the option, he is treated as having received ordinary income (like salary) in the amount of the difference between the strike price and the exercise price; the employer takes a deduction in the same amount and at the same time. A nonqualified option is thus basically like salary as far as the tax treatment is concerned, only with a displacement between the time of performance of service and the payment and receipt of compensation. The attractiveness of deferral in this form would presumably be positively related to the difference between the employee's and the corporation's marginal rate.

A similar treatment applies to nonqualifying pensions (no current inclusion by the recipient; deduction and inclusion when the pension is paid out).

To isolate the role of the marginal tax rates in the tax planning between employer and employee, consider the case in which no variation over time is anticipated in the tax rates of the corporation or employee. The corporation's tax rate is constant over time at τ, and the employee's tax rate is constant at m. Relative to ordinary salary, fringe benefits that do not involve deferral are the more attractive the higher m, regardless of τ. If we looked at the same economy with different values of the tax parameters, we would expect to see less income at the personal level in the one with the higher value of m.

Qualified pensions present a slightly more complicated picture because they affect the timing of income at the personal level. Current personal income includes an element reflecting past corporate deductions. If we were to look across identical economies with different tax parameters, the difference would be mainly due to differences in m. Whether more or less income appears at the corporate or individual level in the economy with the higher m would depend on factors such as the worker's life cycle.

The availability of nonqualified pensions (and, I think, other forms of deferred compensation) brings the corporation tax rate into the equilibrium condition. Higher values of $(\tau - m)$ should induce larger current corporation income (because the deduction is postponed) and smaller current personal income at the time services are rendered. Because of the subsequent reversal when the benefit is paid, again, life-cycle elements would affect the predicted difference between two economies differing only in $(\tau - m)$.

The qualified stock option form of compensation should be chosen more as $(\tau - m + g)$ decreases, where g is the rate of tax applicable to capital gains. Where this form of compensation is used, current corporation income is higher, current personal income lower, and future personal income higher.

It seems to me rather difficult to translate most of these conclusions into clear hypotheses about the time series of corporation and personal income in a single economy with changing tax parameters, except that one might expect the elimination of or sharp reduction in the difference between ordinary and capital gains rates to show up in a substantial reduction in the use of qualified stock options and an increase in nonqualified options. Since the individuals who might be involved in such transactions are likely to be at the very top of the income distribution, one might expect to find an effect in personal incomes in that range. They would show more ordinary income when the capital gains rate is high. A noticeable effect at the company level would be surprising, however, except for small C corporations.

The employee never has an incentive to shift income toward the corporation except to take advantage of a possible lower rate of tax on the intertemporal return. (So I found it hard to understand statements by Gordon and Slemrod such as, "Since small firms faced very low corporate tax rates, most employees gained by shifting income into the corporations, whereas the higher marginal corporate rate faced by larger firms implies that employees on net shifted money out of the firm.") For the non-owner employee, this advantage is organized through deferred compensation arrangements of one sort or another. The problem posed for inference from time series is that the timing of tax rate changes matters. Anticipated changes produce strong incentive effects. Furthermore, even with fixed tax parameters, to any shift of income into the corporation there must ultimately correspond an apparent shift *out* of the corporation, as deferred compensation, including the payout of an appropriate interest factor.

How Should Corporate Owner-Employees Reward Themselves, Given Corporate Business Receipts?

The story is somewhat different when it is the reward to owners of the business that is involved. (The condition "given corporation business receipts" is intended to abstract from the possibility of changing the extent to which assets remain in C corporation hands.) The possibilities are best understood for the case in which there is a single shareholder. The problem for him is to fix up the flow of payments from corporation to owner to maximize something like the discounted present value of the implied after-tax cash flow.

The standard method, like the payment of salary to an employee, is for the corporation to pay dividends, which are not deductible by the corporation and are includible by the owner. This method is dominated in most cases by payments labeled rent, salary, interest, and so on, which are also includible by the owner but deductible by the corporation. For the single-owner case, we would expect such forms of compensation of the owner to be chosen to the extent allowable by the rules designed to prevent just this route. Although it would pay to press the harder against the boundary the higher the corporation rate, the advantage is insensitive to the personal rate.

Any of the devices available to a corporation in relation to its employees, in the sense discussed earlier, are presumably available as well in relation to dividends disguised as salary to the owner.

Although I am trying to sidestep the question of how to make the choice between C corporation form and forms taxed like partnerships, it is worth noting that if the owner's reward can be provided in a form that is deductible to the corporation and not includible by the owner, it may be worthwhile for an individual to structure his affairs in C corporation form. (C corporations might, for example, be eligible to set up better pension plans than could an individual.)

The main new element introduced to the corporation-to-owner transactions, relative to the corporation-to-employee transactions, is the incentive to disguise dividends. Here the corporation tax rate does enter the calculations in a way that it does not in most of the corporation-to-employee transactions. The higher the corporation tax rate, the greater the incentive to structure rewards to the owner in a way that results in deduction by the corporation. The effect of adding shareholders who are insufficiently related to the firm to be compensated in the same fashion must act as a check on disguising dividends, which alters the relative payouts to owner-employees and other shareholders. We would therefore expect to see dividend disguising used not at all by large, publicly held firms, and less even among small firms, the larger they are and the more complex their ownership patterns.

To sum up, most of the effects of the tax system on "shifting" between corporations and non-owner employees are hardly related to the corporation tax rate. The corporation tax rate does seem likely to affect shifting between corporations and owners. All of the effects seem unlikely to have much bearing on the reported income of larger and public corporations. The importance of timing renders even predictions about the relationship between tax rates and personal income rather difficult.

THE EMPIRICAL ANALYSIS
Corporate Rates of Return

The authors study the determinants of the ratio of income before interest deductions to corporate assets. It is not clear just what to expect of this ratio if the greatest impact of tax law changes is to induce changes in the extent of assets "in corporate solution." How, for example, should changes in financial structure play out? What about shifts to S corporations? As I understand it, the authors' expectations about tax effects are based only on corporation-employee, including owner-employee, manipulations. Might not the simultaneous systematic variation in behavior along other dimensions matter?

I found the time series on the ratio of income before interest deductions to corporate assets, shown in table 8.5, interesting in its own right. The authors do not give details of the composition of the sample. Assuming that the sample represents something like the corporate sector of the United States, I was surprised at how low have been the reported rates of return.[4] How, for example, do they relate to the returns "at least as high as 10 percent at least through the mid-1970s" attributed by the authors to Feldstein and Summers (1977)?

I understand that C and S corporations are both included in the sample; I do not know about the other forms of organization mentioned by Boris Bittker and James Eustice (1987). The inability to separate out S corporations may be an important problem, since arguably the most important type of income shifting is between C corporate and other organizational forms.

As noted by the authors, the income measure used in table 8.5 is based on the tax law as it changed though time. In particular, depreciation rules varied substantially over the period studied. Furthermore, both numerator and denominator suffer from failure to index for inflation. Year dummies are used to control for deficiencies in the data as measures of the same economic concept through time.

It is clear from table 8.5 that smaller firms report, on average, a higher ratio of income before interest to assets. This fact shows up in the regressions as well. The authors take this as suggestive of income shifting (presumably owners accumulating within rather than outside of their corporations), although one can think of other reasons (risk premium? moral hazard hurdle for small firms in raising capital? larger element of "labor income" in profits of smaller firms?) that might apply.

Given my earlier remarks about the likely strength of the tax effects, their haphazard impact on the time path of incomes at the corporation and personal levels, and the strong expectation that large firms will show no effect of the phenomenon of income shifting, I was not surprised by the finding that the estimated effect of tax rate differentials is small for large corporations. Rather, I was surprised by the authors' success in finding a measurable effect on small firms.

Income Reported on Individual Tax Returns

In their analysis of corporate "rates of return," the authors use a clever specification to relate outcomes to the size of the business. Similar creativity is applied to the study of individual incomes, whereby the authors take as a null hypothesis the constancy of the relative distribution of "labor compensation." This is interpreted to include wages, salaries, and royalties. A significant problem is how to treat income from proprietorships, partnerships, and S corporations. Given the likely variation in the use of these forms of enterprise in response to tax changes, the ad hoc assumption that two-thirds of such noncorporate business income represents labor compensation has to be a serious weakness in the analysis. The treatment of pensions is not specified.

The basic strategy is to regress the average (real?) labor compensation in fractiles located in the upper half of the distribution on $(\tau_t - \theta_{it})$, where τ_t is the corporate rate and θ_{it} is the marginal personal tax rate in the ith fractile in year t.

If I understand the setup, because year dummies are used, the specification is actually unable to identify the effect of the corporation tax rate. All of the action is in the individual marginal rate. That action is remarkably strong, apparently picking up the same effects that others in the NTR literature have been finding. Taking the results of the corporation rate-of-return analysis at face value suggests that, if income shifting is a major part of the story, it must be mainly through the vehicle of changes in the locus of activity out of C corporations and into other forms. Perhaps a closer examination of the forms of compensation other than wages, salaries, and royalties would offer some clues?

NOTES

1. There is a more recent edition, but for present purposes it is not necessary to be absolutely up to date.

2. There might be shifting between employee-employer combinations, both of whom are individuals, with different marginal tax rates.

3. Some years ago (1990) I estimated that the ratio between the market and book value of the aggregate U.S. nonfinancial corporate sector had ranged between 37 percent and 110 percent over the period from 1945 to 1998.

4. It is also striking how financial accounting smooths out the stochastic path of returns, measured by the value of companies in the capital market. For an example of the volatility in market-value income figures, see Bradford (1990).

REFERENCES

Bittker, Boris I., and James S. Eustice. 1987. *Federal Income Taxation of Corporations and Shareholders.* New York: Warren, Gorham and Lamont.

Bradford, David F. 1990. "What Is National Saving?: Alternative Measures in Historical and International Context." In *The U.S. Savings Challenge: Policy Options for Productivity and Growth,* edited by Charles E. Walker, Mark A. Bloomfield, and Margo Thorning. Boulder, Colo.: Westview Press.

Feldstein, Martin, and Lawrence Summers. 1977. "Is the Rate of Profit Falling?" *Brookings Papers on Economic Activity* 1: 211–27.

9

Portfolio Responses to Taxation:
Evidence from the End of the Rainbow

Andrew A. Samwick

In the pursuit of revenue and equity, taxes induce inefficiencies. Resources devoted to tax avoidance (and tax compliance) are clear examples of deadweight loss to the economy. The simple fact that the wealthiest households have the most at stake when the taxman comes and the most flexibility in managing their tax liabilities suggests that their behavior changes the most when taxes change. Since portfolio choices involve small costs in comparison to changes in labor supply and saving, it is reasonable to expect that portfolio choices would be among the most tax-sensitive household decisions. The economic importance of portfolio responses is demonstrated by simulation studies of tax reform, such as Harvey Galper, Robert Lucke, and Eric Toder (1988), that find potentially large efficiency costs of portfolio distortions.

The effect of taxes on the portfolio decisions of the wealthy has received less attention than other decisions, such as labor supply, in large part because there are few data sets in which wealth can be accurately measured.[1] For the United States the most comprehensive source of data is the Survey of Consumer Finances (SCF) conducted by the Federal Reserve Board every three years since 1983. With the release of the 1995 SCF, the sample period includes both the Tax Reform Act of 1986 (TRA86) and the Omnibus Budget Reconciliation Act of 1993 (OBRA93). The former was an attempt to lower the marginal tax rate by broadening the tax base; the latter increased marginal tax rates substantially at the upper end of the income distribution. The study that most closely resembles the present one was carried out by John Karl Scholz (1994), who used the SCFs from 1983 and 1989 to analyze the effect of taxes on portfolio composition. The additional years of data allow for a more comprehensive analysis that can distinguish the effects of marginal tax rate changes—which showed a reversal over the longer time period—from secular trends that may have affected portfolio choices.

The methodological contribution of this chapter is to calculate marginal tax rates for SCF households and estimate the extent to which changes in portfolio allocations over time can be attributed to changes in marginal tax rates. The primary unit of analysis is percentile ranges of the net worth distribution, such as the top 1 percent. The main conclusion is that marginal tax rates provide a limited explanation for the actual portfolio changes of households at all points in the net worth distribution. For example, predicted changes in the portfolio allocations of the wealthiest households based solely on changes in their tax rates appear to explain about one-tenth of the actual changes *over time*. This conclusion holds true despite the significant role that marginal tax rates on both ordinary and capital gains income play in the *cross-sectional* distribution of portfolio holdings.

This surprising result is reinforced by a less parametric test for the effect of taxes on portfolio allocations of financial assets. This test is based on the time series changes in portfolio allocations at different points in the distribution of marginal tax rates. Between 1983 and 1989 the distribution of tax rates across households converged, with the highest and lowest tax rates moving in toward the middle of the distribution. Between 1992 and 1995 the opposite happened, with the highest tax rates getting substantially higher. However, financial portfolios grew more distinct across households during the early period, and more similar across households during the later period. Portfolio allocations diverged when tax differentials converged, and converged when tax differentials diverged. This pattern again suggests that marginal tax rates are not the primary explanation for the observed time series changes in portfolio allocations.

The next section presents the basic classification scheme for the components of household portfolios as measured in the Survey of Consumer Finances and discusses the tax treatment of different assets. That is followed by a discussion of the aspects of the tax changes over the sample period that would be expected to affect portfolio allocations. The algorithm for computing tax liabilities is also presented in this section. The next section documents the changes in portfolio allocations for net worth categories over time. That discussion is followed by a presentation of an econometric framework similar to that in James M. Poterba and Andrew A. Samwick (1999) to determine the extent to which tax changes were responsible for these portfolio changes. The next section analyzes the response of portfolios to marginal tax rate changes at different points in the distribution of marginal tax rates.

SURVEY OF CONSUMER FINANCES

The Survey of Consumer Finances (SCF) is a series of triennial surveys of the U.S. population designed to collect comprehensive data on household wealth holdings. The original survey in 1983 was designed to be the first of a panel, but the reinterview survey in 1986 yielded only two-thirds of the original sample, and only one-third in 1989. The 1989 sample was supplemented by new households, and all waves since 1989 have been conducted as unrelated cross-sections using the same survey questionnaire and sample design. Although the study of tax policy has not been the main application of the SCF, the timing of the survey is ideal for the task. The three important tax reforms in 1986, 1990, and 1993 all lie squarely in the intervals spanned by the SCF of 1983 to 1989, 1989 to 1992, and 1992 to 1995.[2]

Another important aspect of the SCF is the oversampling of high-income households. Each SCF sample comprises an area-probability sample of the U.S. population and a sample of households drawn from an Internal Revenue Service file of high-income returns. Oversampling based on income helps to equalize the probability of each dollar of wealth in the economy—rather than each household in the population—appearing in the sample.[3] The distinction is important when analyzing the distribution of assets and liabilities that are highly concentrated. A limitation of the SCF that is introduced or exacerbated by the presence of the high-income sample is that the household's state of residence is not available on the public release of the survey (except for the area-probability sample in 1983). This precludes the calculation of the household's state income tax rates as part of a more complete measure of tax incentives.

Table 9.1 presents a breakdown of the sample by net worth category (to be defined later in the chapter) for each of the four survey years. Each cell of the table contains the number of sample observations and their proportion of the total observations in each category. The 1989 survey is somewhat anomalous in having only 3,143 observations, about 1,000 fewer than the other waves. The oversampling of high-income households can be seen clearly by comparing the proportions of the sample in the highest wealth categories to the range of percentiles in those categories. For example, the households in the top 1 percent of the wealth distribution in 1983 make up 7.07 percent of the sample. This proportion increases substantially to 14.60 in 1989 and then exceeds 16 percent in the 1992 and 1995 surveys. The ninety-fifth to ninety-ninth percentiles are also disproportionately represented in each year (though by a lower factor than the top percentile), as is the remainder of the top decile in all but the 1983 survey. Although oversampling is a feature of all the surveys, there is a possibility that the change in the sampling design after the 1983 survey may contribute to changes in the measured distribution of wealth holding between 1983 and the later surveys (see Kennickell and Woodburn 1997).

A growing literature has compared the SCF to other sources of data on household wealth. Richard T. Curtin, F. Thomas Juster, and James N. Morgan (1989) compare the 1983 SCF to the wealth data from the Panel Study of Income Dynamics and the Survey of Income and Program Participation (SIPP) from 1984. They find that, of the three, only the SCF adequately represents the upper tail of the wealth distribution. Other papers, most notably by Edward N. Wolff (1987, 1994, this volume), have compared the SCF to the household sector of the Flow of Funds

Table 9.1   Frequency Counts and Sample Shares by Year

Net Worth Percentiles	1983	1989	1992	1995
99 to 100	290	459	662	698
	7.07	14.60	16.95	16.24
95 to 99	273	348	428	472
	6.65	11.07	10.96	10.98
90 to 95	203	211	242	304
	4.95	6.71	6.20	7.07
80 to 90	364	315	355	392
	8.87	10.02	9.09	9.12
60 to 80	747	482	538	596
	18.21	15.34	13.77	13.86
00 to 60	2,226	1,328	1,681	1,837
	54.25	42.25	43.04	42.73
Total	4,103	3,143	3,906	4,299
	100	100	100	100

Source: Author's tabulations from the Surveys of Consumer Finances, 1983 to 1995.
Notes: The top number is the number of observations in the specified percentiles of the net worth distribution. The bottom number is the proportion of the observations in the specified percentiles of the net worth distribution.

accounts and suggested modifications to the asset holdings in the SCF to reconcile the disparities.[4]

Table 9.2 provides an indication of the magnitude of the changes involved with reweighting. The left panel tabulates the average, total, and share of net worth by percentiles of the net worth distribution for each survey year using the survey weights. All dollar figures are reported in constant 1992 dollars. Average wealth rose from $174,000 to $192,000 between 1983 and 1989, lost about half of that gain by 1992, and rebounded to the same level by 1995. Although not uniform across wealth categories, the pattern of changes for each range of percentiles is not far from the average. The third column depicts the concentration of wealth by category. The share of wealth held by the wealthiest 1 percent is often used to characterize the inequality of wealth. This fraction increased from 30.86 in 1983 to 33.50 in 1989, fell to 29.52 in 1992, and then rose substantially to 35.13 in 1995. The time pattern of changes in the remainder of the top decile moved opposite to those for the top percentile.

The right panel of the table presents the analogous calculations using a set of reweightings based on Wolff (1987, 1994, this volume).[5] The reweightings increase the measures of wealth in all cases and do so disproportionately at the highest percentiles of the distribution, largely because the reweightings increase the values of assets that are typically held primarily by wealthy households. The reweightings do not substantially alter the comparisons between successive surveys, but the comparison of the wealth distributions in 1983 and 1992 are quite sensitive to them. Since the analysis presented later in the chapter depends primarily on comparison of successive surveys (1983 to 1989, 1992 to 1995, and, to a lesser extent, 1989 to 1992), the discrepancies between the SCF and the Flow of Funds may not be too important. All further tabulations use the unadjusted sample weights.[6] The remainder of this section gives a detailed description of the components of financial assets and net worth and briefly discusses their tax treatment.

The overall decomposition of net worth into portfolio components is as follows. Net worth is equal to total assets less total debt. There are five components to total assets: financial, owner-occupied housing, other property, miscellaneous, and business equity. Total debt has four analogous components: financial, owner-occupied housing, other property, and miscellaneous. Financial assets are further disaggregated into interest-bearing accounts, taxable bonds, taxable equity, retirement accounts, tax-exempt bonds, and other financial assets. Assets in retirement accounts are further distinguished as bonds or equity.

COMPONENTS OF FINANCIAL ASSETS

Interest-Bearing Accounts: Checking accounts, saving accounts, certificates of deposit, and money market accounts (excluding tax-exempt accounts). Returns on these assets are taxed each year at the household's marginal tax rate on ordinary income.

Taxable Bonds: Federal government bonds, corporate bonds, and foreign bonds, whether held directly or in mutual fund accounts but not in retirement accounts. Interest payments on these assets are taxed each year at the household's marginal

Table 9.2 Summary Statistics on Net Worth and Tax Rates

Net Worth Percentiles	Unadjusted SCF					Wolff Adjustments[a]		
	Mean (Thousands)	Sum (Billions)	Share (Percentage)	Marginal Tax Rate[b]	Tax Rate Percentile	Mean (Thousands)	Sum (Billions)	Share (Percentage)
1983								
99 to 100	5,343	4,495	30.86	36.51	81.73	6,236	5,251	32.55
95 to 99	992	3,329	22.86	26.86	67.62	1,063	3,570	22.13
90 to 95	420	1,765	12.12	24.46	64.64	456	1,916	11.87
80 to 90	227	1,905	13.08	21.89	60.18	252	2,111	13.08
60 to 80	117	1,957	13.44	19.86	56.51	126	2,107	13.06
00 to 60	22	1,113	7.64	14.29	43.23	23	1,178	7.30
All	174	14,563		17.40		192	16,133	
1989								
99 to 100	6,413	6,002	33.50	23.37	74.07	7,739	7,207	35.27
95 to 99	1,017	3,787	21.13	21.86	70.52	1,187	4,427	21.67
90 to 95	449	2,104	11.74	19.76	65.11	514	2,392	11.71
80 to 90	256	2,386	13.32	17.86	59.38	282	2,633	12.89
60 to 80	132	2,450	13.68	15.42	53.56	138	2,567	12.56
00 to 60	21	1,187	6.62	11.88	44.25	22	1,207	5.91
All	192	17,916		14.10		219	20,433	
1992								
99 to 100	5,301	5,132	29.52	27.06	83.08	7,199	6,910	34.64
95 to 99	1,061	4,068	23.40	24.74	77.54	1,190	4,570	22.91
90 to 95	454	2,186	12.57	21.46	68.00	484	2,306	11.56
80 to 90	248	2,379	13.68	19.07	61.99	257	2,458	12.32
60 to 80	123	2,360	13.58	16.39	54.87	126	2,417	12.12
00 to 60	22	1,262	7.26	11.97	42.51	22	1,289	6.46
All	181	17,387		14.70		209	19,952	

(Table continues on p. 294.)

Table 9.2 *Continued*

Net Worth Percentiles	Unadjusted SCF					Wolff Adjustments[a]		
	Mean (Thousands)	Sum (Billions)	Share (Percentage)	Marginal Tax Rate[b]	Tax Rate Percentile	Mean (Thousands)	Sum (Billions)	Share (Percentage)
1995								
99 to 100	6,688	6,678	35.13	32.11	85.80			
95 to 99	1,020	4,031	21.20	25.88	75.34			
90 to 95	453	2,251	11.84	21.25	65.94			
80 to 90	239	2,364	12.43	18.24	58.86			
60 to 80	120	2,370	12.47	15.88	53.36			
00 to 60	22	1,316	6.92	12.27	43.81			
All	192	19,010		14.78				

Source: Author's calculations.

Notes: All dollar values are in constant 1992 dollars.

a. Wolff adjustments are detailed in Wolff (1987, 1994, this volume).

b. Marginal tax rates are the average of the "first-dollar" marginal tax rates on ordinary income for the households in the specified percentiles of the net worth distribution.

tax rate on ordinary income. Capital gains and losses on these assets are taxable at the household's capital gains tax rate only if the assets are sold before maturity.

Taxable Equity: All holdings of stocks outside of trusts and retirement accounts, including brokerage accounts, mutual funds, investment clubs, and shares in a company where a household member is employed. Unlike interest payments, retained earnings are first taxed at the corporation's marginal tax rate. Dividend payments to households are further taxed each year at the household's marginal tax rate on ordinary income. Taxation of capital gains and losses on these assets is at the household's capital gains tax rate but is deferred until the assets are transferred in a taxable transaction.

Retirement Accounts: All assets held in individual retirement accounts (IRAs), Keogh plans for the self-employed, and defined contribution (DC) pension plans, including 401(k) plans and employee stock ownership plans (ESOPs). Equity holdings may take any of the forms listed under "taxable equity." Bond holdings include all of the forms listed under "taxable bonds" and "tax-exempt bonds," as well as all responses not specifically coded as equity.[7] Interest, dividend, and capital gain taxes are deferred until withdrawn from the account during retirement (preretirement distributions are taxed at a supplemental penalty rate), when such withdrawals face the household's marginal tax rate on ordinary income. Accrued entitlements under defined benefit (DB) pension plans and Social Security are not included in any measure of wealth.

Tax-Exempt Bonds: All state and municipal bonds, whether held directly, in money market accounts, or in mutual funds, but not in retirement accounts. Interest from these assets is tax-exempt. Capital gains or losses resulting from sales prior to maturity face the household's marginal tax rate on capital gains.

Other Financial Assets: The sum of the cash value of whole life insurance policies and trust accounts. These assets generally receive some form of tax-preferred treatment, typically by exempting the annual gains in the value of the assets from taxation while the policy or trust is in effect.

COMPONENTS OF NET WORTH

Financial Assets: The sum of all financial assets discussed under "Financial Assets."

Owner-Occupied Housing Assets: The gross value of the household's primary residence.

Other Property Assets: The gross value of other properties owned by the household, including amounts owed to the household from the past sale of real estate.

Miscellaneous Assets: The residual component of total assets, including the value of all other assets not classified as financial, real estate, or business-related.

Business Equity: The value of the household's share in unincorporated businesses (including farms), whether the household is self-employed and actively manages the business or holds a passive interest.

Financial Debt: The outstanding balances on credit cards and lines of credit not secured by the value of the household's residence.

Owner-Occupied Housing Debt: The outstanding balances on loans secured by the household's residence, including first and second mortgages, home equity loans, and home equity lines of credit.

Other Property Debt: The outstanding balances on loans related to the purchase of real estate other than the household's primary residence.

Miscellaneous Debt: The residual component of total debt, including the outstanding balances on loans taken out for the purchase of consumer durables or investment securities.

Net Worth: The sum of all assets (financial, owner-occupied real estate, other property, miscellaneous, and unincorporated businesses) less the sum of all debts (financial, owner-occupied real estate, other property, and miscellaneous).

There are two main sources of tax advantages with regard to the components of net worth other than financial assets. The first is the deductibility of interest payments on real estate at the household's ordinary income tax rate. Prior to the Tax Reform Act of 1986, interest on non-real-estate loans was also deductible. TRA86 phased out full deductibility, so that by 1989 only 20 percent of such interest payments were deductible and by 1992 payments were not deductible. Interest payments on real estate loans retained their tax deductibility. Sales of real estate and business assets generate capital gains and losses, which are preferentially taxed at the household's capital gains tax rate. The second advantage is the popularity of limited partnerships for tax shelters, which may be classified in the SCF as passively managed businesses or other property. The tax shelter industry largely disappeared after TRA86 owing to narrower differentials between ordinary and capital gains tax rates as well as new passive loss limitations.[8] The undoing of TRA86's rate reductions in subsequent tax legislation may have reintroduced incentives to use these assets to reduce tax burdens.

TAX CHANGES IN THE 1980S AND 1990S

This section discusses the tax changes that have been implemented over the sample period of 1983 to 1995 and the algorithms used to calculate marginal tax rates in the SCF. The main focus of the analysis is on the marginal tax rate (MTR) that each household faces on an additional dollar of ordinary income from investments. The algorithms also permit the calculation of the statutory marginal tax rate on realized capital gains. Although these are not the only relevant aspects of tax policy for portfolio decisions, many of the tax incentives—and especially the differences in these incentives across households—are the direct result of cross-sectional variation in these rates.[9] The estimates are made from the income, balance sheet, and demographic data that are reported by the household.

The algorithm for calculating marginal tax rates in each survey proceeds line by line down the form 1040 and the relevant schedules. Filing status is determined by the household's marital status, with all married households assumed to file a joint return. Personal exemptions are estimated based on marital status and the number of dependents in the house under age eighteen. The SCF reports information on many of the components of total income. Wages and salaries, taxable interest, tax-exempt interest, dividends, alimony received, rents and royalties, business income, and farm income are all straightforward and similarly defined in the SCF and on the tax return.

Other components of income required for the 1040 are not reported in the SCF. The approach followed here is to treat some of these items as zero and others as fully taxable. Refunds of state and local income taxes, other gains, and IRA distributions are not reported in the SCF and are assumed to be zero. All pension and unemployment compensation reported is assumed to be taxable.[10] Social Security benefits are taxed according to the formula appropriate to each year. Reported capital gains are assumed to be taxable as long-term gains, but no adjustments can be made in the calculations for any losses carried forward to or from the current year.

The remaining component of adjusted gross income (AGI) is adjustments to total income. The self-employment tax is applied to all business and farm income. Households are assumed to claim the maximum IRA deductions consistent with their reported balances and individual earnings. Alimony paid is also reported by the SCF. All other adjustments, such as moving expenses, are not reported in the survey and are assumed to be zero. Subtracting the total adjustments from total income gives the household's AGI.

The next step in the computations is to estimate the household's possibility of itemizing deductions on schedule A. The SCF reliably reports information on interest payments and charitable contributions. Deductions for local taxes are based on the reported value of real estate and personal property subject to tax. Itemization is determined by comparing the sum of these deductions to the standard deduction appropriate for the household's age and filing status. The lack of reported information on other possible deductions, such as medical expenses, state and local income taxes, casualty losses, and job expenses, is the biggest handicap in calculating tax rates in the SCF. The household's exemptions and deductions are then subjected to the limits based on income in the later survey years. Subtracting them from AGI yields the household's taxable income. Applying the appropriate tax rate schedule to taxable income gives the household's tax liability. Total taxes include this amount plus self-employment and alternative minimum taxes. Credits such as the earned income credit were not computed.

The household's marginal tax rate on any type of income can be calculated by running this algorithm twice—once with a base amount and then with the base amount plus an increment. The difference in the total taxes divided by the increment gives the marginal tax rate. Following Poterba and Samwick (1999), the base amount is chosen to be the household's taxable income assuming that it had no income from interest, dividends, tax-exempt interest, and capital gains. The increment is set equal to a constant fraction (5 percent) of the household's total financial assets, with a minimum of $100. This "first-dollar" marginal tax rate therefore does not depend on the particular portfolio allocation that the household has chosen, but it does allow for the possibility that if a household invested all of its financial assets in taxable interest-bearing accounts or realized them all as taxable capital gains, it might move into a higher tax bracket. The analysis later in the chapter utilizes marginal tax rates on ordinary income and on capital gain income calculated in this way.

There were three major changes to the relationship between a household's taxable investment income and its tax liability over the sample period. The most comprehensive of these was the Tax Reform Act of 1986. Marginal rates were reduced for most of the income distribution, with the MTR on the highest incomes falling from 50 to 28 percent. Lower down in the income distributions, there was only one other nonzero MTR of 15 percent. TRA86 also introduced a "bubble" MTR of 33 percent over a range of taxable income in order to recapture the benefits of the 15 percent bracket and personal exemptions from high-income taxpayers. Although it retained its progressivity, the tax schedule had far fewer brackets than before.

TRA86 also made substantial changes to the definition of taxable income and eliminated the capital gains exclusion (for an overview, see Hausman and Poterba 1987). In 1989 the statutory rate on capital gains was the same as that on ordinary income. Another change was to include up to 50 percent of Social Security benefits in taxable income for sufficiently high-income recipients. Since the definition of income for this provision includes investment income, it changes the tax treatment of returns to financial wealth. Although not the focus of this analysis, the tax-calculating algorithms do take all of these changes into account.

TRA86 also lowered the top marginal tax rate on corporate income from 46 to 34 percent, so that for the first time the top personal rate exceeded the top corporate rate. As analyzed in Roger H. Gordon and Jeffrey K. MacKie-Mason (1990), this inversion of tax rates affected the financing decisions and organizational form of corporations. More generally, Martin S. Feldstein and Joel Slemrod (1980) show that the position of the marginal tax rate on corporate income in the distribution of personal income tax rates is an important determinant of the portfolio allocations of investors under a progressive tax system. The role of changes in the corporate income tax rate on the analysis of household portfolio allocations will be discussed in more detail later.

The other two tax reforms were the Omnibus Budget Reconciliation Acts (OBRA) of 1990 and 1993.[11] These reforms were more limited in scope than TRA86, affecting primarily the taxpayers with the highest incomes. OBRA90 replaced the marginal tax rate bubble with a new top bracket of 31 percent and revised the phaseout of the personal exemptions. Itemized deductions were also partially phased out for high-income taxpayers. OBRA90 also increased the alternative minimum tax (AMT) rate from 21 to 24 percent. The maximum statutory tax rate on capital gains was capped at 28 percent. OBRA93 added two new tax rate brackets of 36 and 39.6 percent and further increased the rate on the AMT. With an increase in the top corporate rate to only 35 percent, the top personal rate was again higher than the top corporate rate. The act further increased the share of Social Security benefits that could be subjected to tax to 85 from 50 percent. An important feature of the analysis is that OBRA90 and OBRA93 worked in opposition to the base broadening and rate reductions of TRA86. This feature allows differences over time in response to tax reforms to be distinguished from secular trends that may exist in asset allocations.

The effect of the tax reforms is evident in figure 9.1. In this figure, the horizontal axis represents the percentiles of the distribution of the marginal tax rate on ordinary income in each year. The vertical axis represents the actual value of the MTR in percentage points. The four curves trace out the average value of the MTR in each percentile separately for each of the four sample years. The distribution of MTRs in each year is the result of applying the tax-calculating algorithm for that

Figure 9.1   Marginal Tax Rate Distributions, by Year

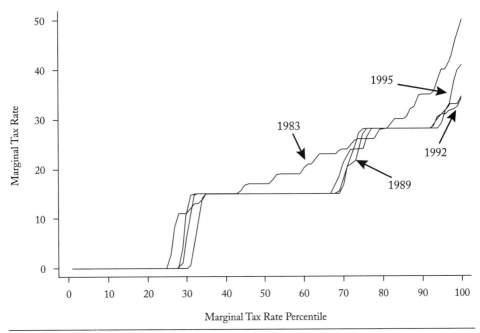

Source: Author's calculations.

year to the corresponding sample of SCF households.[12] In each year roughly 25 percent of the households face a zero MTR. These are households whose current income is low enough that they do not have to pay tax. Beyond this point, the 1983 schedule is substantially different from the other three years, with many short, flat portions denoting tax brackets, on the way up to a top rate of 50 percent. The effect of TRA86 in compressing the tax brackets is shown by the long, flat portions of the 1989 schedule, first at 15 percent and then at 28 percent, rising up to a top rate of 33 percent. Over most of the distributions, the values for 1992 and 1995 are quite close to those for 1989.

Figure 9.2 expands the top quintile of the graph to show the differences between the later three years more clearly. After about the ninetieth percentile, the 1992 and 1995 graphs increase to reflect the 31 percent bracket. The 1995 schedule increases rapidly thereafter, owing to the 36 and 39.6 percent brackets as well as the phase-out of exemptions and deductions. The 1992 schedule drifts upward only to reflect the phaseout of exemptions and deductions. The similarity of the 1992 and 1995 schedules is the result of an indexed tax code, low intervening real wage growth, and the targeting of OBRA93 on taxpayers with the highest taxable incomes.

The fourth column of table 9.2 shows the average value of household MTRs on ordinary income by net worth category and year. The average MTR fell from 17.40 percent in 1983 to 14.10 in 1989 as a result of TRA86. The tax rate reductions ranged from a low of about two and a half percentage points for the bottom 60 percent to 13 percent for the top 1 percent of the net worth distribution. The effect of

Figure 9.2   Top Quintile of Marginal Tax Rate Distributions, by Year

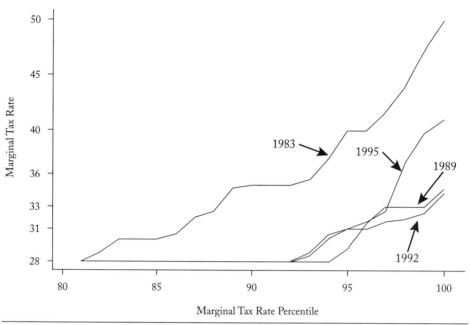

Source: Author's calculations.

OBRA90 was to increase average MTRs by one to three percentage points for all categories above the sixtieth percentile and to 14.70 percent overall. OBRA93 further increased the sample average to 14.78 percent, primarily owing to a large five-point increase for the highest category. For net worth categories below the top decile, the magnitudes of the changes are less than one percentage point in magnitude and mixed in sign.

In an economy in which households face different tax rates, a household's optimal portfolio allocations in equilibrium depends not only on its own tax rate but on where that tax rate falls in the distribution of tax rates. As in Miller (1977), the households with the highest tax rates form the natural "clientele" for the most tax-advantaged assets, and those with the lowest tax rates are the clientele for the least tax-advantaged assets.[13] The fifth column of table 9.2 shows the average percentile in the MTR distribution for households in each net worth category. In 1983 the households in the top 1 percent of the wealth distribution were at the eighty-second percentile of the MTR distribution, on average. After TRA86, the average for the top percentile fell to 74.07. The effect of TRA86 was to reduce the variation in marginal tax rates, with the top and bottom categories moving toward the center and the four middle categories moving toward the extremes between 1983 and 1989.

This effect was largely undone by OBRA90 and OBRA93. Between 1989 and 1992 the average MTR percentile increased for all but the bottom wealth category. By 1992 the average MTR percentile for the top net worth percentile was higher than it had been in 1983. Between 1992 and 1995 the average MTR percentile for the top wealth decile increased again, and the average MTR percentile fell for all lower categories except the bottom 60 percent of the net worth distribution. Given the compression in tax rates due to TRA86, even the smaller changes to MTRs in the later legislation were enough to reintroduce substantial variation in MTRs across net worth categories.

PORTFOLIO ALLOCATIONS BY WEALTH CATEGORIES

This section documents portfolio allocations by net worth categories and shows the magnitudes of changes in these allocations over the period from 1983 to 1995. The basic data on portfolio allocations by net worth category and year are presented in tables 9.3 and 9.4, which correspond to the components of financial assets and net worth, respectively. The next section estimates the share of those changes that can be attributed to the changing cross-sectional pattern of tax rates that occurred over the same period.

Table 9.3 shows the portfolio holdings of each net worth category from table 9.2 in each of the survey years, along with average marginal tax rates on ordinary income and tax rate percentiles (weighted by financial asset holdings). The columns are arranged by tax status, with relatively more heavily taxed assets (interest-bearing accounts) on the left and relatively less heavily taxed assets (tax-exempt bonds) on the right. Because it is not exactly clear where the "other financial assets" belong on this spectrum, they are reported in the last column. The bottom row in each group of numbers (marked "All") gives the aggregate portfolio allocation of the whole population. This row is analogous to the "market" portfolio in the sense that if every household held the same portfolio, then it would have to be equivalent to this allocation. Changes in tax policy may affect this allocation through the financing decisions of firms, banks, and governments as well as the decisions by firms to sponsor defined contribution pension plans. However, the composition of the market portfolio is exogenous to the decision-making process of each individual household. The logical way to analyze household portfolio choices is therefore relative to the benchmark of the aggregate portfolio in each year.

Between 1983 and 1989 the share of equities fell and there was a pronounced shift of allocations toward retirement accounts. Interest-bearing accounts and bonds, both taxable and tax-exempt, made up a greater share of the portfolio compared to other financial assets. In subsequent surveys, allocations moved away from interest-bearing accounts and bonds and into equities. The share in retirement accounts surged again between 1989 and 1992 but leveled off after that.

The other rows in each group of numbers depict the portfolio allocations by net worth percentiles. Comparing the top 1 percent to the benchmark shows that in all years the rich hold less of their assets in interest-bearing accounts and retirement accounts. They hold correspondingly more in taxable equities and tax-exempt bonds. Over the sample period the pattern of increases and decreases in their allocations to interest-bearing accounts, taxable bonds, tax-exempt bonds, and taxable equity reflect the changes in the aggregate portfolio. The magnitudes of these changes are typically larger, however. Their allocations to retirement accounts show less steady growth, and their allocations to other financial assets become steadily smaller over time.

Table 9.3 Portfolio Allocation of Financial Assets, by Net Worth Percentiles and Year

Net Worth Percentiles	Interest-Bearing Accounts	Taxable Bonds	Taxable Equity	Retirement Accounts			Tax-Exempt Bonds	Other Financial Assets	Average Marginal Tax Rate	Marginal Tax Rate Percentile
				All	Bonds	Equity				
1983										
99 to 100	9.04	5.13	45.08	8.36	5.30	3.07	12.50	19.89	42.81	90.77
95 to 99	24.81	9.81	29.04	14.11	8.62	5.49	8.54	13.69	30.23	73.71
90 to 95	39.10	10.53	16.42	19.71	12.07	7.63	5.09	9.14	26.53	68.25
80 to 90	48.67	3.96	13.59	18.97	11.86	7.12	0.84	13.97	22.13	60.75
60 to 80	47.29	3.00	6.30	23.20	13.82	9.38	0.36	19.85	21.96	61.04
00 to 60	45.06	3.45	6.31	19.41	9.49	9.93	1.01	24.77	19.11	54.84
All	27.73	6.27	27.32	14.67	5.80	8.86	7.15	16.87	31.59	74.83
1989										
99 to 100	21.34	10.95	23.87	12.27	6.45	5.64	17.14	14.44	24.59	78.00
95 to 99	27.76	7.70	23.38	20.80	12.99	7.33	9.98	10.37	24.06	76.12
90 to 95	31.54	6.67	12.43	27.18	16.73	9.46	7.62	14.57	21.02	68.78
80 to 90	36.62	5.32	12.11	30.57	17.09	13.05	4.26	11.11	19.49	63.43
60 to 80	43.35	4.84	6.41	26.23	16.39	9.59	3.19	15.97	15.22	53.81
00 to 60	44.10	4.73	5.91	25.86	15.73	9.93	1.92	17.47	16.62	56.37
All	30.59	7.68	17.07	21.44	8.38	12.67	9.68	13.53	21.54	69.75

1992										
99 to 100	17.49	7.56	34.57	13.70	5.38	8.17	16.02	10.66	27.97	86.03
95 to 99	17.97	7.34	21.16	29.67	14.54	14.60	11.30	12.56	26.33	81.51
90 to 95	31.01	5.94	13.19	31.91	18.50	13.41	7.32	10.63	21.41	67.22
80 to 90	31.66	4.39	13.34	34.46	16.88	15.86	3.94	12.20	20.27	65.23
60 to 80	34.97	6.03	7.57	33.80	18.29	15.49	3.93	13.70	18.78	61.16
00 to 60	41.53	4.38	6.92	26.27	15.04	11.07	1.53	19.36	16.83	55.54
All	25.37	6.41	19.77	26.82	12.81	13.57	9.34	12.28	23.61	74.04
1995										
99 to 100	15.60	8.96	38.05	12.78	5.10	7.11	13.34	11.26	34.11	90.39
95 to 99	16.47	5.85	27.42	31.96	10.98	20.72	6.26	12.03	28.10	80.04
90 to 95	21.00	7.35	16.79	36.29	14.62	20.02	3.51	15.06	22.05	68.63
80 to 90	27.37	6.13	13.36	33.52	15.52	16.54	3.02	16.61	19.81	63.17
60 to 80	27.19	4.99	10.80	36.86	15.98	19.49	1.41	18.74	18.86	60.74
00 to 60	30.89	3.45	7.17	37.70	15.29	21.21	0.92	19.86	16.86	55.98
All	20.00	6.93	25.18	26.85	15.28	10.70	7.18	13.86	26.82	76.77

Source: Author's calculations.

Notes: Each entry in the first eight columns represents the share of the aggregate financial assets held in the form of the asset specified at the top of the column by the households in the percentiles of the net worth distribution specified at the left of the row. The entries in the last two columns are the dollar-weighted marginal tax rates on ordinary income and percentiles of that tax rate's distribution for the households in the specified net worth percentiles. The weights are the sample weights multiplied by the household's level of financial assets.

The rightmost two columns present the weighted averages of the ordinary marginal tax rate and its percentile for each net worth category. The difference between these numbers and those in table 9.2 is that the weights here are the household's amount of financial assets. In comparison, the changes in the tax rates over time for the highest wealth categories are more pronounced when the focus is on the marginal tax rate on the average dollar rather than the average household. The goal of the econometric estimation to follow is to determine the extent to which the greater relative changes in the portfolio allocations of the rich are commensurate with the greater relative changes in their tax rates.

Table 9.4 presents the analogous portfolio shares for components of net worth, expressed as percentages of total assets held in each asset or debt category. Looking first at the asset categories, the rich clearly have more in financial, other property, and business assets and less in owner-occupied housing. The latter constitutes over half the total assets of the bottom 80 percent of the wealth distribution in every year, and its share in the total remains fairly stable across years. Over time the movements in the population share of financial assets follows that of equities described in table 9.3, with the rich again having larger portfolio swings than the rest of the population. The share of business equity grows over time for the rich relative to the share for the population as a whole. For other property, the allocations by the rich relative to the population grew between 1983 and 1992 and then fell sharply by 1995. One tax-related factor that may explain some of these movements is that while TRA86 severely curtailed tax shelter opportunities in all types of investments, the cutbacks were less severe in real estate than in other sectors.

The leverage ratios in the right panel of table 9.4 show that the rich have less debt relative to their total assets in every form except for other property. The table clearly shows the dramatic increase in indebtedness between 1983 and 1989 and a smaller decrease in subsequent years. The magnitude of the increase is substantial in all types of debt for the bottom 60 percent of the wealth distribution, and after a small retreat in 1992, this group achieved a 52 percent leverage ratio in 1995. For the next 20 to 30 percent of the wealth distribution, the increases were more limited to owner-occupied housing over the whole sample period. For higher wealth groups, other property debt generated most of the time series variation, and unlike with the lower wealth groups, their overall level of indebtedness decreased substantially after 1989. In interpreting these leverage ratios, it is important to note that the changes may be due as much to changing levels of total assets as to active changes in the dollar amounts that households choose to borrow.

THE ECONOMETRIC FRAMEWORK

The simple tabulations discussed in the previous section document the variation in both the changes in tax rates and portfolio allocations of the rich over the sample period. The purpose of this section is to specify an econometric model that allows for marginal tax rates to affect the portfolio allocations chosen by households. The results can then be used to predict how the portfolio allocations of each net worth group would have changed across each tax reform as a function only of the changes in their tax rates. The end result is a set of comparisons of predicted to actual changes

Table 9.4 Portfolio Allocation of Total Assets, by Net Worth Percentiles and Year

Net Worth Percentiles	Assets					Debt				
	Financial	Owner-Occupied	Other Property	Miscellaneous	Business	Financial	Owner-Occupied	Other Property	Miscellaneous	Total
1983										
99 to 100	37.23	9.16	18.39	1.34	33.87	0.39	1.09	3.11	1.17	5.76
95 to 99	30.93	21.22	19.18	2.71	25.95	0.38	2.46	3.01	0.81	6.66
90 to 95	28.09	32.32	16.09	4.92	18.57	0.56	5.52	2.28	1.44	9.80
80 to 90	29.44	42.51	15.15	4.80	8.10	0.45	9.15	3.45	1.79	14.84
60 to 80	22.28	58.28	8.77	6.58	4.09	0.73	13.28	2.27	2.65	18.92
00 to 60	19.04	60.88	5.28	12.91	1.88	1.71	25.33	1.84	8.49	37.37
All	29.69	31.49	15.08	4.50	19.25	0.61	7.32	2.78	2.20	12.90
1989										
99 to 100	27.48	9.83	23.79	5.47	33.43	0.24	1.31	6.51	0.56	8.63
95 to 99	28.38	24.74	20.76	6.41	19.71	0.13	3.78	5.53	1.12	10.56
90 to 95	35.11	36.52	12.45	6.11	9.82	0.37	6.57	2.87	1.20	11.01
80 to 90	28.89	48.97	10.79	6.61	4.74	0.38	10.65	2.50	1.80	15.33
60 to 80	22.21	58.16	6.66	8.39	4.58	0.68	17.22	2.44	3.25	23.58
00 to 60	16.69	60.96	5.57	15.54	1.23	2.21	28.33	7.05	11.98	49.56
All	26.71	33.59	15.71	7.41	16.58	0.53	8.91	4.84	2.55	16.84
1992										
99 to 100	29.68	8.84	23.20	3.54	34.75	0.22	1.50	4.34	0.68	6.74
95 to 99	34.91	23.98	17.63	4.72	18.75	0.10	5.49	4.64	0.64	10.87
90 to 95	37.64	33.07	14.70	4.18	10.41	0.28	8.43	3.39	0.43	12.53
80 to 90	32.84	45.98	9.04	6.02	6.11	0.44	12.28	1.83	0.91	15.47
60 to 80	24.69	55.76	7.28	8.17	4.10	0.64	18.67	1.48	2.10	22.89
00 to 60	16.98	61.86	4.55	15.20	1.41	2.67	32.54	1.83	8.00	45.04
All	30.08	32.93	14.61	6.19	16.19	0.56	10.65	3.25	1.69	16.15

(*Table continues on p. 306.*)

Table 9.4 *Continued*

Net Worth Percentiles	Assets					Debt				
	Financial	Owner-Occupied	Other Property	Miscellaneous	Business	Financial	Owner-Occupied	Other Property	Miscellaneous	Total
1995										
99 to 100	39.29	7.74	12.45	3.46	37.07	0.11	1.47	2.45	0.64	4.67
95 to 99	42.55	21.96	16.78	5.95	12.76	0.11	5.20	2.83	0.58	8.71
90 to 95	40.13	32.25	14.35	5.79	7.48	0.21	7.50	3.79	0.95	12.45
80 to 90	32.70	45.01	9.37	8.23	4.69	0.49	10.47	2.14	1.30	14.41
60 to 80	26.27	55.34	5.83	9.69	2.86	1.06	19.30	1.25	2.47	24.08
00 to 60	17.20	61.30	3.24	16.73	1.53	3.01	37.22	1.46	10.39	52.08
All	34.74	30.92	11.10	7.26	15.97	0.65	10.78	2.35	2.18	15.97

Source: Author's calculations.

Notes: Each entry in the left panel represents the share of the aggregate total assets held in the form of the asset specified at the top of the column by the households in the percentiles of the net worth distribution specified at the left of the row. The entries in the right panel are the ratio of the outstanding balances on the type of debt specified at the top of the column to the gross value of all the assets owned by households in the percentiles of the net worth distribution specified at the left of the row.

that suggests whether tax considerations play an important role in the changes in portfolio allocations of households in each category of the wealth distribution.

Although a full structural model of portfolio allocations lies beyond the scope of this chapter, theoretical considerations can still motivate a reasonable reduced form specification.[14] The first consideration is simply that a household's demand for any given asset is a function not just of the tax rate on that asset but of the tax rates on all other assets in which the investment could be made. Since relative prices are what matter, the specifications presented here include the marginal tax rates on both ordinary and capital income.

Another consideration is that the levels of the household's tax rates are not by themselves sufficient to determine its optimal portfolio allocations. According to the certainty version of the clientele model of Merton Miller (1977), for example, the tax incentives for a household to hold an asset are determined by the household's tax rate on the asset *relative* to the distribution of all households' tax rate on the asset. Feldstein and Slemrod (1980) further show that the household's marginal tax rate relative to the corporate income tax rate is also relevant in determining its portfolio allocations in general equilibrium.

Considerations of the entire schedule of personal and corporate tax rates suggest that in testing a specific model of portfolio allocation, the real unit of observation is the entire distribution of household allocations in a given year. Given only four such observations, the approach followed in the reduced-form model here is to include dummy variables for each sample year in the econometric specification. These dummy variables can account for the household's position in the marginal tax rate distribution and its position relative to the corporate tax rate. The entire marginal tax rate distribution may well have an important effect on the relative supplies of assets in the aggregate, but this analysis cannot identify that effect. What the results can determine is whether the household level variation in marginal tax rates *around their sample averages each year* is related to the household level variation in portfolio allocations around their sample averages each year. When comparing predicted and actual changes in allocations by net worth group, the actual change in the market proportion of each asset must be deducted from the observed change in the group's proportion.

There are also factors other than tax rates that affect portfolio allocations. Some of them are related to the preferences of the household, such as risk aversion. Others pertain to aspects of the household's budget constraint, such as borrowing restrictions or other risks that the household may have to bear (see Kimball 1993). In a reduced-form specification, these effects are proxied by including other variables that would at least partially reflect the differences in these factors across households. In the analysis that follows, these other covariates include gender, marital status, age, income, education, occupation, and industry. Each of these variables is entered as a set of dummy variables.[15] Note that the inclusion of age and year effects incorporates the variation in portfolio holdings by cohort estimated by Poterba and Samwick (1997), even if all three effects cannot be separately identified. Additionally, the specification includes six dummy variables representing each of the net worth categories from tables 9.2 through 9.4: zero to sixtieth percentile, sixtieth to eightieth, eightieth to ninetieth, ninetieth to ninety-fifth, ninety-fifth to ninety-ninth, and ninety-ninth to one hundredth. The inclusion of a dummy variable for each net worth group ensures that the predicted tax effects for each group are unaffected by any factor that is idiosyncratic to that net worth group.

Because portfolio shares are censored at values of 0 and 100 in the data, the appropriate econometric model is a two-limit tobit, provided that the assumption of normally distributed errors in portfolio shares is acceptable. A refinement to this model would be to impose the constraint that the marginal effects of taxes on the portfolio shares must sum to zero at the estimation stage. For simplicity, this constraint is not imposed for the components of either financial assets or net worth. Each asset demand equation is assumed to be a function of the same explanatory variables, and the equations for different assets are estimated independently. In each regression, all observations from all sample years are pooled (see table 9.1), yielding one set of coefficients for each asset share.

It is important to note that the identification of the tax effects comes from two sources of variation. The first is the cross-sectional variation across households in each survey year. The coefficients on marginal tax rates could be estimated with a single year of data. The second source of variation is in the different tax rate schedules (relative to the average tax rate) across sample years. Figures 9.1 and 9.2 show that there is substantially more variation within cross-sections than across cross-sections, suggesting that the first source of variation is more important in the identification of the estimates than the second.

The econometric results are summarized in table 9.5. Each row corresponds to a tobit model for a different asset or liability's share of financial assets (top panel) or total assets (bottom panel). The first four columns are the coefficients and standard errors on the ordinary and capital gain marginal tax rates. The fifth column is the p-value for the test of the joint significance of the two tax rate variables.

Consider the first three assets, all of which are subject to at least partial taxation in the current period. For interest-bearing accounts, the coefficients are jointly but not individually significant. The negative coefficient on the ordinary MTR is consistent with a higher tax rate on these accounts leading to lower portfolio allocations to them. However, these accounts never generate capital gains or losses, so a higher capital gains MTR should reduce allocations in other assets and increase them in these accounts, contrary to what is implied by the negative coefficient.[16] For taxable bonds, the tax rate variables are neither individually nor jointly significant, and the point estimates are of the wrong signs. For taxable equity, a higher ordinary MTR leads to significantly greater allocations in taxable equity, and a higher capital gain MTR leads to lesser allocations. This result is consistent with investors choosing equities to hold for the long term, to achieve capital gains rather than to receive immediate dividends.

The next three rows show the results for holdings of retirement accounts overall, by bonds and equities. These results are harder to interpret because neither of the tax variables exactly measures the effective marginal tax rate on income earned within the retirement account. In all cases, a higher ordinary MTR leads to greater allocations, with statistical significance in the case of bonds and the total balances. A higher capital gain MTR leads to greater shares of financial assets in tax-deferred equity and lower shares of financial assets in tax-deferred bonds. One possible

Table 9.5   Summary of Econometric Results for Portfolio Allocations, Coefficients on Tobits for Asset Shares

Asset	Ordinary MTR		Capital Gains MTR		Joint Significance (p-Value)
	Coefficient	Standard Error	Coefficient	Standard Error	
Shares of financial assets					
Interest-bearing accounts	−0.0742	0.0881	−0.1774	0.1073	0.0000
Taxable bonds	0.0534	0.0673	−0.0291	0.0825	0.5747
Taxable equity	0.1877	0.0935	−0.1093	0.1163	0.0298
Retirement accounts					
All	0.4814	0.1093	−0.1996	0.1331	0.0000
Bonds	0.7733	0.1103	−0.6494	0.1344	0.0000
Equity	0.0983	0.1172	0.2116	0.1436	0.0000
Tax-exempt bonds	0.2927	0.1251	0.0841	0.1570	0.0000
Other financial assets	0.0040	0.1033	0.0898	0.1269	0.3524
Shares of total assets					
Financial assets	0.2642	0.0622	−0.0110	0.0755	0.0000
Owner-occupied	−0.3018	0.0750	0.1364	0.0912	0.0000
Other property	−0.7937	0.0849	0.3635	0.1055	0.0000
Miscellaneous	0.1778	0.0506	−0.1514	0.0613	0.0012
Business	0.4854	0.1061	−0.1907	0.1343	0.0000
Financial debt	0.1885	0.0481	−0.2544	0.0574	0.0001
Owner-occupied debt	−0.3522	0.0690	0.0689	0.0839	0.0000
Other property debt	0.7389	0.0721	−1.1217	0.0861	0.0000
Miscellaneous	0.2382	0.0713	−0.1917	0.0863	0.0017
Total debt	0.1608	0.0614	−0.4258	0.0741	0.0000

Source: Author's calculations.

explanation is that the higher capital gain tax rate prompts households to take their equity holdings inside the retirement account, and this shift results in less scope for bond holdings in those accounts, which in most cases have contribution limits. However, this explanation does not account for the negative (though insignificant) coefficient on the capital gain MTR for retirement accounts overall.

The next two rows pertain to tax-exempt bonds and other financial assets (whole life insurance and trusts); both categories are tax-preferred relative to the other asset categories. This tax preference should lead to positive coefficients on both tax variables. For both asset shares, the coefficients on both variables are in fact positive, though in the case of other financial assets the estimates are neither individually nor jointly significant. For tax-exempt bonds, the ordinary MTR is significant and the capital gains MTR is not. A possible explanation for the poor empirical performance of the capital gains MTR is that it uses the statutory rate rather than the effective rate, which would take into account any household-specific factors that might influence the timing of realizations. This allows less inclusion of identifying variation in the construction of the variable.

The theoretical predictions for how taxes should affect the allocation of total assets into components are less clear. The specification includes two marginal tax rates for potential substitutes (in the form of financial assets) but none for the asset itself. A convenient way to summarize the role that taxes might play is to classify these assets as similar to the financial asset components that would exhibit the same pattern of coefficients. The results indicate that the tax effects on financial assets, miscellaneous assets, and business equity resemble those that would be predicted for equity. In contrast, both owner-occupied and other real estate exhibit the tax effects that would be predicted for bonds.

The theory of tax arbitrage gives some indication of how tax rates should affect the leverage ratios in the bottom portion of the table. In a tax arbitrage, the investor borrows funds, deducting the interest payments, and uses the proceeds to purchase tax-preferred assets. The tax preference on the assets typically comes in the form of taxing the gains at a capital gains tax rate that is lower than the ordinary income tax rate. This "conversion" of income from ordinary to capital through the use of debt is at the heart of a tax shelter.[17] Given this, we should see higher leverage ratios when the ordinary MTR is high (making the deductions of interest payments more valuable) and when the capital gains MTR is low (lowering the eventual tax liability). This pattern of a positive coefficient on the ordinary MTR and a negative coefficient on the capital gain MTR is present and statistically significant for every type of debt except for owner-occupied real estate. Mortgage debt on the primary residence is intuitively less likely to be determined by tax arbitrage considerations. Consistent with the tax arbitrage explanation, the coefficients are particularly large for other property debt.

The results in table 9.5 suggest that portfolio allocations respond to marginal tax rates in a way that is consistent with basic economic prescriptions. Based on these results, it is reasonable to conjecture that the dramatic tax changes over the sample period are responsible for a portion of the observed changes in household portfolio allocations. To determine how important tax changes were, the tobit equations can be used to predict how much the portfolio allocations of each net worth category would have changed across the survey years if only its tax rates were changed. For example, the tobit equation can be used to generate a predicted asset share for each household based on its explanatory variables. The tobit equation can also be used to predict what each household's asset share would be if it instead faced the (dollar-weighted average) marginal tax rates that its net worth category had faced in the previous survey. The difference between the two predicted values is the effect of taxes for that time period.

This prediction can then be compared to the actual change in that net worth category's asset share to determine how important tax changes were to the overall change. The appropriate measure of the actual change is net of the change in the asset share in the entire population. The difference between the actual and predicted changes represents the effect of factors that are not related to the households' relative positions in the tax rate distributions. Some of this difference is due to the other factors in the model. The rest is due to factors that were not explicitly modeled, but note that such factors are orthogonal to the predicted effect by net worth category, owing to the inclusion of the net worth dummy variables in the model.

Table 9.6 lists the actual and tax-related changes in portfolio allocations of financial assets relative to the population average for each of the three intervals in the sample period. For interest-bearing assets, tax effects are predicted to be less than one percentage point, compared to actual changes that are typically four percentage points or more. The tax effects for taxable bonds are even smaller, with none exceeding one-fifth of a percentage point. Taxes appear to be a slightly larger component of the actual changes in taxable equity shares but still less than 10 percent of the observed magnitudes. There is also a better match between the signs of the effects. For retirement account shares, the magnitudes of the tax effects are now comparable to the actual effects. The matchup is better for bonds than for equity in these accounts. For tax-exempt bonds, the predicted magnitudes are less than one percentage point, and for other financial assets, all predicted effects are small.

The correspondence between actual and predicted changes for the components of net worth is more robust, as shown in table 9.7. For financial and other property assets, the matchup in the signs of the effects is generally close, with magnitudes of predicted changes around 10 percent of the actual changes. For all four asset measures, the comparisons are closest for the 1992 to 1995 interval and for the bottom, not the top, of the wealth distributions. The predicted and actual changes for the debt measures are less clearly related. Financial debt shows the closest match, largely because both actual and predicted effects are small. For owner-occupied debt, the magnitudes are comparable but the signs are unrelated. For other property, the magnitudes are comparable only for the change from 1983 to 1989, and the signs are not obviously related.

The comparisons in tables 9.6 and 9.7 suggest some very general conclusions about the role of tax changes in explaining the actual changes in portfolio allocations. First, there is no evidence that tax changes play a greater role in the portfolio changes of the high net worth groups relative to the low net worth groups. This is especially true for the components of net worth. Second, the correspondence between predicted and actual is generally the best for the period from 1992 to 1995 and worst for the period from 1989 to 1992, although this is not uniformly true across net worth categories and asset types. Among financial asset components, taxes seem to play the largest role for asset shares in retirement accounts. Among net worth components, taxes have fairly consistent effects on all components except for owner-occupied and other property debt.

There are several caveats to this type of analysis that must be acknowledged. The first is that tables 9.6 and 9.7 present a particular type of "marginal" effect calculation in which the change in tax rates is chosen to be the observed historical change. As long as the econometric model is consistent, the divergence between actual and predicted effects based on tax changes simply suggests that the primary explanation for the magnitudes of the changes lies elsewhere. The second is that the comparisons are measuring the changes in portfolio allocations for subgroups of the population *relative* to the population average. This is appropriate for a household-level analysis of the effect of taxes, but it does not preclude the important role of the overall tax schedule, including the corporate income tax, in determining the population average itself. The link is that the financing decisions of firms, governments, and pension plans determine the aggregate portfolio and may be very sensitive to tax changes in the overall tax schedule. In this analysis, taxes are allowed to determine explicitly only the deviations of net worth groups' holdings from the market portfolio.

Table 9.6   Comparison of Actual and Predicted Changes in Portfolio Allocations of Financial

Net Worth Percentile	Interest-Bearing Accounts		Taxable Bonds		Taxable Equity	
	Actual	Tax	Actual	Tax	Actual	Tax
1983 to 1989						
99 to 100	9.44	0.67	4.41	−0.18	−10.96	−0.89
95 to 99	0.09	−0.69	−3.52	0.04	4.59	0.18
90 to 95	−10.42	−0.47	−5.28	0.08	6.26	0.31
80 to 90	−14.91	−0.66	−0.05	0.13	8.77	0.50
60 to 80	−6.80	0.04	0.43	0.09	10.36	0.27
00 to 60	−3.81	−0.55	−0.12	0.10	9.85	0.23
1989 to 1992						
99 to 100	1.37	−0.11	−2.12	0.03	7.99	0.14
95 to 99	−4.57	0.03	0.91	0.00	−4.92	0.04
90 to 95	4.69	0.26	0.55	−0.02	−1.95	−0.07
80 to 90	0.26	0.17	0.34	−0.02	−1.47	−0.05
60 to 80	−3.17	−0.43	2.46	0.02	−1.54	0.05
00 to 60	2.64	0.00	0.92	−0.01	−1.70	0.00
1992 to 1995						
99 to 100	3.48	−0.09	0.88	0.08	−1.92	0.42
95 to 99	3.88	0.20	−2.02	−0.02	0.85	−0.10
90 to 95	−4.64	0.20	0.88	−0.05	−1.80	−0.21
80 to 90	1.08	0.33	1.21	−0.05	−5.40	−0.22
60 to 80	−2.41	0.21	−1.57	−0.04	−2.18	−0.12
00 to 60	−5.27	0.08	−1.46	−0.03	−5.15	−0.07

Source: Author's calculations.
Notes: The "Actual" column is the difference in the portfolio allocation of the specified asset over the time interval for the specified net worth category net of the difference in the portfolio allocation of all households over that time period. The raw data are presented in table 9.3. The "Tax" column is the predicted change in the portfolio allocation of the specified asset over the time period based on the difference between the households' tax rates in the later year and the weighted average tax rates for the same percentile group in the earlier year. Predictions are based on the estimated coefficients in table 9.5.

THE DISTRIBUTION OF ASSET OWNERSHIP BY TAX RATE

The results of the previous section suggest that although marginal tax rates have significant effects on portfolio allocations in the cross-section, their role in explaining time series changes in allocations is limited. Another way to assess the role of taxes is to consider changes in allocations at different points in the marginal tax rate distributions. The simple intuition is that in models of portfolio choice under uncertainty such as the standard capital asset pricing model, all households have the same portfolios of risky assets. They hold the market portfolio in order to diversify optimally. The introduction of differential tax rates across assets and investors prompts them to deviate from the market portfolio, with the size of the deviation determined at least in part by how different the investor's tax rates are from the average tax rates in the population.[18]

Assets, by Net Worth Percentiles and Time Period

| Retirement Accounts | | | | | | Tax-Exempt Bonds | | Other Financial Assets | |
| All | | Bonds | | Equity | | | | | |
Actual	Tax	Actual	Tax	Actual	Tax	Actual	Tax	Actual	Tax
−2.88	−1.81	−2.65	−2.05	0.00	−0.38	2.11	−1.26	−2.13	−0.11
−0.09	0.68	0.57	0.18	−0.74	0.51	−1.09	0.62	0.01	0.18
0.69	1.22	0.86	1.10	−0.74	0.53	−0.01	0.35	8.76	0.09
4.82	2.14	1.44	2.12	3.36	0.80	0.89	0.36	0.48	0.10
−3.74	1.53	−1.23	1.85	−2.36	0.39	0.30	0.09	−0.55	−0.07
−0.34	1.89	2.44	1.95	−2.57	0.46	−1.62	0.07	−3.97	0.03
−3.95	0.31	−1.98	0.29	−1.90	0.12	−0.77	0.23	−2.52	0.02
3.48	0.26	0.65	0.21	2.83	0.21	1.66	0.00	3.44	0.00
−0.65	−0.02	0.86	−0.07	−0.49	0.19	0.04	−0.17	−2.69	−0.05
−1.49	0.08	−1.12	−0.12	−1.63	0.32	0.03	−0.09	2.34	−0.02
2.19	0.60	1.00	0.03	1.46	0.69	1.08	0.07	−1.02	0.11
−4.95	0.10	−1.59	−0.12	−3.30	0.24	−0.05	−0.01	3.14	−0.01
−0.95	0.90	2.59	0.97	−3.54	0.15	−0.52	0.49	−0.97	0.00
2.28	−0.07	−0.69	−0.04	3.65	0.12	−2.88	−0.13	−2.10	−0.03
4.36	−0.45	−1.01	−0.60	4.14	0.21	−1.65	−0.12	2.85	−0.01
−0.97	−0.54	1.51	−0.71	−1.79	0.20	1.24	−0.12	2.83	−0.03
3.04	−0.39	0.56	−0.65	1.53	0.30	−0.35	−0.05	3.46	0.00
11.39	−0.41	3.11	−0.58	7.67	0.20	1.56	−0.02	−1.07	0.01

As suggested by figures 9.1 and 9.2, the SCF sample period contains two intervals during which the distribution of marginal tax rates changed substantially. Between 1983 and 1989 TRA86 compressed the distribution so that the highest marginal tax rates were closer to the population average. With a smaller tax wedge, the portfolio allocations of the highest MTR households should more closely resemble the population proportions in 1989 than in 1983. Conversely, OBRA93 raised marginal rates at the top of the distribution relative to the average. Portfolio allocations of the households at the top of the distribution should adhere to the market proportions to a lesser degree in 1995 than in 1992.

Tables 9.8 and 9.9 provide the data necessary to analyze these propositions informally. The rows of the tables refer to different percentile ranges in the yearly distributions of the ordinary income marginal tax rates. The groups were chosen so that the average MTR by category, weighted by financial assets (shown in the last column),

Table 9.7   Comparison of Actual and Predicted Changes in Portfolio Allocations of Total Assets,

Net Worth Percentile	Financial Assets		Owner-Occupied		Other Property		Business	
	Actual	Tax	Actual	Tax	Actual	Tax	Actual	Tax
1983 to 1989								
99 to 100	−6.78	−1.11	−1.43	0.76	4.76	2.23	2.23	−1.43
95 to 99	0.41	0.75	1.43	−0.60	0.94	−1.36	−3.58	0.71
90 to 95	9.98	1.02	2.10	−1.01	−4.28	−1.83	−6.09	0.88
80 to 90	2.42	1.24	4.37	−1.37	−5.00	−2.09	−0.69	0.78
60 to 80	2.91	1.05	−2.21	−1.39	−2.74	−1.49	3.15	0.50
00 to 60	0.62	1.42	−2.02	−1.69	−0.34	−0.91	2.01	0.19
1989 to 1992								
99 to 100	−1.16	0.47	−0.33	−0.25	0.51	−0.75	1.70	0.54
95 to 99	3.17	0.36	−0.10	−0.22	−2.03	−0.50	−0.57	0.37
90 to 95	−0.83	−0.01	−2.79	0.01	3.35	−0.04	0.98	0.15
80 to 90	0.59	−0.14	−2.33	0.12	−0.65	0.13	1.76	0.08
60 to 80	−0.88	−0.24	−1.75	0.20	1.72	0.07	−0.09	0.03
00 to 60	−3.07	−0.21	1.55	0.15	0.07	0.01	0.57	0.00
1992 to 1995								
99 to 100	4.95	0.59	0.91	−0.46	−7.24	−1.15	2.54	1.01
95 to 99	2.98	−0.35	−0.02	0.25	2.66	0.68	−5.77	−0.16
90 to 95	−2.17	−0.75	1.19	0.66	3.16	1.10	−2.71	−0.42
80 to 90	−4.81	−0.83	1.03	0.79	3.84	0.93	−1.20	−0.28
60 to 80	−3.09	−0.74	1.59	0.75	2.07	0.53	−1.02	−0.17
00 to 60	−4.43	−0.63	1.45	0.60	2.20	0.21	0.34	−0.07

Source: Author's calculations.
Notes: The "Actual" column is the difference in the portfolio allocation of the specified asset over the time interval for the specified net worth category net of the difference in the portfolio allocation of all households over that time period. The raw data are presented in table 9.4. The "Tax" column is the predicted change in the portfolio allocation of the specified asset over the time period based on the difference between the households' tax rates in the later year and the weighted average tax rates for the same percentile group in the earlier year. Predictions are based on the estimated coefficients in table 9.5.

changed very little over time for the bottom four groups. As in the previous tables, the other columns are the shares of financial assets allocated to each asset type. Table 9.8 compares allocations in 1983 and 1989; table 9.9 compares them for 1992 and 1995. The basis of comparison is shown in the bottom group of rows, labeled "Change," in each table. For each MTR category j, the change in allocations is given by:

$$\left| x_{j,t} - \bar{x}_{j,t} \right| - \left| x_{j,t-1} - \bar{x}_{j,t-1} \right|$$

where x is either a portfolio allocation or marginal tax rate and the bar denotes the population mean. A positive value of this change indicates that the portfolio share of asset x in category j's portfolio got further away from the market portfolio over the time interval from t − 1 to t. A negative value indicates the opposite. The test of the proposition is whether the signs of these changes were the same for the MTR as for each asset's portfolio share.

by Net Worth Percentiles and Time Period

			Debt				
Financial Debt		Owner-Occupied		Other Property		Total	
Actual	Tax	Actual	Tax	Actual	Tax	Actual	Tax
−0.08	−0.04	−1.38	0.54	1.40	−0.87	−1.02	0.14
−0.18	0.04	−0.28	−0.56	0.51	0.58	0.02	−0.16
−0.13	0.13	−0.54	−0.95	−1.42	1.69	−2.67	0.06
−0.01	0.23	−0.10	−1.32	−2.96	2.43	−3.39	0.31
0.02	0.35	2.34	−1.48	−1.84	2.85	0.78	0.76
0.63	0.65	1.39	−1.76	2.65	3.94	7.75	1.38
−0.06	0.00	−1.54	−0.24	−0.64	−0.02	−1.27	−0.15
−0.06	−0.02	−0.02	−0.43	0.65	−0.11	0.93	−0.31
−0.12	−0.04	0.12	−0.35	2.06	−0.14	2.13	−0.33
0.03	−0.06	−0.10	−0.32	0.87	−0.12	0.76	−0.34
−0.07	−0.09	−0.28	−0.39	0.58	−0.08	−0.07	−0.40
0.43	−0.11	2.48	−0.26	−3.14	−0.08	−3.28	−0.29
−0.19	0.10	−0.17	−0.32	−0.99	0.70	−1.85	0.33
−0.08	−0.01	−0.43	−0.05	−0.91	0.04	−1.95	0.00
−0.16	−0.09	−1.06	0.20	1.30	−0.13	0.13	−0.13
−0.03	−0.15	−1.94	0.15	1.20	−0.20	−0.85	−0.33
0.33	−0.21	0.51	0.13	0.67	−0.16	1.40	−0.45
0.24	−0.31	4.54	0.27	0.53	−0.22	7.07	−0.49

Consider first the change in allocations from 1983 to 1989 in table 9.8. The last column of the bottom panel shows that MTRs got closer to the population averages for the top 5 percent and bottom 75 percent of the distribution and slightly further away for the seventy-fifth to ninety-fifth percentiles. The first column shows that for all but one MTR category, the signs of the changes in interest-bearing account shares were the same as those for MTRs—negative at the top and bottom and positive in the middle. The same is true for taxable equity, shown in the third column. For no other asset is there any pattern of signs on the asset share changes that aligns well with those of the MTR changes. When examined by MTR category, the bottom quartile and the sixtieth to seventy-fifth percentiles have the most consistent matches. For the top 5 percent, the deviations in portfolio allocations in 1989 are larger, as often as not, than they were in 1983.

Table 9.9 presents the analogous changes for the interval from 1992 to 1995. The pattern of signs on the MTR changes is directly opposite to that found in table 9.8.

Table 9.8   Portfolio Allocation of Financial Assets, by Marginal Tax Rate Percentiles for 1983 to 1989

Tax Rate Percentiles	Interest-Bearing Accounts	Taxable Bonds	Taxable Equity	Retirement Accounts			Tax-Exempt Bonds	Other Financial Assets	Average Marginal Tax Rate
				All	Bonds	Equity			
1983									
99 to 100	11.22	5.16	41.91	11.67	7.28	4.39	9.07	20.96	50.00
95 to 99	17.53	5.52	33.47	20.17	13.22	6.95	9.43	13.87	45.08
90 to 95	22.00	3.93	24.73	18.11	9.15	8.97	12.16	19.07	37.49
75 to 90	29.74	6.60	18.60	20.16	11.94	8.22	3.55	21.34	30.44
60 to 75	34.10	11.74	15.80	19.40	11.16	8.24	2.41	16.55	23.42
25 to 60	42.73	7.54	21.51	9.02	5.34	3.68	6.84	12.36	13.43
00 to 25	55.09	3.54	19.84	5.37	4.08	1.29	2.21	13.95	0.00
All	27.73	6.27	27.32	14.67	8.86	5.80	7.15	16.87	31.59
1989									
99 to 100	31.53	2.05	15.19	39.73	34.02	5.18	7.34	4.16	34.50
95 to 99	23.57	3.85	17.68	28.23	12.78	15.13	9.85	16.82	32.06
90 to 95	30.77	11.04	25.22	15.01	8.98	5.62	9.29	8.67	28.63
75 to 90	24.30	8.48	16.36	26.55	16.41	9.83	11.23	13.08	28.00
60 to 75	25.58	8.69	16.17	19.49	11.68	7.52	12.07	18.00	21.58
25 to 60	43.71	7.38	15.45	13.81	8.58	4.53	7.71	11.94	9.44
00 to 25	45.01	5.80	12.07	24.83	16.14	8.23	3.81	8.49	0.00
All	30.59	7.68	17.07	21.44	12.67	8.38	9.68	13.53	21.54
Change									
99 to 100	−15.57	4.52	−12.71	15.29	19.77	1.79	0.42	5.28	−5.45
95 to 99	−3.18	3.08	−5.54	1.29	−4.25	5.60	−2.11	0.29	−2.97
90 to 95	−5.55	1.02	5.56	2.99	3.40	−0.41	−4.62	2.66	1.20
75 to 90	4.28	0.47	−8.01	−0.38	0.66	−0.97	−2.05	−4.02	5.30
60 to 75	−1.36	−4.46	−10.62	−2.78	−1.31	−1.58	−2.35	4.15	−8.13
25 to 60	−1.88	−0.97	−4.19	1.98	0.57	1.73	1.66	−2.92	−6.07
00 to 25	−12.94	−0.85	−2.48	−5.91	−1.31	−4.36	0.93	2.12	−10.05

Source: Author's calculations.

Notes: The first eight columns contain the share of the aggregate financial assets held in the form of the asset specified at the top of the column by the households in the percentiles of the distribution of marginal tax rates on ordinary income specified at the left of the row. The last column lists the dollar-weighted marginal tax rates on ordinary income for the households in the specified net worth percentiles. The weights are the sample weights multiplied by the household's level of financial assets. The bottom panel marked "Change" is the difference in the column values for the specified percentiles across the two years less the analogous difference for all of the households in the population.

Table 9.9 Portfolio Allocation of Financial Assets, by Marginal Tax Rate Percentiles for 1992 to 1995

Tax Rate Percentiles	Interest-Bearing Accounts	Taxable Bonds	Taxable Equity	Retirement Accounts			Tax-Exempt Bonds	Other Financial Assets	Average Marginal Tax Rate
				All	Bonds	Equity			
1992									
99 to 100	22.72	2.24	18.39	41.43	16.30	25.13	5.26	9.97	34.13
95 to 99	16.98	6.22	23.00	28.08	12.56	15.31	12.14	13.58	31.83
90 to 95	19.27	8.41	24.69	27.89	13.85	13.29	11.28	8.45	29.90
75 to 90	23.16	5.36	17.64	32.12	16.25	15.21	9.80	11.93	27.36
60 to 75	24.15	6.56	20.81	27.53	14.38	12.47	8.76	12.20	21.07
25 to 60	39.13	7.12	14.00	17.48	10.63	6.81	6.27	16.00	11.27
00 to 25	51.41	4.64	12.95	15.79	10.56	5.07	4.29	10.92	0.00
All	25.37	6.41	19.77	26.82	13.57	12.81	9.34	12.28	23.61
1995									
99 to 100	16.50	7.00	26.17	28.01	6.60	19.50	8.27	14.04	41.00
95 to 99	17.40	9.32	32.20	20.32	8.14	11.99	10.70	10.06	36.77
90 to 95	14.71	4.78	32.57	29.74	10.80	18.32	5.55	12.65	29.70
75 to 90	18.72	4.58	11.81	43.97	14.62	28.27	2.98	17.95	28.00
60 to 75	21.44	6.99	22.32	22.24	9.84	11.02	8.35	18.66	21.48
25 to 60	28.25	6.94	16.56	27.30	14.83	11.73	4.19	16.75	10.08
00 to 25	28.31	3.99	25.08	28.70	15.09	12.26	3.22	10.71	0.00
All	20.00	6.93	25.18	26.85	10.70	15.28	7.18	13.86	26.82
Change									
99 to 100	0.85	-4.10	-0.39	-13.45	1.37	-8.10	-2.99	-2.13	3.66
95 to 99	-5.79	2.20	3.79	5.27	1.55	0.79	0.72	2.50	1.73
90 to 95	-0.81	0.15	2.47	1.82	-0.18	2.56	-0.31	-2.62	-3.40
75 to 90	-0.93	1.30	11.24	11.82	1.24	10.59	3.74	3.74	-2.57
60 to 75	0.22	-0.09	1.82	3.90	0.05	3.92	0.59	4.72	2.79
25 to 60	-5.51	-0.70	2.85	-8.89	1.19	-2.45	-0.08	-0.83	4.40
00 to 25	-17.73	1.17	-6.72	-9.18	1.38	-4.72	-1.09	1.79	3.21

Source: Author's calculations.

Notes: The first eight columns contain the share of the aggregate financial assets held in the form of the asset specified at the top of the column by the households in the percentiles of the distribution of marginal tax rates on ordinary income specified at the left of the row. The last column lists the dollar-weighted marginal tax rates on ordinary income for the households in the specified net worth percentiles. The weights are the sample weights multiplied by the household's level of financial assets. The bottom panel marked "Change" is the difference in the column values for the specified percentile across the two years less the analogous difference for all of the households in the population.

The top 5 percent and bottom 75 percent moved away from the average MTR, and those in the intervening 20 percent moved toward the average. The other columns of the table show that with the minor exception of bonds in retirement accounts, there is no asset for which the signs on the allocation changes align well with those on the MTR changes. Although the correspondence across assets is good for the ninety-fifth to ninety-ninth percentiles and the sixtieth to seventy-fifth percentiles, it is very poor for the other categories, especially the top percentile. The key factor seems to be that there is remarkably little variation in financial asset portfolio allocations in 1995.

The results in tables 9.8 and 9.9 do not constitute strong evidence that changes in portfolio allocations over time were determined by changes in marginal tax rates across groups. Furthermore, the restriction on the data that were being tested—that changes in deviations from the sample average should be correlated with analogous changes in MTRs—was a fairly weak one to impose. There are, however, two potential problems with this methodology. The first is that, as in the case of changes by net worth category, the proper specification is a multivariate one that accounts for other possible changes in the optimal allocations of each MTR group. However, based on the explanatory power of other covariates such as age, education, and occupation in the estimates in table 9.5 and in Poterba and Samwick (1999), this is not likely to be an important omission. The second is that there are other factors that determine the extent to which differential tax rates change portfolio allocations. An important one is the degree of systematic risk among all the financial assets. The lack of variation in portfolio allocations across groups in 1995, for example, may be due to a higher degree of systematic risk in that year.

CONCLUSION

Simple cross-tabulations of portfolio allocations by net worth or marginal tax rate group in any year clearly show that marginal tax rates are correlated with the ownership of tax-preferred assets in a way that is consistent with standard economic theory. More careful multivariate analysis, such as that in table 9.5 and in Poterba and Samwick (1999), upholds this result in the cross-section. The analysis in this chapter shows that the ability of taxes to explain the time series changes of portfolio allocations of net worth groups relative to the economy as a whole is more limited. Predicted effects from tax changes constituted about 10 percent of the observed changes, although this number varies considerably across time periods and assets. Within this framework, the predicted portfolio responses of the wealthy, though larger in magnitude, do not seem to be any more tax-related than the responses of other net worth categories.

The primary methodological improvement made in this analysis relative to previous studies of portfolio responses to taxation is the calculation of marginal tax rates for a sample period that spans multiple tax reforms. An important feature of the tax environment was that the later OBRAs undid much of what was accomplished in TRA86. This allows for conclusions to be based not just on trending variables, which would probably be correlated with several factors that are not modeled explicitly.

Nonetheless, there are several reasons why the analysis here could yield predicted effects that are smaller than the actual effects. The first is that the metric for comparison—the similarity of the predicted effect by group to the actual effect observed in the data—is analogous to an R^2 in a regression. Measurement error lowers any such "goodness of fit" measure. In this analysis, it is quite likely that survey responses to portfolio questions are measured with error. The tax-calculating algorithm, though very detailed, also introduces measurement error.

The second is that the true relationship between tax rates and asset shares may be nonlinear. For example, the highest marginal tax rate investors are the natural clientele for tax-exempt bonds in every sample year. Lowering the marginal tax rate on the top marginal tax rate group may not induce the same change in portfolios as increasing the marginal tax rate on a low marginal tax rate group by the same amount. The impact of such a change is reflected in price changes rather than quantity changes. Scholz (1994) examines the period from 1983 to 1989 in more detail and shows that the yield spread between tax-exempt and taxable bonds narrowed over the period. His observations on the quantities of assets held by income and wealth groups match those presented here. Welfare analysis of tax reforms must be made based on changes in both quantities and prices.

A third reason for the low predicted effects of tax rate changes is that transaction costs may prevent portfolios from fully reflecting contemporaneous tax rates. In addition to the well-known problems of "lock-in" due to taxation of gains on realization rather than accrual, all purchases and sales of assets incur transaction fees. These fees may be large relative to the welfare gains that can be obtained from immediate portfolio rebalancing. In this respect, the second test for tax effects provides useful reinforcement for the main results. Where tax differentials narrowed, differences in portfolio allocations across households widened, and where tax differentials widened, portfolio allocations narrowed.

This finding is similar to that of Slemrod (1994), who compared the portfolios of the affluent in the low-tax 1980s and the high-tax 1960s and found no noticeable shift out of tax-exempt securities and into taxable securities.

There are three principal shortcomings in this analysis that point to improvements that could be made in future work. One is the need to calculate more carefully effective tax rates that explicitly incorporate the deferral and conversion of tax liabilities for equity-like investments. Alternative methods of imputing the determinants of taxable income and itemized deductions based on information in tax return data might also refine the analysis. A second improvement would be to use a structural model of portfolio allocations that can generate sharper predictions to be tested. Such a model would incorporate nontax factors for portfolio allocations, most notably risk and borrowing constraints, and allow for nonlinear effects of tax rates on portfolio allocations. A third improvement would be to test the same basic propositions as in this chapter using a panel data set on wealth holdings such as the SCF panel from the period 1983 to 1989. A panel dimension would overcome the problem that the identity of the richest households changes over time. Distributions of household well-being based on marginal tax rates or net worth could be defined based on more than one year of data and thereby be more robust to transitory components of wealth and income. A panel would also permit the use of greater time series variation in estimating the tax elasticities.

The responsiveness of the portfolios of the rich to taxation appears to be limited. This phenomenon may be the result of another factor, such as systematic risk, that makes it worthwhile for the rich to hold a portfolio that is not optimal based on tax considerations alone. The absence of appreciable variation in financial portfolio allocation by marginal tax rates in 1995 in particular suggests the strong desire to diversify risk across asset types. The presence of other factors over which households must optimize in choosing their portfolio allocations reduces the scope for the rich to lessen their tax liabilities by changing their portfolios in response to tax reforms.

I thank Jim Hines, Jim Poterba, Joel Slemrod, Ed Wolff, and conference participants at Michigan and Dartmouth for helpful comments. Arthur Kennickell provided assistance with the Survey of Consumer Finances data. Financial support from the Nelson Rockefeller Fund at Dartmouth College for my ongoing research on taxation and portfolio choice is gratefully acknowledged. Any errors are my own.

NOTES

1. Prominent examples include Feldstein (1976), King and Leape (1998), Agell and Edin (1990), and Scholz (1994). See Poterba and Samwick (1999) for a review of the literature.

2. The SCF 1986 is not used in this analysis owing to its small sample size and the possibility that it represents a transition to the regime implemented by TRA86, which was actively discussed during the months when the survey was conducted.

3. The sampling design and construction of the sample weights that allow the two samples to be used together is discussed in Avery, Elliehausen, and Canner (1984a, 1984b), Heeringa, Conner, and Woodburn (1994), Kennickell and Woodburn (1992), Kennickell, McManus, and Woodburn (1996), and Kennickell and Woodburn (1997).

4. See also Avery, Elliehausen, and Kennickell (1988), Scholz (1994), and Antoniewicz (1996).

5. I am indebted to Ed Wolff for summarizing the changes necessary to reweight the data. The reweighting factors are as follows. For 1983 the factors are checking accounts (1.68), savings and time deposits (1.50), financial securities (1.20), stocks and mutual funds (1.06), and nonmortgage debt (1.16). The Wolff calculations use the full sample composite weight rather than the extended income weight, as in the unadjusted calculations. For 1989 the factors are checking accounts (1.361), thrift and other accounts (1.111), stocks, bonds, and trusts (1.795), and household income (1.123). The Wolff calculations use the average of the two design-based weights, whereas the unadjusted calculations use the design-based weights from Kennickell and Shack-Marquez (1992). For 1992 the factors are all deposits (1.32) and trusts (1.41). The Wolff calculations also reweight the sample weights by income category (increasing the representation of very high-income households in the SCF) to match the proportion of the sample with income over $1 million to published tabulations based on tax return data, as described in Wolff (this volume).

6. Two other factors support the use of the unadjusted weights. First, Antoniewicz (1996) shows that some discrepancies between the SCF and the Flow of Funds for 1989 and 1992 are attributable to different populations and definitions of items. Her comparisons yield estimates of wealth aggregates that are within one standard error of each other when these differences are eliminated. Second, even if the wealth reported in the Flow of Funds is deemed to be the correct number, it is not clear that all adjustments should be proportional. Such adjustments assume that the discrepancies in the SCF are due entirely to (proportional) underreporting by households that report they own the asset in question rather than misreporting by households that report they do not own the asset. Wolff's (this volume) comparisons of the high end of the income distributions in the SCF 1992 and the corresponding Statistics of Income are more troubling and clearly merit further study.

7. Asset allocations for retirement accounts are not directly reported in the SCF 1983 and so are imputed (conditionally on equity ownership outside of retirement accounts) from the allocations in the SCF 1989.

8. See Samwick (1996) for an analysis of the effect of TRA86 on tax shelters.

9. Two other important sources of MTR differences across households are due to state taxes and the estate tax.

10. Another approach would be to impute aggregate amounts or taxable shares based on reports of analogous quantities in the IRS Statistics of Income. Refining the precise calculations of marginal tax rates is the subject of work in progress.

11. See Sammartino and Weiner (1997) for a thorough discussion of OBRA90 and OBRA93 and an analysis of their effects on reported taxable income.

12. The effects of the tax reforms on aspects of the tax code other than the MTR, such as the base broadening that occurred during TRA86, are therefore reflected in the position of each household in the yearly distribution. Had the definition of taxable income remained the same between 1983 and 1989, many households in 1989 would have had lower marginal tax rates. This would have shifted the 1989 schedule to the left, abstracting from complications introduced by the marginal tax rate bubble in 1989.

13. The formation of clienteles is complicated by the presence of retirement accounts, which attach the tax preference to any asset held in the account. See Samwick (1997) for an elaboration of this point.

14. The econometric framework here is a slight variant of the one that Poterba and Samwick (1999) used to analyze the effects of taxation on household portfolios more broadly.

15. The gender variable is a dummy variable for a female-headed household. The marital status variable is a dummy variable for married households. The age categories are: under twenty-five, twenty-five to thirty-four, thirty-five to forty-four, forty-five to fifty-four, fifty-five to sixty-four, and sixty-five and over. The income categories are (in 1992 dollars): $0 to $15,000, $15,001 to $25,000, $25,001 to $50,000, $50,001 to $75,000, $75,001 to $100,000, $100,001 to $250,000, and $250,001 and over. The education categories are: less than high school, high school diploma, some college, college degree, and some graduate work. The occupation categories are: executives and professionals; clerical, technical, and sales; services; crafts; laborers; farmers; retired; and homemakers or other not in the labor force. The industry categories are: agriculture, forestry and fisheries; mining, construction, and manufacturing; services; and public administration.

16. When the model is estimated using the ratio of (1-ordinary MTR)/(1-capital gain MTR), the coefficient is positive with a p-value of 0.27, suggesting that the effect of the ordinary MTR is more important when the two tax rates are included separately in the regression.

17. Cordes and Galper (1985) discuss the market for tax shelters in the period before TRA86.

18. There is also an effect of taxes through the induced change in the variance of risky asset returns. See Auerbach and King (1983) for a derivation.

REFERENCES

Agell, Jonas, and Pers Anders Edin. 1990. "Marginal Taxes and the Asset Portfolios of Swedish Households." *Scandinavian Journal of Economics* 92: 47–64.

Antoniewicz, Rochelle L. 1996. "A Comparison of the Household Sector from the Flow of Funds Accounts and the Survey of Consumer Finances." Finance and Economics Discussion Series Paper 96-26. Washington, D.C.: Federal Reserve Board (July).

Auerbach, Alan J., and Mervyn A. King. 1983. "Taxation, Portfolio Choice, and Debt-Equity Ratios: A General Equilibrium Model." *Quarterly Journal of Economics* 98: 587–609.

Avery, Robert B., Gregory E. Elliehausen, and Glenn B. Canner. 1984a. "Survey of Consumer Finances, 1983." *Federal Reserve Bulletin* 70: 679–92.

————. 1984b. "Survey of Consumer Finances, 1983: A Second Report." *Federal Reserve Bulletin* 70: 857–68.

Avery, Robert B., Gregory E. Elliehausen, and Arthur B. Kennickell. 1988. "Measuring Wealth with Survey Data: An Evaluation of the 1983 Survey of Consumer Finances." *Review of Income and Wealth* 34: 339–69.

Cordes, Joseph J., and Harvey Galper. 1985. "Tax Shelter Activity: Lessons from Twenty Years of Experience." *National Tax Journal* 38: 305–24.

Curtin, Richard T., F. Thomas Juster, and James N. Morgan. 1989. "Survey Estimates of Wealth: An Assessment of Quality." In *The Measurement of Saving, Investment, and Wealth*, edited by Robert E. Lipsey and Helen Stone Tice. Chicago: University of Chicago Press.

Feldstein, Martin S. 1976. "Personal Taxation and Portfolio Composition: An Econometric Analysis." *Econometrica* 44: 631–49.

Feldstein, Martin S., and Joel Slemrod. 1980. "Personal Taxation, Portfolio Choice, and the Effect of the Corporation Income Tax." *Journal of Political Economy* 88: 854–66.

Galper, Harvey, Robert Lucke, and Eric Toder. 1988. "A General Equilibrium Analysis of Tax Reform." In *Uneasy Compromise: Problems of a Hybrid Income-Consumption Tax*, edited by Henry Aaron, Harvey Galper, and Joseph Pechman. Washington, D.C.: Brookings Institution.

Gordon, Roger H., and Jeffrey K. MacKie-Mason. 1990. "Effects of the Tax Reform Act of 1986 on Corporate Financial Policy and Organizational Form." In *Do Taxes Matter?: The Impact of the Tax Reform Act of 1986*, edited by Joel Slemrod. Cambridge, Mass.: MIT Press.

Hausman, Jerry A., and James M. Poterba. 1987. "Household Behavior and the Tax Reform Act of 1986." *Journal of Economic Perspectives* 1: 101–19.

Heeringa, Steven G., Judith H. Conner, and R. Louise Woodburn. 1994. "The 1989 Surveys of Consumer Finances Sampling Design and Weighting Documentation." Unpublished paper. Survey Research Center, University of Michigan, Ann Arbor.

Kennickell, Arthur B., Douglas A. McManus, and R. Louise Woodburn. 1996. "Weighting Design for the 1992 Survey of Consumer Finances." Unpublished paper. Federal Reserve Board (December), Washington, D.C.

Kennickell, Arthur B., and Janice Shack-Marquez. 1992. "Changes in Family Finances from 1983 to 1989: Evidence from the Surveys of Consumer Finances." *Federal Reserve Bulletin* 70: 1–18.

Kennickell, Arthur B., and R. Louise Woodburn. 1992. "Estimation of Household Net Worth Using Model-Based and Design-Based Weights: Evidence from the 1989 Survey of Consumer Finances." Unpublished paper. Federal Reserve Board, Washington, D.C.

————. 1997. "Consistent Weight Design for the 1989, 1992, and 1995 Surveys of Consumer Finances and the Distribution of Wealth." Unpublished paper. Federal Reserve Board, Washington, D.C.

Kimball, Miles S. 1993. "Standard Risk Aversion." *Econometrica* 61: 589–611.

King, Mervyn A., and Jonathan I. Leape. 1998. "Wealth and Portfolio Composition: Theory and Evidence." *Journal of Public Economics* 69: 155–93.

Miller, Merton. 1977. "Debt and Taxes." *Journal of Finance* 32: 261–76.

Poterba, James M., and Andrew A. Samwick. 1995. "Stock Ownership Patterns, Stock Market Fluctuations, and Consumption." *Brookings Papers on Economic Activity* 2: 295–371.

————. 1997. "Household Portfolio Allocation over the Life Cycle." Working paper 6185. Cambridge, Mass.: National Bureau of Economic Research (September).

————. 1999. "Taxation and Household Portfolio Composition: U.S. Evidence from Tax Reforms of the 1980s and 1990s." Working paper 7392. Cambridge, Mass. National Bureau of Economic Research.

Sammartino, Frank, and David Weiner. 1997. "Recent Evidence on Taxpayers' Response to the Rate Increases in the 1990s." *National Tax Journal* 50: 683–705.

Samwick, Andrew A. 1996. "Tax Shelters and Passive Losses After the Tax Reform Act of 1986." In *Empirical Foundations of Household Taxation*, edited by Martin S. Feldstein and James M. Poterba. Chicago: University of Chicago Press.

————. 1997. "The Tax-Adjusted Capital Asset Pricing Model." Unpublished paper. Dartmouth College, Hanover, N.H.

Scholz, John Karl. 1994. "Tax Progressivity and Household Portfolios: Descriptive Evidence from the Surveys of Consumer Finances." In *Tax Progressivity and Income Inequality*, edited by Joel Slemrod. Cambridge: Cambridge University Press.

Slemrod, Joel B. 1994. "On the High-Income Laffer Curve." In *Tax Progressivity and Income Inequality*, edited by Joel Slemrod. Cambridge: Cambridge University Press.

Wolff, Edward N. 1987. "Estimates of Household Wealth Inequality in the United States, 1962–1983." *Review of Income and Wealth* 33: 231–56.

———. 1994. "Trends in Household Wealth in the United States, 1962–1983 and 1983–1989." *Review of Income and Wealth* 40: 143–74.

Commentary on Chapter 9

James R. Hines Jr.

This very interesting study by Andrew Samwick comes to the intriguing conclusion that tax changes had little to do with observed portfolio reallocations over the period from 1983 to 1995 in the United States. Although this finding in no way demonstrates that tax rates have unimportant effects on asset holding patterns, it can easily be misread to this effect—and therefore the results may carry considerable shock value. For this reason alone, Samwick's study warrants close examination. It does so for other reasons as well, since the methods and data are quite interesting and may well lead to additional work that extends these efforts in several directions.

One of the difficulties in interpreting the chapter's results is that it does not offer a test of the proposition that taxes influence portfolio allocations. Indeed, it is virtually certain that any such test, properly conducted, would fail to reject the null hypothesis. A quick perusal of table 9.3 indicates that consumers with the greatest net worth, who face the highest marginal tax rates, tend to hold disproportionate fractions of their wealth in tax-preferred forms such as equities and tax-exempt bonds. Although it is possible that these asset clienteles reflect something other than tax-avoiding behavior, their existence is also consistent with very simple tax incentives that high-income investors understand perfectly well.

In order to understand the contribution of the analysis in this chapter, it is helpful first to review the data and measurement issues that it confronts, to evaluate the estimation procedure, and to consider the theoretical method employed by the study.

DATA AND MEASUREMENT

The primary data consideration is that the components of personal wealth are measured by surveys with considerable noise. Many individuals are unaware of the market values of their asset holdings (simple introspection usually serves to verify this)—and those who have such information may be unwilling to share it with survey questioners. This issue confronts almost all empirical studies of portfolio allocation.

There are several implications of inaccuracy in reported components of wealth. The first is the obvious point that mismeasurement of asset holdings reduces the explanatory power of variables that explain the components of wealth holding. Classical measurement error generally reduces the partial R^2 of a regression, in this case making it appear that tax incentives explain less of asset-holding patterns than they in fact do. Taken into first differences, measurement error makes tax changes appear to account for smaller fractions of changes in asset holdings than they in fact do.

A second implication is that mismeasurement introduces bias in estimated tax coefficients if tax rates are correlated with measurement error in market values of assets. Although it is difficult to evaluate the empirical significance of this point, it is easy to construct simple examples in which the bias may be quite large. Consider the (very plausible) case in which higher marginal tax rates among top-bracket taxpayers raise the prices of tax-exempt bonds. When the government raises top marginal tax rates, individuals in the top tax brackets generally respond by shifting greater fractions of their portfolios into tax-exempt bonds. Market values of tax-exempt debt change in response to the same tax changes. Top-bracket individuals with some long-term holdings of tax-exempt debt may underreport the values of their total holdings of such debt owing to the induced differences between market and book values. As a consequence, standard regression methods underestimate the effect of taxes on total tax-exempt debt holdings.

A different type of measurement problem stems from the serious difficulty of obtaining reliable information on the marginal tax rates of individual investors. The data used in the Samwick study omit state identifiers, thereby making it impossible to adjust properly for differences in marginal tax rates imposed by state governments. There is nothing that one can do about this problem (which is by no means unique to this study) other than to hope that whatever errors it introduces are orthogonal to tax and other important variables of interest.

Tax schedule nonlinearity creates a separate measurement problem. The marginal tax rate on investment income is generally a function of the character and amount of investment income and other income. As a consequence, the marginal tax rate is potentially endogenous to portfolio allocation decisions (as well as labor supply decisions). The Samwick study is fully cognizant of the econometric problems that such endogeneity poses and therefore uses in the econometric analysis, not the marginal tax rates that households actually face, but a "first-dollar" marginal tax rate that applies to the first modest amounts of ordinary capital income. The idea is that this first-dollar marginal tax rate is unaffected by actual portfolio allocations.

This is a sensible approach to the nonlinearity problem, albeit one that introduces other difficulties. The first associated difficulty is that first-dollar marginal tax rates are not what investors face, so in a sense they serve as instruments for actual marginal tax rates. Given that, one might consider using first-dollar marginal rates as instruments for actual marginal rates in an IV equation that would then be a more efficient and direct method of estimating the effect of taxes on portfolio allocations. The second difficulty with first-dollar marginal tax rates is that they are not actually exogenous to portfolio allocation decisions, since labor and other income sources used to distinguish consumers on the basis of first-dollar tax rates are themselves endogenous to portfolio decisions. The third difficulty has to do with the nonlinearity of the tax schedule for which the alternative minimum tax (AMT) and other provisions are responsible. These tax features can be of great importance to consumers with significant capital income. High-income taxpayers who have multiple tax preference items and earn significant amounts of interest from tax-exempt bonds may find themselves subject to the AMT. These taxpayers have incentives to limit their holdings of tax-exempt bonds. This incentive is reflected in demands for tax-exempt bonds that are nonlinear functions of first-dollar tax rates.

ESTIMATION

The econometric estimates presented in the Samwick study are based on pooling observations from several years and then estimating relationships between tax rates and asset holdings both within and between periods of analysis. An alternative method of analyzing asset demands would be to treat the sample as a panel of income types (ignoring that the identities of taxpayers in different income classes change over the sample period) and to identify tax effects through relative changes in tax rates between different income classes over time. The cost of such a procedure is that information contained in the correlation of cross-sectional asset holdings and tax rate differences is thereby discarded; the advantage of such a procedure is that the effect of tax rates on asset holdings is thereby better distinguished from the effect of income on asset holdings. As the estimates are currently obtained, most of the tax rate variation, and therefore most of the identification of the effect of tax rates, comes from cross-sectional rather than time series variation—and as a result it is extremely difficult to distinguish tax rate and income effects.

A more modest alternative is to estimate asset-holding patterns for a single base year and then use the estimated coefficients to predict changes in asset holdings induced by subsequent tax changes. The current method, in which projected changes in asset holdings are based on coefficients estimated using data for periods both before and after tax changes, permits the estimated coefficients to be influenced by asset holdings after the tax changes. This makes projected asset holdings endogenous to actual holdings, thereby complicating the interpretation of the fraction of variation explained by tax rate changes.

The Samwick study estimates demands for each asset category separately in evaluating the contribution of tax rate changes to asset-holding patterns. This estimation procedure is somewhat inefficient in not evaluating asset demands jointly as a system. Another way of putting the same point is that the estimation does not impose the identity that asset-holding shares sum to unity, thereby implying that shocks to demands for one asset category are negatively correlated with demands for assets in other categories. The advantage of imposing this identity is that the resulting estimates would be more efficient than the current estimates. The disadvantage of imposing the identity is that methods that do so are typically more parametric than the two-limit tobit procedure used currently and may therefore impose excessive structure on the estimates.

There is a diagnostic issue that concerns the interpretation of the joint significance of the two separate tax rates (marginal rates on ordinary income and on capital gains income) included as regressors in the specifications reported in table 9.5. The reported p-values indicate the level at which it is possible to reject the hypothesis that both tax rate coefficients are zero. In cases such as this one, however, it is perhaps equally important to characterize the full 95 percent confidence ellipse, since the very high degree of correlation between marginal tax rates on ordinary income and those on capital gains income raises the possibility that the estimated coefficients could be individually significant, in that one could reject the hypothesis that both coefficients are zero, but at the same time one might not be able to reject the hypothesis that both coefficients have signs that differ from those of the point estimates. Such cases arise when there is a high degree of correlation between the variables in question, a condition that is surely satisfied here. If, in fact, the 95 percent confidence interval has this feature, then one should be reluctant to draw strong conclusions from the sign pattern of the coefficient estimates.

METHOD

The Samwick study analyzes the effect of taxes on portfolio demands by considering the effect of tax changes on the distribution of asset holdings by asset class. This method relies on the idea that the relevant attributes of asset classes do not change in response to tax changes. In fact, tax-related asset attributes are probably endogenous to the tax structure. For example, high-tax-bracket individuals generally have stronger incentives to hold corporate stock than do low-tax-bracket individuals. If a tax reform increases top personal tax rates, then shares of firms that pay higher fractions of their profits as dividends become even less attractive to top-bracket taxpayers than they were before tax rates rose. Top-bracket taxpayers are likely to respond to higher tax rates in two ways: by shifting additional assets into corporate stock, and by changing the nature of the shares they hold in order to economize on dividend receipts (and take more of the return in the form of capital gains). Analysis of the effect of tax rates on shares of wealth invested in different categories of assets captures the first effect and omits the second.

The inclusion of year fixed effects in the estimation serves the useful function of abstracting from the effects of omitted variables that change over time but in so doing may also remove important economywide responses to tax changes. Changes in personal tax rates may induce firms to change their borrowing and dividend payout policies, encourage state and local governments to alter the amount of tax-exempt debt that they issue, and have other effects on financial markets generally. Year fixed effects in the estimation incorporate all of these responses to tax changes, leaving tax rate variables to capture only those tax effects that are idiosyncratic to taxpayers in particular income categories. There is nothing wrong with analyzing this subset of tax rate variation, but it is important to bear in mind that it captures only part of the impact of tax rate changes on asset markets and investment patterns.

Another methodological concern stems from the possible inappropriateness of the linear specification of the effect of tax rates on asset demands. For example, in a Miller equilibrium, economywide asset pricing guarantees that the highest-tax-bracket individuals have incentives to hold assets generating capital gains and other tax-preferred returns, and taxpayers facing lower marginal rates have incentives to hold assets generating ordinary income. A personal tax change that increases tax rate differences (such as an increase in the top marginal tax rate) does not actually affect this asset-holding pattern, since it serves merely to reinforce incentives that are already present. An econometric study might conclude that tax rate changes have no effect on asset holdings—even though the tax system *fully determines* the pattern of asset holding in the economy. Other types of tax changes in a Miller equilibrium might induce only a small subset of taxpayers—typically those who are close to indifferent between holding tax-preferred and tax-disadvantaged assets—to change their asset holdings. A simple linear specification of the effect of tax rates on asset hold-

ings incorrectly captures the effect of tax changes and might foster the erroneous conclusion that taxes have far less effect on asset demands than they actually do.

The method of evaluating the role of taxes in portfolio allocations by estimating
the fraction of portfolio changes for which tax changes appear to be responsible
evokes a process of evaluating the importance of a variable by its partial R^2 in a
regression. We would not want to recommend the widespread use of such a procedure in a cross-sectional regression context, for the obvious reason that a partial R^2
is generally uninformative concerning hypotheses. This is not at all to say that the
R^2 is uninteresting—only that it should not be taken in isolation to be anything like
a rigorous test of the hypothesis that a true coefficient is zero. Instead, the R^2 is a
supplemental piece of information that can be useful in judging the extent to which
variation is unexplained. So I believe that the evidence reported in this study is
appropriately evaluated as a supplement to other, more direct methods of evaluating the impact of tax changes on asset demands. This evidence is interesting and
intriguing, and it suggests a number of new directions for future studies of the effect
of tax policy on portfolio allocation.

10

The Estate Tax and After-Tax Investment Returns

James M. Poterba

Federal estate and gift taxes collected $17.5 billion in 1996, and state and local taxes on gifts and estates raised another $5.6 billion, according to the National Income and Product Accounts (table 3.4). Just over thirty thousand taxpayers filed federal estate tax returns for the most recent year (1995) for which data are available, so average estate taxes per taxpayer average several hundred thousand dollars. The top marginal estate tax rate is 60 percent, one of the highest statutory tax rates in the federal tax code.

To place the estate tax in perspective, it can be compared with another tax on capital income, the capital gains tax. In 1993 federal revenues from the individual income tax on capital gains totaled $33.1 billion. The Congressional Budget Office (1997) indicates that 17.7 million taxpayers reported capital gains income. Thus, the estate and gift tax raised half as much revenue as the capital gains tax, with much higher per-taxpayer burdens on a much smaller set of taxpayers.

Despite the high marginal tax rates that apply to taxable estates, there has been relatively little research on the economic effects of the estate tax. Henry Aaron and Alicia Munnell (1992) provide a recent survey of the literature in economics. There is a larger legal literature concerning the rationale for estate taxation, illustrated, for example, by Michael Graetz (1983) and Edward McCaffery (1994). With a few notable and recent exceptions, including Gerald Auten and David Joulfaian (1997), Joulfaian (1991), and Kathleen McGarry (1999), there are few theoretical studies of the incentive effects associated with estate taxation or of the empirical effects of estate taxation on the saving and portfolio allocation decisions of wealthy households. In part, this reflects the difficulty of obtaining survey data on the high-income, high-net-worth households that are affected by the estate tax. In part, it also reflects the lack of professional consensus, discussed, for example, by Louis Kaplow (1997) and Andre Masson and Pierre Pestieau (1997), on why households leave bequests. Some models postulate that bequests are accidental, others specify that they are intentional and motivated by intergenerational altruism, and still others view bequests as intentional but motivated by a "joy of giving." The efficiency cost associated with estate taxation depends on which of these models is the best description of transfer decisions by high-net-worth households.

Many analysts hold the view that the estate tax can be avoided by the use of sophisticated tax planning. George Cooper (1979) described some of these strategies, and recent articles in the popular press, such as Christopher Drew and David Cay Johnston (1996), have contributed to this perception. If the tax is easily avoided, however, it is not clear why it does raise substantial revenue, and why there was substantial political outcry in recent congressional debates to increase the floor below which estates are exempt from taxation.

This chapter presents an exploratory analysis of how the estate tax affects after-tax returns to capital accumulation. It attempts to place the estate tax in context so that it can be considered, along with taxes on interest, dividends, and capital gains, as an investor-level tax on capital income. The chapter is divided into four sections. The first section begins with a description of the pre-1997 structure of the U.S. estate tax as well as the changes that were enacted in the Taxpayer Relief Act of 1997 (TRA97). It also presents summary information on the characteristics of estate tax returns in recent years and on the concentration of estate tax payments.

The second section sketches a simple framework for evaluating the effect of the estate tax on expected returns from asset holding. It views the estate tax as a random tax on both the principal and the income associated with individual investments. The effective tax rate facing a given potential taxpayer depends on the statutory estate tax rate as well as the potential taxpayer's mortality risk. Because mortality rates rise with age, the effective estate tax burden is greater for older than for younger individuals.

The third section uses data from the 1992 and 1995 Surveys of Consumer Finances (SCFs) to evaluate the effective estate tax burden on households of different ages. The estate tax adds 0.3 percentage points to the average tax burden on capital income for households headed by individuals between the ages of fifty and fifty-nine. For households headed by individuals between the ages of seventy and seventy-nine, however, the estate tax increases the tax burden on capital income by approximately three percentage points. The effects are even greater for older households. This section also compares the flow of taxable estates that are recorded on estate tax returns with the flow that one would expect to observe given mortality rates and the current age-specific distribution of wealth in the U.S. population. This calculation provides an estimate of the degree to which end-of-life estate tax avoidance strategies, such as underestimation of the value of assets for estate tax purposes, are used to reduce estate tax burdens.

The fourth section explores the extent to which a simple estate tax avoidance strategy—making gifts to children and grandchildren—can reduce household estate tax burdens. Although households that are potentially liable for estate taxes could transfer roughly one-quarter of their net worth to their heirs through a systematic program of planned giving, the observed flow of inter vivos giving is substantially smaller than such a tax avoidance program would imply. This suggests the need for further study of the factors that determine inter vivos giving. A brief concluding section suggests several directions for additional research.

THE ESTATE TAX IN THE UNITED STATES:
CURRENT RULES AND SUMMARY STATISTICS

The federal estate tax has been integrated with the federal gift tax since 1977. This means that tax is levied on the value of assets transferred at the taxpayer's death, plus the value of taxable gifts that were made during the decedent's lifetime. There are two significant exemptions to these general rules. First, interspousal gifts and bequests are exempt from estate taxation. As a result, the transfers that occur when the first spouse dies are often untaxed, and estate taxes are due when the surviving spouse dies. Given the progressive structure of the estate tax, one strategy used by estate planners working with high-net-worth households involves *avoiding* the higher taxes that may be associated with passing all of a couple's assets to the surviving spouse, and then to the next generation. Second, each individual may make a tax-free gift of $10,000 per year per recipient. A married couple can transfer $20,000 per year to each child, grandchild, or other beneficiary. The $10,000 annual exemption will be indexed for inflation beginning in 1999.

In addition to the two exemptions described here, each household receives a credit against lifetime estate and gift taxes. Under pre-1997 law, each taxpayer received a tax *credit* of $192,800 against estate and gift tax liability: this was precisely the amount of estate tax liability on an estate of $600,000.[1] TRA97 gradually raises the threshold on the size of estates to which estate tax liability applies. The unified credit rises to increase the effective exempt amount to $625,000 in 1998, to further increase the threshold in intermittent increments to $700,000 in 2000, and then to $1,000,000 in 2006.[2] This increase in the exempt amount is recaptured in the form of a surcharge on estates valued at between $10,000,000 and $21,040,000, so that estates valued at more than $21,040,000 will not experience any reduction in taxes paid as a result of TRA97. TRA97 also includes a special provision for estates that include family-owned businesses and farms. Family-owned businesses valued at up to $1.3 million will be exempt from estate taxation effective January 1, 1998.

Table 10.1 reports the tax rates that apply to taxable estates and gifts for tax year 1996. Although the schedule shows tax rates for estates valued at less than $600,000, decedents whose estates and cumulated lifetime taxable gifts are valued at less than $600,000 do not pay any estate tax. The value of the unified estate and gift tax credit exceeds the estate tax liability for such decedents. For decedents whose taxable estates were valued at more than $600,000, the marginal estate tax rate on the 600,001st dollar of taxable estate is 37 percent. The highest statutory marginal estate tax rate is 55 percent. As a result of a surcharge that phases out the unified estate and gift tax credit, however, as well as the inframarginal estate tax rates of less than 55 percent, the highest effective marginal estate tax rate is 60 percent. This rate applies on estates valued at between $10 million and $21.04 million.

In addition to federal estate taxes, many states levy taxes on estates or inheritances. These taxes raise roughly one-third as much revenue as federal taxes. State death taxes are usually creditable against federal estate tax liability for those taxpayers with federal estate tax liability, but not all decedents whose estates pay state death taxes pay federal estate taxes. State death tax credits against federal estate tax liability are roughly half of the value of state estate tax revenues. In calculating the burden of estate taxes, however, it is important to recognize that state taxes raise the total revenue collected on transfers at death.

The 1997 legislative changes are the latest in a long history of changes, described in Pechman (1987), in the real value of the threshold below which

Table 10.1   Federal Unified Estate and Gift Tax Rates, 1996

Taxable Transfer	Marginal Tax Rate
$0 to $10,000	18
$10,001 to $20,000	20
$20,001 to $40,000	22
$40,001 to $60,000	24
$60,001 to $80,000	26
$80,001 to $100,000	28
$100,001 to $150,000	30
$150,001 to $250,000	32
$250,001 to $500,000	34
$500,001 to $600,000	37
$600,001 to $750,000	37
$750,001 to $1,000,000	39
$1,000,001 to $1,250,000	41
$1,250,001 to $1,500,000	43
$1,500,001 to $2,000,000	45
$2,000,001 to $2,500,000	49
$2,500,001 to $3,000,000	53
$3,000,001 to $4,000,000	55
$4,000,001 to $5,000,000	55
$5,000,001 to $10,000,000	55
$10,000,001 to $21,040,000	60[a]
Over $21,040,000	55

Source: Luckey (1995) and author's calculations.

[a.] The 60 percent marginal tax rate on estates valued at between $10 million and $21.04 million is the result of the phaseout of the unified estate and gift tax credit and inframarginal tax rates of below 55 percent for estates in this valuation range.

estates are not subject to federal tax. These movements have been associated with time series fluctuations in the fraction of estates that are subject to estate taxation. Table 10.2 shows how the variation in the real value of the estate tax exemption, or the combined estate and gift tax exemption since the estate and gift taxes were unified in 1976, has corresponded to changes in the fraction of deaths that are subject to the estate tax. Although roughly 1.5 percent of decedents in the mid-1990s could expect to pay estate tax, this percentage was as high as 7.7 percent in the late 1970s, before the Tax Reform Act of 1976 raised the estate tax exemption.[3]

Forecasts made prior to the 1997 tax reform suggested that the fraction of decedents paying estate taxes would rise in the next decade, as the entries in the bottom rows of table 10.2 suggest. The TRA97 reforms will reduce the fraction of future decedents who pay estate tax relative to pre-TRA97 law.

Table 10.3 provides descriptive information on the estate tax base and on the deductions that may be claimed against estate tax liability. The table relates the total value of assets held in estates for which estate tax returns were filed in 1995 to the federal estate tax revenue collected from these estates. The first row, "gross estates,"

Table 10.2   Taxable Estates as a Percentage of Deaths

Year	Taxable Estates/Deaths
1935	0.74
1940	1.04
1945	1.12
1950	1.33
1961	2.93
1970	5.20
1977	7.65
1982	1.81
1991	1.15
1995	1.37
2005 (projected, pre-TRA97)	2.64
2005 (projected, post-TRA97)	1.63[a]

Source: U.S. Congress Joint Committee on Taxation (JCT) (1997, tables 13 and 15).

[a.] The estimate of the fraction of deaths that will lead to taxable estates in 2005 is based on the author's estimate, multiplying the JCT estimate under pre-1997 law by the fraction of estates with net value of more than $600,000 in 1995 that were valued at more than $950,000. This fraction was estimated from data reported in Eller (1996) as the fraction of estates valued at more than $1 million, plus one-eighth times the fraction of estates valued at between $600,000 and $1 million.

indicates the gross value of the assets in estates with a gross value of greater than $600,000. The total value of these assets was $117.7 billion. Because the estate tax is unified with the gift tax, the relevant tax base also includes $3.3 billion in taxable gifts. Bequests to surviving spouses, which are not subject to estate tax, reduce the estate and gift tax base by $35.7 billion. Other deductions from the estate tax base, notably those for charitable deductions and outstanding debts, reduced the estate tax base by another $17.8 billion. The resulting value of taxable estates was $68.9 billion.

Tentative estate tax on the base of $68.9 billion is $27.01 billion, which suggests an average estate tax rate of 39.2 percent. This value is calculated by applying the tax rates shown in table 10.1 to the taxable estate and gift tax base for each estate. There are several credits, however, that reduce federal estate tax collections. The most important is the unified estate and gift tax credit, which reduces tax collections by $13.29 billion and removes a substantial number of estates with gross value of more than $600,000 from the category of "taxable estates." Federal credits for state death taxes reduce estate tax revenue by another $3.02 billion, and other credits lead to a further reduction of $0.79 billion. The result is a federal estate tax liability of $11.84 billion, or 17.1 percent of the value of taxable estates. The fact that federal credits for state death taxes are only about half as great as the value of these taxes suggests that state taxes do affect the total tax burden on estates.

Many of the decedents who face estate taxation have estates that are close to the current estate tax threshold, although most of the estate tax is paid by decedents with gross estates well above the threshold. Table 10.4 presents relevant informa-

Table 10.3 Distribution of Taxable Estate Tax Returns by Size of Gross Estate: 1995 Estate Tax Filings

Size of Gross Estate	Number of Taxable Returns	Net Estate Tax (Billions)
$600,000 to 1,000,000	13,830	$0.65
$1,000,001 to $2,500,000	12,710	3.00
$2,500,001 to $5,000,000	3,298	2.75
$5,000,001 to $10,000,000	1,105	2.05
$10,000,001 to $20,000,000	390	1.38
Over $20,000,000	231	2.00
Total	31,564	11.84

Source: Eller (1996, table 1d).

tion drawn from estate tax returns filed in 1995. Of the 31,564 taxable estate tax returns filed, 43.8 percent (13,830) had gross estates valued at between $600,000 and $1 million. If TRA97 had been phased in fully in 1995, these decedents would not have been liable for estate tax. Some decedents have very high net worth, and this leads to substantial concentration in estate tax payments. The 231 estate tax returns filed for estates valued at more than $20 million, which represented only 0.7 percent of the estate tax returns (and roughly one-ten-thousandth of all deaths) accounted for 17 percent of all estate tax payments. By comparison, the 44 percent of estate tax returns with gross estates between $600,000 and $1 million in 1995 accounted for only 5.5 percent of total estate tax revenue. Estate tax liability is highly skewed because the underlying distribution of net worth is highly skewed, and because the progressive tax schedule accentuates this skewness.

The estate tax exemption for interspousal transfers implies that estate tax is often deferred until the death of the longest-surviving partner in a married couple. Table

Table 10.4 Relationship Between Gross Estate Value, Deductions, and Federal Estate Tax Revenue for Estate Tax Returns Filed in 1995

Accounting Concept	Magnitude (Billions)
Gross estates	$117.74
Adjusted taxable gifts	3.31
(Bequests to surviving spouse)	(35.73)
(Charitable deductions)	(8.71)
(Debts and mortgages)	(6.10)
(Other deductions)	(2.99)
Adjusted taxable estates	68.92
Tentative estate tax	27.01
(Gift tax)	0.62
(Allowable unified credit)	13.29
(State death tax credits)	3.02
(Other tax credits)	0.17
Net estate tax	11.84

Source: Eller (1996).

10.5 reports information on the age distribution for 1992 decedents whose estates paid estate tax.[4] The table shows that 16,805 (62 percent) of the 27,243 taxable estate tax returns were for decedents who were over eighty years of age, and that these tax returns accounted for 66 percent of the estate taxes paid. In contrast, decedents who were less than seventy years of age accounted for only 13 percent of estate tax liability. This concentration of estate tax liability at extreme ages is reflected in the age-specific pattern of effective tax rates shown later in the chapter.

ESTATE TAX AND THE EXPECTED AFTER-TAX RETURN TO SAVING: A FRAMEWORK

Estate taxes are taxes on capital. An individual who earns labor income and consumes this income over the course of his lifetime is not liable for estate taxes, but an individual who saves part of his labor income and accumulates a stock of capital assets may face estate tax liability. This could occur if the individual dies unexpectedly, thereby leaving assets that he planned to consume if he had lived longer, and it could also be the result of a planned decision to transfer some assets to succeeding generations.

Most research on capital income taxation does not consider estate taxes as part of the capital tax burden. Estate taxes are typically omitted in formulating the user cost of capital for corporations and in estimating the total tax burden on corporate capital income, as in Feldstein and Summers (1979) or Poterba (1998). Yet even though estate taxes are small by comparison to household net worth, they are not trivial by comparison to total capital income. In recent years federal estate tax payments have been between 2 and 3 percent of the sum of personal interest receipts, dividends, cap-

Table 10.5   Age Distribution, 1992 Decedents Whose Estates Filed Estate Tax Returns

Age	Number of Returns	Gross Estate (Billions)	Taxes Paid (Billions)
Men			
Under fifty	390	$2.59	$0.10
Fifty to fifty-nine	534	4.96	0.14
Sixty to sixty-nine	1,468	11.96	0.52
Seventy to seventy-nine	2,859	19.10	1.14
Eighty and over	6,351	25.53	2.83
Total men	11,602	64.14	4.73
Women			
Under fifty	132	0.61	0.04
Fifty to fifty-nine	307	1.49	0.09
Sixty to sixty-nine	1,241	4.71	0.48
Seventy to seventy-nine	3,507	8.73	1.10
Eighty and over	10,454	24.48	4.07
Total women	15,641	40.01	5.78
Total (men and women)	27,243	104.15	10.51

Source: Eller (1996, 60–64).

ital gains, trust income, partnership and S corporation income, rent, and royalties. Adding state death taxes would raise this value to more than 3 percent. Thus, estate taxes are large enough to represent a substantial component of the capital income tax burden. Their concentration among a small set of taxpayers, moreover, raises the possibility of substantial incentive effects on taxpayer behavior.

One way to address the effective tax burden associated with the estate tax is simply to divide estate tax revenue by a measure of pre-tax capital income in the U.S. economy. As table 10.4 shows, federal estate tax returns filed in 1995 yielded $11.8 billion in federal estate taxes and were credited for another $3.0 billion in state death taxes. Total state death taxes in 1995, as reported in the national income and product accounts, were $5.5 billion. To estimate the flow of capital income, I start with a stock of assets and apply a rate-of-return measure. I assume a two-year lag between the date of death and the date at which an estate tax return is filed. The Federal Reserve *Balance Sheets of the U.S. Economy* estimate that the net worth of taxable individuals, defined as net worth of the household sector as shown in table B.100 less net financial assets of nonprofit institutions as shown in table L.100a, to be $22.6 trillion at the end of 1992. If the real rate of return on assets were 6 percent per year, then the capital income flow generated by household net worth would be $1.36 trillion. Estate taxes of $17.3 billion would therefore equal 1.27 percent of the capital income flow. If the real return on assets were greater, the effective tax burden due to the estate tax would be lower, and vice versa.[5]

This simple calculation does not provide any information on the effective tax burden on different asset classes or on different types of households. With respect to asset classes, the portfolios of decedents who face estate tax differ in important ways from the portfolios of the household sector as a whole. Martha Britton Eller (1996) reports that on estate tax returns filed in 1995, 32.7 percent of the gross value of taxable estates was accounted for by closely held stock or other corporate stock investments. At the end of 1992, however, the Federal Reserve *Balance Sheets* data suggest that closely held and traded equities accounted for 26.5 percent of net worth for the household sector. Personal residences correspondingly figure more prominently in household net worth than in the portfolios of decedents who face estate tax. These disparities suggest that the burden of the estate tax may fall more heavily on some asset classes than on others. However, the potential endogeneity of household portfolio structure makes it difficult to model this effect.[6]

It is more straightforward to explore differences in estate tax burdens across households, at least those that may be due to exogenous factors such as household age. I now consider a simple model of the effect of estate taxation on an investor's expected after-tax return; in the next section, I apply this model to data from the Survey of Consumer Finances. To fix ideas, the analysis begins with a two-period setting, in which mortality is random. Let p denote the probability that a dynastic family "head" dies between periods 1 and 2, W_1 the initial dynastic wealth, r the pretax return on investment assets, τ the income tax rate that applies to capital income flows, τ_e the estate tax rate, and C_1 the dynastic head's consumption in period 1. Let S_1 denote saving by the dynastic head ($W_1 - C_1$) in period 1. Dynastic wealth in period 2 depends on whether the family head dies before period 2. The analysis implicitly assumes an altruistically linked dynasty, for which the value of dynastic wealth is a summary statistic for dynastic utility. The expected value of period 2 wealth is given by:

$$E(W_2) = (W_1 - C_1) \times \{[1 + r(1 - \tau)](1 - p) + (1 - \tau_e)[1 + r(1 - \tau)]p\}. \qquad (10.1)$$

The presence of the estate tax reduces the expected value of dynastic wealth in period 2 for any level of saving in period 1.

If there were no taxes on estates or capital income, then the return to saving, measured as the change in the expected value of period 2 wealth per dollar of saving in period 1, would be:

$$d\{E(W_2)\}/dS_1 = 1 + r. \qquad (10.2)$$

With a capital income tax as well as an estate tax, this becomes

$$d\{E(W_2)\}/dS_1 = [1 + r(1 - \tau)](1 - p) + (1 - \tau_e)[1 + r(1 - \tau)]p$$
$$= 1 + r - r\tau - p\tau_e[1 + r(1 - \tau)] \qquad (10.3)$$

The third term on the right hand side of equation (10.3), $-r\tau$, is the standard effect of capital income taxation in reducing the rate of return to savers. The last term is the estate tax term, which generates a further reduction in the after-tax return to saving. This term is proportional to p, the saver's mortality probability.

To illustrate the potential importance of the estate tax effect, consider a simple example in which $\tau = .40$, $r = .10$, $\tau_e = .50$, and $p = .05$. This would correspond to an elderly household, since the one-year mortality rate for men does not reach 5 percent until their seventies, and for women not until their early eighties. The late marginal estate tax rate of 50 percent would correspond to an estate of more than $2 million. In this example, the return to saving in the absence of any capital income taxes or estate taxes would be 10 percent. With the capital income tax, the return declines to 6 percent, and with the estate tax and the capital income tax, it declines to 3.4 percent. Thus, the estate tax raises the effective tax rate in this example by twenty-six percentage points, from 40 percent to 66 percent. Even if the marginal estate tax rate is set at 10 percent, rather than 50 percent, as a possible "correction" for taxpayer opportunities to avoid the tax, the effective tax rate rises from .40 to .45.

This analysis simply describes the potential impact of the estate tax on the rate of return. To evaluate its impact on saving, one would need estimates of the interest elasticity of saving on the part of affected households. It is widely recognized that changes in after-tax returns have income, substitution, and wealth effects, and that the net effect of such changes on consumption and saving decisions can be theoretically ambiguous.[7] One particular difficulty with respect to the estate tax is that the key saving elasticities are those that apply to high-net-worth households, a population subgroup that is often not represented in any substantial way in the randomly drawn cross-sectional and panel data bases used to estimate the behavioral effects of tax policy.[8]

ESTIMATED ESTATE TAX BURDENS: EVIDENCE FROM THE SURVEY OF CONSUMER FINANCES

This section uses the 1992 and 1995 Surveys of Consumer Finances to estimate the effective estate tax burden described in the last section. The Surveys of Consumer Finances are stratified random samples of households in the U.S. population. The surveys include a random population sample, as well as a sample that is drawn from information on tax returns overweight to households with high levels of capital income. The SCF is generally regarded as the best data available on the asset and liability positions of U.S. households, and the best information on the high-net-worth segment of the population.

To perform calculations regarding the effective estate tax rate on capital income, one needs information on mortality probabilities as well as on the cross-sectional distribution of wealth holdings. There are two "life tables" that one might use for these calculations. The first is the population life table, reported by the Social Security Administration Office of the Actuary (Bell et al. 1992). It describes the probability of death at various ages for individuals chosen randomly from the population at large. The potential limitation of the population life table is the well-documented fact that high-income, high-wealth individuals have lower mortality rates than low-income, low-wealth individuals (see Attanasio and Hoynes, forthcoming; Guralnik et al. 1993). Because the estate tax affects only households with substantial net worth, calculations about estate tax burdens may be more revealing if they are based on mortality tables that apply to this segment of the population.

A second mortality table that may better describe the mortality rates facing high-net-worth households is the Individual Annuitant Life Table, which is described in Mitchell, Poterba, and Warshawsky, and Brown (1999). The annuitant life table describes the mortality experience of individuals who purchase single-premium annuities from life insurance companies. These individuals typically have sufficient accumulated resources to purchase policies with initial premiums of between $50,000 and $100,000, so they are from the upper tail of the wealth distribution. Age-specific mortality rates in the individual annuitant table are between 25 percent and 35 percent lower than those in the population life table.

To compute the effective burden of the estate tax, the SCF data can be used to evaluate the following expression, which is the sum over all households of their expected estate tax liability:

$$E(\text{Estate Tax}) = \Sigma_h \, q_h \times \tau_e(NW_h). \tag{10.4}$$

The term q_h denotes the probability that the older generation in a household will "die off" during the year, NW_h denotes the net worth of household h, including the face value of any life insurance policies, and $\tau_e(NW_h)$ denotes the estate tax function, which determines estate tax liability as a function of household net worth. For single households, q_h is just the probability of dying during the year: it depends on the age and sex of the household member. For married couples, q_h is the probability that both spouses will die within the year.

Given an estimate of the expected value of estate tax payments, this can be compared with an estimate of the rate of return on household net worth ($\Sigma_h \, r_h \times NW_h$

where r_h denotes the rate of return earned by household h and H is the total number of households) to estimate the effective estate tax burden. Alternatively, in the framework developed in equations (10.1) through (10.3), the effective estate tax burden is $p\tau_e[1 + r(1 - \tau)]/r$. The numerator of this expression is the expected estate tax payment, and the denominator is the pre-tax return on each unit of capital.

The treatment of term life insurance in computing net worth in equation (10.4) deserves comment. Many young and middle-aged households have net worth that would not place them above the threshold for estate tax liability, but they also have substantial amounts of term life insurance. Consider the case of a married couple with $400,000 of net worth but $1,000,000 of term life insurance in force. If both spouses were to die, at least under simple assumptions about the structure of their will and estate plan, their estate would pay estate taxes. The foregoing calculations therefore include the face value of term life insurance in estimating the expected value of estate tax payments. Because most wealth, however, is held by older households, most of which have modest holdings of life insurance, this assumption is not central to the analysis.

The first column of table 10.6 reports the estimated net federal estate tax liability for households in the 1995 Survey of Consumer Finances. This estimate assumes that each estate claims the average level of charitable deductions and funeral expense deductions for estates in its gross estate value category.[9] This leads to an estimate of gross federal estate tax liability for each estate, which is then reduced by the aver-

Table 10.6   Estimated Estate Tax Liability and Effective Tax Rates, 1995 Survey of Consumer Finances

Age of Household Head	Estimated Federal Estate Tax	Effective Total Tax Rate	Tax Rate
Population life table			
Under fifty	$0.4	0.1	0.1
Fifty to fifty-nine	0.9	0.3	0.4
Sixty to sixty-nine	2.8	1.0	1.4
Seventy to seventy-nine	5.1	2.7	3.5
Eighty and over	13.8	19.0	25.0
Total	23.0	1.9	2.5
Annuitant mortality table			
Under fifty	0.2	0.1	0.1
Fifty to fifty-nine	0.5	0.2	0.2
Sixty to sixty-nine	1.5	0.5	0.7
Seventy to seventy-nine	3.3	1.7	2.3
Eighty and over	10.2	13.9	18.4
Total	15.7	1.3	1.7

Source: Author's calculations.
Notes: Calculations include the face value of life insurance policies in the estimate of net worth for estate tax purposes, but not in the calculation of net worth for the denominator calculations. in column 2. The effective tax rate calculation assumes that households earn a 6 percent real return, on average, on their net worth. To compute effective tax rates at other rates of return (say X), multiply the last column by .06/X. The net worth held by households in the various age categories is $6.9 trillion (under fifty), 4.9 (fifty to fifty-nine), 4.5 (sixty to sixty-nine), 3.2 (seventy to seventy-nine), 1.2 (eighty and over), for a total net worth of $20.7 trillion.

age level of state death tax credits for estates in the decedent's gross estate valuation class. The estimate of net federal estate taxes is sensitive to the mortality table that is used. With the annuitant life table, estimated federal estate taxes are $15.7 billion, compared with $23 billion with the population life table. These estimates are of the same order of magnitude as federal estate tax collections.

The second column of table 10.6 presents the effective federal tax rate calculation under the assumption that households can earn an average real return of 6 percent on assets in their portfolios. The effective estate tax rate varies from an average value of 1.3 percent in the case that assumes that wealth-holders face the annuitant mortality table to an average of 1.9 percent using the population mortality table.

The calculations in the first two columns of table 10.6 focus on net federal estate taxes, but they do not include state death taxes. In 1996 the National Income and Products Accounts show that state estate taxes (S) collected $5.6 billion, when net federal estate taxes (F_N) were $17.5 billion.[10] To compute the total tax burden on decedents I therefore multiply the effective net federal estate tax burdens in column 2 of table 10.6 by 1.32, which equals $(S + F_N)/F_N$, to obtain total effective tax burdens. These are shown in the last column of table 10.6. The combined federal and state effective estate tax rate ranges from an average value of 1.7 percent using the annuitant mortality table, and 2.5 percent using the population life table.

Table 10.6 also shows that there is substantial heterogeneity in the effective estate tax burden across age categories, with those aged eighty and above facing the most substantial burdens. Even in the most conservative case, the total effective estate tax burden on households with heads who are eighty or more years old is 18.4 percent; in the less conservative case, it rises to 25 percent. These high rates simply reflect the higher mortality rates faced by households headed by those aged eighty and above.[11] For households headed by individuals between the ages of sixty and sixty-nine, the estimates suggest an effective estate tax rate of 0.7 and 1.4 percent. These effective tax rates are net-worth-weighted-averages over all households in a given age category. As such, they recognize that most of the households headed by persons in each age category will not face estate tax liability, but that a small fraction of households, with a substantial fraction of the age group's net worth, will face estate taxation.

The estimate of a effective estate tax rate of between 1.7 and 2.5 percentage points is somewhat larger than the estimate of a tax burden of 1.3 percentage points that resulted from dividing total estate taxes by an estimate of total capital income. This may reflect a somewhat smaller total asset base in the Survey of Consumer Finances than in the Federal Reserve *Balance Sheets,* or it could reflect the use of discounted asset valuations in filing actual estate tax returns. If the values of assets reported in the Survey of Consumer Finances are higher than the values that would be reported for the same assets if they appeared on an estate tax return, this could explain the pattern of results.

The estimates in table 10.6 provide new information on an issue raised by Edward Wolff (1996), namely, the relationship between taxable estates in a given year and the expected value of taxable estate wealth that would be generated by applying standard mortality tables to age-specific wealth data. The expected value of intergenerational wealth transfers and the associated estate taxes can be compared with observed transfers and estate taxes, and the difference between the two can be attributed to estate tax avoidance *at death*.[12] This is an imperfect measure of estate tax avoidance, because successful tax planning would transfer resources from the older generation to younger heirs so that the reported net worth of the older households, those with substantial mortality probabilities, would be reduced.

The estimated estate tax liability in table 10.6 corresponds quite closely to actual estate tax liability in recent years. This stands in contrast to Wolff's (1996) claim that projected estate tax liability based on the 1992 SCF was $44 billion, compared with $10.3 billion in estate tax collections for 1993. There are a number of potential explanations for this divergence. One is that Wolff uses the population mortality table, which yields a higher estimate of intergenerational transfers and estate tax liability than the annuitant mortality table. A second is that Wolff relies on a reweighted version of the 1992 SCF, with weights that generate a larger total wealth stock than the public-use weights, particularly among high-net-worth households. Further analysis of the source of these differences is left to future research.

THE POTENTIAL FOR ESTATE TAX AVOIDANCE: PLANNED GIVING

Estate tax avoidance is one of the most complicated aspects of tax planning. Many of the tools that high-net-worth households use to avoid estate taxes are not advertised to the general public, in part out of concern for IRS action that might limit their use. Yet there are some estate-planning tools that are widely recognized and understood: the most prominent of these is the use of inter vivos giving. The extent to which inter vivos giving reduces estate tax collections depends on the age at which those with wealth begin to make such gifts, the size of such gifts, and the number of beneficiaries who are the recipients of such gifts. Even taking full advantage of such gifts, many very high-net-worth households may be unable to avoid estate tax liability.

This point can be illustrated as follows. Consider a married couple, both of whom are forty years old. They currently have two children, each of whom will marry and bear two grandchildren when the couple is sixty-five. The current forty-year-olds are interested only in transferring wealth to their children and grandchildren. How much can they expect to transfer? Assume that each of the forty-year-olds faces the "life table" for which $S_{b,j}$ denotes the probability that both spouses are alive when they are aged $40 + j$, $S_{h,j}$ denotes the probability that only the husband is alive at age $40 + j$, and $S_{w,j}$ denotes the probability that only the wife is alive. Further assume that the children and grandchildren are certain to survive both spouses, and that the real interest rate is constant at r. In this case, assuming (as it will be after 1999) that the $10,000 annual limit is specified in real terms, the present value of the transfer that the married couple can make is given by:

$$EPDV = \sum_{j=1}^{25} \frac{S_{bj} \times 40 + \left(S_{hj} + S_{wj}\right) \times 20}{\left(1+r\right)^{j}} + \sum_{j=26}^{\infty} \frac{S_{bj} \times 160 + \left(S_{hj} + S_{wj}\right) \times 80}{\left(1+r\right)^{j}} \quad (10.5)$$

By comparing this expected present discounted value to the amount of wealth that the household currently holds, we can obtain an estimate on the fraction of wealth that can be transferred to the next generation through inter vivos gifts.

This calculation focuses on the fraction of *current wealth* (Wealth$_0$) that can be transferred with a program of planned giving, that is, on PDV$_0$(Transfers)/Wealth$_0$. This is not necessarily the same as the fraction of a household's net worth at the time of death, inclusive of the present value of past gifts, that will have been transferred (this would equal PDV$_T$(Transfers)/[PDV$_T$(Transfers)+Wealth$_T$].

The latter calculation may seem like the more natural way to measure the potential estate tax avoidance associated with inter vivos gifts, but it is also problematic for several reasons. The most important is that to calculate the second ratio, one must project the wealth that *will be accumulated (or decumulated)* in the decedent household's remaining years. If the household is likely to accumulate substantial additional assets by saving out of labor income, then the measure proposed here will be greater than the ratio measured at the time of death. On the other hand, if the household is likely to decumulate a substantial fraction of its assets through nursing home expenses, medical costs, or other outlays, then the calculation presented here will yield a "transfer ratio" that is smaller than the ratio that would be computed at the decedent's death. As an extreme example of this, it is possible that some households that have enough wealth at the time of the survey to be classified as potential "estate tax households" will have drawn down their wealth to finance their own consumption in the years before their death, and that they will no longer be affected by the estate tax.[13]

The ideal database for performing these calculations would combine information on the value of the taxable estate at the time of the decedent's death with a lifetime record of gifts made by the decedent. With such data, it would be straightforward to compute the ratio of the present discounted value of past gifts (that is, past gifts would have their value increased to reflect the value of subsequent returns on these gifts) to the value of the decedent's estate. Unfortunately, the data to perform such calculations do not appear to exist in any public-use data file.

The SCF data can be used to develop a crude estimate of the prospective power of planned giving to reduce estate tax burdens. In addition to data on household net worth, the SCF contains information on the ages of the household head and other household members and on the number of children who live both inside and outside the household. There is unfortunately no information on the total number of grandchildren who are related to household members, and there is only crude information on the ages of children who no longer live in the household. The SCF does provide information on grandchildren who live in the respondent's household, but that is likely to represent only a small fraction of the grandchildren who might receive inter vivos gifts.

By making several additional assumptions about family structure and household behavior, one can use the SCF data to estimate the present discounted value of the inter vivos transfers that households can make over the remainder of their lifetimes. The auxiliary assumptions include:

1. The mortality rates of husbands and wives are independent, and they are described by the Annuity 2000 mortality table "backcast" to apply to 1995.

2. Single individuals make gifts of $10,000 per year to each of their children and grandchildren each year; married couples make gifts of $20,000 to each potential recipient. The amount of these gifts is indexed for the calculations that consider the $1 million threshold for estate tax liability, since TRA97 raised this threshold and also indexed the $10,000 gift limit.

3. Children (grandchildren) always outlive their parents (grandparents).

4. The real discount rate is 3 percent per year.[14]

5. Children of the household head who live outside the household and are at least eighteen years old are assumed to have 1.8 children.

These "grandchild imputations" are based on average family sizes as reported in the *Statistical Abstract of the United States, 1996* (table 106). The assumption that all children outside the household have this average number of children may overstate the opportunity for inter vivos transfers, so I report estimates of transfers with and without the grandchild imputation. The limitation to lineal descendants, however, is an offsetting bias that may understate the extent to which high-net-worth households can transfer resources to younger generations.

The results of calculations based on these assumptions are shown in table 10.7. The first three rows present summary tabulations based on the 1995 SCF. They

Table 10.7   Impact of Inter Vivos Giving on Estate Tax Liability

| | | Age | | | |
	Population	Over Forty	Over Fifty	Over Sixty	Over Seventy
Number of households (millions)	99.0	63.1	41.3	28.1	15.4
Net worth (trillions)	$20.7	18.6	13.8	8.9	4.4
Net worth plus face value of life insurance (LI) (trillions)	$29.6	24.2	16.1	9.8	4.7
Households with net worth plus life insurance greater than $600,000					
Number (millions)	9.5	7.9	4.9	2.8	1.2
Net worth (trillions)	$13.3	12.6	9.4	5.7	2.7
Taxable net worth including life insurance (trillions)	$11.9	11.1	7.9	4.6	2.1
Taxable wealth reduction from program of giving to children					
Starting immediately (trillions)	$2.7	2.5	1.6	0.9	0.3
Starting at age sixty (trillions)	$1.9	1.8	1.4	0.9	0.3
Taxable wealth reduction from program of immediate giving to children and grandchildren (trillions)	$3.9	3.6	2.7	1.6	0.6
Households with net worth plus life insurance greater than $1,000,000					
Number (millions)	4.6	4.1	2.5	1.5	0.6
Net worth (trillions)	$10.9	10.4	7.9	4.8	2.2
Taxable net worth including life insurance (trillions)	$9.3	8.8	6.4	3.8	1.8
Taxable wealth reduction from program of giving to children					
Starting immediately (trillions)	$2.0	1.9	1.3	0.7	0.2
Starting at age sixty (trillions)	$1.6	1.5	1.1	0.7	0.2
Taxable wealth reduction from program of immediate giving to children and grandchildren (trillions)	$3.0	2.9	2.2	1.2	0.5

Source: Author's calculations using 1995 Survey of Consumer Finances.

show that roughly 90 percent of household net worth, which totals $20.7 trillion, is held by households in which the household head is over the age of forty. (Note for comparative purposes that at the end of 1994 the *Balance Sheets* reported household net worth, exclusive of financial assets held by nonprofits, of $23.7 trillion.) In the SCF, the total of net worth and the face value of life insurance is $29.6 trillion.

The next set of tabulations in table 10.7 presents information on households whose net worth plus outstanding life insurance policies totaled more than $600,000 in 1995. There were 9.5 million such households, with net worth of $13.3 trillion, or approximately two-thirds of outstanding net worth. These are the households that might be liable for estate tax. Their taxable net worth, which equals net worth and life insurance in excess of $600,000 per household, is $11.9 trillion.

The next three rows in the table consider the reductions in taxable net worth that follow from various tax reduction strategies. The first is a policy of immediate inter vivos giving to children. The present discounted value of these gifts is $2.7 trillion; this represents a 23 percent reduction in the taxable net worth of these households. If the household head does not begin to make inter vivos gifts until he or she turns sixty, then the corresponding wealth transfer is smaller: the expected present discounted value is $1.9 trillion, or 16 percent of initial wealth. If transfers to grandchildren are allowed and grandchildren are imputed according to the algorithm already described, then the present value of inter vivos gifts rises to $3.9 trillion, or 33 percent of taxable net worth.

The lower panel of table 10.7 presents similar information for the case in which the threshold for estate tax liability is $1 million, as it will be after 2006, rather than $600,000. Raising the estate tax threshold reduces taxable net worth and the face value of life insurance from $11.9 trillion to $9.3 trillion. The share of net worth that can be transferred with an immediate planned giving program targeted only to the household's children would allow the transfer of $2 trillion (in present discounted value), or 22 percent of taxable net worth.

The foregoing calculations suggest the substantial power of inter vivos gifts to reduce the value of taxable estates, but they also raise a question about the extent to which households take advantage of such gift opportunities. If each of the 9.5 million households with current net worth plus life insurance in excess of $600,000 made $10,000 transfers ($20,000 transfers in the case of married couples) to all of their children, the annual transfer flow would be approximately $443 billion.[15] Data on actual transfers from the Survey of Consumer Finances suggest much smaller financial transfers from the old to the young. The magnitude of such transfers depends on whether one uses reports by donors or recipients as the basis for estimation; William G. Gale and John Karl Scholz (1994) note that in the 1983 SCF donors report larger transfers than recipients. The aggregate value of transfers, as reported by donors, is $62.3 billion. SCF gift *recipients* report average inter vivos transfers received over the period from 1993 to 1995 of $18.9 billion per year. This may understate actual transfer receipts because an additional $41.4 billion of "gifts" over this three-year period are coded ambiguously, either as "other" or without information on whether they were inheritances or inter vivos gifts. Even including these transfers as representing inter vivos gifts would raise the annual reported flow of receipts to only $32.7 billion per year. Nevertheless, whether one takes $62.3 billion, $18.9 billion, or some value in between as the best estimate of inter vivos gifts, it is clear that transfers are much lower than one would predict if estate tax avoidance were the only objective of these households.

These findings comport with results from special Treasury tabulations of estate tax returns in 1945, 1951, 1957, and 1959, as reported in Pechman (1987, 244). These data show that among millionaire decedents in these years, the fraction of wealth transferred with lifetime gifts ranged from 9 percent (1957) to 24 percent (1945). Although these special tabulations suggest a decline in the importance of gifts between 1945 decedents and 1959 decedents, subsequent tabulations have not revisited this question.

The cross-sectional data in the Survey of Consumer Finances do provide some support for the hypothesis that households that are more likely to face estate taxes are also more likely to engage in inter vivos giving. The 1995 SCF shows, for example, that among households with heads aged sixty-five or over, the probability of making any financial transfer to persons not in the household was 9.8 percent for households with a net worth of less than $600,000, compared with 24.2 percent for those with a net worth above $600,000 and hence potentially subject to the estate tax. Kathleen McGarry (1999) presents additional evidence on greater use of gifts of $10,000 per year by households in the AHEAD data file who have net worth greater than the threshold at which they would face estate taxation. Whether the higher probability of transfers at net worth levels above the estate tax threshold can be attributed to the incentive effects of the estate tax, or whether it is simply the result of a positive net worth elasticity of transfer-making, is unclear. What is clear is that nearly three-quarters of the elderly households for whom the estate tax may loom as a potential burden are *not* making transfers. This suggests the need for further attention to the issues raised in Bernheim, Shleifer, and Summers (1985) about the reluctance to use inter vivos transfers rather than transfers-at-death.

CONCLUSION AND FUTURE DIRECTIONS

This chapter suggests that the effective tax burden that estate taxes impose on capital income recipients averages between one and two percentage points, but that the effective tax rates are much higher for very old households. Because estate taxes are a nontrivial source of revenue, they should be included in future attempts to calculate the average tax burden on corporate and other types of capital income. The analysis of the pattern of planned giving further suggests that although inter vivos giving can substantially reduce estate tax burdens for many households, especially those with net worth near the estate tax liability threshold, households do not take full advantage of this estate planning tool.

One important limitation of this analysis is that it does not explore a range of other estate tax avoidance strategies that might be pursued by high-net-worth households. These include transferring control rights in family businesses at estimated values that may fall below true market value, creative use of trusts, and a host of other mechanisms. There may be substantial heterogeneity across households in the extent to which they can use such strategies, and there is little data that can be used to gauge their importance.

This analysis has considered the estate tax in isolation, even though there can be important interactions between the estate tax and other parts of the tax system. One reason for holding appreciated assets until death is to avoid capital gains tax on unrealized gains. In the period from 1986 to 1996, when the federal capital gains tax rate was 28 percent, holding appreciated assets until death could reduce the combined decedent and heir's capital gains tax burden substantially. Transferring the same assets as inter vivos gifts would lead to carry-over basis, and therefore to potentially higher income tax liabilities, if the recipients realized these gains. If the marginal estate tax rate is, say, 45 percent, the *net* tax cost of bequeathing rather than transferring while alive is therefore 17 percent rather than 45 percent. Poterba (forthcoming) explores the interplay of capital gains taxes and estate taxes in more detail.

Another example of the interaction between the estate tax and other aspects of the tax system is B. Douglas Bernheim's (1987) discussion of the relative capital income tax rates on donors and recipients of inter vivos gifts. Such gifts can transfer assets from taxpayers with high marginal tax rates on capital income (prospective decedents) to those with lower capital income tax rates (prospective recipients). Such estate tax-induced transfers may reduce federal income tax receipts.

This chapter has also considered *implicit taxes,* defined and discussed in Scholes and Wolfson (1992), only in passing. When households follow strategies that divide the control of family businesses, or when they place assets in trusts, there may be distortions to the pre-tax return that they earn.[16] These distortions can be large before they outweigh the tax benefits associated with estate tax avoidance. Further recognition of the implicit taxes associated with estate tax avoidance, and of the potential nontax costs associated with estate planning strategies, could result in estimates of effective estate tax burdens that are greater than those reported here.

I am grateful to Jeff Brown and especially Scott Weisbenner for outstanding research assistance; to Martin Feldstein, William Gale, Salvatore Lazzari, Joel Slemrod, and numerous conference participants for helpful comments; and to the National Science Foundation for research support.

NOTES

1. The exempt amount of estates and gifts was set in the Tax Reform Act of 1976 at $120,667 for 1977. This amount was phased up to $175,625 by 1981 under the 1976 law. The Economic Recovery Tax Act of 1981 raised the unified credit to exempt estates and lifetime gifts of less than $225,000 in 1982, and it phased in increases in the exemption that reached $600,000 in 1987.

2. The exemption rises to $625,000 in 1998, then to $650,000 in 1999, $675,000 in 2000 and 2001, $700,000 in 2002 and 2003, $850,000 in 2004, $950,000 in 2005, and $1,000,000 in 2006.

3. In the 1930s, even though the fraction of decedents paying estate taxes was only half that in 1995, estate taxes represented more than 5 percent of federal tax receipts.

4. Information from estate tax returns is typically presented in one of two forms: for all estate tax returns filed in a given year, and for all decedents who died in a given year. Because there are inherent time lags in the probate and estate valuation processes, the estate tax returns for decedents who die in a given year are typically filed over a span of several years.

5. The procedures used in Feenberg, Mitrusi, and Poterba (1997) and by the U.S. Congress Joint Committee on Taxation (1993) to allocate estate taxes across households for the purposes of "distribution tables" are closely related to this aggregate calculation. Those studies use various measures of a household's capital income flow as well as information on whether any taxpayers filing a given return are over the age of sixty-five to allocate aggregate federal estate tax payments to individual tax returns.

6. Because capital gains tax liability is extinguished through basis-step-up at death, one would expect to find a higher concentration of capital-gain-generating assets in the portfolios of decedents than in the portfolios of randomly selected households. This factor may contribute to some of the differences observed between the estate tax returns and the *Balance Sheets*.

7. Wolff (1995), in discussing expanded wealth taxes, notes that such taxes would reduce the rate of return to savers, but that the impact of such rate-of-return changes is difficult to quantify.

8. This discussion also presumes that the ultimate incidence of the estate tax falls on capital. Stiglitz (1978) and others have developed models in which some of the burden of the estate tax is shifted to labor through a reduced level of capital accumulation.

9. The average deduction and average state estate tax credit on estate tax returns with different gross estate values are shown below:

Gross Estate Value	Average Deduction (Millions)	Average State Credit (Millions)
$600,000 to 1,000,000	$0.047	$0.009
$1,000,001 to 2,500,000	0.111	0.027
$2,500,001 to 5,000,000	0.263	0.099
$5,000,001 to 10,000,000	0.737	0.265
$10,000,001 to 20,000,000	1.437	0.655
Over $20,000,000	12.458	2.269

10. Although the SCF data are for 1995, deaths that occurred in 1995 would in all likelihood have resulted in estate tax filings in 1996 or 1997, so it is natural to use the 1996 NIPA data. I am grateful to William Gale for substantial help in clarifying the interaction of state and federal estate taxes.

11. These results suggest that when searching for evidence of behavioral distortions associated with the estate tax, it is essential to focus on portfolio and other behaviors of the very old, since this is the group for whom this tax looms largest.

12. Estate tax avoidance is only one of the explanations for divergences between these two magnitudes. Underreporting of wealth data in sample surveys would tend to bias the estimated ratio of paid to projected estate taxes up, and lower mortality rates for very wealthy individuals than for middle-income households would bias this ratio in the opposite direction.

13. To project future wealth accumulation or decumulation profiles for the households in the Survey of Consumer Finances that are likely to face estate taxation, one would need a model of saving and consumption behavior for high-income, high-net-worth households. Unfortunately, such models are difficult if not impossible to estimate from existing household surveys.

14. One could also perform these calculations using a discount rate of 6 percent, the assumed rate of return to capital elsewhere in this chapter. The present discounted value of lifetime inter vivos transfers is somewhat smaller in this case.

15. This calculation assumes that all households with *current* net worth, including the face value of life insurance, make gifts of $10,000 per child. This may overestimate the actual gifts that might be made in a program of planned giving, because some households with current net worth above the estate tax threshold might plan to decumulate assets before death. For other households, how-

ever, that have current net worth *below* the threshold but expect to have net worth above the estate tax threshold by the time they die, this algorithm understates tax-minimizing transfers.

16. One of the common arguments for raising the estate tax threshold is that the tax may force a sale of family farms and other closely held businesses. Burman (1997) presents some evidence on the empirical importance of this issue.

REFERENCES

Aaron, Henry J., and Alicia Munnell. 1992. "Reassessing the Role for Wealth Transfer Taxes." *National Tax Journal* 45: 119–43.

Attanasio, Orazio, and Hilary Hoynes. Forthcoming. "Differential Mortality and Wealth Accumulation." *Journal of Human Resources.*

Auten, Gerald, and David Joulfaian. 1997. "Bequest Taxes and Capital Gains Realizations." Unpublished paper. U.S. Treasury Department, Office of Tax Analysis.

Bell, Felicitie, A.Wade, and S. Goss. 1992. "Life Tables for the United States Social Security Area 1900 to 2080." Actuarial Study 107. Social Security Administration, Office of the Actuary.

Bernheim, B. Douglas. 1987. "Does the Estate Tax Raise Revenue?" In *Tax Policy and the Economy,* edited by Lawrence Summers, vol. 1. Cambridge, Mass.: MIT Press.

Bernheim, B. Douglas, Andrei Shleifer, and Lawrence Summers. 1985. "The Strategic Bequest Motive." *Journal of Political Economy* 93: 1045–76.

Burman, Leonard E. 1997. "Estate Taxes and the Angel of Death Loophole." *Tax Notes* (August 4): 675–78.

Congressional Budget Office. 1997. *Perspectives on the Ownership of Capital Assets and the Realization of Capital Gains.* Washington, D.C.: CBO.

Cooper, George. 1979. *A Voluntary Tax?: New Perspectives on Sophisticated Tax Avoidance.* Washington, D.C.: Brookings Institution.

Drew, Christopher, and David Cay Johnston. 1996. "For Wealthy Americans, Death Is More Certain Than Taxes." *New York Times,* December 22, 1, 30.

Eller, Martha Britton. 1996. "Federal Taxation of Wealth Transfers, 1992–1995." *Statistics of Income Bulletin* (Winter 1996–97): 8–63.

Feenberg, Daniel, Andrew Mitrusi, and James M. Poterba. 1997. "Distributional Effects of Adopting a National Retail Sales Tax." In *Tax Policy and the Economy,* edited by James Poterba, vol. 11. Cambridge, Mass.: MIT Press.

Feldstein, Martin S., and Lawrence H. Summers. 1979. "Inflation and the Taxation of Capital Income in the Corporate Sector." *National Tax Journal* 32: 445–70.

Gale, William G., and J. Karl Scholz. 1994. "Intergenerational Transfers and the Accumulation of Wealth." *Journal of Economic Perspectives* 8 (Fall): 145–60.

Graetz, Michael. 1983. "To Praise the Estate Tax, Not to Bury It." *Yale Law Journal* 93: 259–86.

Guralnik, Jack M., Kenneth C. Land, Dan Blazer, Gerda Fillenbaum, and Laurence Branch. 1993. "Educational Status and Active Life Expectancy Among Older Blacks and Whites." *New England Journal of Medicine* 329: 110–16.

Joulfaian, David. 1991. "Charitable Bequests and Estate Taxes." *National Tax Journal* 44: 169–80.

Kaplow, Louis. 1997. "Transfer Motives and Tax Policy." Unpublished paper. Harvard Law School, Cambridge, Mass.

Luckey, John. 1995. "Federal Estate, Gift, and Generation-Skipping Taxes; A Description of Current Law." Congressional Research Service Report.

Masson, Andre, and Pierre Pestieau. 1997. "Bequest Motives and Models of Inheritance: A Survey of the Literature." In *Is Inheritance Legitimate?,* edited by G. Erreygers and T. Vandevelde. Berlin: Springer-Verlag.

McCaffery, Edward J. 1994. "The Uneasy Case for Wealth Transfer Taxation." *Yale Law Journal* 104: 283–365.

McGarry, Kathleen. 1999. "Inter Vivos Transfers and Intended Bequests." *Journal of Public Economics* 73: 321–51.

Mitchell, Olivia S., James M. Poterba, Mark J. Warshawsky, and Jeffrey R. Brown. 1999. "New Evidence on the Money's Worth of Individual Annuities." *American Economic Review* 89 (December).

Pechman, Joseph A. 1987. *Federal Tax Policy:* 5th ed. Washington, D.C.: Brookings Institution.

Poterba, James M. 1998. "The Rate of Return to Corporate Capital and Factor Shares: New Estimates Using Revised National Income Account and Capital Stock Data." *Carnegie-Rochester Conference Series on Public Policy* 48(June): 211–46.

———. Forthcoming. "Estate and Gift Taxes and Incentives for Inter Vivos Giving in the United States." *Journal of Public Enconomics.*

Scholes, Myron, and Mark Wolfson. 1992. *Taxes and Business Strategy.* Englewood Cliffs, N.J.: Prentice Hall.

Stiglitz, Joseph E. 1978. "Notes on Estate Taxes, Redistribution, and the Concept of Balanced Growth Incidence." *Journal of Political Economy* 86: S137–50.

U.S. Congress Joint Committee on Taxation. 1993. *Methodology and Issues in Measuring Changes in the Distribution of Tax Burdens.* Washington, D.C.: U.S. Government Printing Office.

———. 1997. *Description and Analysis of Tax Proposals Relating to Savings and Investment (Capital Gains, IRAs, and Estate and Gift Tax).* Washington, D.C.: U.S. Government Printing Office.

Wolff, Edward N. 1995. *Top Heavy: A Study of the Increasing Inequality of Wealth in America.* New York: Twentieth Century Fund.

———. 1996. "Discussant Comment on Douglas Holtz-Eakin, 'The Uneasy Case for Abolishing the Estate Tax.'" *Tax Law Review* 51 (Spring): 517–22.

Commentary on Chapter 10

William G. Gale

The estate tax is one of the most controversial parts of the tax law, but its economic effects are poorly understood. James Poterba's paper helps to address that deficiency. The chapter provides a variety of useful information and several interesting findings on how estate taxes affect the taxation of capital income and the extent to which households avoid such taxes.

Poterba models the effective tax rate imposed by the estate tax as household-specific and dependent on household wealth and one-year mortality risk. Overall, the estate tax is estimated to raise capital income tax rates by 1.7 to 2.5 percentage points (table 10.6). The effective tax rate rises dramatically with age and the associated increase in one-year mortality risk but does not exceed two percentage points until household heads reach the age of seventy. For people who are eighty years old or older, the effective tax rate skyrockets to between eighteen and twenty-five percentage points.

These results suggest that the overall burden of the estate tax may not be large. Before reaching such a conclusion, however, it would be interesting to extend the findings in a number of directions. First, estate tax burdens vary as a function of household wealth. A large portion of households in each age category are likely to have less than $600,000 in wealth (including the face value of life insurance) and therefore face a statutory estate tax rate of zero. It would be of interest to see the effective tax rate for, say, the top 20 (10, 5, or 1) percent of households in each age group. These households are likely to undertake a disproportionate share of aggregate private saving, and the impact of the estate tax on these households should prove larger than the figures reported in table 10.6.

Second, the effective tax rate imposed by the estate tax can also depend on the investment horizon and other existing taxes. For example, suppose an asset generates an annual gross return of r, the asset's income is taxed at rate t, and the asset is held for H periods. At the end of H periods, the asset balance resulting from an initial one-dollar investment is $(1 + r(1 - t))^H$. Suppose the asset holder dies at the end of H periods. If an estate tax at rate e is also imposed, the net-of-tax balance is $(1 + r(1 - t))^H(1 - e)$. The effective tax rate imposed by the estate tax in this situation is calculated by determining the tax rate s, such that $(1 + r(1 - t - s))^H = (1 + r(1 - t))^H(1 - e)$. Clearly, the effective tax rate depends on t, e, and H. For example, if r = 10 percent, t = 40 percent, e = 50 percent, and the asset is held until death, the estate tax imposes an effective tax rate on capital income of 71 percent if H = ten years, 36 percent if H = twenty years, and 24 percent if H = thirty years.[1] If t = 0, the effective tax rates are somewhat higher.

These calculations show that the effective tax rate imposed by the estate tax can vary with the holding period and the taxation of other assets. The actual quantitative estimates, however, are not intended to be comparable to the estimates in table 10.6. The table gives estimates that apply to all households, whether their bequeathable wealth exceeds $600,000 or not, and examines mortality risk over a single year. The estimates reported earlier focus on households with a high estate tax rate and assume that the holding period extends until the death of the asset holder.

Another interesting case occurs if the asset in question generates income in the form of capital gains. Taxes on capital gains are paid only when an asset is sold. Notably, if an asset is held until its owner dies, all previously accrued but unrealized capital gains on that asset are exempted entirely from income tax. This is the so-called angel-of-death loophole (Burman 1997). Under these circumstances, the effective tax rate created by the estate tax is lower than in the estimates cited here, since triggering the estate tax (by dying) also triggers the elimination of all taxes on previously accrued but unrealized capital gains.

The effective tax rate may also depend on the extent and nature of tax avoidance. Douglas Bernheim (1987a) argues that many estate tax avoidance strategies effectively reduce income tax payments by shifting funds from high-income to low-income households or nonprofit organizations. He estimates that the overall revenue effects of the estate tax are plausibly in the neighborhood of zero. Regardless of the exact revenue effect, however, Bernheim shows that the effective tax rate created by the estate tax may not correlate well with either the direct revenue yield of the estate tax or the marginal statutory rates.

The link between tax avoidance and effective tax rates leads directly into the second set of results in the chapter, summarized in table 10.7. A well-known, simple way to reduce estate taxes is to provide annual gifts of up to $10,000 from each parent to each child, son- or daughter-in-law, and/or grandchild. Through this mechanism, for example, a couple with two married children and four grandchildren could transfer up to $160,000 per year tax-free. Poterba makes a series of reasonable assumptions needed to construct an estimate and finds that households generally do not exploit this particular mechanism to any great degree. Causal empiricism suggests that this result is not surprising, but as Poterba shows, an examination of the financial incentives to avoid the estate tax implies that the result needs to be explained.

One possibility is that people are engaged in other, preferred forms of estate tax avoidance. Although there is a substantial amount of estate tax avoidance activity, it nevertheless appears that people could avoid a large amount of estate tax liabilities but do not. A second possibility is that, despite the tax advantages, people choose not to make such transfers. There are clearly financial benefits for parents who retain the funds. Parents may also perceive costs in making large inter vivos transfers. Parents may fear that such transfers could hurt relations between family members, reduce the work ethic of their children, or have other adverse effects. Many discussions of estate tax avoidance (see, for example, Bernheim 1987a; Pechman 1987) emphasize the importance of nontax factors in estate planning.

This suggests a somewhat different perspective on the issue, mentioned by Poterba and many others, of whether estate taxes are truly "voluntary." In economic terms, a tax may be termed voluntary if it can be avoided. Poterba's results show that this is an appropriate characterization of at least a portion of estate tax revenues. However, the estate tax is clearly not voluntary in the word's common meaning. That is, people do not pay the estate tax only if they feel like doing so. Rather, they pay it when the marginal costs of tax avoidance exceed the marginal benefits. This perspective helps explain both why the estate tax is viewed as voluntary for many people and why reducing the estate tax is so strongly favored in some sectors of society.[2]

By considering estimates of the effective tax rate and of the extent of tax avoidance, Poterba provides significant new information on the estate tax. An important direction for further research is to consider how the results might matter to broader economic outcomes, such as impact of the estate tax on saving. These effects underlie much of the interest in the effective tax rate created by the estate tax.

Although there appears to be a general presumption that estate taxes reduce saving and capital accumulation, this issue has received virtually no systematic analysis by economists. To at least some degree, the impact of the estate tax on saving and investment is likely to depend on why people give bequests in the first place. These motives are considered later in this discussion.

The effect should also depend on how inheritances affect the saving behavior of the recipients (Holtz-Eakin, Joulfaian, and Rosen 1993; Joulfaian and Wilhelm 1994; Weil 1994), as well as on the disposition of the revenues collected by government. There may also be general equilibrium effects (Stiglitz 1978).

Christopher Carroll (this volume) constructs a model in which people obtain utility from giving a bequest. In his model, an increase in the estate tax raises the parent's consumption and thus reduces the gross estate. Several models provide different motives for bequests. These include: accidental bequests due to uncertain life span (Davies 1981; Abel 1985; Hurd 1987), altruistic bequests (Barro 1974; Becker 1974), exchange-related, or strategic, transfers (Bernheim, Schleifer, and Summers 1985), and "warm glow" giving (Andreoni 1989). It would be of interest to examine the effects of transfer taxes on saving in these models as well.[3]

It is worth noting, however, that none of these models receive strong empirical support from the literature.[4] This is due in part to data limitations and the difficulty of distinguishing rejection of the underlying behavioral model from rejection of the assumptions maintained in order to generate testable hypotheses. In addition, households' behavior is probably influenced by more than one of the motives listed, and the relative importance of each motive may vary across households. Perhaps surprisingly, the most notable empirical finding to date regarding estates—that is, that bequests tend to be divided equally among all surviving children—does not appear to be a strong prediction of any of the theories and actually contradicts several of them (see the discussion in Wilhelm 1996).

In summary, then, the estate tax raises many significant and as yet unanswered questions. Poterba has identified several key issues and presented new empirical analyses of important aspects of these taxes. These findings will prove useful in developing further knowledge of the economic effects of estate taxation. However, a fuller understanding of how the estate tax affects the economy will also require more insights and tests concerning the motives for, and patterns of, intergenerational linkages.

NOTES

1. The effective tax rate that the estate tax imposes on capital income can exceed the statutory estate tax rate because the estate tax applies to asset balances rather than to just the income flow from the assets.

2. Similar considerations apply to capital gains taxes, which are voluntary in the economic sense that they can be avoided by never selling assets.

3. Holtz-Eakin (1996) and Metcalf (1995) contain discussions of related issues.

4. See, for example, Altonji, Hayashi, and Kotlikoff (1997), Barro (1989), Bernheim (1987b), Bernheim (1989), Laitner and Juster (1996), Masson and Pestieau (1997), Perozek (1998), and Wilhelm (1996).

REFERENCES

Abel, Andrew B. 1985. "Precautionary Saving and Accidental Bequests." *American Economic Review* 75: 777–91.

Altonji, Joseph G., Fumio Hayashi, and Laurence J. Kotlikoff. 1997. "Parental Altruism and Inter Vivos Transfers: Theory and Evidence." *Journal of Political Economy* 105: 1121–66.

Andreoni, James. 1989. "Giving with Impure Altruism: Applications to Charity and Ricardian Equivalence." *Journal of Political Economy* 97: 1447–58.

Barro, Robert. 1974. "Are Government Bonds Net Wealth?" *Journal of Political Economy* 82: 1095–117.

———. 1989. "The Ricardian Approach to Budget Deficits." *Journal of Economic Perspectives* 3: 37–54.

Becker, Gary S. 1974. "A Theory of Social Interactions." *Journal of Political Economy* 82: 1063–93.

Bernheim, B. Douglas. 1987a. "Does the Estate Tax Raise Revenue?" In *Tax Policy and the Economy*, edited by Lawrence H. Summers, vol. 1. Cambridge, Mass.: National Bureau of Economic Research and MIT Press.

———. 1987b. "Ricardian Equivalence: An Evaluation of Theory and Evidence." In *NBER Macroeconomics Annual*, edited by Stanley Fischer. Cambridge, Mass.: MIT Press.

———. 1989. "A Neoclassical Perspective on Budget Deficits." *Journal of Economic Perspectives* 3: 55–72.

Bernheim, B. Douglas, Andrei Schleifer, and Lawrence H. Summers. 1985. "The Strategic Bequest Motive." *Journal of Political Economy* 93: 1045–76.

Burman, Leonard E. 1997. "Estate Taxes and the Angel of Death Loophole." *Tax Notes* (August 4): 675–78.

Davies, James B. 1981. "Uncertain Lifetime, Consumption, and Dissaving in Retirement." *Journal of Political Economy* 89: 561–77.

Holtz-Eakin, Douglas. 1996. "The Uneasy Empirical Case for Abolishing the Estate Tax." *Tax Law Review* 51: 496–515.

Holtz-Eakin, Douglas, David Joulfaian, and Harvey S. Rosen. 1993. "The Carnegie Conjecture: Some Empirical Evidence." *Quarterly Journal of Economics* 108: 413–35.

Hurd, Michael D. 1987. "Savings of the Elderly and Desired Bequests." *American Economic Review* 77: 298–312.

Joulfaian, David, and Mark O. Wilhelm. 1994. "Inheritance and Labor Supply." *Journal of Human Resources* 29: 1205–34.

Laitner, John, and F. Thomas Juster. 1996. "New Evidence on Altruism: A Study of TIAA-CREF Retirees." *American Economic Review* 86: 893–908.

Masson, Andrew, and Pierre Pestieau. 1997. "Bequest Motives and Models of Inheritance: A Survey of the Literature." In *Is Inheritance Legitimate?*, edited by Guido Erreygers and Toon Vandevelde. Berlin: Springer-Verlag.

Metcalf, Gilbert E. 1995. "The Lifetime Incidence of a Consumption Tax." In *Distributional Analysis of Tax Policy*, edited by David F. Bradford. Washington, D.C.: American Enterprise Institute Press.

Pechman, Joseph A. 1987. *Federal Tax Policy.* Washington, D.C.: Brookings Institution.

Perozek, Maria G. 1998. "Comment: A Reexamination of the Strategic Bequest Motive." *Journal of Political Economy.* 106(2): 423–45.

Stiglitz, Joseph. 1978. "Notes on Estate Taxes, Redistribution, and the Concept of Balanced Growth Path Incidence." *Journal of Political Economy* 86: S137–50.

Weil, David N. 1994. "The Saving of the Elderly in Micro and Macro Data." *Quarterly Journal of Economics* 109: 55–81.

Wilhelm, Mark O. 1996. "Bequest Behavior and the Effect of Heirs' Earnings: Testing the Altruistic Model of Bequests." *American Economic Review* 86: 874–92.

11

Capital Gains Taxation and Tax Avoidance: New Evidence from Panel Data

Alan J. Auerbach, Leonard E. Burman, and Jonathan M. Siegel

In the United States, capital gains taxes have long sparked interest among economists and policymakers. The Taxpayer Relief Act of 1997 (TRA97) contains the latest changes in the taxation of capital gains. The act has lowered the tax rate on most gains and made the tax rate dependent on the holding period. As amended by the Internal Revenue Service Restructuring and the Reform Act of 1998, the law provides that assets held for at least twelve months qualify for a long-term treatment and maximum tax rate of 20 percent, and assets held for at least five years (and purchased after the year 2000) will face a top rate of just 18 percent. The act also exempts from tax almost all gains from sales of owner-occupied housing.

Other provisions of the act are aimed at reducing tax avoidance associated with the already favorable treatment of capital gains. These include changes that lessen the favorable tax treatment of real estate investments through a change in recapture provisions and the elimination of the ability of investors to hedge open positions by "shorting against the box" (taking an offsetting short position) without realizing their locked-in gains. Such restrictions build on those introduced by the Tax Reform Act of 1986 (TRA86), which limited the ability of taxpayers to deduct losses associated with real estate investments and other "passive" investment activities.

This legislation, which reduces capital gains tax rates in general but also seeks to eliminate certain advantages of holding assets subject to capital gains taxation, reflects an underlying tension in how the capital gains tax is perceived. On the one hand, a low rate of capital gains tax is seen as facilitating the efficient turnover of investor portfolios and encouraging venture capital investment and entrepreneurship. On the other hand, the favorable rate of tax and the ability of investors to time realizations is understood to generate opportunities to avoid not only capital gains taxes but other taxes as well. The continued existence of the annual $3,000 limit on capital loss deductions reflects the perceived need to limit such activity.

The same tension is evident in the economics literature. Theoretical analysis (for example, Constantinides 1984; Stiglitz 1983) has elucidated strategies to avoid taxes on capital gains and to generate capital losses to offset ordinary income. Much empirical research, however, has emphasized the potentially large response elasticities to capital gains tax reductions (see, for example, Feldstein, Slemrod, and Yitzhaki 1980). Subsequent empirical work (including Auten and Clotfelter 1982; Auerbach 1988; and Burman and Randolph 1994) distinguishes between short-run and long-run responses but thus far has failed to focus on the more sophisticated avoidance strategies detailed in the theoretical literature. This remaining gap between theory and evidence has been due in part to data limitations. Complicated avoidance transactions may be difficult to discern without considerable information about the behavior of the high-income individuals who realize most capital gains. But it also seems clear that the theory offers an inadequate description of taxpayer behavior. As James Poterba (1987) shows, relatively few taxpayers realizing capital gains appear to utilize the avoidance strategies that theory would predict.[1] Put simply, over $100 billion of capital gains are realized every year, and most of them face a positive rate of tax.

This chapter aims to bring theory and evidence closer together by examining more closely the behavior of individual taxpayers over time. We follow Poterba in searching for the presence of avoidance activity, but our analysis is facilitated by the use of a rich data set that tracks every capital gains realization for a large number of high-income individuals over a decade, from 1985 through 1994. Having a relatively long panel also allows us to consider changes in avoidance behavior over time and to ask whether growing taxpayer sophistication, perhaps aided by the increasing efficiency of financial markets, has led to an increase in avoidance activity. In addition, with information on individual transactions, we can explore the extent to which avoidance behavior is a function of portfolio composition. The theoretical arguments made by Stiglitz, Constantinides, and others assume that transaction costs are negligible—that assets are highly liquid—but this may not be a good assumption for some assets, such as real estate and business property. Thus, the ability of taxpayers to shelter their gains from tax may depend on the kinds of assets they own.

In a sense, our investigation is complementary to the typical empirical investigation in that we focus especially on a period, 1987 to 1994, during which there were no important changes in the treatment of capital gains taxes (other than an increasing differential created by higher tax rates on ordinary income). Our view is that further analysis of the response of aggregate capital gains realizations to changes in the capital gains tax rate requires a better understanding of the underlying behavior generating these realizations.

A useful starting point for our analysis is a simple description of the relevant capital gains tax provisions in effect during the period we analyze. Figure 11.1, based on one presented in Poterba (1987), shows four distinct tax regimes that apply to marginal short-term gains and losses (applicable during the sample period to sales of assets owned less than one year) and long-term gains and losses (on those assets held for at least one year), based on a taxpayer's overall levels of gains and losses.[2] It distinguishes between long-term gains and losses (those on assets held for more than one year) and short-term gains and losses (those on assets held for less than one year).

The "normal" situation, in which the rates on long-term and short-term gains are equal to their distinct statutory rates, applies only in the region labeled A in the figure. In region A taxpayers have both positive long-term and short-term gains. These net short-term gains are taxed at the same rate as ordinary income, τ. In 1987 the maximum tax rate on ordinary income was 38 percent. From 1988 to 1990 the maximum tax rate on ordinary income was 33 percent, because of the phaseout of the 15 percent bracket for some moderately high-income taxpayers. In 1991 the top rate on ordinary income increased from 28 to 31 percent. In 1993 the maximum

Figure 11.1   Regions of Taxpayer Behavior

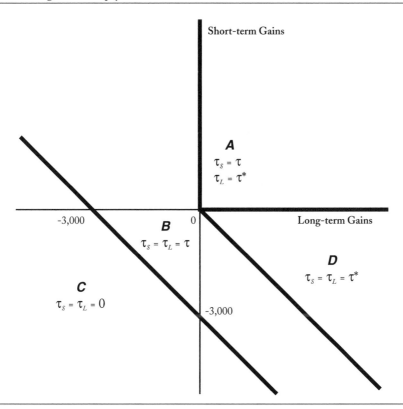

Note: τ_S and τ_L are the applicable tax rates in each region on short-term gains and long-term gains, respectively. τ and τ^* are the statutory tax rates on ordinary income and long-term gains.

ordinary income tax rate increased again to 39.6 percent. The tax rate on net long-term gains was capped at 28 percent in 1987, and from 1991 to 1994. From 1988 to 1990 the tax rate on capital gains was the same as that on ordinary income—as high as 33 percent—owing to the bubble. The resulting tax rate on long-term gains is denoted τ^*.[3]

Taxpayers with net long-term losses but net short-term gains are required to net the long-term losses against the short-term gains; they are taxed fully on the difference if positive and allowed a full deduction of any net loss up to $3,000. Thus, the effective marginal tax rate on both long-term and short-term gains is τ. Similarly, taxpayers with both long-term and short-term losses, or short-term losses in excess of long-term gains, are allowed to deduct any net loss up to $3,000. These taxpayers fall into the region denoted B in the figure, in which the effective tax rate on both short- and long-term gains is τ.

Region C includes those taxpayers with total (short-term plus long-term) losses in excess of $3,000. These taxpayers face no *current* tax on marginal short-term or long-term gains because such gains simply reduce the amount of losses that cannot be deducted. However, because capital losses may be carried forward indefinitely and used to offset gains realized in later years, gains realized while in region C may affect a taxpayer's *future* tax liability. We return to this point later. Note also that the gains calculated in the current year are net of any losses carried forward from earlier years.

The final region in figure 11.1, labeled D, includes those taxpayers with long-term gains in excess of short-term losses. In this case, the long-term gain is reduced by the short-term loss, and the difference is taxed at the long-term gain rate, τ^*. Thus, on the margin, all gains are taxed at the same rate, τ^*.

Poterba (1987) shows that the successful use of capital gains tax avoidance strategies should lead investors to be in the vicinity of region C and to stay there over time, but most investors he observed did not appear in region C. Recent press reports indicate that this might have changed, however. Henriques and Norris (1996) argue, for example, that by exploiting devices like shorting-against-the-box transactions, which (until 1997) allowed constructive realization of a capital gain without triggering capital gains tax liability, many high-income taxpayers had learned how to escape taxation. That is, they approached region C by reducing their taxable gains to near zero. Several prominent economists quoted by Henriques and Norris agreed that high-income taxpayers employed successful tax avoidance strategies.[4]

We are interested in understanding the behavior of those who are near region C and determining whether that behavior has indeed changed over time. We stress the word *near* because there is no clear division between taxpayers who actively use avoidance strategies and those who do not. A taxpayer who annually realizes $1 million of gross gains and $995,000 of gross losses will always be in region A but is qualitatively similar to investors who hit the $3,000 loss limit. Indeed, there may be some taxpayers who enter and remain in region C as the result of a single, unplanned loss and who should not be included in the group identified as successful tax avoiders. Our methodology attempts to take account of these and other issues of classification.

Before discussing this approach further, we turn to a brief discussion of the data set on which this analysis is based.

THE DATA

In our analysis we use the Internal Revenue Service's 1985-based Sales of Capital Assets (SOCA) panel study.[5] This panel was initially selected as a subsample of the 1985 Statistics of Income (SOI) cross-section of tax returns. The tax returns of panel members were then collected and linked for subsequent tax years through 1994. The data include full federal individual tax return information for approximately thirteen thousand filers. In addition to the form 1040 information that is in the standard SOI file, the panel also includes extensive detail on each capital transaction reported on schedule D, form 4797 (sale of business property) and several other forms on which capital gains are reported.

Several features of this panel make the data uniquely appropriate for the analysis of capital gains tax avoidance. First, the sample was highly stratified by income, creating an unusually large sample of wealthy taxpayers. Additionally, the fact that the data are a true panel allows observation of persistence of gains realization behavior and changes in behavior over time. Finally, the detail on individual transactions allows an analysis of heterogeneity by asset types of investors realizing capital gains and losses.

The SOI cross-section oversamples the returns of high-income individuals, and the subset of returns selected for the SOCA panel was even more top-heavy. Table 11.1 shows the resulting distribution of panel members by permanent income. Permanent income is defined here as the individual's mean over the panel years of the positive components of income expressed in 1982 dollars.[6] The top panel in the table indicates that over half of the panel members have permanent income above $200,000 and more than two thousand members have permanent income above $1 million. Comparing the unweighted counts to the population-weighted counts reveals the extent to which these data oversample high-income taxpayers. The population weights account for the panel's sampling stratification and transform the panel aggregates to nationally representative levels in 1985.[7]

The importance of using a high-income sample of taxpayers for capital gains tax analysis is apparent in table 11.2, which shows the distribution of net capital gains realizations by income for each year of the panel. In nearly every year more than half of all net gains were realized by taxpayers with permanent income above $200,000, or the top 2 percent of all taxpayers. Note that, unlike similar results based on cross-sectional data, these conclusions do not represent transitory or timing effects. They represent, as a first approximation, the long-run relationship between capital gains and permanent income.

Table 11.3 summarizes the distribution of gains and losses over time between long-term and short-term. The dramatic timing effect of the capital gains tax rate changes in TRA86 is clear. Realizations of long-term gains nearly doubled in 1986 and fell sharply in 1987 (see Burman, Clausing, and O'Hare 1994). Over the panel time frame, long-term losses grew relative to long-term gains. Short-term gains and losses both also grew substantially relative to long-term gains. These trends may reflect a lagged response to the 1987 rise in the long-term capital gains tax rate and the end of the distinction in tax rates between long-term and short-term gains.

A drawback of this panel (and all other tax panels) is that exiting members are not replaced. Thus, the aggregate numbers may not represent the national population in later years for at least two reasons. The panel suffers from attrition because some members die, some stop filing income tax returns because their incomes fall below the filing threshold, some taxpayers report the wrong Social Security number, and some returns are lost owing to processing errors. A potentially more important source of panel nonstationarity is the aging of panel members. For those reasons, we compare the later years of the SOCA panel to SOI cross-sections from the same years to test such panel drift. We find that attrition does affect the aggregate totals but does not affect the qualitative conclusions in any apparent way. (See note 10 for an example.) There is also now a new 1993-based SOCA panel, which eventually can be used as a further check on panel drift.

For each taxpayer in the panel, the SOCA data contain detailed information on every asset with capital gain or loss that is sold, including: the type of asset by

Table 11.1   Filers by Year and Permanent Income, SOCA Panel, 1985 to 1994

Permanent Income	1985	1986	1987	1988	1989	1990	1991	1992	1993	1994
Unweighted										
Less than $20,000	1,184	1,041	1,008	1,000	984	966	932	893	885	837
$20,000 to $50,000	2,051	2,014	2,007	2,004	1,995	1,991	1,982	1,962	1,943	1,904
$50,001 to $100,000	1,367	1,348	1,342	1,338	1,337	1,330	1,319	1,313	1,311	1,293
$100,001 to $200,000	1,497	1,489	1,482	1,472	1,469	1,461	1,452	1,439	1,428	1,393
$200,001 to $500,000	2,821	2,799	2,791	2,792	2,784	2,771	2,753	2,747	2,723	2,663
$500,001 to $1,000,000	1,764	1,751	1,740	1,740	1,732	1,720	1,713	1,711	1,692	1,663
Greater than $1,000,000	2,381	2,371	2,359	2,358	2,351	2,335	2,313	2,302	2,280	2,240
All	13,065	12,813	12,729	12,704	12,652	12,574	12,464	12,367	12,262	11,993
Population weighted										
Less than $20,000	50,897	46,954	44,995	44,168	42,992	42,837	41,178	39,214	38,436	36,115
$20,000 to $50,000	40,639	40,285	40,067	40,091	39,864	39,802	39,649	39,279	39,109	38,213
$50,001 to $100,000	7,918	7,893	7,880	7,876	7,875	7,836	7,804	7,794	7,756	7,698
$100,001 to $200,000	1,481	1,475	1,458	1,456	1,456	1,464	1,458	1,446	1,439	1,424
$200,001 to $500,000	553	551	550	550	492	549	490	543	541	536
$500,001 to $1,000,000	110	108	104	104	104	103	104	103	103	98
Greater than $1,000,000	38	38	38	38	38	38	38	38	37	37
All	101,637	97,304	95,093	94,283	92,821	92,630	90,719	88,418	87,422	84,121

Source: Author's calculations.

Table 11.2 Distribution of Net Gains by Permanent Income

Permanent Income	1985	1986	1987	1988	1989	1990	1991	1992	1993	1994
Less than $20,000	2.4%	1.5%	3.0%	2.5%	3.0%	3.5%	1.5%	4.3%	3.5%	4.0%
$20,000 to $50,000	11.9	12.0	8.8	11.2	20.3	21.5	10.6	9.5	23.4	17.0
$50,001 to $100,000	16.9	16.0	23.8	14.4	15.2	14.3	16.6	21.9	17.0	16.7
$100,001 to $200,000	16.7	11.2	11.0	13.3	9.2	11.9	12.8	9.5	10.4	11.9
$200,001 to $500,000	17.8	13.9	22.0	23.3	19.4	11.1	27.0	10.7	10.8	12.0
$500,001 to $1,000,000	11.9	18.8	8.3	12.1	10.7	10.4	7.5	9.2	9.3	12.7
Greater than 1,000,000	22.5	26.7	23.1	23.3	22.3	27.3	23.9	34.9	25.7	25.8

Source: Author's calculations.

Table 11.3 Capital Gains and Losses by Term and Year (Millions)

	1985	1986	1987	1988	1989	1990	1991	1992	1993	1994
Long-term gains	$166,354	$308,121	$137,576	$160,675	$163,998	$105,312	$100,961	$115,611	$151,630	$129,074
Long-term losses	13,589	16,586	34,726	24,438	26,054	26,017	30,430	21,972	25,319	35,441
Short-term gains	7,608	11,631	18,704	16,252	21,916	14,606	20,501	20,990	25,586	22,073
Short-term losses	6,058	14,138	20,023	9,127	22,187	20,559	13,916	21,688	15,415	28,748
Net gains	154,314	289,028	101,531	143,361	137,672	73,343	77,115	92,940	136,482	86,959

Source: Author's calculations.

twenty-one classifications, the gain or loss, the sale price, and the purchase and sale dates. In order to utilize this information in a panel data set organized by individual, we summed each taxpayer's gains and losses, separately by asset type, term (long or short), and year. So, for example, we created variables for the individual's long-term stock gains, short-term stock gains, long-term stock losses, and short-term stock losses in each year of our sample.[8] Additionally, we recorded the number of transactions and consolidated several of the asset classifications.

EVIDENCE ON TAX AVOIDANCE BEHAVIOR OVER TIME

The panel data provide an extraordinarily detailed picture of the kinds of gains and losses people realize, and how they have changed over time. The earlier discussion suggests several working hypotheses to be examined using these data:

- Wealthier taxpayers are more likely to avoid tax on their capital gains than the less wealthy (because the former have larger, more diversified portfolios and access to better tax advice).
- Gains on liquid assets, such as shares of corporate stock, should be more lightly taxed than gains on illiquid assets, such as real estate.
- Tax avoidance may have increased over time, because taxpayers, prodded by higher tax rates, learned successful techniques to shelter gains from tax.

To test these hypotheses, we examine how capital gain realization patterns vary by wealth or income, by asset type, and over time. We start out by examining how successful taxpayers are at sheltering gains from tax in individual years, and then we look at how such tax avoidance affects the distribution of taxes paid on capital gains.

Evidence on Tax Avoidance Activity

The perfect tax planner (in the frictionless world with complete financial markets) would have net capital losses of at least $3,000 every year. In this region, denoted C in figure 11.1, both long-term and short-term capital gains are untaxed and losses have sheltered the maximum possible amount of ordinary income from tax. One simple test of whether investor behavior has been moving in this direction is to examine whether more taxpayers (or more gains) have been moving into region C over time.

Table 11.4 shows the percentage of taxpayers in each of the marginal tax rate regions over the ten years of the panel, based on three different weighting schemes.[9] The top panel of the table uses population weights. In this panel we find, as did Poterba, that the majority of taxpayers with a capital gain or loss had both positive net short-term and long-term gains. Poterba reported that, in 1982, 64 percent of taxpayers were in that situation (region A in figure 11.1). In 1985 we find that an even larger share of taxpayers—77 percent—are in region A, but the percentage varies considerably from year to year, reaching a low of 56 percent in 1990.

There is nonetheless a clear break in 1987—when the tax rate on long-term gains increased for most taxpayers. The percentage of investors in region A never approaches its 1985 level in the subsequent years. It is tempting to conclude that

Table 11.4 Distribution of Taxpayers with Capital Gain or Loss, by Marginal Tax Rate Region

	1985	1986	1987	1988	1989	1990	1991	1992	1993	1994
Population weighted										
Region A ($\tau_S = \tau, \tau_L = \tau^*$)	77.4%	78.7%	70.3%	65.5%	65.9%	56.2%	63.9%	65.5%	69.8%	64.5%
Region B ($\tau_S = \tau_L = \tau$)	12.3	11.0	15.8	19.1	15.0	23.5	18.8	19.3	15.4	18.8
Region C ($\tau_S = \tau_L = 0$)	5.4	4.3	9.2	11.4	14.6	15.8	13.8	11.9	9.5	11.6
Region D ($\tau_S = \tau_L = \tau^*$)	4.9	6.1	4.8	4.1	4.6	4.5	3.5	3.3	5.4	5.1
Permanent dividend weighted										
Region A ($\tau_S = \tau, \tau_L = \tau^*$)	68.8	75.7	62.8	62.5	67.3	47.3	58.5	53.8	65.5	43.3
Region B ($\tau_S = \tau_L = \tau$)	6.5	5.6	7.5	12.9	11.0	13.2	10.7	11.8	6.8	11.3
Region C ($\tau_S = \tau_L = 0$)	5.3	4.1	9.6	13.3	13.1	21.8	17.4	22.5	17.2	22.1
Region D ($\tau_S = \tau_L = \tau^*$)	19.5	14.7	20.1	11.3	8.6	17.6	13.4	11.9	10.5	23.3
Gross gains weighted										
Region A ($\tau_S = \tau, \tau_L = \tau^*$)	75.4	78.5	61.6	72.0	75.0	67.4	69.6	64.6	73.1	55.3
Region B ($\tau_S = \tau_L = \tau$)	0.7	1.4	3.3	2.1	3.3	3.6	3.0	5.7	3.8	3.7
Region C ($\tau_S = \tau_L = 0$)	1.3	0.9	5.2	3.2	4.5	7.6	6.6	11.0	5.5	8.6
Region D ($\tau_S = \tau_L = \tau^*$)	22.6	19.3	29.8	22.7	17.3	21.5	20.9	18.7	17.6	32.5

Source: Author's calculations.

this is a permanent response to the higher tax rates on capital gains, but many other factors make it hard to draw firm inferences. For example, the sharp decline in the stock market at the end of 1987 and the decline in real estate prices at the end of the 1980s both would have generated losses, although the stock market was generally robust through most of the ten-year span. Moreover, the huge sell-off of assets in 1986 in anticipation of the increase in capital gains tax rates would have left investors with few capital gains for the years following enactment of TRA86. All of these, however, were temporary phenomena.

The percentage of taxpayers in region A plummeted immediately after enactment of the Omnibus Budget Reconciliation Act of 1990 (OBRA90), which raised tax rates on ordinary income but capped rates on long-term gains. The higher tax rates on both long- and short-term gains should have deterred taxpayers from region B as well, but that percentage increased by the same amount that the percentage in A decreased. Thus, the drop may be coincidental.

The perfect tax planner should be in region C and stay there. Poterba (1987) reported that about 10 percent of investors in 1982 were in that region. We find that the percentage had fallen to 5 percent in 1985 but jumped to the levels found by Poterba after passage of TRA86. Nonetheless, there does not seem to be a clear trend—the peak percentage was actually in 1990 (16 percent).[10]

Under the working hypothesis, wealthier taxpayers are more likely to be in region C. A simple control for wealth is to weight the number of observations in each region by the average dividends earned from 1985 to 1994, which we refer to as "permanent dividends."[11] We use average dividends to smooth out transitory variations over time. Absent clientele effects, average dividends would be a good proxy for holdings of corporate stock over the ten-year period. If there is a clientele effect, this measure will cause tax-conscious investors in high marginal tax brackets to be underrepresented in the averages. In that sense, it will understate the impact of weighting by wealth.

The second panel of table 11.4 reports the populations of the four regions, weighted by dividends. In this case, the movement into region C seems to demonstrate a clear trend that starts in 1987 and continues for the next seven years (peaking in 1992). The dividend-weighted percentage of investors in region C is not much different from the sample-weighted total in 1985 (4 percent versus 5 percent), but by the period 1992 to 1994, the dividend-weighted percentage is about twice the percentage using sample weights. These trends suggest that wealthier investors became more likely to optimize their portfolio behavior over the ten-year period.

Finally, the table also shows the percentages weighted by average gross capital gains over the ten years. This weighting scheme tells us the fraction of gross capital gains in each year that fell into each of the four regions. In 1985 and 1986 only 1 percent of capital gains were in the tax-free zone (region C). In 1987 this percentage jumped to 5 percent. The percentage grew still larger in later years, though it bounced around considerably from year to year.

We would expect taxpayers with higher incomes to be more likely to be in region C, and that turns out to be the case. Table 11.5 repeats the calculations of table 11.4, grouping investors according to their permanent incomes, as defined in the last section. The table shows that taxpayers with incomes under $100,000 were much less

Table 11.5 Percentage of Taxpayers with Gains or Losses in Region C, by Permanent Income

Permanent Income	1985	1986	1987	1988	1989	1990	1991	1992	1993	1994
Less than $20,000	1.8	1.5	2.3	5.5	10.1	8.1	3.3	3.4	3.9	1.9
$20,000 to $50,000	5.5	4.2	8.3	9.1	15.8	14.4	11.6	11.8	7.5	9.5
$50,001 to $100,000	5.1	5.0	10.9	17.5	14.2	18.2	20.1	13.5	12.2	15.5
$100,001 to $200,000	9.0	8.3	20.0	14.2	15.1	27.4	25.1	22.7	20.6	32.3
$200,001 to $500,000	12.6	6.3	19.5	16.5	16.2	26.3	20.8	18.5	22.7	23.7
$500,001 to $1,000,000	10.4	5.7	21.0	16.1	17.3	30.3	24.7	34.0	23.5	27.3
Greater than $1,000,000	13.7	4.9	17.5	19.0	19.9	32.1	29.7	27.7	21.4	29.9
All	5.4	4.3	9.2	11.4	14.6	15.8	13.8	11.9	9.5	11.6

Source: Author's calculations.

likely than higher-income taxpayers to be in region C in 1985. By 1994 the percentage of lower-income people in region C increased, but the percentage of people with higher incomes in that region increased much more.

The distribution of taxpayers in region C by the level of their imputed wealth (the construction of which is described in appendix 11A) follows the same pattern. As table 11.6 shows, wealthier people are more likely to shelter their gains from tax than less wealthy people, although the increase is not monotonic. The differences by wealth generally grow after 1986. The pattern is perhaps clearest if one compares the highest and lowest wealth categories. In 1985, 5 percent of taxpayers with a capital gain or loss and wealth below $500,000 were in region C, compared with 8 percent of taxpayers with wealth greater than $50 million. In 1987, 8 percent of the low-wealth taxpayers were in region C, compared with 12 percent of those with high wealth. But during each year between 1990 and 1994, from 27 to 34 percent of the wealthiest taxpayers were in region C, compared to a range of 7 to 13 percent of the least wealthy.

Because of high transaction costs, sales of illiquid assets such as businesses and real estate are likely to be motivated more by nontax factors and harder to shelter from tax (especially for undiversified investors).[12] Thus, we would expect more gains on liquid assets such as corporate stock and mutual funds to be in region C than gains on illiquid assets. Table 11.7 shows this to be the case, although the differences are not overwhelming. With the exception of 1986, a larger share of gains on stock, mutual funds, and bonds is in region C than on real estate and business assets.[13] The table also shows that gains from short sales, options, commodoties, and futures contracts are much more likely to be in region C in most years. This may be because such investments are much riskier than typical assets, so a taxpayer who engages in such transactions is more likely to realize large capital losses than one who sticks with safer investments. Or it could be that relatively sophisticated investors are more likely to engage in successful tax planning. For example, as explained earlier, short sales against the box were, until 1997, one of the major techniques for avoiding the realization of large taxable gains.

Based on these data, we created a measure of investor "sophistication"—an indicator of whether the investor ever traded options, commodoties, or future contracts, or sold short. Sophisticated investors by this measure were more than twice as likely to end up in region C as unsophisticated investors (see figure 11.2). Both sophisticated and unsophisticated investors were much more likely to be in region C after 1986 than before, but the trends of the two groups diverge after 1987. The percentage of sophisticated investors in region C remained roughly constant at around 20 percent, a remarkable stability compared to the volatile time series of region C probabilities reported in tables 11.5 through 11.7. However, the share of unsophisticated investors in region C declines after 1990. A possible explanation for this peak is the recession of 1990 and 1991. Losses are much more prevalent in a recession, and the pattern among unsophisticated investors seems to reflect that fact. The cyclical stability of the pattern for sophisticated investors suggests that their losses are driven by a different process—not so much by exogenous macroeconomic forces as by tax planning.

To what extent might differences in investor sophistication explain the patterns of the previous tables, which showed that investors with higher income and wealth

Table 11.6 Percentage of Taxpayers with Gains or Losses in Region C, by Imputed Wealth Level

Imputed Wealth	1985	1986	1987	1988	1989	1990	1991	1992	1993	1994
Less than $500,000	4.5	4.1	7.7	9.5	13.5	13.3	11.5	8.4	6.7	8.5
$500,000 to $1,000,000	6.6	2.0	11.5	18.5	14.8	18.9	13.6	22.1	18.9	21.5
$1,000,001 to $5,000,000	7.9	8.8	15.8	16.4	21.5	27.3	30.2	26.9	19.6	28.5
$5,000,001 to $10,000,000	13.4	4.4	11.8	14.1	14.0	30.3	20.2	32.4	25.3	28.0
$10,000,001 to $50,000,000	9.0	9.3	25.9	18.9	20.1	30.9	25.2	15.1	13.7	15.8
Greater than $50,000,000	8.0	6.4	11.8	15.2	22.0	27.3	31.3	33.8	31.4	27.9
All	5.4	4.3	9.2	11.4	14.6	15.8	13.8	11.9	9.5	11.6

Source: Author's calculations.

Table 11.7 Percentage of Gross Gains in Region C, by Asset Type

Asset Type	1985	1986	1987	1988	1989	1990	1991	1992	1993	1994
Corporate stock	1.9	0.8	7.7	4.0	7.1	11.3	8.0	14.5	6.9	8.4
Mutual funds	1.4	0.5	7.1	5.9	6.4	21.1	8.0	15.8	9.5	15.9
Bonds	4.0	0.5	15.3	18.2	6.7	19.2	14.9	14.4	12.5	21.5
Real estate	1.3	0.7	3.0	0.7	4.0	2.8	3.8	3.4	3.4	5.9
Business property	0.7	1.2	1.8	0.7	0.9	6.7	3.0	13.5	1.8	2.5
Short sales	5.3	3.1	28.0	29.5	31.5	21.0	15.5	36.9	12.7	2.0
Options, futures, and so on	8.5	16.8	18.1	14.7	41.8	12.7	28.5	35.3	17.1	37.9

Source: Author's calculations.

Figure 11.2   Sophisticated Versus Unsophisticated Investors

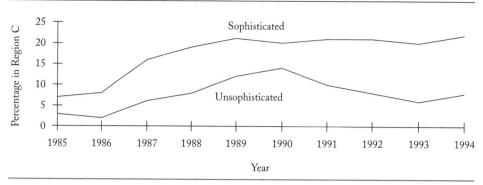

Source: Author's calculations.
Note: Sophisticated investors are those who have ever traded in options or future contracts or sold short.

were more likely to be in region C? Table 11.8 sheds light on this, showing that our measure of sophistication (here, based on annual participation in these markets) is strongly related to income.

Determinants of Tax Avoidance

The previous analysis suggests that successful tax avoidance is related to income, wealth, and the types of assets held in portfolio. We now bring these results together and consider the simultaneous effects of all of these factors, as well as demographic variables such as age and family status and a time trend, on the likelihood of being in region C, modeled using a probit equation. The results are presented in table 11.9. Because of the considerable volatility in capital gains realizations associated with TRA86, we consider only the postreform period 1987 to 1994. Also, we present two sets of estimates, the first based on sample-weighted observations, the second based on unweighted observations. The former approach may seem more appropriate if we wish to characterize the behavior of the representative individual, but the vast majority of capital gains are realized by people with high incomes. Thus, the unweighted data, which primarily represent higher-income taxpayers, better represent the population of those with substantial gains.

Based on the weighted data, people with higher permanent income (net of endogenous capital gains) are much more likely to be in region C, as are people with many capital transactions, another potential measure of an investor's sophistication and portfolio liquidity. Sophisticated investors (defined, as before, as those who have ever traded commodities or options or engaged in short sales) are 9 percent more likely to be in region C than others. The share of mutual fund distributions in gross capital gains has a strongly negative effect.[14] This may reflect the fact that capital gain distributions (typically from mutual funds) are involuntary, and that investors with large mutual fund holdings are less actively involved in portfolio management and tax planning. Growth in GDP and the stock market have the expected

Table 11.8 Percentage of Taxpayers with Gains or Losses with "Sophisticated" Transactions, by Permanent Income

Permanent Income	1985	1986	1987	1988	1989	1990	1991	1992	1993	1994
Less than $20,000	3.1	1.7	0.0	0.6	1.7	2.2	2.7	9.4	1.8	0.8
$20,000 to $50,000	3.5	8.2	8.9	9.7	11.5	5.3	10.8	5.8	3.9	4.8
$50,001 to $100,000	5.3	9.8	12.1	10.5	13.6	7.3	13.4	13.6	12.1	11.2
$100,001 to $200,000	13.6	17.4	18.1	19.8	21.5	18.7	23.9	16.8	17.8	22.4
$200,001 to $500,000	14.8	16.2	28.0	23.3	20.1	16.9	21.3	19.5	18.0	29.1
$500,001 to $1,000,000	14.1	23.7	32.0	24.3	27.1	25.6	31.2	24.1	37.6	33.0
Greater than $1,000,000	21.0	27.7	31.8	31.8	29.9	33.2	36.2	37.5	30.6	35.3
All	5.3	8.6	9.5	10.0	11.7	6.9	11.6	9.7	7.1	7.7

Source: Author's calculations.

Table 11.9 Probit Estimates of the Probability of Being in Region C, 1987 to 1994

	Population Weighted			Unweighted		
	Coefficient	Standard Error	∂F/∂x	Coefficient	Standard Error	∂F/∂x
Constant	-3.4932	0.6554	—	-1.3584	0.1790	—
Log (permanent income less capital gains)	0.1937	0.0623	0.0350	-0.0182	0.0151	-0.0058
Log (imputed wealth)	0.0179	0.0448	0.0032	0.0320	0.0108	0.0102
Stock share of wealth	-0.1531	0.2562	-0.0276	-0.2761	0.0524	-0.0884
Business property share of wealth	0.3024	0.2910	0.0546	0.0352	0.0441	0.0113
Rental property share of wealth	0.3582	0.2978	0.0647	0.0027	0.0488	0.0009
Farm property share of wealth	-0.2926	0.5806	-0.0528	-0.9813	0.2275	-0.3141
Earns tax-exempt interest	-0.1038	0.1035	-0.0184	-0.1528	0.0249	-0.0499
Log (number of capital transactions)	0.1090	0.0401	0.0197	-0.0057	0.0075	-0.0018
Sophisticated	0.4363	0.1251	0.0881	0.2908	0.0231	0.0906
Mutual fund share of capital gains	-0.9908	0.2357	-0.1789	-0.3729	0.0590	-0.1194
Single	0.2226	0.1129	0.0431	0.1291	0.0268	0.0425
Married filing separate	0.0365	0.1751	0.0068	0.0535	0.0497	0.0174
Head of household	-0.0436	0.3179	-0.0077	0.1511	0.0602	0.0506
Number of dependents	0.0101	0.0401	0.0018	0.0103	0.0090	0.0033
Age of primary taxpayer	-0.0025	0.0182	-0.0005	0.0134	0.0053	0.0043
(Age of primary taxpayer)²	0.0000	0.0002	0.0000	-0.0001	0.0000	0.0000
Real GDP growth rate	-2.6139	1.5694	-0.4721	-3.0170	0.3132	-0.9657
Standard & Poors 500 growth rate	-0.1213	0.2661	-0.0219	-0.2636	0.0438	-0.0844
Calendar time trend	0.0024	0.0141	0.0004	0.0335	0.0028	0.0107

Source: Author's calculations.

Note: ∂F/∂x is the partial derivative of the probability of being in region C with respect to the covariate. It is evaluated at mean values, *x*, for nonbinary data, and evaluated for a discrete change in dummy variables from 0 to 1. Italics indicate dummy variable.

negative impact on the probability of a net loss, but neither effect is significant. Wealth, the shares of different asset types, and the demographic variables, with the exception of marital status, are insignificant. Finally, note that, with all the other factors accounted for, the probability of being in region C does not change significantly over time.

However, one should use caution in interpreting these results, because the process of weighting, though appropriate for characterizing the behavior of the overall population, gives relatively low weight to the higher-income investors who realize most capital gains. In the unweighted estimates, permanent income has a negligible and statistically insignificant effect, but the wealth effect becomes large and significant. The shares of wealth accounted for by stock and farm property now have significant negative effects on the probability of having a net capital loss. Although the impact of farm wealth is not surprising, given the illiquidity of such property, the effects of the stock share are less easily explained. One possibility is that during this period of rapid stock market growth individuals with large stock portfolios had especially high accrued gains, some of which were realized. Although this effect should be picked up in part by the growth rate in the Standard & Poors index—the coefficient of which becomes large and highly significant—that index is not a perfect measure of broader stock market wealth. Municipal bond interest also has a significantly negative impact, possibly reflecting the use of a more passive strategy to avoid taxes.

One important result that does carry over from the weighted estimates is the impact of our measure of sophistication. Although the coefficient is somewhat smaller than before, the effect of sophistication on the probability at the mean of being in region C is virtually identical—approximately 9 percent. A final difference from the weighted estimates is the large and statistically significant positive effect of the time trend. The trend accounts for about a twelve-percentage-point increase in the probability of being in region C from 1987 to 1994.[15] The explanation for this trend appears to be the greater weight given to "sophisticated" investors in the unweighted estimates, whose region C population remains steady after 1990 even as that among unsophisticated investors falls (see figure 11.2).

To test this theory, we reestimated the weighted probit with interaction terms for sophistication with the time trend and GDP growth (not shown in the table). After these additions, GDP growth has negligible effect for sophisticated investors, suggesting that their presence in region C is insensitive to cyclical variation, unlike that of unsophisticated investors. In this alternative specification, the time trend for sophisticated investors is positive and nearly as large as that reported for the unweighted specification in table 11.9.

The Duration of Tax Avoidance

The benefit of realizing additional capital gains while in region C depends on how long a taxpayer expects to stay there. An individual who is in region C in one year and in region A the next is not really untaxed on marginal gains—he is only deferring tax for a year. That is, if the taxpayer realizes a gain of g while in region C, he incurs no current tax liability now, but his tax liability increases in the following year because he has that many fewer losses to carry over. So his effective tax rate is $\tilde{\tau}/(1+r)$, where r is the investor's nominal discount rate, and $\tilde{\tau}$ is the tax rate applicable to gains realized in the second year. If he stays in region C for two years, his effective tax rate is $\tilde{\tau}/(1+r)^2$, and so on (assuming his tax rate stays unchanged). Since future gains and losses are uncertain, his effective tax rate is stochastic.

Although this uncertainty makes a full analysis quite complex, a taxpayer's decisions presumably depend on an expected effective tax rate, $\bar{\tau}$, defined as

$$\bar{\tau} \equiv \sum_{t=1}^{\infty} f(t|X_0) \frac{\tilde{\tau}(X_0)}{(1+r)^t} \qquad (11.1)$$

where $f(t|X_0)$ is the probability of staying in region C for exactly t periods conditional on being in region C in period 0 and other information known at time 0, X_0.[16]

We estimate the duration in region C using an exponential hazard function,

$$h(t|X_0)e^{\beta_{0t}+X_0\beta}, \qquad (11.2)$$

where β_{0t} is a parameter that varies with duration, t, and β is a vector of constants. The hazard function is the probability of exiting region C in period t given X_0.[17] This specification allows for arbitrary duration dependence, because the β_{0t} are not constrained. The parameters are estimated by maximum likelihood.[18]

The probability of a duration of t may be derived from the estimated hazard functions. It is the product of the probability of remaining in region C for t periods—the survival function, $s(t|X_0)$—and the hazard in period t. The survival function, in turn, is simply the probability of not exiting region C in each of the previous periods, which is

$$s(t|X_0) = \prod_{i=1}^{t-1} \left(1 - h(j|X_0)\right), \qquad (11.3)$$

with the initial condition that $s(1|X_0) = 1$. Substituting $f(t|X_0) = s(t|X_0)\,h(t|X_0)$ into equation (11.1) yields

$$\bar{\tau} \equiv \sum_{t=1}^{\infty} h(t|X_0)s(t|X_0) \frac{\tilde{\tau}(X_0)}{(1+r)^t} \qquad (11.4)$$

We estimate the hazard function $h(\cdot)$ for the period 1987 to 1994, again using both weighted and unweighted samples and most of the same covariates (some time-varying) as those used in the probit estimation earlier. Table 11.10 presents the estimation results. One effect that is not surprising is that a large capital loss carry-over significantly reduces the hazard rate. All else equal, the larger this loss overhang, the longer it takes an investors to use it up.

In comparing the remaining hazard model results to those in table 11.9, one should keep in mind that variables that increase the rate of departure from region C have a positive coefficient. Thus, variables that are associated with tax avoidance

Table 11.10   Exponential Hazard Estimates of the Duration in Region C, 1987 to 1994

	Weighted		Unweighted	
	Coefficient	Standard Error	Coefficient	Standard Error
Log(permanent income less capital gains)	−0.0838	0.0779	0.0570	0.0175
Log(imputed wealth)	−0.0995	0.0462	−0.0608	0.0135
Stock share of wealth	−0.0330	0.2621	0.3967	0.0604
Business property share of wealth	0.0950	0.2835	0.2599	0.0545
Rental property share of wealth	0.1583	0.2662	0.2777	0.0597
Farm property share of wealth	0.1876	0.4093	0.7585	0.2554
Earns tax-exempt interest	0.3348	0.1116	0.1625	0.0290
Size of initial loss carry-over[a]	−0.2533	0.0326	−0.1415	0.0068
Log(number of capital transactions)	0.0130	0.0748	−0.0368	0.0105
Sophisticated	−0.4566	0.1355	−0.0908	0.0273
Mutual fund share of capital gains	0.2721	0.2749	0.1886	0.0808
Age of primary taxpayer	0.0140	0.0212	−0.0041	0.0066
(Age of primary taxpayer)^2	−0.0001	0.0002	0.0000	0.0001
Real GDP growth rate	−0.1399	2.5710	1.2777	0.7129
Standard and Poors 500 growth rate	0.2861	0.5203	0.2628	0.1358
Calendar time	0.0356	0.0271	0.0320	0.0060
Constant	1.1200	0.7507	−0.7990	0.2210
Duration = 2	−0.3699	0.1153	−0.2846	0.0292
Duration = 3	−0.6009	0.1873	−0.4924	0.0411
Duration = 4	−0.5217	0.2515	−0.8053	0.0624
Duration = 5	−1.5208	0.4134	−0.8931	0.0800
Duration = 6	−0.2631	0.4653	−0.8172	0.0950
Duration = 7	−1.7515	0.5835	−1.2528	0.1573

Source: Author's calculations.
Note: Italics indicate dummy variable.
[a.] The size of the initial loss carry-over variable is defined in appendix 11.1.

by contributing not only to presence in region C but also to longer duration in region C would have a positive sign in table 11.9 but a negative sign in table 11.10. Among the variables in this category are wealth and our measure of investor sophistication, each of which is negative and significant in both weighted and unweighted estimates. Other variables with consistent effects across the two tables are shares of mutual funds and (for the unweighted specification) farm property and stock, which reduce presence in and increase the rate of exit from region C. The trend over the period is positive and significant, indicating an increase in exit rates over time, perhaps reflecting the impact of stock market growth (or growth in other assets) not fully accounted for by the growth rate of the Standard & Poors 500 index.

What is the net impact of these individual effects, taken together, on the hazard rate? The answer, of course, varies across individuals, but we can get an idea of the aggregate picture by considering the hazard rates predicted at the mean values of all the covariates. Table 11.11 presents these predicted hazard rates for the weighted and unweighted estimates. For comparison, it also presents observed ("empirical")

Table 11.11   Typical Hazard Functions, Evaluated at Mean Values of Covariates, and Empirical Hazard Function

Duration in Region C (Years)	Weighted Hazard Model		Unweighted Hazard Model		Kaplan-Meier Empirical Hazard	
	Hazard	Survival	Hazard	Survival	Hazard	Survival
1	0.50	1.00	0.43	1.00	0.45	1.00
2	0.34	0.50	0.32	0.57	0.33	0.55
3	0.27	0.33	0.26	0.39	0.26	0.37
4	0.29	0.24	0.19	0.29	0.19	0.27
5	0.11	0.17	0.17	0.23	0.18	0.22
6	0.38	0.15	0.19	0.19	0.20	0.18
7	0.09	0.09	0.12	0.16	0.13	0.14

Source: Author's calculations.

hazard rates for the unweighted sample that, not surprisingly, are quite close to the predicted values. Except for an unexplained blip at the six-year duration in the weighted sample, the two sets of estimates exhibit very strong negative duration dependence. Close to half of all investors in region C depart after one year, but hazard rates fall nearly monotonically thereafter.

One possible explanation for this apparent duration dependence is unobserved heterogeneity of the region C population. Not all individuals in region C exercise a tax avoidance strategy. Some, perhaps, follow simpler realization strategies but occasionally realize losses. Those investors probably have much higher exit rates than those vigorously pursuing tax-reduction strategies. The investors who remain in region C for more years are more and more likely to be the aggressive tax avoiders.

Another possible explanation for duration dependence is noise in our measure of tax avoidance. We identify individuals as being tax avoiders only if they are in region C, taking the maximum allowable deduction for capital losses. However, as noted early in the chapter, it may not make sense to distinguish this behavior from that of a taxpayer who shelters all or nearly all of his capital gains every year without hitting the exact $3,000 limit. The presence of taxpayers hovering "near" region C and randomly hitting the limit exactly could well introduce a spuriously high exit rate at short durations. In fact, as figure 11.3 illustrates, the distribution of investors is bimodal. Two-thirds of taxpayers with gains or losses are able to shelter less than 10 percent of their gains. (Actually, the denominator in the figure is gain plus $3,000, defined this way so that a taxpayer must reach the boundary of region C to offset 100 percent of gains.) About 12 percent of taxpayers shelter all their gains—that is, they are in region C—but only 1 percent shelter between 90 and 100 percent. The figure also shows the percentage of gains actually sheltered by losses. The bimodality remains, although considerably more gains than taxpayers are in the 0 to 10 percent sheltered category. In addition, only 6 percent of gains are fully sheltered (compared with 12 percent of taxpayers). This suggests that taxpayers who fully shelter their gains have smaller than average gross gains. This would be expected, because it is easier to generate enough losses to shelter a small gain than

Figure 11.3   Percentage of Gross Gains Offset: Distributions of Taxpayers and Gross Gains

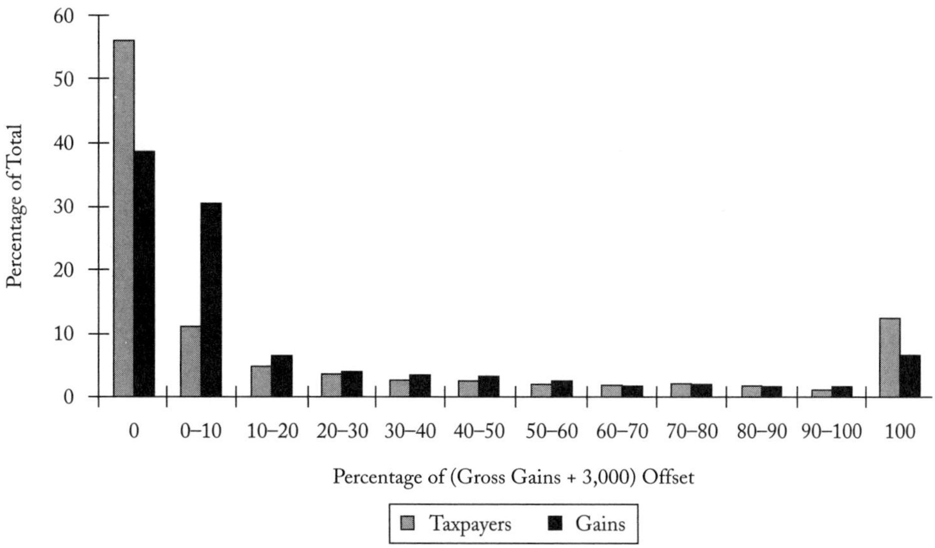

Percentage of (Gross Gains + 3,000) Offset

☐ Taxpayers   ■ Gains

Source: Author's calculations.

a large one. But it is also consistent with the idea that some taxpayers are in region C because they use the tax-avoidance strategies mentioned earlier to reduce the amount of their gross taxable gains.

We tested the sensitivity of our empirical hazard estimates by using a variety of different definitions of tax avoidance, adding to region C each taxpayer who offset at least x percent of his gross capital gains in a particular year. The results of one such specification, with x = 100, are given in appendix 11B. These results are quite similar to those based on the stricter definition.

Effective Tax Rates on Realized Capital Gains

Using the hazard rates presented in table 11.10, we may use the formula given in equation (11.4) to calculate effective tax rates on realized gains for each individual in our sample.[19] We focus on long-term capital gains, as these have been the subject of the greatest policy discussion over the years. Before doing so, however, we must resolve a number of technical issues.

First, since our hazard estimates do not go beyond a duration of seven years, we assume that the hazard rate (which already is very low) remains constant thereafter. Second, we must make assumptions about the values of time-varying covariates (such as GDP growth). We set the values of such variables equal to their sample means, with the exception of the time trend, which we assume equals its value at the end of the sample period (7). Third, we must make some allowance for sample attrition. Our estimates simply exclude longer durations for individuals who disappear from the sample. Using these estimates to calculate tax rates implicitly assumes that attrition is uncorrelated with individuals' hazard rates. An important case in which this is not true is when attrition is due to the death of the taxpayer. Because capital gains taxes are permanently forgiven at death, the correct treatment of a taxpayer who dies is to impose a hazard rate that is permanently equal to zero. Unfortunately, we cannot identify the reason for attrition. Therefore, we performed the calculation under two extreme assumptions: that attrition is random, and that attrition is always due to death. The results are virtually identical for the two cases (primarily because attrition while in region C is relatively unimportant). Thus, we present only those based on the former assumption. Finally, to apply equation (11.4), we need a discount rate and a value for $\tilde{\tau}$, the tax rate on long-term gains in the year the taxpayer leaves region C. We assume a value of 7 percent for the nominal discount rate. As for the value of $\tilde{\tau}$, it is important to keep in mind that exit can occur into one of three regions, A, B, or D. Although the tax rate on long-term gains equals τ^* in regions A and D, it equals the ordinary tax rate, τ, in region B. We assume that each individual's probability of exit into each region equals the observed sample probabilities. And further, since the value of τ in future years is not necessarily the same as in the year of a gain realization, we assign the expected future ordinary income tax rate based on permanent income.

The results of these calculations are presented, for selected years, in table 11.12, which shows the distribution of effective marginal tax rates on realized long-term capital gains broken down by the taxpayer's marginal tax rate on ordinary income. Gains realized in regions A, B, and D are assigned the rate appropriate to the taxpayer, region, and year, and those realized in region C are based on the methodology just described.

The median effective tax rate on long-term capital gains is identical to the statutory rate in every year. Though this may appear surprising, it is implied by the fact that a minority of taxpayers at each income level are in region C (for which the tax

Table 11.12   Effective Marginal Tax Rates on Long-term Capital Gains in Selected Years, by Ordinary Income Tax Rate (Weighted by Population)

Year	Ordinary Income Tax Rate (Percentage)	Percentiles of Marginal Tax Rate Distribution					Mean	
		1	10	50	90	99	By Tax Rate	Overall (Long-Term Gains Weighted)
1988	15	7.6	15.0	15.0	15.0	18.8	14.8	
	28 (low)	14.5	19.6	28.0	28.0	28.0	26.6	26.9
	33	12.6	18.8	33.0	33.0	33.0	30.6	
	28 (high)	13.4	21.3	28.0	28.0	28.0	26.9	
1991	15	7.0	15.0	15.0	15.0	19.7	14.9	
	28	8.9	17.8	28.0	28.0	28.0	26.1	25.0
	31	13.5	18.7	28.0	31.0	31.0	26.8	
1994	15	8.8	15.0	15.0	15.0	20.3	15.0	
	28	15.1	21.5	28.0	28.0	28.0	26.9	
	31	12.8	23.7	28.0	28.0	31.0	27.2	25.3
	36	16.6	19.1	28.0	36.0	36.0	27.5	
	39.6	16.7	19.9	28.0	39.6	39.6	27.5	

Source: Author's calculations.

rate is lower) or in region B (for which the tax rate may be higher). Thus, in all years, more than half of those who realize capital gains are avoiding no tax at all on the gains they realize. Indeed, this identity holds for the twenty-fifth and seventy-fifth percentiles of the distribution of tax rates in every year except 1990 (when the tax rate at the twenty-fifth percentile is 23 percent [not shown]).

Not surprisingly, taxpayers in the lowest tax bracket (15 percent) are least likely to avoid capital gains tax. In most years fewer than 5 percent have an effective rate below their statutory rate—and about an equal number manage to have their gains taxed at rates above the statutory rate. This occurs because some people who enter region C when their marginal tax rate is 15 percent may expect their rate to be higher when they exit region C. In addition, lower-income taxpayers who enter region C do not stay there very long. As a result, the overall average marginal tax rate for people in the 15 percent bracket is very close to 15 percent in every year.

In the higher tax brackets, a somewhat larger fraction of the population faces effective tax rates below the statutory rates. The lowest 1 percent of effective rates is more than ten percentage points below the statutory rate, but the overall effective capital gains tax rate is still very close to the statutory rate in every tax bracket, with the difference never exceeding three percentage points. Indeed, in 1991 and 1994 more than 10 percent of taxpayers in the top bracket face effective rates above the statutory long-term capital gains rate. This is because the tax rate on long-term capital gains in region B equals the tax rate on ordinary income, a rate that after the 1990 act exceeded the statutory rate on long-term gains for higher-bracket taxpayers.

In part because of this factor, the overall effective tax rate on a dollar of long-term capital gains has declined only slightly between 1988 and 1994, despite the increased likelihood of being in region C. Perhaps more important is the fact that presence in region C exerts a relatively small impact on an investor's effective tax rate. Given that roughly half of all investors in region C depart in one year, and about two-thirds within two years, the typical tax rate reduction is relatively small, perhaps five percentage points. For, say, a 10 percent increase in the share of capital gains in region C (an upper bound, based on the numbers given in the bottom panel of table 11.4), this would induce a drop of merely half a percentage point in the average marginal effective tax rate, a change small enough to be lost amid other changes occurring simultaneously over the period.

This is apparent in table 11.13. Investors in region C in 1994 can expect an effective tax rate only slightly below their statutory rate if they are in the 15 percent bracket. Taxpayers in the higher brackets can expect greater discounts from the statutory rate, but the difference is not dramatic. The largest difference is only about ten percentage points for taxpayers in region C in the 28 or 31 percent brackets. Taxpayers in the highest brackets, starting from region C, actually face higher effective tax rates than those in the intermediate brackets, because if they exit into region B, they are likely to face tax rates as high as 39.6 percent.

Tax Avoidance, Progressivity, and Fairness

Our findings dispel two contentions made about the fairness of capital gains taxation. The first is that high-income people can avoid the tax at will, thus subverting the slight progressivity designed into long-term capital gains tax rates. The second

Table 11.13   Effective Tax Rates on Long-term Capital Gains for Taxpayers in Region C Compared with all Taxpayers, by Ordinary Income Tax Rate in 1994

Ordinary Income Tax Rate	Tax Rate on Long-Term Gains	Effective Tax Rate	
		In Region C	All Taxpayers
15	15	14.8	15.0
28	28	17.9	26.9
31	28	17.4	27.2
36	28	19.4	27.5
39.6	28	20.5	27.5

Source: Author's calculations.

is that the loss limitation is especially unfair to lower-income taxpayers with only a single asset (for example, a mom-and-pop grocery store), who can never fully deduct a catastrophic loss against other gains or their other income.

In fact, average effective tax rates on realized capital gains are very close to statutory rates. Furthermore, Mom and Pop seem to be least likely to be constrained by the $3,000 loss limit. People in the 15 percent bracket are least likely to enter region C, and when they do, they do not stay there long. That is why their effective tax rate on long-term capital gains is nearly identical to the statutory rate.

EVIDENCE FROM THE SURVEY OF CONSUMER FINANCES

An important limitation of all the results presented thus far is that they relate only to tax avoidance associated with realization behavior. Thus, we have not focused on investors who fail to offset realized gains with realized losses. But this downplays the effect of an alternative avoidance mechanism, namely, the deferral of accrued gains, possibly until they receive favorable treatment at death or through a charitable contribution. Because such taxpayers may have little or no gross long-term gains, we understate the effect of such strategies on the overall effective tax rate. Even if the effective tax rate on realized gains is high and not strongly related to income or wealth, this may not be true of the rate on accrued gains.

To gain a more complete picture of the relationship between realized and accrued gains, we look at the only available evidence on unrealized gains, from the Survey of Consumer Finances (SCF). Figures 11.4 and 11.5 compare the distribution of average realized gains from 1988 to 1994 on the SOCA (omitting 1987 to eliminate timing behavior around TRA86) with the distribution of accrued gains from the 1992 SCF.[20] If higher-income people more successfully avoid realizing taxable gains, then accrued gains should be more concentrated among high-income people than realized gains. However, this pattern is not in evidence in these two data sets. For corporate stock, taxpayers with over $100,000 of income realized about 87 percent of gains in the average year of the period, whereas their accruals accounted for only 70 percent of gains. For business assets, the respective values for realizations and accruals are 76 percent and 61 percent.

Figure 11.4   Percentage of Gains in Each Income Class: Stock

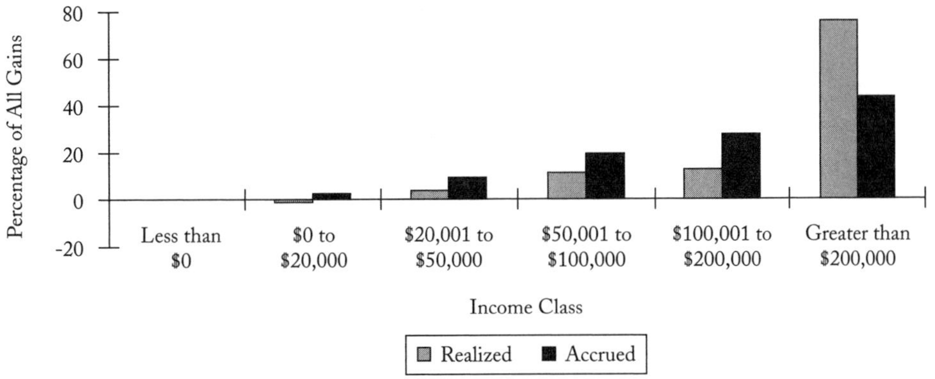

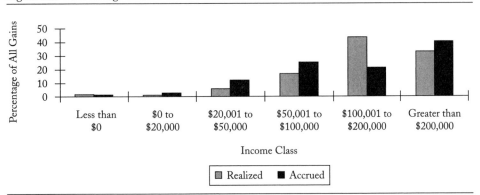

Source: Accrued gains: 1992 SCF; realized gains: 1988–1994 Average, Sales of Capital Assets.

These comparisons should be regarded with caution for several reasons. The SCF has relatively few very high-income respondents, and aggressive tax avoiders might have been less inclined to participate in the survey. The definitions of income are similar, but not identical. Finally, the long-run ratio of realizations to accruals need not be accurately pictured by data from a relatively short panel. Nonetheless, the lack of significant evidence of capital gains tax avoidance of high-income people is consistent with our general results.

CONCLUSIONS

Our analysis has extended the work of Poterba (1987) to look at more recent panel data. We find evidence consistent with his general conclusion—that tax avoidance

Figure 11.5   Percentage of Gains in Each Income Class: Business Assets

Sources: Accrued gains: 1992 SCF; realized gains: 1988–1994 Average, Sales of Capital Assets.

is not prevalent, even after passage of tax reform, and that most high-income people realize gains that are not sheltered by losses. Like Poterba, we also find that a minority of taxpayers—mostly with higher incomes and wealth—manage to shelter all or most of their gains with losses.

We find evidence that tax avoidance increased after 1986, and that it increased most for high-income, high-wealth taxpayers. As many as one-third of the wealthiest taxpayers were able to realize their gains without immediate tax (that is, they were in region C, as we have defined it) in the early 1990s. Moreover, we found that a subset of sophisticated investors were consistently more likely to be in region C than others. Through multivariate probit analysis, we demonstrated that this result persisted after controlling for other variables, such as income and wealth, and was robust with respect to weighting.

But the efficacy of tax avoidance strategies depends on being able to remain in region C for long periods. We found that most taxpayers exited quickly. Only about half of taxpayers are still in region C after one year; about one-quarter make it for at least three years. Combined with the small proportion of taxpayers in region C in the first place, this implies that the overall effective tax rate on realized capital gains is much closer to the statutory rates than is apparent based on a single year's perspective. Again, however, it is the sophisticated investors who consistently remain in region C longer than others, so a subset of taxpayers are able to shelter more of their gains from tax than most people.

Much further research is needed in this area. Our analysis focused primarily on realized capital gains. We could make only indirect inferences about the gains that are never realized but represent the most successful avoidance strategy. Since our analysis is inherently based on a reduced-form model, it is hard to draw firm inferences about the structural parameters involved in people's decisions, and about how they may have changed over time. These questions have proved daunting because of a lack of data and difficult conceptual problems but are still worth pursuing.

APPENDIX 11A: DATA AND METHODOLOGY

This appendix describes the construction of the variables and methodology we use in our estimations. Most of the data come from the 1985-based SOCA panel, which is introduced in the data section of this chapter.

Nearly all of the variables in the SOCA panel are obtained directly from individual federal tax returns for the panel members. Although the data do not include every conceivable supplementary IRS form, the data do include all the line-by-line entries from:

- Form 1040
- Schedule D (Capital Gains and Losses)
- Form 4797 (Sales of Business Property)
- Form 2119 (Sale of a Residence)
- Form 6252 (Installment Sales)
- Form 8824 (Like-Kind Exchanges)

The only data in the SOCA panel that do not originate from the federal income tax returns of the filers are the birthdates for both the primary and secondary taxpayers. This information was obtained through a merger with the Social Security Administration records of the taxpayers.

We linked the panel by matching the Social Security numbers in the separate files from each year and IRS form. A complication that arose in this process was that joint filers in 1985 did not always remain as joint filers (in the same combinations) throughout the panel: a result of death, divorce, marriage, and other changes in filing status. Where possible, the IRS included in the SOCA data files the returns from both Social Security numbers. This forced us to make a decision about what constitutes the appropriate panel observation. In general, when there was a conflict, we chose to follow the Social Security number listed as primary in 1985.

Constructed Variables

We created from the tax filings a variable for permanent income. This measure is not directly dependent on changes in tax code definitions of gross income and is not sensitive to transitory income variations. Permanent income is defined in all of the tabular results we present as the mean of real, positive income over the ten years of the panel. For taxpayers not in the sample for all years, we use the mean over the available years. Positive income is the sum of the positive components of income from: wages, taxable and tax-exempt interest, dividends, alimony, business income, capital gains, supplemental gains, schedule E (rental and royalty) income, IRA distributions, pension income, farm income, unemployment insurance benefits, taxable Social Security benefits, and other income. We use only the positive components since large business and capital losses are usually realized by only the wealthy; if included, these losses would make some individuals with high lifetime income appear to have low income. We normalized prices using the consumer price index (CPI), with a base period of 1982 to 1984. In the probit and duration models, we removed capital gains from permanent income to purge that variable of a source of endogeneity.

We imputed wealth by capitalizing capital income reported on tax forms. Taxable and tax-exempt interest are capitalized based on the three-month Treasury bill rate. Dividends are capitalized by the average dividend payout rate. We used the same rate to capitalize realizations of positive business income, schedule E income, and farm income. To prevent transitory income shocks from causing volatility in this imputation, the average wealth over the panel years is used for each individual. The variables for the shares in wealth of stock, business property, rental property, and farm property are the panel-year averages of the fractions of the total wealth imputation attributable to capitalized dividends, business income, schedule E income, and farm income, respectively. The indicator variable for earning tax-exempt interest is set to 1 if the panel member earns such income in any year.

There are several well-known limitations to this method of imputing wealth. Even if average total returns to capital are similar across individuals, capital income payout rates may differ across individuals and capital types and may depend on tax-related variables. For example, if there is a substantial dividend clientele effect, the wealth of the high-tax-rate individuals is systematically underestimated.

Three variables are constructed from the characteristics of the taxpayers' capital gains realizations. The mutual fund distributions' share of gains is the simple ratio of mutual fund gains to total gross gains plus $3,000 (to avoid dividing by zero for taxpayers with no gains). The measure of taxpayer sophistication is set to 1 if the panel member ever engages in a gain or loss transaction involving a stock short sale, option, commodity, or futures contract. Our logic in defining it this way is that individuals who for at least one time have access to such markets are likely to have a permanently higher level of access. (We tested this assumption by using a sophistication measure based on only the current year's activity, and it did not change any of the results significantly.) On the SOCA data set, short sales of stock are identifiable because the dates of sale and purchase are reversed. Options, commodities, and futures are coded as an asset type in the transactions data. The variable for the number of capital transactions is the total count of asset sales (both gains and losses) of all types in a year. In some cases, such as mutual fund distributions, the number of sales was not distinguishable (and perhaps not relevant) and therefore counted as one transaction.

The variable for the size of loss carry-overs in the hazard model is constructed as the log of the ratio of the amount of the carry-over to $3,000 plus the average size of current and recent gross gains. The specific formula used is

$$x_t = \log\left(\frac{C_t}{3000 + \frac{1}{3}\sum_{t-2}^{t} G_t}\right) \tag{11A.1}$$

where C_t is the amount of loss carry-over, G_t is the amount of gross capital gains, and 3,000 is added to the denominator to ensure that the variable is meaningful when gains are small (or zero).

Probit Estimation of Probability of Presence in Region C

The estimation of the probability of being in region C, reported in an earlier section, was done by commonly used methods for modeling discrete choice. The data used are the pooled observations of each taxpayer in each year reporting a capital gain or loss. The dependent variable is a binary variable equal to 1 when the taxpayer is in region C.

We chose a probit model, which assumes that the values of the independent variables, in vector x, relate to the probability of being in region C in the following manner:

$$\Pr(\text{Individual in Region C}) \equiv F(x) = \int_{-\infty}^{\beta'x} \phi(z)dz - \Phi(\beta'x), \tag{11A.2}$$

where $\phi(\cdot)$ and $\Phi(\cdot)$ are the density and cumulative distribution functions of a standard normal, respectively.

The parameters were estimated by maximum likelihood. The robust standard errors are estimated by assuming that observations for the same individual are not independent (and estimating their covariance). To aid in interpretation, the partial derivatives of the probability function with respect to the independent variables, $\partial F/\partial x$, are evaluated at the mean values for each independent variable. In the case of binary indicator variables, $\partial F/\partial x$ reported is calculated as the change in probability associated with a change in the variable from 0 to 1 holding all other variables constant at their mean values.

Estimation of Duration in Region C and Computation of Effective Tax Rates

We used a proportional hazards model to estimate the probabilities of exiting region C at various durations. Rather than making a specific assumption about the form of the hazard function's dependence on duration, we used the semiparametric approach of estimating a separate constant at each duration. Thus, our form for the hazard function is

$$h(t|X) = \exp(\beta_{0t} + X\beta), \tag{11A.3}$$

where β_{0t} is a constant for duration t.

Most of the variables included in X are not time-varying. Permanent income, wealth, wealth shares, and sophistication are all defined as permanent variables. We use the values only for the initial year in region C for the carry-over, mutual fund distributions share, and age variables. However, we use time-varying values of the GDP and Standard & Poors 500 growth rates, as well as a time trend, that do not remain constant through the duration of an individual's spell in region C.

The coefficients of the hazard model, including the duration constants, are estimated by maximum likelihood. From these estimates, we can construct an estimated hazard function for each individual. We can also look at the hazard function for any set of values for the covariates in X. In table 11.11, we did so for the mean values of the covariates, $h(t|\overline{X})$.

We use the formula in equation (11.4) to convert hazard estimates to effective tax rates, making the assumption that the constant in the hazard function at durations beyond the reach of our sample (seven years) is equal to the constant at seven years. The survival function, $s(\cdot)$, is a function of the hazard rates

$$s(t|X) = \prod_{v=1}^{t-1}[1 - h(v|X)] \quad \text{for } t > 1, \text{ and } s(1|X) = 1. \tag{11A.4}$$

Since we are computing ex ante effective tax rates with our hazard model, we do not assume that the variation in GDP and Standard & Poors 500 growth is known, and we replace the realized values for those variables with their means over the sample years. The trend variable is allowed to vary within the sample years in this calculation but is kept at its 1994 level for subsequent years.

APPENDIX 11B: ALTERNATIVE DEFINITIONS OF REGION C

Theory suggests that people who successfully avoid capital gains tax should be found in region C, the area bounded by the net loss offset limitation of $3,000. However, for many investors there may be only a small financial difference between facing that constraint, and being near it, while offsetting most or all of their gross capital gains. To examine a broader definition of region C than that used earlier, we redefined the region to include those taxpayers who offset high percentages of their gross gains, considering four alternative levels: 100, 90, 75, and 50 percent offset.

Tables 11A.1 (for unweighted and weighted samples) and 11A.2 and 11A.3 (for the unweighted sample only) present results from the estimations with the region

Table 11A.1   Results of the Estimation, Probability of Offsetting 100 Percent of Gross Gains, 1987 to 1994

	Population Weighted			Unweighted		
	Coefficient	Standard Error	$\partial F/\partial x$	Coefficient	Standard Error	$\partial F/\partial x$
Constant	−0.6605	0.5236	—	−0.0360	0.1443	—
Log(permanent income less capital gains)	0.0800	0.0494	0.0257	0.0106	0.0123	0.0036
Log(imputed wealth)	−0.0289	0.0299	−0.0093	−0.0480	0.0087	−0.0165
Stock share of wealth	0.0885	0.1597	0.0284	−0.0924	0.0436	−0.0318
Business property share of wealth	0.2584	0.1926	0.0830	0.3112	0.0368	0.1072
Rental property share of wealth	0.3061	0.2028	0.0983	0.2199	0.0418	0.0758
Farm property share of wealth	−0.5808	0.4369	−0.1865	−0.6660	0.2076	−0.2295
Earns tax-exempt interest	0.0245	0.0807	0.0079	−0.0907	0.0205	−0.0315
Log(number of capital transactions)	0.1375	0.0294	0.0442	−0.0581	0.0063	−0.0200
Sophisticated	0.2219	0.0858	0.0732	0.2838	0.0189	0.0957
Mutual fund share of capital gains	−1.9102	0.3091	−0.6134	−0.5402	0.0580	−0.1861
Single	0.2398	0.0916	0.0798	0.1251	0.0227	0.0441
Married filing separate	−0.0603	0.2170	−0.0190	−0.0035	0.0458	−0.0012
Head of household	−0.0367	0.1739	−0.0116	0.1155	0.0504	0.0409
Number of dependents	0.0041	0.0330	0.0013	0.0064	0.0073	0.0022
Age of primary taxpayer	−0.0193	0.0130	−0.0062	−0.0013	0.0042	−0.0004
(Age of primary taxpayer)^2	0.0001	0.0001	0.0000	0.0000	0.0000	0.0000
Real GDP growth rate	−3.9212	1.5585	−1.2592	−3.9947	0.3115	−1.3764
Standard & Poors 500 growth rate	−1.0099	0.2224	−0.3243	−0.5156	0.0447	−0.1776
Calendar time trend	0.0234	0.0121	0.0075	0.0452	0.0022	0.0156

Source: Author's calculations.
Note: $\partial F/\partial x$ is the partial derivative of the probability of being in region C with respect to the covariate. It is evaluated at mean values, $\bar{x}$, for nonbinary data, and evaluated for a discrete change in dummy variables from 0 to 1. Italics indicate dummy variable.

Table 11A.2   Results of the Estimation, Duration of Remaining in State
of Offsetting 100 Percent of Gross Gains, 1987 to 1994 (Unweighted)

	Coefficient	Standard Error
Log (permanent income less capital gains)	0.0600	0.0135
Log (imputed wealth)	−0.0256	0.0094
Stock share of wealth	0.1701	0.0494
Business property share of wealth	0.0405	0.0422
Rental property share of wealth	0.0405	0.0483
Farm property share of wealth	0.2255	0.2029
Earns tax-exempt interest	0.0886	0.0230
Size of initial loss carry-over[a]	−0.0672	0.0021
Log (number of capital transactions)	−0.0050	0.0087
Sophisticated	−0.0585	0.0216
Mutual fund share of capital gains	0.2406	0.0727
Age of primary taxpayer	−0.0010	0.0051
(Age of primary taxpayer)	0.0000	0.0000
Real GDP growth rate	0.8132	0.5663
Standard & Poors 500 growth rate	0.3086	0.1060
Calendar time	0.0174	0.0049
Constant	−1.4173	0.1704
Duration = 2	−0.2195	0.0247
Duration = 3	−0.4546	0.0371
Duration = 4	−0.6894	0.0527
Duration = 5	−0.7862	0.0718
Duration = 6	−0.6783	0.0841
Duration = 7	−1.1433	0.1487

Source: Author's calculations.
Note: Italics indicate dummy variable.
[a] The size of the initial loss carry-over variable is defined in appendix 11.1.

Table 11A.3   Typical Hazard Functions, Evaluated at Mean Values of Covariates, for Exiting
State of Offsetting 100 Percent of Gross Gains

Duration State of 100 Percent Gain Offset (Years)	Unweighted Hazard Model	
	Hazard	Survival
1	0.45	1.00
2	0.36	0.55
3	0.28	0.35
4	0.22	0.25
5	0.20	0.29
6	0.23	0.16
7	0.14	0.12

Source: Author's calculations.

C boundary repositioned at full (100 percent) offset of gross gains; they correspond to tables 11.9 through 11.11. A comparison of the estimates for the alternative definitions suggests that the choice does not change any of the results significantly and has no effect on our qualitative conclusions.

We are grateful to the staff of the Tax Analysis Division of the Congressional Budget Office for help in analyzing and interpreting the data used in this paper, to our discussant Jane Gravelle and other conference participants for comments on an earlier draft, and to the Robert D. Burch Center for Tax Policy and Public Finance for financial support. Views expressed in this paper are the authors' alone and do not necessarily reflect the views or policies of the institutions with which we are affiliated.

NOTES

1. See also Seyhun and Skinner (1994).

2. The figure is adapted from Poterba (1987) for changes in the treatment of capital losses introduced by TRA86. Poterba's figure reflecting pre-1986 law had seven distinct regions. A comparable figure for present law, when fully phased in, would require four dimensions to graph.

3. Our analysis accounts for the 33 percent bubble region in effect from 1988 to 1990, but not the quantitatively less significant phaseouts of itemized deductions and personal exemptions in effect after 1990, which also raised effective tax rates. We ignore as well the effects of the alternative minimum tax (AMT).

4. Henriques and Norris (1996) quote David Bradford: "The simple fact is that anyone sitting on a big pot of money today probably isn't paying capital-gains taxes and the government can adopt rule after rule after rule—but the people who will get stuck paying capital-gains taxes will be the ordinary investors who own mutual funds."

5. See U.S. Congressional Budget Office (1997) for a discussion of these data. All tabulations and estimations based on confidential tax return data were conducted by Jonathan Siegel while he was employed by the Congressional Budget Office.

6. Income in each year is calculated independent of the tax code by summing the positive components of income, rather than using adjusted gross income (AGI), which depends on the tax code.

7. For a discussion of some of the stratification and weighting issues, see Czajka (1994) and Holik (1989).

8. Since the SOCA transactions data come directly from the tax forms on which they originate, we excluded from this summation some gains and losses in the data set that are either nontaxable or subject to ordinary income treatment. For example, nontaxable personal residence gains from form 2119 were not included, nor were section 1231 losses and recaptured gains and losses. Furthermore, wherever detail by transaction is not needed in our analysis, we use the totals for gains and losses from schedule D, which reflect only those realizations subject to capital gains treatment.

9. As mentioned in note 2, the region definitions changed slightly after 1986. To allow comparison between the period 1985 to 1986 and subsequent years, we use the post-1986 region definitions to classify taxpayers in all years. This procedure has the effect of increasing the fraction of taxpayers in region C in the period 1985 to 1986, but only very slightly.

10. As mentioned earlier, the results may be distorted by the effects of attrition in the panel. For example, if the people who leave the panel (because they do not file a tax return, die, or misreport their Social Security number) are primarily the less tax-motivated investors, these data may sug-

gest more tax planning than really occurs in the population. We compared the estimates with data for the large SOI sample, which is drawn every year and intended to be representative of the population of taxpayers. As in the SOCA data, about 5 percent of investors were in region C in 1985; however, the percentage in the SOI increases only to 8 percent by 1994, compared with 12 percent in the SOCA panel, suggesting that attrition may alter our numerical estimates. Nonetheless, the qualitative conclusions are the same in the representative cross-sections as in the panel.

11. Poterba (1987), out of necessity, uses annual dividends to weight his data.

12. Gravelle (1991) shows why assets with high transaction costs should be less sensitive to tax rates on capital gains than more liquid assets.

13. The large changes in year-to-year percentages for some assets, notably business property, short sales, and options, appear to be attributable to two factors. First, the denominator of the calculation, aggregate net gains for the asset class, can be quite small in any given year for such volatile investments. This magnifies small absolute fluctuations in the level of gains in region C. Second, the weights chosen in 1985 were based on a single year's income. As a result, some apparently low-income people with very high weights were actually quite wealthy with high incomes in most years, a combination that can lead to volatility.

14. This variable equals the ratio of mutual fund distributions to gross gains plus $3,000.

15. The trend effect is calculated by comparing the probabilities (at the mean values of the other variables) with the trend set to 0 and 7, respectively.

16. This approach is similar to that used to calculate the effective tax rate for firms with tax loss carryforwards (see, for example, Altshuler and Auerbach 1990) but is simpler in part because capital losses may be carried forward indefinitely and may not be carried back.

17. See appendix 11A for more discussion of the hazard model.

18. Note that this is a continuous time model but is often used in the economic literature as an approximation for discrete data. See, for example, Blank (1989) and Meyer (1990).

19. Keep in mind that the effective tax rates computed in this section do not account for the nontaxation of accrued but unrealized capital gains held at death. This issue is addressed in a subsequent section.

20. We are grateful to Jeff Groen, formerly of the Tax Analysis Division of the Congressional Budget Office, for providing the tabulations from the SCF as well as useful advice about how to interpret them.

REFERENCES

Altshuler, Rosanne, and Alan J. Auerbach. 1990. "The Significance of Tax Law Asymmetries: An Empirical Investigation." *Quarterly Journal of Economics* 105(February): 61–80.

Auerbach, Alan J. 1988. "Capital Gains Taxation in the United States: Realizations, Revenue, and Rhetoric." *Brookings Papers on Economic Activity* 19 (Fall): 595–631.

Auten, Gerald E., and Charles T. Clotfelter. 1982. "Permanent Versus Transitory Effects and the Realization of Capital Gains." *Quarterly Journal of Economics* 97 (November): 613–32.

Blank, Rebecca M. 1989. "Analyzing the Length of Welfare Spells." *Journal of Public Economics* 39(August): 245–73.

Burman, Leonard E., Kimberly A. Clausing, and John O'Hare. 1994. "Tax Reform and Realizations of Capital Gains in 1986." *National Tax Journal* 47 (March): 1–18.

Burman, Leonard E., and William C. Randolph. 1994. "Measuring Permanent Responses to Capital Gains Tax Changes in Panel Data." *American Economic Review* 84(September): 794–809.

Constantinides, George M. 1984. "Optimal Stock Trading with Personal Taxes." *Journal of Financial Economics* 13(March): 65–89.

Czajka, John. 1994. "Income Stratification in Panel Surveys: Issues in Design and Estimation." In American Statistical Association, *Proceedings of the Section on Survey Research Methods.* Alexandria, Va.: American Statistical Association.

Feldstein, Martin, Joel Slemrod, and Shlomo Yitzhaki. 1980. "The Effects of Taxation on the Selling of Corporate Stock and the Realization of Capital Gains." *Quarterly Journal of Economics* 94(June): 777–91.

Gravelle, Jane G. 1991. "Limit to Capital Gains Feedback Effects." Report 91–250RCO (March). Washington, D.C.: Congressional Research Service.

Henriques, Diana B., and Floyd Norris. 1996. "Wealthy, Helped by Wall Street, Find New Ways to Escape Tax on Profits." *New York Times*, December 1, 1996.

Holik, Dan. 1989. "The 1985 Sales of Capital Assets Study." In American Statistical Association, *Proceedings of the Section on Survey Research Methods*. Alexandria, Va.: American Statistical Association.

Meyer, Bruce D. 1990. "Unemployment Insurance and Unemployment Spells." *Econometrica* 58(July): 757–82.

Poterba, James M. 1987. "How Burdensome Are Capital Gains Taxes?" *Journal of Public Economics* 33(July): 157–72.

Seyhun, H. Nejat, and Douglas J. Skinner. 1994. "How Do Taxes Affect Investors' Stock Market Realizations?: Evidence from Tax-Return Panel Data." *Journal of Business* 67(April): 231–62.

Stiglitz, Joseph E. 1983. "Some Aspects of the Taxation of Capital Gains." *Journal of Public Economics* 21(June): 257–94.

U.S. Congressional Budget Office. 1997. "Perspectives on the Ownership of Capital Assets and the Realization of Capital Gains." Washington, D.C.: CBO (May).

Commentary on Chapter 11

Jane G. Gravelle

Alan Auerbach, Leonard Burman, and Jonathan Siegel have provided an interesting chapter that examines the tax-avoidance behavior among high-income individuals for the source of income thought to be most under the straightforward control of the taxpayer: capital gains. This study is particularly significant because, if high-income taxpayers are not successfully practicing tax avoidance for this source of income, they are unlikely to be more successful with other types of income.

I find very little to criticize about this study in a technical sense. Ideally, a cross-sectional study should not be affected by other sources of disturbance. In particular, the panel should cover a period with no current or recent tax changes, no unusual asset price changes, and no speculation about impending changes. Such ideal conditions rarely occur, and they do not in this panel. Moreover, data derived from tax returns always suffer from difficulties in determining true income and wealth, the former because taxable and economic income differ, and the latter because wealth must be imputed from imperfect capital income data.

Nevertheless, these problems, which are common to most empirical studies of tax policy using tax data, are not likely to change the central conclusion—that losses do not offset more than a small fraction of gains, even for very high-income taxpayers.

In fact, this study both suggests that the wealthy do not avoid much capital gains tax and may present more evidence that the realization response is not very powerful. In order to evaluate these points and assess the meaning of the authors' findings, it is helpful to consider some other sources of information and the various reasons for realization.

These are two necessary conditions if the offsetting of gains with losses is to be significant. First, realization motives must be consistent with using losses to the maximum extent allowed. Second, most accrued gains must not be realized.

The second condition is required because losses are naturally small relative to gains. In the case of corporate stock, the normal expectation is for gain due to the growth arising from reinvested earnings and inflation. Gains also typically occur in real estate sales, because accelerated depreciation reduces basis and because these assets are likely to rise in nominal value over time, since inflation typically outweighs economic depreciation. Thus, the only way to have taxpayers offset most of their gains with losses is to realize very few accruals.

We have independent evidence, however, that a significant fraction of gains are realized. A detailed study of accruals and realizations over a long period of time indicated that about half of accruals are realized (Gravelle 1991). Auerbach, Burman, and Siegel present evidence from the Survey of Consumer Finances suggesting that this degree of realization occurs across the income spectrum, and that higher-income individuals tend to have the same, or larger, shares of realizations as they have of accruals. These data are, however, for only a single year; examining other years would be desirable to confirm this finding.

In addition to loss offsets being limited by the realization of a substantial amount of accruals, their realization may be limited if they are not part of the realizations strategy.

There are three motives for realizing a capital gain: consumption, speculative behavior, and portfolio rebalancing.

Within a life-cycle model, gains might be realized in order to finance consumption. With such a motive, it would be expected that assets with losses would be realized first (at least up to loss limits and thereafter offsetting gains) in order to minimize tax liability. There is reason to believe, however, that consumption is not an important realization motive. First, if consumption were the major motive for realizations, losses would be negatively correlated with age, since it is optimal to realize losses initially and gains later. This study finds no evidence of that effect. Second, capital gains assets are concentrated among higher-income individuals, who are the most likely to save rather than dissave in old age and to pass their wealth to their heirs (where capital gains taxes can be avoided altogether).

The second motive is speculative, that is, buying and selling in anticipation of different rates of return from current market expectations. Such activity requires selection of stocks to sell based on their expected yield. If there is no correlation between past yield and expected future yield by the investor, there is no reason to prefer the sale of assets with losses. In fact, investors may be reluctant to sell assets with losses if they believe these assets are experiencing the downside of a fluctuation.

The third motive, to rebalance portfolios, would also not necessarily be consistent with selling loss assets. Portfolio rebalancing would typically occur when a given asset mix shifts through prior gains and losses in a way that is inconsistent with risk and return preferences, or when the preferences of the investor change. There is no obvious reason to expect the selling of assets with losses for this purpose.

Since the motives for realizations do not appear especially consistent with realizing losses, and since losses tend to be small relative to accruals, the real question is why high-income individuals realize so much capital gain when there are many sophisticated techniques to avoid tax while still obtaining cash and the risk characteristics desired. Moreover, we may wish to know how much realization (for tax purposes) is avoided by using these techniques. The authors present some evidence on the use of these sophisticated techniques and find them not very widely used.

One explanation may be that transaction costs are too large to permit the shielding of gains in this alternative way. Setting up such avoidance vehicles requires not only payment of fees but also time and attention. Especially for the speculator, who may do substantial numbers of transactions, use of such schemes may not be feasible. They may be reserved for the large significant transactions in which time and money spent will be handsomely rewarded with tax payments.

In any case, this failure to use tax-avoidance techniques tends to provide additional evidence that the realizations response is not very large. There is already some evidence to suggest that, at the very least, the long-term permanent realizations response is not very large, despite a number of empirical studies finding large responses. The relatively high ratio of realizations to accruals not only provides evidence that gains are realized despite significant tax consequences but also precludes the large responses previously estimated in some studies, since realizations cannot exceed accruals (Gravelle 1991). There had long been speculation that the higher elasticities in cross-sectional studies, and even in panel studies, were reflecting transitory rather than permanent responses. Leonard Burman and William Randolph (1994), using variation in state tax rates, found a high transitory, but a low permanent, elasticity.

The apparently limited use of sophisticated techniques of capital gains avoidance, even among very high-income individuals, is further evidence of a limited sensitivity to tax factors. If individuals are not willing to take the time to arrange tax-avoidance transactions to allow them to realize without paying tax, how much less willing would they be to forgo sales altogether in order to minimize tax liability? These observations give us some reasons to believe that the realizations response itself is not responsive to tax considerations. If realizations elasticities are small, then much of the efficiency impetus for capital gains reduction is eliminated, and the claims that the lower rates can be adopted with little or no revenue loss cannot be true. Small realizations elasticities also suggest that the recent cuts in capital gains taxes will be much more costly than predicted by the revenue estimators at either the Joint Committee on Taxation or the Treasury, and that the efficiency benefits are less significant than the distributional consequences.

REFERENCES

Burman, Leonard E., and William C. Randolph. 1994. "Measuring Permanent Responses to Capital Gains Tax Changes in Panel Data." *American Economic Review* 84: 94–809.

Gravelle, Jane G. 1991. "Limits to Capital Gains Feedback Effects." Congressional Research Service Report 91–250. Reprinted in *Tax Notes* 51(April 22): 363–71.

12

Taxes and Philanthropy Among the Wealthy

Gerald E. Auten, Charles T. Clotfelter, and Richard L. Schmalbeck

Although it may not be the most visible manifestation of wealth, charitable giving is and has long been a hallmark of affluence. Among the most notable for their philanthropic activities are Andrew Carnegie, John D. Rockefeller, and, more recently, John Paul Getty, George Soros, and Ted Turner.[1] Wealthy patrons occupy a prominent place in the life of the nonprofit sector. They volunteer in fund-raising campaigns, serve on governing boards, have buildings named for them, and receive honorary degrees. As a class, they are almost entirely responsible for the existence of private foundations. Those occupying the top rungs of the income and wealth distributions make a disproportionate share of all charitable gifts. The 1 percent of American households with the highest incomes made more than 16 percent of all contributions in 1994. Charitable bequests are even more concentrated, with the wealthiest 1.4 percent of decedents accounting for about 86 percent of all charitable bequests.[2]

The charitable behavior of the affluent is clearly a matter of significance to the nonprofit sector. Owing to the central role that nonprofit organizations play in education, health, the arts, and human services, the sector, and thus its support, are also matters of public policy importance. Including the value of its volunteer labor, the nonprofit sector accounts for roughly 6 percent of national income.[3] Many observers expect the sector to take on an increasingly important role in the wake of government devolution. Charitable contributions remain an important source of funding for nonprofit organizations. In 1994 they represented about 18 percent of the sector's total revenues, and about a one-third of total revenues outside the health subsector (Hodgkinson and Weitzman 1996, 40, 189). And in light of the increased concentration of income at the top, one would expect that the role of the wealthy in the sector would grow. In particular, the prospect of a massive transfer of wealth over the next few decades includes the likelihood of some very large individual transfers, which in the past have often taken the form of new private foundations.[4]

The purpose of this chapter is to investigate the tax and financial environment of the rich as it relates to contributions, both during life and in bequests. We begin, in the next two sections, by describing the legal and institutional landscape, looking at the options for wealthy individuals who desire to make charitable gifts, and at changes in those options. The first section deals with the tax code, paying particular attention to gifts of appreciated property, the alternative minimum tax, and the gift and estate tax. The next section focuses on giving techniques of the wealthy, including private foundations. That discussion is followed by a section that reviews the social science research on the question of motivations for giving. The following section describes the charitable giving of the wealthy both in life and in their bequests. It examines variations in the percentage of income and wealth given, the concentration of giving, the types of organizations supported, and the pattern of giving over time. It also examines differences in bequest giving between men and women. A final section examines the issue of permanent and transitory price effects of the income tax on charitable giving and presents new evidence on the effects of the tax law changes in the 1980s on giving.

THE TAX ENVIRONMENT OF THE RICH

The federal tax system offers a variety of incentives to make charitable gifts, largely by allowing a deduction of the amount of a charitable gift from the base of the federal income and transfer taxes. We discuss the relevant provisions in this section, paying particular attention to their effects on high-income taxpayers.

Individual Income Tax

Marginal Tax Rates   The marginal income tax rate faced by wealthy taxpayers is the central variable in any analysis of their incentives to make charitable gifts. The conventional formula describing the cost of giving as $(1 - m)G$, where G is the amount of the gift and m the marginal tax rate, highlights the role of rates.[5] The rate structure, and thus the price of giving, has changed many times, with no fewer than four major changes in the last sixteen years alone.

Figure 12.1 illustrates the changes in the price of giving for high-income taxpayers since 1960. The figure depicts the cost of giving in each year for a gift of cash and of zero-basis appreciated property, respectively, per dollar of gift, for a taxpayer in the highest marginal rate bracket. The long-term downward trend in top rates and the consequent upward trend in the cost of giving are clearly discernible.

The Omnibus Budget Reconciliation Act of 1993 (OBRA93), which modestly countered these trends, introduced a 36 percent rate that applied in 1993 and 1994 to taxable incomes of married couples between $140,000 and $250,000, and a 39.6 percent rate that applied to incomes above $250,000.[6] This is, of course, exclusive of any state or municipal income taxes.[7]

Provisions Regarding Deductions for Charitable Gifts   The basic rules governing charitable contributions are reasonably straightforward. Deductible gifts are those made to governmental units or to qualifying organizations that are organized and operated primarily for religious, charitable, or educational purposes (or a few other purposes of less general import). Deductible gifts can be made in cash or in property, with the amount of the deductible contribution in the latter case being ordinarily equal to the fair market value of the property. Current deductions can be taken in some cases for contributions of future interests in property.[8]

Generally, taxpayers may deduct their charitable gifts in any one tax year only to the extent that total gifts do not exceed 50 percent of adjusted gross income (AGI). However, limitations of 20 or 30 percent of AGI apply under some circumstances.[9]

Figure 12.1   The Price of Giving Cash and Appreciated Property, 1960 to 1997

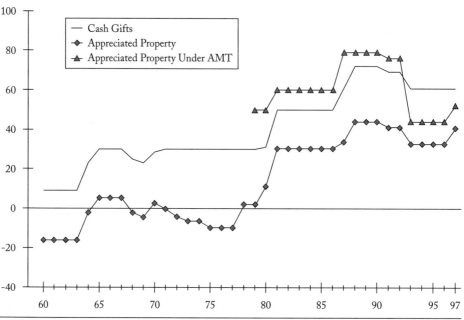

Source: Authors' calculations.
Note: The price of giving cash equals 100 minus the tax rate in the top tax bracket. The price of giving appreciated property equals the price of giving cash less the capital gains tax rate. Gifts of appreciated property are assumed to be gifts of stock with 100 percent appreciation that would otherwise be sold in that year.

To what extent these limitations affect the amount of contributions is uncertain, but some observers have speculated that they constrain the size of gifts by the wealthy.[10]

Deduction amounts barred by these limits may be carried over to up to five subsequent tax years. One might imagine that, with limits as high as these, taxpayers would very rarely exceed them. And as a general matter, that is true. However, in the very top brackets carry-overs are important: for those with incomes in excess of $2.5 million in 1995, nearly 28 percent of the 1995 charitable contributions deductions were for amounts that had been carried over from prior years. Indeed, it can be accurately said that the carry-over of disallowed charitable contributions is essentially a high-bracket phenomenon, since less than 2 percent of the contributions deductions taken by taxpayers with incomes below $200,000 represented amounts carried over from prior years.[11]

Charitable gifts of appreciated property have constituted a particularly problematic aspect of the tax rules from the inception of the charitable contributions deduction. For most of the history of the tax system, for most gifts, a donor could deduct the full market value of a gift regardless of the donor's original investment in the asset. In the case of appreciated property, this is simply an accounting error: the amount of the gain should not be both excluded from capital gains and deducted as part of a charitable contribution.[12] In partial recognition of the abuse possibilities created by the fair market value rule, Congress in 1969 attached some significant limitations to such deductions; with minor modifications, these limitations continue to constitute the major constraints in this area. Under present law, taxpayers are limited, in effect, to deduction of their tax basis for gifts of appreciated property in several situations: gifts to "private foundations" (with some exceptions noted later); gifts of property that would not be "long-term capital gain" property; and gifts of tangible personal property whose use is unrelated to the exempt purposes of the charitable organizations to which the property was given. Although the 1969 act eliminated some abuses, it actually left the larger part of the problem intact, since donors can still generally deduct gifts of appreciated property to public charities.

The Alternative Minimum Tax   Since 1979 the federal income tax has been followed by its shadow tax, the alternative minimum tax (AMT).[13] Concerned that some taxpayers with very high incomes might arrange their affairs in such a way that they had little or no taxable income, Congress created a separate—and generally more inclusive—set of income and deduction rules that would define the base of this minimum tax. High-income taxpayers are essentially required to compute their tax liabilities under both taxes, and to pay the larger liability.

The significance of the AMT for present purposes is limited to two unrelated points. First, taxpayers whose circumstances expose them to the alternative minimum tax generally face decisions influenced more by the AMT marginal rate than by the regular marginal tax rate. Currently, the AMT rates are 26 percent of the first $175,000 of AMT income, and 28 percent of incomes in excess of that amount, regardless of filing status.

Second, at various times in our recent tax history, certain kinds of charitable contributions involving gifts of property have been only partly deductible for AMT purposes. During those times, the AMT has had a dramatic impact on the incentive to make such gifts. These rules are explained later.

Appreciated Property Gifts and the Alternative Minimum Tax   In writing the Tax Reform Act of 1986 (TRA86), Congress decided that the portion of a charitable contribution that represented the excess of fair market value over basis would be treated, beginning in 1987, as a "tax preference item." The effect of this, for taxpayers exposed to the AMT, was generally to limit the deduction to the amount of the basis in the property. And in the case of a taxpayer who was making a very large gift, or who was, prior to making the gift, close to the point of AMT exposure, a gift of appreciated property could actually create an AMT liability. This was particularly troublesome for high-income taxpayers, since the AMT is, more or less successfully, targeted at them.[14]

Museums, and to a lesser degree universities, believed that this feature inflicted serious damage on their acquisition and development prospects. Efforts to undo this small piece of tax reform began almost immediately and bore fruit—at least for museums—in 1990, when Congress temporarily suspended AMT preference treatment of charitable gifts of appreciated tangible personal property. This suspension was allowed to expire on July 1, 1992, but the continued lobbying by museums and universities ultimately led, in 1993, to a retroactive repeal of the preference treatment for contributions of tangible personal property made after June 30, 1992, and for all appreciated property contributions made after December 31, 1992.

Federal Transfer Taxes

The American transfer-tax system was substantially revised by the Tax Reform Act of 1976 (TRA76), which integrated previously separate taxes into a unified transfer tax applying to all gratuitous transfers during life and at death, supplemented by a special excise tax on so-called generation-skipping transfers, by which assets could be passed, for example, to grandchildren rather than to children. In this way, Congress hoped to tax dynastic wealth transfers to each succeeding generation. This tax regime purports to cover all gratuitous transfers; however, several important exceptions effectively limit the applicability of the tax only to transfers of relatively large amounts. The first is the annual exclusion from the gift tax of up to $10,000 per year, for each particular combination of donor and donee.[15] The second is the "unified credit"—that is, a credit that can be used against either gift or estate taxes—of $192,800, which is the amount of tax liability generated by transfers totaling $600,000.[16] Thus, effectively, the gift and estate taxes apply only to individuals whose lifetime and at-death transfers exceed that latter sum. The third exception allows unlimited tax-free transfers to a spouse during life or at death, provided that the spouse is a U.S. citizen. Finally, there is a lifetime exemption of $1 million per transferor from the generation-skipping transfer tax. The rate schedule applying to total lifetime and at-death transfers rises to a marginal rate of 55 percent on transfers to the extent that they exceed $3 million.[17] The generation-skipping transfer tax also has a top rate of 55 percent, resulting in a total tax rate of nearly 80 percent on transfers subject to both taxes.

The rules regarding transfer-tax deductions for charitable contributions are quite straightforward: under both the estate and the gift tax rules, the value of property given to a qualified charitable entity is simply subtracted from gross transfers, reducing the amount of taxable transfers to the full extent of the gift.[18] There is no explicit deduction for charitable gifts in the generation-skipping transfer-tax rules; however, the definition of taxable transfers makes it clear that only transfers to natural persons, or trusts for the benefit of natural persons, are to be taxed.

Relatively few deceased individuals are actually subject to federal transfer taxes. In recent years, of the more than 2 million adult Americans who have died each year, only about 70,000, or about 3 percent, have filed estate tax returns, and fewer than half of those were actually taxable.[19] Most of the top 1 percent of income taxpayers are presumably subject to transfer taxes.[20]

It appears that the majority of decedents—even relatively wealthy ones—do not make charitable bequests. In 1995 only about one-fifth of decedents filing estate tax returns made any deductible contributions. This percentage rose with the size of the estate but reached 50 percent only for the 272 estates with net worth exceeding $20 million.[21] Nevertheless, those estates that do include charitable bequests convey substantial wealth to charities: the total value of such bequests in 1995 was $8.7 billion.

The failure of many estates to make any charitable bequests may reflect one obvious tax consideration: a charitable bequest reduces the taxable estate by the amount of the bequest but confers no other tax benefits. A gift of the same amount given to charity during the donor's life, however, not only reduces the taxable estate but confers an income tax benefit in the year of the contribution. Thus, those wealthy individuals who wish to make significant contributions to charity would generally benefit from making the bulk of such gifts during their lifetimes.

GIVING TECHNIQUES OF THE WEALTHY: THE INSTITUTIONS AND MECHANISMS

Although wealthy individuals and families can and do make contributions by simply writing a check to a charitable organization, tax and estate planning and certain other nontax goals can frequently be optimized by more complex transfers. In this section, we consider some of the institutions used by the wealthy in making more sophisticated charitable transfers, along with some of their preferred gift techniques, concluding with some historical examples of apparently philanthropic behavior that was in fact probably motivated more by tax considerations than by charitable ones.

Control-Preserving Institutions

Private Foundations   The federal tax law distinguishes between those charitable entities that are "public charities," receiving contributions and program revenues from a wide range of sources, and those that are "private foundations," created by one or a few large gifts, typically from a single family. Except for a minority of foundations that are "operating" private foundations (about 10 percent of the total), the activities of private foundations are limited to investing and managing their capital and making grants to other charitable organizations out of their income. Contributions to private foundations are generally fully deductible. Because private foundations are privately funded and controlled, however, opportunities for public scrutiny have been limited until recently.[22] The considerable potential for abuse in this situation has led over time to a wide variety of restrictions on all aspects of the organization and operation of private foundations. These provisions are numerous and elaborate; even a brief summary is beyond the scope of this chapter. However, the most important of these require distribution for charitable purposes of 5 percent of the assets of the foundation each year; prohibit a broad range of self-dealing transactions between the foundation and "disqualified persons"(its donors, their family members, and the foundation's board members); and prohibit the foundation from holding, in conjunction with the holdings of disqualified persons, controlling interests in corporations. There is also a 2 percent excise tax on the annual net investment income earned by private foundations, which can be reduced to 1 percent in certain cases when the foundation increases its distribution rate.

For those who propose to transfer assets of great value, the restrictions may be worth enduring in exchange for the ability to continue indefinitely to control the flow of funds to their ultimate charitable uses. Indeed, in part because it is cumbersome and expensive to create and maintain, a private foundation with an individual or family's own name on it has been something of a hallmark of great wealth.[23] Collectively, these organizations represent a significant portion of the charitable sector. In 1995 the 48,000 private foundations reporting for that year held assets of more than $263 billion and made distributions for exempt purposes of about $13 billion (Arnsberger 1999, figure A).

Congress has in recent years made it much more attractive for entrepreneurs to fund a private foundation with appreciated stock. As noted in the previous section, deductions for gifts in kind to private foundations are generally limited to the basis in the property. There are, however, some exceptions. The first exception applies to operating foundations. Gifts in kind to these foundations have always been fully deductible at the fair market value of the property given.

Another exception was added in 1984 for gifts made before January 1, 1995, to private foundations of certain corporate stock. Although Congress allowed this provision to expire, a window for full deduction of appreciated stock contributions to private foundations was reopened in 1996 for the period from July 1, 1996 through May 31, 1997; extended until June 30, 1998 in the Taxpayer Relief Act of 1997; and finally extended permanently in the Internal Revenue Service Restructuring and Reform Act of 1998.

Short of creating a private foundation, individuals who wish to make an immediate transfer for charitable purposes (and thereby to generate an immediate tax deduction) but who also wish to continue to have some control over the future flow of charitable benefits have a number of options. They can contribute to a "donor-advised fund" held by a community foundation or other charitable entity. These funds allow donors to recommend periodically the direction in which they would like their share of the foundation's income to flow. Such directions are not legally binding on the community foundation, but the level of voluntary compliance with such directives is reportedly high.[24]

Another possibility is the "supporting organization," commonly established by educational institutions and other public charities. This is an entity that would typically not qualify as a public charity, for lack of a broad base of support. However, because it is operated in conjunction with a public charity, it is exempt from the burdens associated with free-standing private foundations. Supporting organizations may maintain their own grant-making operations as long as there is a sufficient operational or supervisory relationship with a public charity.

Split-Interest Trusts

A "split-interest" gift is one by which property is given to a trust, under the terms of which either the remainder interest or the income interest in the property is conveyed to one or more charitable entities, while other interests are given to specified individuals, often including the grantor of the trust. The actuarial value of the interest given to charity is allowed as a current income tax deduction in the year of funding of the trust.

Remainder Trusts   The Internal Revenue Code recognizes three types of deferred gift trusts: the charitable remainder annuity trust (CRAT), the charitable remainder unitrust (CRUT), and the pooled income fund. CRATs and CRUTs are distinguished chiefly by the fact that the trust agreement governing the former calls for payment of a particular sum each year to the income beneficiaries, while the latter fixes the income payments in terms of a stated percentage of the then-current trust assets. A pooled income fund is a trust maintained by the target charitable organization. Multiple donors can contribute remainder interests in property to such a fund and enjoy annual income payments determined by the overall rate of return earned by the fund.

The principal tax advantage in using a remainder trust is that the trust is itself exempt from income taxation. It is thus free to engage, without tax consequences, in transactions—such as the sale of the trust assets—that would be taxable if done directly by the grantor. For example, individuals who were founders or early participants in a very successful venture may find themselves with a great deal of wealth, but in a portfolio that is exposed to an unacceptable degree of risk. For a relatively young entrepreneur, a lifetime income interest in such a venture may well amount to as much as 90 percent of its total value.[25] In such a case, creation of a charitable remainder trust may be motivated at least in part by a desire to achieve a more diversified portfolio without exposing accrued gains to a capital gains tax; nevertheless, some value is passed to a charitable organization, and only what is so passed is allowed as a deduction.

Considerable flexibility is permitted in the design of charitable trusts, especially in the case of CRATs and CRUTs. And the ingenuity of tax planners has found in these vehicles a range of opportunity that is paralleled in few other areas of tax law. An example would be to create a trust in which the grantor is the income beneficiary, which invests in growth stocks during the working years of the grantor, shifting to income-producing assets during the grantor's retirement years. Because such trusts can include "makeup" provisions, the income payments during retirement can be structured to provide total lifetime payments that approximate the present value of a more traditional life estate but are timed to better meet the tax and financial planning preferences of the grantor.[26]

Charitable Lead Trusts   These trusts are another form of split-interest gift, but they involve the direction of some form of income interest to the charitable organization, with the remainder interest going ultimately to a noncharitable party, most typically an heir of the grantor of the trust. The periodic distributions to the charitable organization may be fixed as to either dollar amount or percentage of the assets then in the trust. Although the creation of such a trust can generate a current income tax deduction equal to the actuarial value of the interest transferred to charity, trust accounting rules generally require that the income from the trust continue to be taxed to the grantor, significantly limiting the income tax advantages associated with the transfer. There are some transfer-tax advantages associated with these trusts, however, inhering essentially in the fact that the valuation for transfer-tax purposes of the remainder interests ultimately transferred to the heirs will be discounted to their present value as of the date of the funding of the trust, thus yielding a much lower taxable transfer value than the simple transfer of the same assets at death.

Abuse Possibilities

At various times in the history of our income tax, it has been possible to generate enough tax savings with certain types of charitable gifts that the "gift" actually has a negative cost; that is, a taxpayer could be better off—even without accounting for the joy of giving—by giving away valuable assets than by selling them. Before 1969, for example, it was particularly advantageous for a taxpayer to give away highly appreciated assets. Such a gift generated a current income tax deduction of the fair market value of such property and also avoided imposition of a tax on the realization of the gain position of the asset. When marginal tax rates were as high as 70 percent (as they were in the mid- to late sixties, when this device was most often employed), this would have meant that gifts of highly appreciated assets generated as much as $1.19 of tax savings for every dollar of value transferred.[27]

An abuse opportunity closed by the Taxpayer Relief Act of 1997 involved the use of a CRUT with a very high payout rate and a very short term. For example, a CRUT could be arranged with a principal consisting of $1 million of appreciated stock, an 80 percent payout rate, a two-year term, and the grantor as the income beneficiary. In the first year the trust would sell no stock; it would meet its 80 percent payout obligation by selling $800,000 of stock before April 15 of the following year, since a trust generally has until that time to make distributions of income or principal from the preceding year to its beneficiaries. Because the trust had no income in its first year, however, this distribution would be treated as a tax-free return of capital to the grantor-beneficiary. At some point in its second year the trust would sell the remaining $200,000 of stock and distribute $160,000 (80 percent) to the grantor-beneficiary and the $40,000 remainder to charity. The trust itself would not be taxable on its sales of stock, but the character of the income generated in the second year would be passed through to the grantor-beneficiary. Thus, the $160,000 distributed would be taxable to the recipient as capital gain income. The taxpayer thus hoped to pay as little as little as $44,800 on the $160,000 taxable distribution and also sacrificed—albeit on a deductible basis—the $40,000 value going to the charitable remainder. If the $1 million of appreciated assets had been sold directly rather than through the trust device, the capital gains tax would have been $280,000. Therefore, by making a charitable gift of $40,000, the taxpayer could emerge from the transaction more than $200,000 better off compared with a straightforward sale of the stock.[28]

As noted, this device was a target of the Taxpayer Relief Act of 1997, which limited payout rates on trusts of this sort to a maximum of 50 percent of the value of the corpus. The same act also lowered the maximum capital gains rate to 20 percent. These changes appear to preclude the possibility that a gift of this sort could have a negative cost, though the use of a CRUT may still significantly reduce the positive cost of charitable gifts.

WHY DO THEY GIVE?

Economists tend to believe that in dealing with individual behavior in general the question of motivation is best left to the psychologists and theologians; they prefer to limit their attention to the effects of changes in prices and incomes on that behavior. With minor exceptions, this generalization also applies to economists' empirical work on charitable contributions. Yet the question of motivation in this context is both interesting and significant. For our purposes, the most useful research on what motivates the wealthy to give is based on interviews with donors. Because of the difficulty in obtaining such interviews, the studies have necessarily relied on small samples, and the findings have tended to be qualitative rather than statistical in form. Using such evidence, researchers can draw conclusions with respect to the motivations of donors either from the donors' own statements—an approach seldom favored by the skeptic—or from inferences based on the donors' behavior.

Before noting the conclusions of scholars who have examined the question of motivation, it is useful to note three observable respects in which the charitable behavior of the affluent differs from that of other individuals. First, the wealthy tend to favor different types of tax-exempt organizations than those supported by the majority of donating individuals. As noted in the next section, the wealthy, in comparison to other taxpayers, devote a much smaller share of their contributions to religious organizations and a much larger share to education, health, and arts and culture.

The second distinctive aspect of the charitable behavior of the wealthy is the considerable influence that they tend to exert in the charitable organizations to which they contribute. Although it is not uncommon for donors to be active participants in the organizations they support—either as volunteers or as users of services—wealthy donors are greatly overrepresented on governing boards and at high-profile gatherings of supporters (Ostrower 1995, 30). Odendahl (1990, 34, 35), noting the "self-enclosed" nature of governing boards and the high degree of crossover among board members of various organizations, declares, "Only those people who can make or raise large contributions are allowed access to policy-making positions." Moreover, the capacity to make large gifts opens the door to particular forms of philanthropy in which donor control is inherent.

A third observable aspect of the charitable behavior of the affluent is their widespread use of advisers. Attorneys and personal advisers are commonly used by wealthy donors to advise them on the tax consequences, other legal ramifications, and administrative alternatives connected with their giving. According to Francie Ostrower (1987), attorneys are the more important class of advisers. They are employed most often in connection with the estate and gift tax and the establishment of private foundations. In practice, the effect of their advice is often to encourage wealthy donors to use community foundations or split-interest trusts rather than set up their own foundations because of the cost and complexity of the foundation form (see especially Ostrower 1987, 251–52).

As to the motivations that underlie these patterns of giving, any statements must necessarily be speculative. However, the literature on this subject, especially regarding giving by the affluent, does feature several themes worth noting. One is the importance of personal connections—what Paul Schervish and John Havens (1997) call the "social networks of invitation and obligation." A recent study by Ostrower (1995) of ninety-nine wealthy donors in the New York City area illustrates the importance of donors' personal association with the recipient organizations. She finds that personal contact—as alumni, audience members, special guests, honorees, volunteers, or board members—is of paramount importance for these donors. In the same way that religious congregations provide many Americans with a sense of community, she argues, the nonprofit organizations that these donors support provide the venue for much of the community of the wealthy: "Nonprofit organizations are focal points around which upper-class life revolves. Through their philanthropy, wealthy donors come together with one another and sustain a series of organizations that contribute to the social and cultural coherence of upper-class life" (36). Through gatherings ranging from board meetings to gala receptions, the social and economic elite sustain social networks that tend to be both exclusive and prestigious. This exclusivity appears to be especially pronounced in the case of cultural institutions, according to Ostrower, although wealth has increasingly become a substitute for social standing even in those institutions, as suggested by the decline in the percentage of the board of the Metropolitan Museum of Art listed in the *Social Register*.[29]

Not surprisingly, one theme that runs through some scholarly speculations about motivation is the degree to which donative behavior is self-serving. At one extreme, contributions and other involvement with nonprofit organizations may bring personal rewards, a possibility illustrated by respondents who cite the prestige associated with board membership or the social connections made possible from inclusion in gala dinners (see, for example, Ostrower 1995, 36, 93–95). Large contributions can also bring with them considerable fanfare and publicity, although, as Ted Turner complained, often not as much public approbation as wealth itself.[30] Another kind of payoff, especially in connection with cultural organizations, is the aesthetic enjoyment of attendance at concerts or special showings of art.

Other scholars emphasize the desire of donors in their giving to repay institutions that helped them or to "make a difference" (see, for example, Schervish, forthcoming). One survey conducted in 1982 sought to address the question of motivation directly in the case of foundations. Of the twenty possible motivations for establishing a foundation listed on the form, those judged to be the strongest were personal philosophy, systematic giving, and welfare of others.[31] At its extreme, "making a difference" becomes a desire to exert control, and this is an objective certainly within reach of wealthy donors in certain cases. But as Eugene Steuerle (1987) points out, giving money away deprives donors of the possibly greater control made possible by holding wealth. That the urge to retain such power is strong, he argues, can be inferred from the small size of charitable contributions in life made by the wealthy compared to their charitable bequests, despite the clear tax advantages from lifetime giving.[32]

As this brief review of the social science research makes clear, the question of motivation remains both complex and ultimately resistant to scientific proof. Although it may well be the case that some donors seek recognition or even more tangible rewards from their philanthropy, it is clear that other donors want no recognition at all. The purely altruistic instinct to advance a cause or assist others must surely play a major role for many of the donors whose giving is included in the statistics presented in this chapter. Likewise, some wealthy donors appear to be motivated by a sense of obligation to share their wealth. And to these considerations must be added the role of solicitations by charitable organizations, which probably stimulate as well as inform giving, further complicating any attempt to determine motivation. Therefore, in a spirit of humility with respect to those things still unknown about the motivations behind this behavior, we press on to that which is measurable.

PATTERNS OF GIVING BY THE RICH

Charitable giving is a form of expenditure whose patterns vary dramatically by income level. In order to compare the behavior of the most affluent taxpayers to taxpayers at lower income levels, table 12.1 presents information for broad income classes beginning with those earning between $25,000 and $50,000.[33] (This information is presented graphically in figure 12.2.) As the table makes evident, average giving rises with income for 1995, to the lofty average of $248,000 for the 20,352 taxpayers with incomes of $2.5 million or more, a group representing roughly 0.02 percent of all taxpayers.[34] As shown by the table's third column, almost all taxpayers at these income levels made some contribution in 1995, and an even higher share made a gift between 1991 and 1995.

Besides the magnitude of their giving, those in the top income brackets are distinctive in two ways. First, a much larger share of their contributions are not in cash. Over one-third of all contributions from those with incomes over $1 million were not in cash. Presumably, the bulk of these noncash gifts were in the form of appreciated assets, as opposed to used household items. The second distinguishing mark for this high-income group is seen in the portion of contributions that were not deductible in the filing year. More than one-quarter of all reported contributions in 1995 by those in the top class exceeded the percentage limits and were thus subject to carry-over to future years. This could suggest that some gifts, perhaps including a relatively few very large gifts, were made in a lumpy form, such as interests in closely held businesses or real estate.

Previous work on charitable contributions contains occasional references to a U-shaped curve of giving as a percentage of income, implying that the proportion of income given as contributions tends to rise with income among the rich. The table's sixth column confirms this pattern, with the average propensity to give rising from 2.4 percent in the $100,000 to $200,000 class to 4.0 percent in the highest income class.[35] It is instructive to note, however, that what applies to the mean propensity is not the case for another common measure, the median. For 1995 the median propensity falls with income throughout the income range, with the majority of taxpayers with incomes over $1 million giving less than 1 percent of their income in contributions. Looking at average giving over the five-year period changes this pattern slightly, with the median percentage falling only to 1.2 percent and then rising slightly in the highest class. It is clear that taxpayers differ markedly in the percentage of income donated. As illustrated by the last column, it is the very big givers who cause the mean propensity to rise with income. When ranked by percentage of income given, those in the top 5 percent are very generous indeed, especially at the top of the income distribution. In the highest income class, those in that top 5 percent gave away at least 18 percent of their income.[36]

Besides its size and asset composition, the giving of the wealthy is also distinguished by the types of organizations supported. The little previous research on

Table 12.1 Charitable Contributions by Itemizers by Income Class

Adjusted Gross Income Class	Number of Returns	Average Giving	Percentage of Returns with Contributions	Noncash Percentage of Giving	Percentage of Giving Over Limits	Giving as a Percentage of Income		
						Weighted Average	Median	Ninety-Fifth Percentile
1995 data								
$25,000 to $49,999	10,480,338	$1,230	87.0	13.3	2.0	3.2	1.5	12.4
$50,000 to $99,999	14,197,579	1,823	93.5	14.7	2.2	2.6	1.4	10.0
$100,000 to $199,999	3,868,976	3,140	95.3	16.7	1.2	2.4	1.3	8.5
$200,000 to $499,999	956,204	7,442	96.2	19.5	8.2	2.6	1.2	9.0
$500,000 to $999,999	165,789	18,297	97.2	26.2	7.4	2.7	1.0	9.7
$1,000,000 to $2,499,999	60,024	46,418	97.6	34.3	15.5	3.2	0.8	14.0
$2,500,000 and over	20,352	248,069	97.8	43.9	27.6	4.0	0.7	20.9
All itemizers	34,235,743	2,155	89.3	14.6	6.3	2.9	1.5	12.5
1991 to 1995 panel								
$25,000 to $49,999	5,642,697	1,477	96.9	12.7	1.8	3.8	2.0	14.0
$50,000 to $99,999	10,813,584	1,928	98.4	13.3	1.0	2.8	1.6	10.0
$100,000 to $199,999	3,063,305	3,624	99.3	17.2	3.8	2.8	1.6	9.1
$200,000 to $499,999	746,781	8,225	99.6	21.2	8.3	2.8	1.4	9.9
$500,000 to $999,999	132,239	19,533	99.8	23.5	12.7	2.9	1.2	11.1
$1,000,000 to $2,599,999	47,309	53,487	99.9	34.5	25.5	3.6	1.2	16.1
$2,500,000 and over	14,040	288,791	99.8	47.5	34.0	5.0	1.3	18.1
All itemizers	21,610,373	2,633	97.9	18.6	6.7	3.5	1.7	11.8

Source: Tabulations by the authors of IRS Statistics of Income Individual Income Tax Returns samples.
Notes: The 1995 data are from the 1995 SOI sample, including some prior year returns filed during the 1995 filing season. The 1991 to 1995 panel includes tax returns of taxpayers who itemized deductions in all five years. All dollar amounts are in constant 1995 dollars.

Figure 12.2   Mean, Median, and 95th Percentile Giving as a Percentage Income, 1991 to 1995

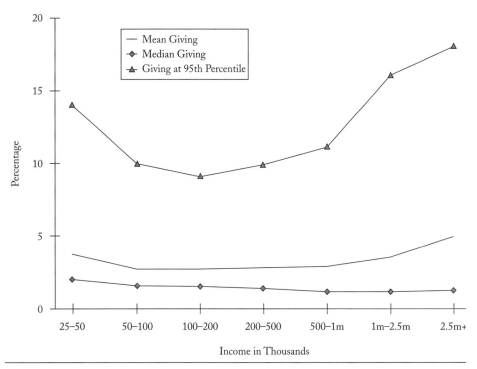

Source: Tabulations by authors of IRS statistics of Income Individual Income Tax Returns samples as shown in table 12.1.
Note: The price of giving cash equals 100 minus the tax rate in the top tax bracket. The price of giving appreciated property equals the price of giving cash less the capital gains tax rate. Gifts of appreciated property are assumed to be gifts of stock with 100 percent appreciation that would otherwise be sold in that year.

where donors direct their contributions suggests that, although the bulk of individual donations go to religious congregations, federated giving campaigns, and social services, the contributions of the affluent tend to be concentrated in quite different areas: higher education, health, and arts and culture. A 1973 national survey based on respondents' largest gifts made in the previous year showed that, among those donors with incomes over $1.6 million (in 1996 dollars), 24 percent of their largest identified gifts went to colleges and universities and 9 percent went to cultural institutions, with only 9 percent going to religious organizations and the rest to other organizations. By contrast, the shares for higher education and culture for those with incomes between $59,300 and $89,000 were only 5 and 3 percent, respectively; for those with incomes of $30,000 to $59,300, the comparable percentages were 1 percent and less than 0.5 percent.[37]

Although no recent, systematic survey data exist on the distribution of contributions by high-income individuals, a recent compilation provides a profile of the very largest individual gifts. Relying largely on newspaper accounts, a Web-based publication called Slate 60 has begun to compile lists of the largest gifts, with brief descriptions of the gifts appended. Their list for 1996 includes seventy-three gifts by named individuals plus another list of the largest anonymous gifts. Combining the two yields a list of ninety gifts of $5 million or more, some $1.5 billion in all. To provide an idea of how giving at these levels is directed, table 12.2 summarizes these gifts by type of recipient organization. Medical research and higher education dominated this giving. Of the total, 9.3 percent went to university-affiliated medical centers and another 55.6 percent was directed to nonmedical components of universities. Another 7.6 percent went to medical research institutes not affiliated with universities. Of the remaining contributions, cultural organizations garnered the largest share, at 14.1 percent, followed by private foundations, at 7.9 percent. The remaining 5.5 percent of giving by this wealthy group went to a variety of organizations, including a public library and a private school.

An issue of policy importance is the degree to which the contributions made by the wealthy actually end up benefiting the poor. Because the organizations receiving the bulk of the contributions summarized in table 12.2 do not primarily benefit the poor, that table would appear to suggest that the redistributive component in this giving is small. Assessing the distributional impact of this giving is complex, however, and cannot be assessed even from a list of recipient organizations.[38]

One feature of giving by the wealthy that cannot be reflected in annual data such as those in table 12.1 is its variability over time.[39] To give an idea of how widely contributions by individuals do vary from year to year, table 12.3 presents data over a five-year period for a panel of taxpayers, classified by average income. In this table, variability is measured by the five-year range of giving (maximum minus minimum giving, in constant dollars) as a percentage of average giving for the period. Although each class's mean giving rises with income in much the same way it does with annual data, the table clearly shows that the variability of this giving increases

Table 12.2   The Ninety Individual Gifts of $5 Million or More in 1996, by Type of Recipient Organization

Recipient Organizations	Amount (in Millions)	Percentage of Total
Free-standing medical research institutions[a]	$ 115	7.6
University-affiliated medical centers	140	9.3
Other health	0	0.0
Other higher education	837	55.6
Culture	212	14.1
Private foundations	119	7.9
Other	83	5.5
Total[b]	1,505	100.0

Source: "The 1996 Slate 60," June 23, 1997; "The Top Anonymous Gifts of 1996," May 29, 1997; website:www.slate.com.

Note: Figures cover the top seventy-three gifts from named donors plus seventeen anonymous gifts that would have been on the list by virtue of their size (all $5 million or more). The list was compiled from newspaper accounts and other sources. Figures for gifts include pledges.

[a.] Includes the largest single gift of $100 million, to the Scripps Research Institute, which, although it grants a Ph.D. degree, is classified as an independent research institute.

[b.] Due to rounding, the total is not the sum of components.

Table 12.3 Variability of Giving over Time: Five-Year Range of Contributions as a Percentage of Average Contributions, 1991 to 1995

Average Adjusted Gross Income Class	Number of Returns	Range of Giving as a Percentage of Mean Giving					Total	Percentage of Giving by Top 5 Percent
		Less than 25 Percent	25 to 49 Percent	50 to 99 Percent	100 to 199 Percent	More than 200 Percent		
$25,000 to $49,999	5,642,697	15	18	26	28	14	100	24
$50,000 to $99,999	10,813,584	14	19	30	27	10	100	25
$100,000 to $199,999	3,063,305	11	21	34	24	10	100	28
$200,000 to $499,999	746,781	7	17	35	29	13	100	35
$500,000 to $999,999	132,239	5	14	30	35	15	100	38
$1,000,000 to $2,499,999	47,309	3	12	24	35	26	100	42
$2,500,000 and over	14,040	1	5	18	36	39	100	45

Source: Calculations based on a panel of 1991 to 1995 individual income tax returns (see table 12.1).
Note: Income is constant law AGI as defined in table 12.1. Dollar amounts are in constant 1995 dollars.

with average income. One-third of those with average incomes under $100,000 had ranges that were 50 percent or less than their average giving level, but only 6 percent of those in the highest bracket showed this level of consistency. Indeed, the variability at the top was such that for three-fourths of those in the highest bracket the difference between their highest and lowest yearly giving exceeded their five-year average. Not surprisingly, this variability at the top appears to be associated with noncash gifts, which may often take the form of large, indivisible lumps such as real estate parcels and blocks of nontraded stock.

Another dimension of variability is that giving tends to be concentrated among a relatively small number of donors. The last column in table 12.3 illustrates this concentration, showing the percentage of total contributions by each income class made by the most generous 5 percent. Not only is giving quite concentrated, the degree of concentration rises with income. Among those with $2.5 million or more in income, fully 45 percent of all giving is accounted for by this top 5 percent of donors.

Another characteristic of the giving patterns of the wealthy is the apparent sensitivity to changes in tax rates. Any time legislation causes tax rates to change from one year to the next, the change is invariably well publicized. Even if a taxpayer's long-term level of contributions is unaffected, such a situation invites taxpayers to accelerate or delay some of their giving so that more can be deducted in the year with the higher tax rates. Over the period 1991 to 1995, contributions by the top income class ($2.5 million or more in average income) illustrated this kind of timing. The top marginal rate increased from 31 percent in 1992 to 39.6 percent in 1993, setting up the opportunity for taxpayers to save by moving contributions from 1992 into 1993.[40] Measured as a percentage of average income over the period, the average giving for the top income class fell from 6.0 percent in 1991 to 4.4 percent in 1992, and then rebounded to 6.3 percent in 1993 and 1994. The giving rate increased as well from 1992 to 1993 for the next two income classes, but by much smaller amounts.[41]

Tax-sensitive timing is also evident in a special form of giving whose cost was greatly affected by changes in tax law: gifts of artwork to museums. One can see in table 12.4 a clear response to the changing tax environment for gifts of appreciated tangible personal property over the last decade. In fiscal year 1988, the first full fiscal year during which unfavorable AMT treatment applied to such gifts, donations of artworks totaled only 64 percent of the average total over the preceding three years. In fiscal years 1991 and 1992, when the unfavorable AMT treatment was temporarily suspended, average gift levels were about 90 percent higher than the average levels over the period from fiscal year 1988 to fiscal year 1990. When the suspension lapsed in 1992 (so that unfavorable treatment was restored), donations again dried up: of gifts artwork in fiscal year 1993 reverted to levels even below those of the period from fiscal year 1988 to fiscal year 1990. Finally, when the unfavorable AMT provisions were repealed in 1993, the donation levels rebounded, albeit less impressively than they had done in fiscal year 1991. Thus, one can track in donation levels each of the four tax changes in this area between 1986 and 1993, as unfavorable AMT treatment was imposed, suspended, reimposed, and repealed and gift levels bounced up and down accordingly.[42]

Table 12.4   Artworks Donated to American Museums, Fiscal Years 1983 to 1996 (Values in Millions of Constant FY1996 Dollars)

| Fiscal Year | Artworks Donated by Individuals | | | Artworks Bequeathed | | |
	Value	Number of Works	Museums Reporting Gifts	Value	Number of Works	Museums Reporting Gifts
1983	123.8	N/A	72	N/A	N/A	N/A
1984	N/A	N/A	N/A	N/A	N/A	N/A
1985	126.3	27,082	112	N/A	N/A	N/A
1986	204.2	43,258	94	N/A	N/A	N/A
1987	135.3	22,860	112	N/A	N/A	N/A
1988	99.3	19,034	112	N/A	N/A	N/A
1989	210.8	33,069	124	N/A	N/A	N/A
1990	164.9	18,310	133	77.6	1,052	41
1991	302.6	44,908	139	60.5	2,527	43
1992	292.8	54,478	138	27.7	1,878	55
1993	91.6	18,536	145	47.0	1,024	46
1994	156.9	29,522	150	74.8	5,157	64
1995	157.3	32,262	140	45.2	19,251	45
1996	152.2	33,890	142	24.6	2,275	51

Source: Association of Art Museum Directors, unpublished compilations from annual Statistical Surveys, 1984 to 1997. No survey was conducted covering the 1984 fiscal year.
Note: Dollar figures are deflated using the average value of the GDP price deflator for the previous year and the current year corresponding to the year in which each fiscal year ended (U.S. Council of Economic Advisers 1996, 284).

In light of the increased share of income received by the wealthy, it is interesting to examine trends in their share of total giving. Table 12.5 focuses on the top 1 percent of households by income, where income is measured in two consistent ways: by adjusted gross income as defined in the Tax Reform Act of 1986, and by adjusted gross income as defined in the pre-1986 tax law; thus, the latter definition consistently excludes 60 percent of long-term capital gains.[43] Data are presented for four years separated by the major tax acts of 1981, 1986, and 1995.[44] For the most recent year of 1994, the roughly 1 million households at the top, whose average income was about $500,000, received over 9 percent of aggregate income and made more than 16 percent of aggregate contributions. The share of total income accounted for by this affluent group rose over the entire period, reflecting the growing inequality in incomes that has been widely noted. Using the pre-TRA86 income definition, the share of income received by the top 1 percent increased from 8.2 to 12.8 percent, a percentage increase of over 50 percent. Over the same period the share of total giving accounted for by this group also rose, but only by about 18 percent. As a percentage of income, giving by this affluent group declined over the period, from 4.1 to 3.1 percent, before partially recovering to 3.5 percent. This pattern of declining giving is consistent with the existence of a negative price effect, although the magnitude of the price effect is a matter of debate, a point to which we return in the next section.[45]

Table 12.5   Giving by Wealthy Individuals, 1979 to 1994

	1979	1984	1991	1994
Total giving[a]	36,590	56,460	96,100	104,530
Personal income[b]	2,049,700	3,205,500	4,968,500	5,753,100
Total income[e]	1,531,234	2,301,147	3,433,753	3,886,074
Total pre-TRA86 income[e]	1,489,713	2,220,174	3,376,509	3,802,887
Top 1 percent of tax returns by income[c]				
Number of returns	872,011	950,556	1,033,202	1,063,600
Income	143,712	258,091	437,722	530,634
Charitable deductions	4,848	8,535	13,054	17,332
Total giving	5,126	7,982	13,573	17,318
Cash	3,210	5,385	9,828	10,854
Noncash	1,915	2,595	3,745	6,464
Carry-over	760	3,788	1,691	3,381
Nondeductible	1,038	3,234	2,210	3,379
Percentage noncash giving	37.37	32.51	27.59	37.32
Giving as a percentage of income	3.57	3.09	3.10	3.26
Top 1 percent's share of total income	9.39	11.22	12.75	13.65
Top 1 percent's share of total giving	14.01	14.14	14.12	16.57
Top 1 percent of tax returns by pre-TRA86 income[d]				
Number of returns	871,983	950,518	1,033,168	1,063,386
Income	122,802	210,435	410,159	486,610
Charitable deductions	4,830	8,506	12,971	17,134
Total giving	5,075	7,907	13,442	17,100
Cash	3,202	5,382	9,762	10,796
Noncash	1,873	2,524	3,680	6,304
Carry-over	714	3,758	1,701	3,334
Nondeductible	959	3,158	2,173	3,302
Percentage noncash giving	36.91	31.92	27.38	36.87
Giving as a percentage of income	4.13	3.76	3.28	3.51
Top 1 percent's share of total income	8.24	9.48	12.15	12.80
Top 1 percent's share of total giving	13.87	14.01	13.99	16.36

Source: Unpublished data on individual income tax returns, Internal Revenue Service, *Statistics of Income.*
Note: Includes late returns filed in the following year and excludes prior year returns.
[a] *Source: Giving USA* (in millions of dollars).
[b] *Source:* U.S. Council of Economic Advisers (1996, 305) (in millions of dollars).
[c] Income is a constant-law definition of AGI based on TRA86, which includes all long-term capital gains, plus deductions for IRAs, SECA taxes, health insurance, and moving expenses. Dollar amounts are mean values.
[d] Pre-TRA86 income is a constant-law definition of AGI based on pre-TRA86 law, which excludes 60 percent of long-term gains. Dollar amounts are mean values.
[e] In millions of dollars.

Since the marginal tax rate applying to top incomes declined over this period, from 70 percent to 50 percent beginning in 1982, then to 28 percent beginning in 1987, the net price of giving increased markedly. The tax savings from charitable deductions for the top 1 percent declined from 53 percent of giving in 1979 to 35 percent of giving in 1994. As a result, net after-tax giving increased from 2.0 percent of pre-TRA86 income in 1979 to 2.3 percent of pre-TRA86 income in 1994. Thus, as measured by the after-tax cost of their giving, the generosity of the top 1 percent actually increased between 1979 and 1994.

Bequest Giving

Although they amount to much less than contributions from living individuals, charitable bequests constitute an important form of giving by the wealthy. Compared to some $116 billion in total contributions from individuals in 1995, charitable bequests were estimated to be only $10.7 billion (AAFRC Trust for Philanthropy 1998, 154). Yet a disproportionate share of this total came from the wealthy. In 1995, for example, $4.3 billion in charitable bequests—almost half the total in that year—came from 804 returns, representing 0.036 percent of all deaths that year.[46] Table 12.6 summarizes data from estate tax returns filed in 1995. As net worth rises, the average charitable bequest increases markedly, as does the percentage of returns with a charitable bequest and the percentage of net worth given away. The 272 decedents in the top wealth category gave away one-quarter of their net worth to charitable organizations. Besides this heavy concentration of giving at the top, the table also demonstrates that, for most decedents, bequests to surviving spouses are much larger than charitable bequests, a point elaborated upon later.

Trends in bequest giving are shown in table 12.7, which presents data for returns with at least $600,000 in net worth, defined in constant 1987 dollars, for selected years between 1963 and 1995. The general increase in numbers of estates exceeding the constant-dollar threshold reflects the growth and possible increased concentration of wealth at the top. The dropoff in 1995 may be the result of new estate planning devices.[47] Average net worth remained more or less steady over the entire period, but the average charitable bequest was more variable. A most interesting trend is the growing importance of returns, and bequests, from women. As a percentage of all returns, those filed by women held steady at 34 percent from 1963 to 1977, and then began to increase, probably owing to the introduction of the unlimited marital deduction in the Economic Recovery Tax Act of 1981 (ERTA81).[48] As a percentage of net worth, charitable bequests made by female decedents remained higher than those for males. And despite their smaller numbers, returns for females constituted about half of all those reporting any charitable bequests through 1977, after which they represented a generally growing majority of such returns. Most of the higher charitable propensity among women appears to be explained by widowhood rather than by any attributes associated with gender. For both men and women, those who leave behind spouses, and presumably other family obligations, tend to make much smaller charitable bequests than those who were not married at death. Male decedents who were married at death gave an average of 2.4 percent of their net worth in charitable bequests, while those who were not married gave 12.5 percent. Among female decedents, the corresponding percentages were 1.7 percent and 15.0 percent.[49] Although generosity may well differ by gender, most of the differences evident in the previous table appear to be due to differences in marital status between male and female decedents.

Table 12.6 Charitable Bequests by Size of Estate, Marital Status, and Sex, 1995

Net Worth Class	Number of Returns	Average Values		Charitable Bequests	Percentage of Returns with Charitable Bequests
		Net Worth	Bequests to Surviving Spouse		
Under 1,000,000	38,932	711,744	147,417	25,614	15.4
$1,000,000 to $2,499,999	23,412	1,462,154	443,121	79,374	21.3
$2,500,000 to $4,999,999	5,002	3,380,631	1,236,448	189,750	27.0
$5,000,000 to $9,999,999	1,615	6,877,376	2,608,807	636,404	33.3
$10,000,000 to $19,999,999	532	13,836,035	5,704,739	1,337,704	37.0
$20,000,000 or more	272	52,895,254	21,681,227	13,291,015	50.4
All returns	69,766	1,685,930	508,128	131,347	19.0
Marital status and sex					
Married men	24,475	1,802,775	1,198,999	42,595	8.9
Other men	13,579	1,467,283	N/A	183,067	27.1
Married women	7,912	1,446,869	770,770	23,914	7.6
Other women	23,800	1,522,181	N/A	228,823	28.4

Source: Tabulations by the authors of IRS *Statistics of Income* Estate Tax Returns for 1995.

Table 12.7 Net Worth and Charitable Bequests, Selected Years, 1963 to 1995 (Constant 1995 Dollars)

All Returns

Year	Number of Returns	Total Charitable Bequests (Thousands)	Percentage of Returns with Bequests	Average Net Worth	Average Charitable Bequests	Charitable Bequests as Percentage of Net Worth
1963	28,446	$4,274,350	22	$2,202,686	150,262	6.8
1966	32,996	5,563,802	22	2,269,460	168,621	7.4
1970	36,343	8,567,885	21	2,211,722	235,750	10.7
1973	37,886	6,340,131	21	2,117,255	167,436	7.9
1977	32,994	7,061,131	22	1,986,526	214,016	10.8
1983	28,452	7,061,238	18	1,952,687	127,415	6.5
1987	42,274	5,895,473	20	2,182,648	139,458	6.4
1990	49,850	7,403,124	19	2,194,127	148,508	6.8
1995	45,549	8,697,996	21	2,113,989	182,043	8.6

Returns Filed by Women

Year	As Percentage of All Returns	As Percentage of Returns with Charitable Bequests	Percentage of Returns with Bequests	Average Net Worth	Average Charitable Bequests	Charitable Bequests as Percentage of Net Worth
1963	34.0	48.7	31	$2,400,945	256,826	10.7
1966	34.4	50.1	32	2,428,667	255,104	10.5
1970	34.1	48.2	30	2,429,182	424,626	17.5
1973	34.4	50.7	30	2,249,419	256,783	11.4
1977	34.4	49.7	31	2,211,142	191,388	8.7
1983	35.8	54.3	27	1,871,963	184,959	9.9
1987	42.9	55.6	26	1,984,677	159,031	8.0
1990	45.0	60.6	26	2,012,850	176,465	8.8
1995	43.9	53.7	25	1,988,205	258,120	13.0

Source: Rosenfeld (1995) and unpublished IRS *Statistics of Income* estate tax data for 1995.
Notes: Data include all estate tax returns filed in indicated years with gross estates of $600,000 or more in 1987 dollars ($804,930 in 1995 dollars). All dollar amounts are expressed in constant 1995 dollars.

It is instructive to consider the distribution of bequest giving by type of recipient organization. Table 12.8 summarizes data collected from estate tax returns filed in 1995. This tabulation reveals a striking increase in the proportion of bequests directed toward private foundations as estate size grows. By contrast, the share of bequests directed to education, medicine, and science falls, especially in the top category, and the share going to religious organizations drops precipitously, almost disappearing in the highest net worth class. The bottom portion of the table divides returns by gender and marital status. Among the four groups, married men tended to direct their bequests in ways that differed noticeably from the other groups. Collectively, these married male decedents made a smaller share of their charitable bequests to religious and educational, medical, or scientific organizations, instead channeling 60 percent of their charitable bequests into foundations.[50]

A final topic related to bequest giving is its connection to giving during life. As noted earlier, since contributions during life reduce the size of a person's taxable estate, just as charitable bequests do, but offer the added advantage of income tax relief during life, lifetime giving is clearly the tax-minimizing strategy. Yet, as Steuerle (1987) has noted, many wealthy taxpayers do not follow this approach. We examined data for a sample of taxpayers who died in 1982, including information on their charitable bequests as well as their contributions in 1980 and 1981. The data indicate that while almost all reported some charitable contributions, lifetime giving, even in these last two years of life, was only a small fraction of giving at death. Among those whose net worth was $20 million or more, and whose charitable bequests averaged $20.9 million, the average giving for the last two years of life was only $544,000, or about 2.6 percent of the eventual bequest. Among those with net worth between $10 million and $20 million, average giving was 3.8 percent of the eventual charitable bequest.[51] Wealthy individuals thus appear to hold during life to assets earmarked for charitable purposes, forgoing the tax benefits of the personal income tax deduction.

EVIDENCE ON THE INCENTIVE EFFECT OF TAXES

A great deal of empirical research has examined the effect of tax deductibility on individuals' charitable giving.[52] The deduction effectively reduces the price of making donations. Although most studies published before the 1990s concluded that the elasticity of giving with respect to the tax-defined price is greater than one in absolute value, several recent studies have challenged this finding, arguing that donors' efforts to time their contributions have been misinterpreted as indicating permanent price effects.[53] Owing to fluctuations in income over time as well as to periodic changes in the tax law, the net-of-tax price faced by a taxpayer may well vary from one year to the next. In a way analogous to the approach that has been taken in some studies of income, analysts have distinguished permanent from transitory changes in price, a distinction with very important implications for tax policy. One possibility is that taxes have an effect on the timing of charitable gifts—donors may bunch their giving into years when their tax rates are highest and thus when the net cost of giving is the lowest—but not on the lifetime amount of giving. This case would be compa-

Table 12.8   Type of Donee of Charitable Bequests by Size of Estate, Marital Status, and Sex, 1995

Net Worth Class	Number of Returns	Percentage Distribution of Charitable Bequests Amounts						
		Arts and Humanities	Medical and Science	Social Welfare	Private Foundations	Religious	Other	Total
Under $1,000,000	38,932	3.4	39.0	1.2	2.5	26.9	26.9	100.0
$1,000,000 to $2,499,999	23,412	2.4	47.9	2.4	3.3	20.6	23.3	100.0
$2,500,000 to $4,999,999	5,002	3.1	36.0	3.8	13.7	13.2	30.3	100.0
$5,000,000 to $9,999,999	1,615	4.0	37.7	0.9	18.4	6.3	32.7	100.0
$10,000,000 to $19,999,999	532	7.1	26.4	1.9	35.1	5.8	23.7	100.0
$20,000,000 or more	272	2.0	9.8	0.2	73.9	1.0	13.0	100.0
All returns	69,766	3.0	27.8	1.4	36.4	10.0	21.4	100.0
Marital status and sex								
All men	38,054	3.0	29.5	1.5	34.3	8.8	22.9	100.0
Married men	24,475	2.4	17.1	0.6	60.3	4.4	15.2	100.0
Other men	13,579	3.2	34.7	1.9	23.4	10.7	26.2	100.0
All women	31,712	3.0	26.8	1.3	37.6	10.8	20.5	100.0
Married women	7,912	1.0	24.2	0.5	27.6	9.5	37.2	100.0
Other women	23,800	3.0	26.9	1.3	38.0	10.9	19.9	100.0

Source: Tabulations by the authors of IRS Statistics of Income Estate Tax Returns for 1995.

rable to that of a family whose lifetime purchases of lightbulbs are unaffected by price but that nonetheless buys all its bulbs when they are on sale. If taxes, by way of the price effect, influence mainly the timing of gifts and not their long-run level, there would be less reason to believe that tax changes have a significant long-term impact on giving. Compared to most previous empirical work, recent estimates based on this model imply a smaller price effect and a larger income effect, with elasticities of about −0.5 and 1.1, respectively (Randolph 1995).

Such permanent effects are important for the consideration of tax policy, and this is nowhere more true than for the wealthy taxpayers who are the subject of the present volume. To the degree that the long-run donative behavior of these taxpayers is less responsive to the existence of the charitable deduction, smaller and fewer contributions are stimulated per dollar of lost government revenue. As a simple device for assessing the magnitude of the permanent price and income effects among wealthy taxpayers, we examined the relationship between contributions and permanent income and the permanent tax-defined price, using a panel of tax returns. The panel contains returns for approximately 16,000 returns for the period 1979 to 1990, of which about 9,200 itemized in most years. We sought to measure the permanent levels of income and price before and after significant tax reforms, reasoning that such reforms would have altered individuals' subjective values of each. "Permanent" values were based on three-year averages of the three variables of greatest interest: contributions, net income, and tax-defined price. Following the approach taken in previous studies, we defined price as the weighted average of the price of giving cash and giving appreciated property, where the weights are derived from the average proportions of each in the individual's income class and a gain-to-value ratio of 50 percent for appreciated property is assumed.[54] Net income is defined as AGI minus first-dollar tax liability, where AGI is defined as constant-law post-TRA86 AGI. In order to eliminate the effects of individual-specific factors in giving, equations were estimated in first-difference form.

Equations were estimated for two periods spanning major tax law changes: changes between 1979 to 1981 and 1983 to 1985, which spans the 1981 tax reform act, and changes between 1983 to 1985 and 1988 to 1990, which spans the 1986 act. Only taxpayers with average AGI of $20,000 or more in 1990 dollars were included in the sample. Both equations include age dummies and marital status as explanatory variables.[55] Where G_{t-t+2} is a taxpayer's average charitable giving in the years t, t+1, and t+2, P and Y are similarly defined price and net income and M is a dummy variable indicating a married taxpayer, the estimated equation using the panel for the change in giving before and after the Economic Recovery Tax Act of 1981 was:

$$\ln(G_{83-85}/G_{79-81}) = 0.44 - 0.52 \ \ln(P_{83-85}/P_{79-81}) + 0.43 \ \ln(Y_{83-85}/Y_{79-81})$$
$$(7.1) \quad (10.0) \qquad\qquad\qquad (24.1)$$
$$-0.16 \ \text{Age3544} - 0.29 \ \text{Age4554} - \ 0.29 \ \text{Age5564}$$
$$(2.4) \qquad\qquad (4.5) \qquad\qquad\quad (4.5)$$
$$-0.28 \ \text{Age65} + 0.023\text{M}; \ \ R^2 = 0.11; \ \ N = 7,460.$$
$$(4.2) \qquad\qquad (0.7) \qquad\qquad\qquad\qquad\qquad\qquad (12.1)$$

The equation for the change in giving before and after the Tax Reform Act of 1986 was:

$$\ln\left(G_{88-90}/G_{83-85}\right) = 0.58 - 0.95 \ \ln\left(P_{88-90}/P_{83-85}\right) + 0.41 \ \ln\left(Y_{88-90}/Y_{83-85}\right)$$

$$(6.5) \quad (12.3) \qquad\qquad\qquad (23.0)$$

$$-0.23 \ \text{Age}3544 - 0.30 \ \text{Age}4554 - 0.29 \ \text{Age}5564$$

$$(2.4) \qquad\qquad (3.3) \qquad\qquad (3.0)$$

$$-0.22 \ \text{Age}65 + 0.009\text{M}; \ \ R^2 = 0.10; \ \ N = 7,266.$$

$$(2.4) \qquad (0.2) \qquad\qquad\qquad\qquad\qquad (12.2)$$

As the coefficients of the log change in price indicate, the implied price elasticity is −0.52 in the first equation, spanning the 1981 act, and −0.95 in the second equation, spanning the 1986 act. Both point estimates are smaller in absolute value than conventional estimates of the price elasticity, and the first is similar in magnitude to that calculated by Randolph (1995). The implied income elasticities are small by almost any standard, being 0.43 and 0.41.

We present these estimates as a rough and tentative test of the important considerations raised in recent studies of charitable giving. They are based on the notion that the two prominent tax acts of the 1980s had the effect of causing taxpayers to revise their estimates of their own permanent price of giving. The estimated equations are based on the implicit assumption that nothing else changed over these two to affect the giving behavior of taxpayers. In fact, it is possible that the charitable inclinations of donors were aroused by the tax acts themselves and the publicity surrounding their possibly deleterious effect on contributions, causing donors to give more than they otherwise might have. To the extent that such exogenous effects were uncorrelated with changes in prices, however, one would not expect them to bias the estimated price effect. These considerations notwithstanding, however, the present estimates imply that taxes do have a permanent price effect, although not as large as that implied by a number of previous studies.[56]

CONCLUSION

The charitable giving of the wealthy is distinctive on several counts. Most obviously, on a per capita basis, it is very large. The average taxpayer in the highest income class gives away in a year an amount greater than what 99 percent of households earn in a year or give away in a lifetime. To be sure, the wealthy have higher incomes than most. Those at the very top give away a somewhat larger percentage of their incomes than the average household, although this percentage appears to have declined during the 1980s, and only part of this decline has been reversed in recent years. By virtue of their size, the gifts of the wealthy also tend to be prominent, serving as the seeds for grand buildings and new initiatives. Wealthy donors are much more likely than others to be personally involved in the governance and operation of the nonprofit organizations they support. The types of organizations differ as well. Although the mass of individuals tend to allocate most of their giving to religious organizations, the wealthy focus on colleges and universities, arts and cultural organizations, and health-related institutions. The nation's tax laws obviously affect the wealthy in a distinctive way, in that the tax rates under the progressive rate structures of the various laws are higher for them than for other taxpayers. But so too does the whole landscape of laws, administrative mechanisms, and personal relationships. Most of the verbiage in the Internal Revenue Code applying to the charitable deduction is of interest only to the wealthy; seldom are the nonwealthy concerned with percentage limits on contributions, the rules applying to private foundations, or the alternative minimum tax. Nor do those of modest means concern themselves with the gift and estate tax or the various mechanisms for making charitable bequests.

It is probably safe to identify two main consequences of the current taxation of the wealthy for charitable giving. First, it appears to stimulate some charitable giving. In comparison to a situation in which contributions did not receive a deduction, in the individual income tax or the estate tax, actual current giving levels are higher. If, as our preliminary regressions suggest, the elasticities applying to permanent price are smaller than has been believed, the amount of that aggregate stimulus is correspondingly smaller than it might otherwise have been thought. But it is substantial nonetheless. To repeat a point made previously in the economics literature, this is not to suggest that taxes cause people to make contributions, only that the existence of taxes and the associated deduction induce people to give more than they would have otherwise. The second consequence comes in the form of complexity. As a result of high tax rates and serpentine provisions, the wealthy resort to much more elaborate arrangements associated with their charitable donations then they otherwise would.

We are grateful to Julie Harter, Karen Price, and Thomas Sima for valuable research assistance; to Millicent Hall Gaudieri for providing unpublished data; and to Eleanor Brown, Milton Cerny, Lowell Dworin, Joel Fleishman, David Joulfaian, John Piva, William Randolph, Gabriel Rudney, Shannon St. John, Michael Shultz, Joel Slemrod, Eugene Steuerle, Dennis Zimmerman, and other participants at the conference for useful comments and discussions. Neither they nor the institutions with which we are affiliated, however, are responsible for the views reflected in this chapter.

NOTES

1. After reviewing his quarterly financial statement and noting, "Hey, $1 billion is a good round figure," the media magnate Ted Turner recently pledged a donation of that amount to the United Nations (Goshko 1997).

2. There were 31,962 returns with gross estates over $1 million, or about 1.4 percent of all deaths, in 1994. These returns accounted for $8.35 billion in charitable bequests, or about 86 percent of the $9.66 billion estimated by AAFRC Trust for Philanthropy (1998, 154). See also Eller (1996–97, 36, 39) and U.S. Bureau of the Census (1996, 94).

3. Assigning values for volunteer work, the nonprofit sector accounted for $354 billion in 1994, compared to $5,591 billion for national income, a figure that also includes the imputed value of unpaid family workers. By comparison, the direct expenditures of government were $842 billion (Hodgkinson and Weitzman 1996, 40).

4. Owing to the thrift and exceedingly good fortune of the generation that is now at or nearing the end of their working lives, there is now the prospect of a wealth transfer of unprecedented pro-

portions over the next few decades. According to estimates made by Avery and Rendall (1993), total annual bequests will increase from $40 billion in 1990 to over $330 billion in 2015, with total bequests between 1990 and 2040 exceeding $10 trillion. After four years of exuberant increases in stock prices from 1993 to 1997, one would expect that figure to be even higher. According to the *New York Times* of December 2, 1997, from their average values in 1993 to December 1, 1997, the Dow Jones Industrial Average more than doubled, increasing by 128 percent, and the Standard and Poors Composite Index of 500 stocks increased 116 percent; see also U.S. Council of Economic Advisers (1996, 384). What is true for the economy as a whole is likely to be true for the wealthiest households. Since large wealth transfers in the past have been the principal source of foundations and large capital gifts to nonprofits in education, health, and culture, the prospect of an approaching bulk of bequeathable wealth is surely a significant fact in considering the charitable behavior of the affluent.

5. This formula applies to cash gifts, and only for taxpayers who itemize their deductions. A more detailed model of the price of giving is described later in the chapter.

6. This is essentially the rate structure that has prevailed through 1999, except that the indexing provisions resulted by 1999 in an upward adjustment of the two bracket boundaries to $158,550 and $283,150, respectively.

7. Several states have significantly progressive income taxes, with rates up to 12 percent. Most, but not all, states allow charitable contribution deductions on terms similar to those that prevail in the federal income tax.

8. Itemized deductions, including those for charitable contributions, are subject to an overall limitation that effectively reduces total itemized deductions by the lesser of 3 percent of the excess of AGI over a statutory threshold ($121,200 for 1997) or 80 percent of total itemized deductions. In practice, 3 percent of the excess AGI is almost invariably the lesser amount, which means that the reduction is measured in terms of AGI rather than itemized deductions. As such, the limitation does not directly affect the price of giving except in rare cases.

9. The 30 percent limit applies to contributions of appreciated property deducted at fair market value and to contributions to private foundations. The 20 percent limit applies to gifts of qualified appreciated stock to private foundations. See discussion later in the chapter.

10. Steuerle and Sullivan (1996, 772) speculate that the administrative complications of going over the limit discourages such gifts, causing donors to stay below the limit. Odendahl (1987, 11) found that a majority of 135 millionaires in a special survey reported that they give as much as allowed, presumably referring to the deduction limits. A recent lottery winner who wanted to give away all of her $11.8 million in New Jersey winnings was counseled to reduce her donations to about $8 million to cover income taxes on contributions over the limits (Westfeldt 1997).

11. Figures based on the authors' tabulations using the 1995 IRS Statistics of Income Individual Income Tax Return sample.

12. The rule allowing fair market value deductions for appreciated property contributions is not indefensible. An ideal tax system would index each asset's tax basis and tax accrued capital gains of decedents at their deaths (if not before). The failure of our current laws to do either of these things may make the rules on appreciated property deductions an acceptable second-best choice.

13. The AMT was preceded by an "add-on" minimum tax on tax preference items that was enacted in 1969. The structure of that tax, however, was such that it had little impact on charitable contributions.

14. For example, in 1988, the first full year of the new rules, returns showing less than $200,000 of adjusted gross income had less than one chance in one thousand of generating an AMT liability; returns showing more than $200,000 of income had one chance in thirty of showing AMT liability. And the latter figure no doubt greatly understates the effect of the AMT on high-bracket taxpayers, because the structure of the AMT invites careful planning to avoid actual AMT incidence. Thus, many, if not most, high-bracket taxpayers were (and are) likely to be close enough to AMT exposure that concerns about the AMT are never far away. (See Internal Revenue Service, *Statistics of Income* 1988, table 3.3.)

15. This simple statement masks a wide range of complications and refinements. Among the most important are that gifts must be of a "present interest" (not in trust, nor otherwise encumbered), and that the exclusions available to a married couple are $20,000 per donee, regardless of which partner makes the gifts.

16. The tax-free transfer amount noted is scheduled to be increased in several steps, beginning in 1998 and reaching $1 million when the increase is fully phased in by 2006, pursuant to the Taxpayer Relief Act of 1997 (TRA97).

17. The rate structure purportedly begins with an 18 percent rate; however, the unified credit effectively consumes the rates between 18 and 34 percent, inclusive, so that the true rate structure begins with a 37 percent bracket. In the interval between $10 million and $21 million, a surcharge of 5 percent of the taxable transfers in that interval is assessed, creating a 60 percent "bubble" over that range, after which the rate returns to 55 percent.

18. Note that, unlike the case of income tax deductions, there is no particular advantage associated with transferring appreciated property to charity for transfer-tax purposes. The full fair market value of such property would be included in the gross transfers and subtracted at the same value to determine taxable transfers.

19. These data are for 1995, from *SOI Bulletin* 18 (3, 1998–99), table 16, p. 217, and *SOI Bulletin*, 16(3, 1996–97), table 1d p. 42, respectively. By 1997 the number of estate tax returns had increased to 90,000, or about 4 percent of adult deaths (Johnson and Mikow 1999).

20. Of course, some wealthy taxpayers are able—at some cost—to arrange their affairs so as to avoid transfer taxes altogether (see Poterba, this volume).

21. The figures in this paragraph are based on calculations for estate tax returns filed in 1995, as shown in table 3.6 and 3.7.

22. To increase the public accountability of private foundations, Congress subjected them to the same disclosure rules as public charities in the Internal Revenue Service Restructuring and Reform Act of 1998 (IRSRRA98). Thus, in the future private foundations will be required to provide copies of their three most recent tax returns (Form 990-PF) to anyone who requests it.

23. The January 27, 1997, issue of the *Wall Street Journal* quoted Herbert Chao Gunther, president of a nonprofit communications agency: "For rich people who've made a killing in the stock market lately, the ultimate status symbol is creating a foundation with your name on it" ("A Tax Break Prompts Millionaires' Mad Dash to Create Foundations").

24. For example, the 1996 annual report of the Chicago Community Trust, one of the older and larger community foundations, describes its donor-advised funds as affording "the opportunity to . . . remain actively engaged in the grant-making process through periodic recommendations to the Trust's Executive Committee regarding the use of fund income, and limited amounts of principal" (23). In 1996 over 63 percent of the trust's funds consisted of donor-advised funds (11). There are costs associated with the administration of such funds, however, in the form of gathering information for donors about giving options as well as time taken with donors to explain those options.

25. It is, of course, actuarially possible that the remainder interest of such a trust could be less than 10 percent of the value of the corpus, especially if the life interest is spread among two or more people. Under limitations enacted in TRA97, however, an interest having an actuarial value of at least 10 percent of the current value of the assets placed in trust must pass to the charitable entity in order for the gift to generate a charitable deduction.

26. However, the IRS is studying this and similar devices that allow the donor to control the timing of the trust distributions and has recently announced that it will not issue private letter rulings on the tax treatment of any such charitable remainder trusts. See Revenue Procedure 97–23, 1997–1 CB 654.

27. The $1.19 is simply the sum of the maximum capital gains tax avoided (49.125 percent) plus the value of the current income tax deduction available to offset other income, a calculation that assumes that the alternative to giving away the asset is to sell it immediately. Although the top

marginal tax rate continued to be 70 percent until 1981, the Tax Reform Act of 1970 (TRA70) denied deductions after 1969 of the full market value of assets that would not have generated long-term capital gain if sold. In some circumstances, however, gifts of long-term capital gain property could have a tax cost that was slightly negative, until the capital gains rate was lowered to 28 percent by the Revenue Act of 1978.

28. The facts of this example are taken from Notice 94–78, 1994–2 CB 555, in which the IRS announced its intention to attack CRUTs of this type. This particular avoidance stratagem has in common with the best of that breed an aesthetic elegance that makes it difficult for the IRS to provide any definitive statement of why the device does not work to produce the results intended by the taxpayer. The IRS offers four different lines of attack, none of which is particularly convincing. Nevertheless, the abuse is patent enough that one or more of the arguments might well be accepted by a court sympathetic to the IRS position. The results of the IRS attack, if any, have not yet shown up in any reported cases.

29. Ostrower (1995, 47) reports that the percentage of the board of the Metropolitan Museum listed in the *Social Register* declined from 67 percent in 1972 to 44 percent in 1982, to 33 percent in 1992. An alternative explanation, of course, is that wealth has always been the variable determining influence in these institutions, but that it has simply become less correlated with social standing over time.

30. Noting that the prominence of the Forbes 400 list of the wealthiest Americans, and the fear of falling off of it, constitutes a deterrent to giving by the very wealthiest, Ted Turner suggested that there be a list of the most generous Americans (Dowd 1996). In apparent response to this idea, one organization has begun compiling and publicizing lists of the top charitable gifts. See the archives for the Slate website (www.slate.com) for December 12, 1996, and later articles by Ann Castle and Jodie Allen. Turner reiterated his views in announcing his $1 billion pledge to the United Nations: he suggested the establishment of an "Ebenezer Scrooge Prize" for the least generous among the country's wealthiest (Hofmeister 1997).

31. The 435 respondents rated each motivation from "strong" (5 points) to "none" (1 point). Of twenty possible motivations listed on the survey form, those judged to be strongest, in order of importance, were personal philosophy, systematic giving, welfare of others, social responsibility, flexibility of foundation, and tax incentives, with mean scores ranging from 3.83 to 3.12. Those motivations reported to be weakest, in order of increasing importance, were "control business assets" (1.14), political beliefs, social pressures, and memorial to self (1.78) (Boris 1987, 78).

32. We offer more recent evidence on this point in our discussion of bequest giving.

33. Data are not presented for itemizers with incomes below $25,000 because itemization is much less prevalent at lower incomes and those who do itemize at lower incomes include a disproportionate share of taxpayers whose adjusted gross income understates their capacity to make contributions. There were 4.6 million itemizers with incomes below $25,000, representing about 7 percent of all taxpayers in that income class in 1995. Itemizers at these lower incomes tend to be older and wealthier than others in the class, and more likely to have income that is not subject to tax.

34. There were 119 million tax returns filed for tax year 1995 (Internal Revenue Service, *Statistics of Income*).

35. One explanation that has been given for the lower proportion of income given at middle-income levels is the possibility that in the lowest income brackets annual income tends to understate economic income.

36. Taxpayers who give a very high proportion of their current income to charity may be unusual in either or both of two ways. It may be that their charitable giving is high relative to their economic circumstances and the habits of their peers; these would be taxpayers of extraordinary generosity. Alternatively, it may be that their current AGI is low relative to their wealth or permanent income and thus may understate their ability to give.

37. Calculated from Clotfelter (1997, table 5) and GDP price deflator for 1994, 105.0 (U.S. Council of Economic Advisers, 1996, 284). See also Morgan, Dye, and Hybels (1977, 208).

38. The problem is illustrated by the fact that most higher education aid is directed at the disadvantaged, as are some arts programs and those medical research programs on diseases that disproportionately affect the poor. For a fuller discussion of the distributional effects of nonprofit activities, see Clotfelter (1992).

39. For an earlier study of the variability of giving, see Auten and Rudney (1990).

40. The 1993 rate changes were not signed into law until August 10, 1993. However, the 1992 elections, which resulted in Democratic Party victories in races for the White House and a majority of the seats in both houses of Congress, had led many to predict that tax rates in 1993, especially at the top end, would not be lower, and might well be higher, than they had been in 1992.

41. For the $1 million to $2.5 million class, the rate rose from 3.3 to 3.8 percent; for the $500,000 to $1 million class, it rose from 3.1 to 3.5 percent.

42. Although data such as these provide strong evidence of tax-induced timing of charitable giving, they are not conclusive on the question of whether taxes have a permanent price effect on giving.

43. A number of adjustments were made to the income measure to account for statutory changes. The most important change was to put capital gains on a consistent pre-TRA86 or post-TRA86 basis. Before TRA86 only 40 percent of long-terms gains were included in AGI, but all long-term gains were included after TRA86. The post-TRA86 definition is a more complete measure of realized income. Because of the transitory nature of much capital gain income, the pre-TRA86 measure may more accurately reflect permanent income.

44. For each indicated year, the sample includes late returns filed in the following year and excludes late returns filed for the prior year.

45. This pattern would also be consistent with a lower propensity to give out of recent increases in income (or transitory income). For discussions of both price and income effects, see, for example, Auten, Cilke, and Randolph (1992) and Randolph (1995).

46. In 1995 there were 2,252,471 adult deaths from all causes (*SOI Bulletin* [Winter 1998–99], table 16, p. 217). As shown in table 12.6, there were 804 returns that showed net worth of $10 million or more.

47. New estate planning devices include the family limited partnership (partnerships formed to facilitate the transfer of wealth to family members over time at discounted values) and the principal residence trust. Declining real estate prices in the early 1990s may also have contributed to the drop-off after 1990.

48. Rosenfeld (1995) makes this point.

49. Calculations based on unpublished estate tax returns filed in 1995.

50. Eller's (1996–1997) analysis of returns for 1992 decedents also showed men in general giving larger shares to foundations and smaller ones to religious organizations. Unmarried decedents gave a larger percentage than did married ones to educational, medical, and scientific organizations.
    With respect to the share of gifts made to foundations, it is worth noting that, because foundations are essentially intermediaries that make grants themselves to nonprofit organizations, any analysis of shares of giving by type of organization tends to understate the shares eventually going to organizations that will receive those grants by foundations.

51. Calculations based on the 1982 IRS Statistics of Income Estate Tax Collation Study. It should be noted that one obstacle to taking fuller advantage of the favorable effects of contributions during life is the percentage limitations on charitable deductions, as noted earlier. For example, someone who has wealth of $20 million and plans to give away all or most of it at death, may have income in each of the years immediately preceding death of only $1 million or less if that wealth is invested in stocks with low dividend payouts or in conservative, money market investments. This limits such a taxpayer to deduction of no more than $500,000 of charitable contributions. However, these limits do not appear to be binding for most decedents in the sample.

52. For a brief review of this literature, see Clotfelter (1997).

53. Randolph (1995), for example, argues that by using annual data on income and prices, most statistical studies of giving incorrectly ascribe permanent significance to variations in prices that are

in fact heavily influenced by transitory fluctuations in income. He argues that, although people appear to smooth their giving in response to transitory variations in income, the effect on price is just the opposite: they tend to bunch their gifts into years when transitory income is the highest to take advantage of the unusually high tax rate in those years. He also presents statistical estimates consistent with this argument, although the difficulty in finding appropriate instruments in the instrumental-variables estimation argues for caution in placing undue reliance on any one set of statistical findings. See also Barrett et al. (1997).

54. Where m is the individual's marginal tax rate on ordinary income, gm is the rate on capital gains income, and c is the proportion of the income class's contributions in the form of cash, the weighted average price is $P = c(1-m) + (1-c)(1-m-0.5 gm)$. For taxpayers subject to the alternative minimum tax, in years in which contributions were treated as a preference item, thus eliminating the advantage of the nontaxation of capital gains, the price is simply $P = 1-m^*$, where m^* is the applicable alternative minimum tax rate. The 0.5 is the standard discount factor to account for the ratio of gains to value and differral of capital gains taxes.

55. Age3544 corresponds to the age thirty-five to forty-four group, Age4554 to the age forty-five to fifty-four group, Age5564 to the age fifty-five to sixty-four group, and Age65 to the age sixty-five and older group. Age is measured in the center year of the post-change period, that is, 1984 and 1989.

56. Conference participants suggested several additional regression equations. To illustrate that our data provide cross-section results similar to those in previous studies, a cross-section regression for 1981 yields a price elasticity of −1.04 and an income elasticity of 0.76. Estimating the equations in the text using an instrumental-variables procedure yielded similar price elasticities but smaller income elasticities. Adding the log of initial period income to the change regressions reported in the text as a control variable increases the estimated price elasticities (from −.52 to −.61 in the first equation, and from −0.95 to −1.18 in the second equation) but has little effect on the estimated income elasticities. Another suggestion was to isolate the income elasticity of giving by using a sample limited to those in the top tax rate bracket. A regression of the log of average giving for 1983 to 1985 on the log of average income and dummy variables for the age class and marital status yields an income elasticity of 0.94, considerably larger than in the change equations.

REFERENCES

AAFRC Trust for Philanthropy. 1998. *Giving USA 1998*. New York: AAFRC Trust for Philanthropy.

Arnsberger, Paul. 1998–99. "Private Foundations and Charitable Trusts." *Statistics of Income Bulletin* 18(3): 60–104.

Auten, Gerald E., James M. Cilke, and William C. Randolph. 1992. "The Effects of Tax Reforms on Charitable Contributions." *National Tax Journal* 45(September): 267–290.

Auten, Gerald E., and Gabriel Rudney. 1990. "The Variability of Individual Charitable Giving in the U.S." *Voluntas* 1(2): 80–97.

Avery, Robert B., and Michael S. Rendall. 1993. "Estimating the Size and Distribution of Baby Boomers' Prospective Inheritances." *Proceedings of the Social Statistics Section*, American Statistical Association, 11–19.

Barrett, Kevin, Anya McGuirk, and Richard Steinberg. 1997. "Further Evidence on the Dynamic Impact of Taxes on Charitable Giving." *National Tax Journal* 50(June): 321–34.

Boris, Elizabeth T. 1987. "Creation and Growth: A Survey of Private Foundations." In *America's Wealthy and the Future of Foundations;* edited by Teresa Odendahl. New York: Foundation Center.

Chicago Community Trust. 1996. Annual report.

Clotfelter, Charles T. 1997. "The Economics of Giving." In *Giving Better, Giving Smarter: Working Papers of the National Commission on Philanthropy and Civic Renewal*, edited by John W. Barry and Bruno V. Manno. Washington, D.C.: The National Commission on Philanthropy and Civic Renewal.

————— ed. 1992. *Who Benefits from the Nonprofit Sector?* Chicago: University of Chicago Press.

Dowd, Maureen. 1996. "Ted's Excellent Idea." *New York Times*, August 22.

Eller, Martha Britton. 1996–97. "Federal Taxation of Wealth Transfers, 1992–1995." *SOI Bulletin* 16(Winter): 8–63.

Goshko, John M. 1997. "Gift Idea Just Came to Him, Turner Says." *Raleigh News and Observer*, September 20.

Hodgkinson, Virginia Ann, and Murray S. Weitzman. 1996. *Nonprofit Almanac 1996–1997*. San Francisco: Jossey-Bass.

Hofmeister, Sallie. 1997. "Ted Turner Increases Philanthropy Stakes." *Raleigh News and Observer*, September 20.

Internal Revenue Service. Various years. *Statistics of Income: Individual Income Tax Returns.*

———. 1997. *Statistics of Income Bulletin* 17(Summer).

Johnson, Barry, and Jacob Mikow. 1999. "Federal Estate Tax Returns, 1995–1997." *Statistics of Income Bulletin* 19 (1, Summer).

Morgan, James N., Richard F. Dye, and Judith H. Hybels. 1977. "Results from Two National Surveys on Philanthropic Activity." In Commission on Private Philanthropy and Public Needs, *Research Papers*, vol. 1. Washington, D.C.: U.S. Treasury Department.

Odendahl, Teresa, ed. 1987. *America's Wealthy and the Future of Foundations*. New York: Foundation Center.

———. 1989. "The Culture of Elite Philanthropy in the Reagan Years." *Nonprofit and Voluntary Sector Quarterly* 18(Fall): 237–48.

———. 1990. *Charity Begins at Home: Generosity and Self-interest Among the Philanthropic Elite*. New York: Basic Books.

Ostrower, Francie. 1987. "The Role of Advisors to the Wealthy." In *America's Wealthy and the Future of Foundations*, edited by Teresa Odendahl. New York: Foundation Center.

———. 1995. *Why the Wealthy Give: The Culture of Elite Philanthropy*. Princeton, N.J.: Princeton University Press.

Randolph, William C. 1995. "Dynamic Income, Progressive Taxes, and the Timing of Charitable Contributions." *Journal of Political Economy* 103(August): 709–38.

Rosenfeld, Jeffrey P. 1995. "Charitable Giving 1963–1990 (Selected Years)." U.S. Treasury Department. Unpublished paper.

Schervish, Paul G. Forthcoming. *The Modern Medicis: Strategies of Philanthropy Among the Wealthy*. San Francisco: Jossey-Bass.

Schervish, Paul G., and John J. Havens. 1997. "Social Participation and Charitable Giving: A Multivariate Analysis." *Voluntas* 8(3, September): 235–60.

Steuerle, C. Eugene. 1987. "Charitable Giving Patterns of the Wealthy." In *America's Wealthy and the Future of Foundations*, edited by Teresa Odendahl. New York: Foundation Center.

Steuerle, C. Eugene, and Martin A. Sullivan. 1996. "Toward More Simple and Effective Giving: Reforming the Tax Rules for Charitable Contributions and Charitable Organizations." *Exempt Organization Tax Review* 13(May): 769–87.

U.S. Bureau of the Census. 1996. *Statistical Abstract of the United States 1996*. Washington, D.C.: U.S. Government Printing Office.

U.S. Council of Economic Advisers. 1996. *Economic Report of the President 1996*. Washington, D.C.: U.S. Government Printing Office.

Westfeldt, Amy. 1997. "Woman Gives Away $11.8 Million Lottery Prize, Says 'God Takes Care of Me,'" *Bradenton Herald*, November 29.

Commentary on Chapter 12

John B. Shoven

The chapter by Gerald Auten, Charles Clotfelter, and Richard Schmalbeck offers an excellent analysis of many aspects of the charitable giving of the wealthy. It summarizes the form of such gifts (cash, appreciated assets, private foundations, and so on), the recipient organizations (predominantly higher education, health organizations, and the arts), the tax rules regarding philanthropic donations, and the nature of the social and management involvement of rich donors in the organizations they support. It presents new and interesting data regarding the distribution of giving at different income and wealth levels. Notable in their findings is the concentration of giving among those in all income classes. For instance, 45 percent of all donations by the super-rich (those with incomes exceeding $2.5 million) are due to the generosity of only 5 percent in that situation. The authors also show that only about 20 percent of taxable estates make any charitable bequests at all. Although the rich are an important source of support for many nonprofit activities, it does appear that many wealthy people refrain from significant giving.

It is difficult to criticize the material of this chapter. It contains a great deal of useful information and presents it clearly. However, it may commit some sins of omission. First, the deductibility of giving to qualified charitable organizations could be characterized as a government matching grant program. For the rich, the federal and state governments provide roughly half of the funds, with the donor providing the other half. The governments (or more accurately, the general taxpayers) may pay for an even higher share if the donor receives both income and (in the long run) estate tax relief. Interestingly, despite providing only half or less of the money, the donor gets complete control of how the money is used. Certainly, this matching grant idea causes one to look differently at table 12.2, which shows the recipients of the largest gifts in 1996. Although all these institutions are worthwhile, it is not at all clear that taxpayers or even their congressional representatives would have allocated their (or should I say, our) half of the resources in this precise way.

Second, the chapter assumes that the deductibility of taxes lowers the price of charity. Although that is the usual formulation, it does raise the issue of whether payments to the Treasury over and above the absolute minimum that a crack tax lawyer could achieve should not themselves be thought of as charity. Certainly one motivation for giving is to help others, perhaps particularly future generations. To the extent that people have such motivations, it is not clear that extra payments are not an efficient way to help others (and to the extent that such extra taxes result in more capital infrastructure or a lower national debt, help future generations). I realize that this is a somewhat novel, perhaps radical, perspective, but it still deserves consideration. Consider two identical estates—one leaves $3 million for the construction of a fountain at a major university, and one does not (and therefore pays

$1.65 million more in estate taxes). Which person provided more for others and for future generations in his or her estate plan? I would argue that the answer to that question is not obvious.

Third, giving unspent pension assets in an estate to charity is very tax-efficient—at least as tax-efficient as setting up a private foundation. (I am going to ignore the previous point about the desirability of tax efficiency for the moment.) Although the extremely rich may not rely on pensions as a major source of wealth, cumulatively there are several trillion dollars in defined contribution accounts today. The initial contributions into pension accounts are tax-deductible (subject to a number of limitations). The money compounds free of tax and free of the excise tax on private foundations. If and when pension money is given away to charity late in life (or from an estate), there is no net tax owed. A bequest from a pension account can cost the otherwise-heir only 17 percent of the amount of the gift. The other 83 percent comes from the government in forgone estate taxes and income taxes that otherwise would have been paid by the heir. I do not know how much charitable giving is currently done from pension accounts, but with the rising popularity of 401(k) and Keogh accounts it may be an increasingly large phenomenon.

To again illustrate the tax efficiency of giving from pensions from an estate, consider a large estate with three $100,000 accounts—cash, appreciated securities, and a 401(k) account. If only one of these is going to be given to charity, which one costs the heir the least to give away? The answer is the 401(k) account. It is the only one of these assets on which the heir would still be liable for personal income taxes. What this seems to indicate is that pensions are a great combination investment. Although their primary purpose is to provide retirement support, unspent or unneeded money in a pension provides for a tax-efficient pool of charitable money.

In terms of additional research, I wonder whether state income taxes are not sufficiently different to help get a better fix on the responsiveness of charitable giving to taxes. We know that the marginal state income tax rates for the rich range from zero to 12 percent, although these additional taxes must be multiplied by roughly 0.6, due to the deductibility of state income taxes from the federal income tax base. Still, a top-income person in the state of Massachusetts has an effective marginal income tax rate of 48 percent compared to 40.8 percent in New Hampshire or Washington. I do not know whether the data are available to study this (it certainly is to the IRS), but such a study could be very interesting.

My mention of what is not in the chapter should not detract from what is there. I certainly recommend this article for anyone who wants a thoughtful and thorough treatment of the charitable giving of the rich. I will be adding it to my reading lists for all relevant courses.

13

Entrepreneurs, Income Taxes, and Investment

Robert Carroll, Douglas Holtz-Eakin, Mark Rider, and Harvey S. Rosen

Some of America's richest people are entrepreneurs.[1] Much of the public policy interest in these individuals has surrounded their putative roles as "creators" of jobs and new products. More specifically, it has been argued that tax policy should encourage entrepreneurs to invest in their businesses. Such arguments influenced the Omnibus Budget Reconciliation Act of 1993 (OBRA93), which contained a number of provisions favoring investment in small businesses, including a 50 percent exclusion of long-term capital gains from certain small business investments. At the same time, there are concerns that the high marginal tax rates embodied in that law have discouraged investment by entrepreneurs. As one business economist opined in the *Wall Street Journal* on January 11, 1994, after high-end personal income tax rates had been raised in 1993: "It means their cash flows will not grow as fast, and they will not have as much to plow back into their business" ("Sticker Shock: Increased Taxes Prompt Wealthy to Cut Spending").

Does tax policy affect the investment decisions of small businesses? Interestingly, most of the voluminous literature on taxes and investments focuses on aggregate business investment, or investment undertaken by large firms of the type represented, say, in the Compustat database.[2] Eric Engen and Jonathan Skinner (1996) point out that there has been little systematic investigation of whether the tax system adversely affects entrepreneurial investment behavior. This is a significant omission given that entrepreneurial enterprises account for at least 10 percent of the economy's nonresidential fixed investment.[3]

The purpose of this chapter is to analyze entrepreneurs' investment behavior and how it is affected by their tax situations. We analyze the income tax returns of a large group of sole proprietors before and after the Tax Reform Act of 1986 (TRA86) and determine how the substantial reductions in marginal tax rates associated with that law affected whether and how much they invested in their enterprises.

The next section presents the framework for our analysis, which is based on a conventional user cost of capital model. That section is followed by a description of the data and a preliminary investigation of the issues using simple tabulations. The next section presents a multivariate analysis of the decision to invest and also considers the impact on the quantity of investment spending. Our results indicate that taxes exert a statistically and quantitatively significant influence on the probability that an entrepreneur invests. For example, a five-percentage-point rise in marginal tax rates would reduce the proportion of entrepreneurs who make new capital investments by 10.4 percent. Further, such a tax increase would lower mean capital outlays by 9.9 percent.

WHY TAXES MIGHT MATTER

Consider an entrepreneur organized as a sole proprietor who is considering a marginal investment in his enterprise.[4] There are two possible ways in which his personal income tax situation can affect his decision. First, taxes affect the demand for investment through their impact on the user cost of capital. Following Jason Cummins, Kevin Hassett, and R. Glenn Hubbard's (1994) exposition of the neoclassical investment model, the investment of entrepreneur i during year t, I_{it}, is

$$I_{it} = E_{it-1}(\gamma c_{it}) + \varepsilon_{it}, \tag{13.1}$$

where E_{it-1} is the expectations operator given information available at time $t-1$, c_{it} is the user cost of capital γ is a parameter, and ε_{it} is a white-noise error. The user cost, in turn, is

$$c_{it} = \frac{r_t - \pi_t + d}{1 - \tau_{it}}(1 - k_t - a_{it}\tau_{it}z_t), \tag{13.2}$$

where r is the nominal after-tax discount rate, π is the (constant) inflation rate, d is the exponential rate of economic depreciation, k is the rate of investment tax credit, τ is the entrepreneur's personal income marginal tax rate, a is the percentage of basis entitled to statutory depreciation allowances, and z is the present value of depreciation allowances per dollar of marginal investment.[5] (See appendix 13B for a detailed discussion of the construction of the user cost.) Clearly, changes in the personal tax rate alter the user cost and may thereby influence investment decisions. The magnitude of the effect depends on the elasticity of investment with respect to the user cost. This discussion presumes an interior solution for the desired amount of investment. As will become apparent later in the chapter, many entrepreneurs are at a corner solution involving zero investment. If so, equation (13.1) is best interpreted as determining the latent index of desired investment.

The other channel through which the entrepreneur's tax rate may affect his investment decision relates to liquidity constraints.[6] An increase in taxes reduces the entrepreneur's cash flow. To the extent that liquidity constraints are present, this leads to a reduction in the demand for capital. The user cost and liquidity constraint stories are not mutually exclusive, and we will investigate both.

To make equation (13.1) operational, we need to establish a link between expected and observed user costs. Cummins, Hassett, and Hubbard (1994) show that if a change in user costs generated by a tax reform is expected to last indefinitely, then the change in expected user costs can be represented by the actual change. Our identifying variation in user costs is generated by TRA86, so we make this strong and useful assumption later.

DATA

Description

Our data are drawn from the Statistics of Income Individual Income Tax Returns files for 1985 and 1988, a panel consisting of over 62,100 tax returns for taxpayers present in both years.[7] These files contain detailed information on taxpayers' income and deductions taken from their form 1040. Of those taxpayers with complete information on their schedule C, we exclude those taxpayers who filed more than one tax return for any year, those who changed filing status between 1985 and 1988, those who reported income on a fiscal year basis, and those who reported farm or rental income.[8] We include only people between twenty-five and fifty-five years of age in order to avoid complications that would arise because of entry into the labor market by the young and impending retirement by the old. We also eliminate taxpayers who had negative marginal tax rates or who were subject to the alternative minimum tax (AMT). The tax situations of the former group are complicated by the interaction of the earned income tax credit (EITC) with the ordinary income tax, while the members of the latter group are in effect subject to an entirely separate tax base and rate schedule. Figure 13A.1 and 13A.2 provide information on the sample distributions of adjusted gross incomes (AGIs) and marginal tax rates, respectively.

Sole proprietors do not report annual investment on their schedule C. However, they do report depreciation deductions. Moreover, using the detailed information regarding the computation of these deductions reported on form 4562, it is possible to identify which of these deductions are associated with capital purchased during the tax year under consideration.[9] Thus, we can determine whether the entrepreneur made any investment during the year and the associated expenditure. (To compute expenditures, we simply add up the amounts listed on form 4562 indicating the cost or basis of investments made during the current year.) Detailed summary information on the types of investment expenditures undertaken by sole proprietors is contained in tables 13A.1 and 13A.2.[10]

Our basic sample consists of individuals who filed a schedule C in both 1985 and 1988. In principle, this might engender selectivity bias—sole proprietors who survive until 1988 may not be a random sample of the 1985 group. However, as noted later in the chapter, when we expand our analysis of investment decisions to include individuals who exited from entrepreneurship between 1985 and 1988, no important differences emerge.

An important implicit assumption in this discussion is that we can equate sole proprietors with "entrepreneurs." Is this sensible? In the nonstatistical literature on this topic, entrepreneurs are typically identified by their daring, risk-taking, animal spirits, and so forth. However, statistical work forces us to settle for more prosaic, observable criteria for classifying someone as an entrepreneur. With tax return data, the most sensible proxy for entrepreneurship is the presence of a schedule C in the return.[11]

It has been suggested that the presence of schedule C is more indicative of tax-sheltering activity than entrepreneurial activity. For example, some economists may report their consulting incomes and honoraria on schedule C solely in order to be eligible for certain deductions. However, data from the 1985 Statistics of Income suggest that such personal service activities are undertaken by only a small portion of schedule C filers, about 16 percent.[12] And surely at least some of these activities reflect classical entrepreneurial behavior.

One might be tempted to implement an algorithm for identifying which schedule C filers are "serious" entrepreneurs. For example, one could require that business income be above some threshold level. But many start-up enterprises have low or even zero receipts. Another possibility is that the ratio of schedule C income to earned income be above some threshold. But as already suggested, "serious" entrepreneurs can have low incomes from their enterprises. Further complications result from using annual data. A serious entrepreneur who starts his or her business late in the year is likely to resemble a full-year, but nonserious, entrepreneur.

We conclude that trying to weed out ersatz entrepreneurs from the population of schedule C filers is not likely to be terribly fruitful. Nevertheless, we experiment a bit later in the chapter with alternative thresholds for business revenues as criteria for being classified as an entrepreneur and find that they have no serious impact on our substantive results. Finally, we note that even if all sole proprietors are entrepreneurs, it is clearly not true that all entrepreneurs are sole proprietors. Analysis of the behavior of entrepreneurs who are organized in other forms of business is beyond the scope of this chapter.

A Preliminary Look at the Data

Tables 13.1 and 13.2 provide some information on the number of sole proprietorships in 1985 and 1988, and the extent to which they made capital purchases, Table 13.1 exhibits a three-by-three matrix comparing combinations of filing status and investment decisions in 1985 (rows) with corresponding measures for 1988 (columns). Consider, for example, the center entry. It indicates that 1,705 observations are sole proprietors who did not make any investment in either 1985 or 1988. The second entry in this cell indicates that these observations constitute 57.3 percent of the entrepreneurs who did not have capital outlays in 1985. In contrast, 459, or 15.4 percent, moved from zero to positive investment, and 812, or 27.3 percent, exited from sole proprietorship entirely.

For the matrix as a whole, a couple of observations stand out. First, those who made an investment in 1985 are more likely to stop acquiring physical assets than to leave sole proprietorship (40.6 percent versus 12.3 percent). Second, those who made no investment in 1985 are more likely to cease operations than add capital (27.3 percent versus 15.4 percent).

As already noted, we focus mostly on individuals who were sole proprietors in both 1985 and 1988, that is, those in the lower righthand two-by-two submatrix.

Table 13.1   Sole Proprietors and Investment Decisions

		1988	
	No Schedule C	Schedule C No Investment	Schedule C Investment
1985			
No schedule C	13,252	1,222	304
	(0.897)	(0.083)	(0.020)
Schedule C,	812	1,705	459
no investment	(0.273)	(0.573)	(0.154)
Schedule C,	185	609	707
investment	(0.123)	(0.406)	(0.471)

Source: Authors' calculations
Note: The first entry in each cell is the number of observations. The second entry is the number of observations as a fraction of the total number of observations in the corresponding *row*.

Table 13.2   Investment Among Sole Proprietors in 1985 and 1988

	1988	
	No Investment	Investment
1985		
No investment	1,705	459
	(0.788)	(0.212)
Investment	609	707
	(0.463)	(0.537)

Source: Authors' calculations.
Note: The first entry in each cell is the number of observations. The second entry is the number of observations as a fraction of the total number of observations in the corresponding *row*.

Table 13.2 replicates these cells but provides frequencies contingent on remaining a sole proprietor. Within this sample, 79 percent of the individuals who made no investment in 1985 also made no investment in 1988, and 54 percent of those who invested in 1985 also did so in 1988. Thus, there appears to be substantial persistence in the propensity to invest, a feature of the data that influences the design of our statistical analysis. Another critical implication of the data in table 13.2 is that only a relatively small proportion—about one-third—of the sole proprietors make any capital investments. This is consistent with earlier findings using different data suggesting that most small enterprises have no capital at all (see Meyer 1990).

In tables 13.3 and 13.4, we divide our entrepreneurs into two groups, those with "lower" tax rates in 1985 (below 34 percent) and those with "higher" rates (34 percent and above). Relatively affluent people in the upper tax brackets received the largest tax rate reductions under TRA86. Hence, if there is anything to the story about higher tax rates discouraging entrepreneurs from investing, then we would expect those individuals who were initially in the higher brackets to have the largest increase in their propensity to make capital outlays. The figures in tables 13.3 and 13.4 appear to be consistent with this story. Of the sole proprietors who made no investment and had lower tax rates in 1985, 18.7 percent made capital purchases in 1988. For those with higher tax rates in 1985, the figure was 23.9 percent. Similarly, 55.7 percent of the lower-tax-rate sole proprietors who made capital expenditures in 1985 made no investment in 1988; for the higher-tax-rate sole proprietors, the figure was only 41.0 percent.[13]

Table 13.3   Investment Decisions and Tax Rates: Lower Tax Rate in 1985

	1988	
	No Investment	Investment
1985		
No investment	923	213
	(0.813)	(0.187)
Investment	263	209
	(0.557)	(0.443)

Source: Authors' calculations.
Note: The first entry in each cell is the number of observations. The second entry is the number of observations as a fraction of the total number of observations in the corresponding *row*.

Table 13.4   Investment Decisions and Tax Rates: Higher Tax Rate in 1985

	1988	
	No Investment	Investment
1985		
No investment	782	246
	(0.761)	(0.239)
Investment	346	498
	(0.410)	(0.590)

Source: Authors' calculations.

Note: The first entry in each cell is the number of observations. The second entry is the number of observations as a fraction of the total number of observations in table 13.3 includes all sole proprietors with 1985 marginal tax rates below 34 percent. Table 13.4 contains the remainder.

Of course, our theory suggests that investment decisions depend on the user cost of capital, of which marginal tax rates are only one component. Indeed, as documented in appendix 13B, the tax reform affected not only marginal tax rates but also depreciation allowances and the investment tax credits (the variables z and k in equation [13.2]). It turns out, however, that in our data, changes in the user cost are primarily driven by changes in tax rates—the correlation between changes in the two variables is 0.99. That said, the user cost framework is more desirable in principle because it allows one to estimate how the change in any relevant tax parameter affects investment. An additional limitation of the simple tabulations in tables 13.3 and 13.4 is that variables other than marginal tax rates (or user costs) may influence an entrepreneur's propensity to invest, and some of these could be correlated with marginal tax rates. Hence, although the preliminary calculations in tables 13.3 and 13.4 are suggestive, we turn now to a multivariate approach in which the focus is on changes in the user cost of capital.

MULTIVARIATE ANALYSES
The Investment Decision

Investment functions are typically estimated using aggregate data or data from established corporations. Hence, it can be taken for granted that each observation is associated with at least *some* investment. However, as tables 13.3 and 13.4 demonstrates, most sole proprietors make no investments in physical capital, so understanding the dichotomous decision, to invest or not to invest, is itself of considerable importance. Hence, our first goal is to estimate the determinants of the probability that a sole proprietor made any investment in 1988 (Prob [$I_{88} > 0$]).

What are the determinants of this probability? In light of the strong persistence in the propensity to invest evident from tables 13.3 and 13.4, one variable that belongs is an indicator for whether there was investment in 1985. Conditional on the 1985 investment decision, the discussion of the previous section suggests that the 1988 decision is influenced by changes in the user cost of capital between the two years.

Finally, and unlike the case in conventional analyses of investment using corporate data, it makes sense to include some demographic and economic information about the individual who is actually making the decison.[14] (For example, even conditional on past investment, an individual's decision may depend on his or her stage in the life cycle.) All of this suggests that the probability that the entrepreneur acquires some capital in 1988 can be written as

$$\text{Prob } (I_{88} > 0) = \alpha_0 + \alpha_1 (\%\Delta c) + \alpha_2 (\%\Delta c \times I_{85}) + \alpha_3 I_{85} + X\beta, \tag{13.3}$$

where $\%\Delta c = [\ln(c_{88}) - \ln(c_{85})]$ and c_s is the entrepreneur's user cost in year s (as defined in equation [13.2]); $I_{85} = 1$ if the firm had positive capital outlays in 1985 and is 0 otherwise; and X is a vector of personal and economic characteristics of the entrepreneur for which β is the associated parameter vector. The interaction term permits us to determine whether taxes affect differently those entrepreneurs who did and did not initially purchase capital, a possibility suggested by tables 13.3 and 13.4. If $I_{85} = 0$, the effect of the change in user cost is given by α_1. In contrast, for those entrepreneurs who had investment in 1985 ($I_{85} = 1$), the effect is $\alpha_1 + \alpha_2$. To estimate the parameters of equation (13.3) requires that we make some assumption about the error term associated with the investment decision. We assume normality, which yields the conventional probit statistical model.

The specification of equation (13.3) gives rise to several questions. First, what personal and economic characteristics are to be included in the X vector? Tax returns do not contain as rich a set of personal variables as some other data sets, but some useful controls are available. These variables, along with their means and standard deviations, are listed in table 13.5. Age is included because it is related to one's experience in the job market, human capital accumulation, and, hence, the structure of the business; previous research on entrepreneurial decision-making suggests that a quadratic term is also appropriate.[15] Marital status and the number of dependents may be related to attitudes toward risk.

We include capital income in 1985 as a measure of the individual's assets, which should affect entrepreneurial decision-making in the presence of capital market constraints.[16] However, one should note that tax return data on capital income are quite limited. Our variable is the sum of reported dividends and interest; it omits capital gains and municipal bond interest, inter alia.[17] Hence, one must be cautious in interpreting the coefficient on this variable as a test of the liquidity constraint hypothesis. Finally, using the principal business codes reported on schedule C, we develop a set of dichotomous industry variables. These are intended to take into account the fact that the capital-intensity of the production technology differs across industries. Further, as suggested by Andrei Shleifer and Robert Vishny (1992), investment opportunities within industries tend to move together, suggesting that a firm's industrial classification is a useful proxy for its investment opportunities.

The second major issue associated with equation (13.3) is the potential endogeneity of the user cost variable. Marginal tax rates, of course, vary with taxable income. As capital investment goes up, taxable income and the marginal tax rate decline, as does the user cost of capital, ceteris paribus. This may induce a positive relationship between $\%\Delta c$ and the probability of investing that has nothing to do

Table 13.5   Sample Statistics

I_{85} (= 1, if investment in 1985)	0.378
	(0.485)
I_{88} (= 1, if investment in 1988)	0.335
	(0.472)
%Δc (log-difference in user cost)	−0.00695
	(0.0785)
Age (age in years)	40.2
	(7.93)
Age^2 (age squared)	1,679
	(648)
Capinc (interest and dividend income $\times 10^{-6}$)	0.0248
	(0.156)
Married (= 1, if married)	0.914
	(0.281)
Dependents (number of dependents)	0.159
	(0.127)
Mfg (= 1, if manufacturing sector)	0.0250
	(0.156)
Wholesale (= 1, if wholesale sector)	0.0207
	(0.142)
Retail (= 1, if retail sector)	0.0934
	(0.291)
Finance (= 1, if finance sector)	0.0948
	(0.293)
Service (= 1, if service sector)	0.602
	(0.490)
N (number of observations)	3,480

Source: Authors' calculations.
Note: Table entries are means and, in parentheses, standard deviations. The sample consists of individuals who were sole proprietors in 1985 and 1988.

with economic behavior, a problem ubiquitous in investigating the behavioral effects of taxation (see Feenberg 1987). A remedy is to estimate the equation using instrumental variables; to do so, we must first find a variable that is correlated with %Δc but is unlikely to be correlated with the error term.

We construct an instrumental variable that takes advantage of the most prominent feature of our data: the exogenous decline in marginal tax rates due to TRA86 itself.[18] To do so, we begin by computing each individual's marginal tax rate and user cost of capital using the data and tax law for 1985. Next we compute each individual's marginal tax rate using the data for 1985 (inflated to 1988 levels) but employing the tax law for 1988. Clearly, the change between the 1985 rate and the synthetic 1988 tax rate computed in this fashion is due entirely to modifications of the tax code. We then use this synthetic marginal tax rate together with 1988 values of the interest rate and the economic depreciation parameter to compute a synthetic user cost for 1988.[19] Our instrumental variable is the percentage change between the synthetic 1988 user cost and the actual 1985 value. (Similarly, the instrumental variable for $I_{85} \times \%\Delta c$ is I_{85} times the synthetic percentage change in the user cost.) Essentially, this procedure removes the endogenous component of tax rate movements from $\%\Delta c$, leaving only the part due to the exogenous change in the tax law associated with TRA86.[20] Prior to estimating our probit model with these instrumental variables, we can use them to implement the test suggested by Douglas Rivers and Quang Vuong (1988) to assess whether the potential endogeneity of $\%\Delta c$ is in fact a significant problem.[21]

Results To begin, we present in column 1 of table 13.6 a simple specification that includes on the righthand side only $\%\Delta c$, an indicator variable for whether the firm made any investment in 1985 (I_{85}), and the interaction of the two. In effect, this represents a more structured variant of the comparisons presented in tables 13.3 and 13.4 that exploits all changes in the user cost. Not surprisingly, the coefficient on I_{85} is positive and highly significant—those entrepreneurs who invested in 1985 are more likely to have done so three years later. Given the discussion surrounding tables 13.3 and 13.4, it is equally unsurprising that the coefficient on $\%\Delta c$ is also highly significant and has the expected negative sign. The greater the percentage increase in a sole proprietor's user cost of capital between 1985 and 1988, the lower the probability that he or she undertook capital outlays in 1988. Finally, the negative sign on the interaction term suggests that increases in the user cost are even more important for firms that already had some capital outlays.

In column 2 we augment the specification to include our other control variables. The coefficients on both $\%\Delta c$ and the interaction of $\%\Delta c$ with I_{85} remain negative and statistically significant. They are essentially identical to their counterparts in column 1. Thus, the apparent importance of taxes (embodied in the user cost) found in column 1 is not an artifact of any correlations between $\%\Delta c$ and other variables. Turning to these other variables, the effect of Age is initially positive but subsequently declines (the quadratic term is negative). Although Age and Age^2 are individually insignificant, a joint test reveals that the effect of age as a whole is statistically significant.[22] The effect of Age is positive until the age of twenty-nine, and after that is negative. Our other demographic variables, marital status and number of dependents, do not have a statistically significant impact. The coefficients on the industry dichotomous variables suggest that entrepreneurs engaged in the service sector are more likely to have undertaken investment than their counterparts in other sectors.[23]

As stressed earlier, the negative coefficient on $\%\Delta c$ might simply be a reflection of the fact that marginal tax rates increase with taxable income, ceteris paribus. To investigate this phenomenon, we implemented the Rivers-Vuong test for endogeneity described earlier. The chi-square test statistic associated with the hypothesis that the coefficients of the relevant residuals are both zero is 13.2, which easily rejects at any conventional level of significance. Thus, we reestimated both of our equations using instrumental variables. These results are reported in columns 3 and 4 of table 13.6. The results in these columns are essentially the same as their counterparts in columns 1 and 2. In particular, the coefficient on $\%\Delta c$ in column 4 is still negative (−1.86, with a standard error of 0.536), as is the coefficient on the interaction term (−1.88 with a standard error of 0.722).

Table 13.6   Probit Analysis of Investment Decisions

Intercept	−0.795	−1.38	−0.794	−1.27
	(0.0304)	(0.607)	(0.0304)	(0.611)
%Δc	−1.26	−1.33	−1.71	−1.86
	(0.400)	(0.419)	(0.500)	(0.536)
%Δc × I_{85}	−1.47	−1.41	−1.96	−1.88
	(0.584)	(0.586)	(0.716)	(0.722)
I_{85}	0.822	0.814	0.800	0.790
	(0.0472)	(0.0474)	(0.0478)	(0.0481)
Age	—	3.13	—	2.81
	—	(3.07)	—	(3.09)
Age^2	—	−4.58	—	−4.35
	—	(3.76)	—	(3.78)
Capinc	—	0.0605	—	−0.0066
	—	(0.153)	—	(0.156)
Married	—	0.0739	—	0.0727
	—	(0.0887)	—	(0.0892)
Dependents	—	−0.354	—	−0.404
	—	(0.203)	—	(0.205)
Mfg	—	0.0754	—	0.0911
	—	(0.155)	—	(0.156)
Wholesale	—	0.159	—	0.162
	—	(0.171)	—	(0.171)
Retail	—	−0.0641	—	−0.0506
	—	(0.0979)	—	(0.0984)
Finance	—	0.0245	—	0.0149
	—	(0.0956)	—	(0.0960)
Service	—	0.137	—	0.122
	—	(0.0650)	—	(0.0655)
N	3,480	3,480	3,480	3,480

Source: Authors' calculations.
Note: Figures in parentheses are standard errors. Variables are defined in table 13.5. The dependent variable takes a value of 1 if the sole proprietor purchased capital in 1988, and 0 otherwise. Columns 3 and 4 show the results when the specifications in columns 1 and 2, respectively, are estimated using instrumental variables.

Implications   We turn now to the quantitative significance of our results, using the instrumental variable results (column 4 of table 13.6) to simulate the effect of a change in the user cost on the probability of purchasing capital. Specifically, we consider a 10 percent rise in the user cost. To begin, we evaluate all the righthand variables at their actual values. We then use the coefficients in column 4 to find the predicted probability of investing for each observation in the sample. Next, we raise the value of %Δc by 0.1 for every observation and recompute the probabilities leaving all other variables at their initial values. These calculations suggest that the increase in the user cost lowers the mean probability of undertaking investment from 0.335 to 0.251, a decline of 0.084 or 25 percent.

An alternative approach to assessing the quantitative significance of our results is to focus directly on tax rates. To do so, we again begin by evaluating each of the righthand variables at their actual values and computing the predicted probability of investment for each observation. Next, we raise the 1988 marginal tax rate of each individual in the sample by five percentage points, compute the implied user cost for 1988, and calculate the resulting value of %Δc. Using this value of %Δc and the actual values of the other righthand variables, we recompute the implied probability of investment. In this instance, the mean probability of investment falls from 0.335 to 0.300, a decline of 0.035 or 10.4 percent. Using either metric, the estimates imply a substantial response of investment decisions to tax rates.

Alternative Specifications   We now discuss a number of exercises that we conducted in order to assess the robustness of our results.

Statistical model   One possible problem with our results is that they are a consequence of the assumptions underlying the statistical model. In the probit model, the two-stage procedure generates consistent estimates only if the error terms in both the first- and second-stage equations are joint normally distributed, and both equations are correctly specified. In a linear probability model, the conditions are less stringent—the righthand variables in the first-stage equation have to be uncorrelated with the error term in the second-stage equation, but consistent estimates may be obtained even if some variables that belong in the first-stage equation are omitted. Therefore, despite the well-known limitations of the linear probability model, it seemed worthwhile to use it to check our estimates.

   The linear probability results are very similar to those obtained using the probit. Specifically, using the linear probability model, the estimated coefficients on %Δc and %Δc $\times$ I_{85} in both the parsimonious and fully specified models (analogous to columns 1 and 2 of table 13.6, respectively) are negative and statistically significant. As before, we can reject the null hypothesis of exogeneity of the user cost variables, leading us to estimate the linear probability model using two-stage least squares. The resulting estimates for the coefficients of the user cost, -0.554 (standard error = 0.169), and the interaction term, -0.901 (standard error = 0.238), provide nearly precisely the same qualitative *and* quantitative message regarding the impact of user costs and tax policy on the probability of investment. Specifically, the estimated coefficients imply that an increase of 0.1 in %Δc would reduce the mean probability of investment by 0.089, or 27 percent.

Control variables   As noted earlier, tax-based data provide relatively few candidates for controls. However, we subjected our equation to a variety of checks to determine whether the estimated relationship is sensitive to the specification. To begin, we included the 1985 value of family wage and salary earnings (they are not reported separately for each spouse). More than one interpretation of this variable is possible. To the extent that earnings are attributable to the entrepreneur's spouse, they may create an income effect for the entrepreneur. To the extent that they are attributable to the entrepreneur, they may be an indicator of the opportunity cost of time that is spent in sole proprietorship activity. If so, they are also likely to be endogenous to business decisions generally, the primary reason for not including earnings in the baseline specification. In any event, the estimated coefficient of the earnings variable was positive but insignificant, and its inclusion had essentially no impact on the character of the results.

An important feature of TRA86 is that it embodied changes in the tax base as well as in marginal tax rates. (For example, the itemized deduction for state sales taxes was eliminated.) Ceteris paribus, the changes in after-tax income induced by such "tax-base effects" might alter the propensity to invest either by influencing the entrepreneur's own labor supply or by changing the cash flow of a liquidity constrained venture.[24] To investigate this possibility, we augmented the specification in table 13.6 with the change in after-tax income between 1985 and 1988. Of course, this variable may be endogenous for the same reasons as our tax price variable. Hence, we constructed an instrument analogous to that used for our tax price variable (by computing 1988 after-tax income using the 1985 income data and 1988 tax structure). We find that augmenting the equation with this variable does not appreciably alter our other estimates. In the analog to column 2 of table 13.6, the coefficient of the user cost variable is -1.32 (standard error $= 0.419$) and that of the interaction variable is -1.47 (standard error $= 0.587$). Somewhat surprisingly, the coefficient on change in after-tax income itself is negative. We do not regard this finding as serious evidence against the hypothesis that liquidity constraints affect the decisions of small firms. Taxable income, after all, poorly measures the total financial resources available to the entrepreneur. Our data set allows us to get a good fix on the effects of marginal tax rates but is not much help in learning about the independent effect of liquidity constraints.

Another possible problem with our canonical specification is that it ignores possible state-based differences in investment incentives. For example, states differ considerably in their tax and regulatory environments. To control for such differences, we added a set of dichotomous state variables to our basic specification. The inclusion of these controls has little effect as the coefficient on %Δc remains negative (-1.54) and statistically significant (standard error $= 0.434$), as does that on %$\Delta c \times I_{85}$ (-1.30, standard error $= 0.596$).

Sample   The estimates so far are based on a sample that includes only individuals who were sole proprietors in both 1985 and 1988. The propensity to exit from schedule C status is not random. Indeed, TRA86 embodied incentives to alter the organizational form of a business. The main thrust was to make taxation under the individual income tax (sole proprietorship, partnership, subchapter S corporation) more attractive relative to the corporation tax (see Carroll and Joulfaian 1997; Plesko 1994). Hence, TRA86 was more likely to induce "entry" than "exit." One possible econometric strategy for dealing with this phenomenon would be to estimate a sequential bivariate probit model, which would jointly estimate the probability of survival as an entrepreneur with the probability of having investment, conditional on survival. However, this model requires very strong identification assumptions (see van Praag and van Ophem 1994) that cannot be made convincingly in our context.

Instead, we simply expand the sample to include all individuals who were sole proprietors in 1985, even if they ceased being so in 1988. The dependent variable in the probit equation in effect becomes "stayed a sole proprietor *and* purchased capital." This exercise allows us to see whether ignoring nonrandom entry and exit changes the character of our results. We find that the coefficients on the user cost variable and the interaction of user cost and lagged investment are still negative and significant. For example, in the specification corresponding to column 4 of table 13.6, the coefficient of %Δc is -2.09 (standard error = 0.509) and the coefficient on the interaction term is -2.04 (standard error = 0.681).

Another issue in constructing the sample is the possibility that the process determining investment differs between those who already have a history of investment and those who do not. That is, it may not be desirable to pool observations for which $I_{85} = 1$ with those for which $I_{85} = 0$. To see whether our pooling of the data was driving the results, we estimated separate probits for those who had investment in 1985 and those who did not. This yielded results similar to those reported in table 13.6; %Δc significantly affects the probability of investment in both cases. For those with $I_{85} = 1$, the estimate is -3.59 (standard error = 0.564), while for those with $I_{85} = 0$, the result was -2.04 (standard error = 0.556).

Last among the sample issues is that, as discussed earlier, one may wish to tighten the criteria for classifying schedule C filers as entrepreneurs. To do so, we imposed the requirement that sole proprietors reported $1,000 of gross business receipts and repeated our analysis using this smaller (2,556 observations), more select sample. The basic tenor of our results is unchanged; both %Δc and the interaction variable continue to be negative (-1.21 and -1.40, respectively) and statistically significant (standard error = 0.444 and 0.615, respectively). As further checks, we raised the minimum threshold to $5,000 of business receipts, and then to $10,000. In each case, the estimated coefficients remain negative and jointly significant.

Equipment versus structures   Our canonical specification determines the probability that an entrepreneur makes any kind of investment. However, one might wish to distinguish between investment in structures and equipment. Indeed, TRA86 had different provisions for each type of investment. For structures, depreciation allowances were made less generous, and for equipment, the major innovation was elimination of the investment tax credit. In short, both the underlying demands and the magnitudes of price changes may have differed across the two types of investment.

We therefore estimated separate probits for equipment and structures. For equipment, the estimated coefficient for %Δc in the instrumental-variables probit is -3.57 (standard error = 1.11), and the coefficient on %Δc $\times$ I_{85} is -3.43 (standard error = 1.47). For structures, the corresponding coefficients are -3.73 (standard error = 0.443) and 1.94 (standard error = 1.53). Thus, increases in the user cost reduce the propensity to invest both in equipment and in structures. (Although the point estimate for the interaction term in the structures model is positive, it is estimated somewhat imprecisely, and the combined effect of both coefficients indicates a negative impact of the user cost on structures investment even when $I_{85} = 1$.)

In summary, our finding of an inverse relationship between tax rates and entrepreneurs' propensity to invest is quite robust. It emerges in the face of a variety of alterations to our assumptions regarding the specification and estimation of the model.

Investment Expenditures

As noted earlier, the supporting information associated with tax returns enables us to compute the dollar value of investment outlays in each year, thereby permitting a parallel analysis of the quantity of investment expenditure in 1988, E_{88}. The mean value of E_{88} was \$1,699.[25] Recall from table 13.5, however, that only 33.5 percent of the firms had positive investment outlays in 1988. The large number of zeros affects both the interpretation of the mean—among those with positive spending, the mean outlay was \$5,070 (with a standard deviation of \$15,933)—and our econometric strategy.

To begin, we estimate an ordinary least squares (OLS) regression in which the dependent variable is E_{88} and the righthand variables are the same as in the probit equations discussed earlier, except that we replace the indicator variable for investment expenditures in 1985, I_{85}, with the value of investment expenditures in 1985, E_{85}. We restrict the analysis to those 3,480 observations that included a schedule C in both 1985 and 1988 because it is not possible to impute the appropriate level of investment expenditure for those that exited from sole proprietorship status.

The results are shown in the first column of table 13.7. The coefficient on $\%\Delta c$ is negative (−17.4, with a standard error of 2.44), and the coefficient on the interaction variable $\%\Delta c \times E_{85}$ is positive, (6.48, with a standard error of 0.142). Thus, the impact of changes in the user cost becomes smaller as the amount of investment in 1985 gets larger. In keeping with the pattern established in table 13.6, the lagged value of investment expenditures has a positive and statistically significant coefficient. Also consistent with our analysis of the dichotomous decision, only Age (which along with its square is jointly significant) among the demographic variables influences the magnitude of investment spending. In contrast to the earlier findings, however, of the industry indicator variables only Finance is statistically significant in determining the quantity of investment.

A potentially serious technical problem arises with OLS because of the large number of zeros among the observations for the dependent variable. Hence, it is appropriate to employ the tobit estimator, the results of which are shown in the second column of table 13.7. Clearly, accounting for the distribution of the zeros has a substantial impact on the estimates. The coefficient on the user cost is now −54.4, and that of the interaction variable is 7.13. Both are statistically significant. Thus, moving to the tobit model strengthens our main qualitative result—increases in the user cost of capital decrease entrepreneurs' expected investment expenditures.

As before, it is important to account for the potential endogeneity of the user cost. Implementing the Rivers-Vuong test in the tobit context yields a test statistic of 280.2 (distributed as a chi-square with two degrees of freedom), an overwhelming rejection of the null hypothesis of exogeneity. Thus, we turn in the third column to a two-stage tobit (2STobit) estimator that employs our instrumental variable for the change in the user cost. The 2STobit estimate of the coefficient on $\%\Delta c$ is −67.0 and highly statistically significant. As before, the coefficient on the interaction variable has the opposite sign, 8.24, and is statistically significant.

Table 13.7   Analysis of Investment Expenditures

	OLS	Tobit	Two-Stage Tobit
Intercept	−4.84	−27.7	−22.2
	(4.69)	(10.3)	(9.80)
%Δc	−17.4	−54.4	−67.0
	(2.44)	(5.26)	(6.30)
%Δc × E_{85}	6.48	7.13	8.24
	(0.142)	(0.262)	(0.259)
E_{85}	0.888	1.05	1.05
	(0.0160)	(0.0295)	(0.0283)
Age	37.8	93.0	74.0
	(23.7)	(52.2)	(49.5)
Age^2	−48.6	−130.0	−108.0
	(29.0)	(63.9)	(60.5)
Capinc	−0.555	−0.194	−0.856
	(1.18)	(2.45)	(2.32)
Married	−0.832	−0.607	−0.633
	(0.686)	(1.49)	(1.41)
Dependents	1.040	−2.41	−3.24
	(1.57)	(3.39)	(3.23)
Mfg	0.868	3.38	3.58
	(1.21)	(2.57)	(2.44)
Wholesale	−1.04	−0.355	−0.407
	(1.31)	(2.89)	(2.73)
Retail	−0.283	−1.26	−0.868
	(0.733)	(1.66)	(1.57)
Finance	−1.74	−2.53	−3.54
	(0.728)	(1.63)	(1.54)
Service	−0.877	0.202	−0.0905
	(0.500)	(1.10)	(1.04)
N	3.480	3,480	3,480

Source: Authors' calculations.
Note: Figures in parentheses are standard errors. The sample consists of individuals who were sole proprietors in 1985 and 1988. The dependent variable is the value of purchased capital in 1988.

In sum, the results in table 13.7 complement our analysis of the dichotomous
decision, showing that changes in the user cost and, thus, changes in tax rates have
a statistically significant impact on entrepreneurs' investment expenditures. But how
large is the impact? In the presence of the interaction term, the answer clearly
depends on the distribution of 1985 investment expenditures in the sample. Indeed,
given that the coefficient on the interaction term is positive, there is a possibility
that the response to an increase in the user cost will be positive. However, this is
unlikely. With a coefficient on %Δc of −64.0 and a coefficient on E_{85} × %Δc of 8.24,
the net impact becomes positive only when 1985 investment expenditure exceeds
$8,131. However, mean expenditures in 1985 were only $1,536 ($4,064 among
those with positive expenditures).

In any case, it is clear that to gain a feel for the quantitative implications of our sample, we need to conduct some simulations. We begin by evaluating each of the righthand variables at their actual values and computing the predicted value of E_{88} for each observation in the data. Then we raise the value of %Δc by 0.1 (ten percentage points) and recompute the predicted E_{88}. We find that, evaluated at the means, the implied elasticity of investment expenditure with respect to the user cost is −1.78. This is quite a bit higher than the elasticity estimates based on corporate data that, according to Eric Engen and Jonathan Skinner (1996), range from −0.25 to −1.0. We conjecture that small businesses of the type in our sample are more likely to be liquidity-constrained than corporations and that the user cost may be picking up some of this effect.[26]

As before, it is useful to provide a more direct measure of the impact of changes in tax rates. Following our previous strategy, we first compute the predicted value of investment using the actual values of the righthand variables. Next, we increase the 1988 marginal tax rate of each individual member of the sample by five percentage points, compute the implied user cost, and the corresponding value of %Δc. Using the implied value, along with the actual values of the remaining variables, we calculate the new predicted value of investment for each observation. We find that a five-percentage-point increase in marginal tax rates leads to a 9.9 percent decline in the mean predicted value. In short, our estimates imply that changes in the user cost of capital induced by increases in marginal tax rates have a substantial impact on entrepreneurs' investment spending.

CONCLUSION

Policymakers have long been concerned with tax policy toward high-income individuals, the health of small businesses, and the impact of tax policy on investment. But little is known about the intersection of these concerns, how the taxes levied on the owners of such enterprises influence their investment decisions. In this chapter, we have focused on the impact on sole proprietors' investments of their personal income tax situations. Do high-income tax rates discourage entrepreneurs from making capital outlays? On the basis of tax return data for sole proprietors from before and after the Tax Reform Act of 1986, we conclude that the answer is yes. When a sole proprietor's marginal tax rate goes up, the probability that he or she buys capital assets goes down, as does the expected amount of investment expenditures. Further, the magnitudes of the estimated responses are quite substantial. Our response to the question posed by the title of this volume is that these particular Atlases do indeed shrug.

APPENDIX 13A: FURTHER DESCRIPTION OF THE DATA

The computations in this chapter are based on confidential Treasury data. This appendix provides some additional summary information about the sample of sole proprietors on whom the results in tables 13.6 and 13.7 are based. Figure 13A.1 is a histogram of the distributions of taxpayers by AGI for 1985 and 1988; figure 13A.2 similarly shows the distributions of taxpayers by marginal tax rate in the two

Figure 13A.1   Distribution of Taxpayers by Adjusted Gross Income (Thousands)

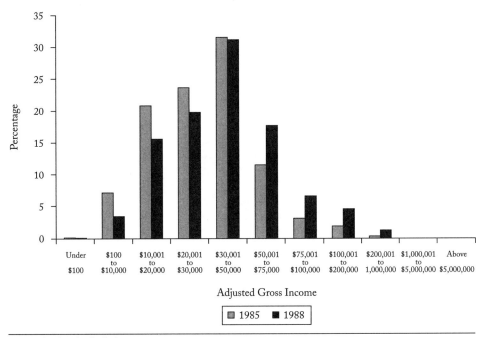

Source: Authors' calculations.

Figure 13A.2   Distribution of Taxpayers by Marginal Tax Rate (Percentage)

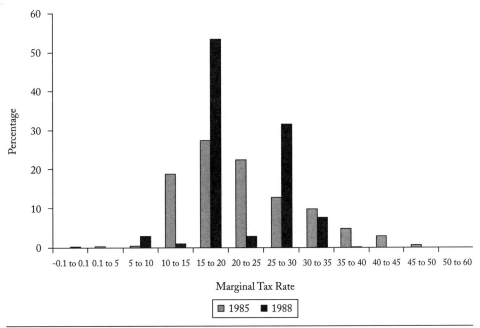

Source: Authors' calculations.

Table 13A.1   Composition of Investment

	All	Agriculture	Mining	Construction	Manufacturing
1985					
Equipment	6,527	4,559	6,956	4,090	7,505
	(1,283)	(23)	(44)	(87)	(37)
Structures	24,193	*	*	16,396	*
	(126)	—	—	(10)	—
1988					
Equipment	8,108	6,759	18,373	10,530	9,045
	(957)	(17)	(18)	(59)	(27)
Structures	27,874	*	44,634	18,367	26,460
	(496)		(22)	(33)	(12)
N	3,480	67	102	242	87

Source: Authors' calculations.
Note: The first number in each cell is the conditional weighted mean of expenditure in the associated category. The second number (in parentheses) is the number of returns on which the calculation is based. (The total number of observations in the sample is 3,480.) The sample consists of individuals who were sole proprietors in 1985 and 1988.
*Mean investment is positive but based on nine or fewer observations. The Treasury's confidentiality rules require that the mean not be published. The last row shows the number of observations. There were nine returns in which no industry was indicated.

years. (In each case, the observations are weighted so that the histograms reflect the underlying population.) Table 13A.1 displays mean spending on structures and equipment by industry. Table 13A.2 provides a more detailed breakdown of the type of investment expenditures.

The investment figures are based on form 4562, which taxpayers use to claim the current year's deduction for depreciation and amortization, inter alia. Form 4562 is divided into three parts. Part I of form 4562 is used to calculate the expensing deduction, in the case of section 179 property, and the depreciation deduction for assets other than automobiles and other listed property placed in service only during the current tax year. In general, part I requests that the taxpayer provide the following information: class of property, date placed in service, cost or other basis, recovery period, depreciation method, and deduction. Part II is used to report amortization for the current tax year. Amortizable property includes pollution control facilities, bond premiums, amounts paid for research or experiments, business start-up expenses, qualified forestation and reforestation costs, organizational expenses for a corporation, certain railroad property, construction period interest and taxes on real property, and certain rehabilitation expenses of historic property. Part III is used to report the depreciation deduction for automobiles and other listed property regardless of the tax year such property was placed in service. Such items include automobiles, property used for amusement or entertainment, and computers or peripheral equipment.

Transportation	Wholesale Trade	Retail Trade	Finance, Insurance, Real Estate	Services	Other
19,634	4,274	6,363	4,461	5,014	5,547
(34)	(22)	(98)	(94)	(827)	(16)
*	*	*	9,572	28,011	—
—	—	—	(10)	(80)	(0)
36,845	6,288	5,852	7,138	5,709	2,337
(21)	(20)	(65)	(69)	(643)	(15)
*	*	37,624	46,281	27,172	*
		(34)	(40)	(324)	
91	72	325	330	2,094	61

In order to compute total current year investment, we use the cost information reported in part I of form 4562 as provided for tax year 1985 and 1988 filings. For the dichotomous choice regressions, the dependent variable is given a value of 1 if the sum of the line items, as provided in table 13A.3 in tax year 1988, was positive, and 0 otherwise. For the analysis of investment expenditures, total investment is the sum of the line items reported in table 13A.3. The definitions of equipment and structures are also indicated in the righthand column of the table.

APPENDIX 13B: COMPUTING THE USER COST OF CAPITAL

We measure investment incentives using the cost of capital approach of Hall and Jorgenson (1967). Consider a price-taking entrepreneur contemplating a new investment in a world with no uncertainty. Assume that the enterprise has sufficient tax liability to take associated credits and deductions, and that he or she does not resell the asset. Investment receives a tax credit in year t at rate k_t. The rental return increases at the constant inflation rate π, and decreases because of constant exponential depreciation of the asset at rate d. The return is subject to the federal personal income tax of individual i in year t at rate τ_{it}. These net returns are discounted at the nominal discount rate r, which represents the opportunity cost of funds. The present value of depreciation allowances per dollar of marginal investment in year t is z_t. The percentage of basis entitled to statutory depreciation in year t is a_t. Assuming debt finance at the margin, in equilibrium the user cost of capital for individual i in year t is

Table 13A.2   Detailed Composition of Investment

	All	Agriculture	Mining	Construction
1985				
Structures				
ACRS, low-income	—	—	—	—
housing	—	(0)	(0)	(0)
ACRS, eighteen-year	21,126	*	*	*
real property	(76)			
Fifteen-year real	16,969	—	*	*
property	(16)	(0)		
Recovery property,	33,458	—	*	*
undefined type	(40)	(0)		
Equipment				
Section 179	4,109	*	4,528	5,987
	(647)		(19)	(37)
ACRS three-year	6,773	*	*	9,074
	(223)			(35)
ACRS five-year	5,536	3,947	4,838	6,321
	(812)	(14)	(36)	(50)
ACRS ten-year	13,879	—	*	*
	(22)	(0)		
1988				
Structures				
Residential rental	59,812	*	*	*
property	(99)			
Nonresidential	27,605	*	*	15,182
rental property	(139)			(12)
MACRS, twenty-year	—	—	—	—
	(0)	(0)	(0)	(0)
MACRS, seven-year	6,696	*	8,871	3,997
	(337)		(19)	(16)
MACRS, fifteen-year	8,247	—	—	*
	(21)	(0)	(0)	
Recovery property,	59,166	—	—	—
undefined type	(10)	(0)	(0)	(0)
Equipment				
Section 179	5,542	*	3,477	6,378
	(770)		(13)	(44)
MACRS, three-year	8,220	*	*	*
	(41)			
MACRS, five-year	8,204	*	*	10,505
	(311)			(28)
MACRS, ten-year	28,149	*	—	*
	(32)		(0)	(0)

Source: Authors' calculations.

Note: The first number in each cell is the conditional weighted mean of expenditure in the associated category. The second number (in parentheses) is the number of returns on which the calculation is based. (The total number of observations in the sample is 3,480.) The sample consists of individuals who were sole proprietors in 1985 and 1988.

* Mean investment is positive but based on nine or fewer observations. The Treasury's confidentiality rules require that the mean not be published.

Manufacturing	Transportation	Wholesale Trade	Retail Trade	Finance, Insurance, Real Estate	Services
—	—	—	—	—	*
(0)	(0)	(0)	(0)	(0)	
*	*	*	*	*	22,011
					(48)
*	—	—	*	*	25,846
	(0)	(0)			(10)
*	—	*	*	*	40,391
	(0)				(25)
2,733	12,323	3,105	3,784	3,439	3,417
(23)	(15)	(12)	(34)	(48)	(442)
*	8,505	*	7,503	13,423	4,339
	(15)		(23)	(10)	(118)
8,390	15,551	2,252	5,839	1,805	4,399
(22)	(24)	(14)	(64)	(58)	(521)
—	*	—	*	*	14,846
(0)		(0)			(14)
—	*	*	*	90,772	57,205
(0)				(12)	(63)
*	*	*	16,494	*	30,546
			(14)		(93)
—	—	—	*	—	*
(0)	(0)	(0)		(0)	
27,178	*	*	4,648	1,872	6,430
(10)			(21)	(25)	(227)
*	—	*	*	*	11,479
	(0)				(16)
*	—	—	—	—	*
	(0)	(0)	(0)	(0)	
7,718	22,372	5,602	3,148	3,433	4,779
(21)	(13)	(18)	(48)	(54)	(537)
*	*	*	*	*	3,421
					(22)
*	25,847	*	2,766	43,755	4,621
	(14)		(24)	(23)	(190)
—	—	*	*	*	21,693
(0)	(0)				(14)

Table 13A.3   Construction of Investment from Form 4562

Line	Column	Description	Category
Tax year 1985			
1	(b)	Cost of section 179 property	equipment
4a	(c)	Cost of three-year ACRS property	equipment
4b	(c)	Cost of five-year ACRS property	equipment
4c	(c)	Cost of ten-year ACRS property	equipment
4d	(c)	Cost of fifteen-year ACRS public utility	structure
4e	(c)	Cost of ACRS low-income housing property	structure
4g	(c)	Cost of eighteen-year real property	structure
4f	(c)	Cost of fifteen-year real property	structure
SOI balancing item		Cost of recovery property, undetermined type	structure
Tax year 1988			
1	(c)	Cost of section 179 property	equipment
6a	(c)	Cost of three-year MACRS property	equipment
6b	(c)	Cost of five-year MACRS property	equipment
6d	(c)	Cost of ten-year MACRS property	equipment
6g	(c)	Cost of residential rental property	structure
6h	(c)	Cost of nonresidential property	structure
6f	(c)	Cost of twenty-year MACRS real property	structure
6c	(c)	Cost of seven-year MACRS real property	structure
6e	(c)	Cost of ten-year MACRS real property	structure
SOI balancing item		Cost of recovery property, undetermined type	structure

Source: Authors' calculations.

$$\rho_{it} = \frac{r - \pi + d}{1 - \tau_{it}} \left(1 - k_t - a_t \tau_{it} z_t \right). \tag{13B.1}$$

The marginal federal individual income tax rates τ_{it} are computed for each observation, using detailed tax calculators developed by the U.S. Treasury Office of Tax Analysis. These calculators account for both the statutory rate schedule and the many implicit tax rates that arise from special features of the tax code.

The values used for the remaining parameters (r, π, a_t, k_t, z_t, and d) are provided in table 13B.1.[1] The discount rate r and inflation rate π are assumed to be equal to 8 percent and 4 percent, respectively, in both 1985 and 1988, as shown in table 13B.1. The parameters a_t, k_t, z_t, and d are summary values computed using values from the thirty-five asset types listed in table 13B.2, weighted by their respective shares of the noncorporate capital stock. The capital stocks used to compute the weights are provided in the column labeled "CAP" in table 13B.2 and were obtained from the Bureau of Economic Analysis.

In table 13B.1, the column labeled "Equipment and Structures" provides the parameter values used to calculate the aggregate user cost of capital, combining both equipment and structures. Table 13B.1 also provides the parameter values used to compute separate user costs for equipment and structures. In order to compute the parameter values for the user cost of equipment, the capital stock weights for assets 1 through 20 are applied to the corresponding values in table 13B.2 for a_t, k_t,

Table 13B.1   Parameter Values Used to Compute the User Cost of Capital

| Asset Type | 1985 | | | 1988 | | |
| | 1 to 35 | 1 to 20 | 21 to 35 | 1 to 35 | 1 to 20 | 21 to 35 |
	Equipment and Structures	Equipment	Structures	Equipment and Structures	Equipment	Structures
a	0.90	0.50	0.99	1.00	1.00	1.00
r	0.08	0.08	0.08	0.08	0.08	0.08
π	0.04	0.04	0.04	0.04	0.04	0.04
d	0.04703	0.15932	0.02142	0.04703	0.15932	0.02142
k	0.01978	0.09840	0.00185	0.00	0.00	0.00
z	0.63721	0.80819	0.59821	0.50805	0.83770	0.43288
MCAP	1.00	0.19	0.81	1.00	0.19	0.81

Source: Authors' calculations.
Note: Variables are defined in appendix 13B.

z_t, and d. In order to compute the user cost of structures, we use the corresponding values for assets 21 through 35.

The percentage of basis entitled to statutory depreciation a_t is 90 percent in 1985, as shown in the top panel of table 13B.1. This value is obtained by taking the sum of the percentage of basis eligible for statutory depreciation for each assets, weighted by their respective shares of the capital stock. In 1985 the percentage of basis eligible for depreciation is 50 percent for assets eligible for an investment tax credit (ITC), and 100 percent otherwise. The column labeled "ITC" of table 13B.2 indicates the ITC rates for the thirty-five asset types in 1985. The Tax Reform Act of 1986 eliminated the ITC for assets placed in service after 1986. Therefore, the percentage of basis eligible for statutory depreciation in 1988 is 100 percent, as shown in the lower panel of table 13B.2.

The investment tax credit k_t is assumed to be 0.01978 in 1985, as shown in the upper panel of table 13B.1. This value is the capital-stock-weighted average of the statutory investment tax credits in 1985 for the thirty-five asset types. The investment tax credit k_t is equal to zero in 1988.

We assume a constant value of 0.04703 for economic depreciation d in both 1985 and 1988, as shown in the upper and lower panels, respectively, of table 13B.1. This rate is computed by taking the sum of the thirty-five asset depreciation rates, provided in the column labeled "HWDEP" of table 13B.2, weighted by their respective shares of the capital stock. The depreciation rates HWDEP are summary measures, computed by Don Fullerton, Yolanda Gillette, and James Mackie (1987). They, in turn, use capital-stock-weighted averages of more disaggregated depreciation rates, obtained from Charles Hulten and Frank Wykoff (1981) and Dale W. Jorgenson and Martin A. Sullivan (1981), to calculate the economic depreciation rates for the thirty-five asset types in table 13B.2. For a more complete account, see Fullerton, Henderson, and Mackie (1987).

The present value of one dollar of depreciation allowances per dollar of marginal investment in the noncorporate sector, z_t, is 0.63721 in 1985 and 0.50805 in 1988, as shown in table 13B.1. The variables z_{85} and z_{88} are computed as capital-stock-weighted averages of Z85 and Z88, respectively, for the thirty-five asset types pro-

Table 13B.2 Parameter Values for User Cost of Capital (by Asset Type)

Number	Asset Type	HWDEP	ITC	Z85	Z88	CAP
1	Furniture and fixtures	0.1100	0.10	0.8081920	0.8237391	19,186
2	Fabricated metal products	0.0917	0.10	0.8081920	0.8237391	6,090
3	Engines and turbines	0.0786	0.10	0.8081920	0.8237391	2,167
4	Tractors	0.1633	0.10	0.8081920	0.8721278	38,212
5	Agricultural machinery	0.0971	0.10	0.8081920	0.8237391	67,654
6	Construction machinery	0.1722	0.10	0.8081920	0.8237391	26,372
7	Mining and oil field machinery	0.1650	0.10	0.8081920	0.8721278	5,182
8	Metalworking machinery	0.1225	0.10	0.8081920	0.8237391	3,473
9	Special industry machinery	0.1031	0.10	0.8081920	0.8237391	6,779
10	General industrial machinery	0.1225	0.10	0.8081920	0.8237391	11,349
11	Office and computing machinery	0.2729	0.10	0.8081920	0.8237391	8,432
12	Service industry machinery	0.1650	0.10	0.8081920	0.8237391	11,786
13	Electrical machinery	0.1179	0.10	0.8081920	0.8237391	12,568
14	Trucks, buses, and trailers	0.2537	0.10	0.8081920	0.8721278	48,081
15	Autos	0.3333	0.06	0.8081920	0.8721278	12,926
16	Aircraft	0.1833	0.10	0.8081920	0.8721278	4,740
17	Ships and boats	0.0750	0.10	0.8081920	0.7588973	12,071
18	Railroad equipment	0.0660	0.10	0.8081920	0.8237391	59

19	Instruments	0.1500	0.10	0.8081920	0.8237391	11,794
20	Other equipment	0.1500	0.10	0.8081920	0.8237391	13,356
21	Industrial buildings	0.0361	0.00	0.5846580	0.3728805	27,938
22	Commercial buildings	0.0247	0.00	0.5846580	0.3728805	341,797
23	Religious buildings	0.0023	0.00	0.5846580	0.3728805	8,456
24	Educational buildings	0.0188	0.00	0.5846580	0.3728805	6,423
25	Hospital buildings	0.0233	0.00	0.5846580	0.3728805	9,226
26	Other nonfarm buildings	0.0454	0.00	0.5846580	0.3728805	19,470
27	Railroads	0.0176	0.10	0.5975897	0.5432431	0
28	Telephone and telegraph	0.0333	0.10	0.5975897	0.5432431	836
29	Electrical light and power	0.0300	0.10	0.5975897	0.5432431	19,467
30	Gas facilities	0.0300	0.10	0.6931839	0.6226086	5,886
31	Other public utilities	0.0450	0.10	0.6931839	0.6226086	0
32	Farm structures	0.0237	0.00	0.5846580	0.5432431	108,048
33	Mining, shafts, and wells	0.0563	0.00	0.8612461	0.8475169	66,009
34	Other nonfarm facilities	0.0290	0.00	0.5846580	0.3728805	37,502
35	Residential structures	0.0150	0.00	0.5846580	0.4124012	762,149

Source: Authors' calculations.
Note: Variables are defined in appendix 13B.

vided in table 13B.2. To estimate the present value of depreciation allowances, we classify assets into statutory depreciation categories and calculate Z_{85} and Z_{88} using the statutory depreciation rules.

APPENDIX NOTE

1. A complication that arises in the computation of the user cost relates to the fact that eligible investments below a cap may be expensed, so that $z_t = 1$. However, even for individuals whose current level of eligible investment is below the cap, one cannot know whether the marginal investment would be expensed. To obtain some sense of the potential importance of this issue, we set $z_t = 1$ for individuals whose eligible investments were below the cap and who also had no ineligible investments. With the user cost calculated in this way, the qualitative results reported in table 13.6 were basically unchanged, although the magnitudes were somewhat smaller.

We thank Esther Gray, Ann Wicks, and Jodi Woodson for their aid in preparing the manuscript. We are grateful to Lowell Dworin, Bo Honoré, Joel Slemrod, and attendees at both the April 1997 preconference and October 1997 conference for useful suggestions. Rosen's research was supported by the Center for Economic Policy Studies at Princeton University and was conducted in part during his term as a Visiting Scholar at the Russell Sage Foundation. Holtz-Eakin's research was supported by the Center for Policy Research at Syracuse University's Maxwell School. The views in this chapter are the authors' alone and, in particular, do not represent those of the U.S. Treasury.

NOTES

1. Vincenzo Quadrini's (1996) tabulations of data from the 1984 Panel Study of Income Dynamics indicate that the average wealth of entrepreneurs was $240,249 compared to $71,481 for workers.

2. Robert Chirinko (1993) provides an extensive survey of this literature.

3. For purposes of this calculation, we think of entrepreneurial enterprises as consisting of sole proprietorships plus some partnerships, S corporations, and small C corporations. We are able to calculate only the sole proprietors' investment outlays, which thus serve as a lower bound for the total. From the Statistics of Income (SOI) 1993 individual sample, we added up the investments recorded by sole proprietors on form 4562 (Depreciation and Amortization) and arrived at a figure of $63.3 billion. This is 10.6 percent of nonresidential fixed investment in 1993, which was $598.8 billion, according to the November-December 1995 *Survey of Current Business*. Note, however, that the definition of investment in the National Income and Product Accounts is not quite the same as the tax definition. A reconciliation is contained in the *Survey of Current Business*.

4. See Mitchell and Cowling (1996) for a careful theoretical analysis of the demand for inputs by an entrepreneurial firm.

5. As Anthony Atkinson and Joseph Stiglitz (1980, 136) note, there is some ambiguity associated with selecting the appropriate discount rate, because the investor's perceived opportunity cost of funds is not observed. Our specification of equation (13.2) follows the assumption in Fullerton, Gillette, and Mackie (1987) that the opportunity cost is a tax-exempt investment opportunity.

6. Fazzari, Hubbard, and Petersen (1988) argue that corporate investment decisions are limited by lack of access to capital; Holtz-Eakin, Joulfaian, and Rosen (1994b) document the same phenomenon for sole proprietorships. (Also see Lindh and Ohlsson 1994.)

7. The panel is constructed from returns common to the 1985 and 1988 cross-sectional files, that is, the "overlap" between these two files. Matches between the two years are based on the Social Security number of the primary filer. Sample stratification is based on a number of variables, including the presence of a schedule C, but not on capital expenditures.

8. The instructions that accompany individual income tax returns state: "Use Schedule C to report income or loss from a business you operated or a profession you practiced as a sole proprietor. . . . An activity qualifies as a business if your primary purpose for engaging in the activity is for income or profit and you are involved in the activity with continuity and regularity" (Internal Revenue Service, 1996, 105).

9. A number of our sole proprietors were also involved with partnerships or S corporations. In these cases, we are not able to distinguish between investment done in the sole proprietorship and investment done in one of the other entities. To the extent that the tax reform affected businesses' choices of organizational form, the inclusion of investment from S corporations and partnerships could bias our results. Partnerships are unlikely to be important in this context—C corporations converting to pass-through status probably tend not to become partnerships because limited liability is still available if they remain in corporate form as S corporations. Although switches from C to S corporations are potentially important, when we excluded returns with any S corporation income in either year, it had little effect on our substantive results.

10. Two classes of investment, computers and vehicles ("listed property"), are often used for consumption as well as investment purposes. We therefore exclude them from our measure of investment.

11. This, for example, is the criterion used in the Bureau of the Census Characteristics of Business Owners survey (see Holmes and Schmitz 1991).

12. This figure includes "business services" (advertising, management consulting, public relations, computer services, and so on) and "accounting and bookkeeping services."

13. In each case, these differences are statistically significant at the 5 percent level.

14. The entrepreneur's investment decision is presumably made jointly with other input decisions, including the owner's supply of labor to the enterprise, which in turn depends on his personal characteristics.

15. Taxpayers' ages are not reported on individual income tax forms. Ages are added to the Individual Tax File through the use of data provided by the Social Security Administration.

16. See Evans and Jovanovic (1989), Holtz-Eakin, Joulfaian, and Rosen (1994a, 1994b), and van Praag and van Ophem (1994) for evidence on the impact of liquidity constraints on entrepreneurial decision-making.

17. We have data only for realized capital gains and no data on municipal bond interest. Of course, other conventional data sets also lack information on important components of capital income such as accrued capital gains.

18. We calculate our marginal tax rates using detailed tax calculators developed by the U.S. Treasury Office of Tax Analysis and tailored for our panel. These calculators account for both the statutory rate schedule and the many implicit tax rates (for example, the post-TRA86 phaseout of tax benefits associated with the 15 percent tax bracket and the personal exemption) that arise from special features of the tax code. The distribution of marginal tax rates in our sample is shown in figure 13A.2.

19. As noted in appendix 13B, computation of the user cost requires weighting across different types of assets. We employ 1985 weights in the computation of the 1988 synthetic user cost so that the instrumental variable cannot be contaminated by endogenous changes in the composition of capital outlays.

20. The identification strategy here is essentially the same as that used by Cummins, Hassett, and Hubbard (1994).

21. Rivers and Vuong's test is a generalization of Wu's (1973) test in a limited dependent variable setting. In the first stage, the potentially endogenous variable is regressed on the instrumental variables. In the second stage, the residuals from the first-stage equation are included in the probit model. If the residuals are statistically significant, then one may reject the null hypothesis of exogeneity. An endogenous component of changes in tax rates of particular interest is that stemming from tax evasion. One possibility is that a cut in tax rates reduces evasion, raises reported taxable income, and as a consequence raises observed marginal tax rates, ceteris paribus. Our instrumental variable is constructed to eliminate any behavior-based changes in marginal tax rates, including those associated with evasion.

22. The chi-square test statistic (with two degrees of freedom) is 5.21, which is significant at the 5 percent level.

23. The omitted industry category includes transportation, construction, mining, agriculture, and miscellaneous other industries. They are grouped together because, on an individual basis, each accounts for a very small proportion of the observations. See tables 13A.1 and 13A.2 for details on investment expenditures by industry.

24. TRA86 might also have changed the interest rate, r, in the user cost. To investigate this possibility, we reestimated the model using the 1985 and 1988 values of Moody's Aaa corporate bond rate when computing $\%\Delta c$. The instrumental-variable estimates were basically unchanged, although a bit smaller in absolute value. The coefficient on $\%\Delta c$ was -1.344 (standard error = 0.337), and on the interaction term -1.096 (standard error = 0.457).

25. We measure investment in 1985 dollars, using the CPI-U to adjust for changes in the price level.

26. Our investment expenditures elasticity takes into account both the change in the probability of investing (the extensive margin) and the change in expenditures conditional on investing (the intensive margin). In contrast to our sole proprietors, corporations never make extensive-margin decisions—they more or less always do *some* investment. Our finding that sole proprietors' decisions on the extensive margin are quite sensitive to tax considerations may account for the difference between our results and those from previous studies using corporate data. Note the analogy to the labor supply literature: married women's labor supply is more elastic than that of prime-age males, but most of the difference is due to the responsiveness of married women's participation rates (the extensive margin) to changes in the net wage.

REFERENCES

Atkinson, Anthony B., and Joseph E. Stiglitz. 1980. *Lectures on Public Economics*. New York: McGraw-Hill

Carroll, Robert, and David Joulfaian. 1997. "Taxes and Corporate Choice of Organization Form." U.S. Department of Treasury. Unpublished paper.

Chirinko, Robert S. 1993. "Business Fixed Investment Spending: Modeling Strategies, Empirical Results, and Policy Implications." *Journal of Economic Literature* 31(December): 1875–1911.

Cummins, Jason, Kevin Hassett, and R. Glenn Hubbard. 1994. "A Reconsideration of Investment Behavior Using Tax Reform as Natural Experiments." *Brookings Papers on Economic Activity* 2: 1–59.

Engen, Eric, and Jonathan Skinner. 1996. "Taxation and Economic Growth," *National Tax Journal* (December): 617–42.

Evans, David S., and Boyan Jovanovic. 1989. "An Estimated Model of Entrepreneurial Choice Under Liquidity Constraints." *Journal of Political Economy* 97: 808–27.

Fazzari, Steven M., R. Glenn Hubbard, and Bruce C. Petersen. 1988. "Financing Constraints and Corporate Investment." *Brookings Papers on Economic Activity* 1: 141–195.

Feenberg, Daniel. 1987. "Are Tax Price Models Really Identified?: The Case of Charitable Giving." *National Tax Journal* 40(4, December): 629–33.

Fullerton, Don, Robert Gillette, and James Mackie. 1987. "Investment Incentives Under the Tax Reform Act of 1986." In Office of Tax Analysis, *Compendium of Tax Research 1987*. Washington, D.C.: U.S. Government Printing Office.

Fullerton, Don, Yolanda Henderson, and James Mackie. 1987. "Investment Allocation and Growth Under the Tax Reform Act of 1986." In Office of Tax Analysis, *Compendium of Tax Research 1987*. Washington, D.C.: U.S. Government Printing Office.

Hall, Robert, and Dale W. Jorgenson. 1967. "Tax Policy and Investment Behavior." *American Economic Review* 57: 391–414.

Holmes, Thomas J., and James A. Schmitz. 1991. "Measuring Small Business Dynamics When Owners and Their Businesses Can Be Separately Identified." Unpublished paper. Dartmouth College, Hanover, N.H.

Holtz-Eakin, Douglas, David Joulfaian, and Harvey S. Rosen. 1994a. "Sticking It Out: Entrepreneurial Survival and Liquidity Constraints." *Journal of Political Economy* (February): 53–75.

———. 1994b. "Entrepreneurial Decisions and Liquidity Constraints." *RAND Journal of Economics* 23(2, Summer): 334–47.

Hulten, Charles, and Frank Wykoff. 1981. "The Measurement of Economic Depreciation." In *Depreciation, Inflation, and the Taxation of Income from Capital*, edited by Charles R. Hulten. Washington, D.C.: Urban Institute.

Internal Revenue Service. 1996. *Package X-Reference Copies of Federal Tax Forms and Instructions*. Vol. 1.

Jorgenson, Dale W., and Martin A. Sullivan. 1981. "Inflation and Corporate Capital Recovery." In *Depreciation, Inflation, and the Taxation of Income from Capital*, edited by Charles R. Hulten. Washington, D.C.: Urban Institute.

Lindh, Thomas, and Henry Ohlsson. 1994. "Self-employment and Self-financing." Unpublished paper. Uppsala University, Uppsala, Sweden.

Meyer, Bruce. 1990. "Why Are There So Few Black Entrepreneurs?" Working Paper 3537. Cambridge, Mass.: National Bureau of Economic Research.

Mitchell, Peter, and Marc Cowling. 1996. "Developing the Theory of Labor and Capital Inputs to the Self-employed Entrepreneurial Firm." Unpublished paper. University of Warwick, Coventry, England.

Plesko, George. 1994. "The Role of Taxes in Organizational Choice: S Conversions After the Tax Reform Act of 1986." Unpublished paper. Northeastern University, Boston.

Quadrini, Vincenzo. 1996. "Entrepreneurship, Saving, and Social Mobility." Unpublished paper. University of Pennsylvania, Philadelphia.

Rivers, Douglas, and Quang Vuong. 1988. "Limited Information Estimators and Exogeneity Tests for Simultaneous Probit Models." *Journal of Econometrics* 39: 347–66.

Shleifer, Andrei, and Robert Vishny. 1992. "Liquidation Value and Debt Capacity: A Market Equilibrium Approach." *Journal of Finance* 47: 1343–66.

Van Praag, C. Mirjan, and Hans van Ophem. 1994. "Determinants of Willingness and Opportunity to Start as an Entrepreneur." Unpublished paper. University of Amsterdam.

Wu, De-Min. 1973. "Alternative Tests of Independence Between Stochastic Regressors and Disturbances." *Econometrica* 41: 733–50.

Commentary on Chapter 13

R. Glenn Hubbard

Robert Carroll, Douglas Holtz-Eakin, Mark Rider, and Harvey Rosen have written a thought-provoking chapter that investigates the effects of entrepreneurs' personal income tax situations on their capital investment decisions. Applying models of business investment generally used to study determinants of capital expenditures by publicly traded corporations, the authors point up an under researched dark side of increases in individual marginal income taxes—a higher cost of capital and lower investment by entrepreneurs. Indeed, they conclude that a five-percentage-point increase in marginal tax rates would reduce the fraction of entrepreneurs making new fixed capital investments by more than 10 percent and reduce mean fixed investment expenditures by about 10 percent.

An underlying question raised by many of the chapters in this volume is whether there are links between tax changes and income changes for the "rich" (and further, whether those links represent "real" decisions). Simply put, does Atlas shrug, or does Atlas have a good tax lawyer? This chapter's findings place it squarely in the former camp.

I generally like the chapter, and I find its results interesting. In the remainder of this discussion, I focus on three questions. Who is an "entrepreneur"? How should we model "investment" decisions by entrepreneurs? And finally, are there efficiency consequences of lower investment by entrepreneurs?

WHO IS AN "ENTREPRENEUR"?

Entrepreneurs occupy a prominent place in popular presentations of the "good rich"—say, Bill Gates (at least before his recent battle with the U.S. Department of Justice). In fact, to understand the decisions of the "rich," one must often understand the decisions of "entrepreneurs." William Gentry and I have documented (Gentry and Hubbard 1997) that only 8.6 percent of households (in the 1989 cross-section of the Federal Reserve Board Survey of Consumer Finances [SCF]) have active business assets of more than $5,000, but that those households own about 40 percent of household wealth. Moreover, the higher one goes in the wealth distribution, the greater is the importance of business owners and business assets. Entrepreneurs own 68 percent of the net worth held by the top 1 percent of households in the wealth distribution.

If entrepreneurs are so important, who is an entrepreneur? Someone who is self-employed? Someone who has some self-employment income? Someone who makes active business investments? Someone who creates jobs? As the authors' quote from Joseph Schumpeter reveals, many descriptions of entrepreneurship (even by economists) are quite broad, leaving the impression that, as with pornography, one will know it when one sees it. Unfortunately, such a standard is not promising for meaningful empirical work. Moreover, one's choice of a definition of entrepreneurship is linked to one's decision about which source of data to use in empirical tests of links between the rates of business owners and investment decisions.

Carroll and his colleagues have chosen to use schedule C filings for federal income tax purposes as an indicator of business ownership. Such data have clear strengths, including rich longitudinal information and (presumably) minimal reporting error. These data and this definition of entrepreneurship are not without problems, however. First, schedule C status does not necessarily mesh well with a definition of business ownership centered on studying fixed investment decisions. Second, tax return data contain little information related to wealth. Third, shifts in organizational form for tax purposes (for example, between unincorporated and incorporated businesses) may spuriously change the entrepreneurship status of households. Although other definitions and data are possible (see, for example, Quadrini 1997; and Gentry and Hubbard 1997), the approach taken by Carroll et al. is a reasonable starting point for studying the investment decisions of business owners.

HOW SHOULD WE MODEL ENTREPRENEURIAL "INVESTMENT"?

In principle, taxation may affect three margins of entrepreneurial investment: entry (business formation and entrepreneurial entry), the choice of technology (capital intensity), and the level of fixed investment (capital expenditures). Carroll and his colleagues focus on the third area (and to a much lesser extent, on the second). Studying these "investment" decisions requires one to define a "business" (see the foregoing discussion) and to define empirically relevant measures of determinants of investment decisions.

How might tax policy affect entry or entrepreneurial selection? Absent taxes, one could imagine a condition that a household would select into entrepreneurship if:

$$\theta f(k) - r(k - a) \geq w + ra, \tag{13C.1}$$

where k represents business fixed capital, f(k) represents business output (as a function of capital employed), θ indexes entrepreneurial ability, a represents assets of the would-be entrepreneur, r represents the gross interest rate (or opportunity cost of funds), and w represents the wage that the individual would earn if he or she worked for someone else (as a function of, inter alia, education and experience). Condition (13C.1) simply states than an individual would become an entrepreneur if net entrepreneurial income exceeded net income from being a wage employee.

A proportional income tax would not affect the selection condition (13C.1). Two channels for tax effects are possible, however. First, a progressive tax schedule could affect entry depending on the relative variability of entrepreneurial and wage income. Second, if, in contrast to condition (13C.1), financing constraints affect entrepreneurial selection (as in Evans and Jovanovic 1989; Holtz-Eakin, Joulfaian, and Rosen 1994; and Gentry and Hubbard 1997), the effects of tax policy on collateralizable assets and saving can affect entry.

Tax policy can also affect the continuous investment decisions of business owners. To continue the example presented above, let $f(k) = k^\alpha$. Then, abstracting from taxes and complications arising from capital-market imperfections, the entrepreneur would choose a business capital stock k such that:

$$K = (\theta\alpha/r)^{1/(1-\alpha)}, \tag{13C.2}$$

so that, letting i index entrepreneurs and t index time:

$$\ln k_{it} = (1/[1-\alpha])\ln\theta_i + (1/[1-\alpha])\ln(\alpha/r_{it}). \tag{13C.3}$$

That is, the capital stock chosen depends on technology (α), entrepreneurial ability (θ), and the cost of capital (r). If entrepreneurial ability, which is unobservable to the econometrician, is time-invariant, then

$$\Delta \ln k_{it} = -(1/[1-\alpha]) \Delta \ln r_{it}. \tag{13C.4}$$

To study the effects of tax parameter on entrepreneurial investment, one could incorporate the tax variable in the "cost of capital" in equation (13C.4). As noted by Jason G. Cummins, Kevin A. Hassett, and R. Glenn Hubbard (1994) and Hassett and Hubbard (1997), problems of measurement error and simultaneity make "investment" equations such as (13C.4) difficult to estimate meaningfully. To the extent that tax reforms offer significant exogenous cross-sectional variation in the user cost (as argued by Cummins, Hassett, and Hubbard 1994), one may be able to estimate the responsiveness of investment to the user cost.[1] This is in large part the estimation strategy followed by Carroll et al.

Before presenting their "investment equations," Carroll et al. find that, using data for 1985 and 1988: there is substantial persistence in entrepreneurs' propensity to invest; only about one-third of the sole proprietors make any capital investments; and entrepreneurs subject to high marginal tax rates in 1985 appear to have the greatest response to the Tax Reform Act of 1986.

More formally, they estimate:

$$\text{Prob}(I_{88} > 0) = \alpha_0 + \alpha_1(\%\Delta c) + \alpha_2(\%\Delta c \times I_{85}) + \alpha_3 I_{85} + X\beta, \tag{13C.5}$$

where I is an indicator variable equaling unity if the entrepreneur made a capital investment decision in the given year, c is the user cost of capital, and X is a vector of other covariates. In table 13.4, they represent results indicating a negative relationship between the user cost and the likelihood of investing. Carroll and his colleagues find no effect of capital income on the probability of investing, but, as they note, their variable is a very noisy proxy for collateralizable net worth.

The results of the authors' empirical analysis of the effects of tax parameters (through the user cost of capital) on the level of investment are presented in table 13.5. Although they estimate large and statistically significant effects of changes in marginal income tax rates on investment, at least three caveats are in order. First, returning to equation (13C.3), one might worry that unobserved heterogeneity in entrepreneurial ability (θ) is influencing the results. That is, high-ability entrepreneurs may have experienced a more substantial change in the marginal tax rates than other entrepreneurs. If one had data on assets, one could use initial assets as a proxy for the unobserved ability, but such data are lacking. Second, the fact that investment by high-previous-investment entrepreneurs is less sensitive to changes in the user cost than investment by low-previous-investment entrepreneurs is a bit odd under a null hypothesis of perfect capital markets. One possibility is that the high estimated responsiveness for low-previous-investment entrepreneurs reflects both the effect of tax change on the user cost and the effect of the tax change on financing constraints. Third, when Carroll et al. evaluate the responsiveness of investment at the means, the implied plasticity of investment expenditure with respect to the user cost is −1.78, more than twice as large in absolute value as the (sometimes-thought-to-be-high!) estimate by Cummins, Hassett, and Hubbard (1994) for publicly traded corporations. One possible explanation for this difference is financing constraints, as described earlier. Another is that large corporations are always on the intensive margin (always investing, by varying amounts) but the estimated effects for individual business owners may be combining extensive and intensive margins.

These concerns notwithstanding, the findings in this chapter are strongly suggestive of a significant effect of changes in marginal income tax rates on investment by individual business owners. This finding indicates that analysis of the impact of tax policy on investment that focuses only on the links between tax parameters, the use of capital, and investment for large corporations is likely to be incomplete.

SHOULD WE CARE ABOUT FOREGONE ENTREPRENEURIAL INVESTMENT?

Although the authors offer interesting findings about the effects of changes in marginal tax rates on physical investment by business owners, a broader question remains: What are the efficiency consequences of the tax consequences they identify? Two lines of inquiry seem promising: investigating consequences for entrepreneurial selection and for investment by financially constrained entrepreneurs.

In the first line, specialists in public finance often focus on "labor supply" distortions caused by income taxation—in particular, the effects of tax policy on "hours worked." Using this definition of labor supply, losses in economic well-being from progressive labor income taxation are generally estimated to be modest for men (whose hours worked tend to be relatively insensitive to changes in marginal tax rates) and greater for married women. Recently, Martin Feldstein (1995) has argued for shifting the focus to income in order to measure the effects of tax distortions on job selection, effort, and amenities; his estimates imply much greater deadweight losses as a result of higher marginal tax rates. For potential entrepreneurs, the effects of progressive taxation on entry offer another source of deadweight loss.

The second line focuses more directly on investment, conditional on selection into entrepreneurship. Conventional analysis of tax policy—and the approach taken by Carroll et al.—stresses the effects of income taxes on the marginal return to investing. That is, an increase in marginal income tax rates, all else being equal, reduces the marginal return to investing and decreases business investment. Vencenzo Quadrini (1997) and William M. Gentry and R. Glenn Hubbard (1997) argue that the high saving rates and undiversified portfolios of entrepreneurial households are consistent with a role for financing constraints in entrepreneurial investment decisions. To the extent that entrepreneurs face costly external financing, an additional tax effect emerges; higher marginal tax rates reduce collateralizable resources and internal funds, reducing the ability to finance desired investment. Recent evidence for corporations suggests that this adverse effect of higher marginal income tax rates can be substantial (see, for example, the review in Hubbard 1998).

Exploring this latter line further is likely to be important in shedding light on the extent of efficiency consequences of foregone entrepreneurial investment. If capital markets were perfect and no rents were associated with business ownership, investment "lost" by one entrepreneur might easily be made elsewhere. With imperfect markets and scarce entrepreneurial talent, however, high marginal tax rates may reduce entry and investment by talented entrepreneurs. Sorting this out is a significant area for future research.

CONCLUSION

To summarize, Carroll, Holtz-Eakin, Rider, and Rosen have made an important first step in analyzing the effect of taxes on entrepreneurial investment decisions. Atlas shrugs. The authors have focused attention, not on the slope of Atlas's shoulders, but, more importantly, on who Atlas is. This observation may open the door to a profitable line of inquiry into the savings, investment, and asset allocation habits of the business "rich."

NOTE

1. Carroll et al. appeal to the static user cost definition (as in Hall and Jorgenson 1967). In contrast, Cummins, Hassett, and Hubbard (1994) focus on tax reforms as representing "permanent" changes in the tax components of the sequence of expected future values of the user cost of capital in a forward-looking investment model.

REFERENCES

Cummins, Jason G., Kevin A. Hassett, and R. Glenn Hubbard. 1994. "A Reconsideration of Investment Behavior Using Tax Reforms as Natural Experiments." *Brookings Papers on Economic Activity* 2: 1–59.

Evans, David S., and Boyan Jovanovic. 1989. "An Estimated Model of Entrepreneurial Choice Under Liquidity Constraints." *Journal of Political Economy* 97: 808–27.

Feldstein, Martin. 1995. "The Effect of Marginal Tax Rates on Taxable Income: A Panel Study of the 1986 Tax Reform Act." *Journal of Political Economy* 103: 551–72.

Gentry, William M., and R. Glenn Hubbard. 1997. "Why Do the Wealthy Save So Much?: Saving and Investment Decisions of Entrepreneurs." Columbia University, New York. Unpublished paper.

Hall, Robert E., and Dale W. Jorgenson. 1967. "Tax Policy and Investment Behavior." *American Economic Review* 57: 391–414.

Hassett, Kevin A., and R. Glenn Hubbard. 1997. "Tax Policy and Investment." In *Fiscal Policy: Lessons from Economic Research*, edited by Alan J. Auerbach. Cambridge, Mass.: MIT Press.

Holtz-Eakin, Douglas, David Joulfaian, and Harvey S. Rosen. 1994. "Entrepreneurial Decisions Under Liquidity Constraints." *RAND Journal of Economics* 23: 53–75.

Hubbard, R. Glenn. 1998. "Capital-Market Imperfections and Investment." *Journal of Economic Literature* 36: 157–86.

Quadrini, Vincenzo. 1997. "Entrepreneurship, Saving, and Social Mobility." Discussion paper 166. Institute for Empirical Macroeconomics, Federal Reserve Bank of Minneapolis.

Part III
Alternative Perspectives

Why Do the Rich Save So Much?

Christopher D. Carroll

F. SCOTT FITZGERALD TO ERNEST HEMINGWAY: "The very rich are different from you and me."

ERNEST HEMINGWAY TO F. SCOTT FITZGERALD: "Yes. They have more money."

The saving behavior of the wealthy has received remarkably little academic atten- tion in the past twenty years or so. This is probably largely attributable to a rel- ative lack of good data: the Survey of Consumer Finances is virtually the only pub- licly available source of detailed data on wealthy households, and even the SCF has only a few hundred really wealthy households in each triennial wave. Despite recent neglect, the topic is an important one for scholars of saving behavior, for at least two reasons. First, wealthy households should provide a powerful means of testing whether the standard model of consumer behavior, the Life-Cycle/Permanent-Income Hypothesis, is adequate as a universal model of saving and consumption. This is an application of the general scientific principle that models should be test- ed under extreme conditions; if they do not hold up, a new model (or an extended version of the old one) is called for. The second reason for studying the wealthy is that they account for a large share of aggregate wealth. In fact, some understanding of the saving behavior of the wealthy is probably indispensable to any credible attempt to account for the magnitude of aggregate wealth.

The primary sources of evidence in this chapter are the four Surveys of Consumer Finances conducted in 1983, 1989, 1992, and 1995, but the inevitable limitations of those data are apparent. The chapter therefore also relies to a considerable extent on unorthodox kinds of evidence, ranging from information in the annual Forbes 400 tabulation of the richest American households to quotations from and about the very rich, to the results of a "focus group" meeting with a set of wealthy indi- viduals who were directly asked their reasons for saving.

The chapter begins by considering whether the standard model of household consumption and saving decisions, the Life-Cycle model, provides an adequate description of the behavior of wealthy households. I argue that the Life-Cycle model, or at least the traditional incarnation in which the decision-maker saves mainly to finance his own future consumption, cannot simultaneously explain both the behavior of the median household and the behavior in the upper tail of the wealth distribution. The next section of the chapter considers whether a "dynastic" model, in which the wealthy save mainly for the benefit of their heirs, performs better. Although the dynastic model can explain some observations, and probably does roughly apply to some households, I argue that it still does not explain some important facts about the saving behavior of the wealthy. Furthermore, the dynastic model conflicts with the self-reported motives for saving that many wealthy people voice. Finally, I consider a model in which the wealthy save because, either directly or indirectly, they obtain greater pleasure from possessing an extra dollar of wealth than they would get from an extra dollar of consumption. Following Max Weber (1958) as interpreted by Heng-Fu Zou (1994) and Gurdip Bakshi and Zhimu Chen (1996), I call this the "capitalist spirit" model. I argue that a direct wealth accumulation motive is indispensable in explaining at least some of the observed behavior of the very wealthy.

CAN THE LIFE-CYCLE MODEL EXPLAIN THE BEHAVIOR OF THE WEALTHY?

A provocative recent paper by R. Glenn Hubbard, Jonathan Skinner, and Stephen Zeldes (1994) (henceforth HSZ) argues that an expanded version of the Life-Cycle model, in which uncertainty is modeled realistically, can generate patterns of wealth accumulation that are roughly consistent with average data from household surveys, and amounts of aggregate wealth that are similar to observed aggregate household wealth in the United States. If such a model did indeed produce roughly correct predictions for household wealth holdings, there would be little need to study the very wealthy in detail, since they would merely be scaled-up versions of everyone else.

Behind the scenes of the HSZ model, however, all is not well. Although it is true that the model can predict approximately correct average values for wealth or the wealth-to-income ratio, it achieves this average by making large but offsetting errors in predicting the underlying distribution of wealth. Specifically, the HSZ model predicts, at most ages, that the household with median wealth actually holds substantially more wealth than the median household in SCF data holds, and at the same time, the model greatly *underpredicts* the amount of wealth held by the households at the top of the wealth distribution.

Figure 14.1 presents data on the age profile of the ratio of total wealth to permanent income for the median household in a stochastic Life-Cycle model very similar to that of Hubbard, Skinner, and Zeldes.[1] The figure also presents data on the age profile of the actual median household's wealth—permanent income ratio from the 1992 and 1995 Surveys of Consumer Finances (dashing lines) during the working lifetime.[2] The figure makes clear that the HSZ model substantially *overpredicts* the wealth of the median household in the SCF data.[3]

How, then, can the HSZ model produce overall averages that resemble the means of the SCF data? The answer lies in the wealth holdings of the top few percent of the distribution. The solid line in figure 14.2 shows, for each age group, the average ratio of wealth to permanent income for households at the ninety-ninth percentile (by age) in the HSZ model. The dashing line shows the corresponding calculation using the actual data from the 1992 and 1995 SCFs. Clearly, the richest SCF households own enormously more wealth, in relation to their permanent income, than the richest consumers in the HSZ model.

Figure 14.1   Median Wealth to Permanent Income Ratio, HSZ Model

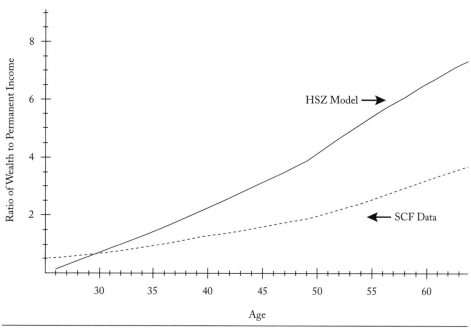

Source: Author's calculations using the model described in the text.

Figure 14.2   Ninety-ninth Percentile of Wealth to Permanent Income Ratio, by Age, HSZ Model

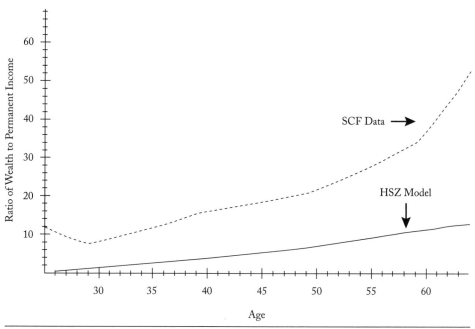

Source: Author's calculations using the model described in the text.

Taken together, figures 14.1 and 14.2 show that the stochastic Life-Cycle model under HSZ parameter values matches the aggregate and average data only because it makes two offsetting errors: overestimating the wealth of the typical household and underestimating the wealth of the richest households.

These simulations indicate that even the extended Life-Cycle model misses some crucial features of household behavior. However, the model's overprediction of the wealth of the median household is easily rectified; Christopher D. Carroll (1992, 1997) argues that the model captures the main features of the behavior of the median household very well if consumers are assumed to be slightly more impatient than Hubbard and his colleagues assume, and if the income process is modified to include the benefits of aggregate productivity growth. (Hubbard et al. assume that households expect, and experience, zero aggregate productivity growth over their lifetimes.)

If assuming that consumers are somewhat more impatient can make the stochastic Life-Cycle model match the behavior of the median household, a natural question is whether assuming that consumers are somewhat more *patient* can make the model match the richest households. If so, then it might be possible to argue that the only modification needed to make the stochastic Life-Cycle model match the facts is to assume that consumers with higher lifetime incomes are also more patient. Figure 14.3 examines this possibility by showing the pattern of wealth over the working life of consumers who are the same as the consumers in the baseline HSZ model except that they have a time preference rate of zero rather than the baseline HSZ time preference rate of 3 percent annually. Although the age-wealth

Figure 14.3   Wealth Profiles for Baseline and More Patient Consumers, by Age

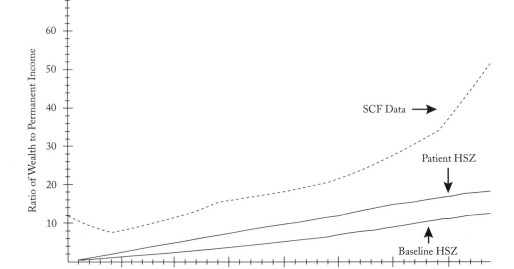

Source: Author's calculations using the model described in the text.

profile is certainly higher than in the standard HSZ model, it remains far below the profile for the consumers in the top 1 percent of the SCF data. Plausible modifications of other parameter values also fail to raise the model profile to the level found in the data. In other words, the richest households are saving more than can be justified even in a version of the Life-Cycle model that allows for very patient consumers with a strong precautionary saving motive.

The evidence presented thus far has concerned the saving behavior and wealth profiles of consumers during the working period of life. The Life-Cycle model has another set of testable implications for behavior in the latter stages of life, after retirement. In particular, according to the standard Life-Cycle model, even patient consumers want to spend all of their wealth before they die. Of course, an uncertain date of death makes this difficult to achieve on one's own. However, there is a financial instrument that accomplishes exactly the goal implied by the model: annuities. One test of the rough accuracy of the basic Life-Cycle model is therefore whether the wealth of retired households is largely annuitized.

Carrying out such a test requires some methodology for calculating annuity wealth. I assume that the annuity is fixed in real terms (primarily because the largest form of annuity income, Social Security, is inflation-adjusted). I assume a real interest rate and use the mortality tables from HSZ to construct the expected present discounted value of a one-dollar-per-year annuity as:

$$\Gamma_a = \sum_{i=a}^{T} \left(\prod_{j=a}^{i} \Lambda_j \right) R^{a-i} \tag{14.1}$$

where Λ_j is the probability of surviving from year $j - 1$ to year j and $R = 1 + r$ is the gross interest rate. (I assume $R = 1.03$, but results would be similar for other plausible interest rates.) The wealth value of the observed annuity income YANN at age a is then Γ_a YANN$_a$.

Using this method, and including home equity in annuitized wealth, the mean household over age sixty-five has approximately 55 percent of its wealth in annuitized form. However, among the richest 1 percent of households, the mean annuitization rate is only 10 percent.

This evidence on annuitization is suggestive but hardly conclusive. Annuity markets are probably far from perfect; as in other insurance markets, adverse selection may distort the market sufficiently to make inference hazardous. Furthermore, annuities are the perfect financial vehicle to counter only one kind of risk, mortality risk. If other kinds of risk are important, it is no longer obvious that even selfish life-cycles consumers should annuitize most or all of their wealth. For example, if there is a small probability of a very expensive medical problem, it may be important to have access to a large chunk of nonannuitized wealth in order to pay the bills (assuming that no health insurance will fully cover every possible medical catastrophe or every potentially desirable experimental treatment).

An extreme assumption would be that annuity markets are so imperfect that, for practical purposes, we can assume that annuities cannot be purchased. This assumption would obviously vitiate the argument that the failure of the wealthy to annuitize

their wealth proves that they are not life-cyclers. However, in the absence of annuities, the Life-Cycle model has other implications. In particular, it implies that selfish life-cycle consumers, even patient ones, will eventually begin running down their
wealth as they age. Figure 14.4 shows that by around age eighty the HSZ model
implies that consumers should be dissaving at a fairly substantial pace. (The simulations here follow the assumptions of Hubbard et al. about mortality rates, which they
derived from actuarial data, with the modification that they assume that death occurs
for certain at age one hundred if it has not happened yet.) However, figure 14.5 shows
the actual average age profile of wealth across the four SCF surveys. Although wealth
accumulation slows, or perhaps halts, around age sixty-five, there is no noticeable
decumulation of assets for consumers in the top percentile of the wealth distribution.[4]

Of course, nothing in economics requires us to believe that the only purpose of
saving is to finance one's own future consumption; that is merely a hypothesis of the
basic Life-Cycle model. One natural idea is that the wealthy do not run down their
assets because they want to leave bequests to their children. This thought leads to
the next model.

THE DYNASTIC MODEL

I would as soon leave my son a curse as the almighty dollar.

—Andrew Carnegie

In the 1995 issue of the annual Forbes 400 count of the richest Americans, there
are at least eleven households that contain descendants of Pierre du Pont (who died
in 1817). This might seem to be compelling evidence that at least some of the very

Figure 14.4   Age Profile of Log Wealth for the Ninety-Ninth Percentile, HSZ Model

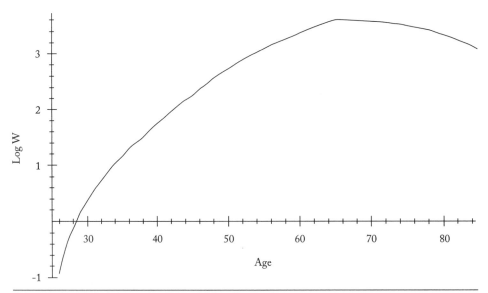

Source: Author's calculations using the model described in the text.

Figure 14.5   Age Profile of Log Wealth for the Ninety-ninth Percentile, SCF Data

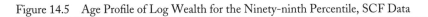

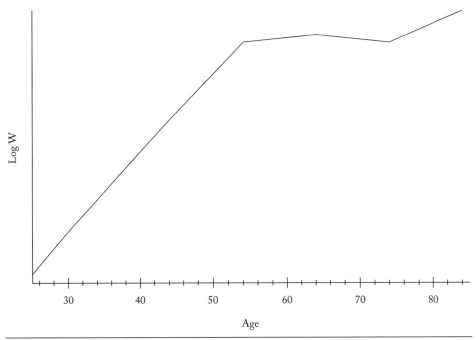

Source: Author's calculations using the model described in the text.

rich have a powerful bequest motive. On the other hand, apparently no members of the four hundred trace their wealth to Robert Morris, reputed to be the wealthiest man in America at the time of the Revolutionary War. And Andrew Carnegie gave away over 90 percent of his fortune before he died. Furthermore, the fact that large bequests to children do occur does not prove that provision of such bequests is the primary motivation for accumulation.

This section considers a particular model of bequests proposed by Robert Barro (1974). The dynast alive at time t is assumed to solve the intertemporal maximization problem:

$$\max_{C_t} \quad U(C_t) + \sum_{i=t+1}^{\infty} \beta^{i-t} U(C_i) \tag{14.2}$$
$$\text{s.t.} \quad W_{t+1} = R[W_t - C_t] + Y_{t+1},$$

where C_t corresponds to the lifetime consumption spending of the generation living at time t, W is the dynasty's wealth, Y is the (noncapital) income earned by that generation, R is the intergenerational interest rate, and β is the discount factor. The implications of this equation for macroeconomics spawned the large literature on Ricardian equivalence in the 1970s and 1980s. More recently, Altonji, Hayashi and Kotlikoff (1992) have tested the dynastic model with household-level data from the

Panel Study of Income Dynamics (PSID) and rejected its strong implication that only dynastic resources should matter for any individual family's consumption. The typical PSID family, however, is not particularly wealthy, so those results do not necessarily imply that the dynastic model is a poor one for the wealthiest families.

Although intuition suggests that the dynastic model might be interchangeable with other models in which leaving a bequest yields utility, in fact the model has distinctive implications, such as Ricardian equivalence, that need not follow from other models of bequests. As a result, the economic literature has drawn a distinction between dynastic models like the one specified in equation (14.3) and "joy of giving" models in which the bequest yields utility directly. For example, the dynastic model implies that the size of the bequest should be a function of the ratio of the parent's lifetime income and the child's lifetime income; that parents should give larger bequests to poorer children; and that childless wealthy people should leave no bequests. All of these implications of the dynastic model have been tested in population-representative data sets, and none has received consistent empirical support. This section provides evidence that the dynastic model is also a poor description of the behavior of the richest households.

To begin with some very informal evidence, Arthur B. Kennickell, M. Starr-McCluer, and Annika Sunden (1995) report some results from a "focus group" session on saving motivations that was convened as part of the preliminary work in designing the questions for the 1995 SCF.[5] The eight members of the group were all wealthy individuals, mostly in their fifties.[6] Participants were asked, "Thinking about your reasons for saving, what sorts of reasons are most important to you?" In the entire course of a three-hour conversation about saving behavior, providing a bequest was not mentioned once as a reason for saving.[7]

A group of eight individuals is obviously too small a sample to demonstrate convincingly the general absence of a bequest motive among the wealthy. Somewhat more persuasive evidence is provided in the results of survey questions on the 1992 SCF. Respondents were asked to list their five most important reasons for saving. As shown in table 14.1, only 3 percent of the general population, and 2 percent of the wealthy households, indicated that providing an inheritance was the most important reason to save.[8] Furthermore, only 5 percent of the total population and 4 percent of the wealthy households indicated that providing an inheritance was one of their *top five* reasons for saving. (The differences between the wealthy households and the general population are not statistically significant here.)

Another obvious test of the model is to see whether the childless elderly tend to dissave more than those with children. This hypothesis has been tested using population-representative data; Michael D. Hurd (1986) found that in the popula-

Table 14.1   Percentage Who Say Inheritance Is Important Reason to Save

	Most Important Reason	One of the Five Most Important Reasons	Number of Observations
Entire sample	.03	.05	3254
Richest 1 percent	.02	.04	652

Source: Author's calculations using 1992 survey of consumer finances.

tion as a whole there is no tendency for elderly without children to decumulate faster than those with children. Unfortunately, even when the data from the four SCFs are combined, the number of childless, elderly, wealthy households is too small to permit reliable estimation of age profiles of wealth. (Only about 10 percent of elderly couples are childless.)

Another option is to consider what childless elderly people say about their saving and spending behavior. Respondents to the 1992 and 1995 SCFs were asked whether their spending was greater than, equal to, or less than their income over the past year, and how spending usually compared with income. The results are presented in table 14.2.[9] The childless elderly were *less* likely to say that they dissave than those with children, by this crude measure, either as a general rule or in the current year in particular. Of course, it is possible that some of the "spending" of the elderly with children consists *of* inter vivos transfers to those children. The real problem for the Life-Cycle model is the testimony of the childless, wealthy elderly, essentially none of whom say that their spending exceeds their income. This is all the more impressive given the comparatively small fraction of their income that is annuitized.

Given the paucity of publicly available data on the very wealthy, it is not surprising that the economic literature contains almost no empirical studies that shed any light on the behavior of the childless, wealthy elderly. (There have been several studies, however, that examined the behavior of *nonwealthy*, childless, elderly households and found that they do not dissave; see, for example, Menchik and David [1983] and the references therein.) I was able to find only one study that contains even tangential information on the subject, a paper by Gerald Auten and David Joulfaian (1996) that uses a proprietary data set compiled by the Internal Revenue Service on 1982 decedents who paid estate taxes. From those IRS figures (table 1, p. 62), it is possible to calculate that the mean wealth of the childless decedents was virtually identical to that of those with children—hardly what would be expected if those with children had a powerful dynastic saving motive that the childless (presumably) did not share.[10] Furthermore, those *with* children actually contributed slightly *more* to charity during their lifetimes than the childless. Again, a dynastic motive would suggest the opposite. Finally, Auten and Joulfaian found no significant effect of children's income on the size of charitable bequests. This finding is consistent with evidence reported by Mark O. Wilhelm (1996), who found little support for the altruism model's implication that the size of bequests in families with more than one child should be related to the relative lifetime income of the children. Instead, Wilhelm found roughly equal bequests in about 80 percent of cases.

Table 14.2   Saving by the Wealthy Elderly With and Without Children

	Spending Usually Exceeds Income	Spending Exceeded Income This Year
With children	.05	.23
No children	.00	.00

Source: Author's calculations using 1992 survey of consumer finances.

THE CAPITALIST SPIRIT

This section presents a model in which wealth enters consumers' utility functions directly, and it argues that such a model is both consistent with the available data on the saving behavior of the wealthy and plausible on grounds other than its consistency with these facts. Zou (1994) and Bakshi and Chen (1996) have recently noted that Weber (1958) long ago argued that the pursuit of wealth for its own sake was the "spirit of capitalism," and so I call this the "capitalist spirit" model.

The Model

Consider a consumer entering life with wealth w_T. Suppose the utility function for consumption is a standard CRRA utility function, $u(c_t) = \dfrac{c^{1-\rho}}{1-\rho}$ and suppose the consumer also obtains utility from wealth in a modified Stone-Geary form, $v(w_t) = \dfrac{(w+\gamma)^{1-\alpha}}{1-\alpha}$. Formally, the consumer's maximization problem is:

$$\max_{c_t} \quad u(c_T) + v(w_{T+1}) \tag{14.3}$$

$$\text{s.t.} \quad w_{T+1} = w_T - c_T.$$

The problem as described thus far can be interpreted in either of two ways. The first interpretation is that the model describes a consumer deciding how to allocate lifetime resources between consumption and wealth, with wealth yielding utility directly. The second interpretation is of a consumer deciding how to allocate lifetime resources between lifetime consumption and end-of-lifetime wealth. (The reasons end-of-period wealth might yield utility include the "joy of giving" bequest motive mentioned earlier and several others. These issues are discussed further later in the chapter.)

The first-order condition for an interior solution to this problem is:

$$u'(c_T) = v'(w_{T+1})$$

$$c_T^{-\rho} = (w_T - c_T + \gamma)^{-\alpha}. \tag{14.4}$$

Call the c_T that satisfies this equation c_T^*. It is clear that for sufficiently small w_T the equation is satisfied only by choosing a c_T larger than w_T, that is, by ending with negative wealth. If we impose the condition that consumers may not die in debt, the solution to the problem is:

$$c_T = \text{Min}\left[c_T^*, w_T\right] \tag{14.5}$$

If $\rho > \alpha$, end-of-period wealth is a luxury good. Furthermore, if γ is positive, there is a range of initial wealth such that the marginal value of an extra dollar of consumption always exceeds the marginal value of an additional dollar of wealth. In this range, the consumer will choose to spend all available resources and end the period (and life) with zero wealth.

The problem can be solved analytically if we choose $\rho = 2$ and $\alpha = 1$. If we set $\gamma = 1$, the solution is

$$c_T = \text{Min}\left[\frac{-1 + \sqrt{1 + 4(1 + w_T)}}{2}, w_T\right]. \tag{14.6}$$

Define the saving rate as the fraction of beginning-of-period total assets the consumer ends up holding at the end of the period, w_{T+1}/w_T. Figure 14.6 shows the saving rate of this consumer as initial wealth goes from 0 to 10. For initial wealth between 0 and 1 the consumer saves nothing, but above initial wealth of 1 the saving rate rises monotonically. Furthermore, as $w_T \to \infty$ the saving rate approaches 100 percent.

The essential insights from this model carry over when the model is extended to many periods and when labor and capital income are incorporated: consumers with permanent income below a certain threshold behave like standard life-cycle consumers and try to spend all their assets before death; consumers with permanent incomes above the threshold save at ever increasing rates as lifetime income rises.

Figure 14.6   Saving as a Function of Wealth in the Capitalist Spirit Model

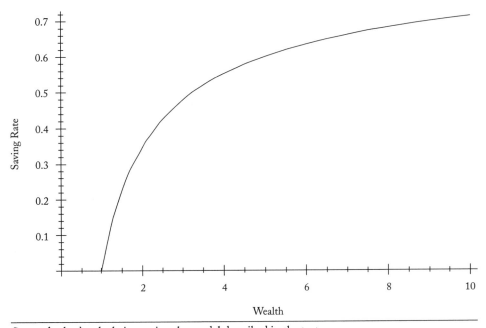

Source: Author's calculations using the model described in the text.

The idea that bequests (charitable or otherwise) are insignificant for most of the population but become increasingly important in the upper reaches of the lifetime income distribution has been informally expressed by several authors. Indeed, Modigliani (1986) himself has argued that, to the extent that bequests must be included in the life-cycle framework, they should be incorporated in precisely this "luxury good" manner. There is also a growing body of empirical evidence in support of the proposition. Karen E. Dynan, Jonathan Skinner, and Stephen P. Zeldes (1996) examine data from several microdata sets and find consistent and strong evidence that households with higher lifetime income leave larger bequests; Lee Lillard and Lynn Karoly (1997) find similar results. And most directly, Auten and Joulfaian (1996) find an elasticity of bequests with respect to lifetime income well in excess of 1. (Their point estimate is 1.3.)

In theoretical terms, the value added in this chapter relative to the previous literature is simply the proposal of a specific and simple functional form for the consumer's utility function that captures the informal idea that rich people save more in a way that is at least roughly consistent with the empirical evidence marshaled earlier. But such consistency may not be a high enough standard.

Informal Evidence

Utility maximization is a metaphysical concept of impregnable circularity.

—Joan Robinson

The essence of Joan Robinson's complaint about utility theory was that it is possible to construct a utility function to justify any conceivable behavior: just assume that the behavior in question yields more utility than its alternatives. Any postulated utility function, or proposed modification to a standard utility function, should therefore be defensible on grounds other than its ability to match the facts it was created to match. This section argues, using a variety of informal evidence, that most qualitative descriptions of the behavior of the wealthy, both by the wealthy themselves and by outside observers, can be interpreted at a fundamental level as implying that wealthy people derive utility either directly from the ownership of wealth, or indirectly, either from the activities that lead to wealth accumulation or from a flow of services that is closely tied to the ownership of that wealth.

The first important argument about the plausibility of the capitalist spirit model concerns the assumption that the marginal utility of consumption decreases sharply with the level of consumption. What matters critically here is the assumption that there is an alternative way to employ wealth whose marginal utility decreases more slowly than that of consumption (and hence is a luxury good relative to consumption). It is important to recall that the kind of consumption treated in the model is for strictly nondurable goods and services. Sidney L. Carroll and Herbert Inhaber (1992) note that the "luxury" goods generally associated with the wealthy, such as art, estates, jewelry, even sports teams, are almost all assets. Indeed, beyond a certain level of wealth it becomes difficult to imagine how one could spend even the earnings on one's wealth on nondurable goods and services for personal enjoyment. For example, recent press accounts have estimated Bill Gates's net worth at $100 billion. Assuming a 10 percent annual rate of return, Gates would have to spend $10 billion a year, or over $25 million a day, on nondurable goods and services simply to avoid further accumulation.

The proposition that the marginal utility of consumption approaches zero as the level of consumption rises is also lent credence by the statements of wealthy people themselves. Andrew Carnegie, Cornelius Vanderbilt, and other fabulously wealthy people have referred to their "surplus" wealth and spoken about how to determine when one has "enough" wealth. H. L. Hunt, then the richest man in the world, once said that, "for practical purposes, someone who has $200,000 a year is as well off as I am." Similar statements (appropriately adjusted for inflation) have been attributed to William Henry Vanderbilt and John Jacob Astor, two nineteenth-century plutocrats.

One of the appealing features of the idea that rich people eventually reach near-satiation in their consumption of nondurables is that this means one need not assume that a towering and obsessive greed lies behind their continuing accumulation. If "greed" is defined as a desire to possess wealth for its own sake, even a modest amount of greed will suffice so long as greed does not diminish with wealth as fast as the marginal utility diminishes with consumption. Or to put the idea more concretely, if ownership of extra houses, yachts, artwork, or, for that matter, corporations has even a modest intrinsic appeal, eventually that appeal is likely to exceed the waning lure of an extra dollar of nondurable consumption. This is merely another way of saying that ownership of these kinds of wealth yields utility directly, as the basic capitalist spirit model assumes.

Of course, towering and obsessive greed cannot always be ruled out. In *Trump: The Art of the Deal* (1988), Donald Trump pronounces "you can't be too greedy." The infamous Ivan Boesky told Berkeley business school students in 1987 that "greed is good." The idea is expressed with greater irony in the epigram: "The one with the most toys when he dies, wins." Among the nineteenth-century plutocrats, according to the historian Frederic Cople Jaher (1980),

> Money-making and keeping, not adorned or rationalized by nobler explanations, actually constituted a powerful force in the lives of the very rich. As boys, [the mining magnate William Boyce] Thompson and [John D.] Rockefeller vowed to accumulate a fortune. Thompson . . . and [Andrew] Carnegie promised themselves to retire after reaching a certain level of wealth, but kept pushing onward. Rogers, a Rockefeller disciple and associate, said that the Standard Oil partners made the profit motive a "religion," a faith "taught" them by "Mr. Rockefeller."

To the extent that these quotations express the general truth about the motivations of the wealthy, the capitalist spirit model can be said to apply directly. However, the view that all wealthy people are motivated solely by a love of wealth for its own sake is surely extreme. A variety of other plausible, and apparently very different, motivations are commonly proposed, ranging from job satisfaction to status-seeking, to philanthropic ambitions, to power lust. The remainder of this section argues that, from a modeling standpoint, these other common ideas—different though they may be from a psychological perspective—are essentially indistinguishable from each other and from the basic capitalist spirit model in terms of their implications for individual behavior. The argument, therefore, is that if any of these several proposed motivations is correct, the capitalist spirit model constitutes an appropriate mathematical model of the behavior of the wealthy.

Perhaps the most obvious example of a psychologically very different model that would be behaviorally indistinguishable from the wealth-in-the-utility-function model is the idea that the wealthy enjoy doing their jobs well, and that they view the accumulation of wealth as the principal measure of job performance. This idea appears frequently both in the statements of the wealthy themselves and in commentary by others on the behavior of the wealthy. Two statements are particularly direct:

> The rich man's "duty," such as it is, is not to society but to his art, and his art is making money.
>
>   —Michael Lewis, *New York Times Magazine* (July 1995)

> Money's just a way of keeping score. It's the game that matters.
>
>   —H. L. Hunt, cited in Jaher (1980, 215)

A closely related idea is suggested by the work of Robert Frank (1985), who has argued that an intrinsic component of human nature is a tendency to judge oneself by comparison with others. If for some wealthy people wealth is the metric of comparison, the utility function should contain not the absolute level of their wealth but some function of the relationship of their wealth to that of others. Bakshi and Chen (1996), Cole, Mailath, and Postlewaite (1992), and Zou (1994) have also argued that wealth matters because it is an index of social status.[11] For practical purposes of analysis of household-level data, however, both of these ideas are virtually indistinguishable from the proposition that wealth enters the utility function directly, and both ideas should produce essentially identical results in a model of saving. (Although they might have different implications for optimal tax policy; see the discussion later in the chapter; and Frank, this volume).[12]

It is also possible that wealthy people continue accumulating because greater wealth yields some other benefit that is more difficult to measure, such as power. In particular, the view that wealth brings power is commonplace among both the wealthy themselves and observers of the wealthy. (The idea that power is desirable appears to be taken for granted.)

> The ultimate gift of colossal wealth, at least for the founders of the richest families, was power (Jaher 1980, 215)

> Money is the measuring rod of power.   —Howard Hughes

> 'Twasn't the money we were after, 'twas the power. We were all playing for power. It was a great game.
>
>   —The Gilded Age financier James Stillman, cited in Jaher (1980)

If you give away the surplus [money], you give away the control.

—Cornelius Vanderbilt, cited in Jaher (1980)

'Tis a sort of duty to be rich, that it may be in one's power to do good, riches being another word for power.

—The English society figure Lady Mary Wortley Montagu (1689–1762)
in a letter to her husband, c. September 24, 1714, cited in Jaher (1980)

The last quotation raises a final idea that crops up frequently in the statements of the wealthy themselves: that their purpose in accumulating wealth is ultimately to be able to pursue philanthropic activities or to establish institutions to carry out such activities. Although such an evidently self-serving interpretation should be subject to considerable skepticism, there are many prominent examples of philanthropy that bear out the proposition. The Ford Foundation, the Rockefeller Foundation, Carnegie-Mellon University, Duke University, Johns Hopkins University, the Getty Museum, and a host of other prominent institutions owe either their existence or a substantial part of their endowments to the munificence of wealthy individuals (often, although not always, manifested through bequests). Morally, socially, and psychologically this motivation for wealth accumulation is very different from pure greed. However, if more wealth allows one to establish a larger foundation or to endow more institutions, the implications for saving behavior are again virtually indistinguishable from the idea that wealth enters the utility function directly.

DEATH AND TAXES

Assuming that the capitalist spirit model provides a roughly correct description of the behavior of wealthy households, it is natural to ask what the model implies about the relationship between accumulation behavior and taxes.[13] Returning to the parameterized version of the model in which $\rho = 2$ and $\alpha = \gamma = 1$, if bequests (or wealth) are taxed at rate τ then the equation for optimal consumption becomes:

$$c_T = \min\left[\frac{-1 + \sqrt{1 + 4(w + \gamma / (1 - \tau))}}{2}, w_T\right] \tag{14.7}$$

Figure 14.7 shows the effect on consumption if bequest taxes are increased from 40 percent to 80 percent. Consider first the curve labeled $\tau = .4$, which shows the optimal amount of consumption for consumers facing a 40 percent bequest tax if bequests are not constrained to be positive. The actual consumption function, of course, is the minimum of the 45-degree line and this curve. The point of intersection of this curve and the 45-degree line, labeled ω_1, reveals the level of lifetime wealth at which consumers begin to leave positive bequests.

When the bequest tax is raised to 80 percent, the amount of consumption shifts up, as indicated in the curve labeled $\tau = .8$. The point at which consumers begin

Figure 14.7   Effect on Consumption of an Increase in Bequest Taxes

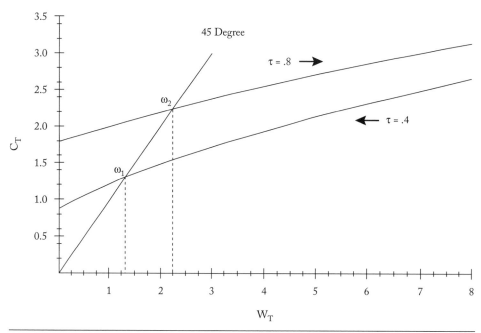

Source: Author's calculations using the model described in the text.

leaving bequests, ω_2, is substantially higher than when the tax rate was 40 percent.

Hence, it is useful to think of the effects of raising the bequest tax by considering three categories of consumers. The first are those with lifetime wealth less than ω_1. They leave bequests under neither tax regime, so their behavior is unaffected by the tax increase. The second region is occupied by those consumers with lifetime wealth between ω_1 and ω_2. These are the consumers who would leave bequests if the bequest tax were only 40 percent, but who prefer to consume all of their lifetime wealth when the bequest tax rises. Finally, consumers with lifetime wealth greater than ω_2 will leave bequests even when the bequest tax is 80 percent. However, at any level of lifetime wealth the size of the bequests they leave is reduced by an amount equal to the gap between the two consumption curves. It is simple to show that as lifetime wealth goes to infinity the fraction of lifetime wealth bequeathed approaches 100 percent even with the higher bequest taxes. This is the region of the model that presumably corresponds best to the circumstances of fabulously wealthy people like Bill Gates.

Because the effect of taxes on consumption depends on the distribution of consumers across the different levels of lifetime income, the aggregate effect of bequest taxes in this model is impossible to judge in the absence of evidence (or assumptions) about the distribution of lifetime income (and information about the parameters of the model). If most bequests come from people with $\omega_1 < w_T < \omega_2$, then an increase in the bequest tax could reduce bequests almost to nothing. If, on the other hand, most bequeathed wealth comes from consumers with very large amounts of lifetime income, increasing the bequest tax might have very little effect on either consumption or (pre-tax) bequests.

In principle, it should be possible to tease out estimates of the relevant parameter values from available data on wealth, consumption, and income, using methods like those employed in an impressive recent paper by Gourinchas and Parker (1996). Those authors assume a "residual value function" that characterizes the utility experienced during the last part of life that is mathematically very similar to the "bequest utility" function postulated in the model here. Gourinchas and Parker assume that the coefficient of relative risk aversion for the residual value function is the same as for the period utility function, and they do not incorporate a Stone-Geary term like my γ, but their estimation methodology could easily be adapted to estimate those two additional parameters. Having estimated those parameters, they could then perform simulations to gauge the predicted impact of changes in bequest taxes on consumption.

CONCLUSIONS

A variety of evidence, both qualitative and quantitative, strongly suggests that people at the top end of the wealth and income distributions behave in ways that are substantially different from the behavior of most of the rest of the population. In particular, it is difficult to explain the behavior of these consumers using the standard Life-Cycle model of consumption. A leading alternative to (or perhaps just an extension of) the Life-Cycle model is the dynastic model, in which the decisionmaker cares about the utility of his descendants. The dynastic model, however, has problems of its own, starting with the testimony of many wealthy households that providing an inheritance is not a principal motivation for saving and ending with the fact that childless, wealthy, old people do not appear to dissave. I argue that the simplest model capable of fitting all the facts is a model in which either wealth enters the utility function directly as a luxury good or wealth yields a stream of services that enter the utility function in ways that would be virtually indistinguishable in any formal way from a model in which wealth enters the utility function directly.

In a way, the model reconciles Fitzgerald and Hemingway. Fitzgerald was right that the rich do not behave simply like scaled-up versions of everyone else. They choose to save more and to accumulate faster because they can "afford" the luxury of doing so. But Hemingway was right to suggest that the rest of us would probably behave the same way, if only we had more money.

I am indebted to Sidney Carroll, Elizabeth B. Carroll, and Elizabeth I. Carroll for many of the insights in this chapter. Any errors are my own. The STATA programs and SCF data used in the empirical work in this paper are available online at ftp://sun1.econ.jhu.edu/pub/ccarroll/rich.

NOTES

1. The most important differences are, first, that this model incorporates shocks to permanent income, while the HSZ model has only transitory (but very persistent) shocks (they estimate an AR(1) coefficient greater than .90); second, this model ignores health risks; third, I assume that in every period there is a small (p = .03) and serially uncorrelated chance of unemployment; and finally, I do not extensively model the social welfare system that applies to households at the bottom of the income distribution. (However, I assume that unemployment insurance replaces 50 percent of permanent income for unemployed consumers.) Hubbard and his colleagues found that labor-income risk was far more important than health risk in determining the age profile of wealth and saving, and the details of the social welfare system are not very important in determining the behavior of the median households (much less the rich households). Hence, these modeling differences should not matter much for my purposes. I have adopted the assumptions of Hubbard et al. about parameter values: time preference rate equal to the interest rate at 3 percent annually; coefficient of relative risk aversion of 3; and a similar age-income profile. The definition of permanent income here is the annual income that a household would receive if there were no transitory shocks to income. Except for the incorporation of unemployment insurance and stochastic mortality, and the use here of HSZ parameter values, this model is the same as that in Carroll (1997); see that paper for further discussion of the model's characteristics and implications.

2. Of course, permanent income is not directly observed in the SCF. However, the survey does ask consumers whether their income over the last year was unusually high, unusually low, or about normal. The figure shows the median of the ratio of wealth to actual income for the set of consumers who reported that their income was about normal. Arthur Kennickell (1995) argues that this question appears to provide a very effective way of identifying households that have recently experienced transitory shocks to income. I excluded SCF households that report ever having received an inheritance, so the difference in the SCF and HSZ models cannot be due to inheritances.

3. The SCF profiles were generated by a quantile regression of the log (wealth-permanent income) ratio on a set of age indicator variables that produce a smooth approximation to a ten-year centered moving average of the actual log (wealth-permanent income) ratio. For further details, see the programs that generated the data, available at the URL listed in the acknowledgments.

4. The methods for constructing this figure draw on a literature dating at least to Browning, Deaton, and Irish (1985), with contributions by Attanasio and Weber (1985). These authors have shown how to construct "synthetic panels" from a series of cross-section surveys like the four SCFs used in this chapter. That literature has noted that age, time, and cohort effects cannot be independently distinguished using such data, because age, time, and cohort are linearly related. The assumptions I made to identify age effects were, first, that cohort effects can be captured by a single term reflecting the lifetime level of permanent income of each cohort (which I assume increased on average by 1.5 percent per annum for the cohorts in question—if anything an underestimate of the relevant average productivity growth rate and therefore a source of downward bias in the slope of the estimated age profile); and second, that the time effects averaged to zero over the four SCF surveys.

5. Focus groups are commonly used in the preliminary stages of survey design to test sample questions and to explore whether respondents interpret questions in the intended way; to identify plausible ranges of behavior that might be exhibited by survey respondents; and to suggest the most important sources of variation across individuals.

6. They were required to have a minimum annual income of $250,000, minimum net worth of $600,000, or both.

7. A woman made the only remark even tangentially related to inheritance: "When I die, my daughter's reaction is going to be, 'Mother's dead? That's too bad. *Where's the jewelry?'*"

8. A similar question was asked in the 1995 SCF, with similar results.

9. There is a strong correlation between the level of net worth and the answer to these questions. The median net worth of consumers who said their consumption regularly exceeded their income

was $47,599; that of consumers who said their consumption did not usually exceed their income was $154,079.

10. Of course, one might argue that the "dynasty" of the childless couples could be carried on by nephews and nieces, or second cousins, or any other heir who might be found. However, such an argument only intensifies the problems with the dynastic model pointed out by Bagwell and Bernheim (1988): to wit, that sexual reproduction and nonperfectly assortative mating imply that eventually one's own descendants are so intermixed with everyone else's that there is no plausible sense in which a "dynasty" can be said to exist at all.

11. There is also a growing literature that explores the consequences if the utility obtained from consumption depends on a comparison of consumption to a reference stock determined either by one's own past consumption (Carroll, Overland, and Weil, forthcoming; Campbell and Cochrane 1995; Constantinides 1990) or the consumption of others (Abel 1990; Carroll, Overland, and Weil 1997).

12. One problem with the particular specifications of Bakshi and Chen (1996) and Zou (1994) is that their specifications imply that consumers with zero wealth would have negative infinite utility. According to the SCFs, however, about 10 percent of the population has zero or negative net worth. Furthermore, their model does not necessarily predict that high lifetime income consumers will save more than those with low lifetime income. Finally, there is a growing consensus that the standard Life-Cycle model, with an appropriate treatment of uncertainty, does a fairly good job of describing the behavior of the typical household without any need for important direct effects of wealth on utility. Only at the upper reaches of the wealth distribution does behavior unmistakably diverge from the model's predictions.

13. I should note here that the following analysis is only correct for those interpretations of the model in which consumers care about the absolute level of wealth or consumption. If, instead, utility from w_{T+1} depends on how large one's own w_{T+1} is compared to the w'_{T+1}s of others, bequest taxes would probably have a much smaller effect than that discussed in the text. For an analysis of related issues in income taxation, see Frank (this volume).

REFERENCES

Abel, Andrew B. 1990. "Asset Prices Under Habit Formation and Catching up with the Joneses." *American Economic Review* 40(2): 38–42.

Altonji, Joseph G., Fumio Hayashi, and Laurence J. Kotlikoff. 1992. "Is the Extended Family Altruistically Linked?" *American Economic Review* 82(5): 1177–98.

Attanasio, Orazio P., and Guillermo Weber. 1985. "Is Consumption Growth Consistent with Intertemporal Optimization?: Evidence from the Consumer Expenditure Survey." *Journal of Political Economy* 103: 1121–57.

Auten, Gerald, and David Joulfaian. 1996. "Charitable Contributions and Intergenerational Transfers." *Journal of Public Economics* 59(1): 55–68.

Bagwell, Kyle, and B. Douglas Bernheim. 1988. "Is Everything Neutral?" *Journal of Political Economy* 96(2): 308–38.

Bakshi, Gurdip, and Zhimu Chen. 1996. "The Spirit of Capitalism and Stock-Market Prices." *American Economic Review* 86(1): 133–57.

Barro, Robert J. 1974. "Are Government Bonds Net Worth?" *Journal of Political Economy* 82: 1095–1117.

Browning, Martin, Angus Deaton, and Margaret Irish. 1985. "A Profitable Approach to Labor Supply and Commodity Demands over the Life Cycle." *Econometrica* 53: 503–44.

Campbell, John Y., and John H. Cochrane. 1995. "By Force of Habit: A Consumption-Based Explanation of Aggregate Stock Market Behavior." Working paper 4995. Cambridge, Mass.: National Bureau of Economic Research.

Carroll, Christopher D. 1992. "The Buffer-Stock Theory of Saving: Some Macroeconomic Evidence." *Brookings Papers on Economic Activity* 2: 61–156.

———. 1997. "Buffer-Stock Saving and the Life Cycle/Permanent Income Hypothesis." *Quarterly Journal of Economics* 112(1): 1–56.

Carroll, Christopher D., Jody R. Overland, and David N. Weil. Forthcoming. "Saving and Growth with Habit Formation." *American Economic Review.*

———. 1997. "Comparison Utility in an Endogenous Growth Model." *Journal of Economic Growth* 2(4): 339–67.

Carroll, Sidney L., and Herbert Inhaber. 1992. *How Rich Is Too Rich?* New York: Praeger.

Cole, Harold. L., George J. Mailath, and Andrew Postlewaite. 1992. "Social Norms, Savings Behavior, and Growth." *Journal of Political Economy* 100(6): 1092–1125.

Constantinides, George M. 1990. "Habit Formation: A Resolution of the Equity Premium Puzzle." *Journal of Political Economy* 98: 519–43.

Dynan, Karen E., Jonathan Skinner, and Stephen P. Zeldes. 1996. "Do the Rich Save More?" Unpublished paper. Board of Governors, Federal Reserve System.

Frank, Robert H. 1985. *On Choosing the Right Pond: Human Behavior and the Quest for Status.* New York: Oxford University Press.

Gourinchas, Pierre-Olivier, and Jonathan Parker. 1996. "Consumption over the Life Cycle." Unpublished paper. University of Michigan, Ann Arbor.

Hubbard, R. Glenn, Jonathan S. Skinner, and Stephen P. Zeldes. 1994. "The Importance of Precautionary Motives for Explaining Individual and Aggregate Saving." In *The Carnegie-Rochester Conference Series on Public Policy,* vol. 40, edited by Allan H. Meltzer and Charles I. Plosser.

Hurd, Michael D. 1986. "Savings and Bequests." Working paper 1708. Cambridge, Mass.: National Bureau of Economic Research.

Jaher, Frederic Cople. 1980. "The Gilded Elite: American Multimillionaires, 1865 to the Present." In *Wealth and the Wealthy in the Modern World,* edited by William D. Rubinstein. London: Croon Helm.

Kennickell, Arthur B. 1995. "Saving and Permanent Income." Finance and Economics Discussion Series 95–41. Board of Governors, Federal Reserve System.

Kennickell, Arthur B., M. Starr-McCluer, and Annika Sunden. 1995. "Saving and Financial Planning: Some Findings from a Focus Group." Unpublished paper. Board of Governors, Federal Reserve System.

Lillard, Lee, and Lynn Karoly. 1997. "Income and Wealth Accumulation over the Life Cycle." Unpublished paper. RAND Corporation.

Menchik, Paul L., and Martin David. 1993. "Income Distribution, Lifetime Savings, and Bequests." *American Economic Review* 73(4): 672–90.

Modigliani, Franco. 1986. "Life Cycle, Individual Thrift, and the Wealth of Nations." *American Economic Review* 76(3): 297–313.

Trump, Donald, with Tony Schwarz. 1988. *Trump: The Art of the Deal.* New York: Random House.

Weber, Max M. 1958. *The Protestant Ethic and the Spirit of Capitalism.* New York: Charles Scribner's and Sons.

Wilhelm, Mark O. 1996. "Bequest Behavior and the Effect of Heirs' Earnings: Testing the Altruistic Model of Bequests." *American Economic Review* 86(4): 874–982.

Zou, Heng-Fu. 1994. "The 'Spirit of Capitalism' and Long-Run Growth." *European Journal of Political Economy* 10(2): 27–93.

Commentary on Chapter 14

Stephen P. Zeldes

A challenge for modern models of consumption and saving is to explain the large degree of heterogeneity in individual wealth holdings. True, large numbers of households hold levels of assets that appear consistent with conventional life-cycle motives for wealth accumulation. But a sizable fraction of households have wealth levels far below what would be predicted by standard life-cycle models. Finally, some households, typically high-income ones, have wealth levels in excess of what would be predicted in nearly any (no-bequest) life-cycle model. In this discussion, I first briefly review some recent attempts to explain why some people save so little, relative to the life-cycle model. I then turn to the main objective of Christopher Carroll's chapter, which is to explain why some households hold much more in wealth than would be suggested in a conventional life-cycle model.

Carroll's chapter is separated into two parts. The first appears to be a comment on a series of papers by Glenn Hubbard, Jonathan Skinner, and myself (Hubbard, Skinner, and Zeldes 1994a, 1994b, 1995) in which we attempted to construct a realistic stochastic life-cycle model to explain why some households appear consistent with the first group (that is, those who hold levels of wealth consistent with life-cycle models) while others are consistent with the second group (those with little or no assets). We did this by modeling uncertainty about earnings, length of life, and medical expenses, as well as means-tested social insurance programs. We have argued that while the uncertainty leads to higher levels of wealth for all (for precautionary reasons), the effective tax on saving imposed by means-tested social insurance programs leads many optimizing households to save considerably less. As we show in Hubbard, Skinner, and Zeldes (1995), our model is able to match the actual wealth distribution found in the Panel Study of Income Dynamics (PSID) surprisingly well. For example, the model matches the twentieth, fortieth, sixtieth, and eightieth percentiles of the wealth distribution extremely well for college graduates. We also capture the fact that the bottom 20 percent of the population with no high school degree has virtually no wealth. One problem we recognize with the model is that the predicted wealth of the median (and higher-income) households headed by a high school dropout is considerably higher than what we observe in the PSID.

Carroll has attempted to revisit this debate by running, as a benchmark model, something he calls an HSZ (Hubbard, Skinner, Zeldes) model; he claims that his results do not match well with actual data. One reason for his inability to match the empirical data could be that he has not replicated the HSZ model; in particular, his model does not include the feature of asset-based means testing, which, we have argued, is crucial to matching the actual distribution of wealth (see, for example, Hubbard, Skinner, and Zeldes 1995, table 3). Although I recognize the limitations of the HSZ model, it is important to understand that it is the only model that can explain the heterogeneity of wealth described earlier, as well as a variety of other empirical observations about consumption and wealth accumulation, without recourse to varying the time preference rate by education or income group.[1]

The second and main part of Carroll's chapter focuses on a different topic: why does the third group—people with wealth far in excess of what would be predicted by the life-cycle model—hold so much wealth? Carroll's criticisms of the HSZ model are more appropriate here: we predict some people in our model with wealth accumulation in excess of $1 million (in 1984 dollars), but we do not come close to explaining the wealth of people like Bill Gates, whose monthly interest earnings probably exceed their yearly current consumption expenditures. (The same criticism could be made, of course, of other standard life-cycle models.) One could try to patch up more conventional models by including income data for the very high-income households; for example, if Hubbard, Skinner, and Zeldes (1995) had estimated the earnings distribution using the SCF, with its panel of high-income recipients, instead of the PSID, which includes just a few people who make more than $200,000 annually, they would have predicted somewhat higher levels of wealth accumulation. But Carroll is on the mark when he suggests the need for thinking about the wealth accumulation motives of the super-rich that transcend typical life-cycle motives.

One way to start to understand this puzzle is to examine how the rich got the way they are. There are a number of possible explanations. The first is that they had very high labor income and, like others, saved in order to consume later in life or in states of the world where income is lower, leading to high wealth. As noted earlier, this cannot be the entire explanation, however, because not only is wealth high, but it is high relative to income for high-income households.

A second possibility is that those with a great deal of wealth earned very high rates of return (either anticipated or unanticipated) on what they saved, perhaps because they had access to better investment technologies, or perhaps because they were lucky. A third possibility is that they may have inherited substantial resources from their parents or other family members.

A fourth possibility is that the rich may have higher propensities to save. In some recent work (Dynan, Skinner, and Zeldes 1999), my coauthors and I have reexamined an old but unanswered question: Do households with higher lifetime income save a greater fraction of that income? We use three household data sets—the Consumer Expenditure Survey (CEX), the Survey of Consumer Finances (SCF), and the Panel Study of Income Dynamics (PSID)—to look at households across the entire income distribution, including the top 5 percent and the top 1 percent of households (from the SCF). In order to overcome the transitory income problem described by Milton Friedman (1957) and others, we use a variety of instruments for permanent income, including lags and leads of labor earnings, consumption, and education. We find strong evidence that the higher the lifetime income, the higher the saving rate. At moderate income levels, the size of the effect is about one and a half percentage points per $10,000 of income.

In practice, all of these are probably contributing factors. If the fourth possibility is important, it leads us to ask what motivates these households to save more, and how might we modify our models to account for this? Any theory put forth should be able to explain not just how the rich got their wealth, but what they do with it once they have it: Do they consume it over their lifetimes? Give it away to others during their lifetime? Leave it to others after they die?

Carroll argues that the rich do not annuitize much of their wealth, and that they do not run it down during old age. This suggests a need to include a bequest motive, in which individuals care about the utility of their children. But Carroll provides some suggestive evidence that the standard bequest motive is not the explanation. He cites evidence that bequests are almost always split evenly between multiple children, and that those with children are more likely to dissave in a given year than those without.

Carroll then proposes an alternative, what others have called the "capitalist spirit" model: that people get utility from the wealth per se, rather than the consumption that it enables—in other words, that wealth is intrinsically desirable. He sets forth a simple two-period model in which the household receives utility from lifetime consumption and second-period wealth. The utility function is modified Stone-Geary, with wealth being a luxury. I think that this is a promising model, but I do not think that it is the capitalist spirit model. Since the utility comes at the end of life, the model is indistinguishable from a model that includes a "joy of giving," which for many purposes (with the notable exception of Ricardian equivalence) is indistinguishable from a model with an altruistic bequest motive of a certain functional form. In other words, in a two-period model, it is impossible to distinguish between utility coming from the stock of wealth owned in each year the person is alive and utility coming from wealth at the end of life. Judging from his descriptions and the many interesting quotes from the rich and observers of the rich, I think what Carroll has in mind is the idea that the utility comes from consumption in each period of life and from wealth in each period of life.

Carroll is correct when he argues that we need something else in the model to explain the behavior of the super-rich. There are limits to how much money one can fruitfully spend on traditional goods and services, particularly since most consumption also involves time, which is limited to twenty-four hours a day even for the rich. Once the rich have bought large wardrobes of expensive clothes and more houses than they can spend time in, the marginal utility of extra consumption in this form is very low. Other needs and desires may then arise that are satisfied in different ways: respect, status, power, control. These may come from having the opportunity to run one's own company or being invited to important social events. I agree with Carroll that achieving many of these goals is related to wealth, but I am not sure I agree with the hypothesis that people get utility from wealth per se. Instead, such goals may essentially be purchased by the person with the wealth. It is probably not the wealth per se, but the promise of spending it or giving it away in certain states of the world that leads to attention, power, and invitations. If a person has a great deal of wealth but is not allowed to spend it or give it away in any state of the world, it seems unlikely that it would lead to attention or power.

Carroll's work is a very interesting first step in largely uncharted terrain: what motivates the very wealthy to save. A theory is only compelling, however, if it can explain a wide range of facts, not just the single one around which it was designed. In other words, the next step is to derive additional testable implications of the theory. For, example, can the theory explain why many high-income people are not tremendously wealthy? Although it is very difficult to get good data on the rich, it is still important that any theory have implications that are in principle testable.

The final step is to examine the policy implications of the theory. Let's consider a few of them. A model in which wealth generates utility says that if you give a household a large sum of money and tell the members of the household that they cannot spend any of it or give any of it away in any state of the world, that money would still generate utility. This is not observationally equivalent to a model in which wealth buys things or is simply a metric of success. Carroll's type of model implies, for example, that capital income taxation hits households especially hard, taxing something that is directly providing utility. Any taxes that come late in life would be preferable. Think how much better an estate tax would be, therefore, because members of a household continue to get utility from wealth while they are alive and do not really care about what happens when they die.

Along the same lines, even though in traditional theory front-loaded and back-loaded IRAs are equivalent, here they are certainly not. Front-loaded IRAs give individuals additional wealth during their working years but take it away later in life, an arrangement that would be vastly preferred in this model.

Carroll claims that understanding the behavior of the very rich is a powerful way of learning about the rest of the population. I like the modeling strategy of assuming a single form of preferences for all households, but in his model the motive takes effect only above a certain level of affluence. This suggests that we are unlikely to learn much about the rest of the population from the behavior of the rich.

Overall, I agree with Carroll that standard life-cycle models cannot explain the extremely high wealth-income ratios at the high end of the wealth distribution, and that we need to consider some other motives for these households. I think that the bequest or "joy of giving" motives, considered as luxuries, are an important piece of this, and I think that the ownership of wealth facilitates another kind of satisfaction of needs. Carroll has provided us with a very thought-provoking chapter that forces us to think harder about what is actually motivating the accumulation behavior of the rich. My hope is that we can further develop testable implications of this and other related models of the saving of the rich and improve our access to high-quality data in order to test these implications.

NOTES

1. By appealing to a relatively high time preference rate, the buffer stock model of Carroll and Samwick (1997) can explain the wealth holdings of the second group (the low-wealth households). However, their model is unable to explain the first group of households (the conventional life-cycle households), since virtually no one is predicted to hold wealth of more than half of their income prior to age fifty.

REFERENCES

Carroll, Christopher D., and Andrew Samwick. 1997. "The Nature of Precautionary Wealth." *Journal of Monetary Economics* 40(1, September): 41–71.

Dynan, Karen, Jonathan Skinner, and Stephen P. Zeldes. 1999. "Do the Rich Save More?" Unpublished paper. Columbia University.

Friedman, Milton. 1957. *A Theory of the Consumption Function.* Princeton, N.J.: Princeton University Press.

Hubbard, R. Glenn, Jonathan Skinner, and Stephen P. Zeldes. 1994a. "Expanding the Life-Cycle Model: Precautionary Saving and Public Policy." *American Economic Review* 84(2): 174–79.

———. 1994b. "The Importance of Precautionary Motives in Explaining Individual and Aggregate Saving." *Carnegie-Rochester Conference Series on Public Policy* 40(June): 59–125.

———. 1995. "Precautionary Saving and Social Insurance." *Journal of Political Economy* 103(2): 360–99.

Progressive Taxation and the Incentive Problem

Robert H. Frank

All taxes are a drag on economic growth. It's only a question of degree.
—Federal Reserve Chairman Alan Greenspan,
quoted in the *Wall Street Journal*,
March 26, 1997

The setting of personal tax rates is widely believed to confront policymakers with an agonizing trade-off between equity and efficiency. Most liberals, and even many conservatives, believe that a more progressive tax structure would be desirable on equity grounds. Yet most liberals and conservatives also believe that greater progressivity would entail significant penalties to economic growth.

In the United States and the United Kingdom, concerns about efficiency appear to have trumped concerns about equity. Strongly influenced by supply-side rhetoric, legislators in both countries voted to cut top marginal tax rates sharply in the 1980s, and despite slight upward revisions in the United States in the 1990s, these rates remain the lowest among industrialized nations.

My aim in this chapter is to question the conventional wisdom about the agonizing trade-off. My critique comprises two simple departures from the conventional neoclassical model: first, that the rewards in many of the labor markets in which top earners toil depend more on relative performance than on absolute performance; and second, that a person's utility depends not only on absolute but also on relative consumption. There is a solid evidentiary basis for both modifications. Using conventional neoclassical models modified in these ways, I suggest that greater tax progressivity may enhance rather than reduce economic efficiency.

THE BASIS FOR THE CONVENTIONAL WISDOM

The conventional view that tax equity comes at the expense of efficiency is predicated on the time-honored belief that people respond to incentives. Thus, say the supply-siders, when the rewards for effort and risk-taking are reduced by the imposition of higher taxes, people expend less effort and take fewer risks. In the standard rhetorical flourish of trickle-down theory, the problem with steeply progressive taxes is that they kill the geese that lay the golden eggs. Or as Benjamin Higgins (1992, 38) put it, "The rate of development is reduced, possibly to the point where even the very level of welfare of the underdog, which the equity measures are designed to help, is lowered instead."

The supply-siders are surely right that incentives matter. When the price of gasoline doubled in the late 1970s, for example, the proportion of cars sold with fuel-efficient four-cylinder engines rose sharply, with corresponding declines in the proportions sold with six- and eight-cylinder engines. By the same token, when the price trajectory of gasoline reversed itself in the ensuing years, falling sharply relative to the price trajectories for other goods, the market for cars with larger engines began a robust comeback. We may not be perfect rational maximizers, but most of us know enough to rearrange our spending patterns when relative prices move sharply.

Yet the fact that we respond to incentives in a self-interested way does not, by itself, imply that higher tax rates at the top will cause a slowdown in economic growth. It is true that an increase in the tax rates facing top earners reduces the economic rewards for taking risks and expending effort, just as the supply-siders insist. As every basic economics textbook makes clear, however, a fall in the after-tax wage rate simply does not lead to an unambiguous prediction about the quantity of effort supplied. Thus, whereas the substitution effect of a lower real wage is a reduction in effort, the income effect pulls in the opposite direction: by making the individual poorer than before, it provides an incentive to work more in order to recoup his loss. Economic theory is completely silent on the question of which of these two opposing effects will dominate. The case for the conventional position must therefore be made on empirical grounds.

There are a number of episodes that appear, at least superficially, to support the supply-siders' central premise. Perhaps the most vivid of these consist of responses to changes in state and local income tax rates. For example, conservatives in New York have warned since the 1950s that rising personal and corporate tax rates would prove costly to the state's economic vitality, and by most criteria these warnings have been remarkably on target. Thus, as one corporation after another has moved its headquarters from New York to some other jurisdiction with lower tax rates, the state's per capita income has continued a pattern of long decline in relative terms. At the same time, southern states with low tax rates have enjoyed a sustained economic boom. At the local and even state levels, at any rate, the fundamental premise of supply-side economics appears largely confirmed. Higher tax rates seem to translate into lower rates of economic growth. And this, we may suspect, is an important reason for the widespread support that the fundamental premise of supply-side economics currently enjoys.

Yet the observed responses to state and local tax changes tell us only that people are willing to substitute one location for another in response to tax incentives. They tell us nothing about their willingness to substitute leisure for effort, or about their reluctance to take risks for economic gain. If the top tax rates were increased significantly in *every* jurisdiction, would people work less, or would they be less willing to risk their capital? Or more important, in view of the reduction in barriers to labor mobility across national borders, would top earners in a given country either flee or work less in response to an increase in their nation's highest tax rates?

For sufficiently high tax rates, the answer to even this question appears to be yes, at least if the early experience of countries like England and Sweden is any guide. With marginal tax rates above 90 percent in the 1960s, both countries experienced costly out-migrations of talent.

Yet international labor flight is probably not an important constraint at the moment in the United States and the United Kingdom, both of which now have top marginal tax rates of roughly 40 percent—far lower than those in other industrial nations. For these countries, the important question for policymakers considering higher marginal tax rates is not whether top earners will flee, but whether their domestic economic decisions will be significantly distorted.

The case for such distortions is difficult to make on empirical grounds. If the net effect of a real wage reduction were to induce most people to supply significantly less labor, then the opposite should be true in the case of a real wage increase. Thus, the cumulative effect of the last century's dramatic rise in real wages should have been a significant increase in hours worked. In fact, however, the length of the workweek is significantly lower now than in 1900 (see Ehrenberg and Smith 1994, 33).

What is more, the downward trend in hours worked leveled out shortly after World War II in the United States and has actually turned slightly upward over the last two decades. This observation also casts doubt on the fundamental premise of supply-side economics, for the after-tax wage of the median earner has declined slightly during the last twenty years; according to supply-siders, that decrease should have caused a reduction in work hours instead of an increase. By many accounts, the recent increase in hours worked is an attempt to recoup the loss of purchasing power that stems from lower wage rates.

Although cross-country comparisons are inherently difficult to interpret, on balance we would also expect to see more effort supplied in countries with higher real after-tax wage rates if the fundamental premise of trickle-down economics were correct. Yet here too the numbers tell a different story. For example, even though Japanese CEOs earn less than one-fifth as much as their U.S. counterparts and face substantially higher marginal tax rates, there is no evidence that Japanese executives log shorter workweeks.

I stress again that none of these observations are inconsistent with the claim that people respond to incentives. They do not rule out the possibility that people work less if the top tax rate rises beyond some point. Nor do they contradict the claim that some people will go on welfare if they can earn more that way than by going to work. But taken as a whole, the empirical evidence is consistent with the claim that increases in the top U.S. and British marginal tax rates would not cause wholesale reductions in effort.

TAX AVOIDANCE AND TAX EVASION

Another claim by supply-siders is that high marginal tax rates compromise economic efficiency by channeling talent and effort into tax avoidance and tax evasion rather than productive work. Several writers saw evidence for this claim in the fact that the reduction in the top U.S. tax rates that was enacted in 1986 was followed by a large increase in the amount of income declared by top earners (see, for example, Feldstein 1995).

No one can dispute that the payoff from a dollar invested in tax avoidance is higher when tax rates are high than when they are low. But the Tax Reform Act of 1986 (TRA86) not only cut top tax rates but also broadened the tax base significantly by eliminating a large number of deductions and exemptions. If a rational tax avoider knows about the existence of a legal deduction or exemption, he will almost

surely claim it whether his tax rate is 40 percent or 60 percent. He may spend a little more effort searching out exemptions when the tax rate is higher, but his tax consultant is unlikely to advise him differently in the two cases. The post-1986 increase
in reported income appears to be explained more plausibly by the fact that the act
eliminated many existing loopholes.

Another potential efficiency loss stems from the greater incentives that corporations have to compensate executives with expensive perks when tax rates are higher.
For instance, when top British marginal tax rates were higher than 90 percent, it
was apparently not uncommon for companies to provide top executives with
chauffeur-driven Rolls-Royces. For each executive, this perk might cost the company $50,000 per year, an amount the executive would never see fit to spend on
himself. But since the after-tax value of an extra $50,000 in pay would have been
less than $5,000 for the executive, a company-provided Rolls might have loomed
as an attractive option.

Tax evasion is a serious problem. Yet in-kind compensation and other similar
behaviors must be monitored and controlled even with tax rates at their current, relatively low levels. More important, tax evasion of every sort would be sharply
reduced if we taxed consumption rather than income. Rather than spend $50,000
to provide an executive with a chauffeur-driven Rolls, a company can give her an
extra $50,000 in cash, 100 percent of which she can then shelter by simply putting
it into a mutual fund. By allowing people to shelter their savings completely from
taxation, we thus eliminate much of the incentive to engage in tax evasion. Indeed,
we have every reason to expect that tax evasion would be a less serious problem
under a steeply progressive consumption tax than under today's only moderately
progressive income tax. (More on the advantages of consumption taxation follows
later in the chapter.)

GROWTH AND INEQUALITY ACROSS NATIONS

A growing empirical literature casts further doubt on the presumed trade-off
between equity and efficiency (see, for example, Alesina and Roderick 1992; Garrison and Lee 1992; and Persson and Tabellini 1992). Several studies, for example,
have found a negative correlation between the various measures of income inequality and economic growth in cross-national data. Using World Bank and Organization for Economic Cooperation and Development (OECD) data for a sample of
industrial nations, Andrew Glyn and David Miliband (1994) examined the relationship between income inequality (as measured by the ratio of the income of the
top 20 percent to the income of the bottom 20 percent for each country in 1980)
and economic growth (as measured by the annual percentage growth rate in labor
productivity between 1979 and 1990). Their findings, which are shown in figure
15.1, reveal a sharply negative association between income inequality and growth
thus measured.

In another study, Alberto Alesina and Dani Roderick (1992) found that national
income growth rates in sixty-five countries were negatively related to the share of
national income going to the top 5 percent and the top 20 percent of earners, and
that, by contrast, larger shares for poor and middle-income groups were associated

Figure 15.1   Growth Versus Inequality in Cross-National Data

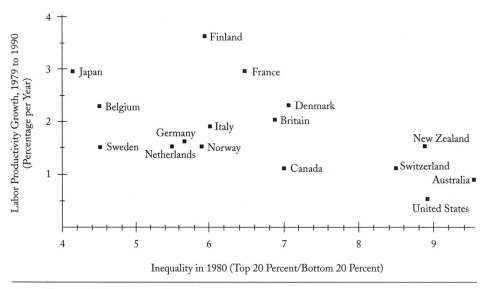

Source: Glyn and Miliband (1994, 3).

with higher rates of growth. Essentially the same pattern has been confirmed in several other independent studies (Garrison and Lee 1992; Persson and Tabellini 1992).

Of course, the mere fact that inequality and growth are negatively correlated in cross-national data does not imply that greater inequality is necessarily a cause of slower growth. A multitude of other factors that affect growth rates differ sharply across nations, and a positive correlation of some of the most important of these with income inequality might explain the pattern. One way to check for this possibility is to see whether the negative relationship between inequality and growth holds up when we examine these two variables within countries over time.

GROWTH AND INEQUALITY OVER TIME

Several recent studies have found that the correlation over time between inequality and economic growth is also negative. For example, as Don Corry and Andrew Glyn (1994) note in their recent survey, the postwar experience in most industrial countries may be partitioned neatly into two periods for the purpose of describing variations in economic growth and income inequality. The first, from roughly the end of World War II until about 1973, has been called the golden age of economic growth. National income growth during that period averaged 5 percent and more in many developed countries. By contrast, the growth rates of national income in the OECD countries have been only about half as large during the post-1973 period. Corry and Glyn also note that, by virtually any measure, income inequality during the golden age was low by historical standards, and in most countries it fell throughout the period. They go on to point out that the degree of income inequality in most countries has risen significantly since 1974, although the change began at different times in different countries. As in the cross-national data, higher growth rates are associated not with higher income inequality, as predicted by supply-siders, but with lower inequality.

Here again, however, the observed negative correlation does not necessarily imply that growing inequality is the cause of slower growth. As before, it could be that other factors positively correlated with inequality are the real causal agents. Yet it seems most unlikely that the same unobserved causal agents that might have explained the pattern in cross-national data could also have been at work in the time series data. It *could* have happened that way. But now we need two coincidences, not just one, to get inequality off the causal hook.

On balance, it thus appears that the supply-siders' case for the agonizing trade-off between equity and economic growth is far from compelling. There was never any solid theoretical support for the existence of this trade-off, and the empirical evidence, such as it is, would never change a skeptic's mind.

OCCUPATIONAL CHOICE: A MORE IMPORTANT MARGIN?

Perhaps conventional labor supply measures—typically, the number of hours worked during the year—simply cannot capture the richness of the supply-siders' economic vision. Thus, we might imagine a world in which most people work more or less full-time, independently of tax rates, and yet still imagine circumstances in which taxes might introduce important distortions. For example, suppose we assume, plausibly, that the most important labor supply decision is not how many hours to work but which occupation to pursue. And suppose further, again plausibly, that in some occupations the work is stressful and difficult but pays well, while in others it is less stressful but also pays less well. Supply-siders might then argue that the effect of higher marginal tax rates will be to divert people from the first occupation to the second, and that the resulting decline in income will be an efficiency loss properly attributable to the higher tax rates.

Fine so far. But now let us explore a variation on this basic story. This time, suppose we divide occupations not according to how stressful their tasks are but according to the extent to which additional talent translates into additional productivity.[1] For concreteness, imagine a world in which there are only two occupations, production workers and singers. The market for production workers can absorb indefinitely many workers at a constant wage of w that is independent of talent. The market for singers, by contrast, requires only a single individual to record a compact disc that will be sold in the world market. Talent, which is unobservable ex ante, is revealed in a contest for the recording contract. To enter this contest, one must forfeit the opportunity to be a production worker. As the number of people who enter this contest grows, the higher, on average, will be the quality of the winning singer's voice. The wage of a contestant in the singing market is V > w if she wins the contract, and 0 otherwise. V is assumed an increasing, concave function of N_1, the number of people who compete for the recording contract.

Since talent is unobservable ex ante, potential contestants for the recording contract think of themselves ex ante as being equally likely to win it. If the worker's utility is equal to his wage, the equilibrium allocation of labor across occupations must satisfy

$$(1/N_1)V(N_1) = w, \tag{15.1}$$

and the result is that the expected utility of workers in each occupation will be equal to w in equilibrium. In brief, we have a standard tragedy of the commons. All potential rent from the recording market is squandered in the competition to see who lands the recording contract.

On the assumption that V measures not just the winning singer's pay but also the social value of the recording she produces, we can calculate the optimal allocation of labor across the two occupations. To find this allocation, we first write

$$GNP = V(N_1) + (N - N_1)w, \tag{15.2}$$

and then solve

$$dGNP/dN_1 = V'(N_1) - w = 0 \tag{15.3}$$

for N_1.[2] Thus, at the socially optimal value of N_1, denoted N_1^{**}, the slope of V is equal to w.

For purposes of comparison, note from the private equilibrium condition (equation [15.1]) that the slope of the ray to $V(N_1)$ at the private equilibrium, N_1^*, is given by

$$V(N_1^*)/N_1^* = w \tag{15.4}$$

The conditions that define the socially optimal and private equilibrium values of N_1 are compared graphically in figure 15.2.

Note in figure 15.2 that the payment to the winning contestant is higher under the private equilibrium allocation (V^*) than under the socially optimal allocation (V^{**}), reflecting the fact that the quality of the top-ranked singer—and hence the value of his or her services to the buying public—rises when more people compete for the recording contract. The fact that GNP is higher at N_1^{**} than at N_1^*, however, implies that the private equilibrium quality of music is "too high" from a social welfare perspective.

Now suppose the government taxes the earnings of the winning singer at the rate of t and distributes the resulting tax collections in equal lump-sum amounts to all workers. Labor market equilibrium now obtains when

$$w = (1 - t)V(N_1)/N_1 \tag{15.5}$$

The optimal tax rate t^* is the one for which

$$w = (1 - t^*)V(N_1^{**})/N_1^{**}, \tag{15.6}$$

Figure 15.2   The Private Equilibrium and Socially Optimal Allocations to the Winner-Take-All Sector

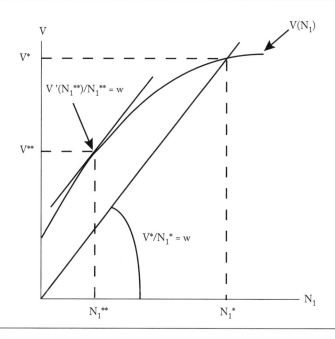

which yields

$$t^* = 1 - w\, N_1^{**}/V(N_1^{**}), \tag{15.7}$$

where N_1^{**} is again the socially optimal number of contestants for the recording contract, as defined by equation (15.3). This tax rate maximizes GNP and also each worker's ex ante expected utility. In this model, the effect of a progressive tax is thus to increase efficiency rather than reduce it.

The model just discussed does not assume that individuals care about rank per se. The payoff to rank is strictly a result of a nonconvexity in technology. A progressive tax improves efficiency in this model because it curbs overcrowding in the market in which reward depends on rank.

In our recent book (Frank and Cook 1995), Philip Cook and I have argued that winner-take-all payoff structures, long prevalent in entertainment, sports, and the arts, have increasingly permeated law, journalism, consulting, medicine, investment banking, corporate management, publishing, design, fashion, and a host of other high-wage labor markets. Indeed, it is fair to say that virtually all top-decile earners in the United States are participants in labor markets in which rewards depend heavily on relative performance. In view of the growing prevalence of such labor markets, it is hardly fanciful to suppose that progressive taxes may dominate flat taxes on both equity *and* efficiency grounds.

THE IMPORTANCE OF RELATIVE CONSUMPTION

Standard models of the labor-leisure choice assume that the individual derives utility from the consumption of goods and of leisure. In models in which the substitution effect dominates the income effect, taxes on income lead the individual to supply less labor than would be socially optimal—and hence, in part, the presumed trade-off between equity and efficiency.

The picture changes significantly if utility depends not just on leisure and absolute consumption but also on relative consumption.[3] Suppose, for example, that the ith individual's utility is given by

$$U_i = U_i[C_i,L_i,R(C_i)], \tag{15.8}$$

where C_i denotes the individual's consumption of goods, L_i denotes his consumption of leisure, and $R(C_i)$ is his rank in the consumption distribution, $0 \le R(C_i) \le 1$. If $f(C)$ is the density function for the observed values of consumption in the population, then $R(C_i) = \int_{C_o}^{C_i} f(C)dc$, where C_0 is the consumption expenditure of the population member who consumes least. Let w be the wage rate and 1 the price of consumption goods, and suppose for simplicity that individuals have only wage income. If individuals take $f(C)$ as given, the first-order condition for maximum utility is given by

$$U_{i1}/U_{i2} + (U_{i3}/U_{i2})f(C_i) = 1/w, \tag{15.9}$$

where U_{ij} denotes the first partial derivative of U_i with respect to its jth argument.

The expression $(U_{i3}/U_{i2})f(C_i)$ on the lefthand side of equation (15.9) reflects the fact that when an individual sacrifices an additional hour of leisure, his payoff is not just the additional w units of consumption goods he can buy but also the fact that he moves forward in the consumption ranking. Other individuals also perceive this second reward from selling leisure, however, and when all respond to it, the resulting consumption ranking remains unchanged. In the end, consumers end up selling more than the socially optimal quantity of leisure. Thus, suppose consumers could agree collectively to ignore the effect of selling leisure on their consumption rank—that is, suppose they agreed to assume that $U_{i3} = 0$. The first-order condition then simplifies to

$$U_{i1}/U_{i2} = 1/w, \tag{15.10}$$

and the amount of leisure individuals choose to sell declines. The solution to equation (15.10), not that to equation (15.9), defines the socially optimal allocation.

In this model, the effect of a tax on wages is, as in conventional models, to lower the reward for selling leisure. But whereas in conventional models this introduces a distortion, in this model the same tax mitigates an existing distortion. Here again, a plausible modification of the conventional model suggests that progressive taxation may enhance efficiency rather than reduce it.

CHOOSING BETWEEN THE TWO MODELS

The case for the agonizing trade-off between equity and efficiency is weak. This trade-off is not predicted on theoretical grounds, even in conventional models, nor does its existence appear to enjoy any significant empirical support. What is more, if we modify conventional models to incorporate the dependence of important individual payoffs on rank, these models imply that efficiency may actually *require* more equitable tax rates.

These observations notwithstanding, it seems fair to say that most policymakers continue to believe that the goals of equity and efficiency are squarely in conflict. People with such beliefs obviously tend to favor tax policies different from those favored by those who believe these goals are complementary. The issues involved in the current tax debate are important. How is a neutral observer to choose between the competing views? On what evidence, for example, might she decide whether interpersonal comparisons loom large in the utility function?

In a recent paper, David Neumark and Andrew Postlewaite (1996) approach this question by examining how individual labor supply decisions depend on the incomes of important reference group members. The difficulty in such efforts has always been that it is hard to know which others a person includes in her reference group. Neumark and Postlewaite solve this problem by examining the behavior of sisters. Does a woman's decision about whether to work outside the home depend on her sister's economic circumstances? In conventional models, it would not, but Neumark and Postlewaite find differently for a sample of women whose sisters are not employed. Specifically, they find that sister A is 16 to 25 percent more likely to work outside the home if sister B's husband earns more than sister A's husband (Neumark and Postlewaite 1996, table 3).

Some of the most striking evidence concerning interdependencies in demands comes from markets for collectible items. Kenneth Koford and Adrian Tshoegl (1996), for example, show that the prices of rare coins are often dramatically higher than prices for otherwise identical coins that were minted in large quantities. Jacob Zahavi (1995) reports that the Franklin Mint, a private issuer of collectibles, had over 3 million active customers and sales of more than $600 million in 1992. Exclusivity also appears to help explain why the Ferrari 456 GT sells for twice the price of the Porsche 911 Turbo, even though the Porsche is faster, handles better, and is more reliable.

In my 1985 book *Choosing the Right Pond,* I described additional behavioral evidence consistent with the view that status concerns have significant weight in economic decisions. There I showed that the wage distributions within firms are typically much more compressed than we would expect if workers did not care about relative income (Frank 1985b, ch. 4). Likewise, the incidence of piece-rate pay schemes is much lower, and the frequency with which workers go on strike is much higher, than we would expect if relative income did not matter. In addition, the observed structural differences between the compensation packages of unionized firms and nonunionized firms are difficult to explain without reference to collective action problems that arise from concerns about status (Frank 1985b, ch. 8).

Sheryl Ball and her coauthors (1996) have shown that even simple laboratory manipulations of status can have profound implications for the terms of market exchange. In one experiment, for example, they awarded half of their subjects "stars" on the basis of their performance on a transparently meaningless quiz. These subjects consistently received better terms when they exchanged goods with subjects who had not received stars.

Another important source of relevant evidence on the nature of the utility function is found in the burgeoning psychology literature on the factors that explain variations in subjective well-being. For present purposes, subjective well-being is the psychologist's term for what economists call utility. But whereas the economist's strategy is to try to infer the determinants of utility from patterns of choice, the psychologist tries to measure subjective well-being directly.

By far the most popular approach has been simply to ask people how satisfied they are (for a discussion, see Easterlin 1974). For example, people may be asked to respond on a numerical scale to a question like, "All things considered, how satisfied are you with your life as a whole these days?" Another approach measures the frequency and intensity of positive affect by asking people the extent to which they agree with such statements as: "When good things happen to me, it strongly affects me"; "I will often do things for no other reason than that they might be fun"; "When I get something I want, I feel excited and energized"; "When I'm doing well at something, I love to keep at it"; and so on (reported by Goleman 1996).

More recently, neuroscientists have also used brainwave data to assess positive and negative affect. Subjects with relatively greater electrical activity in the left prefrontal region of the brain are likely to indicate strong agreement with statements like the ones in the preceding paragraph, while those with relatively greater electrical activity in the right prefrontal region are much more likely to disagree with these statements (Davidson 1992). The left prefrontal region of the brain is rich in receptors for the neurotransmitter dopamine, higher concentrations of which have been shown independently to be correlated with positive affect (reported by Goleman 1996).

Satisfaction as identified by any of these measures is predictive of a variety of observable behaviors that most of us take to be indicative of well-being. For example, people who describe themselves as highly satisfied, or who have relatively high levels of electrical activity in the left prefrontal region, are: more likely to be rated as content by friends; more likely to initiate social contacts with friends; more likely to respond to requests for help; less likely to suffer from psychosomatic illnesses; less likely to be absent from work; less likely to be involved in disputes at work; less likely to die prematurely; less likely to attempt suicide; and less likely to seek psychological counseling.[4] In short, it seems that what the psychologists call subjective well-being is a real phenomenon. Empirical measures of it have high consistency, reliability, and validity (Diener and Lucas 1999).

Richard Easterlin (1974) was the first to call economists' attention to survey data that illuminate the relationship between material living standards and subjective well-being.[5] Easterlin saw three significant patterns in the self-reported happiness data. First, he noted that satisfaction levels across individuals within a given country vary directly with income—richer people, on the average, are more satisfied than their poorer countrymen. This relationship is illustrated in figure 15.3, which plots average satisfaction against annual income for a U.S. sample of 4,942 persons surveyed between 1981 and 1984.

Second, Easterlin noted that the average happiness levels within a given country tend to be highly stable over time, even in the face of significant economic growth. Figure 15.4, for example, plots the percentage of Americans surveyed whose response was "very happy" when asked, "Taken all together, how would you say things are these days—would you say that you are very happy, pretty happy, or not too happy?" Figure 15.5, which plots mean subjective well-being over time for Japan, tells a similar story.

And finally, Easterlin noted that average happiness levels across countries are not strongly correlated with average levels of GNP.

Easterlin argued that these patterns are consistent with the hypothesis that relative income is far more important than absolute income as a determinant of individual happiness levels. His pessimistic conclusion was that economic growth does not improve the human condition, since no matter how prosperous a society becomes in absolute terms, the frequency with which people experience relative deprivation is not much affected.

Subsequent work suggests that Easterlin was perhaps too pessimistic. For example, most careful studies find a clear relationship between subjective well-being and absolute income at extremely low levels of absolute income. Thus, in a country in which most people lack minimally adequate shelter and nutrition, across-the-board increases in income appear, not surprisingly, to yield significant and lasting improvements in subjective well-being (Diener and Suh 1999). In the same vein, it

Figure 15.3   Income Versus Satisfaction in the United States, 1981 to 1984

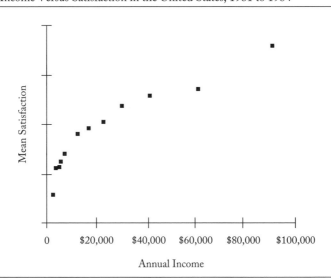

Source: Diener, Sandvik, Seidlitz, and Diener (1993).

Figure 15.4   Percentage of Americans Who Are "Very Happy," 1972 to 1991

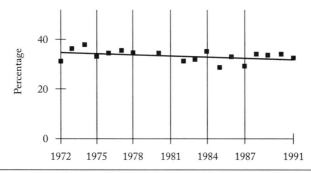

Source: National Opinion Research Center (1991).

now appears that average satisfaction levels are in fact significantly lower in extremely poor countries than in rich ones (Argyle 1997). But it still does not appear that average satisfaction levels within a country are significantly correlated over time with income.

This is not to say that having additional economic resources could not lead to greater well-being. On the contrary, the literature identifies many forms of consumption that contribute in significant and lasting ways to human well-being. For example, it appears that most people would be more satisfied with their lives if the

Figure 15.5   Mean Subjective Well-Being, Japan, 1958 to 1987

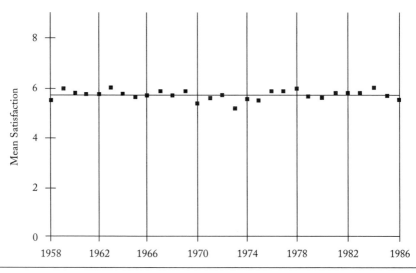

Source: Veenhoven (1993).

resources that are currently used to build bigger houses and more expensive cars were instead used to support more convenient public transportation and a cleaner, safer environment. The evidence also suggests that people would be more satisfied if they had fewer goods but more time to spend with family and friends or more time for exercise (for a summary of this evidence, see Frank 1997). That these are not the choices people actually make can be understood as the result of the collective action problems that arise when payoffs depend on rank.

INCOME TAXES VERSUS CONSUMPTION TAXES

Interpersonal comparisons are not likely to apply with equal force with respect to all categories of consumption. For example, we might expect such comparisons to be more important, on average, for goods that are readily observed than for goods that are not readily observed. Expenditures on cars and houses thus tend to generate stronger consumption externalities than does money deposited in savings accounts. This suggests yet another reason to favor consumption taxation over our present system of income taxation.

Many of the current consumption tax proposals call for a flat tax rate irrespective of how much a family consumes. But these proposals can be easily modified to incorporate marginal rates that rise with total consumption. For example, taxable consumption could be defined as the difference between taxable income and current savings, with rates then rising as this difference grows.

As Martin Feldstein and others have argued, steeply progressive rates applied to income may lead to inefficiency to the extent that they create incentives for payments in kind and other forms of tax avoidance. But if savings are fully tax-deductible, the individual's incentive to engage in such behavior is sharply reduced.

ARE POSITIONAL EXTERNALITIES A LEGITIMATE CONCERN OF TAX POLICY?

Most economists accept the proposition that market allocations may be suboptimal when production is accompanied by the discharge of environmental pollutants. Most tend also to be enthusiastic in their embrace of effluent taxes as a solution to the problem of environmental pollution.

The dependence of utility on relative performance and relative consumption gives rise to what I have elsewhere called positional externalities (Frank 1992). Analytically, these externalities are no different from ordinary environmental pollutants. My proposal to tax consumption is thus precisely analogous to an effluent tax.[6]

Many economists may accept the existence of positional externalities as a purely descriptive matter.[7] Yet these same economists often question whether such externalities are proper targets for public policy intervention. On its face, this is a curious position for the profession that has always insisted that "a taste for poetry is no better than a taste for pushpins."

Of course, it is one thing to say that a person's tastes are her own business, and quite another to say that A's discomfort from B's consumption constitutes grounds for restricting B's consumption. As parents, most of us try to teach our children not to worry about what others consume, and perhaps this is the best posture for the state to assume as well. And yet many forms of consumption cause not only injured feelings in others but also more tangible economic losses.[8] The job seeker gains a leg up on his rivals, for example, by showing up for his interview in a custom-tailored suit. The best response for others may be to show up in custom-tailored suits as well. Yet all job seekers might prefer the alternative in which each spent less on his professional wardrobe. Likewise, when A sends his child to an expensive private school, he may not intend to reduce the likelihood that the children of others will be accepted to top universities, but that is an effect of his action nevertheless, and it may be the best response of others to send their children to private schools as well. And yet all might find that outcome less attractive than when all send their children to the public schools.

Not even a steeply progressive consumption tax can fully neutralize the externalities that arise from competition for spots atop various local hierarchies. At best, it can reduce some of the costs of those externalities. Even with such a tax, it will still prove useful to ameliorate those externalities through a variety of less formal means—adoption of social norms, choice of personal reference groups, introspection, and so on. As policy interventions go, a consumption tax is not especially intrusive. After all, we have to tax something. And the evidence is strong that across-the-board consumption reductions do not entail significant utility losses for middle- and upper-income citizens.

CONCLUDING REMARKS

The United States and the United Kingdom are unique among industrialized nations in the enthusiasm they have shown for supply-side tax policies. And in both countries there has also been sharp growth in earnings inequality in recent years. For example, whereas an American at the ninety-fifth percentile of the income distribution earned slightly less than twelve times as much as one at the fifth percentile in 1973, the corresponding ratio in 1993 was more than twenty-five to one (Burtless 1996). The incomes of the top 1 percent of U.S. earners more than doubled in real terms since 1979, a period during which the median income was roughly stable and the bottom one-fifth of earners saw their incomes actually fall by more than 10 percent (for a detailed discussion, see Krugman 1992). In Britain, according to *The Economist* on November 5, 1994 (19), the richest 20 percent earned seven times as much as the poorest 20 percent in 1991, as compared with only four times as much in 1977. And as the *Guardian* reported on November 25, 1996, the poorest one-tenth in Britain are 13 percent worse off in real terms than they were in 1979, but the richest one-tenth are now 65 percent better off. The gap between males with the highest wage rates and those with the lowest wage rates is larger now in Britain than at any time since the 1880s, when statistics on wages were first gathered systematically.

The social costs associated with pronounced earnings inequality have long been recognized. The supply-siders' implicit message is that these costs are worth bearing in return for the gains in efficiency that accompany lower marginal tax rates. Where liberals have reached a different conclusion on this issue, it has almost always been because they assign different weights to the two goals, not because they dispute the premise that the goals are in conflict.

Yet as we have seen, there is no compelling theoretical or empirical evidence for this conflict. What is more, if we accept plausible modifications to the standard rational choice model, it turns out that the very same tax policies that promote equity may also promote efficiency. These modifications rest on two assumptions: that monetary rewards in many of the top-paying occupations depend on relative, in addition to absolute, performance; and that people care not just about absolute but also about relative consumption. There is considerable evidence for both assumptions. I am aware of no credible evidence against them. Absent such evidence, economists should stop advising policymakers that a more equitable tax structure will entail a loss of efficiency.

NOTES

1. For a much more detailed exposition of the model to follow, see Frank and Cook (1993).

2. Concavity of V(K) assures that equation 15.3 is also a sufficient condition for maximum GNP.

3. The model discussed in this section is more fully elaborated in Frank (1985a).

4. For surveys of this evidence, see Frank (1985a, ch. 2) and Clark and Oswald (1996).

5. Easterlin (1995) updates his earlier study.

6. Many others have suggested taxes to mitigate the externalities that arise from the dependence of utility on relative income or relative consumption. See, for example, Boskin and Sheshinski (1978), Layard (1980), Ng (1987), Oswald (1983), Haavelmo (1971), Kosicki (1987), Seidman (1987), and Ireland (1994, 1997).

7. Indeed, there is an extensive literature in which economists have discussed the dependence of satisfaction on relative living standards. In addition to the authors cited in note 6, see Kapteyn and van Herwaarden (1980), van Praag (1993), Easterlin (1974, 1995), Sen (1983, 1987), Hirsch (1976), Robson (1992), and Scitovsky (1976).

8. Sen (1987) emphasizes this point.

REFERENCES

Alesina, Alberto, and Dani Roderick. 1992. "Distribution, Political Conflict, and Economic Growth." In *Political Economy, Growth, and Business Cycles,* edited by Alex Cuckierman, Zvi Hercowitz, and Leonardo Leiderman. Cambridge, Mass.: MIT Press.

Argyle, Michael. 1997. "Causes and Correlates of Happiness." In *Understanding Well-being: Scientific Perspectives on Enjoyment and Suffering,* edited by Daniel Kahneman, Ed Diener, and Norbert Schwartz. New York: Russell Sage Foundation.

Ball, Sheryl, Catherine Eckel, Philip Grossman, and William Zame. 1996. "Status in Markets." Working paper. Department of Economics, Virginia Polytechnic Institute.

Boskin, Michael, and E. Sheshinski. 1978. "Optimal Redistributive Taxation When Individual Welfare Depends on Relative Income." *Quarterly Journal of Economics* 92: 589–601.

Burtless, Gary. 1996. "Trends in the Level and Distribution of U.S. Living Standards: 1973–1993." *Eastern Economic Journal* 22(Summer): 271–90.

Clark, Andrew, and Andrew Oswald. 1996. "Satisfaction and Comparison Income." *Journal of Public Economics* 61: 359–81.

Corry, Don, and Andrew Glyn. 1994. "The Macroeconomics of Equality, Stability, and Growth." In *Paying for Inequality: The Economic Costs of Social Injustice,* edited by Andrew Glyn and David Miliband. London: Rivers Oran.

Davidson, Richard J. 1992. "Emotion and Affective Style: Hemispheric Substrates." *Psychological Science* 3: 39–43.

Diener, Ed, and Richard E. Lucas. 1999. "Personality and Subjective Well-being." In *Understanding Well-being: Scientific Perspectives on Enjoyment and Suffering,* edited by Daniel Kahneman, Ed Diener, and Norbert Schwartz. New York: Russell Sage Foundation.

Diener, Ed, and Eunkook Suh. 1999. "National Differences in Subjective Well-being." In *Understanding Well-being: Scientific Perspectives on Enjoyment and Suffering,* edited by Daniel Kahneman, Ed Diener, and Norbert Schwartz. New York: Russell Sage Foundation.

Diener, Ed, Ed Sandvik, Larry Seidlitz, and Marissa Diener. 1993. "The Relationship Between Income and Subjective Well-being: Relative or Absolute?" *Social Indicators Research* 28: 195–223.

Easterlin, Richard. 1974. "Does Economic Growth Improve the Human Lot?" In *Nations and Households in Economic Growth: Essays in Honor of Moses Abramovitz,* edited by Paul David and Melvin Reder. New York: Academic Press.

———. 1995. "Will Raising the Incomes of All Increase the Happiness of All?" *Journal of Economic Behavior and Organization* 27: 35–47.

Ehrenberg, Ronald E., and Robert S. Smith. 1994. *Modern Labor Economics.* New York: Harper-Collins.

Feldstein, Martin. 1995. "The Effect of Marginal Tax Rates on Taxable Income: A Panel Study of the 1986 Tax Reform Act." *Journal of Political Economy* 103(June): 551–72.

Frank, Robert H. 1985a. "The Demand for Unobservable and Other Nonpositional Goods." *American Economic Review* 75(March): 101–16.

———. 1985b. *Choosing the Right Pond.* New York: Oxford University Press.

———. 1992. "Positional Externalities." In *Strategy and Choice: Essays in Honor of Thomas C. Schelling,* edited by Richard Zeckhauser. Cambridge, Mass.: MIT Press.

———. 1997. "The Frame of Reference as a Public Good." *Economic Journal* 11: 1832–1847.

Frank, Robert H., and Philip J. Cook. 1993. "Winner-Take-All Markets." Unpublished paper. Cornell University.

———. 1995. *The Winner-Take-All Society.* New York: Free Press.

Garrison, Charles, and Feng-Yao Lee. 1992. "Taxation, Aggregate Activity and Growth." *Economic Inquiry* 20: 172–76.

Glyn, Andrew, and David Miliband, eds. 1994. *Paying for Inequality: The Economic Cost of Social Injustice.* London: IPPR/Rivers Oram Press.

Goleman, Daniel. 1996. "Forget Money; Nothing Can Buy Happiness, Some Researchers Say." *New York Times,* July 16, C1, C3.

Haavelmo, Trygve. 1971. "Some Observations on Welfare and Economic Growth." In *Induction, Growth, and Trade: Essays in Honour of Sir Roy Harrod,* edited by W. A. Eltis, M. Scott, and N. Wolfe. Oxford: Oxford University Press.

Higgins, Benjamin. 1992. "Equity and Efficiency in Development." In *Equality and Deficency in Economic Development,* edited by Donald L. Savoie. London: Intermedia Technology Publications.

Hirsch, Fred. 1976. *Social Limits to Growth.* Cambridge, Mass.: Harvard University Press.

Ireland, Norman. 1994. "On Limiting the Market for Status Signals." *Journal of Public Economics* 53: 91–110.

———. 1997. "Status-Seeking, Income Taxation, and Efficiency." *Journal of Public Economics* 70: 99–113.

Kapteyn, Arie, and F. G. van Herwaarden. 1980. "Interdependent Welfare Functions and Optimal Income Distribution." *Journal of Public Economics* 14: 375–97.

Koford, Kenneth, and Adrian Tshoegl. Forthcoming. "The Market Value of Rarity." *Journal of Economic Behavior and Organization.*

Kosicki, George. 1987. "Savings as a Nonpositional Good." *Southern Economic Journal* 54 (October): 422–34.

Krugman, Paul. 1992. "The Right, the Rich, and the Facts." *American Prospect* 11(Fall): 19–31.

Layard, Richard. 1980. "Human Satisfactions and Public Policy." *Economic Journal* 90(December): 737–50.

National Opinion Research Center. http://www.icpsr.umich.edu/GSS/trend/happy.htm.

Neumark, David, and Andrew Postlewaite. 1996. "Relative Income Concerns and the Rise in Married Women' Employment." Unpublished paper. Department of Economics, University of Pennsylvania.

Ng, Yew-Kwang. 1987. "Diamonds Are a Government's Best Friend: Burden-Free Taxes on Goods Valued for Their Values." *American Economic Review* 77: 186–91.

Oswald, Andrew J. 1983. "Altruism, Jealousy, and the Theory of Optimal Nonlinear Income Taxation." *Journal of Public Economics* 20: 77–87.

Persson, Torsten, and Guido Tabellini. 1992. "Growth, Distribution, and Politics." In *Political Economy, Growth, and Business Cycles,* edited by Alex Cuckierman, Zvi Hercowitz, and Leonardo Leiderman. Cambridge, Mass.: MIT Press.

Robson, Arthur J. 1992. "Status, the Distribution of Wealth, Private and Social Attitudes to Risk." *Econometrica* 60: 837–58.

Seidman, Laurence. 1987. "Relativity and Efficient Taxation." *Southern Economic Journal* 54: 463–74.

Scitovsky, Tibor. 1976. *The Joyless Economy.* New York: Oxford University Press.

Sen, Amartya. 1983. "Poor, Relatively Speaking." *Oxford Economics Papers* 35(July): 153–67.

———. 1987. *The Standard of Living.* Cambridge: Cambridge University Press.

Van Praag, Bernard M. S. 1993. "The Relativity of the Welfare Concept." In *The Quality of Life,* edited by Martha Nussbaum and Amartya Sen. Oxford: Clarendon.

Veenhoven, Ruut. 1993. *Happiness in Nations: Subjective Appreciation of Life in Fifty-six Nations.* Rotterdam: Erasmus University.

Zahavi, Jacob. 1995. "Franklin Mint's Famous AMOS." *OR/MS Today* 22, 18–23.

Contributors

JOEL B. SLEMROD is Paul W. McCracken Collegiate Professor of Business Economics and Public Policy at the University of Michigan and research associate of the National Bureau of Economic Research. He is also director of the Office of Tax Policy Research at the University of Michigan Business School.

JAMES ALM is professor of economics in the Andrew Young School of Policy Studies at Georgia State University.

ALAN J. AUERBACH is Robert D. Burch Professor of Economics and Law and director of the Burch Center for Tax Policy and Public Finance at the University of California, Berkeley.

GERALD E. AUTEN is an economist with the U.S. Treasury Department's Office of Tax Analysis.

DAVID F. BRADFORD is professor of economics and public affairs at Princeton University and adjunct professor of law at New York University. He is also research associate of the National Bureau of Economic Research and adjunct fellow of the American Enterprise Institute.

W. ELLIOT BROWNLEE is professor of history at the University of California, Santa Barbara.

LEONARD E. BURMAN is deputy assistant secretary (tax analysis) of the U.S. Department of the Treasury, on leave from the Urban Institute, Washington, D.C.

CHRISTOPHER D. CARROLL is associate professor of economics at Johns Hopkins University and faculty research fellow of the National Bureau of Economic Research.

ROBERT CARROLL is an economist with the Treasury Department's Office of Tax Analysis.

CHARLES T. CLOTFELTER is Z. Smith Reynolds Professor of Public Policy Studies and professor of economics and law at Duke University. He is also research associate of the National Bureau of Economic Research.

DANIEL FEENBERG is research associate of the National Bureau of Economic Research.

ROBERT H. FRANK is the Goldwin Smith Professor of Economics, Ethics, and Public Policy at Cornell University.

WILLIAM G. GALE is Joseph A. Pechman Fellow in the Economic Studies Program at the Brookings Institution.

AUSTAN GOOLSBEE is associate professor of economics at the University of Chicago Graduate School of Business. He is also research fellow of the American Bar Foundation and the National Bureau of Economic Research.

ROGER H. GORDON is Reuben Kempf Professor of Economics at the University of Michigan. He is also research associate of the National Bureau of Economic Research and the Centre for Economic Policy Research.

JANE G. GRAVELLE is senior specialist in economic policy at the Congressional Research Service of the Library of Congress.

JAMES R. HINES JR. is professor of business economics at the University of Michigan and research associate at the National Bureau of Economic Research. He is also research director of the Office of Tax Policy Research at the University of Michigan.

DOUGLAS HOLTZ-EAKIN is professor of economics at Syracuse University and research associate of the National Bureau of Economic Research. He is also editor of *National Tax Journal*.

R. GLENN HUBBARD is Russell L. Carson Professor of Economics and Finance at Columbia University and research associate of the National Bureau of Economic Research. He is also director of the Program on Tax Policy at the American Enterprise Institute.

ROBERT A. MOFFITT is professor of economics at Johns Hopkins University and research affiliate of the National Bureau of Economic Research, the Institute for Research on Poverty, and the Joint Center for Poverty Research.

JAMES M. POTERBA is Mitsui Professor of Economics at the Massachusetts Institute of Technology and director of the Public Economics Research Program at the National Bureau of Economic Research.

MARK RIDER is associate professor of economics at Kennesaw State University.

HARVEY S. ROSEN is John L. Weinberg Professor of Economics and Business Policy at Princeton University.

ANDREW A. SAMWICK is assistant professor of economics at Dartmouth College and faculty research fellow of the National Bureau of Economic Research.

RICHARD L. SCHMALBECK is professor of law at Duke University School of Law.

DOUGLAS A. SHACKELFORD is professor and Arthur Anderson Distinguished Tax Scholar at the University of North Carolina's Kenan-Flagler Business School. He is also research associate of the National Bureau of Economic Research.

TERRY SHEVLIN is Deloitte & Touche Professor of Accounting and director of the doctoral program at the School of Business at the University of Washington, Seattle.

JOHN B. SHOVEN is Charles R. Schwab Professor of Economics at Stanford University.

JONATHAN M. SIEGEL is a doctoral candidate in economics at the University of California, Berkeley.

CHRISTOPHER R. TABER is assistant professor in the Economics Department and research associate of the Institute of Policy Research at Northwestern University.

SALLY WALLACE is associate professor of economics in the Andrew Young School of Policy Studies at Georgia State University.

MARK O. WILHELM is associate professor of economics at Indiana University and Purdue University at Indianapolis. He is also faculty affiliate of the Indiana University Center on Philanthropy.

EDWARD N. WOLFF is professor of economics at New York University and senior scholar of the Jerome Levy Institute of Bard College.

STEPHEN P. ZELDES is the Benjamin Rosen Professor of Economics and Finance at the Graduate School of Business, Columbia University, and research associate of the National Bureau of Economic Research.

Index